SLAVERY IN CHINA DURING THE
FORMER HAN DYNASTY

SLAVERY IN CHINA DURING THE

FORMER HAN DYNASTY

206 B.C.—A.D. 25

BY

C. MARTIN WILBUR

CURATOR, CHINESE ARCHAEOLOGY AND ETHNOLOGY

FIELD MUSEUM OF NATURAL HISTORY

NEW YORK / RUSSELL & RUSSELL

FIRST PUBLISHED IN 1943
REISSUED, 1967, BY RUSSELL & RUSSELL
A DIVISION OF ATHENEUM HOUSE, INC.
L. C. CATALOG CARD NO: 66-27181
PRINTED IN THE UNITED STATES OF AMERICA

CONTENTS

CONTENTS

LIST OF ILLUSTRATIONS

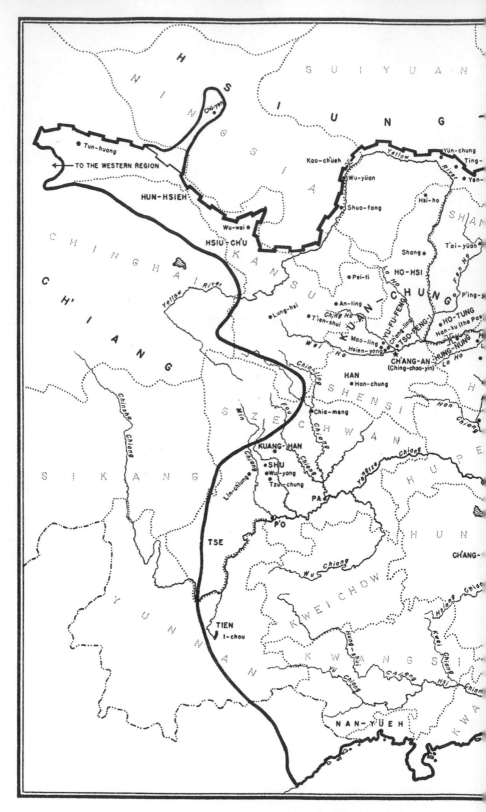

CHINA DURING THE FORMER HAN DYNASTY, CA. 100 B.C.

PREFACE

The economic history of Greece and Rome, and of our own nation before 1860, cannot be understood without a knowledge of slavery. China, too, had a slavery system, but it has never been adequately described by Western historians. Noting many similarities between ancient China and the classical world, modern Chinese scholars have recently devoted considerable attention to this subject, and their research has fostered an ardent dispute concerning its importance in successive periods. How important was slavery in ancient China? Is the social and economic history of that country, or of any of the periods in its development, also unintelligible without a clear picture of slavery and its function there?

Chinese slavery may be studied either extensively or intensively. The first method would seek to describe the institution throughout a period longer than that from Homeric times down to the middle of the nineteenth century. More than a hundred years ago Edouard Biot used the extensive method in his "Mémoire sur la condition des esclaves et des serviteurs gagés en Chine." Toni Pippon used the same approach in his "Beitrag zum Chinesischen Sklavensystem," published in 1936. The present work employs the intensive method, concentrating entirely upon the first period for which native historical literature allows a detailed examination of the system in its historical and economic setting. Chinese slavery did not originate during the Former Han dynasty (206 B.C.–A.D. 25), but it expanded rapidly at that time. Slaves probably then achieved their greatest numbers in proportion to the total population, and the period is the first in which it is possible to suppose, on the basis of historical texts, that slavery had an important place in Chinese economy.

This study of Chinese slavery is divided into two sections:

Part I seeks the solution to two general questions. What was the nature of Chinese slavery in Former Han times? What were the position and function of slaves in Han society and economics? Since these problems relate to a particular epoch in China's development, the period itself must be described from the point of view of its unfolding history, its society, and its general economic system. The success of the answers depends upon the adequacy of the available source material, the way it is used, the precision with which the term "slave" is defined, and the degree of identity that can be established between our usage and the terminology found in Chinese sources. The first question asks for a descriptive answer, and requires

11

an analysis of the sources of slaves, acquisition by owners, the slave trade, hereditary slavery and manumission—everything that might be called the "life cycle" of slaves in the abstract. The position of slaves in Former Han society is illustrated by their status, both customary and legal. Servile status depends to a considerable degree upon the kinds of people that owned slaves, the purposes for which slaves were owned, and the proportion of slaves to the total population. When we know what kinds of people owned slaves it is possible to ask why they owned them, that is to say, what functions the slaves fulfilled: whether they were important to their masters or to the state as producers of wealth—that is, as labor—or whether they were more important in other ways.

The response to the two major questions raises a third. What were the place and function of the whole slavery system in China as a whole, during the Former Han period? But is it permissible to discuss China during two and a quarter centuries "as a whole"? What evidences are there of rigidity or of historical change in the slavery system? Answers to such queries should contribute to a solution of the controversy, namely: Was the society of the Former Han period a "slavery society," and was the economic system a "slavery economy"?

Part II, which was prepared first, translates and annotates some 140 passages on slaves discovered in historical literature written during the Former Han period or shortly thereafter. When all the basic documents are placed in one section they retain their independent validity (except for that personal factor of translation), and therefore may be employed by any investigator without regard to the analysis of them in Part I. Aside from being the foundation, of this book, the documents are an integral part of it, constantly referred to by number in substantiation of all descriptions and conclusions. Many reveal, *inter alia*, fascinating details about life in the imperial palaces or patrician households, the political system of the dynasty, and the rise and fall of Chinese statesmen, generals, or relatives of the imperial house by marriage. For casual readers I venture to recommend document Number *14*, which poignantly describes the reunion of a young slave and his elder sister after she unexpectedly became Empress; Number *27*, which tells how a chorus girl captivated Emperor Wu and ultimately became his consort; the revealing account of jealousy and intrigue in a royal household, detailed in Number *37*; the report, in Number *55*, of an imperial investigating commission which substantiated the claim that a rustic old dame was the maternal grandmother of Emperor Hsüan; the lurid story of a pathologically jealous queen, recounted in Number *64;* and document Number *75,* the confidential report of a detective who had been commissioned to spy upon a man deposed from the imperial throne and suspected of plotting a *coup d'état.* There are many other passages of general interest, but perhaps the most revealing of all is Number *107,* which gives an eye-witness description of the machinations of an imperial concubine. She so dominated Emperor Ch'eng that he weakly submitted to her wishes and destroyed his only sons, thus dying without an heir, and most calamitous of all, leaving no direct line to carry on his ancestral worship!

Many people and institutions have assisted in the preparation of this book. I wish to record first my gratitude to Hollis Adelbert Wilbur and Mary Matteson Wilbur, my parents.

At Columbia University Professor William Linn Westermann, himself an authority on ancient slavery, provided the first inspiration for the study, and his continued interest and critical advice have been very stimulating. Dr. Luther Carrington Goodrich, Executive Officer of the Department of Chinese and Japanese at Columbia, provided unflagging encouragement for my research, and has read the entire manuscript, making numerous suggestions for improvement. Professor Jan Julius Lodewijk Duyvendak, Director of the Sinologisch Instituut at Leiden and Visiting Professor of Chinese at Columbia, went through most of the translations with infinite care, correcting errors, and proposing many felicitous renderings. Two other friends of long standing in the same department, Dr. Cyrus Henderson Peake and Mr. Chi-chen Wang, have read the manuscript and made numerous useful suggestions.

During several years of extensive correspondence, Dr. Homer H. Dubs, Professor of Philosophy at Duke University and translator of the Imperial Annals in the *History of the Former Han Dynasty,* has thrown light on a number of vexing problems concerning the China of those ancient days. He has meticulously read most of the manuscript, suggesting innumerable corrections and offering additional information from his storehouse of knowledge and notes. Likewise, during a period of more than two years Mr. Charles Y. Hu 虎矯如, a gifted graduate student in the University of Chicago, worked with me on the translations and their analysis.

It is also a genuine pleasure to express my gratitude to Dr. Charles Sidney Gardner, of Harvard University; to Dr. Herrlee

Glessner Creel, of the University of Chicago; to Dr. A. W. Hummel, Chief of the Division of Orientalia of the Library of Congress; and to Mr. and Mrs. Carl Whiting Bishop of the Freer Gallery of Art. Mrs. John King Fairbank kindly made the delicate and accurate restoration of the rubbing which is reproduced on Plate 2. Mr. Robert Yule 游佑生, of Field Museum, Assistant in Archaeology, drew the map, and greatly improved the legibility of the sixteenth century copy of the contract for a slave, reproduced in document *83*. Miss Rose Harris and Mrs. Anna Pfeiffer did the tedious work of typing, and patiently checked and rechecked citations through several recensions. There is also my wife, who would prefer to see no mention of her part; and indeed there is no way to describe the extent of her aid and of my gratitude.

Through the good offices of Mrs. Emily M. Wilcoxson, Librarian at Field Museum, I have been freely allowed to borrow books in Chinese and Japanese from the Division of Orientalia, Library of Congress, and from the Far Eastern libraries of Columbia University, the University of Chicago, and the Harvard-Yenching Institute. Some of the preliminary work on this book was done during after-hours when I was a Fellow of the Social Science Research Council; its support is gratefully acknowledged here again. By a happy arrangement, the American Friends of China, Chicago, enabled me to continue work with Mr. Charles Hu longer than would have been otherwise possible. To the American Council of Learned Societies I am indebted for a grant which provided the electrotypes of the Chinese texts printed in the second part of the book. Mr. Mortimer Graves, Administrative Secretary of the Council, aided greatly by working out the technical details. Dr. George A. Kennedy, of Yale University, supervised the setting of the Chinese type, which was made doubly difficult by the frequency of archaic forms.

Finally, there is Field Museum of Natural History, whose Director, Colonel Clifford C. Gregg, allowed me to devote the greater part of the past year, and some of my Museum time previously, to this study. Dr. Paul S. Martin, Chief Curator of Anthropology, constantly encouraged me and, by lightening my routine tasks, allowed me more uninterrupted time for study and writing. Miss Lillian Ross, Associate Editor of Scientific Publications, has greatly improved this book in seeing it through the press.

C. MARTIN WILBUR

August 1, 1941

SLAVERY IN CHINA DURING THE FORMER HAN DYNASTY

PART I

ABBREVIATIONS USED IN PART I

BEFEO	*Bulletin de l'Ecole Française d'Extrême-Orient*
BMFEA	*Bulletin of the Museum of Far Eastern Antiquities*
CHHP	*Ch'ing Hua hsüeh pao (Tsing Hua journal)*
CHS	*Ch'ien Han shu*
CLHP	*Chin Ling hsüeh pao (Nanking journal)*
HFHD	*The history of the Former Han dynasty by Pan Ku,* translated by Homer H. Dubs
HHS	*Hou Han shu*
HJAS	*Harvard journal of Asiatic studies*
JAOS	*Journal of the American Oriental Society*
JNCBRAS	*Journal of the North China Branch of the Royal Asiatic Society*
MH	*Les mémoires historiques de Se-ma Ts'ien,* translated by Edouard Chavannes
MRDTB	*Memoirs of the Research Department of the Toyo Bunko*
MSOS	*Mitteilungen des Seminars für orientalische Sprachen*
SC	*Shih chi*
TP	*T'oung pao*
YCHP	*Yen Ching hsüeh pao (Yenching journal of Chinese studies)*

LIST OF RULERS DURING THE FORMER HAN DYNASTY

	B.C.
EMPEROR KAO (KAO-TSU)	206–195
EMPEROR HUI	194–188
THE EMPRESS DOWAGER *née* LÜ	187–180
EMPEROR WEN	179–157
EMPEROR CHING	156–141
EMPEROR WU	140– 87
EMPEROR CHAO	86– 74
EMPEROR HSÜAN	73– 49
EMPEROR YÜAN	48– 33
EMPEROR CH'ENG	32– 7
EMPEROR AI	6– 1

	A.D.
EMPEROR P'ING	1– 5
WANG MANG (Regent)	6– 8
WANG MANG	9– 23

Ascension to the throne usually occurred in the year preceding the official commencement of the reign.

I. HAN HISTORY AND SOCIETY[1]

Storming down from Tibet, arching into a great northward loop around the Ordos, racing south between Shensi and Shansi, the Yellow River finally cuts its way eastward through loess-covered hills to flow sluggishly across its delta, the rich north-China plain, to the sea. The lower basin of the river and the valley of its affluent, the Wei, are the arena of early Chinese history. Screened behind the Tibetan massif, which has deserts to the north and jungles to the south, China stands at the eastern end of the great Eurasian continent, her history the central history of eastern Asia. The deserts and steppes of Mongolia fix northern limits to the spread of China's economy of intensive agriculture. But southward lie no natural barriers, and century after century the Chinese pushed their way and spread their culture from the Yellow River, first to the Yangtze, then slowly southward to the sea.

The southward expansion had only begun in early Han times. The political center of the Former Han empire was in the northwest, where the fertile valleys of the Wei and the Ching rivers served during most of the period as the main economic base. Blest with strong natural defenses, this region "within the pass" was populous, and rich in agricultural and grazing land. Set in the heart of an irrigated, mountain-surrounded plain, Ch'ang-an, the capital, kept its watchful eye upon the strategic eastward passes from the south bank of the Wei. Outside those passes were the regions which had been independent feudal kingdoms only a few decades before the Han dynasty commenced.

DECLINE OF FEUDALISM AND BEGINNING OF EMPIRE

History always begins *in medias res*. The Han dynasty arose from the ruins of the Ch'in empire, which was originally only one of many states into which China was divided along feudal lines. The two centuries prior to the beginning of the Han empire saw a

[1] This chapter is designed as a historical and societal framework for the rest of the book. Much that would be important from some other point of view has been omitted, and only primary historical trends and the essentials of the social system are discussed. In order that a conception of the period may be presented in broad outline and without interruption, the documentation has been placed in a long note at the end. There is no attempt to cover every statement with exact citation, but many assertions made here are more fully developed and better substantiated in later chapters.

revolution in Chinese society. Shortly after 400 B.C. feudal government began to assume a regional quality, presaging empire. One
evidence of this regionalism was the building of great walls which
apparently attempted to define "forever" the maximum areas that
could be ruled by feudal forms: walls not only between China and
the slowly emerging steppe society on the north, but also interior
barriers between the great states, between Wei and Ch'in, Ch'i and
Ch'u, and between Ch'u and the smaller states of the middle Yellow
River Valley. Within the great states a system of administration
was developing which increased state power at the expense of the
various vassal lords. Ch'in dominated the northwest, Ch'i lorded
over a group of small states in the east, while Ch'u controlled most
of the area in the south between the Yellow River and the Yangtze,
and the coastal area northward to Shantung. Disunited, Chao,
Wei, and a different Han, the succession states of the once powerful
Chin in the north, were in danger of being rolled up from the west
by Ch'in. Warfare was changing in both technique and objective.
Mounted archers, trained infantry, and crossbowmen gradually
replaced the clumsy feudal chariots surrounded by poorly armed
serfs, and the objective was no longer to assert leadership among
vassals, but to destroy defeated ruling houses and to absorb defeated
states. Ch'in, the protagonist of this non-feudal way of fighting,
succeeded little by little in consolidating adjacent areas, west, east,
and south, into one ever-expanding empire.

Among the internal reforms of Ch'in, giving it superiority over
all rivals, was its change in the system of land tenure, ascribed to
Shang Yang, to whom in the capacity of Chancellor was intrusted
the rule of Ch'in state. In feudal China the owning of land had
been almost a religious matter, and only nobles could hold it either
in fee or in domain. The actual farmers were serfs working part
of the land for the overlord and part for themselves. Shang Yang,
who is stylized by formal Chinese history as the originator of changes
going forward in many regions, is credited with permitting private
ownership of land by the common people, thereby shattering the
foundations of feudalism and forwarding the subjugation of the
nobility to an absolute monarch. By introducing direct taxation
in kind, Ch'in helped to transform the actual farmers from serfs
to free peasants, who no longer owed their lord stated amounts of
labor, but owed only a tax to the state and perhaps rent to a landlord. For administration and law-enforcement, families were grouped
into fives and tens, the members of which were severally responsible

for the conduct of all the others. By direct taxation, emphasis on agriculture, and encouragement of immigration, Shang Yang endeavored to increase the amount of surplus grain, and thus support a large professional army solely in the service of the state.

Ch'in used its new military machine ruthlessly, encouraged its troops to slaughter defeated enemies, and gave bonuses according to the number of heads taken in battle. At the same time it slowly suppressed its great feudal families, and created a new but honorary aristocracy of fighters and people of wealth. As its old nobility was shorn, or as new territory was conquered, Ch'in established commanderies or prefectures whose officials were directly appointed by the Ch'in king.

During the fourth and third centuries B.C., other states also were altering their political, economic, and social forms. A whole class of "political scientists," men like Shang Yang, traveled from court to court advising on statecraft and war. Ch'in seems to have had the edge on its rivals by an early start and by a more thoroughgoing economic reform which made its base more productive than any of the other great regions, with the possible exception of Ch'u. In war Ch'in had the great advantage of nearly impregnable natural defenses on the south and east, together with control of passes and head-waters leading into the territories of its rivals.

The climax of the last two centuries before Han came during the reign of the First Emperor of the Ch'in dynasty, who ruled (246–210 B.C.) first as King of Ch'in, then as the Emperor of a consolidated China. The breath-taking speed with which he mastered all the rival kingdoms is shown by the following chronology of conquest and annexation: 230 B.C., Han; 228, Chao; 225, Wei; 223, Ch'u; 222, Yen; 221, Ch'i—all of China conquered. Principally on the advice of his great minister, Li Ssu, the First Emperor crushed the old feudalism wherever he found it and established the Chinese imperial system whose main forms endured for two millenniums. He further encouraged private landowning and introduced a standard coinage. He tried to enforce a detailed and harsh criminal code, emphasizing legalism in place of the essentially feudal customary morality. He unified the forms of the written characters, and attempted to remove from circulation the ancient historical literature employed by scholars to oppose his reforms. He established an administrative system using a civil bureaucracy, and divided the country into thirty-six commanderies, laying the basis for the provincial and prefectural system of today.

The Han Dynasty

FIRST PHASE: FOUNDING, CONSOLIDATION, AND RECUPERATION

The First Emperor enjoyed his empire for only a dozen years. After his death in 210 B.C. it burst apart. Rebellion sprang up in southern Honan and spread quickly all over eastern China. It began as a mêlée of regional armies and rival generals, some of whom were members of the old aristocracy, others mere commoners who gave their local revolts the color of legitimacy by sponsoring various royal scions. In this respect the rebellion was a re-assertion of feudalism. But it was also a popular movement arising from the masses. As the rebellion progressed, the aristocracy proved incapable, while commoners fought their way to the top. The capture of the Ch'in capital late in 207 B.C. was the signal for a bitter struggle between Hsiang Yü, descended from famous generals of Ch'u, and Liu Chi, a former village official who turned bandit and then became a rebel leader. This struggle lasted until 202, when Liu Chi finally slew his rival, absorbed his army, and was made Emperor by his nobles and adherents. Thus the Han dynasty began. Liu Chi is known historically by his temple name, Kao-tsu, "the Eminent Founder," or by his posthumous title, Emperor Kao; and the dynasty officially begins in 206 B.C., the first year after the Ch'in dynasty fell.

During nearly seven years of rebellion and civil war, rival armies had crossed and recrossed north China, conscripted troops, besieged towns, burned stores of grain, looted, and fought pitched battles. Disrupting agriculture and trade, they brought on cruel famines which in some areas cut the population in half. Emperor Kao therefore faced the colossal problem of organizing an empire, demobilizing and rewarding his troops, and returning his country to a productive, peace-time basis. Fortunately he had competent advisers for, though he was a good leader of troops and a shrewd politician, he had had no experience in governing. One of his first acts was to claim Shensi for himself and to establish there his capital. Other regions he awarded as kingdoms and marquisates to his best generals and to some of Hsiang Yü's leaders who had surrendered to him. This policy quickly spelled trouble, and Kao-tsu had to devote much of his reign to quelling revolts among seven kings not of the house of Liu. At his death, nine of his sons or relatives occupied kingdoms, while men from his native prefecture held practically all the important government positions.

Thus, while the early years of the dynasty witnessed a return to regionalism, with political administration in several important areas controlled by virtually independent nobles, it was not a return to Chou feudalism. Organization of society and developments in economics, especially land ownerships, prohibited that. In areas not controlled by kings, Kao-tsu set up commanderies and prefectures just as the Ch'in rulers had done. Furthermore, the new nobility was not descended from the old aristocracy, but was composed entirely of members of his own clan and of his followers, some of whom had risen from very humble station. During the course of the next century actual control over the whole country, including the feudal fiefs, was wrested from the nobility and lodged again with the central government.

The first serious threat to Kao-tsu's imperial line came from his Empress *née* Lü, a forceful and scheming woman who had considerably aided Kao-tsu in his conquests. She succeeded in getting her son made Heir-apparent, although he was neither the oldest nor the favorite son of the Emperor. She closely controlled Emperor Hui during his seven years on the throne, and after his death appointed a child for whom she ruled as Regent. When this child died she appointed another, asserted to be a son of Emperor Hui, but in reality from her own clan. Some members of the Lü clan had assisted in Kao-tsu's conquest and had been awarded marquisates. During her regency the Empress ennobled many others from her own clan, even making some of them kings; she placed one of her nephews in charge of the civil government, and another in command of the army. This conspiracy to steal the empire was crushed within six weeks after her death in 180 B.C., when Kao-tsu's relatives and old followers, supported by the army, massacred the entire Lü clan. Yet the fear that a consort family might usurp the throne haunted every ruler thereafter.

Emperor Hui had no living male descendant. The Liu clan therefore selected the oldest living son of Kao-tsu to be the next Emperor. Canonized as Emperor Wen, he gave China a long and model reign. It was under his successor, Emperor Ching, that there arose the second threat to the dynasty: the Rebellion of the Seven States, in 154 B.C. This was a contest between central control and the regional power lodged in a group of kings, all from the house of Liu. Both Emperors Wen and Ching had systematically limited the authority of their kingly relatives whenever a suitable opportunity arose. Thus, when the King of Ch'i died without a son in 164 B.C.,

Emperor Wen divided Ch'i into seven parts, placing one of the King's brothers over each district, thereby automatically weakening that important region. Emperor Ching reduced the territory of Chao, Ch'u, and Chiao-hsi, and planned to do the same with Wu, the richest and strongest of all. But the King of Wu rebelled, and was quickly joined by the Kings of Chao, Ch'u, and four divisions of the former Ch'i. The imperial armies quelled the revolt, but it cost thousands of lives, including those of the seven rebels, whose kingdoms were abolished and made into commanderies. Thereafter, the imperial government methodically reduced the power of the kings by directly appointing for each noble a chancellor who actually governed the fief, and by dividing fiefs among all the sons of a deceased noble, thus finally settling for that dynasty the question of regionalism versus empire.

The first seventy years of the dynasty was a period of rest and recuperation for the people, marred only by the revolts during Kao-tsu's reign, the Rebellion of the Seven States, and sporadic conflict with the Hsiung-nu. Most of the harsh, exacting laws of Ch'in were revoked. Empress Dowager née Lü gave a good administration, and the long, frugal reign of Emperor Wen was a golden period for the common people. In 195 B.C. the basic tax on agricultural products was set at one part in fifteen, a reduction from the Ch'in tithe; in 167 it was entirely abolished, and in 156 it was restored at only half the earlier rate. Emperor Wen insisted on lighter corvée duties for the people; his edicts, and the memorials of such great statesmen as Chia Yi and Ch'ao Ts'o, show real solicitude for the condition of the farmer. Developments in irrigation brought increased yields, while an edict of 163 B.C., stating that the amount of farm land per person was greater than in ancient times, suggests that over-crowding of the land was not yet the problem it later became. Peace and reconstruction brought a general prosperity and an ever-increasing flow of taxes to the government. Ssu-ma Ch'ien pictures economic conditions after the first six decades of peace in glowing terms, and reports treasuries and granaries bursting with unspent revenue.

SECOND PHASE: EXPANSION AND DEPLETION

Emperor Wu's long reign (141–87 B.C.) was a period of foreign wars and territorial expansion, but also of economic depletion and frantic experiment in government finance. Although a map of the Han Empire after Emperor Wu's wars shows nearly all of south

China and even part of northern Annam under Chinese control, this is deceptive. Between 135 and 110 B.C. the imperial armies did conquer the principal coastal states, and even parts of present Yunnan, by costly and sometimes ingenious military campaigns. But these wars were not the central effort, and China was not yet ready to absorb the south into its economic system. It is doubtful whether the government collected there more than enough taxes to support Chinese officials stationed in a few occupied towns. Chinese armies also conquered a fringe of southern Manchuria and northern Korea, but the colonies established there had little importance in the empire's structure or internal economy. The south and northeast were the fringes; the central drama of Emperor Wu's reign was the wars against the Hsiung-nu on the north and northwest.

Contemporary Chinese described the Hsiung-nu as war-like nomads inhabiting the steppes of Mongolia from Manchuria west into Chinese Turkestan. Their whole economy revolved about sheep and cattle, horses and camels, and the search for fresh pasture determined their seasonal migrations. During the Ch'in period they had been welded for the first time into a confederacy of tribes, each with its traditional grazing land, and all acknowledging the suzerainty of one ruler, the *Shan-yü*. Probably not numbering more than a few million, they were nevertheless a formidable enemy, masters of the powerful Asiatic bow, expert horsemen, and highly mobile.

From the beginning of the dynasty, China had been subjected to frequent plundering raids by swift-moving Hsiung-nu cavalry units which penetrated deep into the frontier commanderies, looting, slaughtering, and kidnaping. During Emperor Wen's reign one such band of raiders actually came within sight of the capital. The first wars under the "Martial Emperor" were at least partly punitive, but there must have been other reasons, not all of which are understood. Lattimore has adduced one such cause of conflict, emphasizing the wide marginal terrain supporting a people of mixed Chinese and Hsiung-nu culture who employed a mixed economy neither intensively agricultural nor entirely nomadic. The necessity of holding this border region within the Chinese political orbit, and the pull of this frontier region, led China into vastly expensive campaigns both into the steppe and into the desert.

Emperor Wu was drawn by his early successes into larger and larger campaigns against the Hsiung-nu. Many of his best generals came from the frontier and were adept at border fighting. The

Chinese armies often numbered from fifty to a hundred thousand cavalry with even larger infantry and supply columns. Equipping and provisioning such armies cost the government enormous sums, not to speak of hidden costs in forced labor for transporting provisions and military supplies. Rewards to victorious troops mounted into hundreds of millions of cash. The government furthermore fed and clothed surrendered Huns, on one occasion numbering 40,000, till they could be established in new colonies.

Chinese armies wrested from the Hsiung-nu all the area of what is now southern Suiyuan, eastern Kansu, and Ningsia, within and adjacent to the great northward bend of the Yellow River, and also the lengthy Kansu corridor leading out to the "Western Regions" of Chinese Turkestan. This territory, though not agriculturally important, became a strategic part of the empire, populated, it is said, by more than 700,000 Chinese colonists who were moved there at government expense and mixed with surrendered allies of the Hsiung-nu. Between 129 and 119 B.C. China crushed the armies of the *Shan-yü* in the east, the west, and the center, but conflict still flared up sporadically until 51 B.C. By controlling the Kansu corridor the imperial armies were able to penetrate the Tarim basin, subjugating and loosely attaching various oasis kingdoms to the empire, till China dominated all of Chinese Turkestan politically. Chinese leaders became aware of other nations and other cultures to the west, of India, of Persia, and dimly of the Roman Orient.

This warfare drained the abundant treasury with which the "Martial Emperor" had begun his reign. His advisers were fertile with schemes to replenish the coffers. One attempted method was the creation of eleven ranks of new nobility based on war chest donations ranging from 170,000 to 370,000 cash—the higher the donation the higher the rank. The central government exacted large contributions from the old nobility, and levied property taxes on merchants and speculators. Those who failed to report their total wealth had their fortunes confiscated, while informers were encouraged by the promise of one-half the confiscated property. By this device so many people were impoverished that the government, in addition to getting large amounts of cash, was temporarily embarrassed with less negotiable things, such as land, houses, and slaves. Several novel and sub-standard issues debased the monetary standards of the day, and then, because of a wave of counterfeiting, the central government instituted a monopoly on the coinage of money. Probably the greatest revenue-producing agency, however, was the government monopoly of those indispensable commodities, salt and iron, reinstituted in 119 B.C. after the pattern of the Ch'in dynasty.

The reign of Emperor Wu was a period also of intensive canal building, an activity designed primarily to improve transport of tax grain from regions not adequately tapped. A secondary purpose, but one which became increasingly important as mounting expenses cancelled the gains of better transport facilities, was to increase production in those areas from which the central government could economically collect its thirtieth part of the harvests. The greatest canal-digging enterprise was naturally in Shensi and nearby areas, from which the government could profit immediately. Cutting a canal from Ch'ang-an south of the Wei to meet the Yellow River, for example, greatly reduced the time and difficulty of that stage in the transit up the Wei which brought grain from Honan, Shansi, and regions farther east; but it also irrigated thousands of acres close to the capital. Other canals were dug, with increased production the primary aim. Furthermore, reorganization of the grain transport from the lower Yellow River basin quadrupled the yield from that area. Not till this improvement had made eastern China directly important to the capital did Emperor Wu tackle a twenty-year-old problem of flood control at Ku-tzu on the lower Yellow River.

As the tempo of foreign wars decreased, the various financial schemes and the increasing flow of tax grain began to refill the treasury. Thus, by the closing years of Emperor Wu's long reign, China's political boundaries were roughly staked out. The central government firmly commanded the territory between the Yangtze and the Great Wall, and it controlled by military power other areas which only later were fully absorbed into the Chinese social and economic pattern; but the people were economically exhausted.

THIRD PHASE: GRADUAL ECONOMIC DECLINE

The century from 87 B.C., which covers the reigns of Emperors Chao, Hsüan, Yüan, Ch'eng, Ai, and P'ing, is not easy to generalize. A second period of recuperation, with only sporadic foreign wars, it also developed into an age of great luxury for the upper classes and increasing poverty for the masses, of corruption among rulers and officialdom, and of the labor-pains of peasant revolt. Young Emperor Chao was supported by wise ministers, who noted and tried to ameliorate the suffering of the masses; during his reign the country began to recover from the costs of previous wars. Emperor Hsüan, who had grown up among the people, gave an enlightened rule. His reign was perhaps the zenith of the dynasty, the high point of Chinese diplomatic success, and a period of general economic stability. Early in the reign of his son, Emperor Yüan, the economic balance seems to have turned. This ruler and some of his ministers tried to halt the mounting expenses of government, to reduce the tax-fed bureaucracy, and to lighten the burdens on the people.

But there was a fundamental maladjustment between population and land, which the economic system could not solve. Steady growth in population began to crowd the land, offsetting all gains through reclamation and irrigation, opening of state lands to the poor, slow peopling of new marginal territory, and improvements in farming techniques. Theoretically Chinese farmers had an unlimited frontier southward, but practically this frontier was limited by the need for extensive drainage works, and government projects are not reported south of the Huai River Valley. Farming techniques were still far below what they later became. The use of iron tools and plowing with animal power were apparently not very widespread. As late as about 90 B.C. the government attempted to increase production by teaching selected local officials and outstanding farmers the methods of crop rotation, and by giving them sample tools designed separately for plowing, planting, and harvesting. Spread of this knowledge was apparently slow except near the capital and in northern state-supervised agricultural colonies. Furthermore, an important part of the best-irrigated land passed gradually into the hands of nobles, officials, merchants, and gentry, who owned it for investment and rented it to share-cropping tenants. It was the landlords who benefited most by the low tax on agricultural produce. The "average" peasant, working a smaller plot than his ancestor early in the Han period, or paying half his produce to the town-dwelling landlord, had small reserves against endemic north-China famine. Successive droughts or sudden floods sent swarms of refugees trooping along the highways in search of food and work in unaffected regions. Concurrently the tax-fed bureaucracy grew in numbers, while the nobility, higher officials, and merchants vied with one another in luxury.

This contrast was not the event of a single decade but a trend, already noted by ministers of Emperor Wu, which grew sharper and sharper as the dynasty reached its decline. During the weak reign of Emperor Ch'eng, four popular revolts, each starting with a few scores of desperadoes, rapidly spread to dangerous proportions before they were quelled. They were the storm signals of disaster. A few farsighted ministers tried to persuade Emperors Ch'eng and Ai to enforce sumptuary laws and break up the landed estates. Where only Draconian measures could have sufficed, Emperor Ch'eng relied upon exhortations to his officials, while the ordinances drawn up for Emperor Ai were prevented from becoming law by the objections of his affinal relatives and his favorite, Tung Hsien. The dynasty had reached that stage when the officials and the great landlords were indivisible, when the personal stake of those who administered the government and enjoyed its bounties compelled them to resist any reform that touched the substructure of their wealth.

Tung Hsien is a singular example of that inner circle of imperial favorites and affinal relatives who strove to pile up family fortunes during a precarious heyday of power. During the brief reign of Emperor Ai, Tung Hsien rose from a mere court attendant to the rank of marquis, and held the office of Commander-in-Chief of the armed forces. After Tung Hsien was forced to commit suicide on the death of his imperial paramour, his property was confiscated and sold by the government for four billion three hundred million cash. In about five years he had acquired this fabulous wealth out of imperial grants, presents and bribes from officials, and the salaries and perquisites of office, all compounded by incomes from his investments and estates.

FOURTH PHASE: LAST MINUTE REFORM, AND COLLAPSE

The threat of consort families, first raised against the dynasty by relatives of the Empress *née* Lü, was finally fulfilled by Wang Mang. His father's half-sister was the Empress of Emperor Yüan and mother of Emperor Ch'eng. The Wang family rose to great political heights during the reign of Emperor Ch'eng, but was eclipsed during the reign of Emperor Ai. When the latter died without an heir in 1 B.C., the Grand Empress Dowager *née* Wang reasserted her family's power, and called the most competent man of the family, Wang Mang, to take charge of the government. By skilful manipulation he continually augmented his power, first as Regent, then as "Acting Emperor," until he was strong enough to seize the throne in A.D. 9.

Wang Mang is perhaps the most controversial figure in Chinese history. Some modern writers consider him a farsighted reformer, while the traditional view excoriates him as a political scoundrel who lusted only for personal power. No man is so entirely lofty or so completely base as Wang Mang is variously portrayed. He unquestionably committed a great political crime by overthrowing an imperial house *impermanently*. His "reforms" failed, and his dynasty was swept away by *popular* rebellion. His greatest misfortune, coloring all historical judgment, was to have the succeeding dynasty established by a member of the old Liu house, making it a *continuation* of the Han dynasty. Although his biographer quotes archival materials both favorable and damning, they are interlarded with caustic comments which unconsciously prejudice our judgment. Publicly writing a story of the dynasty Wang Mang overthrew, and writing it during the continuation of that dynasty, the historian could not possibly have given Wang Mang a favorable treatment even had he so desired. But judgment of Wang Mang's political crime must be made, not from the viewpoint of those who supplanted him, but by considering the quality of the last weak and infamous rulers whom he supplanted. Likewise, his "reforms" cannot be fairly judged by how wise or foolish, how humanitarian or avaricious, they now appear. They must be judged against the background of economic and social conditions of his own day. These conditions he neither created nor successfully changed, although some of his reforms temporarily dug at the roots of the problems. Only the holocaust of his downfall, which greatly reduced the population and broke up the landed estates, ameliorated the economic unbalance and gave the house of Han another two centuries of grace.

When Wang Mang assumed the throne in A.D. 9, he issued a remarkable imperial order (translated in document *122*). The introduction explains the reasons for instituting reform. He described how the Ch'in dynasty had made possible the accumulation of both land and offices in the hands of the same people, on the one hand by overtaxing the peasantry, on the other by abolishing the ancient communal land system. Not only did greed for wealth arise from this, but also the strong annexed the fields of the poor to such an extent that they did not even have enough land upon which they "could stand an awl." He also described the evils of slavery, and quoted the *Book of History* to prove that in antiquity only the government possessed slaves, and they were criminals. Admitting that the house of Han had reduced the tax on produce to one-third the Ch'in tithe, he called attention to the corvée service and extra poll-taxes levied on old and weak alike. Worst of all was the "usurious" rental charge, whereby tenants paid five parts in ten when the tax on produce was only one part in thirty. The reforms he proposed were these: All fields were to be nationalized and thereafter called "the King's fields"; private slaves were to be called "private retainers." Neither fields nor slaves could be bought or sold. Furthermore, land was to be equitably distributed. Each family comprising less than eight males but owning more than 102 acres was to distribute its excess land among its clansmen and neighbors. Conversely, those without land were to receive it according to the regulations. Anyone who dared to oppose the new law would be banished to the frontier.

This was fundamental but it was not entirely novel, for elements of the reform had been openly advocated by Confucianists in the reigns of Emperors Wu and Ai. Introduced by executive decree, in an age when free ownership and free sale of land had long been legal, such a sweeping reformation could never have been enforced. To effect it anywhere would require a bloody revolution. From the nobility and the highest officials down to the commoners, innumerable people were punished for refusing to obey, but the plan came to nothing in the end. Wang Mang was persuaded to repeal the law in three years.

In the shadow of this failure all the other measures were mere tinkering. The alteration and debasing of the coinage enriched the treasury but caused great hardship. The "six state controls" included several well-tried monopolies and new types of taxation. The "controls" also attempted to stabilize prices of basic commodities by a novel method, and made loans available to the poor without interest or at low rates. These acts were primarily designed to raise revenue, but some of them did benefit the poor. Even Wang Mang's defamers admit that he worked tirelessly, but he could not enforce his grandiose schemes, which, furthermore, were continually perverted by his officials. Every new law created a host of enemies. Expensive wars and famines produced a rebellion whose seeds had been sprouting long before Wang Mang entered public life.

A rebellious movement called the Red Eyebrows first became active in Shantung about A.D. 18. A little later two pretenders from the house of Liu organized regional revolts. Strife followed the classic pattern. China fell apart into constituent regions all at war with the central authority and each ultimately opposing the other. By A.D. 22 all of eastern and southern China was lost to Wang Mang. Finally one rebelling army captured Shensi, invested the capital, and Wang Mang was killed in October, A.D. 23.

One of the rival pretenders, who had earlier been made Emperor, fixed his capital at Lo-yang, then in the next year moved it to Ch'ang-an.   His two years were anarchy.   The Red Eyebrows devastated eastern China, and several rival emperors established themselves elsewhere.   Then the Red Eyebrows, who had become the worst sort of plunderers, captured Ch'ang-an and took the first pretender captive.   It was their pillage and burning that destroyed the old capital beyond repair.   The city is said to have burned for three months.   It is hard to understand how any of the imperial archives survived, although it is said that some hundreds of cartloads of books were later taken to the new capital at Lo-yang.   The ultimate victor among all the rivals was Liu Hsiu, who is lauded for his humanitarian reign and brilliant victories by the posthumous title "Emperor Kuang-wu."   Although he accepted the throne in A.D. 25, he still had years of warfare ahead, both against the Red Eyebrows and against rival political areas in China.   Not till A.D. 36, when he conquered Szechwan, did he really control all of China, a country that had suffered nearly two decades of brutal civil war.

The census of A.D. 2 lists the population at 59,594,978.   This was two decades before the death of Wang Mang.   The earliest Latter Han census reported 21,007,820.   This was in A.D. 57, almost thirty-five years after the death of Wang Mang, and following two decades of internal peace.   Figures for the Latter Han period rose to more than 49,000,000 in A.D. 140 but never achieved the Former Han total.   While Chinese census figures are always inaccurate in detail, this tremendous drop in the half-century between A.D. 2 and 57 eloquently bespeaks the leeching which relieved the fever if it did not cure the malady of China's ancient agrarian economy.

DISTRIBUTION OF POPULATION, AND URBANIZATION

What was the structure of Chinese government and society during the Former Han dynasty, and in what manner did people live?   The census which recorded a population just under sixty millions shows a distribution very different from that of modern times.   The basin of the Yellow River stands out darkly on a map of population density.   A great black nebula centers between Loyang and Kaifeng, blanketing eastern Honan, southern Hopei, and western Shantung.   West of this area there is a heavy concentration around the capital, near modern Sian, in the irrigated region between the Ching and Wei rivers.   Northeast and southeast of the nebula the distribution is fan-like, covering the northern coastal plain. South of the Yangtze is almost a vacuum, and so too are the northern and western frontiers.

Most of the people were peasant farmers, settled in tiny hamlets and concentrated where wheat, kaoliang and millet could be grown most abundantly. These regions were southern Shensi in the valleys of the Lo, the Ching, and the Wei, and the Honan-Shantung segment of the Yellow River, bordered by southern Shansi and Hopei, and northern Kiangsu and Anhwei. Because Han dynastic history is concerned primarily with the metropolitan upper classes and locates occurrences with reference to administrative centers, it suggests a degree of urbanization which probably did not exist. With a low level of industrial development and a primarily agricultural economy, most "cities" were merely walled towns, focal points for administration, grain-storage, garrisons, services, handicrafts, and market trade, and probably did not have more than ten or twenty thousand residents.

A few important cities there were. Lin-tzu, former capital of Ch'i, in the heart of silk-producing Shantung, bustled with processors and traders of silk. Yen, near Peking, was the emporium for trade in the north. Han-tan in modern Hopei, once capital of the state of Chao, and Yüan near modern Nan yang in Honan, were centers of iron-smelting. The capitals of the commanderies of Pa and Shu, corresponding to Chungking and Chengtu in Szechwan, gathered the trade of the southwest, while Lo-yang maintained a certain importance as an old cultural center. All roads led, like the ribs of a fan, to the capital district, with a population of nearly two and a half millions. But the capital district was not a city; it was a congregation of fifty-seven towns, each with its tributary agricultural terrain, which together composed three commanderies. Ch'ang-an itself claimed a population less than a quarter of a million, and where individual figures exist no other Han metropolis (including surrounding farm land) is credited with more than three hundred thousand souls.

LOCAL AND CENTRAL ADMINISTRATION

The basic geographic unit of government was the prefecture or *hsien*, an area of agricultural land, villages, and towns, whose borders were seldom more than two days' walk from a central walled "city." The lowest extension of empire and the widest expansion of Chinese familism was the point where prefectural government, in the hands of a prefect or chief and his staff, met local government, typified by the *San-lao*, or "Thrice Venerable." Hamlets were often composed of single clans or groups of families, each with its clan or family elder. According to a decimal scheme, perhaps more theoretic than real, ten hamlets made up a commune, or *t'ing*, with a chief in charge of civil and military affairs, and ten *t'ing* composed a district (*hsiang*). Early in his reign the first Han Emperor, who himself had been chief of a *t'ing*, adopted the system of *San-lao*, whereby venerable men of cultivated personality, "able to lead the masses and do good," were selected, one in each district. Among the district *San-lao* one was chosen to serve as consultant for the Prefect and his staff.

Somewhat equivalent to prefectures in function, but more military in nature, were the *tao*, or border marches, primarily inhabited by barbarians. Many prefectures were designated as marquisates or as estate-cities of female nobles, but they were apparently not governed directly by the nobles.

Prefectures, border marches, marquisates, and estate-cities were grouped into commanderies or kingdoms that roughly corresponded in function to modern Chinese provinces, though they were smaller and much less populous. Each commandery was under an administrator in charge of civil affairs, and a military governor. Kingdoms were actually independent of the central government early in the Han period. As the dynasty progressed, however, the kings, all of the house of Liu, were slowly shorn of political power, and their royal bureaucracies were controlled by chancellors appointed by the central government and approximating commandery administrators in function and power. Toward the end of the dynasty, groups of commanderies and kingdoms were loosely joined together into thirteen *chou*, or provinces, but these were not administrative divisions so much as circuits under inspectors who reported to the central government on the administration and activities of officials. The "Treatise on Geography" in the *Ch'ien Han shu* gives population figures for each commandery and kingdom during the reign of Emperor P'ing, and lists all the constituent divisions by name. At the end of the dynasty there were 103 commanderies and kingdoms, 83 and 20 of each. They were made up of 1,314 prefectures and estate-cities, 32 marches, and 241 marquisates.

The government of the empire centered in the capital district around the Emperor at Ch'ang-an. There resided the Chancellor, in charge of civil government, the Grand Marshal and Commander-in-Chief, in charge of military affairs, the Grandee Secretary, who acted as a check upon the Chancellor, and many other high officials. There, too, were the many departments and bureaus that administered state finances, justice, affairs of the nobility and dependent or foreign states, agriculture and commerce, and public lands. There, also, was that part of the government more directly connected with the imperial household, the dynasty as distinguished from the empire. Officials of various departments administered the affairs of the privy purse, the palaces, and the ancestral ceremonies, and cared for the needs of the imperial family. The capital district was a special administrative area, organized by commanderies and prefectures, and having officials and bureaus that were a part of the central government. By the time of Emperor Ai, the bureaucracy numbered some 130,285 officials, counting from junior clerks up through the Chancellor.

CLASS SYSTEM

COMMONERS

In Han times, just as recently, the Chinese "large family," rather than the individual or the marriage group, was the basic unit of society from the Emperor down to the bottom of the social scale.

The structure of society was already complex in Former Han times, but the class system was fairly simple as referred to by contemporary writers. The mass of the people was called "commoners" (*shu-jen*), or "the people" (*min*), being thus differentiated from two higher classes, the officials and the nobility, and two lower groups, convicts and slaves.

Commoners included all the peasantry, as well as artisans, shopkeepers, merchants and the like. They were the governed, who supported the state and enriched the upper classes by their taxes, their corvée labor, and their industry. Taxes of the common people varied greatly during the two and a quarter centuries of the Former Han epoch. They depended also upon occupation and place of residence—whether, for example, on the frontier, in a marquisate, or near the capital. The average adult commoner during most of the dynasty paid a poll-tax of 120 cash annually to the state and 63 cash for the uses of the imperial family, while children were charged 20 and 3 cash per year, respectively. Households in marquisates and kingdoms paid 200 cash to the overlord, but were relieved of the poll-tax and the tax on children. Farmers paid one-thirtieth of their crops; merchants paid double poll-taxes, heavy market dues, and assessments on their capital; artisans paid income taxes. Furthermore, common people were subject to four kinds of forced labor or corvée duty. The most important was labor for the prefectural government on roads, canals, embankments, buildings, and tombs, one month a year. Military duty, frontier duty, and service at the capital were usually commuted by payment of money for a permanent force. These taxes and services were a heavy burden, and supplied considerably more revenue than the government normally required. This made it possible for the Emperor, in his magnanimity, frequently to pass up one or another of the taxes to win the people's gratitude, and also to hand out gifts to widows, the aged, and the poor. Such devices were only a palliative, and thoughtful statesmen regularly urged reduction of the burdens on the people.

Within the broad status group of commoners there were, of course, different economic and professional groups. Among these, merchants and the landed gentry were most important. Because of the peculiarly cellular structure of China's political and economic geography, in which each district or prefecture contained a walled city surrounded by tributary agricultural terrain, each prefecture fed itself and produced in its own trade center most of the goods needed for everyday life. Unification of north China in a single empire, abolition of most trade barriers, and the increasing use of coined money did, however, produce in Han times an inter-regional trade in certain essentials not everywhere produced, particularly salt and iron, and a luxury trade in fine silks, furs, bronze and gold, jade and pearls, lacquer, bamboo, exotic foods and spices, herbs and medicines. Besides merchandising, many fortunes of the Han period were based on mining, smelting, grain-dealing, and money-lending.

The chief evidence of the growth of commerce is contained in memorials of statesmen deploring the fact, and in laws penalizing and disfranchising merchants. The prevalent economic philosophy held merchants to be the enemies of farmers, and trade the natural rival of agriculture. Popular metaphor described farming as the root or trunk, and manufacturing and trade as the end branches of the national economy. Emphasis on agriculture maintained what was fundamental, while trade drew people away from the basic pursuit. Merchants imposed on farmers, fleecing them of their produce at low prices and selling them finished goods at exorbitant rates; they lived luxuriously in towns and cities, while farmers suffered privation and want on their land. This philosophy squared with the fact that a money economy, though not far advanced in Han times, was apparently upsetting the rural economy based on grain, and with the fact that many merchants also dealt in grain. They handled the farmer's surpluses in good years and advanced seed grain and food in bad. Organized, sophisticated, and in touch with crop conditions and prices elsewhere, local dealers had a tremendous advantage over the peasants, and there is little reason to doubt their depressing effect on rural economy, which many Han memorialists described. The government legislated against merchants and encouraged the agricultural class by pious edicts and frequent remission of taxes, because the financial structure of the state was built primarily upon taxes levied on produce. Furthermore, the policy-making bureaucracy came from the landed gentry, and the nobility acquired its principal revenue from taxes paid by the peasants. Thus, any group adversely affecting the taxpaying potential of the farmer imperiled both the state and the ruling class. Merchants were therefore heavily taxed, denied in theory the right to hold office, and above all forbidden to invest in farm land. Indirectly, the government attacked commercial profits by monopolizing salt and iron, experimenting with price-stabilizing granaries, and lending seed and food. The prohibition against merchants owning farm land, though never entirely effective, was crucial because there were no other important forms of capital investment.

Land was the property to own. It brought security, influence, and regular income from tenants who paid—what seems to have been considered excessive—a half share of the harvests. Produce taxes fell lightly on landlords in comparison with their income. Money taxes, so heavy for poor peasants, were minuscule for the well-to-do, and anyone who could afford to pay the fee escaped corvée duty. Landed gentry and local officials naturally clung together. Officials were recruited partly from the landed gentry and when sent to the provinces to govern they found in the local landlords people of their own kind. The most important and most active line of cleavage in Han social structure was not that between the free and the slave, or between the nobleman and the commoner, but that between landlords, officials, and the nobility on the one hand, and small farmers, tenants, and laborers on the other.

THE BUREAUCRACY

Most government positions required a fair knowledge of the written language, and the better civil positions demanded a quoting

familiarity with the classics. To learn the written language and the
contents of ancient books required leisure and security, and these
were made possible by landholding. Several roads led to the lower
and middling offices. People of wealth other than merchants could
buy the honorary ranks, which made them eligible for selection.
High officials were privileged to propose candidates, and they
naturally promoted their relatives or fellow townsmen. Scholars
and men of special ability might recommend themselves by some
clever scheme for government, or be recommended by commandery
or prefectural officials. The government was constantly searching
for local worthies and students, astute interpreters of omens and
portents, military strategists and border fighters, or loyal underlings
who smelled out plots against the throne. For the top positions only
two things counted: special distinction in administration, which
usually meant a long, slow climb, or affinal relationship to the
imperial house.

Salaries of important officials were generous. Men of the highest
brackets received 9,000 cash and 72 *hu* (40 bushels) of grain monthly.
From that figure the scale of payments descended by sixteen stages
to junior clerks, who received only 8 *hu* (4.5 bushels) monthly.
Higher officials and their families had special benefits aside from
salaries, perquisites, and opportunities for graft: the right to introduce
relatives for official position, and freedom from certain taxes.
Families of some officials were exempted from implication in crimes
committed by the official, and others could appeal directly to the
Emperor for leniency, a favor otherwise reserved to members of the
imperial clan.

THE NOBILITY

The aristocracy consisted of a titular nobility of eighteen ranks,
and an enfeoffed nobility of several types. The first spanned the
commoner and official classes. Lower honorary ranks were handed
out rather liberally to officials and deserving plebeians, and all could
be purchased. Imperial edicts celebrating enthronement, appointment of an heir-apparent, selection of an empress, or some auspicious
omen frequently also announced general grants of the first grade to
heads of families or eldest sons. The principal advantage accorded
those of the lower grades was reduction in sentence for crime; men
in the ten higher brackets were exempt from taxes and corvée duty,
and occasionally received money grants from the Emperor. This
titular aristocracy, though appearing to be all-inclusive, probably
comprised collateral descendants of noblemen, scholars, landed

gentry, local worthies, lesser officials, and people of some financial
pretensions. It was, in other words, the upper middle class surrounding the throne and the enfeoffed nobility.

The enfeoffed nobility came from three sources: members of the
imperial family by blood, the most valorous warriors and highest
officials, and members of consort families or imperial favorites.
Normally one son of each emperor was selected heir-apparent and
the rest were appointed vassal kings. Ranking first in the nobility,
they lived in their kingdoms away from the capital, and, during
the early part of the dynasty, were rulers in fact, holding royal
court, collecting taxes, controlling independent armies and civil
administration. After the radical changes instituted by Emperor
Wu, kings no longer ruled, and they only received the taxes from
their fiefs; still, they were very wealthy, for they continued to own
royal lands that brought rich income.

Early in the dynasty, when a king died one son inherited the
kingdom while others received separate marquisates. Emperor Wen
was the first to divide kingdoms among a number of heirs (in this
case brothers), each of whom became a king. Later still, title to the
kingdom was given to only one son, while others received marquisates
carved from the kingdom. The appointment of "marquises who
were sons of kings" paralleled that of vassal kings. Only one son
of such a marquis inherited the title; others continued on the books
of the imperial clan, and had special privileges, but had to make
their own living as landlords or business men. Vassal kings and
marquises who were sons of kings all had the surname Liu.
Daughters of emperors became princesses, receiving estate-cities
and mansions near the capital. The title was not hereditary.
Princesses generally married marquises of other surnames than Liu
and their daughters could marry emperors.

The second branch of the enfeoffed nobility came from generals
who distinguished themselves in foreign or domestic wars, men who
quelled revolts or uncovered plots against the throne, and enemy
leaders who surrendered to China. At the beginning of the dynasty
Kao-tsu and his followers had sworn a solemn oath that none but
members of the imperial family would be made kings, and only men
of valor would be given marquisates. The early marquises were
men who helped Kao-tsu conquer the empire, and throughout the
dynasty a good proportion of all marquises not sons of kings or
members of consort families were military men. On the death of
the title-holder, the marquisate was normally inherited by the

oldest son and thus the noble line continued, though the estate was reduced by an inheritance tax.

Originally the system of sending away from the capital all the male relatives of the Emperor seems to have been to hold important regions loyal to the dynasty, to compensate disappointed candidates for the throne, and to prevent their intriguing at court. The net result, after the vassal kings and their sons had been shorn of administrative power, was that consanguineal relatives of the Emperor, his uncles, brothers, cousins, and nephews, had no part in ruling. The men of the Liu clan being disqualified, most of the high positions at court went to the Emperor's male relatives by marriage. It was men of the consort families who mostly comprised the third branch of the enfeoffed nobility. This phenomenon is one of the most interesting aspects of Han social structure, and it had far-reaching effects on the dynasty.

CONSORT FAMILIES

The ways in which various consort families rose to power differed in detail but appear to have followed a discernible pattern. The Emperor had in his palace many ladies of high rank and innumerable women of lowly status, as did the Heir-apparent also. Ladies were pushed into the seraglio by their powerful families, but lesser women were chosen from all parts of the empire in beauty contests. Some happened to be noticed and summoned by emperors on their travels. As various women bore children, especially sons, their male relatives were rewarded by positions at court. One son had to be chosen as Heir-apparent; it might be the oldest, the brightest, the Emperor's favorite child, or the son of the woman with the most powerful connections. When a boy became Heir-apparent his mother almost automatically became Empress, and then her family started its climb to power.

The first step was usually appointment of her father, and frequently her brothers, to marquisates, often *kuan-nei* marquisates, which were of low grade but had the advantage of estates located near the capital. The Empress's close relatives slowly acquired important positions and succeeded in placing their clansmen in the bureaucracy. As sons of the Emperor by other women grew up they were sent off to kingdoms, which meant that their maternal relatives lost their chief access to court. Not every boy chosen Heir-apparent actually achieved the throne, however; in several cases a new selection was made, and the first boy deposed. Five emperors died without living sons, so that collateral descendants had to be selected, giving great opportunity for intrigue by consort families.

When an Emperor died, the Heir-apparent ascended the throne, his mother was made Empress Dowager, and the new Emperor's maternal grandfather and some of his uncles or cousins were often granted full marquisates and high positions in the government. If the new Emperor was young, his mother and uncles had control over him, and, through him, of the government. If he was already mature, with several wives and sons, the contest for selection of the next Heir-apparent began once more. Several consort families related to the Dowager Empress, the actual Empress, and the wives of the Heir-apparent, might simultaneously hold high positions and intrigue to perpetuate their influence. Empresses were often much younger than their spouses, and several even outlived their sons, thus helping to protect the family power. For example, Emperor Yüan's Empress *née* Wang entered the court in 54 B.C., bore the Heir-apparent's first son (later Emperor Ch'eng) in 51, became Empress in 49, lived through the reigns of Emperors Ch'eng, Ai, and P'ing, and died in A.D. 13 at the age of eighty-four.

Struggles of the consort families darken the inner political history of the dynasty, especially after the reign of Emperor Wen. Yet the system had its good points along with the bad. It constantly brought vigorous new blood into the nobility, and talent to high administrative positions. It prevented any one consort family from gaining enduring or exclusive control over the palace. The families currently in power had their whole stake in supporting the ruler. While for personal advantage they sought to manipulate him through his grandmother, his mother, or his consort, they had to maintain him in power. Few consort families attempted to overturn the dynasty; it was members of the Liu clan who most often revolted, hoping to seize the throne.

On the other hand, the system led to bitter palace intrigues, sometimes culminating in the assassination of imperial sons or favored ladies. Women wielded great power at court and their rivalries embittered the palace. Some imperial sons were purposely debauched to make them pliable weaklings. The worst evil arose from the fact that most consort families could expect no more than two or three generations of power. Therefore they hastily amassed great fortunes and invested in farm land, hoping to give their descendants security—a vain hope, for many a family was tricked into crime, or accused of lèse majesté and stripped of titles and holdings.

Among great names resounding through the dynastic history or echoing among the documents on slavery are many noble relatives of empresses or imperial concubines. Here are only a few: Lü Lu and Lü Ch'an, Tou Kuang-kuo and Tou Ying, T'ien Fen, Li Kuang-li and Li Yen-nien, Wei Ch'ing, Ho Ch'ü-ping and Ho Kuang, Shang-kuan Chieh and Shang-kuan An, Wang Shang, Shih Tan, Chang Fang, Wang Feng and Wang Yin and Wang Shang and Wang Ken, and, greatest of all, Wang Mang.

The catalogue of noblemen in the Han history classes together those from consort families and high official position, and places military men and their like in a section by themselves. Frequently, however, the distinction between these three paths to enfeoffment is dubious, for affinal relatives often proved to be great generals or excellent officials before they became noblemen. Conversely, important military or civil officials frequently succeeded in placing women from their families in the imperial seraglio and thus became relatives of the house of Liu by marriage.

Sizes of estates given to marquises who were sons of kings are not recorded in terms of households. Marquisates of the other two sorts varied greatly in value. Some possessed less than a hundred households, while the greatest numbered twenty thousand. A sampling of one in ten shows 2,600 to be an average. From each household the marquis collected a fee of 200 cash annually.

In terms of purchasing power, noblemen and high officials received princely incomes from their estates, investments, salaries, perquisites, and imperial grants and graft. Vying with each other to imitate the life of the palace, they sometimes had princely mansions with private parks, slaves and servants dressed in fancy silks, and many ladies in their concubines' quarters. Singers and dancers, acrobats and musicians entertained at their banquets. They watched cock-fights and bear-baiting, and raced dogs and horses for sport. Riding out in their handsome carriages, they were escorted by mounted retainers who officiously cleared the highways. Some noblemen patronized scholarship and the arts, while many high officials were men of distinctive culture and learning. China possessed a rich and complex culture, and the upper classes doubtless matched their Western contemporaries in luxury and sophistication.

THE LOWEST SOCIAL CLASSES

In the recognized divisions of Han society people of plebeian status were by far the most numerous. Above them were the officials, numbering a hundred-odd thousand, and the real nobility, never more than a few hundreds, or a few thousands if their families be counted. Below the commoners were two large groups, convicts and slaves.

Though the Han law code no longer exists, and was indeed lost by the sixth century, some of it has been reconstructed from edicts, recorded cases, citations in commentaries, and later codes based upon the great code of the Former Han period. Apparently it was very detailed. Toward the end of the first century of our era more than six hundred listed crimes involved the death sentence, and there was an almost infinite number of ways people could be sentenced to criminal servitude. The Chou and Ch'in punishments of bodily mutilation were theoretically abolished early in the Han period, and thereafter convicts served sentences varying in length from one to five years. Clad in felons' dress, often shackled and with shaven heads, sometimes even tattooed on the face, convicts worked out their terms in frontier guard duty and in building the Great Wall, transporting army provisions, constructing imperial mausoleums, toiling in state mines or government iron bureaus, and in many other ways. Convicts, during sentence, were much like some government slaves, but after the term was completed they were freed and became commoners. The number of convicts controlled by the government at any one time cannot be estimated, but there were always myriads, and on occasions upward of a hundred thousand.

Slaves, both government and private, formed a distinct and recognized class in society; they are the principal subject of this study.

FLUIDITY OF SOCIAL POSITION

Describing Chinese society according to the components recognized in Han times perhaps creates the impression of rigid stratification. This is the opposite of the facts. Not only was the commoner class so broad as to include most of the population, but also fluidity of social position, the negation of a caste system, was a prime characteristic of the times. Individuals and their whole families rose meteorically from the lowest rank to the highest, while others tumbled as precipitously to the bottom of the social scale.

The founding of the dynasty was itself a great upheaval which brought commoners and even convicts to the top and submerged finally the remnants of the feudal aristocracy. Liu Chi, the founder of the Han House, was an uneducated peasant who became a village official and then turned bandit; his principal followers, who later became marquises, were nearly all commoners, many from his native district. During the whole dynasty, but particularly during the reign of Emperor Wu, men of ability rose from the lowliest origins to high official positions and entered the nobility. Many of the biographies of eminent people go back no farther than one generation to trace the family history or point out an illustrious ancestor. This is the more significant in a land where the cult of ancestors was of cardinal importance.

The following biographical vignettes illustrate the ways in which people of lowly background rose without hindrance to the highest positions in government. Chi Yen, a descendant of the old aristocracy, was only an outrider for the Heir-apparent in the reign of Emperor Ching. He climbed through the ranks of the bureaucracy to be Administrator of part of the Capital District. He was a great champion of the common people, and Emperor Wu's most fearless critic. . . . Kung-sun Hung was a swineherd who first studied the classics at the age of forty, took top honors among a group of scholars examined by Emperor Wu, and rose because of his pliability to be Grandee Secretary, then Chancellor and a marquis. . . . A vagabond, Chu-fu Yen, attracted the attention of General Wei Ch'ing about 134 B.C., became a Palace Grandee and was appointed Chancellor of Ch'i to keep his eye on the King. He successfully expounded to Emperor Wu the clever scheme for weakening kingdoms by dividing them among all the royal sons. . . . Jen An was an orphan whose first positions were assistant thief-catcher, chief of a commune, and then *San-lao*. Entering the service of General Wei Ch'ing as a squire he met another squire, T'ien Jen. Both were poor and could not afford to buy the necessary paraphernalia for introduction to court, so the general grudgingly staked them and they distinguished themselves in the imperial audience. Jen An rose to be Inspector of a province, while T'ien Jen, because of his fearless denunciation of incompetent officials, became Assistant to the Chancellor. . . . Pu Shih, a shepherd, became successful enough to contribute liberally to Emperor Wu's war chest. In reward he was made an official and advanced to chancellorship of a kingdom and then to the position of Grandee Secretary. . . . Chu Mai-ch'en, coming from a poor family, cut firewood to support himself while studying. Because of his literary talents he became a Palace Grandee, then Administrator of a commandery in Chekiang. . . . Sang Hung-yang, the son of a shop-keeper, was drafted into the government because of his business acumen and given the job of provisioning Emperor Wu's armies. Later he was that Grandee Secretary who, having helped to establish certain state monopolies, defended the government's economic policies in the great debate of 81 B.C., immortalized in the *Discourses on salt and iron.* . . . Another successful scholar was the poor farm boy K'uang Heng, who indentured himself in order to study. Passing through many official positions, he became Tutor for the Heir-apparent under Emperor Yüan, then Grandee Secretary, Chancellor, and a marquis. . . . Wang Tsun, starting his career as a petty jailer, became a commandery Administrator, Major in the army, Censor, and Chancellor of a kingdom. Demoted to the rank of a commoner, he rose again to become Inspector of Morals in 33 B.C.

All those men, and many others like them, climbed from obscurity mainly by personal ability. To round out the picture, here are longer sketches of two consort families that rose from the humblest origin.

Emperor Wu's first Empress *née* Wei was the daughter of a slave woman in the household of his older sister. At a banquet given by her, the Emperor spotted the girl singing and dancing in a chorus, was infatuated, took her into his palace, and then forgot her for more than a year. Once when he noticed her weeping, he "pitied" her and granted her his "favors." When she conceived, the Emperor summoned her older brother and her younger half-brother, Wei Ch'ing, to serve in the palace. Wei Tzu-fu bore three daughters and finally a son who was chosen Heir-apparent, as a result of which she was made Empress.

By that time Wei Ch'ing had become a general. The next year he received a marquisate, and later saw his three sons ennobled. One of the greatest Han warriors, Wei Ch'ing was surpassed in his own day only by his brilliant nephew, Ho Ch'ü-ping, the natural son of another of Wei Ch'ing's half-sisters. He, too, became a marquis in recognition of his military feats, and introduced to court his half-brother, Ho Kuang.

When Emperor Wu died Ho Kuang was one of the three regents for the minor, Emperor Chao, to whom he married his granddaughter and whose government he dominated. When Emperor Chao died without issue, Ho Kuang engineered the selection of a successor. Then he led the coalition of ministers who petitioned the Empress Dowager (his own granddaughter, age fourteen or fifteen) to depose his unwise selection, and he helped pick the next ruler, Emperor Hsüan. For his services to the state Ho Kuang was richly rewarded, held the chief military position, and was awarded the largest estate of any Han marquis. His son and two grandnephews also became marquises and high officials, yet two years after his death the family was accused of intrigue and the poisoning of an empress and was stamped out.

The second family of humble origin was related to Emperor Hsüan's mother. Wei Tzu-fu's son was Heir-apparent for thirty-seven years, and had a grown son. A retainer of the Heir-apparent, sent to find female entertainers for his patron's household, secured a quintet of singing and dancing girls, among whom was Wang Weng-hsü. The daughter of a simple village couple, she had been taught her trade in the household of the younger son of a marquis, and then sold by him to a merchant. Entering the Heir-apparent's household, she became the favorite of his son, to whom she bore a male child who much later became Emperor Hsüan.

In 91 B.C., when the child was only a few months old, there occurred a palace intrigue in which the Heir-apparent was accused of conspiring to kill Emperor Wu by black magic. The Emperor was sick and away from his capital, so the accusers were able to slay the Heir-apparent and his whole family. Only the infant son of Wang Weng-hsü was rescued by a loyal official and reared as a plebeian in the family of his grandmother, née Shih. After Emperor Chao died without heir in 74 B.C., this forgotten great-grandson of Emperor Wu was raised to the throne at the age of seventeen. It then became essential to discover whether any relatives of the new Emperor's mother were still alive.

After many disappointments, the commission found an old lady, Dame Wang, and her two sons, Wu-ku and Wu, and brought them to the capital in 67. The people of Ch'ang-an roared with laughter when these rustics rode through the gate, but a careful judicial investigation proved that the woman was indeed the Emperor's grandmother, and the two men his uncles. Dame Wang was made a baroness with an estate of 11,000 households, while the men became marquises, each with 6,000. Wu-ku's son rose from that humble background to become Grand Minister of Agriculture and General of Cavalry and Chariots.

Wu's son, Wang Shang, inherited the marquisate in 52 B.C. and steadily advanced to the top position of Chancellor in 29. But Emperor Ch'eng was only his second cousin once removed, and already another Wang clan, related to Emperor Ch'eng's mother, was gaining power. Blaming an eclipse of the sun on Chancellor Wang Shang, and producing arguments to prove that his family wealth and power were so great as to menace the dynasty, the other

Wang family secured his removal from office in 25. After three days he "fell sick, spat blood, and died."

Fall from glory was easier and often quicker than ascent. A characteristic of Han nobility was its impermanence of tenure. Convenient tables which assemble pertinent data about the nobility can be analyzed by rough statistics. Out of approximately 850 persons who were granted titles—vassal kings, marquises who were sons of kings, marquises of military merit and of consort families— the lines of more than a hundred are said specifically to have expired for lack of an heir, and at least as many more end suddenly for reasons no longer known. Lack of an heir can often be accounted for by death of the title-holder before he reached maturity, but since collateral descendants were appointed by imperial favor (and such cases were not included among the hundred) that does not explain the high figure. Such family dissolution is the more surprising in a polygamous society which put great emphasis on progeny. Almost half the titles, over four hundred, were lost because the holder committed some serious crime. Usually demotion was considered punishment enough; in some 230 cases the noblemen were dismissed and became commoners. In 45 cases, however, the guilty noblemen were sentenced to serve terms as convicts, and 99 others were executed, while a few committed suicide to escape that fate. Another 170 are simply said to have been dismissed, without mention of crime.

Impermanence of tenure is most graphically shown by calculations based upon figures given by Wu Ching-ch'ao. The average period for all the nobility was only 2.31 generations. During the lifetime of the appointee or at the time of his death, 41 per cent of all titles were lost; nearly 63 per cent had been lost by the end of the second generation; and 79 per cent no longer existed after the death of the original nobleman's grandson, if he had one. These calculations are, of course, weighted by the fact that all noble lines were terminated during Wang Mang's reign, so that titles granted toward the end of the dynasty had only a brief course. However, not a single direct or collateral descendant of Kao-tsu's original marquises, the men who helped found the dynasty, had noble title by 86 B.C.; and in 62 Emperor Hsüan bemoaned the fact that descendants of this early aristocracy had fallen to the position of indentured laborers.

If fluidity of social position typified the upper classes it also characterized the lower. Members of any societal group might become convicts at one stroke. Slaves were generally recruited from the commoner class, but sometimes from the nobility itself. Conversely, descent to those classes was no bar to becoming a commoner and even a nobleman. Imperial amnesties of convicts were frequent, and theoretically all convicts became commoners within six years. There were several ways in which slaves could achieve freedom, thus becoming commoners automatically. Thus the upper and lower classes were not rigidly fixed, and their members were incessantly absorbed into the great commoner group.

To place this subject in proper perspective one adjusting observation needs to be made. While there were no unsurmountable walls between the social classes, the number of commoners who ever left that class was trifling in proportion to the total group, which itself made up the bulk of the population.

The educated people of the Han period fell heir to a considerable literature of philosophy, classical texts, poetry, history, and romance belonging to the Chou epoch, and important intellectual activities of the age were discovery, investigation, and annotation of the books which had been driven from circulation by the First Ch'in Emperor. Privileged academicians had access to the imperial library where some of this early literature was preserved. Competing private schools expounded various classical texts and developed the concepts of different Chou philosophers. The period also produced an extensive literature of its own, in history, poetry, political philosophy, military science, arts, divination, belles-lettres, and many other branches. Just as the dynasty was nearing its close, Liu Hsiang and his son Hsin made digests of the extant literature and listed some 600 authors whose works numbered 13,000-odd fascicles.

Ssu-ma Ch'ien compiled the first general history of China, bringing the narrative well down into the reign of Emperor Wu. Other men extended Ssu-ma Ch'ien's chronicle, or wrote histories of particular periods and subjects. Then, during the first century, Pan Ku picked up the research of his father and wrote a history of the dynasty just ended. Others treated special subjects relating to the Former Han period, while commentators, living only a century or two after Wang Mang, added bits of data here and there to explain facts and terms already growing obscure. Only a small part of Han literature remains. Some of it contains the information about slavery on which this book is based.

_____

Only those sources which have been employed and found most useful in preparing this introductory chapter, both as to facts and concepts, are here listed by order of subjects.

For decline of feudalism, unification, and the Ch'in empire see Henri Maspero, *La Chine antique*, Paris, 1927, pp. 361–425 (Book IV, The Warring States); J. J. L. Duyvendak, trans., *The book of Lord Shang, a classic of the Chinese school of law*, Probsthain's Oriental Series, vol. 17, London, 1928, pp. 1–65 (introduction), and *passim;* Edouard Chavannes, trans., *Les mémoires historiques de Se-ma Ts'ien*, 5 vols., Paris, 1895–1905 (cited as MH), vols. IV and V *passim* (sections on the hereditary houses after 400 B.C.), and II, pp. 58–246 (on Ch'in after 400, and Ch'in Shih-huang); Owen Lattimore, *Inner Asian frontiers of China*, American Geographical Society, Research Series, No. 21, New York, 1940, pp. 369–443 (on kingdom and empire in ancient China), and *passim;* Derk Bodde, *China's first unifier, a study of the Ch'in dynasty as seen in the life of Li Ssu (280?–208 B.C.)*, Sinica Leidensia, vol. 3, Leiden, 1938.

From the founding of the Han dynasty, the principal source is the *Ch'ien Han shu* [*History of the Former Han dynasty*], by Pan Ku and others (originally titled *Han shu;* later the prefix *Ch'ien* was added to distinguish it from the *Hou Han shu* or *History of the Latter Han dynasty*). The edition used is the imperial Ch'ien-lung edition (1739–46) of the twenty-four dynastic histories, reprinted at Shanghai in 1908 by the Chi ch'eng t'u shu kung ssu, which has been checked with the monumental *Han shu pu-chu* by Wang Hsien-ch'ien, printed in Changsha in 1900. The *Ch'ien Han shu* is abbreviated throughout this book as CHS. *Chüan* ("chapters") are cited by Arabic numerals; parts of *chüan* that are separately paged are cited by capital letters, A, B, C, etc., in sequence; page numbers follow chapter numbers, and are cited by Arabic numerals, with *a* and *b* for recto and verso. (References to the *Shih chi* (SC), *Hou Han shu* (HHS), and other dynastic histories are to the same edition, and the system of notation is identical.) CHS deals with this period, in ch. 1–5 (emperors); 24A, 1a–6b, and B, 1a–3a (economics); 31–52 (important persons); and elsewhere. The first five chapters of CHS, covering the period 209–141 B.C., have been translated by Homer H. Dubs (Baltimore, 1938; hereafter cited as "HFHD, vol. I." Four other volumes are promised). This covers the "first phase" of my historical account, and the introductions by Dubs to separate chapters were exceedingly useful. Parallel information appears in the *Shih chi* by Ssu-ma Ch'ien, translated in MH, vols. II, pp. 246–510 (on Hsiang Yü, Kao-tsu, and other emperors to Wu), and III, pp. 538–544 (economics).

The reign of Emperor Wu, the "second phase," is covered in CHS, 6 (Emperor Wu); 24A, 6b, and B, 3a–8a (economics); 53–63 (important generals, statesmen, and literary figures); most of 94A, 95, and 96 (on foreign states); 97A, 5a–7b; and many other places. On the period in general, see MH, vol. I, introduction, pp. lxii–cviii. On foreign wars see chapter IV, below, and CHS and SC references there cited; also Lattimore, op. cit., pp. 429–510. On the Hsiung-nu particularly, cf. J. J. M. de Groot, *Die Hunnen der vorchristlichen Zeit* (vol. 1 of his *Chinesische Urkunden zur Geschichte Asiens*), Berlin, 1921; A. Wylie, trans., "History of the Heung-noo in their relations with China," *Journal of the Anthropological Institute of Great Britain and Ireland*, vol. 3, 1873, pp. 401–451. On economic conditions, in addition to CHS, 24, cf. MH, vol. III, pp. 544–600, which translates SC, 30. On canal digging see Chi Ch'ao-ting, *Key economic areas in Chinese history*, London, 1936, pp. 80–86; MH, vol. III, pp. 520–537; M. S. Bates, "Problems of rivers and canals under Han Wu Ti (140–87 B.C.)," JAOS, vol. 55, 1935, pp. 303–306.

Third phase, "economic decline": CHS, 7–11 (emperors); 24A, 7a–8a, and B, 8a–b (economics); 68–87 (statesmen); 93, 4b–7a (Tung Hsien); 97A, 7b ff. and all of B (consort families). On population-growth, landlordism, and famines see chapter IX, below, and CHS references there cited. Also, Ch'en Po-yin, *Chung-kuo t'ien chih ts'ung k'ao* [*An investigation of the Chinese land system*], rev. ed., Shanghai, 1936, pp. 51–55 (hereafter cited by translated title); Wan Kwoh-ting, *Chung-kuo t'ien chih shih* (*An agrarian history of China*), vol. I, Nanking, 1933, pp. 82–88 (hereafter cited by its English title); Wan Kwoh-ting, "Liang Han chih chün ch'an yün-tung (The movement for equal land holdings in the Han dynasty)," CLHP, vol. 1, 1931, pp. 1–25 (see pp. 14–16); T'ao Hsi-sheng, *Hsi Han ching-chi shih* [*An economic history of Western Han*], Shanghai, ed. of 1935, *passim*, esp. pp. 43–73 (hereafter cited by translated title). For contemporary Han descriptions of economic conditions see Esson M. Gale, trans., *Discourses on salt and iron, a debate on state control of commerce and industry in ancient China*, chapters I–XIX, translated from the Chinese of Huan K'uan, Sinica Leidensia, vol. 2, Leiden, 1931; and Esson M. Gale, Peter A. Boodberg, and T. C. Lin, trans., "Discourses on salt and iron (*Yen t'ieh lun:* chaps. XX–XXVIII)," JNCBRAS, vol. 65, 1934, pp. 73–110.

Fourth phase: On Wang Mang, CHS, 98 and 99; 24A, 8a–9a, and B, 9a–11b; and many others. CHS, 99, has been translated by Hans O. H. Stange, *Die Monographie über Wang Mang (Ts'ien-Han-shu Kap. 99)*, Abhandlungen für die Kunde des Morgenlandes, vol. XXIII, pt. 3, Leipzig, 1938; see also his *Leben, Persönlichkeit und Werk Wang Mang's dargestellt nach dem 99. Kapitel der Han-Annalen*, Berlin, 1934. I have also read, in manuscript, a forthcoming translation of CHS, 99A, by Clyde Bailey Sargent, *Wang Mang: A translation of the official account of his rise to power as given in the History of the Former Han dynasty*. On details of Wang Mang's reforms, and widely conflicting appraisals, see Hu Shih, "Wang Mang, the socialist emperor of nineteen centuries ago," JNCBRAS, vol. 59, 1928, pp. 218–230; and Homer H. Dubs, "Wang Mang and his economic reforms," TP, vol. 35, 1940, pp. 219–265. The rebellion against Wang Mang and the establishment of the Latter Han are described in CHS, 99C, and HHS, 1A, and 41 ff. See also L. Vieger, trans., *Textes historiques* (Rudiments, vols. 10–11), 2 vols., Ho-chien Fu, 1903–04, vol. 1, pp. 732–770. Population figures for A.D. 2 are in CHS, 28B, 9a; for Latter Han, in HHS, 33, 8a–b. See also Wan Kwoh-ting, "Han i ch'ien jen-k'ou chi t'u-ti li-yung chih i pan (Population and land utilization in China, 1400 B.C.–200 A.D.)," CLHP, vol. 1, 1931, pp. 133–150 (pp. 138–142) (hereafter cited by its English title).

Population distribution: idem, map, p. 142, based upon CHS, 28. Larger cities, Albert Herrmann, *Historical and commercial atlas of China*, Harvard-Yenching Institute, Monograph Series, vol. 1, Cambridge, 1935, pp. 20, 22 and 23; HFHD, vol. I, inset map; see also Map, this volume.

On political divisions: CHS, 28 (for totals, 28B, 8b). Local and central administration, CHS, 19A (abstracted, MH, vol. II, pp. 514–533); HFHD, vol. I, p. 27, footnote 2, and p. 75. Also for any details, *Hsi Han hui yao*, ch. 31–43. (The *Hsi Han hui yao* is a classified compendium of information in CHS, compiled by Hsü T'ien-lin and completed A.D. 1211. Hereafter cited by Chinese title; page references to Commercial Press edition [*Kuo-hsüeh chi-pen ts'ung-shu*], Shanghai, 1935.)

The section on the commoner class draws on many parts of CHS; see references in chapter IX, below. See also Wu Ching-ch'ao, "Hsi Han ti chieh-chi chih-tu (The class system of the Western Han dynasty)," CHHP, vol. 10, 1935, pp. 587–629 (pp. 598–606) (hereafter referred to by English title). He assembles much useful information, as does the *Hsi Han hui yao*, ch. 47 and 52. On the attitude toward merchants see memorials of Chia Yi, Ch'ao Ts'o, and Tung Chung-shu in CHS, 24; and same, *passim*, for government action. Many modern Chinese writers have discussed merchandising and the Han attitude toward it, but T'ao Hsi-sheng, op. cit., has perhaps gone farthest in making it a central theme.

For the bureaucracy, same references as for local and central administration; see also Wu Ching-ch'ao, op. cit., pp. 613–614.

Concerning honorary ranks, cf. MH, vol. II, pp. 527–528; and Wu Ching-ch'ao, op. cit., pp. 614–615. The basic sources on the nobility are CHS, 14–18, which are Tables of noble houses, with important prefaces; see also SC, 17 (MH, vol. III, pp. 86–92). For vassal kings and marquises who were sons of kings cf. also individual biographies in CHS, 38, 44, 47, 53, 63, 80. CHS, 97, assembles important data on individual consort families and gives cross-references to separate biographies of more important ones such as Tou Ying and T'ien Fen (CHS, 52), Li Kuang-li and Li Yen-nien (61, 93), Wei Ch'ing and Ho Ch'ü-ping (55), Ho Kuang (68), Wang Shang and Shih Tan (82), Chang Fang (59), and the relatives of the Empress of Emperor Yüan (98). These are only a few of many important affinal relatives. Sizes of estates were calculated from CHS, 16–18.

References to criminals are widely scattered; see citations to CHS in chapter X, below. On the Han law code, cf. Ch'eng Shu-te, *Chiu ch'ao lü k'ao [An investigation of the legal codes of the nine dynasties (Han through Sui)]*, Commercial Press one volume ed., 2nd ed., Shanghai, 1935 (hereafter cited by Chinese title), introduction; and also references and citations in chapter III, below. On number of crimes involving death sentence see HHS, 76, 4b.

The section on fluidity of social position is more or less original. Biographical vignettes: Chi Yen (CHS, 50), Kung-sun Hung (58), Chu-fu Yen (64A), Jen An and T'ien Jen (my document *39*), Pu Shih (58), Chu Mai-ch'en (64A), Sang Hung-yang (24B, 5a), K'uang Heng (81), Wang Tsun (76). The careers of most of them may also be traced in 19B; there are many others like them. Full abstracts of the CHS accounts of all important persons are to be published by Dr. Dubs in his final volumes of Glossary and Onomasticon. The accounts of the two consort families, Wei and Wang, are based upon material translated and annotated in my documents *26*, *27*, *29*, *70*, *72*; and *55*, *80*, *98*, in which the basic sources are cited. Calculations on loss of noble title are based on CHS, 14–18, while numbers of generations are figured from Wu Ching-ch'ao, op. cit., pp. 612–613. Ssu-ma Ch'ien himself noted the impermanence of noble title when he pointed out that in his own day (specifically the period 104–101 B.C.) descendants of only five of Kao-tsu's original nobles still enjoyed the title. Cf. MH, vol. III, p. 124.

II. HISTORICAL SOURCES, AND DEFINITION OF TERMS

Source material has different degrees of value depending not only upon its nature and authenticity, but also upon the subjects to which it is applied. The subject here considered is a lowly social group in ancient China—slaves—and the essential problems are social and economic. The sources available, on the other hand, were primarily designed to recount the political history of an empire and the activities of the ruling class. This inconsistency between sources and subject fundamentally delimits the investigation. In what respects are the sources inadequate, wherein are they strong, and how do they restrict this study?

Historical Sources

Most of the slavery documents translated in Part II come from the *Ch'ien Han shu* [*History of the Former Han dynasty*] by Pan Ku (and others), who wrote near the end of the first century of our era. Of four principal divisions in the history in its present form, the first or "Imperial Annals" deals in strictly chronological fashion with the official acts of emperors and the political history of the empire from 209 B.C. to A.D. 6. A classificatory principle underlies the second division, or "Tables," each of which contains terse but pertinent facts about members of the various classes of enfeoffed nobility and about the holders of the highest positions in the bureaucracy. Within each Table noble houses are arranged chronologically by date of appointment, and the inheritors of each title are traced through the several generations; appointments to all higher offices are also treated chronologically. These Tables might be made appendices in Occidental history. Chapter 21 begins the third division, containing the ten "Treatises." Each is a general monograph on ritual and music, jurisprudence, economics, astronomy, geography, literature, and so forth, but only the "Treatise on Economics" is important for material on slavery.

The fourth division, the "Memoirs," is in seventy chapters and accounts for half the total work. It is by far the richest division in a history apparently conceived as a narrative of the deeds of great men. Starting with biographies of those who aided and opposed Kao-tsu, it proceeds chronologically to the end of the dynasty. Chapters 88 through 97 (58 through 68 in the division itself) depart from the chronological principle and give first place to classification. Thus, chapters 88 to 93, and 97, bring together important literati,

50

officials who were champions of the people, others excessively
tyrannical, rich business men, wandering redressors of wrong, imperial male favorites, imperial consorts and such of their relatives
as were not granted individual biographies.   Three important
chapters, 94, 95, and 96, give historical accounts of China's relations
with the Hsiung-nu, with the peoples of the southwest, southeast,
and northeast, and with the peoples of the Western Regions, respectively.   Logically following chapter 97, on consorts and their
families, comes the biography of Wang Mang's aunt, Empress of
Emperor Yüan, and her relatives; then the longest and penultimate
chapter, on Wang Mang.   Chapter 100 is the historian's "preface"
and family history.

Because of the book's cyclopaedic character and classificatory
arrangement, facts about any event are widely scattered; for example, to study the campaigns against the Hsiung-nu during Emperor Wu's reign one must read back and forth through the Annals
of the period, the biographies of leading generals and policy-making
statesmen, the "Memoir on the Hsiung-nu," and the "Treatise on
Economics." Scraps of information appear in the Table of those
marquises who acquired titles for military merit, the "Table of
the Bureaucracy," the "Treatise on Geography," and in many
other places.   Indeed it is impossible to be sure of covering a
problem merely by reading through what appear to be relevant
chapters.   Passages dealing directly with slavery were found in
sixty-eight of the hundred chapters, some in the most improbable
places, others in sections having many long and significant items.

Only second to the *Ch'ien Han shu* is the *Shih chi* by Ssu-ma
Ch'ien and his father Ssu-ma T'an, completed some time between
100 and 90 B.C., but containing important additions by Ch'u Shao-
sun and others.   For the first century of Han the two histories are
parallel, each supplementing the other.   Pan Ku was heavily indebted to Ssu-ma Ch'ien for many of his chapters, while conversely
the present text of the *Shih chi* contains sections which appear to
have been copied back into it from the *Ch'ien Han shu* because they
were lost in transmission.   Nearly half the work deals with the pre-
Han epoch, and since its references to slavery for the Han period
are nearly all found in the *Ch'ien Han shu*, only its unique items
have been translated, the rest being taken from Pan Ku's more
comprehensive work, and textual variants noted.

These two works begin the series of twenty-five (or twenty-six)
Standard Histories which together cover all recorded Chinese history

to 1912. The third of the series, the *History of the Latter Han dynasty*, written in major part by Fan Yeh of the fifth century (but based on many earlier works), supplied a few of the documents, translated because they applied to the Former Han period. The work also contained numerous data which have been used for comparison with and illustration of Former Han conditions. Later dynastic histories down to T'ang were also consulted for illustrative material, but they were used cautiously because of the increasing factors of elapsed time and historical change.

During the half century after Wang Mang, Wei Hung composed the *Han chiu i* to record the governmental system of the period just ended. This book contains some of the most revealing items on slavery included among the documents. Another important source was the long and semi-humorous essay by Wang Pao, dated 59 B.C. The *Discourses on salt and iron* or *Yen t'ieh lun*, compiled by Huan K'uan during the reign of Emperor Hsüan (74–49 B.C.), contained one important passage and a number of minor references to slavery. This work is part of the *Han Wei ts'ung-shu* [*Collection of books on the Han and Wei periods*]; other Han texts there included were consulted and used as reference, but very little material on slavery was found that could be included among the reliable documents upon which this study is primarily based.[1]

[1] These are the basic sources. Problems of textual criticism are not in the province of this book. All the works have passed the exacting examination of Chinese scholarship and (save Wang Pao) of Sinological scrutiny. Historical criticism has been attempted in the footnotes to those documents which presented special problems concerning the type of source material on which they were based, probable accuracy of statements made, and evidences of special bias.

For the *Ch'ien Han shu* Dr. Dubs promises to supply in his introductory volume a translation of the historian's "Introductory Memoir," lives of the author and others who worked on the book, a discussion of the texts and their tradition, and a list of important commentators (HFHD, vol. I, p. ix). His introductions and appendices to the five chapters already published contain important historical criticism; see also items in my bibliography under Dubs. On Pan Ku and other members of the Pan family, the plan and sources of the *Ch'ien Han shu*, and a comparison between it and the *Shih chi*, see Lo Tchen-ying, *Les formes et les méthodes historiques en Chine: Une famille d'historiens et son oeuvre*, Paris, 1931. Another valuable work primarily concerned with Pan Ku's sister, who is supposed to have helped with the CHS, is that by Dr. Nancy Lee Swan, *Pan Chao: Foremost woman scholar of China*, New York, 1932. This also has some valuable notes (pp. 158–161) on the composition of the *History of the Latter Han dynasty*. On the *Shih chi* the most authoritative Occidental textual and historical criticism is still that by Chavannes in his introduction to MH, vol. I, which contains chapters on the authors, the age in which they wrote, their sources, their critical method, and the later history of the text. For its precise discussion of Chinese historical method and native textual criticism, as well as for its convenience and wealth of reference, the work of Charles S. Gardner (*Chinese traditional historiography*, Cambridge, 1938) is unsurpassed.

NATURE AND DEFICIENCY OF SOURCES

"The Chinese," Gardner points out, ". . . conceive of the past as a series of concrete events and overt acts; and of history as a registration of them which should be exact and dispassionate, without any projection across the scene of the personality of the registrar, who must punctiliously refrain from garbling his presentation by his own perhaps imperfect appreciation of the true sequence of causation. It is the function of the Chinese historian to collect the facts and to subject them to a process of discreet filtering which may only suppress those of insignificant importance and present those of greater moment to speak for themselves without interference . . . . And accordingly, verbatim reproduction of the records of earlier historians, no matter how extensive, is to be regarded, not as plagiarism, but rather as the natural and reasonable process by which new histories of previously recorded events should be constructed. [Chinese] historical writing ordinarily involves, not original composition of any considerable length, but compilation of choice selections from earlier works." [1]

There is abundant evidence, internal and historical, that the authors of the *History of the Former Han dynasty*, adhering to the methods of Ssu-ma Ch'ien, used as their basic sources both state archives and existing books such as the *Shih chi*, themselves based upon archives. These sources were not employed merely as the foundation for a synthetic account, but many were copied in entirety or in large part. Thus, the *Ch'ien Han shu* is itself a vast storehouse of documents faithfully reproducing the selected originals, except in so far as errors have crept in through centuries of transmission. Embedded in it are imperial edicts and orders, long memorials on economic conditions, formal recommendations on state policy, reports of investigating commissions summarizing testimony of witnesses, records of trials and judicial verdicts, accusations presented by individuals or groups against other officials, intra-bureau communications, records of administrative acts, memoranda on military campaigns, and other data, almost without end. This eclecticism gives the history a high degree of reliability in the fields it was intended by the historian to cover; the difficulty is that slavery was not one of the subjects considered of historical importance.

There are many references to slavery in the copied archives and in other passages whose sources are no longer evident. These references have a fortuitous character; they were included because

---

[1] Gardner, op. cit., pp. 69–70.

they were integral parts of selected documents, or because they happened to be necessary elements of the larger narrative. As they are entirely unsystematic, they leave great gaps in the picture even when assembled and organized. For example, it is mere chance that we know that slaves could purchase their freedom. There would be no evidence of the practice in Former Han histories if one such case had not been mentioned in connection with the trial of a nobleman. Likewise, it is almost by accident that we know of the enslavement of a certain group of noble folk; we know because fourteen years later they were freed by an imperial edict which only happens to be recorded.

Most historians write for their contemporaries rather than for future generations, and accordingly take much common knowledge for granted. Even writing for the future, one cannot predict what parts of his own culture will change so radically as to need explanation. Most references to slavery in the previous dynasty were self-evident when set down; to explain them would have been pedantic. Yet many of them soon became so obscure as to arouse dispute among Chinese commentators only a few centuries later, while today uncertainties of meaning abound.

Two other general weaknesses arise from the nature of the sources. Because mention of slaves is incidental, the slaves appear chiefly in association with important people or events. The "important" people were those connected with the state (noblemen and high officials), or those who by their acts or accomplishments either influenced the course of national events or won some niche in the historian's hall of fame. About the slaves of these people we are comparatively well informed; but about slaves belonging to "unimportant" people, those who were only somewhat wealthy, somewhat successful in business and scholarship, or somewhat important as administrators, there is little information. If the common folk had slaves, virtually nothing is known about them. This lack of information may greatly distort the picture of Han slavery, especially in regard to its extent and economic importance.

In the second place, where slaves happen to be mentioned in matters of state concern there is a conspicuous lack of detail about them; for example, we read an imperial order freeing government slaves, but nothing indicates whether, or to what extent, the order was carried out. Presuming that it was at least partially executed, there is no answer at all to such natural questions as the effect of the order upon the slaves, the mode of establishing them in plebeian life,

the requisite changes in records of bureau property, sorts of manumission papers, and the like. To give another example, there are
numerous references to trials of noblemen who had ordered their
slaves to murder people, or to do other unlawful acts, and in each case
the verdict against the nobleman is reported. Not one of the cases,
however, gives the slightest indication of what happened to the slave.

This is not a weakness of the material on slavery alone; it is a
characteristic of Han history, and perhaps of all formal history.
Throughout the annals of the Former Han period there is an exasper-
ating lack of information on all the intimate details of administration
and economics. When we read of thousands of prisoners captured
in any particular war, we search in vain for clear-cut evidence of
their disposition, of their having been brought into China, or even
for proof of their having been captured. There is no eyewitness
description of prison camps, no account of triumphal processions,
no report by an official who had actually inspected or counted a
batch of captives. Were they merely prisoners on paper? Are
the reports fabrications? Only by devious means can we learn
that they were not. The Former Han history remains a curious
mixture: archives copied *in extenso*, unexpectedly revealing important
facts about administration, law, and society; biographies recounting
the most intimate matters in the lives of the great; and large statements serenely floating in a vacuum.

ADVANTAGES OF SOURCES

This deficiency, in the last analysis, should not be charged against
the histories but against the attempt to use them for an end they
were not designed to fill. Records of administrative routine, filled
with passing references to government slaves, must have accumulated
in piles and mountains in the archives of various bureaus. Clearly,
they were too unimportant to encumber a grand history. Only
archaeology normally reveals such inconsequential details. Already,
for Han China, as for so many other ancient cultures, archaeology
has unearthed a rich written record that fills some of the gaps left
by native historians. Because of climatic conditions and the types
of writing material used, documents of the Han and later periods
have appeared most extensively at the periphery of the ancient
empire, in the dry sands of Chinese Turkestan among ruined watch
towers and settlements along the now desolate sections of the Great
Wall. Mere scraps of inscribed wood and silk, bamboo and paper,
these memoranda from the rubbish heaps reveal in fine detail the

ordinary affairs of life in military encampments. Some documents discovered by Stein and Hedin, translated by Chavannes and Conrady, do mention slaves, but so fragmentarily as to disclose only that slavery existed also along China's northwest frontier at a time roughly corresponding with the Former and Latter Han periods.[1]

In 1930 the Sino-Swedish Scientific Expedition to Northwest China, organized by Dr. Sven Hedin, discovered "more than ten thousand" inscribed wooden slips, reportedly of Han date, near Estingol (Chü-yen) in Ningsia, while later many others were found by the Chinese archaeologist, Huang Wen-pi, in the Lop-nor region already made famous by discoveries at the ancient Chinese military station of Lou-lan. These documents are said to include many references to slavery, and one bit of information on prices has already been published by Lao Kan.[2] Unfortunately the Chü-yen and new Lop-nor documents are still unavailable. They may not in the end prove very enlightening on problems of Han slavery; or they may by lucky chance supply some of those minute and informal details

[1] Aurel Stein, *Serindia, detailed report of explorations in Central Asia and westernmost China*, 5 vols., Oxford, 1921, vol. 2, pp. 722–790; Edouard Chavannes, *Les documents chinois découverts par Aurel Stein dans les sables du Turkestan oriental*, Oxford, 1913 (English translation of introduction in the *New China Review*, vol. 4, 1922, pp. 341–359); August Conrady, *Die chinesischen Handschriften und sonstigen Kleinfunde Sven Hedin's in Lou-lan*, Stockholm, 1920 (Conrady's transcriptions are reprinted and corrected in the *Bulletin of the National Library of Peiping*, vol. 5, No. 4, July–August, 1931, pp. 25–64).

Documents apparently mentioning slaves are the following: Chavannes, p. 81, No. 356; p. 94, No. 422; p. 95, No. 428 (might be of date 39 B.C.); p. 111, No. 508(?); also a Chin dynasty document, p. 167, No. 770. See also Conrady, p. 81, No. 5.1; p. 97, No. 19.6; p. 107, No. 29.6. Conrady's documents are mostly later than Han. In several other of his documents the term "slave" seems to be part of a tribal name, as [Hsiung]-nu, p. 105, No. 27.2; or Shao-nu (of uncertain meaning), p. 104, No. 25.1; p. 111, No. 33.1 (three times).

[2] "Han tai nu-li chih-tu chi lüeh (The system of slavery during the two Han dynasties)," *Academia Sinica, Bulletin of the Institute of History and Philology*, vol. 5, pt. 1, 1935, pp. 1–11 (hereafter cited by its English title), p. 2.

The vicissitudes of these documents after discovery is almost melodramatic. In 1937 the following statement appeared in the June issue of the *Quarterly Bulletin of Chinese Bibliography:* "After several years study, the thousands of manuscripts on wood discovered by the Sino-Swedish Scientific Expedition to the Northwest have been transcribed. The wooden strips are now in Shanghai, where they are being photographed with a view to publication.

"The manuscripts and other objects discovered by the expedition at Lob Nor have been studied by Huan Wen-pi, a member of the Expedition, whose study is ready for the press. It is reported that this study will be published by the Commercial Press, Shanghai." (English ed., vol. 4, No. 1, 1937, p. 66.)

Almost at the moment that *Bulletin* reached America, China was invaded by Japan. During August and September great parts of Shanghai were destroyed, including the Commercial Press. What happened to the "wooden strips *now in Shanghai*"? Had they been preserved for two millenniums only to be burned on

which transmitted historical literature lacks so lamentably. At present the information on slavery in the Former Han period is much less than that for a period of equal length in Greece after the Persian Wars, and only a trifle of that for the contemporary period in Rome.

In spite of their deficiencies the available sources for this study have at least two advantages. In the first place, the fact that so much of the *Shih chi* and *Ch'ien Han shu* consists of archives copied direct and verbatim means that references to slavery in those passages enjoy nearly the independent validity of excavated records. The high standard of integrity shown by Ssu-ma Ch'ien and Pan Ku in their use of sources, together with the fact that matters concerning slavery were generally incidental, minimizes the dangers of original distortion. Errors in transmission cannot be controlled absolutely, but fortunately textual criticism is the Chinese forte.[1] Whereas records were often copied into the histories intact, and whereas bits on slavery are always intact, most of the excavated material is badly mutilated and in part undecipherable. Furthermore, though dates are rare on such material, most of which cannot be identified more precisely than within a century, the archival remnants in the histories can all be closely dated, usually within a year and sometimes even to the day.

This advantage of authenticity only slightly less than that of original records pertains to some 35 per cent of the texts, not counting many others obviously based on archives. When, for example, an

the eve of publication? In September, 1940, another note in the *Bulletin* finally answered these questions:

"In 1937, plans were well under way for their publication, but they were interrupted by the outbreak of the Sino-Japanese hostilities. All the plates were destroyed during the invasion of Shanghai in August, 1937.

"Through the financial assistance of the Board of Trustees of the Indemnity Funds remitted by the British Government, its publication is now assured. During 1938–40 much time has been spent in the difficult task of photographing these records. The work of photographing having been completed, the Commercial Press is commissioned to publish this book on behalf of the Scientific Mission to Northwestern China. The plates alone will occupy over 600 pages and the book will be bound in the traditional Chinese style." (*Quarterly Bulletin of Chinese Bibliography*, English ed., n.s., vol. 1, No. 3, 1940, p. 284.)

No further report on this publication was received up to the time of the outbreak of the war between the United States and Japan. The original Han documents, however, are known to be in safety.

For information on the discoveries at Lop-nor see Folke Bergman (BMFEA, vol. 7, 1935, pp. 76–77) and two items by Huang Wen-pi and Ma Heng cited in his bibliography (p. 143).

[1] See especially Gardner, op. cit., pp. 18–63, and references there cited. In the "Treatise on Economics," CHS, 24A, Pelliot discovered that one hundred characters differed as between a T'ang manuscript copy preserved in Japan and the modern text. Cf. BEFEO, vol. 2, 1902, p. 335 (also my *45*, footnote 4).

official noted for his integrity is commissioned by the Emperor to
investigate a certain suspicious ex-king and sends back a written
report of his personal investigation, and in this quoted report
casually mentions the ex-king's 183 slaves, that item may be considered accurate. It is even more likely to be true because the
investigator's letter of transmission mentions an appended list of
the slaves and an invoice of palace property. Again, one of the longest translated passages is the official report of a judicial commission,
appointed after Emperor Ch'eng died without leaving an heir, to
investigate the previous suspicious deaths of his two imperial sons.
This was a most serious dynastic matter, and the officials cross-
examined all employees of the palace who knew of the details.
Witnesses are mentioned by name and identified by office. Some
of them were slaves, and some of the facts revealed happened to
concern palace slaves and their work. This report, left in its original
form, is the raw material of history, skilfully woven into the chronicle
by a compiler who knew by long habit when to let official documents
speak for themselves.

Nowhere is there any evidence that the historians themselves
were interested in slavery as such. This is the second advantage
of the sources. There is no abolitionist sentiment, no special pleading. Although the historians quote statements which show that some
thinkers in the Han dynasty opposed slavery, the institution was
apparently a matter of indifference to them historically. A subject
of common knowledge (Pan Ku himself was a slave owner), slaves
are mentioned only when entering naturally into the narrative.
Reports are dry and matter of fact, and only occasionally show
evidence of exaggeration. Thus, even in those numerous passages,
particularly among the biographies, where we cannot determine the
original sources, casual references to slaves have an exceptional
reliability.

Method of Using Sources

How can transmitted literature possessing the inadequacies and
advantages described be used most fruitfully in a study of slavery?
To get the best results every reference from the basic texts pertaining
to the period should be scrutinized, no matter how "inconsequential,"
and each should be placed in its historical setting. To counteract
the Chinese categorical method of writing history, each reference
should be dated (as it refers to slavery) and the whole group arranged
chronologically. The result of using all references is a wider and
surprisingly richer corpus than any other assembled; presentation

of background places most of the documents in the setting essential for understanding; strict chronological arrangement has obvious historical advantages, but strangely enough is a unique feature of the present work.[1]

In the matter of analysis as little as possible was taken for granted about the system of Chinese slavery, and the documents, being assembled topically and compared, were allowed to speak for themselves. Analysis itself, however, involves preconceptions; the materials had to be arranged in some manner to disclose logically the "essential" aspects of Former Han slavery. Questions about the nature and function of this slavery demanded formulation and some attempt at solution. Wherever possible, analyses and conclusions were tested in two ways: by comparing the Former Han data with similar data from later periods (particularly that of the adjacent Latter Han); and by studying the conclusions of modern Chinese scholars—conclusions which conflict among themselves but which all arise from a conceptual background somewhat different from that of an Occidental.

The period studied intensively spans two and a quarter centuries, an elapsed time about equal to that between 1710 and 1940. It was approximately concurrent with the last two centuries of the Roman Republic, from the end of the Second Punic War through the founding of the Empire and part of the reign of Tiberius—a period, incidentally, of great development in the system of Roman slavery. In such a span of time great changes in the slavery system seem likely *a priori*. What justification is there, then, for taking items of information from various parts of the period and combining them in a description of slavery in the Former Han era? Does this not presuppose a static rather than an ever-changing situation, and does it not create a purely artificial something which never existed, as described, at any particular moment?[2] What reality would a description of American slave-trading possess if it were synthesized from references dating: 1644 (a biography of a sometime slave), ca. 1646 (a description, in a geographical text, of an African slave port), 1669–72 (the description of slave markets in a speech in Parliament), 1691–1702 (a remark by a slave owner quoted in a physician's memoirs), 1726 (a biography of a slave owner), 1756–62 (the report

[1] In the preparation of this book all discovered references to slaves were used, but about a quarter of them have now been placed in the appendix or used as footnotes of other documents.

[2] No Chinese writer seems to have considered this deficiency in the method universally employed.

of an investigating commission), 1787 (a slave contract), 1839 (an economic report), 1842 (a petition from a bureau chief to the president about the sale of public bondsmen), 1855 (a president's inaugural address condemning the slave trade), 1860 (a presidential executive order forbidding the sale of slaves), supplemented by many other items showing merely that slave-selling was continuous in that period?

Because materials are too scanty for a detailed study decade by decade there is an obligation to try to detect and emphasize all evidences of historical change. Usually, therefore, references to each topic are treated chronologically, but the assumption of continuity is tested by noting whether the phenomena occur throughout later Chinese history, or better, in the dynasty immediately following the Former Han. When information on important topics is entirely lacking or quite inadequate the fact is pointed out. Unfortunately it is necessary to refer to a few of the documents repeatedly and *ad nauseam*.

Actually, the analogy just made between Han China and North America from 1644 to 1860 is unjustified except as a warning. In ancient China changes in society certainly did not occur with anything like the rapidity that has characterized the Occident shortly before and during the Industrial Revolution. Probably social and economic developments were very gradual, and I believe the Former Han period is not too long to treat as a unit for a description of slavery if evidences of development are conscientiously sought out.

PROBLEMS OF DEFINITION

The fundamental problem of semantics remains. What do we mean by "slave"; and is the Chinese meaning of the terms translated as "slave" close enough to our meaning to approach identity? Words usually connote much more than they denote. And even if the Chinese terms translated as "slave" can be shown to possess in fact essentially the same meaning as our word, used precisely, the Chinese conceptual background of their terms must differ radically from our own today, as well as from that of peoples who practiced enslavement at other times and in other parts of the world.

There is an overwhelming variety and dissimilarity in the aspects of that social institution which has been called "slavery," and which has been analyzed and described by ethnologists and historians. These disparities arise from differences in the social organization and economic system of the various societies that practiced it. Assuming that some core of identity does exist among various systems, the task of defining "slave" is so to emphasize the core that the "universal" qualities—the characteristics—will stand out.

The extremes of difference are greatest among various primitive societies that have used the institution, and between slavery at a primitive cultural level and in more complex civilizations. In general, ethnologists have been much more interested than historians in defining the institution. H. J. Nieboer, who has concerned himself primarily with primitive slavery and has given the question of definition very shrewd analysis, first presents a definition of slave in the popular sense of the term as "a man who is the property of another, politically and socially at a lower level than the mass of the people, and performing compulsory labour." This he sharpens to "a man who is the property of another man, and forced to work for him." Finally he concludes that "slavery is the fact that one man is the property or possession of another." [1] Professor W. L. Westermann has given a somewhat similar definition: "Slavery is a system under which some human beings are chattels. Where this fundamental legal and social fact does not exist another relationship between human groups has arisen which is not slavery." [2]

The following dictionary definitions of slave in the specific rather than derivative sense are still not very precise: "One who is the property of, and entirely subject to, another person, whether by capture, purchase, or birth; a servant completely divested of freedom and personal rights." [3] "A person who is the chattel or property of another and is wholly subject to his will; a bond-servant; a serf." [4] "A person held in bondage to another; one held as a chattel; one whose person and services are under the control of another as owner or master; a thrall; a bondsman." In distinguishing between slave and serf: "A slave is the absolute property of his master and may be sold at will." [5]

[1] H. J. Nieboer, *Slavery as an industrial system: Ethnological researches.* 2nd ed., The Hague, 1912, pp. 5–9.

[2] William Linn Westermann, "Athenaeus and the slaves of Athens," *Harvard Studies in Classical Philology,* Special Volume, Cambridge, 1941, p. 452, footnote 2.

[3] [The Oxford English dictionary], *A new English dictionary on historical principles,* vol. IX, pt. 1, Oxford, 1919, p. 182.

[4] *The Century dictionary and cyclopedia,* rev. ed., New York, 1911 (vol. IX), p. 5687.

[5] *Webster's new international dictionary . . . ,* 2nd ed., Springfield, Mass., 1935, p. 2361.

Finally, it might be useful to note a recent definition formulated for international agreement. Article 1 of the Slavery Convention, Geneva, September 25, 1926, states:

"For the purpose of the present convention, the following definitions are agreed upon: (1) Slavery is the status or condition of a person over whom any or all of the powers attaching to the right of ownership are exercised." [1]

Most definitions stress ownership of a human being, but some emphasize control of his services.[2] Ownership, however, is not necessarily vested in an individual, as some of these definitions imply. It may be vested variously in the state, in a group of individuals such as a family or tribe, or in some such organization or corporate body as a guild, lodge, temple, monastery, or stock company. Slaves must be in the category of property, however the society conceives it, and the abstract right to own humans must in some way be validated by that society. The right may be legally codified or simply recognized generally by customary usage. Individual ownership of individual slaves will be authorized in either way depending upon the society involved.

A pragmatic test of true ownership is the legally or socially recognized right of an owner to transfer his slaves to another owner outright, by sale, barter, gift, or in some other way. This right may be shown to exist by concrete evidences of such transfer openly and legally performed. This is a positive test, but it cannot be applied universally because certain societies forbid transfer of certain types of slaves who are otherwise owned as property. The right to destroy (enjoyed in regard to some sorts of property) is not an essential characteristic of slave-owning, being a good example of those attributes of slavery in which cultures vary.

Control of services derives from ownership. It is secondary and less precise. Depending upon the culture involved it may be very

---

[1] *American journal of international law*, vol. 21, Supplement: Official documents, 1927, p. 174. Also *International conciliation*, Documents for the year 1928, No. 236, p. 13. The other definition is of the slave trade.

[2] For example, Edward Westermark (*The origin and development of the moral idea*, 2 vols., London, 1906, vol. 1, pp. 670–671) takes the compulsory nature of the slave's relation to his master to be the chief characteristic. The nearest he comes to a definition is to say: "Slavery is essentially an industrial institution, which implies compulsory labour beyond the limits of family relations. The master has the right to avail himself of the working power of his slave, without previous agreement on the part of the latter." The weakness of this definition is that by emphasizing compulsory labor alone it does not exclude convict, corvée, or other types of forced labor which cannot be classed as slavery if that term is to have precision.

mild or very strict. It involves the right of the owner to regulate
the habits of his slave and to command performance of duties and
separate acts, even against the slave's will, but only within the limits
allowed by law or sanctioned by customary usage. This right to
regulate and command implies the further right of enforcement by
punishment or penalty imposed by the owner, or, for him, by some
agency such as the state. Customary usage or law denies, however,
the right of the owner to order the slave to do what is considered
injurious to other people's property, other members of society, or
society in general. Often the restriction extends also to acts injurious
to the slave, and the right of punishment and penalty may be
confined—but these latter limitations are not essential elements.

A second characteristic is inherent and may be mentioned as the
clue to the distinction between slaves and other groups in each
society. It is the recognition in custom and/or law of a particular
and distinct status for an individual because he is property.[1]

Against the background of this discussion the following definition
of "slave" is offered tentatively: *A slave is a person who is owned
as actual property by another person, group, corporation, or the state,
whose services are therefore controlled, and who is accorded a distinct
status as one of a group so owned and controlled.* From this definition,
that of "slavery" in reference to the individual, follows as: *The
condition of a slave; the fact of being a slave;* and in reference to the
phenomenon: *The fact of slaves existing as a class in the community.*

There remains the second part of the question: Is the Chinese
meaning of the terms translated as "slave" close enough to our
meaning to approach identity? Chinese students of slavery in the
Han period often give lists of the terms which they believe denote
slavery, or rather, which fall within the Chinese expression *nu-li*

---

[1] Certain discriminations, perhaps not adequately covered by this discussion,
may be suggested. The term "serf" is usually distinguished from "slave" by the
fact that a master can require from his serf only legally specified services or
dues, and by the fact that serfs are bound to the land and not to other men,
and cannot be sold away from the land on which they work. Indentured servants or bondsmen are distinguished by a closer definition of control, an agreed
limit to period of service, and usually by restrictions on the right of transfer.
Convicts for life should be distinguished even though they are completely subjugated to the state, unless no distinction in status is made between them and slaves,
or unless they may be transferred outright to another owner. In societies which
conceive or formulate the relationship of parents to children (or of husbands to
wives) as ownership, including right of transfer, the children would not be the
slaves of their parents because the status group "children" is too broad, and
because the status of an individual child would not derive from ownership but
the other way around, ownership deriving from kinship. Other analogous situations can be distinguished by some reflection. See, for example, "Slavery distinguished from similar phenomena" in the article Slavery (Primitive), *Encyclopedia
of religion and ethics*, vol. XI, p. 596. This is based upon Nieboer, op. cit., pp. 9 ff.

chih-tu 奴隸制度.¹ Usually these lists include several terms which do not prove on close inspection to mean "slaves" as opposed to other groups in society; indeed, Chinese writers dispute among themselves which terms are admissible.

There would appear to be two methods of establishing the basic terminology for the Former Han period: one, to consult Chinese dictionaries; the other, to observe the ways in which the terms are used contextually. The first has the disadvantage that the conceptions of dictionary compilers intervene as extra, uncertain factors between the terms and the investigator. Furthermore, various senses are usually explained by use of synonyms which cannot be exactly identical, and which themselves have to be correlated with some imperfect English equivalent. Studying terms contextually, on the other hand, is comparable to the use of a simple algebraic formula in which the value of an unknown factor, x, is determined by its relation to several known factors. Terms suspected of being equivalent to the word "slave" are thus defined by their context. Neither method escapes the inherent uncertainties of translation, but the second involves fewer filtrations and allows us to search out Han period meanings from contemporary texts. Wherever possible, therefore, the second method has been employed.

SLAVE TERMINOLOGY OF THE FORMER HAN PERIOD

NU 奴

Male Slave.—A few contextual evidences of males being sold and becoming *nu*, or of *nu* being sold, are as follows. Before 207 B.C.: "[Luan] Pu was kidnaped by someone and sold as a *nu* at Yen . . . ." (5.)² In 202 B.C.: "Chu Chia recognized him to be Chi Pu. He bought him and put him in a house among the fields. [Then he

---

¹ The distinction is worth making although the expression may merely be a term coined to translate the Occidental concept. I do not know how early it appears in native literature. For examples of such lists see Liang Ch'i-ch'ao ("Chung-kuo nu-li chih-tu (System of slavery in China)," CHHP, vol. 2, 1925, pp. 527–553 [hereafter cited by its English title], pp. 527–528), Ma Fei-pai ("Ch'in Han ching-chi shih tzu liao [Source material on the economic history of Ch'in and Han]," pt. 6, "nu-li chih-tu [The slavery system]," *Shih Huo*, vol. 3, No. 8, March 16, 1936, pp. 385–400 [hereafter cited by its translated title], pp. 585–586), Ma Ch'eng-feng (*Chung-kuo ching-chi shih [An economic history of China]*, 2nd ed., vol. 2, Shanghai, 1939 [hereafter cited by translated title], pp. 246–247). See also Wu Ching-ch'ao, "Hsi Han nu-li chih-tu [The slavery system of the Western Han]," *Shih Huo*, vol. 2, No. 6, Aug. 16, 1935, pp. 264–270 (hereafter cited by translated title), p. 246.

² Hereafter numbers in italics refer to the translated documents numbered consecutively in Part II. In most cases the whole text and the footnotes add considerably to the part cited or quoted.

enjoined his son, saying: 'In the field work be lenient with this *nu;* you must eat together.']" (*8.*) From a contract dated 59 B.C.: "... the gentleman Wang Tzu-yüan, of Tzu-chung, purchases from the lady Yang Hui of An-chih village in Chengtu, the bearded *nu*, Pien-liao, of her husband's household. The fixed sale [price] is fifteen thousand [cash]. The *nu* shall obey orders about all kinds of work and may not argue." (*83.*) From an excavated fragment from Chü-yen, date uncertain: "Two young *nu*, price thirty thousand [cash]; a grown *pei*, price twenty thousand [cash]." [1] These items fulfill the pragmatic test of ownership.

Slave.—Very rarely *nu* seems to have a generic sense of "slave" rather than the specific sense of "male slave." The generic sense is usually supplied by the combination *nu-pei.* One example is from the "Treatise on Jurisprudence," in its description of criminal laws of the Chou period, and is also found in the present *Chou li,* of uncertain date and authorship: "As to *nu*, males went into criminal servitude; females went into pounding dried grain. No one who had noble title, or was seventy, or had not yet lost the milk teeth became a *nu.*" (*1.*)[2]

Other Uses.—Throughout Han texts, *nu* appears as part of the name of the people on China's northern frontier, the Hsiung-*nu*. Sometimes *nu* clearly stands for them. Elsewhere it appears in place names, such as Lu-*nu*, and in the names or appellations of people, such as Chao Po-*nu*, "Chao, the vanquisher of the [Hsiung]-*nu.*" Such uses are, of course, not included in this study. I have found no other uses of *nu* in Han texts. Aside from these there is no evidence that *nu* signifies anything but "male slave" or "slave," actually or figuratively.

PEI 婢

Female Slave.—Date 10–8 B.C.: "[Wang Mang] once privately bought a serving *pei.* Some of his cousins heard rumors of it.

---

[1] Cited by Lao Kan, op. cit., p. 2.

[2] The *Shuo wen chieh tzu,* the great etymological dictionary presented to the throne in A.D. 121, in its definition of *nu*, says, "*Nu-pei* were all criminals in antiquity (... 皆古之辠人)," and then quotes this citation from the *Chou li.* Among the various editions of the *Shuo wen* assembled in the *Shuo wen chieh tzu ku lin,* the most important for information on the term *nu* (pp. 5554–56) is that cited in abbreviation as 義證 (the *Shuo wen chieh tzu i cheng*), which has nineteen double columns of quotations from early dictionaries, histories, and encyclopaedias, including some passages quoted above. It is a mine of lore from the *Chi chiu p'ien, Feng ssu t'ung, Ch'u hsüeh chi,* and other early works, and is recommended as an example of the definitions of key slavery terms in the numerous Chinese encyclopaedias.

[Wang] Mang thereupon said: 'The General of the Rear, Chu Tzu-yüan, has no sons . . . and so I bought her for him.' He immediately presented the *pei* to [Chu] Tzu-yüan." (*108.*) 3 B.C.: ". . . the Empress Dowager [*neé*] Fu sent an internuncio to buy *pei* from various government bureaus, taking them at a low price; and she also took eight *pei* from the Bureau of the Chief of the Palace Guard. [Mu-chiang] Luṅg memorialized, saying: 'The price is too low. Please readjust it.' " (*116.*)   Earlier evidences of sale are given below.

Other Uses.—There are no uses of *pei* in place names, personal names, or tribal names so far as I have discovered.   Prior to Han times the term *pei* was also used figuratively by women in speaking of themselves, but this has not been noted in texts referring to the Former Han period.

NU-PEI

Male and Female Slaves.—References to the compound term are numerous; herewith are only a few dealing with sale.   In 202 B.C., an edict of Emperor Kao: "Those common people who because of famine have sold themselves to be people's *nu-pei* are all to be freed and become commoners." (*9.*)   Ca. 120 B.C.: "[Ho] Ch'ü-ping liberally bought fields, houses, and *nu-pei* for [Ho] Chung-ju, and then left." (*42.*)   Because of a law proposed in 7 B.C. to limit the amount of farm land and *nu-pei* that might be owned by people in various classes "the price of fields, residences, and *nu-pei* depreciated." (*109.*)   Quoting the inaugural edict of Wang Mang, A.D. 9: "Furthermore, [the Ch'in dynasty] established markets for *nu-pei* [putting humans into] the same pens with cattle and horses." Wang Mang proclaimed that neither land nor *nu-pei* could be bought or sold.   As a result, "the people went so far as to weep in the markets and highways.   Moreover, those who were tried for selling and buying fields, residences, and *nu-pei* . . . were innumerable." (*122.*)

Slaves.—There are no cases where a male is called a *pei* and only the one case quoted above (*1*) where females are called *nu*, in the generic sense.   Wherever sex is shown males are *nu*, females *pei*. Therefore the term *nu-pei* is usually translated "male and female slaves."   However, it probably has the generic meaning "slaves" in many instances where the reference is general.

The legal and customary status of *nu*, *pei*, and *nu-pei* is an involved problem dealt with in considerable detail later in this work.

T'UNG 僮 or 童[1]

Youths.—This term is frequently used in the sense of "slave," but also merely in the sense of "child," especially "young boy." Therefore, it is always translated "youth," though usually it is considered to mean "slave" in the passages accepted. It has the generic sense of slaves, both male and female, and also a specific sense, male, and sometimes, female. Ca. 200 B.C.: "Some of the people of Pa and Shu went out clandestinely for trade, taking their horses from Tse, *t'ung* and yaks from P'o; and because of this [trade] the people of Pa and Shu became prosperous and wealthy." (*10.*) 177–174 B.C.: "Nowadays people who sell *t'ung* dress them up in embroidered clothes and silken shoes with the edges all embellished, and put them into pens." (*16.*) 113 B.C.: "With many attendants [she intends] to go to Ch'ang-an [where they] will be made captives and sold to become *t'ung-nu*...." (*50.*) Wang Pao's essay on the purchase of a *nu*, dated 59 B.C. and using *nu* several times, is entitled "The Contract for a *T'ung.*" (*83.*) Meng K'ang, who lived ca. A.D. 180–260, says, "*T'ung* are *nu-pei.*" (*53*, footnote 5.)

Youth (male).—When Chi Pu was disguised as a slave he was sent to be sold with several tens of household *t'ung*, who were probably males also (*8*). Likewise *t'ung* used as cavalry escorts were probably males (*81, 112*), this being a regular function of *nu*, as described in chapter VIII, below. When the expression "youth horsemen" arises, Yen Shih-ku, A.D. 581–645, explains it as "*t'ung-nu* horsemen" (*112*, footnote 7); again, "[They] made cavalry men of their *t'ung-nu.*" (*81*, footnote 2.) Used thus in conjunction with *nu*, the term may be adjectival, or merely a compound. Shih Tan's wealth and extravagance during the period 33–15 B.C. are described: "... and *t'ung-nu* numbered by the hundred." (*97.*) The extravagance of Wang Mang's uncles is similarly noted: "In their women's quarters each had several tens of concubines, and their *t'ung-nu* were numbered by the thousand or hundred." (*99.*)[2]

---

[1] The second form seems to be the original, and prior to Han times some distinction was made. In extant literature of the period the forms are used interchangeably. The first occurs in fourteen of the translated documents, the second in six; in documents *2, 49,* and *53*, CHS uses the second while the equivalent SC passage uses the first. The *Shuo wen* makes only the second form correct in this sense. See footnote 2.

[2] The *Shuo wen* (op. cit., pp. 1111–12), defining *t'ung* in the second form (above), says: "Males who had undergone criminal punishment were called *nu*, *nu* were called *t'ung*, females were called *ch'ieh* 男有辜曰奴奴曰童女曰妾." Some commentators correct this: "Males who had undergone criminal punishment and become *nu* were called *t'ung* 男有罪為...." I have not found any Former Han dynasty cases of *t'ung* specified as government slaves because of crime.

Youth (female).—Wei Ch'ing's mother was a *t'ung*, and Yen Shih-ku says, "The word *t'ung* is a general term for *pei*-concubines." (*26*, and footnote 5.)   Wang Mang's wife dressed so simply that other women calling on her mother-in-law, in 8 B.C., thought she was a *t'ung* or a servant (*A17*).

TSANG 臧 and HUO 獲

These terms have a variety of meanings, even in reference to slavery, and are not translated.   The first more often refers to males and the second to females, but the terms can be a compound referring to males, or to slaves generically.   The terms appear in only one document which assembles the various definitions (*11*, and footnotes).   Meanings are here listed without attempt to unravel their interrelationships.

(1) In southern and eastern China (of the Former Han period or earlier) "when cursing a *nu*, one says '*tsang*'; when cursing a *pei*, one says '*huo*.' "

(2) In the northeast, "all plebeian males who mate with *pei* are called *tsang*; [plebeian] females who become wives of *nu* are called *huo*."   This use may not mean slave; the status of the plebeians is not made clear.

(3) Runaway *nu* are called *tsang*; runaway *pei* are called *huo*. The author of the *Fang yen* then summarizes by saying: "They are all abusive terms of diverse regions for cursing *nu-pei*."

(4) Chin Shao (fl. ca. A.D. 275) is quoted as having said: "*Tsang-huo* are those defeated enemy who have been captured and made *nu-li*."

(5) Wei Shao (A.D. 204–273) is quoted as having said: "When a good man takes a *pei* as wife and she bears a child, [the child] is called a *huo*; when a *nu* takes a good woman as wife and she bears a child, [the child] is called a *tsang*."   This reverses the terminology for plebeians given in (2), but follows the sense of (1) and (3) that *nu* (here child of a *nu*) is a *tsang*, and *pei* (here child of a *pei*) is a *huo*.

(6) Finally the *Feng su t'ung i*, supposedly by Ying Shao (ca. A.D. 140–206), is quoted as having said: "In the ancient institutes there were originally no *nu-pei*, and then those who committed offenses were the origin of it.   *Tsang-che* are those who have undergone the punishment of *tsang*, being seized and becoming government *nu* [a variant here has a *nu-pei*].   *Huo-che* are runaways who

have been recaptured and become *pei* [variant, *nu-pei*]." The second part of this is a repetition of the second part of (3).

Several terms are used to refer to special kinds of *nu* or *pei*, but they do not occur frequently in the basic texts. Definition of these comes, in the main, from direct statements by writers of the Latter Han period, or from commentators, rather than from contextual evidence.

TS'ANG-T'OU 蒼頭

"Green-head."—Wei Hung, who was active between A.D. 25 and 57, and who wrote the *Han chiu i*, on governmental practices during the Former Han epoch, says: "Government *nu* were selected to give [service] as writers and accountants. Those of [the rank of] Attaché and below were *ts'ang-t'ou*, [wearing] blue-green turbans." (*92.*) A memorial dated ca. 3 B.C. says: "That *ts'ang-t'ou* and *lu-erh* should all be employed [as officials] and become rich, is not Heaven's intention." (*118.*) On this, Meng K'ang remarks: ". . . [people of the] Han period named *nu*, '*ts'ang-t'ou*,' not pure black, in order to differentiate them from good people." The term was also applied to private slaves, as indicated by the report that when Ho Yün, grandnephew of Ho Kuang, should have been attending court he preferred "sending a *ts'ang-t'ou nu* up to court to pay the visit [in his stead]." (*72.*)

The term *ts'ang-t'ou* was used shortly before Han times to designate members of private armies who wore green kerchiefs or turbans around their heads. During Latter Han times it was apparently used quite specifically for male slaves.

LU-ERH 盧兒

"Hut-dweller."—This term is met infrequently, and, like *ts'ang-t'ou*, is a sort of sobriquet. *Lu* were the houses for servants and minor attendants in the imperial palace. In the commentary just cited, Meng K'ang adds: "The place where all those who served in the halls [of a palace or residency] lived was a 'hut' (*lu*). *Ts'ang-t'ou* who were serving attendants were therefore called *lu-erh*." (*118,* footnote 4.)

KUNG-JEN 宮人

Palace-women.—Wei Hung twice speaks of *kung-jen* as a type of *pei*. "*Kung-jen* were selected from among palace *pei* in their eighth year or over. They waited upon [ladies of the palace from] the Empress on down." (*91.*) Also, "In the Inner Apartments [of the palace], Maidservants and Orderlies were all government *pei* selected in their eighth year or over. They dressed in green and were called *kung-jen*." (*92*.) Chao Fei-yen, the Empress of Emperor Ch'eng, "was originally a *kung-jen* of Ch'ang-an." Yen Shih-ku remarks about her, "Originally a *kung-jen*, she was presented to the household of the Princess of Yang-a. '*Kung-jen*' was the name for government *pei* who were servants in the forbidden parts of the palaces." (*101*, and footnote 3.) However, *kung-jen* were not exclusively slaves, and there is one reference, dated 113 B.C., to a *kung-jen* in a king's palace, who was a man. This was Luan Ta, the magician (*91*, footnote 1).

There is a group of words regularly used to modify the terms *nu*, *pei*, *t'ung*, and sometimes *nu-pei*. *Kuan* 官, "government"; *ssu* 私, "private"; *kung* 宮, "palace"; *chia* 家, "household" or "family"; *ta* 大, "senior" or "elder"; *ch'i* 騎, "cavalry"; *ts'ung* 從, "attendant"; *shih* 侍, "serving"; *yü* 御, "personal"; *fu* 傅, "chamberlain"; *t'u* 徒, "convict."

A few of these terms occasionally stand alone, in combination, or with suffixes, in place of the terms they regularly modify.

SHIH 侍

Serving.—*Shih* is used to modify *pei* in documents *79*, *82*, *108*, and *A20*, the last dated about A.D. 9. Yüan Ang's Attendant Secretary, some time between 165 and 157 B.C., "had secret relations with [Yüan] Ang's *shih*-child." Yüan Ang "then presented him with the *shih-che*." After the first reference the commentator Wen Ying (fl. ca. A.D. 196–220) says definitely that she was a *pei* (*23*, and footnote 3). Some time between 164 and 154 B.C. a King summoned a physician to examine "all his girls and *shih-che*." The King said, "... I bought them in the common people's [market] place." Because the King did not believe the diagnosis of one girl's condition, "he did not sell her at the [market] place for nobles." (*21*.) About 142 B.C. Wei Ch'ing's sister, the daughter of a household *t'ung*, was a *shih-che* in the same household (*29*).

The following account equates *shih-che* with *yü-che* and *yü-pei* contextually. (The latter terms are discussed next.) About 125 B.C. the Queen of Heng-shan "had a *shih-che*, a fine dancer, to whom the King had granted his favors." She arranged for her step-son, named Hsiao, to have relations with the girl, and his brother told the King, "Hsiao had relations with the King's *yü-che* ...." Later, "Hsiao was tried for having had relations with the King's *yü-pei*," and was executed (*37*).

YÜ 御

Personal.—*Yü* modifies *pei* in documents *37*, *48*, and *85*. In 82 B.C. Shang-kuan An, when drunk, would "have incestuous relations with his stepmother and various of his father's Ladies and *shih-yü.*" Yen Shih-ku here makes the important statement, "The *shih-yü* were at the same time *pei.*" (*59*, and footnote 3.) In 115 B.C. a marquis "was tried for having had relations with his father's *yü-pei*, and killed himself." The terse account of this trial in the Table of Marquises, CHS, 16, 3a, uses exactly the same words, but drops the one word *pei*, as though it were unessential; it appears, however, in the equivalent SC, 18, 3b (*48*, and footnote 2).

FU 傅

Chamberlain.—*Fu* occurs as a modifier of *pei* in documents *76* and *120*, and much more frequently in the *History of the Latter Han dynasty*. Yen Shih-ku explains the term by saying, "Whenever it says *fu-pei* it means [one who] assists with the affairs of [her master's] clothes and bed." (*120*, footnote 2.) In only one instance has the term been found standing alone—in the quoted accusation that Wang Shang had "had intercourse with his father's *fu.*" There Yen Shih-ku says "*fu* means *fu-pei.*" (*98*, and footnote 5.)

Instances in which these modifying terms stand alone, with suffixes, or in combination, in place of the word they modify are relatively rare. There is no way of telling contextually that they always mean slave. Therefore a few indeterminate references which add nothing to the body of information are not included among the documents in Part II.

T'U 徒

Convict.—In several documents *t'u* precedes *nu* or *nu-pei* in such a way that it might be a modifier. *T'u* occurs innumerable times by itself. Several Chinese writers include it among component terms for their studies of Chinese (or Han period) slavery, while others use it without special comment. There appears to be no contextual evidence for the Former Han period that *t'u* were sold, bartered, given away, or in any other way transferred in a manner that would fulfill the pragmatic test of ownership. While *t'u* were indeed subjugated to the full extent of the word, there seems to have been a distinction in status between *t'u*, on the one hand, and *nu*, *pei*, or *t'ung*, on the other. This, however, is an involved subject, best treated in its appropriate place in the next chapter.

III. ENSLAVEMENT

When the Former Han period was at the height of its luxury there were several hundred thousands to perhaps a million real slaves in China. Many of them passed in various ways from freedom into bondage. What were the methods by which free people became slaves? Which led to government slavery and which to private?

Free people were enslaved for crime, sold because of economic distress, forced into bondage illegally, and imported from foreign regions for sale. Some prisoners of war were perhaps enslaved, but this is a complex question reserved for special discussion in the next chapter. Crime led always to government slavery, while economic distress and illegal bondage produced private slaves by the first sale. Both the government and private individuals acquired imported slaves.

ENSLAVEMENT OF CRIMINALS AND THEIR FAMILIES

Enslavement of criminals and the families of men executed for treason and rebellion has a long history as a typical Chinese mode of punishment. Many writers of the Han period state that this form of punishment was in use during late Chou and Ch'in times. The famous scholar and legal authority Cheng Hsüan (A.D. 127–200) explains in his commentary to the *Chou-li* that in ancient times males and females drawn into trial (i.e. related to people tried) were seized[1] by the government as slaves; also, that contemporary male and female slaves were the descendants of, or the same as criminals of antiquity. His contemporary, Kao Yu, remarked in a commentary to the Ch'in dynasty book, the *Lü shih ch'un ch'iu*, that fathers and older brothers of criminals were tried and seized as slaves. The great dictionary *Shuo wen*, produced around A.D. 121, says that males who underwent criminal punishment were called male slaves (*nu*), while females who underwent criminal punishment were called female slaves (*pei*).[2]

[1] The term 没入, literally "submerged into," is hereafter translated as "confiscated" when it refers to property, and as "seized" or "seized and enslaved" when it refers to people previously free.

[2] There are several other similar references but these most definitely refer to pre-Han conditions, and illustrate the point that Han scholars believed criminals or members of their families were enslaved in pre-Han times. These commentators were men of real scholarship, having access to sources now lost, conversant with customs and laws which developed out of earlier ones, and using a language in

From the end of the Han period until late into Ch'ing times laws specified enslavement as punishment for families of people guilty of crimes classed as treason and rebellion. Legal codes changed, the classes of crimes subject to this form of punishment varied, and occasional attempts to abrogate the system occurred. Perhaps it is impossible to prove for every period that such laws were enforced, but the principle remained a basic feature of Chinese law during most of its recorded history.[1]

A basic social and philosophic principle of family unity and mutual responsibility underlay this practice of enslaving a major criminal's relatives: the whole family was considered responsible for the acts of one of its members. The Chinese family was much larger than the simple marriage group of husband, wife, and children, and therefore it is hard to tell how many living generations and what degrees of relationship comprised the legally responsible family in each criminal situation. The gravity of the offense determined the number of family members and the classes of relatives held responsible.

which legal terminology was still fairly close to that of late Chou and Ch'in times. In the works which they studied certain passages appear to refer to enslavement of criminals, but contextual evidence alone does not prove that they do. Since it is necessary anyway to fall back upon the explanations of the commentators, it is more objective to quote what they said than to try independently to interpret ambiguous passages in works bristling with textual and historical problems.

The above quotations and others like them are conveniently assembled in Ch'eng Shu-te, *Chiu ch'ao lü k'ao* (Han lü k'ao, ch. 3), pp. 81–82. Cf. also Shen Chia-pen, *Li-tai hsing-fa k'ao* [*An investigation into the history of the laws and punishments*], "Fen k'ao," ch. 15, 3a–5b (hereafter cited by Chinese title); and *Yüan chien lei han*, ch. 258 (Jen pu, ch. 17), 2a–b, and 16a.

[1] For citations of the law, modifications of it, or examples of its practice during the period between Han and T'ang, cf. Ch'eng Shu-te, op. cit., pp. 239, 246, 271, 294, 305, 369, 406, 438, 471, and 520. For a discussion of the continuity of the law during T'ang and later periods, cf. Wang Shih-chieh, "Chung-kuo nu-pei chih-tu [The Chinese slavery system]," *She-hui k'e-hsüeh chi-kan (Social Science Quarterly)*, vol. 3, 1925, pp. 303–328 (see pp. 307–308) (hereafter cited by translated title. This article has been translated by Toni Pippon, "Beitrag zum Chinesischen Sklavensystem," *Mitteilungen der Deutschen Gesellschaft für Natur- und Völkerkunde Ostasiens*, Bd. 29, Teil B, Tokyo, 1936, pp. 93–113).

The law on enslavement in the *T'ang lü su i*, ch. 17, section on thieving and robbery, may be translated as follows: "Those plotting rebellion or major crimes shall all be beheaded. Fathers, and sons over sixteen years old, shall be strangled. [Sons] fifteen years old or younger, mothers, daughters, wives, concubines, sons' wives and concubines, grandfathers, grandsons, older and younger brothers, older and younger sisters, and such others as *pu ch'ü* [shall be enslaved], and property, fields, and houses shall be confiscated by the government. Men over eighty or incurably sick, women over sixty or incurably sick, shall all be excused." (Cf. Pippon, p. 100.)

The *T'ang lü su i* is the earliest extant Chinese law code (or, more precisely, a commentary on a code now lost) and dates from A.D. 653–654 (cf. Paul Pelliot, "Notes de bibliography chinois II: Le droit chinois," BEFEO, vol. 9, 1909, pp. 123–152 [see pp. 124–125] and Jean Escarra: *Le droit chinois*, pp. 96–97). Various

Some crimes, for example, were punished by executing three sets of relatives. Commentators disagree in their explanations of "the three sets of relatives." Chang Yen of the third century says that they were the criminal's parents, brothers, wife, and children. Ju Shun (fl. ca. 189–265) says that they were the members of his father's clan, mother's clan, and wife's clan. Other suggestions give his father, sons, and grandsons; or his father and father's brothers (including male cousins?), his own brothers (including male cousins?), and his sons and their brothers (i.e., cousins).[1]

Theoretically this punishment was abolished by an imperial edict of the Dowager Empress neé Lü in 187 B.C., yet in 164 B.C. when Hsin-yüan P'ing plotted rebellion he was exterminated, together with his three sets of relatives. Again in 104 B.C. the relatives of Wang Wen-shu were tried and executed, probably to the *five* degrees of relationship.[2]

It is not unusual to read that a punishment was abolished and then to learn that it was practiced only a short time later. Emperor Wen abrogated all statutes and orders for arresting wives and children of criminals and punishing them also. Yet an apparently contradictory event occurred under his successor some twenty-five years later, when Chi K'uei-yüeh conspired to revolt and kill his father, Chi T'ung-chia. This was pronounced to be "treason and inhumanity." Ju Shun says that according to the Code in cases of "treason and inhumanity" the father, mother, wife, children, brothers, and sisters of the criminal should all be publicly executed. In spite of Emperor Wen's abrogation, Emperor Ching especially pardoned the father, together with his wife and children, "*who should have been condemned with him*," and ordered that Chi K'uei-yüeh, together with his wife and children, should be sentenced "according to the law." [3]

parts of it have been translated by R. Deloustal in his "La justice dans l'ancien Annam," BEFEO, 1909–13, and 1919–20, *passim*, which translates an Annamite code based upon, and in many ways similar to, the T'ang code. It may be pointed out here that the *T'ang lü su i* contains scores, if not hundreds, of references to slaves, either in special laws applicable to them, or in modifications of laws for cases in which slaves are involved. It is invaluable for a legal study of slavery in T'ang times. This multiplication of slave legislation is in marked contrast to the paucity of (extant) similar legislation before T'ang times, especially during the Han period.

[1] Cf. Ch'eng Shu-te, op. cit., p. 59, and *Tz'u yüan*.

[2] HFHD, vol. I, pp. 193 and 260; for Wang Wen-shu see CHS, 90, 4b. Ch'eng Shu-te (op. cit., p. 119) quotes the "Hsing fa chih" of the *Chin shu* as saying that Hsiao Ho abolished the punishment of three sets of relatives and those drawn into trial (*lien tso*) when he took over the Ch'in code.

[3] CHS, 4, 2b; and 5, 2a. Cf. HFHD, vol. I, pp. 233 and 313, respectively.

If whole families, including remote relatives of people guilty of particularly heinous crimes, might be executed, it is obvious that their enslavement was comparatively a mild form of punishment. The *History of the Former Han dynasty* records only a few instances of this form of enslavement, but they involved considerable numbers of people. Furthermore, they are probably typical of a constant series of criminal cases which were either not important enough to be reported, or were reported in such meager detail that the fate of the families was not specified beyond the ambiguous remark that they were punished "according to the law."

The families of the leaders in the Rebellion of the Seven States in 154 B.C. were enslaved. This is the first case recorded for the Han period. It illustrates how the formal histories often lack crucial details for a study of slavery, for it is almost an accident that this instance is on record at all, though the rebellion was the most important one that occurred during the dynasty proper. Although it was quickly suppressed, thousands died on both sides, one of the kings was beheaded, and the others committed suicide.[1]

The biographies of the seven rebellious kings do not indicate what happened to their families. The "Table of the Vassal Kings" shows in each case only that the ruler expired and that the royal line was terminated. Emperor Ching's edict in the "Annals" refers to the extermination of the kings, but also neglects to mention what happened to the families. It only tells that the Emperor "could not bear to apply the law" to Liu Yi (the son of a former King of Ch'u, and an uncle of the rebelling King) and some other imperial clansmen who had joined in the rebellion. Instead, he ordered all their names expunged from the register of the imperial house. He pardoned officials and people who had been coerced to join in the rebellion, although they should have been sentenced as accomplices.[2]

Thus, no record of the events at that time tells what happened to the families of the leading rebels. Yet fourteen years later Emperor Wu "pardoned the families of [the leaders of the rebellion of] Wu, Ch'u, the Seven States, who had been condemned to the government." Ying Shao says explicitly in his commentary: "At the time of the rebellion . . . the wives and children of the leaders had been seized and made government slaves. Emperor Wu, pitying them, pardoned them and sent them all away." (*30*, and footnote 3.)

[1] For a clear summary, cf. HFHD, vol. I, pp. 292–297.

[2] Biographies: CHS, 35, 7a; 36, 2a; 38, 2a and 4b; also SC, 106. Tables: CHS, 14, 3b–8a, *passim*. Edict of Emperor Ching: CHS, 5, 2b; cf. HFHD, vol. I, pp. 314–315.

There is no reason to doubt that this amnesty occurred as recorded. Living in the century after the *Ch'ien Han shu* was written, Ying Shao simply amplified and explained the statement. Chinese encyclopaedias and modern writers on slavery uniformly cite this early example of enslavement. For fourteen years these wives and children were government slaves, but if Emperor Wu had not pardoned them, or if the ten-word record had not been entered in his "Annals," it might not now be known at all that these people became government slaves. How often did the historians fail to record such enslavements in the appropriate places?

Chapters 14 through 18 of the *Ch'ien Han shu* list in tabular form all the important noble families of the Han dynasty, with brief records of succession to and termination of the lines. At least fifty-three of these noble families were abruptly cut off because the title-holder rebelled or plotted to rebel, and was executed or committed suicide. Eliminating the leaders of the Rebellion, and the members of the Empress *née* Lü's clan, which was entirely exterminated "without consideration of youth or old age," there are still some thirty other cases of rebellion in which there is no hint about the fate of the rebels' wives and children. It is reasonable to suppose that in some of these cases also the families became government slaves.

A special case of enslavement of families occurred in 120 B.C. when Wang Wen-shu, one of Emperor Wu's most ruthless officials, was appointed Administrator of Ho-nei Commandery. On taking office he immediately arrested more than a thousand families among the tyrannical gentry of the commandery. "Tyrannical gentry" (豪猾 or 豪強) usually means powerful plebeians who oppressed their neighbors, appropriated property, and accumulated large amounts of farm land which they rented. They were the economically powerful people who manipulated or defied the laws and were the actual bosses of their communities. Emperor Wu had a policy of suppressing these people. He quickly consented when Wang Wen-shu requested permission to execute the major criminals and their families and to enslave the families of the lesser offenders, who would be executed singly. Half the property was to be given to the victims of their oppression, while the government kept the rest. Here is a clear-cut example of enslavement as an alternative for execution, and a punishment one degree less severe. The passage closes with the grim sentence, "Blood flowed over ten or more *li*." (*43.*)

Only one document definitely reports enslavement of criminals *themselves* during the Former Han period. This was during the reign of the usurper Wang Mang, in connection with his currency "reforms." Several times during his regency and reign, Wang Mang altered the monetary system, greatly to the disadvantage of all people who owned money. Many new types of coins were introduced, and their metal content was reduced. People were ordered to adopt and circulate new issues whenever Wang Mang altered the currency, and were supposed to turn in their old bronze coins in exchange for new coins containing much less metal. There was tremendous opposition and many traders refused to accept the new coins at their face value. Almost anyone could coin money, for it was cast rather than struck. Therefore many people melted down their old coins and made new and lighter Wang Mang coins instead of turning in their old coins for exchange at great loss. Widespread counterfeiting greatly reduced the profits Wang Mang expected to obtain by depreciating the metal content of his money.[1]

To enforce circulation of the new coins and to stamp out counterfeiting Wang Mang altered the monetary laws several times. In A.D. 9 he decreed that anyone who clung to the old five-*chu* cash or talked against the new currency would be banished to distant frontiers (*122*). Counterfeiters were executed.[2] Possibly their families were enslaved, for the next year Wang Mang increased the severity of his laws to include the five mutually responsible families (see p. 78) who would be tried along with the counterfeiter and be enslaved by the government (*123*).

When these stringent measures did not stop the evil, he changed and lightened the law. Instead of being executed, those who privately coined money were to be seized with their wives and children and made government slaves; and officials or groups of mutually responsible five families who knew of such counterfeiting and failed to report it were to be punished with them. Instead of banishing people who opposed the new money, he sentenced plebeians to one year of punishment, and dismissed officials from office (*131*).

Leniency was less effective than severity. Offenders were even more numerous. In A.D. 21 a great frost destroyed crops, and in

---

[1] For a clear and detailed summary of Wang Mang's currency reforms, their disastrous economic effects, and the resulting wide-scale counterfeiting, cf. Homer H. Dubs, "Wang Mang and his economic reforms," TP, vol. 35, 1940, pp. 233–237.

[2] I have not found a specific Wang Mang decree that condemned counterfeiters to execution, but CHS, 24B, 11a, reports that the people who died for counterfeiting and were cast to the four bounds of the empire for opposing Wang Mang's new money could not be counted. Emperor Ching's law of public execution for coining cash or making alchemistic counterfeit gold (cf. HFHD, vol. 1, p. 323) was presumably still in effect in Wang Mang's time.

consequence plebeians of eastern China resorted to counterfeiting. They and mutually responsible groups of families tried with them were seized and enslaved to the number of ten myriad. Males were transported in cage carts, while women and children walked with iron fetters dangling on their necks. When they arrived at Ch'ang-an these slaves were set to work in the Bureau of Mint (*131, 132*). An ironic touch, but thoroughly Chinese!

The number reported enslaved need not be taken too literally, nor even perhaps the historian's grim statement that 60 or 70 per cent died of grief and suffering. What is noteworthy is that in this instance criminals, that is, the counterfeiters, were enslaved.

Even more interesting are the references to enslavement of people not actually related to counterfeiters but held responsible for their crimes because they and the counterfeiters were members of the same groups of five families. Each family was held legally responsible for the conduct of four others—a great extension of the fundamental principle whereby a family was responsible for the acts of its own members.

Wang Mang did not originate this system. It had been advocated by Shang Yang in the fourth century before Christ, and may have originated earlier.[1] Not merely a harsh legal measure to extend the terror of the law, it was a far-reaching system of political organization based upon conditions of small, self-contained peasant hamlets and close-knit villages within towns. Schematically this administrative system consisted of five families in a neighborhood, five neighborhoods to a hamlet, five or ten hamlets in a commune, and ten communes to a district. A headman or elder in charge of each division was the focal point of administration and responsibility. Exact quinary or decimal units could not have been followed rigidly, but the principle was applied for purposes of taxation, corvée labor, military levies and self-defense, and the administration of laws. The state of Ch'in, and later the dynasty, charged each family in a neighborhood to denounce crimes committed by members of any of the other families; if certain crimes occurred all five families were implicated and tried together.

The harsh application of that part of the system which made people responsible for the conduct of their neighbors was thoroughly repellent to the subjects of the Ch'in empire—intra-family responsibility was an integral part of Chinese social organization, but

---

[1] Ch'eng Shu-te, op. cit., p. 82; J. J. L. Duyvendak, *The book of Lord Shang*, p. 14 and footnote 7, pp. 57–59; Derk Bodde, *China's first unifier*, pp. 35, 166.

extension of legal responsibility beyond the family was apparently an artificial system imposed from above. The Han dynasty seems to have abandoned the objectionable part of the system while maintaining most of it for administrative purposes.[1] Wang Mang merely re-established mutual legal responsibility among groups of five families in order to enforce his currency reforms.

Thousands of people thereby became slaves in A.D. 21 because they or some of their neighbors were secretly coining money. Ten years later, after Wang Mang had been killed, the new Emperor Kuang-wu freed those who had survived the revolution and were still slaves. Writing finis to this mass enslavement, the imperial edict said: "Those officials and people who, during Wang Mang's time, were seized and became slaves not in accordance with the former laws, are all to be freed and made commoners." (*135.*)

Orthodox enslavement of families of executed criminals (and perhaps of some criminals themselves) continued, however, during the Latter Han dynasty. An edict of A.D. 106, prepared for the infant Emperor Shang, said that many members of the Imperial House had been enslaved since A.D. 25, and ordered the unfortunates all to be freed and made commoners. In 110 Emperor An decreed: "All those who have been tried and banished to the frontiers for monstrous talking and other crimes since the *Chien-ch'u* [reign period (76–83)] are to be returned each to his original commandery; those seized by the government as slaves are to be pardoned and become commoners." [2]

These passages are evidence of enslavement of criminals' families throughout the Han period. Any assertion about the frequency of the practice, or estimate of the number of people thus enslaved during the dynasty, would be without documentary foundation. Considering the nature of the historical sources it seems certain that there were many unreported cases. Such enslavement was always to the government in the first instance.

---

[1] In 179 B.C. Emperor Wen "completely abrogated all statutes and orders for arresting wives and children and punishing them with [the criminals]." (CHS, 4, 2b; HFHD, vol. I, p. 233.) This certainly indicates that the extension of responsibility beyond the family or clan was already obsolete.

[2] HHS, 4, 9a; 5, 4a. The wording of the edict of A.D. 110 leaves some doubt today whether the slaves (1) had been enslaved, rather than banished, for "monstrous talking" and other crimes; whether they were (2) families of people banished; or whether they were (3) all those people seized and enslaved since the *Chien-ch'u* period for any reason. On "monstrous talking" cf. HFHD, vol. I, p. 193, footnote 2.

DISTINCTION BETWEEN CONVICTS AND SLAVES

Several modern Chinese writers on Han slavery treat convicts (*t'u* 徒) as though they were slaves.[1] It is true that convicts were sentenced to hard labor, that they worked side by side with certain types of government slaves, and that both sometimes wore similar clothes, shackles, and marks of identity. But unless convicts were slaves in a legal sense, unless they were property of the government in the same way that slaves were, only confusion results from calling them slaves. Even at the risk of "beating the dead tiger" it is imperative to clear up this point. What are the facts?

The earliest specific definition of *t'u* known to me is that by Wang Ch'ung, who lived A.D. 27 to ca. 97, and was a contemporary of Pan Ku, the author of the *Ch'ien Han shu*. He says: "[Those who] have undergone criminal punishment are called *t'u* 被刑謂之徒."[2] This is so general that only equally general terms such as "convict" or "felon" convey the same meaning. The great etymological dictionary *Shuo wen chieh tzu*, presented to the throne in A.D. 121, offers no hint that *t'u* refers to enslavement, as indeed it would not unless that meaning were considered primary. However, none of the later commentators on the *Shuo wen* suggests the idea of enslavement or equates *t'u* with *nu*.[3] The only early writer who makes such an equation is Li Chi, who flourished ca. A.D. 200. He says: "A general term for male and female *t'u* was *nu* 男女徒總名爲奴." (*1*, footnote 2.) However, Li Chi himself speaks (CHS, 8, 1a) of *t'u* sentenced to one year. People sentenced to a single year of government servitude cannot be called slaves. If Li Chi is correct that *nu* was a general term for *t'u*—and the pre-Han context of

---

[1] Liang Ch'i-ch'ao, "System of slavery in China," p. 532; Ma Fei-pai, "Source material on the economic history of Ch'in and Han," pt. 6, "The slavery system," p. 385; Wu Po-lun, "Hsi Han nu-li k'ao [An investigation of slavery in the Western Han]," *Shih Huo*, vol. 1, No. 7, March 1, 1935, pp. 275–285 (see p. 278) (hereafter cited by translated title); Lao Kan, "The system of slavery during the two Han dynasties," p. 8; Ma Ch'eng-feng, *An economic history of China*, vol. 2, p. 246. This usage is refuted by Wu Ching-ch'ao ("The slavery system of the Western Han," p. 246, footnote 1), who quotes in his support Wang Shih-chieh, who has made the most exhaustive study of Chinese slavery from the legal point of view. Wang points out that in enslavement for crime the basic principle seems to be that the slaves were the people mutually implicated, but not the criminals themselves. It was a punishment for relatives of major criminals, arising from the Chinese family system (op. cit., p. 306; Pippon, p. 99).

[2] *Lun heng*, ch. 23 (sec. 3), 10b; cf. Alfred Forke, trans., *Lun-Hêng*, 2 vols., London, 1907, Berlin, 1911, vol. 2, p. 378. The whole passage concerns *t'u*, yet gives no evidence of enslavement.

[3] See *Shuo wen chieh tzu ku lin*, pp. 736–737.

his commentary should be remembered—it tends rather to diffuse the meaning of *nu* than to sharpen the meaning of *t'u*.

Several passages contextually associate the terms *t'u*, and *nu* or *nu-pei*, but because of the nature of the language it is not always possible to tell whether they are separate items, or form a compound, or whether *t'u* is an adjective indicating a kind of *nu*. The first passage (*3*), referring to men working at Li Mountain who were freed in 209 B.C. to fight one of the rebelling armies, makes a clear distinction between two types of people: convicts, and born male slaves 徒人奴產子. In proposing the scheme Chang Han had only suggested freeing of *t'u*. The second passage, dated 197 B.C. and referring to a plan to free men willing to fight Kao-tsu's Empress and Heir-apparent, is indecisive (*13*). It simply says, "the various bureaus' *t'u nu*" 諸官徒奴. Here "convict" and "male slave" could be either two classes, or one special class of "convict-slaves." The third passage (*46*), dated 119–113 B.C. and telling of the confiscation of property from merchants and others who infringed certain drastic emergency laws, points to an adjectival usage. It seems to distinguish between confiscated slaves 沒入奴婢, that is, slaves confiscated along with other property, on the one hand, and criminals seized and enslaved 徒奴婢, on the other. However, this is only an assumption. The second reference may equally well be read "convicts and male and female slaves," as it is translated in the document. There is an interesting undated passage in the *Han chiu i* (*95*), in which it is said that the government took twelve hundred *t'u nu* from bureaus within the capital city and subordinated them to (or put them under the control of) a single inspectorate. The passage itself could be translated either as "convicts and male slaves," or as "convict-slaves." The interesting point is that in the introductory section to the "Table on the Bureaucracy" in the *Ch'ien Han shu*, under the heading *Ssu-li chiao-wei*, a similar statement leaves out *nu* and mentions only the *t'u*,[1] saying: "Carrying credentials, [the Colonel over the Retainers] was escorted by twelve hundred *t'u* from the bureaus of the capital city. He arrested [those who practiced] *wu-ku*, and judicially investigated major [cases of] licentiousness and treachery." Here *t'u* may be standing for *t'u-nu*; on the other hand there may be a scribal error, or a misunderstanding, or the meaning "foot soldier" may be indicated. This seems most likely in view of the fact that

---

[1] CHS, 19A, 6a (*Han shu pu-chu*, 22a). The passage is translated in *95*, footnote 2.

the next statement is: "Later his soldiers (兵) were abolished. . . ." Finally, there is a usage dated A.D. 19 which reports that Wang Mang made a great enlistment of imprisoned *t'u* and people's male slaves 囚徒人奴 to fight as shock troops against the Hsiung-nu. As it makes a distinction between *t'u* and private slaves, it does not exactly fit the present discussion, but it is interesting because another report of the same event in the same source says Wang Mang enlisted prisoners sentenced to death, and male slaves of officials and plebeians 死罪囚吏民奴. The conjunction of the two passages shows that the imprisoned *t'u* in the first item were criminals sentenced to death, and not government slaves *(130)*.

In summary, two of the passages show a clear distinction, one is indecisive, and two can be argued to mean "convict-slaves."

Now, granting that there is a term "convict-slave," does this mean that *t'u* alone means slave? Obviously it does not. There are many meanings for *t'u*. Referring to citations in two Chinese dictionaries compiled on modern principles, the *Chung-hua ta tzu-tien* isolates twenty-four meanings, and the *Tz'u yüan* gives ten. Not all of these are Han usages, and only a few are nouns such as foot-soldier, commoner giving menial service in government bureaus, and sentenced criminals. But in both dictionaries under the definition meaning a convict the reference to *nu* comes from the "Treatise on Jurisprudence" of the *T'ang shu*, or *History of the T'ang dynasty* (618–906). There are many pre-T'ang historical and legal texts, items from dictionaries, and commentaries, which in one or another way tell of government enslavement of the families or descendants of criminals, and perhaps even of criminals themselves (the distinction is not easy to draw in view of the Chinese family system), but while these employ *nu* or *nu-pei* as the term for such people, none earlier than this *T'ang shu* passage (except Li Chi) equates them with *t'u*.[1]

Liang Ch'i-ch'ao, the most scholarly of those who include *t'u* in their discussions of slavery, speaks of two types of enslavement for crime. He is not so much interested in the Former Han practice as in that throughout Chinese history, but the documents he quotes are the *Chou li* and *Han chiu i*.[2] The first of these dates only shortly

[1] I mean by this that I have not been able to find such references in various Chinese encyclopaedias, legal works, or the *Shuo wen chieh tzu ku lin*, with its extensive quotations of *Shuo wen* commentaries. I may not have looked far enough, but considering that assembling of early references on all subjects is a passion with Chinese scholars, methodically driven to the point of a vice, the search has certainly passed the point of "diminishing returns."

[2] Liang Ch'i-ch'ao, op. cit., pp. 532–533.

before Han (probably edited, or "rediscovered" about the beginning of our era), while the second is an early Latter Han work. His first class of government slaves consists of lightly punished people, those sentenced to servitude for one to five years. Though his citations do not refer to these people as *t'u*, Liang says that they were called *t'u*. Here it is not necessary to go into the types of work such criminals did, or the names of the various kinds of sentences.[1] If, however, *t'u* were people serving criminal sentences from one to five years in length, then they were certainly not slaves any more than convicts in a southern chain-gang are slaves, no matter how slavish their treatment may be.

It must be admitted that a confusion between *t'u* and certain government *nu* or *nu-pei* is understandable, and there may indeed have been points of identity. Wang Mang's slaves were certainly given the treatment of convicts, for that is what they were, though they are called *nu-pei*. Two documents dating very early in the Former Han period describe free people disguising themselves as private slaves, and therefore having their heads shaved, putting on iron collars, and dressing in russet clothes. These were the identifying costume of *t'u* and people sentenced for limited periods.[2] It is probably significant that the only reported instances during the Former Han period of private or government slaves so treated (except for the Wang Mang case), come at the beginning of the dynasty. At this time private slavery was apparently not very extensive, and perhaps reflected the Ch'in and late Chou treatment of the enslaved families or descendants of executed criminals, who seem to have been the most common government slaves in the pre-Han age.

Tattooing the face was another way of distinguishing criminals. It was next to the least of five punishments involving bodily mutilation. Ch'ing Pu, a convict working on Li Mountain at the end of

[1] See HFHD, vol. I, p. 177, footnote 1, for a translation of the *Han chiu i* passage. Ch'eng Shu-te (op. cit., pp. 51–55) assembles the Han material. He does not equate criminals of this sort with *t'u*, just as he does not equate *t'u* and *nu*, yet the passages he quotes when dealing with punishments of one and three year servitude use *t'u* contextually. Dubs does equate *t'u* with slaves and also apparently with people sentenced to servitude from one to five years. In his note on the *t'u* that Kao-tsu was escorting to Li Mountain, he says: "Enslavement or convict labor was a common punishment; a criminal could be sentenced to enslavement for a *number of years*." HFHD, vol. I, p. 34, footnote 1. (Italics mine.)

[2] *8* and *12*. See Ch'eng Shu-te, op. cit., pp. 51–52, for shackling and shaving the heads of criminals; also HFHD, vol. I, p. 177, footnote 1, and Edouard Chavannes, *Les documents chinois*. . . , p. 63. Document *26* describes the meeting of the slave, Wei Ch'ing, with a convict in an iron collar.

the Ch'in period, had been tattooed, and took his name from that fact. The practice was theoretically abolished by an edict of Emperor Wen in 167 B.C., but probably continued to be done at later times.[1] Evidence that enslaved relatives or descendants of executed criminals were tattooed appears in a citation of the Han law code, quoted by the Grand Judge, Chung Yu, toward the end of the Latter Han period. According to the Han code, said Chung Yu, "the wives and children of criminals [罪人] are confiscated as male and female slaves, and tattooed on the face." Amplifying this citation he explained that "the punishment of tattooing the face as practiced by Han was preserved from ancient statutes. The genuine male and female slaves of today had ancestors who originally committed crimes. Even though a hundred generations have gone by, still they have tattooed faces [as a sign of] submission to the government."[2]

There seem to have been differences as well as similarities between *t'u* and government *nu* or *nu-pei*. There is no evidence that *t'u* were sold, or given away, which is a useful pragmatic test of slave-ownership. An affirmative conclusion cannot be drawn from absence of evidence. Therefore, while it cannot be asseverated that *t'u* were not sold, it cannot be proved that they were. There is plenty of documentary proof, on the other hand, that slaves,

---

[1] For example, about A.D. 150 Chu Mu offered to have his face tattooed in expatiation of a misdeed. Cf. HHS, 73, 5b. This could hardly have happened if the custom had been strictly abolished for more than 300 years.

[2] *San kuo chih, Wei chih*, 12, 4a. The statement occurs in the biography of Mao Chieh (ibid., 3b–4b), an important official under T'ai-tsu (i.e., Wu-ti or Ts'ao Ts'ao) shortly before A.D. 220. Someone reported that Mao Chieh had interviewed some "rebels with tattooed faces, whose wives and children had been seized by the government as slaves." (The Chinese construction of the sentence makes it appear that the rebels were the ones whose faces were tattooed, but Chung Yu's statement quoted above, as well as what follows, indicates that it was the enslaved wives and children of *former* rebels who are meant.) Mao Chieh was thrown into prison because he was reported to have said that this sort of treatment was the cause of a current drought. In the trial Chung Yu quoted the *Book of history* and the *Chou li* to prove that such enslaving was an ancient practice, and then cited and explained the Han law code, as quoted above. He asked how many tattoo-faced people Mao Chieh had interviewed, and wanted to know how the ignorant "tattoo-faced male and female slaves" had been able to obtain an interview with Mao Chieh to present their grievances.

Cited by a Grand Judge in an official trial, this quotation of the Han code, and his explanation, constitute good evidence of the treatment of this type of government slave.

Chung Yu's citation is quoted as evidence of Han conditions by such Chinese students of law and slavery as Ch'eng Shu-te (op. cit., p. 81), Shen Chia-pen (op. cit., 5b, 6a–b), Wang Shih-Chieh (op. cit., p. 307), Liang Ch'i-ch'ao (op. cit., p. 532), Ma Fei-pai (op. cit., p. 389), and several others.

Since slaves were tattooed for purposes of identification, the face was the natural place for the marking. The kind of tattoo mark applied in Han times

including government ones, were sold and given away. Many special pardons of *t'u* were recorded, but very few manumissions of government slaves during the Former Han period. *T'u* were often recruited to fight in China's frontier wars, but government slaves are not reported to have been. There were a number of revolts of *t'u*, but none reported for government slaves, which strongly suggests a fundamental difference in treatment.

Because there seems to be no contextual evidence that *t'u* were slaves; because many of those called *t'u* were merely criminals sentenced to labor from one to five years;[1] because the term has a number of other important meanings; and because *t'u* in the sense of criminal cannot be equated with any other Former Han term surely or exclusively meaning "slave"—for these reasons it is unjustifiable to translate the term as "slave." To treat *t'u* as slaves distorts the crucial problems of slave numbers, functions, and economic position. In this work the term is translated "convict."

ENSLAVEMENT BECAUSE OF ECONOMIC DISTRESS

Famine and slavery in China are cause and effect, and the sale of women and children because of economic distress is a constant factor during all Chinese history when slavery was an established institution. Numerous instances of the sale of children from the beginning of Han times through the Ming period appear in the dismal record of famines spread out year by year in the pages of Chinese encyclopaedias, and many Occidental writers attest to the practice during the last dynasty. As late as 1920–21, women and children, and particularly young girls, were sold in large numbers in a north-China famine which cost 500,000 lives. Yet at that time slavery was already legally abolished in China. Sales during famines doubtless still occur.

Extensive warfare almost always causes famine. People flee their homes, trade and communications collapse, crops and grain-

is not known, but a description of the practice in Chin times (A.D. 265–419) perhaps throws a little light on this minor point. An official order stated that male or female slaves who ran away were to be tattooed on both eyes with a copper-green substance like ink; if they ran away a second time they were to be tattooed on both cheeks; and if they ran away a third time they were to be tattooed under each eye with a horizontal mark one and a half (Chinese) inches long and half an inch wide (Ch'eng Shu-te, op. cit., p. 354, quoting the *Yu yang tsa tsu* and the *T'ai p'ing yü lan*).

[1] Instead of being executed, seriously mutilated, dismissed from office or title, or fined. These were the principal types of punishments; cf. Ch'eng Shu-te, op. cit., pp. 42–63.

stores are seized or destroyed to weaken the enemy, able-bodied men forced into the army cannot attend to planting and harvesting, and brigands stalk and pillage in the wake of the troops. At the beginning of the Han period, after four years of rebellion and civil war, a great famine swept the Ch'in stronghold of Shensi, normally a rich and fertile region. Grain cost five thousand cash the picul, people ate human flesh, and over half the population died. In 205 B.C. Kao-tsu permitted people to sell their children and migrate to Szechwan for food (7).

Probably this order merely sanctioned a widespread practice. Famine does not wait for imperial decrees! Three years later, when the country was scarcely pacified, the Emperor decreed: "Those common people who because of famine have sold themselves to be people's slaves are all to be freed and become commoners." (9.) This edict shows that people had sold themselves as well as their children.

The cycle of warfare, famine, and slavery was repeated at the close of the Former Han period. The successful rebellion against Wang Mang degenerated into years of civil warfare. Famine devastated the land, and two edicts of Emperor Kuang-wu evidence the sale of victims. Three years after the murder of Wang Mang, the new Emperor proclaimed that plebeians' wives married and children sold could freely return to their parents (134). In A.D. 31 a more specific edict ordered that those officials and plebeians who had encountered famine and turmoil, thus becoming slaves and lesser wives, should all be allowed to return home if they wished. To put teeth into the edict the Emperor ordered that any master who dared to restrain them from leaving should be tried according to the "law for selling people." (136.)

Records of famine and widespread economic distress caused by droughts, untimely frosts, floods, and wars appear at least twenty times in the "Imperial Annals" of the Ch'ien Han shu during a period of 212 years. Each of these disasters was severe enough to demand government action, or at least imperial solicitude. Four notices report cannibalism. There is no indication in any but the first of these terse and stark records that people sold themselves or their children, but it is likely that every famine produced a new batch of slaves. Several leading statesmen referred to the practice in memorials on general economic conditions.

Thus, in 178 B.C. Chia Yi told Emperor Wen that even after several decades of peace public and private stores of grain were lamentably small. "When there is a lack of timely rains," he said, "the people cast wolfish glances; when the harvest is bad and is not harvested, pleadings to be allowed to sell titles and children have been heard." (*A4.*) Ch'ao Ts'o also addressed to Emperor Wen a long memorial on agriculture, in which he described the hardships of farmers, burdened with year-long labors, corvée duties, charitable obligations, excessive taxes, and ill-timed legislation.[1] When droughts and floods occur, "those who have [grain] sell at half price [sic!], and those who have none get respite by borrowing, to be repaid double; and therefore there are those who sell their lands and houses, and sell their children and grandchildren in order to repay their creditors." (*18.*)

Chia Chüan-chih attempted to dissuade Emperor Yüan from launching a military expedition against the people of Hai-nan Island in 46 B.C. A year before, a famine in Shantung was so severe that people there resorted to cannibalism. Chia Chüan-chih pictured the unhappy condition of the people in eastern China, who for years had suffered and been forced to leave their homes. Although in human nature no family relationship is closer than that between children and their parents, he said, and nothing is more joyous than the relationship of husbands and wives, still the people are driven to the extremity of marrying off their wives and selling their children. Neither laws nor the sense of righteousness could stop them. He argued that to send off a great military expedition at such a time was no way to cope with famine and to preserve the people (*A13*). During Wang Mang's reign famine and warfare against the Hsiung-nu forced the people to flee into the central commanderies, where they were sold as slaves. To prevent this depopulation of the frontiers, Wang Mang ordered public execution for anyone, official or plebeian, who dared to traffic in frontier plebeians (*126*).

An interesting variant of child-selling was "pawning children." Liu An, better known as Huai-nan Tzu, referred to this custom in his letter to young Emperor Wu. He criticized a proposed campaign against the Kingdom of Yüeh because economic conditions were unfavorable. Two years before, a flood of the Yellow River had forced people to practice cannibalism. "For several years," he said, "the harvests have successively not been abundant, and people have had to depend upon selling their honorary ranks and pawning

---

[1] The whole memorial is translated by Herbert A. Giles (*Gems of Chinese literature*, rev. ed., Shanghai, 1922, pp. 70–73) and Georges Margouliès (*Le Kou-wen chinois*, Paris, 1926, pp. 68–73). The essential parts of the famous documents are translated by Duyvendak (op. cit., pp. 54–55).

their children in order to continue to clothe and feed themselves."
(*33.*) Ju Shun, a third century commentator, explains the practice
of pawning children. In Huai-nan people sold children to do slave
work. If, after three years, the parents could not redeem them,
the children then became male and female slaves. A T'ang dynasty
custom is quoted in support of Ju Shun's observation. It was the
custom at one place in Kiangsi province to use boys and girls as
collateral for borrowing money. If the loan was not repaid in the
specified time, or if the interest due equaled the principal, the
children were seized and enslaved (*33*, and footnote 5). Although
there is no other evidence in the Han dynasty of this custom, or of
debtor slavery specifically, it is plausible as a modified and mitigated
form of the well-documented practice of selling children outright.

A poor family that could not afford to rear another child, or
especially another girl, might allow the newborn child to die. Infanticide may be used as a measure of economic distress. A destitute
family might prefer to leave its baby girl on the doorstep of a wealthy
family that could rear her as a slave. Formal histories do not give
much precise information about infanticide, yet there are references
to it in Han times. In one region so many poor people abandoned
their children that Chia Piao announced that parents who let their
children die would be punished for murder.[1]

LEGALITY OF SALE INTO SLAVERY

Two curious facts stand out in the documents regarding enslavement because of economic distress. The first is that the sale of free
people was apparently extra-legal, justified only in special cases.
Kao-tsu gave special permission for people to sell their children.
Chia Yi speaks of people pleading to be allowed to sell their children. Chia Chüan-chih reports that laws could not prevent people
from marrying off their wives and selling their children. The second
fact is that in the early years of both dynasties people who had
been sold into slavery because of famine were ordered to be freed,
as though the enslavement were invalid. Emperor Kuang-wu even
ordered that slave owners who refused to comply would be tried
according to the "law for selling people."

These two facts raise an important question. Was the sale of
free women and children, or voluntary self-sale, recognized by Han
law as a valid transaction? Since Emperor Kuang-wu invoked a
"law for selling people" almost at the beginning of his reign, it must

---

[1] HHS, 97, 11b; cf. also Ch'eng Shu-te, op. cit., p. 134, for other early cases.

be assumed that it was an already existing law dating from the Former Han period. What was this law?

The *Chin shu* or *History of the Chin dynasty* (A.D. 265–419), compiled in the seventh century from eighteen earlier works, has a reference to this "law for selling people" in its "Hsing fa chih." It quotes the preface to the *Hsin lü* or *New code*, by Ch'en Ch'ün, who died in A.D. 236. He and others prepared this *New code* for the Wei dynasty of the Three Kingdoms period some time before 229, and the mention in Ch'en's preface of the "law for selling people" probably refers to the Han law; that is, the law invoked by Emperor Kuang-wu in A.D. 31. The preface said merely: "The law on robbery had items on kidnaping, terrorizing, and selling and buying people by persuasion." The heading "Law on Robbery" was one of the six divisions taken over by the Han dynasty from the Ch'in, and incorporated by Hsiao Ho into his "Law in nine sections," the basic Han code. The details of this law on robbery are mostly lost. But Wang Hsien-ch'ien quotes the eighteenth century commentator Hui Tung as writing that it said: "Those who kidnap people or kidnap and sell people or sell people by persuasion or buy people by persuasion, and make them slaves, shall die." [1]

The law of the Northern Wei dynasty (A.D. 386–534) had virtually the same provision in its section on robbery: "Those who kidnap people or kidnap and sell people or sell people by persuasion, and make them male and female slaves, shall die." This law was cited in the trial of a very interesting case in A.D. 502. A man sold his seven-year-old daughter to be the slave of a fellow townsman. The latter purposely bought her for resale, and did resell her in another region without revealing her background. She was thus in danger of losing her identity as a "good" person. Charged with buying by persuasion, he should, according to the law, have been strangled. The same case affords the earliest extant citation of a law against selling members of the family. It was invoked against the girl's

---

[1] *Chin shu*, ch. 31 ("Hsing fa chih"), 5a. I translate the word "item" in the plural, because in A.D. 37 Emperor Kuang-wu ordered that owners who dared to restrain plebeians kidnaped into slavery should be tried according to the "law on kidnaping people." Obviously the law on selling people was a separate item from the law on kidnaping people, and both were part of the law on robbery. Cf. Shen Chia-pen, op. cit., "Han lü chih i," ch. 2, 9b, ff. On the *Hsin lü* of Ch'en Ch'ün, cf. Ch'eng Shu-te, op. cit., p. 229 (preface to his ch. 2, on the Wei dynasty law). On the "Law in nine sections" of Hsiao Ho, cf. Jean Escarra, *Le droit chinois*, Peking, 1936, pp. 23 and 94. Wang Hsien-ch'ien's commentary is quoted in *136*, footnote 2. Liang Ch'i-ch'ao (op. cit., p. 550) also quotes Hui Tung's statement, and locates it as a commentary to the *Jih chih lu* by the famous scholar Ku Yen-wu. He also points out that this law on robbery was part of "Law in nine sections" by Hsiao Ho.

father, and read: "Those who sell their children shall be punished for one year. [Those who sell] relatives of the same surname, who are their superiors or elders within the five grades of mourning, shall die. Those who sell their near relatives, or their concubines, or their sons' wives, shall be banished.[1]

These citations reflect obscurely the Han attitude toward sale of free people. To judge by later codes, the "law for selling people" —invoked by Emperor Kuang-wu in A.D. 31 against anyone who refused to free slaves who were victims of famine, turmoil, and kidnaping—was part of a law against sale into slavery by force or guile. This was, in turn, part of the larger law on robbery. It is not clear whether the Han code actually had any law against selling members of one's family. But it is evident that such transactions were precarious if brought on by famine and other untoward conditions. The slaves might be ordered to be freed even though permission for sale had formerly been granted. Both Liang Ch'i-ch'ao and Wang Shih-chieh, generalizing from the continuity of Chinese law, assert that sale of free people has never been legally recognized in China, though it was regularly practiced.[2]

In Han times people compelled by starvation to sell themselves or their children had to find some private buyer. Purchase of famine victims is not reported among the various measures adopted by the government to relieve or forestall widespread economic distress, and there is no evidence that the government ever bought people who were free up to the time of purchase, or enslaved people for debt.

ILLEGAL FORCED ENSLAVEMENT

Stringent laws during the Han period did not prevent kidnaping. This indicates that there was a market for slaves which made kidnaping profitable and worth the risk of the death penalty.

Shortly before the beginning of the Han period Luan Pu was kidnaped by someone and sold as a male slave in Yen to do a deed of revenge for his master (5). Luan Pu was not a child, but a homeless wanderer who had hired himself out several years before to serve a wineshop keeper. Perhaps it is an indication of the decadence of law and order in the closing years of the Ch'in rule that a young

---

[1] Cf. Ch'eng Shu-te, op. cit. (ch. 5, "Hou Wei lü k'ao"), p. 415.

[2] Liang Ch'i-ch'ao, op. cit., p. 550; Wang Shih-chieh, op. cit., pp. 311–313. I may add, what is only an opinion, that it was probably the chief source of private slaves throughout the period here discussed, as it seems to have been in later times.

man could be kidnaped in Ch'in, transported to Yen two hundred miles away, and sold there without interference. Since it is not known what kinds of legal papers were necessary for slave transactions it is only a guess that he was sold with the connivance of the civil authorities.

About the year 190 B.C. Tou Kuang-kuo, the four-year-old son of a poor family, was kidnaped and sold by some one, and his family could not find him. Resold about ten times, and traveling several hundred miles from his home, he was finally bought a number of years later by a man living near Lo-yang. Tou Kuang-kuo's later importance explains why a history devoted primarily to matters of state concern reports the kidnaping of a poor boy. His older sister became the consort of Emperor Wen. About the same time Tou Kuang-kuo escaped death almost miraculously. Casting his horoscope, he learned that he would soon become a marquis. Therefore he went with his master to the capital and heard that the new Empress was a lady named Tou, from his native town. How he got in touch with her and proved his identity is a moving story. Eventually he did become a marquis as his horoscope had predicted (*14*).

These are the only specific cases on record of individual Chinese who were kidnaped and sold into slavery. However, strong robber bands are frequently reported from various parts of the empire and often had to be suppressed by military force. These bands doubtless kidnaped many people for sale. Wang Mang, in his edict of A.D. 9, denounced kidnaping of women and children for sale as if it had been a constant occurrence throughout the Han period (*122*). Three edicts of Emperor Kuang-wu in 31, 36, and 37 specifically ordered that people who had been kidnaped and made slaves during the troubled period of founding his dynasty were to be freed (*136*, and footnote 3).

Many other cases of kidnaping are indeed reported but it is not clear that the victims were sold. People could be seized for revenge, hostage, ransom, forced labor, sexual gratification, or other reasons. Why did Fan Ping and his accomplices kidnap officials and plebeians in a brief rebellion in 14 B.C.? They may have been seized for hostages of safe passage.[1] Why did Hsiung-nu bands raid the Chinese frontiers to kidnap plebeians and officials? The Hsiung-nu kept private slaves (*54*), but it is unlikely that they wanted or could absorb the thousands of Chinese reported captured on these recurrent raids. Perhaps they held some of the victims for ransom, but they

----

[1] CHS, 10, 6a.

may have sold many to Chinese slave traders operating on other parts of the frontier, or to various Central Asian kingdoms farther west. Ransom was the primary motive of Chinese officials who, during the reign of Wang Mang, falsely put seals on people's necks, making them youth-servants. They removed the seals only when they received bribes (A21).

Kidnaping was not practiced by disreputable robber-bands or "barbarians" alone. Some of the "best people," relying upon their lofty rank for protection, were guilty. Usually the motive was sexual desire and not sale. Thus, in 130 B.C. the Marquis of Chü-ni kidnaped a man's wife. When this was discovered he was executed and his marquisate abolished. In 74 B.C. the King of Ch'ang-i kidnaped girls on his way to the capital. Chang Fang, the favorite of Emperor Ch'eng, tried to take the daughter of a commoner by force.[1]

Han documents lack information on many questions naturally arising about kidnaping for slavery. Were there large-scale kidnaping rings? If so, by what methods did they operate, what were the profits, and how did they dispose of their victims? Did they work through corrupt officials? What did the government do, beyond passing laws and executing sentences, to prevent kidnaping? Did it scrutinize titles to ownership of slaves, and listen to slaves' complaints? To what extent did kidnaping contribute to the total number of new slaves? These questions must go unsolved because Chinese history concerns itself only with "important" matters.

IMPORTATION OF FOREIGN SLAVES

Foreign slaves were very popular with the cosmopolitan upper classes of the T'ang period.[2] Korean girls were in demand as personal maids for wealthy gentlemen, and piracy along the Korean coast

[1] Cf. CHS, 16, 6b, and 40, 9a, for the Marquis of Chü-ni; documents 67 and 100 for the King of Ch'ang-i and Chang Fang. Several similar cases in Latter Han times indicate that kidnaping of women, under the cloak of imperial protection, was a by-product of nearly unlimited power enjoyed by distaff relatives of the imperial house, by some nobles, and by high officials. Around A.D. 90 Tou Hsien, a brother-in-law of Emperor Shang, and a leading general, kidnaped women and girls (HHS, 53, 8a) as did the powerful eunuch Hou Lan in 170 (HHS, 108, 6b). In A.D. 150, Liang Chi, brother of the Dowager Empress Liang, and one of the most powerful men of his day, not only kidnaped women and girls, but also seized several thousand "good" people and made them male and female slaves, calling them "self-sold people." (HHS, 64, 6a–b.)

[2] The subject is not new. It has been discussed in several works on slavery or on the T'ang period, of which the following are a few more readily accessible: Liang Ch'i-ch'ao, op. cit., pp. 540–542; Chang Hsing-lang, "The importation of negro slaves into China under the T'ang dynasty (A.D. 618–907)," *Bulletin of*

and trade in the seaports of Shantung helped supply this fashionable need. Turkic, Tibetan, and Uighur slaves were captured in raids or sent as tribute by frontier governments. Dancing girls imported from regions even farther west performed novel Iranian dances; they were probably slaves. Dark-skinned K'un-lun slaves, certainly negroid, were very popular; references to them go back to the fourth and fifth centuries. In T'ang times some K'un-lun slaves may have been African negroes imported by Arab traders. The greatest source of new slaves during this period, however, was south China, where much of the population consisted of aboriginal tribes. Edict after edict vainly attempted to prohibit kidnaping or importing of tribespeople from the regions now comprising Fukien, Kwangtung, Kwangsi, Hunan, Kweichow, Yunnan, and Szechwan.

In Former Han times foreign slaves were popular also. Southern Szechwan and Yunnan supplied many non-Chinese youths for the Chinese market. Merchants of Shu and Pa, the regions of modern Chengtu and Chungking, were middlemen in a lucrative trade in slaves taken from P'o and T'ien, and resold in Ch'ang-an (10). P'o, at the juncture of the Yangtze and Min rivers, was a particularly important center for it was the gateway to Yunnan and about equally distant from the capitals of Pa and Shu. T'ien was the region of modern Kunming (Yunnanfu). Whether these slaves were aborigines or members of the gifted T'ai race is uncertain. The men of T'ien and P'o may have been slave traders themselves, capturing people from the surrounding hill tribes for sale to Chinese merchants. Both regions were natural centers for such operations. On the other hand, the term "youth," used for these slaves, usually signifies young boys and girls in the luxury class, and it seems more likely that they would be civilized T'ai children. The passages which describe this trade indicate that it already functioned early in the Han period. Ssu-ma Hsiang-ju, acquainted at first hand with conditions in southwestern China, referred to enslavement of children there in a conversation with Emperor Wu (A7). A remark by Fu Ch'ien of the second century of our era indicates that the trade was continuous. He says: "In the *former* capital"—that is, the Ch'ang-an of his own day—"there are female slaves from P'o." (10, footnote 2.)

the Catholic University of Peking, vol. 7, 1930, pp. 37–59; L. C. Goodrich, "Negroes in China," ibid., vol. 8, 1931, pp. 137–139; Kuwabara Jitzuzô, "On P'u Shou-keng," MRDTB, No. 2, 1928, pp. 61–63; Ishida Mikinosuke, "Etudes sino-iraniennes, I: A propos du *Hou-siuan-wou*," ibid., No. 6, 1932, pp. 61–76; Stefan Balazs, "Beiträge zur Wirtschaftsgeschichte der T'ang-Zeit, II, Der Sklaverei," MSOS, vol. 35, 1932, pp. 2–14.

Yüeh was an ancient coastal state in present Chekiang and northern Fukien, having a cultural element markedly different from that of north China. It is interesting, therefore, to read of a slave woman from Yüeh ordered to "descend to the spirits and invoke curses on Emperor [Wu]." (*38.*) She may have been a sorceress, accomplished in the black arts of the south-China coast. This reference does not prove that Yüeh slaves were common, but another document shows that there was a market for them. In 113 B.C. Lü Chia, Chancellor under the last three kings of Yüeh, issued a statement accusing the Dowager Queen, who was Chinese, of scheming to surrender the kingdom to China. He asserted that she planned to take a large number of her attendants to Ch'ang-an, and there sell them as slaves (*50*). This accusation would have been meaningless unless the people he was seeking to influence knew there was a ready market for Yüeh slaves at the Han capital.

Along the northern frontier the Chinese intensive farming and walled-city type of culture gradually faded off into extensive agriculture and pastoral husbandry. The frontier was not a fixed boundary line between two nations and two antagonistic cultures, despite the Great Wall which symbolized the Chinese desire to create such a line. As determined by climate and terrain, it was rather a broad zone of change from river valley agriculture to steppe nomadism. The frontier was inhabited by people of mixed stock who employed applicable techniques of production, political organization, domestic life, and warfare derived from both cultures, and freely modified to suit local conditions.[1]

From the north the Hsiung-nu constantly harassed the Chinese colonists and indigenes of the frontier, plundering their goods and livestock and kidnaping plebeians. As early as the time of Emperor Wen, Ch'ao Ts'o suggested methods to strengthen the Chinese colonists against these forays. He proposed that the government encourage the colonists to resist the Hsiung-nu and to "recover" what they plundered. If, when the enemy invaded one area, the people of a neighboring region could intercept them and recapture live stock and people kidnaped, then the original owner should give half the plunder, or half its value, to the rescuer. The government would reimburse the owner. Ch'ao Ts'o thought this system would make the Chinese resist the Huns and mutually rescue each other, not for the glory of the Emperor, but for personal gain (*19*). Ch'ao

---

[1] A most instructive work on the northern frontier is that of Owen Lattimore, *Inner Asian frontiers of China*, New York, 1940.

Ts'o phrased his proposal as a purely defensive measure for newly established colonies, but the real frontiersmen certainly needed no official encouragement to retaliate or initiate raids against the people of the "outer frontier," who were merely more nomad and less "Chinese" than themselves. Such raids were part of the technique of frontier life.

In 33 B.C. Hou Ying gave direct evidence of this practice in a ten-point speech against turning over guardianship of the Wall to the then friendly southern Hsiung-nu. He pointed out that a similar policy had been tried with the Ch'iang people inhabiting eastern Tibet, but that peace had been disturbed because greedy Chinese officials and commoners had invaded their territory and stolen their livestock, produce, women and children. Hou Ying argued that the same thing would happen if China ceased to man the Wall and the Hsiung-nu moved in. What he apparently feared was that the zone of "kidnaping" by Chinese, and "rebellion" by the Hsiung-nu, would be moved in closer to the central core of China. Another of his arguments is probably indirect testimony that the Chinese kidnaped and enslaved their northern neighbors. He reported that the male and female slaves of the frontier people were "melancholy and bitter." Many wanted to escape to the Hsiung-nu lands, where they considered life to be happy. Some did indeed escape and the others were restrained only by the oppressive vigilance of the guard-watchers on the Wall (96).[1] Now, slaves who wanted to escape to the happy life of the Hsiung-nu were very likely marginal people or Hsiung-nu themselves. Real Chinese slaves from interior provinces would not only be in general ill-adapted to frontier life, but would be much more likely to long for their own homelands, as did most Chinese colonists.

Two incidents in the first century of the Latter Han reflect a trade in foreign slaves which was probably in operation during the period covered by this study. In A.D. 49 the leader of the Wu-huan people west of the Liao (western Manchuria and eastern Inner Mongolia) came with 900 followers to the Chinese court to present "tribute," which consisted of male and female slaves, cattle and horses, bows, and the furs of tiger, leopard, and sable. Because of

---

[1] The statement that watchers of the Wall prevented slaves from escaping to the Hsiung-nu is a minor corroboration of Lattimore's thesis that the Great Wall had a double function: it was just as important to keep the intra-mural frontier peoples under Chinese political control as to protect China from the nomads outside. Cf. Lattimore, op. cit., pp. 480–482. A treaty of peace with the Hsiung-nu in A.D. 5 stipulated as its first item that Chinese absconding to the Hsiung-nu should not be given asylum (96, footnote 4).

the size of the party the tribute was probably large.   In return they received rich imperial "gifts." [1]   Exchange of "tribute" and "gifts" between rulers of states in Mongolia and Central Asia and the Chinese government was actually trade.[2]   There is every reason to believe that the first historical notice of slaves in this exchange came long after, not before, they were first used in trade at the frontiers.

Shortly before A.D. 90 Li Hsün was appointed internuncio, or director of guests, and sent to be Assistant Protector-General of the Western Regions.   On several occasions hostage princes, ambassadors, and foreign merchants tried to present to him male and female slaves, Ferghana horses, gold, silver, incense, and rugs, but he refused to accept them.[3]   Considering Li Hsün's position, these gifts, part of the stock in trade of visiting foreigners, must have been bribes.   The slaves probably came from Central Asia, since most of the goods listed were unmistakably products of the "Western Regions."   The historian reported Li Hsün's refusal as an illustration of his particularly virtuous character.   It may be concluded, therefore, that officials in similar positions normally accepted such gifts,[4] and that slaves were part of the Central Asian trade in Former Han times just as they were later, in T'ang times.

These are the principal ways by which free Chinese and foreigners became slaves.   Major crimes by family members led exclusively to government slavery; economic distress and kidnaping produced private bondsmen; while foreigners, enslaved by methods generally unknown, went to both categories of owner.

During the 230-year period covered by this study, and particularly during the reign of Emperor Wu, China fought a series of extensive and costly wars on its several frontiers.   In these foreign wars thousands of the enemy were captured.   The custom of enslaving prisoners of war has had a very wide distribution in various historical periods, though it was by no means universal.   Warfare

[1] HHS, 120, 2a.

[2] Cf. Frederick J. Teggart, *Rome and China*, Berkeley, Calif., 1939, pp. 214–216, especially footnote 59; Lattimore, op. cit., p. 175.

[3] HHS, 81, 1a.   On other men who held the position around the same time, and the regions under control, cf. Edouard Chavannes, "Trois généraux chinois de la dynastie des Han orientaux," TP, 2nd ser., vol. 7, 1906, pp. 210–269.

[4] As noted by Ma Fei-pai (op. cit., p. 388).   Lao Kan (op. cit., p. 9), quoting the *Tung kuan chi*, emphasizes that the slaves were Hu, "barbarians."

was probably the main source of Roman slaves at the other side of the Eurasian continent at precisely the period here being examined. Therefore the question arises: Did the Chinese make slaves of enemy soldiers and civilians captured in battle? Without close examination of the historical evidence it cannot be lightly assumed that they did.

IV. WERE PRISONERS OF WAR ENSLAVED?

To this absorbing and perplexing problem there is no decisive answer. Modern Chinese scholars have reached three divergent conclusions: (1) Prisoners captured in war by the Chinese were enslaved; (2) some prisoners of war may have been enslaved, but this was not characteristic, and prisoners were not an important source of slaves; (3) such captives were not enslaved at all.[1]

Obviously we are on very uncertain ground. These contradictory conclusions are possible precisely because historical sources are neither explicit nor decisive on the matter of disposition of prisoners.

[1] (1) Lao Kan ("The system of slavery during the two Han dynasties," p. 9) states that prisoners of war taken from non-Chinese tribes were all enslaved; but he makes the important observation that barbarian peoples who voluntarily surrendered were not enslaved. Wu Po-lun ("An investigation of slavery in the Western Han," p. 281) believes that enslavement of prisoners was universal in Western Han times, and that one of the principal reasons for the wars with the Hsiung-nu was to capture slaves.

(2) Wu Ching-ch'ao ("The slavery system of the Western Han," p. 265) says that prisoners of war were not an important source of slaves in Western Han times. He points out that it is exceedingly difficult to say whether or not Hsiung-nu captured on the field of battle were all enslaved, but considering the large numbers it is hard to believe that they all were. Wang Shih-chieh ("The Chinese slavery system," pp. 309–310 [trans. Toni Pippon, "Beitrag zum Chinesischen Sklavensystem," p. 104]) states that there were several cases during Chinese history when large numbers of prisoners were made slaves, but that this situation usually occurred in times of internal war and dynastic change when Chinese soldiers took soldiers and civilians of rival regions as slaves. Moreover, the practice was more common when non-Chinese ruled the country. He does not discuss Chinese enslavement of non-Chinese enemy. Liang Ch'i-ch'ao ("System of slavery in China," p. 542) does not mention captured enemy as slaves until after T'ang times, when they became common. He considers the practice more typical of northern barbarians who ruled China during much of the time after T'ang. Ma Ch'eng-feng ("Ts'ung hsi Chou tao Sui ch'u chih i-ch'ien-ch'i-pai yü nien ti ching-chi chuan-i [Economic transition during the seventeen hundred years from Western Chou to the beginning of Sui]," *Shih Huo*, vol. 2, No. 9, Oct. 1, 1935, pp. 400–410, [see p. 403]) emphasizes that prisoners of war were not the principal source of slaves.

(3) T'ao Hsi-sheng (*An economic history of Western Han*, p. 56) asserts that captives were not made slaves, and that in fact many thousands of them were supported by the government with food and clothing and received rewards. He cites as evidence the case of the followers of the King of Hun-hsieh (cf. 40, footnote 1), thus failing to distinguish between captives taken on the field of battle, and enemy who voluntarily surrendered (cf. my discussion, pp. 102–103 below). Yet he represents a strong school of thought on Chinese economic history. Apparently T'ao Hsi-sheng held the opposite opinion in his article entitled "A new estimate of the development and process of the forms of Chinese society (Chung-kuo she-hui hsing-shih fa-chan kuo-ch'eng ti hsin ku-ting)," in which he stressed the fundamental position of a slavery economy in Han times. I have not seen this article, but Ma Ch'eng-feng (*An economic history of China*, vol. 2, p. 237) quotes him as saying that the military conquests of the two Han periods—especially the brilliant conquests of Emperor Wu—were a movement for slave-hunting and commercial expansion. Ma refutes this view with numerous arguments and citations, thus placing himself in the camp which believes that prisoners of war were not enslaved (pp. 237–244) or were not an important source of slaves (p. 322).

In regard to most campaigns they record the numbers of enemy killed and captured, but none tells what was eventually done with the captives.[1] This is even more puzzling because a Chinese ethnographical account of the Hsiung-nu, written during the second century B.C., tells explicitly that enemy captured by the Hsiung-nu in battle became the private slaves of their individual captors (54).

RECORDS OF CAPTIVES

How accurate are the records of enemy killed and captured, and was there falsification? Why were records kept? On the whole, reports are quite specific. When the numbers are small they are stated exactly,[2] but when large they are estimated in round numbers. Frequently if a campaign is described in several different chapters, one account will give a precise figure while the others will be general. Thus in reporting the first campaign led by Ho Ch'ü-ping in 121 B.C., two accounts say that he killed or captured over 8,000 Huns, but the laudatory speech by Emperor Wu, probably quoted directly, tells of his killing or capturing 8,960.[3]

Keeping records of enemy losses as accurately as possible was important because rewards of honorary rank in the official hierarchy

[1] I have searched in vain through the memoirs on those foreign nations with whom the Chinese fought, the chronicles of the Han emperors, and the biographies of the great Han generals for any indication of what was done with enemy soldiers and civilians after they were captured. Chinese writers on Han slavery consulted have likewise produced no positive historical references.

[2] Thus CHS, 41, 1a, which tells that Fan K'uai at various times "beheaded 15," "beheaded 23," "beheaded 40 and captured 16," etc.

[3] CHS, 55, 3b, as compared with 6, 6a and 94A, 8b.

It is necessary here to discuss the terminology involved in these reports.

The most important term is *lu* 虜, which means "to capture an enemy" or "an enemy captured alive in warfare." This definition of *lu* is confirmed by the commentators Chin Shao (ca. A.D. 275) and Yen Shih-ku (A.D. 581–645), and is proved contextually, for example, in the biographies of Fan K'uai, Hsia-hou Ying, and Chin Hsi (CHS, 41, *passim*, and SC, 95 and 98, *passim*). Lists of their successes state how many enemy heads were cut off, prisoners captured, enemy surrendered, cities taken, armies defeated, etc., in such a way that *lu* can only mean prisoners. Furthermore, several instances of *lu* giving valuable military information show that they were soldiers taken alive (CHS, 55, 5b, twice; 94B, 10b).

The term has other meanings. The most common is a general designation for the enemy. The Hsiung-nu were often simply called *lu*. This is a potential source of confusion with *lu* meaning "a captured enemy." A third meaning is "male slave." The *Tz'u yüan* explains that "the ancients used captured *lu* as household male slaves. Therefore they also called slave-servants '*lu*.'" *Locus classicus* for this meaning is a passage in the SC biography of Li Ssu, in a memorial addressed to the second Ch'in Emperor, which quotes Han Fei-tzu as saying: "It is the affectionate mother who has the prodigal son, while the severe household is without fierce slaves (*lu*)." (SC, 87, 6b. Derk Bodde, trans., *China's first unifier*,

were given to officers in proportion to their successes. Very successful generals and other commanding officers were given marquisates which carried incomes expressed in terms of households in the fief. In the heat of battle, records of enemy slain or captured by individual soldiers must have been hard to keep accurately, yet men of the ranks sometimes received money rewards after the return of a highly successful expedition. After the campaigns of 124 and 123 B.C., for example, the soldiers who had cut off heads or captured enemy, received grants which were reported to total more than 200,000 catties of gold. Although this may be an exaggeration, there is no reason to doubt the fact that large money rewards helped to bankrupt the government.[1]

p. 40; cf. J. J. L. Duyvendak, *The book of Lord Shang*, p. 291, footnote 1. In Han Fei-tzu the passage appears in ch. 19, [par. 50], p. 26.) *Lu* is also often used in the generalized sense of "despicable person"; cf. the analogous term "caitiff," derived from Latin *captivus*.

The term most commonly used for enemy slain in battle is *shou* 首, "head." In statements of successes of military expeditions or of individual commanders a regular formula was used to report the number slain: "斬首 . . . [number] . . . 級, i.e. heads cut off . . . [so many] . . . degrees [of honorary rank]." This equation of degrees of honorary rank with numbers of enemy slain apparently began with the practice in Ch'in State of granting one degree for each enemy slain in battle. Cf. Duyvendak, op. cit., pp. 63 and 295–303 (cf. p. 147 for a discussion of par. 19); Bodde, op. cit., p. 8. The term *shou* 級, in the combination *shou* . . . *chi*, appears by Han times to have had the value merely of a numerical classifier.

In texts referring to the early part of the Han period, enemy soldiers slain and those captured in battle are normally listed separately (cf. CHS, 41, *passim*). However, reports during and after the reign of Emperor Wu usually give totals of soldiers lost by the enemy. It is impossible to distinguish the number in each category. The formula 斬首捕虜 or 斬獲首虜, followed by the total number, is often abbreviated to 得 (or 獲, or 斬, or 斬, or 捷) 首虜. Furthermore, beginning with the reign of Emperor Wu the word *chi* "degrees [of honorary rank]," is frequently used in the passages which lump enemy slain with enemy captured. In CHS, 55, 2a, Yen Shih-ku explains the use of *chi* for both slain and captured. "Originally," he says, "for one head of a slain enemy [a person] was conferred one degree of honorary rank. Therefore one head was called one degree. Accordingly they also named one [enemy] taken alive as one degree."

For the expression *shou lu*, Chavannes (MH, vol. III, p. 553, footnote 2) adopts the translation "esclaves soumis." This gives *shou* the special meaning of *fu* 服, "to submit." But there appears to be no evidence for this sense before Latter Han times, and it seems incorrect for the previous period to give a special meaning to *shou* in combination with *lu*. Dubs discusses this problem (HFHD, vol. II, footnote 7.8 to chapter VI).

The act of voluntary surrender was called *hsiang* 降. Loot was called *lu* 鹵; but this term sometimes means captives also.

A Latter Han bas-relief of a battle scene shows enemy heads hanging in a rack and prisoners with hands tied behind their backs. Cf. Edouard Chavannes, *Mission archéologique dans la Chine septentrionale*, 2 vols. plates, 2 vols. text, Paris, 1909, 1913, 1915: pl. XXVI, No. 47, lower left, and pl. XXVIII, No. 50, left center.

[1] CHS, 24b, 3b; SC, 30, 2b (MH, vol. III, pp. 552–553). Two hundred thousand catties (*chin*) of "yellow metal" come to 1,568,000 troy ounces, accord-

Since success in killing and capturing enemy brought valuable rewards, records were sometimes falsified. But this was dangerous, for discovery of deceit brought severe punishment. The fact that reports were closely scrutinized and falsification was dangerous adds a certain degree of credibility to the figures finally given by the historian. The following trials illustrate the procedure against falsifiers.

Wei Shang, Administrator of a commandery in present Suiyuan province, fought a whole day with the highest merit for killing and capturing Hsiung-nu; but because the reports by his staff members did not exactly agree he was tried and not rewarded. Considering this a great injustice, Feng T'ang protested to Emperor Wen that the laws were too strict, rewards too light, and punishments too severe. He said that because of a miscalculation of only *six*, the Emperor had turned Wei Shang over to civil officials who had stripped him of his honorary rank. Emperor Wen saw the injustice and immediately ordered Feng T'ang to take credentials pardoning Wei Shang and reappointing him Administrator of Yün-chung. In 117 B.C. Kuo Pu-chih, the Marquis of I-kuan, was tried for increasing the count of heads he had taken in a fight with the Hsiung-nu. He should have been executed but was allowed to pay redemption and was merely dismissed from his marquisate. In 71 B.C. Ch'e Shun, the Marquis of Fu-min, was tried for falsely increasing the amount of loot and number of captives taken in a battle with the Hsiung-nu. He committed suicide.[1]

Yang P'u tried a most interesting variant on this dangerous trick. He had won considerable merit as a general against the southern Yüeh in 112 B.C., and was made Marquis of Chiang-liang. When the Eastern Yüeh "rebelled," Emperor Wu planned to use him again. Because Yang P'u was excessively boastful about his earlier accomplishments, the Emperor sent him a letter of reproof, listing his various faults, the first of which was that in the defeat of P'an-yü (Canton) he had seized people who had surrendered and made them prisoners of war, and had dug up corpses and used them as slain enemy! The significant point in this case is the

ing to a personal communication from Dr. Homer H. Dubs. Today, at a price of $35.00 per ounce, this "yellow metal," if real gold, would be worth $54,880,000 in United States currency.

[1] For Feng T'ang, see CHS, 50, 3a; SC, 102, 3b. For Kuo Pu-chih, CHS, 17, 8a; SC, 20, 9b. Note the commentary by Yen Shih-ku. For Ch'e Shun, CHS, 18, 8b; 66, 3b; and 94A, 14a.

clear distinction between enemy captured in warfare and enemy who voluntarily surrendered.[1]

DIFFERENTIATION BETWEEN SURRENDERED AND CAPTURED ENEMY

This distinction is important, and it is just here that some Chinese writers confuse the whole issue by failing to differentiate between the two. The distinction was much more sharply drawn than that between enemy slain and captured in battle. The disposition of captured enemy is unknown but several cases show what happened to those who surrendered voluntarily.

During the overthrow of the Ch'in dynasty, when a city or a general voluntarily surrendered, the normal procedure was to leave the civilian population alone, but to annex most of the surrendered army. Sometimes defeated soldiers were enlisted in the victorious army.[2] Hsiang Yü executed a reported 200,000 Ch'in soldiers who had been surrendered by their general, perhaps against their will (6). This slaughter, in violation of the accepted code, is one of the blackest crimes charged against him.

Foreigners who surrendered voluntarily were not supposed to be mistreated. For example, Li Kuang, consulting a soothsayer, attributed his failure to be promoted to the fact that he once induced 800 rebellious Ch'iang to surrender, and then killed them. The interpreter of psychic emanations agreed, saying that nothing was more calamitous than killing those who had already surrendered.[3]

There are several examples before the reign of Emperor Wu of enemy being rewarded for surrendering to China. About 166–164 B.C., Han T'ui-tang and Han Ying, grandsons of a Chinese king who had joined the Hsiung-nu, surrendered with their followers and were given marquisates. When Hsiu-lu and four other Hsiung-nu kings surrendered, about 147 B.C., Emperor Ching made them marquises to encourage other alien kings to submit also. Three more became marquises by surrendering during his reign.[4]

---

[1] CHS, 90, 5a. 捕降者以爲虜掘死者以爲獲.

Another irregularity occurred in the same campaign, for in 104 B.C. Sun Hsiang, who inherited the Marquisate of Lin-ts'ai, was tried for having appropriated other people's prisoners (*lu*) and loot in the battle of P'an-yüeh (CHS, 17, 13b).

[2] Cf. HFHD, vol. I, pp. 44, 49, 53–54, 75.

[3] CHS, 54, 3a; SC, 109, 3a.

[4] For Han T'ui-tang and Han Ying, see CHS, 33, 4b; 16, 53a, and 54a. For the eight Hsiung-nu kings made marquises, CHS, 17, 3a–4a.

Between 140 and 119 B.C., ten kings, four chancellors, two majors, a *Tang-hu*, and the Hsiung-nu Heir-apparent, deposed on his father's death by his uncle, voluntarily surrendered and were given marquisates.[1] Such surrenders were natural during a period of Chinese military ascendancy. It is highly significant that there is no correspondence between the names of these Hsiung-nu who were given marquisates and the names of Hsiung-nu leaders captured between 129, when active war commenced, and 119, the year of China's greatest success. None of the Hsiung-nu leaders named as being captured is listed as receiving a marquisate, and all Hsiung-nu who became marquises are specifically stated to have surrendered. Furthermore, accounts of campaigns in those years often mention captured Hsiung-nu officials by title only, yet even these titles are never reflected in the list of marquises appointed in corresponding or succeeding years. Obviously, then, those Hsiung-nu officials who resisted the Chinese and were taken in battle were treated very differently from those who surrendered voluntarily.

The wars against kingdoms in present southwestern and southeastern China and in Korea were of short duration, and the Chinese took relatively few prisoners. But the wars against the Hsiung-nu were of a quite different order. Intermittent punitive expeditions and minor warfare characterize the period before Emperor Wu, the "Martial Emperor." Much of his reign was devoted to successive campaigns against the Hsiung-nu, who lost vast territories in the northwest. After 90 B.C. the armed peace was broken only occasionally until the time of Wang Mang, when the Hsiung-nu succeeded in recapturing much of their lost territory.

TYPICAL REPORTS OF WARS AND CAPTURES

Historical accounts of the Hsiung-nu wars follow a general pattern. A digest of the seven campaig⁻ between 129 and 119 B.C. indicates the nature of the available information about treatment of prisoners of war—Hsiung-nu, Koreans, Cantonese, or any other people. These campaigns[2] are interesting because of the extraor-

[1] CHS, 17, 4b–10a; SC, 20, 1b–14b (MH, vol. III, pp. 161–169).

[2] Information on them is found in CHS, 6, the "Annals of Emperor Wu," 3b–7a, under respective years; in the biographies of Wei Ch'ing and Ho-Ch'ü-ping, CHS, 55, 1b–3a (SC, 111, 1b–3a), and CHS, 55, 3a–6a (SC, 111, 3a–6b), respectively; and in the "Memoir on the Hsiung-nu," CHS, 94A, 7b–9b (SC, 110, 8b–10b). Further facts appear scattered through biographies of lesser commanders, statesmen, and the "Treatise on Economics."

In preparing this description the material in all these sources was translated and collated, but it is impossible to give a continuous and intelligible narrative

dinary totals that are reported of persons killed and captured. Furthermore, unique information on slavery at this particular time appears to bear upon the question of enslavement of prisoners.

Campaign of 129 B.C.—In the fall or winter of 130 the Hsiung-nu invaded Shang-ku. The following spring Emperor Wu dispatched four armies of 10,000 cavalry each, from four bases on the center of the northern frontier: Shang-ku, Tai, Yen-men, and Yün-chung. Only Wei Ch'ing, commander of the eastern army, distinguished himself by going to Lung-ch'eng, the place of the annual Hsiung-nu spring assembly, and killing or capturing some 700 of the enemy. The two central forces under Kung-sun Ao and Li Kuang were badly beaten, Kung-sun Ao losing 7,000 soldiers, most of his army. The western force under Kung-sun Ho achieved nothing significant. How Wei Ch'ing was able to reach Lung-ch'eng in west-central Mongolia, when the other three forces made no headway from points much nearer, is not explained. Perhaps he made a rapid dash behind the Hsiung-nu armies. He could not have encountered much resistance for he killed or captured only 700 of the enemy.

Campaign of 128 B.C.—In the winter of 129 B.C., and again in the autumn of the next year the Hsiung-nu invaded the northeastern frontiers at Yü-yang, Liao-hsi, and Yen-men, killing or kidnaping more than 3,000 people. Wei Ch'ing set out from Yen-men with a force of 30,000 cavalry, and Li Hsi started from Tai,

and at the same time discuss textual differences and debatable terms. The following paragraphs, then, are a synthesis. Figures are quoted as given. A copy of Herrmann's *Historical and commercial atlas of China* (pp. 22–23; p. 17, II; and p. 24) is useful; see also Map, this volume.

PLACE NAMES IN ORDER OF APPEARANCE

Shang-ku	Southern Chahar, just northwest of Peking.
Tai	Southern Chahar, northeast of present Yü hsien.
Yen-men	Northern Shensi, west of Tatung.
Yün-chung	Southern Suiyuan, southeast of Paotow.
Lung-ch'eng	In west-central Mongolia, but not precisely located.
Yü-yang	Northeast of Peking on the road to Kupeikow.
Liao-hsi	Northeastern Hopei near Shanhaikuan.
Kao-ch'üeh	Near northwest bend of the upper Yellow River.
Lung-hsi	Kansu, near Lanchow.
Shuo-fang	Southern Suiyuan, on the west side of the Ordos along the Yellow River.
Ting-hsiang	Northern Shansi, near Yuyü hsien west of Tatung.
Shang	Eastern Shensi, southeast of Suite hsien.
Yu-pei-p'ing	Northeastern Hopei and southern Jehol.
Pei-ti	Eastern Kansu, near Huan hsien.
Chü-yen	Northern Ningsia, southwest of Gashun-gol.
Ch'i-lien Mountains	Or Nan-shan, the range skirting the south of western Kansu.
Hsiu-ch'u	Kansu, around present Wuwei or Lanchow.
Hun-hsieh	Kansu, around present Kiuchuan or Suchow.
Chih-yen Mountain	In Outer Mongolia, but unidentified.

with an army of unreported size. Wei Ch'ing killed or captured several thousand, but considering the force involved this was an unimpressive campaign.

Campaign of 127 B.C.—In the spring, Wei Ch'ing and Li Hsi again set out, this time from Yün-chung, farther west. Following the upper course of the Yellow River, first to the west as far as Kao-ch'üeh and then south to Lung-hsi in Kansu, they defeated the Hun King of Lo-fan, killed or captured several thousand, and took more than a million head of cattle. Farther west they defeated two other kings and captured 3,017 people. Because of these successes China took the land south of the river—that is, within the great bend of the Yellow River: southwestern Suiyuan, western Shensi, and eastern Kansu—and established Shuo-fang Commandery. Using the river for a defense, China restored the Ch'in dynasty wall built by Meng T'ien, and transported a hundred thousand people from the interior to populate the Shuo-fang territory, which became a new base. Emperor Wu made a laudatory speech detailing Wei Ch'ing's victories, and enfeoffed him as the Marquis of Ch'ang-p'ing with the income from an additional 3,800 households.

Campaign of 124 B.C.—The Worthy King of the West, in command of the western Hsiung-nu dominions, contested this loss of his territory by invading Shuo-fang and killing or kidnaping many of the colonists. Other Hsiung-nu raiding parties invaded the central northern frontier at Tai, Yen-men, and Ting-hsiang, and even penetrated to Shang Commandery. At this time the frontiers were obviously very loosely defined and held.

In the spring of 124 China organized more than 100,000 men, led by six generals under Wei Ch'ing, and an attempt was made to demolish Hsiung-nu opposition in the new northwest area. Wei Ch'ing led 30,000 cavalry from Kao-ch'üeh, while Su Chien, Li Chü, Kung-sun Ho, and Li Ts'ai went jointly from Shuo-fang. Far to the east another army under Li Hsi and Chang Tz'u-kung went out from Yu-pei-p'ing with no important results.

The armies of Wei Ch'ing advanced rapidly from the wall six or seven hundred *li*, took the Worthy King of the West completely by surprise, and surrounded his encampment in the night. Although the Hsiung-nu king escaped with a few followers, the Chinese captured some ten petty kings, 15,000 men and women, and several hundred thousand to a million herd animals. Wei Ch'ing then led his troops back to the wall and was greeted by an imperial emissary who conferred on him the title of General-in-Chief. After a review of the troops Wei Ch'ing returned to the capital where the Emperor lauded him, giving him an additional fief of 8,700 households and making his three sons marquises. Various senior officers whose troops had distinguished themselves also received rewards.

This campaign firmly established Chinese control of the region within the great northward bend of the Yellow River, which, in turn, allowed the Chinese to push out through the narrow corridor of Kansu toward the strategic oases in the desert to the west.

Campaign of 123 B.C.—Two successive expeditions against the Hsiung-nu center were successful but not conclusive. Early in the spring Wei Ch'ing and six generals—Kung-sun Ao, Kung-sun Ho, Chao Hsin, Su Chien, Li Kuang, and Li Chü—left Ting-hsiang with more than 100,000 cavalry. The Chinese killed or captured only some 3,000 of the enemy, and the army returned to rest at Ting-hsiang, Yün-chung, and Yen-men.

In the second campaign two months later the main army killed or captured some 15,000. Ho Ch'ü-ping first distinguished himself as a major in charge of 800 light cavalry. He advanced several hundred *li* beyond the main force, killing or capturing 2,028 of the enemy. At the same time, however, a small force of some 3,000 cavalry under Su Chien and Chao Hsin stumbled on a much larger force of the Hsiung-nu, and without support was completely defeated. Su Chien escaped but Chao Hsin surrendered with about 800 of his cavalry and joined the Hsiung-nu *Shan-yü*. Chao Hsin was originally a petty king of the Huns who had surrendered to China some years before and been granted a marquisate. After he went over to the Hsiung-nu he became the principal adviser of their ruler, who gave him a daughter in marriage.

The combined total of enemy killed and captured reached 19,000, but the *Shan-yü* had maintained his own army intact, so the result was not decisive.

Campaign of 121 B.C.—In the spring Ho Ch'ü-ping led a select force of 10,000 cavalry from Lung-hsi some thousand *li* out through the narrow corridor of modern Kansu province. He killed or captured more than 8,000, and seized the sacrificial gold idol[1] of the King of Hsiu-ch'u.

Early in the summer Ho Ch'ü-ping and Kung-sun Ao went out from Pei-ti and Lung-hsi, leading an army of several myriad cavalry.

---

[1] For recent discussions of this event, see H. H. Dubs ("The 'golden man' of Former Han times," TP, vol. 33, 1937, pp. 1–14) and J. R. Ware ("Once more the 'golden man,'" TP, vol. 34, 1938, pp. 174–178).

Kung-sun Ao lost the road and did not meet Ho Ch'ü-ping at the appointed place. Nevertheless Ho Ch'ü-ping pushed out through Chü-yen, then turned south and delivered a crushing blow near the Ch'i-lien Mountains. In his document of praise, Emperor Wu listed 30,200 enemy killed or captured, 2,500 surrendered, and 59 enemy nobility and 63 high military officers captured. Ho Ch'ü-ping lost only 30 per cent of his forces, which was apparently considered low. He was given 5,400 additional households for his marquisate, and two of his subordinates were enfeoffed. Kung-sun Ao was tried for failing to keep his appointment, but was allowed to pay redemption and was made a commoner.

Because of Chinese successes in this campaign the Hsiung-nu kings of Hsiu-ch'u and Hun-hsieh, in western Kansu, decided to submit voluntarily to China. By their surrender the empire acquired areas of great strategic importance.

An expedition on the extreme eastern flank was a dismal failure. A force of 10,000 cavalry under Chang Ch'ien and another of 4,000 under Li Kuang set out by different roads from Yu-pei-p'ing to attack the Worthy King of the East. Li Kuang's force was surrounded and nearly cut to pieces before Chang Ch'ien arrived to rescue the remnants. Chang Ch'ien was tried for delay on the way, but instead of being executed he was allowed to pay redemption and became a commoner.

Campaign of 119 B.C.—This last campaign was the greatest triumph of all, for it shattered the armies of both the *Shan-yü* and the Worthy King of the East. Neither had been really defeated before; the previous great successes had been in the west. Late in the spring an enormous Chinese army of 100,000 cavalry, several hundred thousand infantry and supply columns, and 140,000 horses privately provided, assembled at Ting-hsiang under the joint command of Wei Ch'ing and Ho Ch'ü-ping. Prisoners taken in a preliminary reconnaissance revealed that the *Shan-yü* was farther eastward. It was therefore decided that Ho Ch'ü-ping should take part of the army out from Tai, farther east, making a double thrust by armies operating independently. Chao Hsin devised the strategy of the *Shan-yü*. The Hsiung-nu would withdraw northward and attack the Chinese armies while they were still exhausted from crossing the desert.

Wei Ch'ing split his army into four or five columns, to meet at a predetermined place. Two columns failed to arrive at the rendezvous. Nevertheless, as soon as Wei Ch'ing had crossed the desert with the main force and sighted the Hsiung-nu he prepared for battle. He ordered his baggage train to form a solid ring for an encampment and kept most of his army hidden. Then he led forward a deceptively small body of 5,000 cavalry. Suddenly a great windstorm blew up and the air was filled with sand, so that the armies were invisible to each other. Wei Ch'ing brought up his right and left wings and encircled the Hsiung-nu, who were actually weaker than the Chinese. In the confusion of battle the *Shan-yü* escaped northwestward with a hundred cavalry. A little later the Chinese, learning of his escape from an enemy prisoner, sent a body of light cavalry in pursuit, but they failed to capture the Hsiung-nu ruler. The battle continued in great confusion through the night, with both sides suffering heavy losses. By morning the Chinese had won a decisive victory, killing or capturing more than 10,000 Hsiung-nu and putting the rest to flight.

Wei Ch'ing then advanced with his army to Chao Hsin's base at Chih-yen Mountain in Outer Mongolia, where he captured the Hsiung-nu grain stores. After resting and provisioning his troops, he burned the "city" and enemy stores. While recrossing the desert he met the two generals that had failed to keep their appointment. Li Kuang committed suicide, while the other general was allowed to pay redemption and became a commoner. The total of enemy killed and captured was 19,000.

Ho Ch'ü-ping's army of picked fighters was even more successful, though the details of the campaign are not reported. Riding out from Tai and Yu-pei-p'ing some 2,000 *li*, it defeated the army of the Worthy King of the East, killed or captured more than 70,000 persons, and seized three petty kings and 83 high officials and officers. Chinese casualties were 20 or 30 per cent.

The combined totals for the campaign of 119 B.C. are given as 80,000 or 90,000 Hsiung-nu killed and captured. The Chinese losses were "counted by the myriad." They also lost more than 100,000 horses. Thus, although they won a crushing victory from which the Hsiung-nu did not recover in a century, they won it at great cost in men and material.

Summary.—The biographies of Wei Ch'ing and Ho Ch'ü-ping conclude with summaries of their military achievements: Wei Ch'ing is credited with killing or capturing more than 50,000 in seven campaigns, while Ho Ch'ü-ping is credited with more than 110,000 in six campaigns, during the last four of which he was a general in charge of his own forces.

PRESUMPTIVE EVIDENCE FOR ENSLAVEMENT OF CAPTIVES

Were the Hsiung-nu captured in these seven campaigns enslaved? In the historical sources we can find presumptive evidence that some captives were enslaved. Then other questions arise. How many or what proportion of the captives became slaves? Were they an important part of the slave population? What was done with those who were not enslaved?

Certain facts associated with the surrender of the King of Hun-hsieh and his people lead to the belief that some Hsiung-nu captives were made slaves. In 121 B.C. Ho Ch'ü-ping overran most of present Kansu province, the western stronghold of the Hsiung-nu. The *Shan-yü*, enraged at his heavy losses, summoned the kings of that area to his court, planning to execute them. Instead of going, they decided to surrender to China, and sent an ambassador to announce their decision. Fearing a plot, Emperor Wu sent Ho Ch'ü-ping to meet them. At the last minute the King of Hsiu-ch'u lost heart, and the King of Hun-hsieh murdered him and merged the two hordes. Just before crossing the river some of the King's officers wanted to withdraw, fearing the treatment they would receive. Ho Ch'ü-ping immediately galloped up and slew those who wanted to flee. He must have been attended by a strong force, for it is said that he killed 8,000! Those who surrendered numbered more than 40,000, though they claimed to be 100,000.[1]

The Chinese government issued 30,000 carts to transport these people with their belongings to the capital. Various local governments along the route were taxed heavily to feed them. The King of Hun-hsieh received a marquisate having an income from 10,000 households, while three of his petty kings and his chief *Tang-hu* received marquisates of 500 to 700 households each. The government gave rich rewards to the surrendered people, supplied them with food and clothes, and established them as members of Dependent States in eastern Kansu, Shensi, and southern Suiyüan, at An-ting, T'ien-shui, Shang Commandery, Hsi-ho, and Wu-yüan. The Bureau for Dependent States had to be expanded to handle the increased administrative problems. Presumably the people continued their pastoral economy, for the new territory, though farther east, was similar to that which they had abandoned. They also had to help defend their new homeland. For example, in 111 B.C. other

---

[1] For the account of the surrender see CHS, 6, 6a–b; 55, 4b–5a (SC, 111, 4b); and 94A, 8b (SC, 110, 10a). For marquisates and rewards see also CHS, 17, 8a–b (SC, 20, 10a–11b); 24B, 3b. For the establishments of the Dependent States, see CHS, 6, 6a–b; for their location see Map, this volume; for the Bureau of

Hsiung-nu invaded one of the places where these Dependent States had been established, and cavalry from T'ien-shui and An-ting was mustered to fight them.

This voluntary surrender opened to Chinese political and military control most of that long salient of western Kansu which was the strategic highway to the oases kingdoms of Chinese Turkestan. Without control of this region any further push westward would have been impossible. Moreover, this surrender represented the first major success in the Emperor's policy of splitting up the Hsiung-nu empire.

Now, when the King of Hun-hsieh surrendered he brought along the Queen and the two sons of the King of Hsiu-ch'u as prisoners. The Chinese government seized them and made them slaves (*41*).

Furthermore, one of Emperor Wu's officials proposed that the whole horde be enslaved. This official, Chi Yen, was indignant because 500 Chinese merchants were sentenced to death for trading with these Hsiung-nu at Ch'ang-an. A law which prohibited exporting or selling weapons and iron to the Hsiung-nu at the frontier passes had been invoked against these merchants, though they had traded at the capital. Chi Yen, who was prefect of the western section of the capital, and a noted champion of the people, considered this a great injustice and protested to Emperor Wu (*40*):

> Now, the Hsiung-nu, attacking and blocking the highways and barriers, broke the [treaty of] peace and friendship. China raised troops to punish them, and the [Chinese] killed and wounded were innumerable, while the expenses were counted by the ten billions [of cash]. Your servant foolishly thinks that when Your Majesty obtains northern barbarians they should all be made slaves and be granted to the families of those who died in the army; [also let (whatever)] is captured be given to them, in order to relieve the empire ['s distress] and satisfy the hearts of the people.
>
> Now, supposing You cannot do that. The King of Hun-hsieh comes leading a horde of several myriad [to surrender. You] empty the treasury

Dependent States see CHS, 19A, 5b (MH, vol. II, p. 523). On the use of cavalry from T'ien-shui and An-ting see CHS, 6, 9a. A little later, Chao Po-nu led a large force of "cavalry of the Dependent States" to fight the Hsiung-nu; in 104 B.C. Li Kuang-li used 6,000 "cavalry of the Dependent States" against the city of Erh-shih (CHS, 61, 3b and 4a, respectively). Under later emperors there was considerable use of Yüeh, Hu, and Ch'iang cavalry, but these may have been mercenaries.

At the funeral of Ho Ch'ü-ping in 117 B.C. soldiers from the Dependent States, dressed in black armor, were lined up along the way from Ch'ang-an to the cemetery at Mao-ling (CHS, 55, 6a).

For further information on "Dependent States" during Former Han times see P. A. Boodberg, "Two notes on the history of the Chinese frontier," HJAS, vol. 1, 1936, pp. 283–307 (see pp. 287–288).

and reward them, and send forth good people to wait on them as though serving spoiled children. How can the ignorant people understand that because they traded [with the Hsiung-nu] in Ch'ang-an the civil officials arrest them for exporting goods as though at a frontier pass? If Your Majesty cannot derive benefit out of the Hsiung-nu for relief of the empire, still more [how can You] execute more than 500 ignorant people because of a trifling law? Your servant ventures to suggest that Your Majesty should not take [such a step].

What does the essential proposition in the first paragraph signify? Does it indicate, as some Chinese writers believe, that captured Hsiung-nu were not enslaved? One argument is that since Emperor Wu refused to enslave the followers of the King of Hun-hsieh he did not enslave Hsiung-nu captives. This argument is invalid because these were not captured Hsiung-nu fighters, but a special group who had surrendered. Another argument seems to be that since Chi Yen suggested that the Emperor ought to enslave *all* Hsiung-nu he obtained, therefore it was not customary to enslave *any* Hsiung-nu. This is equally fallacious.

Chi Yen brought forward some unusual suggestion which Emperor Wu rejected. To interpret his suggestion correctly it is necessary to determine which part of it was novel. Since the arrival of the Hun-hsieh horde in Ch'ang-an brought on the trial of Chinese merchants the novelty probably concerned these surrendered people. Chi Yen suggested that, since the Hsiung-nu had broken the peace treaties and caused China enormous expense in men and treasure, all Hsiung-nu that the Emperor obtained should be enslaved. Certainly he did not create the idea of enslaving Hsiung-nu. Prisoners of war had been enslaved during Shang and Chou times, and three Hsiung-nu were made slaves on this very occasion.[1] The novelty of his suggestion must have been, therefore, that these surrendered people be treated like captured Hsiung-nu, and be enslaved.

In view of the general situation, in which Hsiung-nu power was weakened and China had gained important areas in Kansu because

[1] Whether shortly before or after cannot be precisely determined. It should be pointed out that the Queen and two sons of the King of Hsiu-ch'u may have been enslaved as the family of a "rebel" rather than as captives of war. The distinction is probably fictitious, since from the Chinese point of view Hsiung-nu "rebelled" and had to be "chastised" when they broke the peace and fought.

For enslavement of captives in Shang times, cf. H. G. Creel, "Soldier and scholar in ancient China," *Pacific Affairs*, vol. 7, 1935, pp. 336–343 (see pp. 341–342 and references cited), and *The birth of China*, London and New York, 1936, pp. 130, 214, 282, and index (New York ed.) under "Slaves." For Chou, especially Ch'un-ch'iu and Chan-kuo periods, consult references cited by Ch'en Hsien-hsüan, "Ch'un-ch'iu ti nu-li [Slavery of the Ch'un-ch'iu period]," *Shih Huo*, vol. 2, No. 5, Aug. 1, 1935, pp. 234–236; Chang Yin-lin, "Chou tai ti feng-chien she-hui (Feudalism in the Chou dynasty)," CHHP, vol. 10, 1935, pp. 803–836

of their surrender, it is unlikely that Chi Yen thought Emperor Wu really would enslave them. To do so would probably have destroyed at one stroke the possibility of splitting off other parts of the Hsiung-nu empire in the future. People who surrendered had to be rewarded, and the Hun-hsieh folk were treated so liberally as to strain the treasury. Thus, Chi Yen made the suggestion merely as an effective contrast to the proposed execution of 500 ignorant Chinese merchants who had unwittingly broken a frontier law.

His proposition also had a second part: Enslaved Hsiung-nu should be bestowed upon families of those who had died in the Chinese army. This should be done in order to relieve the empire's distress and satisfy the hearts of the people. Here too was a novel suggestion. It must have been an extension of current practice. It would be incredible that Chi Yen should come to court and create the whole idea of enslaving all Hsiung-nu—captives and surrendered alike—and of giving them as recompense to Chinese families. Emperor Wu's rejection of the suggestion does not prove that captured Hsiung-nu were not enslaved. He rejected the preposterous idea of enslaving these surrendered Hsiung-nu, or the idea of giving enslaved Hsiung-nu to the families of slain Chinese soldiers. Whatever elements may have been novel in Chi Yen's proposal it seems evident that the presupposed idea of enslaving Hsiung-nu captives was thoroughly familiar and probably in practice.

Two other documents from this period strengthen the conclusion deduced from Chi Yen's proposal to Emperor Wu. In 127 B.C., because of the costs of the first three campaigns against the Hsiung-nu, the government treasuries and arsenals were empty. As a remedy the government appealed to the people to contribute male and female slaves in exchange for tax exemption or increase in honorary rank (*36*). Since these slaves were to improve the condition of the treasury and arsenals they must have been put to work in the arsenals or at money-making projects, or sold for revenue.[1] The latter is the more probable, since female slaves were also requested.

(see pp. 806–807); Liang Ch'i-ch'ao, op. cit., p. 528; Duyvendak, op. cit., p. 298. I have not emphasized historical precedent here because the whole picture of slavery before 200 B.C. is much more fragmentary and confused than that of Han times when documentary material, scant as it is, becomes relatively abundant. Classical references do not prove by context which terms refer unequivocally to slaves, and which refer to serfs, convicts, and free or semi-free menials of various ranks. It does not clarify a doubtful point in Han slavery to cite the practice of a period which is even more obscure. Nor do we know whether the custom of enslaving prisoners—if actually practiced in Chan-kuo times—carried through the Ch'in period into Han.

1 Wu Ching-ch'ao (op. cit., p. 264) believes they were sold.

Since the government was actively seeking slaves it would seem that it must have enslaved those prisoners—captured in the very wars that had depleted the treasury—who showed most adaptability to servitude, and either sold them for revenue or put them to gainful work.

During the period immediately after the last campaign the government appropriated male and female slaves "by the thousand [even to] a myriad" from wealthy Chinese of the merchant class. These slaves were put to work on government enterprises (46). Can it be assumed that a government, needing thousands of slaves for work, would pass by the prisoners it captured in war?

Aside from these four documents dating from the period of the great campaigns, there is another broad, etymological indication that some prisoners were enslaved. At the end of the Ch'in period Chang Han surrendered his Ch'in army to Hsiang Yü and the rebelling nobles, whose officers and soldiers took advantage of the victory to treat the Ch'in soldiers like slave captives (nu lu). The latter feared that if the nobles were unable to conquer Ch'in they would make captives (lu) of them and take them east (6). What did they fear about being taken east as captives? Having been treated like slave captives, was it not that they would be really enslaved?

Here the term lu is important. Used in combination with nu, "male slave," it has its derivative meaning of "slave" as explained (p. 99, footnote 3) in connection with the saying: "It is the affectionate mother who has the prodigal son, while the severe household is without fierce slaves [lu]." The combination nu lu appears with similar meaning in two other translated documents. The biography of Tiao Chien, who made his fortune from the work of slaves, opens with the statement: "In Ch'i it was customary to look down upon male slave captives [nu lu], but Tiao Chien alone appreciated and valued them. Rascally and crafty male slaves are what men suffer from. But Tiao Chien alone gathered and employed them . . . ." (17.) Ssu-ma Hsiang-ju predicted conditions in the southwest—noted as a source for child slaves—if China did not take over the area, saying: ". . . and children and orphans will be made slave captives [nu lu], bound up and weeping . . . ." (A7.) In both these passages lu has by context the sense of "slave." In another instance, Liu Ch'ü, who had murdered two concubines and their female slaves, said in reference to his fear that they would haunt him: "Those captives [lu] will appear again to terrify me . . . ." (64.)

The fact that the word for "captive" is also used as a term for "slave" is only suggestive. It does not by itself prove that captives were enslaved. There is, however, the additional testimony of Chin Shao, who lived during the third century of our era. He says the terms *tsang* and *huo* mean "those defeated enemy who have been captured and made slaves." (*11*, footnote 5.)

Finally, why did the Chinese take prisoners of war at all? It must have been difficult to bring them back to China, and if they were of no value it would have been much easier to kill them on the spot. No people are more eminently practical or shrewd than the Chinese. The government and officers certainly profited from herds of cattle and other loot captured in warfare.[1] Considering the enormous expense entailed in these wars the conclusion is inescapable that some captives were forced to labor as slaves on government works, or were sold.

PROPORTION ENSLAVED, AND DISPOSITION OF OTHERS

If this be admitted, the next questions concern the numbers enslaved and their proportion to the total slave population. About two hundred Hsiung-nu nobles or officials were taken in the seven campaigns, and Wei Ch'ing captured 3,017 people in 127 B.C., and more than 15,000 men and women in 124. Aside from these specific figures it is quite impossible to know the proportion of the 160,000 killed or captured that were taken alive. The problem thus turns upon the question of how many could have been absorbed.

Elsewhere, it is estimated on the basis of a memorial by Kung Yü (*89*) that the government owned about 100,000 slaves in 44 B.C., when it was both rich and extravagant. This figure is probably close to the maximum for the Former Han period. That the government owned many fewer slaves during the time of Emperor Wu may be deduced from the great confiscation of private slaves during the years 119–113, when it appropriated several thousand "[even to] a myriad." (*46*.)[2] This small number nearly swamped the govern-

---

[1] There may have been a regular system of division of loot between officers and the government. Ch'en T'ang was severely censured, or slandered, for his greed in a campaign of 36 B.C. in which he allowed each person to keep what loot he could get, and himself brought in through the wall more loot than was allowed by military law (CHS, 70, 5a and 5b). In 104 B.C. Sun Hsiang was tried for having appropriated other people's prisoners and loot in the battle of Canton (CHS, 17, 13b). It is told that in preparation for the campaign of 119 B.C., 140,000 *private* baggage and following horses were gathered, aside from the regular cavalry horses and provision wagons supplied by the government (CHS, 94A, 9a). This looks very much as though the generals expected to bring back a great deal of loot.

[2] Possibly this should be read "by the thousand and the myriad," an indefinite figure representing a large number but not yet "several myriad." The point is discussed in *46*, footnote 4. This uncertainty is to be borne in mind whenever this document is cited below.

ment. The slaves were sent off to parks and ranches or given to various bureaus. Many government bureaus had to be enlarged and new ones established. Still, a multitude of slaves (and convicts) was sent away to work on the grain transport. If roughly ten thousand or even several myriad private Chinese slaves, the most useful and tractable type, were absorbed by the government only with difficulty in seven years it seems unlikely that as many Hsiung-nu could have been enslaved in an equivalent period. Yet during the previous seven years, 125–119, the total number listed as "killed and captured" was roughly 138,000, in addition to the 15,000 men and women definitely stated to have been taken alive in 124.

Most adult Hsiung-nu males would have been unsuited for jobs in government bureaus or skilled manufacturing; they could have been used profitably only in ranching and gang labor. Yet multitudes of criminals and the corvée system regularly provided as much forced labor as the government could employ. As for ranches, the *Han chiu i* reports (for some unspecified date, it is true) that 30,000 government male and female slaves tended 300,000 horses on thirty-six imperial ranches scattered on the north and west frontiers (*93*). But could the government have kept many captured Hsiung-nu warriors as actual slaves on ranches near the frontier? They could have escaped almost at will if given the freedom of movement necessary for tending herds of horses. From the purely practical point of view it is doubtful whether the government could have used many Hsiung-nu warriors as slaves under the prevalent system.

If the government was unable to absorb any large number did it sell many into private slavery? Here again there is no evidence, and in speculating it is necessary to anticipate later discussion, which shows that most private slaves were domestics performing service functions that native Chinese could do best. Hsiung-nu warriors, reared in a totally un-Chinese background and speaking a foreign tongue, were fitted for few normal slave occupations. The possibility of their escaping must have made them a risky investment, especially in view of the ill-defined and poorly guarded frontier. Probably only the more attractive Hsiung-nu women and children could have been absorbed naturally into the system of private slavery as it is reconstructed from extant documents. The very fact that numbers of killed and captured are not separately reported even in direct quotations suggests that the distinction was not historically important, and that it did not make an important difference to the state, economically, whether enemy were slain or captured.

Furthermore, there is no observable change in the slavery system during or shortly after the wars. One of the outstanding characteristics of Chinese slavery from the beginning of Han times was the absence of a marked racial character of slaves. Though non-Chinese slaves were fashionable, they apparently comprised only a small element in the slave population. Those from south China were always the most important "foreign" type, and enemy captured in the southwest or southeast are much more likely to have been enslaved than Hsiung-nu. But wars in those regions were brief, comparatively few prisoners were taken, and the texts are equally reticent about disposition of enemy captives. Whatever demand there was could probably have been filled easily by slave raids, or by sale to Chinese traders of captives taken in intertribal wars.

Thus, while large numbers of Hsiung-nu were captured during the Han period, and some were enslaved, it appears altogether unlikely that they constituted an important part of the servile population of China. What became of prisoners who were not enslaved?

The histories do not tell. Prisoners may have been exchanged for Chinese captured by the Hsiung-nu, but this is not reported. If so, the Chinese had the advantage, for on the whole they were more successful in the wars. Perhaps prisoners were ransomed. Neither alternative seems likely in view of the Chinese policy of keeping the Hsiung-nu weak and divided. Captured Hsiung-nu probably could have been sold by the Chinese to Central Asian kingdoms farther west, but there is no report of this. However, the Chinese did sometimes give Hsiung-nu prisoners to their Central Asian allies after a joint campaign. Another alternative would have been for the government to have established them along the inner frontier in regions distant from the place of capture, perhaps among colonies of surrendered Hsiung-nu or their allies. Given grazing land of their own to defend, they could probably have been induced to submit.

Several facts about the frontier make this final hypothesis seem reasonable. It was not a national boundary line peopled on either side by mutually hostile nations, but rather a broad zone of mingled Chinese and Hsiung-nu culture, where intensive agriculture gradually faded off and changed into extensive agriculture and herding, then into pure nomadism. Political control fluctuated with the fortunes of war and the relative strength of the imperial Chinese state and of the confederations in Mongolia. Many of the best Chinese generals came from the frontier; some were even "Hsiung-nu"—which means that they had once recognized the suzerainty of the *Shan-yü*, and then had come over to China. The phenomenon of quick and easy "surrender" to China or "flight" to the Hsiung-nu merely manifests the fluid condition of the frontier. Another evidence is the ease with which Hsiung-nu raiders penetrated deep into territory that the Han empire claimed as its own.

The frontier was most strongly Chinese when China won campaign after campaign, slaughtered and captured Hsiung-nu, split them up into warring groups, and drove them back. When China was on the defensive, or internally weak, the pattern reversed; the frontier turned in upon the empire. Thus it was exactly those periods when China captured far more enemy than it could absorb into slavery that it was probably safest to establish many of them, as we have postulated, along the inner frontier as a buffer and an asset.

V. ACQUISITION, HEREDITARY SLAVERY, AND MANUMISSION

Free people were enslaved either to the government or to private individuals. Initial enslavement, depending on the process, generally led exclusively to one or the other type of ownership, but there was a real fluidity in transfer of slaves, in both directions, between the government and private masters. Individual slaves did not necessarily belong permanently in one category or the other, and the process of acquiring slaves was not identical with the mechanism of enslavement.

Corresponding to the constant recruiting of new slaves was the opposite process of liberation. Enslavement, transfer, and manumission are all part of a fluidity of status which appears to characterize Chinese slavery, and indeed Chinese society, at this epoch. In political, economic, and social matters China was in a period of youth, of rapid change and growth. Slavery was a part of this flux, although we cannot determine the proportion of the slave population, or the number of individuals, involved.

ACQUISITION OF SLAVES

The government acquired privately owned slaves by confiscation, by gift, and probably by purchase. Favored individuals received gifts of slaves but most people got them by purchase.

Laws threatening confiscation of slaves indicate that the process was recognized, even though histories do not report final details.[1] On the other hand, confiscation of property is frequently reported, but only occasionally do we hear of the kinds of property.[2] When the government made a total confiscation, slaves must often have been included, as when on Emperor Wu's order Wang Wen-shu confiscated all the property owned by a thousand families of "tyrannical gentry" in a single commandery (43). Likewise, when important families became too powerful, or when they were successfully accused of menacing the imperial house, the whole clan might be stamped out. In such cases the property was probably taken over,

---

[1] Emperor Wu's counselors advised him to confiscate the fields and slaves of merchants daring to own agricultural land (45). When Emperor Ai considered restrictions on the number of fields and slaves that could be owned by people of various ranks it was proposed that after a specified time excess lands and slaves should be confiscated (109).

[2] Cf., for example, CHS, 45, 6a–b; 51, 11b; 90, 6b.

even though the histories fail to tell.   More than usual detail is accorded to Tung Hsien, the darling on whom Emperor Ai loaded imperial treasures.   After the Emperor died Tung Hsien was forced to commit suicide, and the imperial government confiscated and sold his belongings.   The texts do not itemize the property taken, but we know that Tung Hsien was the owner of many slaves (*109, 117, 118, 119*) so it is fair to assume that the government acquired his slaves even if it sold them immediately for revenue.   The same thing probably occurred when Ho Kuang's wealthy slave-owning family was stamped out; and so, too, with unnumbered families, great and small, throughout the dynasty.

One confiscation was pushed through on a large scale.   As part of the policy of suppressing merchants, and as a scheme to replenish the imperial coffers, investigators all over the empire tried people who had accumulated fortunes in "secondary" occupations.   Between about 119 and 113 B.C. they confiscated personal property by the hundred million cash, slaves by the thousand up to a myriad, and large areas of farm land (*46*).[1]

Some years earlier Emperor Wu tried a different plan to augment the treasury by allowing plebeians to give male and female slaves in exchange for life exemption from taxes and corvée duty.   Those already enjoying exemption could contribute slaves for an increase in rank (*36*).   This is very vague.   How many slaves did a person have to give?   Did anyone accept this offer, and was the condition of the treasury improved?   Information to answer these questions may already have been lacking when Han histories were written, for routine records of fact, invoices, treasury reports, minor census records and the like—the intimate, day-by-day records of government in operation—were of a transitory nature, and were probably easily scattered or destroyed when they became out of date.   Apparently the government found this plan difficult to administer, for a new one, introduced only four years later, allowed people to buy titles of "military merit" at specified prices for various grades. "Military merit" entitled the owner to reduction of two degrees of punishment if he committed a crime.   As early as 167 B.C. Ch'ao Ts'o had advocated to Emperor Wen the plan of granting honorary ranks in exchange for slaves who would be sent to colonize the frontier.   He also suggested that criminals be allowed to atone by giving slaves.   "The Emperor followed his counsel and enlisted

---

[1] Ma Ch'eng-feng (*An economic history of China*, vol. 2, p. 248) considers this a unique case based upon a special emergency law designed simply to authorize confiscation of what the government needed for prosecution of its wars.

people to remove to beneath the Barrier." (*19.*) Does this mean that
the plan was followed in detail? Did the populace and criminals
respond? Again the records are silent.

In the opposite direction, slaves went to private individuals as
customary grants, rewards for outstanding services, or marks of
imperial favor. Probably princesses received a regular allotment
when they left the palace. This is deduced from a document telling
of a pseudo-princess, treated at court like a real one, who was given a
"princess' fields, houses, and male and female slaves." (*88.*) Emperor
Wu gave his long-lost half-sister a million cash, three hundred
male and female slaves, a hundred *ch'ing* (465 acres) of government
farm land, and a first-class mansion (*31*). Because she was not
a daughter of Emperor Ching she was not made a princess, but
instead became Baroness Hsiu-ch'eng. Chao Fei-yen, who later
became Empress, was once given to the Princess of Yang-a (*101*).
Furthermore, princesses are often mentioned as slave owners (*26,
27, 39, 61, 109*). Probably they all owned scores of slaves, for they
were daughters of emperors, maintained elaborate households where
they entertained their royal or imperial brothers, and normally
married marquises of other surnames than Liu.[1]

The government occasionally gave slaves to noblemen in reward
for services to the state, though grants of money and land were
more common. Ho Kuang received 170 male and female slaves,
together with rich gifts of gold, cash, silk, horses, and a first-grade
mansion (*70*). Shih Tan was given slaves "numbered by the
hundred" because two generations previously his family had protected and reared the imperial infant who became Emperor Hsüan
(*97*). The slaves given to the pseudo-princess, mentioned above,
should actually be counted among rewards for services. Sent as
a bride to the Wu-sun ruler, she was the spearhead of Chinese
diplomacy in that far northwestern country for nearly four decades.
Finally at the age of seventy she begged to return to spend her last
years in China and be buried in her native soil. When she arrived
at the capital the Emperor duly rewarded her.

Other imperial grants signalized special favor, and allowed select
people of no private means to live in proper luxury. For a brief
period a charlatan magician named Luan Ta convinced supersti-

---

[1] There is no evidence to show that their brothers, too, received a regular
allotment of government slaves when they were made kings, for no Former Han
record tells of a king granted government slaves. The Latter Han cases all
describe special gifts in no way connected with enthronement. Cf. HHS, 72,
3a; 72, 5b; 80, 4a; 85, 2a.

tious Emperor Wu of his supernatural abilities. The Emperor gave him the title "General of Magicians of the Earth," made him a marquis, presented him with the highest-class mansion for a marquis, a thousand "youths," a princely chariot, extra carriages and horses, and furniture to fill his house. He was even married to one of the Emperor's eldest daughters. Then, convinced that Luan Ta was an imposter, the Emperor had him executed the next year! (*49.*) Other imperial darlings like Chang Fang and Tung Hsien received lavish gifts, and in all likelihood slaves, for they were noted slave owners. When the child Emperor Chao was placed upon the throne his previously unimportant maternal grandaunt received two million cash, male and female slaves, and a mansion and houses to give her "abundance" (*58*). Wang Mang presented slaves and other gifts of enormous value to the inconspicuous family from which he chose his second Empress (*133*). This distribution presumably went on all the time, especially to lowly families of the girls who became empresses or imperial favorites. Slaves were indispensable around the court.

Buying and Selling Slaves

Extant documents on sales of slaves are at once fragmentary and suggestive; they reveal faint outlines and hint at more, but leave the total picture vague. We should like to know who sold slaves and by what methods; about professional dealers and syndicates; about sources of supply, and markets for distribution. We want to know the relative importance, in terms of frequency and volume, of dealer sales and owner-to-owner sales, and of wholesale and retail selling; and whether the government regulated and authenticated transactions, and levied sales taxes. We should also like to know, in relation to general Han economy, something about prices, fluctuations in the market, profits, and speculation, and above all, how important slave-trading was in the nation's commerce.

Sales were made both by direct transactions between one owner and another and by dealers in slave markets. Wang Pao provides the classic account of direct sale in his semi-humorous account of the purchase of Pien-liao (*83*). A resident of Chengtu in Szechwan, Wang Pao went in 59 B.C. on business to the Chien River where he called on the widow Yang Hui, who owned a male slave belonging formerly to her husband. Wang Pao requested that the slave be sent out to buy some wine, but Pien-liao refused to go, claiming that the agreement or contract with his late master specified that he had only to guard the house. Furious, Wang Pao decided on the spot to buy

the slave, and the widow agreed. The sale contract, a unique document, gives the exact date, names and residences of the buyer and
seller, name and description of the slave, and the agreed price of
15,000 cash. These items would form the essential core of any
such transaction—the bill of sale and evidence of ownership.[1]

There is no term for slave dealers, as distinguished from other
sorts of merchants, in Han literature. Information about volume
of transactions is too scanty to judge whether sales of low-priced
slaves supported a group of specialists. Volume, the factor most
important for profits in that field, would be a product of urbanization and the geographical concentration of slave-owning classes,
as well as abundant sources of supply. Probably the demand for
slaves in the capital district, with its congregation of noble and
wealthy slave-owning families, produced such constant turnover that
slaves did not eat up dealers' profits between time of purchase and
sale. A few other thickly populated areas, particularly the western
Shantung and eastern Honan region, might have supported a specialized trade also. Elsewhere, and early in the Han period, most slave
sales were probably handled by agents who simply brought buyer
and seller together, or by merchants and other business men as an
occasionally profitable sideline.

The account of Chi Pu's sale illustrates the point. He was
seeking to escape the wrath of Emperor Kao because he had been
one of Hsiang Yü's generals. A man named Chou, who lived at P'u-
yang on the Shantung-Hopei border, disguised Chi Pu as a slave, and
sent him with a score or more Chou family youths to be sold by
Chu Chia, who lived at Lu about 100 miles east. Careful reading
of Chu Chia's biography, and of this particular incident, reveals

---

[1] The only similar record (cited by Lao Kan, "The system of slavery during
the two Han dynasties," p. 2) is the brief item excavated at Chü-yen, which gives
the price of two young male slaves as 30,000 cash, and of one adult female
slave as 20,000.

Cheng Hsüan of the second century tells in his commentary to a passage in
the *Chou li* concerning government supervision of markets that two kinds of
contracts were used. Long ones covered sales of people, horses, and cattle, while
short ones were used in sales of utensils. Cf. Edouard Biot, trans., *Le Tcheou-li*,
2 vols., Paris, 1851, t. 1, p. 52, footnote 3; also p. 318, footnote 1. This is good Latter
Han evidence on slave contracts, and probably of government supervision. The
T'ang lü su i contains several items showing that in T'ang times sales contracts
for slaves had to be authenticated by the government.

Prices of slaves are interesting only in relation to prices of other commodities,
concerning which little is known. Attempts to figure commodity prices for the
Western Han period are unfortunately almost worthless, for they are generally
based upon two or three references for any single commodity, either undated, or
miscellaneously scattered over a 200-year period. Cf., for example, Ch'ü Tui-
chih, "Hsi Han wu chia k'ao (The prices of commodities during the Western
Han dynasty)," YCHP, vol. 5, 1929, pp. 877–881.

that he was not a professional slave trader. He was most famous as a protector of political refugees, which is the reason why Chou was confident that he would harbor Chi Pu until the Emperor could be induced to pardon the refugee. But the stratagem demanded that every detail of the sale appear perfectly natural, for the Emperor had threatened to execute anyone who aided Chi Pu. Hence we must conclude that there was nothing unusual or suspicious about sending a group of slaves a hundred miles for Chu Chia to sell. By profession, Chu Chia was primarily a large-scale farmer who employed innumerable hired (or indentured) workmen. He recognized and bought Chi Pu, hid him in a shed in the fields, and had him work with other farm-hands so as to appear to be one of them. Being on friendly terms with Kao-tsu's influential associate, Marquis Hsia-hou Ying, he visited the marquis for several days at Lo-yang, and persuaded him to intercede and win Chi Pu's pardon. From these assembled facts it is clear that a well-established landlord-business man might also traffic in slaves (8).[1]

This was at the very beginning of the period. Another transaction eighty years later may indicate a more developed sales system. About 120 B.C. Ho Ch'ü-ping was passing through P'ing-yang in western Shansi to take command of his army. He had never met Ho Chung-ju, his father, so the latter was brought to the hostel. Then the general liberally bought his father fields, houses, and male and female slaves, and hurried on to the wars (42). This quick transaction, involving land, houses, and slaves, may have been handled by agents who knew of real estate for sale and could speedily assemble a group of slaves.

Apparently some merchants did specialize in slaves for the luxury trade. They bought children, especially young girls, trained them as entertainers, and then resold them. Wang Weng-hsü, the mother of Emperor Hsüan, was such a girl. The son of a marquis took her from her parents under an agreement to rear her in exchange for her services, trained her as a singer and dancer, and then sold her to a merchant who was in the business of handling entertainer slaves. A member of the suite of Emperor Wu's Heir-apparent was sent out as an agent to find trained girls for his patron's palace, and bought Wang Weng-hsü with four others from the merchant (55). Well-trained girls commanded very fancy prices, as is suggested by the boastful remark of the King of Chi-pei around 160 B.C., that

[1] See his biography in SC, 124, 2a, and CHS, 92, 1b–2a. The incident appears also in SC, 100, 1a.

he had paid 4,700,000 cash for four girls especially clever at doing tricks (*21*).

He said that he bought the girls at "the common people's place," and even though a doctor pronounced one of them incurably ill, he did not sell her at "the place for nobles." The first of these "places" (*so*) must have been a market where commoners sold goods, and the second, a market for the nobility. Chia Yi described such market places a decade earlier, saying: "Nowadays people who sell youths dress them up in embroidered clothes and silken shoes with the edges all embellished, and put them into pens." (*16*.) Slaves dressed like this must have been for the luxury trade, and the end of the passage shows that the "youths" were singers and entertainers. Wang Mang briefly described slave markets in his fulmination against the evils of the Ch'in dynasty perpetuated by the House of Han. Accordingly, his statement that male and female slaves were sold in the same kind of pens as were cattle and horses (*122*) referred equally to conditions in his own day.

Instances of kidnaping, purchase of famine victims, slave-raiding and importation of foreign slaves indicate a constant demand perhaps exceeding the normal supply. Slave-raiding and transportation of foreign slaves to the capital suggest some sort of professional organization. The youths acquired by people of Chengtu and Chungking from southern Szechwan and Yunnan (*10*) went hundreds of miles overland to reach Ch'ang-an.[1] Wang Mang's order that "those officials or plebeians who dare traffic in frontier people shall be publicly executed" (*126*) suggests organized trade in slaves from the frontier. People who wanted to escape the turmoil and famine there perhaps applied to dealers who arranged for their transportation to, and sale in the interior commanderies. This system may have been operated by a syndicate in co-operation with officials. Since Wang Mang wanted to prevent depopulation of the hard-won frontier, he directed his law against those who made it possible for people to leave rather than against the frontiersmen themselves.

New slaves transported overland were probably convoyed in parties like groups of convicts, who traveled on foot, with shackles, to work at the frontier or on government construction. Both convicts (*t'u*) and male slaves[2] sometimes had their heads shaved

[1] For the routes, cf. Albert Herrmann (*Historical and commercial atlas of China*, p. 20) and L. H. D. Buxton (*China, the land and the people*, Oxford, 1929, map, p. 141, and discussion, p. 144).

[2] For slaves, see *8, 12, 131*, and *132*. For convicts, see CHS, 23, 6a and 10a; 90, 2a; and 97A, 2a; also HFHD, vol. I, p. 117, footnote 1.

and wore coarse clothes and iron collars as marks of identity. There is no mention of special slave guards, but a hint is provided by the story of Liu Chi before he became Emperor Kao. As a petty official he had to escort a group of convicts from northern Anhwei to Li Mountain near the Ch'in capital some 600 miles distant. He was personally responsible for each convict, and when a few escaped he untied the rest and absconded.[1] Later in the period slave traders must have developed a much better system than this primitive method of escorting convicts. Since slaves represented a financial investment it may be assumed that those transported against their will were also closely guarded.

When females and docile young slaves for the luxury trade were sent from one place to another they went in carts (or probably by boat where possible), for it was important that they arrive in good condition. Mr. Chou sent his household youths by cart the hundred odd miles to Lu (8), and the merchant who bought the female entertainer slave, Wang Weng-hsü, sent her by horse to her new home (55). There is no information to show whether the regular land routes were equipped with special lodgings for slaves in transit comparable to the system of guest houses and lodges established along principal highways for the use of the Emperor or members of the nobility, or the post stations which were used by girls being sent to the imperial seraglio.[2]

These fragments of information about contracts, prices, markets, dealers, and trade routes fit together to form only a vague picture of the slave trade. A marked difference must have existed between selling methods at the capital and in the provinces. Furthermore, we must assume a development from the beginning of the Han period, only shortly removed from the feudalistic Warring States period, to the time of Wang Mang after two centuries of economic growth. By the end of the period slaves were regular commodities, freely sold, and commanding standard prices. When Emperor Ai attempted to limit the number of slaves owned by people of various classes in society, stipulating that after three years all slaves over the specified limits would be confiscated, the mere proposal threw prices into a slump (109). A few years later when Wang Mang attempted to abolish buying and selling of fields and private slaves,

---

[1] HFHD, vol. I, p. 34.

[2] When the girl who later became Empress Tou was being sent to the palace she started her journey from such a "transfer house." Cf. 14, and footnote 13 for commentary.

opposition was so great that he had to repeal the law in three years. The antagonism aroused during that short time contributed to his downfall ten years later (*121, 124, A22*).

The slave trade was not a monopoly of private dealers, for the government itself sold slaves. Near the end of the dynasty the Grand Empress Dowager *née* Fu sent an internuncio to various government bureaus to purchase female slaves, buying them at a low price. When he bought eight girls from Mu-chiang Lung's bureau, Mu-chiang Lung formally protested to Emperor Ai, stating that the Grand Empress Dowager had paid too little and asking the Emperor to readjust the price (*116*). The notable point about Mu-chiang Lung's protest is that his only complaint concerned price. Apparently sale was so normal that prices were well-established and understood.

The appeal by Emperor Wu, more than a century earlier, that plebeians contribute private slaves to help meet a grave deficiency in the treasury and arsenals suggests, as noted before, that even then the government sold slaves for revenue (*36*). Secret sale of government slaves and other valuables—a clear case of graft—was cause for executing the governor of northern Annam in 54 B.C. (*86*).

HEREDITARY SLAVERY

In the Chinese family system certain types of property were owned by that part of the family group which clung together as a single economic unit. Control of real estate, particularly farm land, was vested in the family head, who held it in trust as a patrimony and was expected to pass it on intact to his eldest son or successor. Sale of land was decided upon by the adult members of the family. If brothers or nephews of the family head established separate economic households they could demand a share of the land.

Ownership of slaves was apparently of the same order. Many accounts speak of slaves belonging to a family or household. That they were part of the family estate in T'ang times is indicated by the law on freeing private slaves, which specified that the head of the family must give the slave a document, co-signed by the eldest son and others, and turn over a similar document to the local government for validation and filing;[1] that is, the son or others who would normally inherit the slave had to agree to his manumission

---

[1] From the *T'ang lü su i*, ch. 12. See also Liang Ch'i-ch'ao, "System of slavery in China," p. 549, and Wang Shih-chieh, "The Chinese slavery system," p. 324 (translated by Toni Pippon: "Beitrag zum Chinesischen Sklavensystem," p. 127).

in writing and file their agreement with the government to prevent later argument. Several cases in the *Hou Han shu* illustrate the principle of family ownership and the procedure of inheritance at that time. The incidents were recorded to illustrate the character or misfortunes of the individuals in whose biographies they appear, and not to reveal anything about slavery.

When Hsüeh Pao's parents died some time before A.D. 121, his younger brother's son asked for a division of the property. This indicates that Hsüeh Pao had become head of an economic family which included the son of his deceased younger brother. Unable to prevent his nephew from leaving, he divided the male and female slaves into two groups, taking for himself the old ones, to whom he said: "You have worked with me for a long time; you cannot be sent away." He likewise took the poorer fields and sheds and the worn-out household furnishings.[1]

The curious procedure which Hsü Wu used to help his younger brothers become officials is a peculiarly Chinese illustration of character. Hsü Wu was the grandfather of an official who served Emperor Ho (A.D. 89–105); therefore the present event probably occurred early in the Latter Han period. He was already a prefect, but his two younger brothers were not yet noted. He therefore proposed that they take their shares of the patrimony and live separately. In the division Hsü Wu himself took the fertile fields, large houses, and sturdy male and female slaves. The people of the countryside all admired the humility and self-denial of the younger brothers and despised Hsü Wu for his greed. Because of this both younger brothers were selected and advanced for office. Only then did Hsü Wu call the family together and in tears reveal the whole scheme. Under his management the property had increased three times in value. He offered it all to his brothers. "Therefore the whole commandery applauded; far and near proclaimed him; and he advanced to the position of Treasurer of the Ch'ang-lo [Palace]."[2]

Chou Tang, the scion of a very wealthy family, was orphaned as a child and reared by a kinsman who mistreated him and refused to give him his family inheritance when he came of age. He therefore sued in the district court, forcing his kinsman to turn over the estate. Then he distributed his property among his fellow clansmen,

---

[1] HHS, 69, 1b. The *Feng su t'ung i*, 4, 8b, tells the same story, but calls Hsüeh Pao by his *Tzu*, "Meng Ch'ang." This version is presumably earlier than that in HHS, and has the same purpose—that of illustrating virtuous character.

[2] HHS, 106, 5b.

freed all his male and female slaves, and went to Ch'ang-an as an itinerant scholar.[1]   This occurred shortly before Wang Mang usurped the throne, and is evidence that courts upheld the right of a son to inherit family slaves, who were part of the estate to be held in trust during his minority.

Going back earlier in the Former Han period, there is the case of the widow Yang Hui, who had her late husband's slave Pien-liao (who haunts this work!); and the widow of Ho Kuang, who owned her husband's household slaves (*83* and *72*).   Presumably Ho Kuang's widow would have passed them on with the estate to his son and grandnephews had not the whole family been stamped out a few years later.   In 115 B.C. Hsia-hou P'o was tried and deposed for having had sexual relations with his father's personal female slave (*48*).   But his father had been dead eighteen years at the time of the trial.   It is clear that Hsia-hou P'o had inherited the bondswoman, but since she had been his father's mistress his relations with her were incestuous.   Here Chinese customary morality intervened to limit his rights of possession by inheritance.

The converse of slave inheritance is hereditary slave status.   In Han times the child of two slave parents was apparently a slave automatically.   Grand Judge Chung Yu clearly indicated the hereditary status of government slaves late in the Latter Han period, in his statement on the practice of tattooing enslaved families of criminals: "The genuine male and female slaves of today had ancestors who originally committed crimes.   Even though a hundred generations have gone by, still they have tattooed faces [as a sign of] submission to the government." [2]

Already in Ch'in times the government owned hereditary slaves, for in 209 B.C. the last Ch'in ruler ordered the Treasurer of the Privy Purse to free the convicts and "born male slaves" working at Li Mountain (*3*).   Yen Shih-ku used the seventh century expression *chia sheng nu*, "house-born slave," to explain the Han term *nu ch'an tzu*, translated "born male slave."   It is therefore particularly interesting to find his expression used contextually in a T'ang will dated A.D. 865, and discovered by Sir Aurel Stein at Tun-huang. By the terms of the will a nun bequeathed her only property, a "house-born" female slave, to her niece (*3*, footnote 4).

[1] HHS, 113, 2b.

[2] *San kuo chih, Wei chih*, 12, 4a.   See p. 84 and footnote 2 for the context of his statement.

Ts'ao Hsiao, a government slave woman, had a daughter named Ts'ao Kung, who also belonged to the government. Ts'ao Kung was probably born into slavery although the record does not say so. The alternative—that the girl and her mother became government slaves together—is most unlikely because the mother and the girl's best friend testified in the careful judicial investigation about the murder of Ts'ao Kung's son. This child was the son of Emperor Ch'eng, and might have been heir to the throne. Had Ts'ao Kung once been free the fact would have been reported and probably emphasized, in so important a case (107).

Wei Ch'ing complained to a fortune teller that he was "born as another's male slave." (26). He was the son of a slave woman and a free man to whom she was not married. The position of her children gives the clearest internal evidence of hereditary slave status, but is discussed in the chapter on status as part of the subject of marriages between slaves and free people.

MANUMISSION OF GOVERNMENT SLAVES

We do not know what proportion of the slave population at any moment had been born free, nor what part of any generation of slaves won their freedom. Yet references to manumission are casual enough to make the act appear not unusual. This is not to say that individual slaves had mathematically favorable chances of becoming free men. On the basis of historical records we can only describe the methods of liberation without much detail about actual process, and attempt to deduce some of the motives for the cases that are preserved. From these points of view the distinction between government and private slaves is important.

Most manumissions of government slaves affected groups of people in specified categories. Indeed, there are only two records of the liberation of individuals. In the first instance Emperor Wu personally freed Chin Jih-ti, the son of the Hsiung-nu King of Hsiu-ch'u. Noticing the boy because of his dignified bearing and because the horses in his charge were fat and well groomed, the Emperor questioned him and was impressed by the straightforward account of his background and enslavement in 121 B.C. Emperor Wu immediately freed him and granted him a ceremonial bath, robe and cap (41). The ceremony was not part of the process of manumission; it was the process by which a commoner became a Gentleman. Thus Chin Jih-ti rose from enslavement to honorary rank almost in one step.

A woman named Tse, who worked in the palace, was the other government slave known to have been individually freed. About twenty years before, she had assisted in caring for a child (later Emperor Hsüan) whose father and grandfather were killed in the scandalous witchcraft affair in 91 B.C. (p. 44). This child was secretly reared and finally placed on the throne as Emperor Hsüan. In 63 B.C. the slave woman persuaded her commoner husband to submit a memorandum on her case to Emperor Hsüan, who was ignorant about many of the facts of his childhood. After her plea had been investigated and substantiated, she was freed and made a commoner by imperial edict, received a gift of 100,000 cash, and had an imperial audience (*80*). Her claim to historical mention lies solely in the fact that she told the Emperor how Ping Chi had saved his life, and this revelation finally brought Ping Chi his due reward.

In discussing government slaves, Wei Hung states that they could purchase their freedom for a thousand myriad cash (*92*). This figure seems very high, and "thousand" may be a scribal error for "ten." The interesting point is that government slaves had sources of revenue with which to free themselves. The only direct testimony to this is the complaint, lodged by the Worthies in the great debate of 81 B.C., that government male slaves accumulated great fortunes (*60*). Even without such a statement it would be possible to deduce from the duties of government slaves, discussed below, that they had plenty of opportunities for grafts and tips. Whether or not they received stipends, however, is unknown.

Five documents report manumissions of government slaves in groups. Four were specific groups and one was general. How and why did the government free its slaves? The cases are as follows:

> *First.*—In 209 B.C., when Ch'in was imperiled, the Second Emperor ordered the Treasurer of the Privy Purse to free the convicts and male slaves working at Li Mountain and send them out to fight the invaders (*3*).
>
> *Second.*—In 160 B.C. Emperor Wen proclaimed a general amnesty and also freed government male and female slaves, who thereupon were to become commoners (*24*).
>
> *Third.*—In 140 B.C. Emperor Wu pardoned the enslaved families of leaders of the Rebellion of the Seven States (*30*).
>
> *Fourth.*—In 7 B.C. Emperor Ai sent out to be married from his predecessor's seraglio all the Palace Women who were thirty years of age or younger. He freed and made commoners all government slaves fifty years of age or older (*110*).

Fifth.—In A.D. 31 Emperor Kuang-wu freed and made commoners all those who, during Wang Mang's time, had been seized and made slaves not in accordance with the old laws (*135*).

The first amnesty is reported both in the Ch'in Imperial Annals and in a biography. The four from Han times appear only in the Annals, where they are treated as imperial decisions, with no description about the discussion leading up to each, and no suggestion of motive. Nowhere is it stated by what process the slaves were freed; indeed, only the first case, because it is recorded in a biography, contains evidence that the order was carried out. Dry statements of fact are like precipices beyond which there is nothing but mist. What happened after edicts of liberation? Was there any ceremony of manumission? Were names struck from the ledgers of bureau and palace property? Did the slaves get credentials of freedom? Could they work as free men in their old slave jobs? Were they really free to go if they were useful cogs in bureau routine or valued personal retainers? Did they receive cash grants to start life anew?

No single or general motive covers all these manumissions. In the last one Emperor Kuang-wu tried to re-establish justice by freeing people made government slaves under the usurper's laws.

In the first case the government offered a bargain: the slaves and convicts would be freed if they fought to defend the dynasty. They were a tough lot, men who had spent years at hard labor, probably having the *esprit de corps* of convicts; and since they helped Chang Han defeat an army reported as numbering a thousand chariots and a hundred thousand foot, they must have been stout fighters and numerous. Many probably had to stay in the army which Chang Han treacherously surrendered two years later and which Hsiang Yü slaughtered on that grim night before he invaded Ch'in (*6*).

The same reason for manumission, a bargain to be earned by special service, appears several more times during the Former Han dynasty. When Han Hsin planned a revolt against Kao-tsu, who was conducting a campaign against Ch'en Hsi, he plotted to forge an imperial edict pardoning all the government convicts and male slaves, who would then form an army to attack the Empress and the Heir-apparent (*13*). The plot was foiled, but the idea of manumission in return for fighting is clear. Convict levies were used in wars against the southern and western regions, and government slaves may have served with them to win their freedom. Wang Mang "enlisted" levies of criminals sentenced to death and private male slaves to fight as shock troops against the Hsiung-nu (*130*). Whether contributed in exchange for honorary rank or requisitioned, those who survived the assaults against the Hsiung-nu surely won or took their freedom. Likewise, any private slaves contributed to the government as colonists for the frontiers, following the plan proposed by Ch'ao Ts'o (*19*), must have been freed in compensation.

Two liberations of government slaves in the Latter Han period help to establish the motive for the third manumission, in 140 B.C., in which Emperor Wu pardoned the families of rebels. In A.D. 106 all people belonging to the imperial house or noble clans who had been enslaved for crimes since A.D. 55 (and their descendants) were ordered pardoned and sent away.[1] In 110 Emperor An freed all those who had been enslaved since A.D. 76.[2] The decrees of 140 B.C. and A.D. 106 are parallel in two respects: they occurred during the first year of a new ruler, and they freed members of the imperial clan who had been in servitude for many years. Together, the three cases of manumission form a type, falling into the class of imperial amnesties.

During the period before A.D. 9 there were eighty-four general amnesties, or about one every thirty months. Thirty-three others pardoned special classes or groups of criminals.[3] Most general amnesties celebrated imperial enthronement, establishment of an empress or heir-apparent, or the adoption of a new reign period. Others signalized the observance of auspicious omens or the occurrence of Heaven-sent disasters such as earthquakes, fires, and eclipses. Amnesties were considered acts of imperial kindness designed to win popular favor by remitting taxes or corvée duty, halting investigations of crimes, and freeing prisoners. The manumission of enslaved families of rebels fits perfectly into this pattern. Did other government slaves win their freedom in this way, or was Emperor Wu's pardon unique during Former Han times? It is at least unique in having been reported.

---

[1] HHS, 4, 9a. The act was done on behalf of the baby Emperor Shang by the Empress Dowager *née* Teng. Cf. HHS, 10A, 9a, and Nancy Lee Swann, "Biography of the Empress Teng," JAOS, vol. 51, 1931, pp. 138–159 (see p. 146).
    The same edict ordered that the names and duties of all male and female slaves who had the surname Liu, or were old and sick, and who belonged to government bureaus, treasuries, commandery (offices) and households of kings and marquises of states should be sent up for careful investigation. Presumably slaves with the imperial surname who were really related, and old and sick slaves, were to be freed.

[2] HHS, 5, 4a. Cf. p. 79, footnote 2, above.

[3] All are conveniently assembled in the *Hsi Han hui yao*, ch. 63.

Emperor Ai's manumission of Palace Women and old slaves (the fourth case) introduces a new principle, age. Whereas Emperor Ai sent the younger Palace Women out to be married,[1] it was the older government male and female slaves, those over fifty, that he emancipated. A number of later cases[2] in which old slaves were freed suggests that Emperor Ai acted in line with a principle that old slaves deserved to be granted their freedom.

Did slaves over fifty consider this manumission a benevolent act, as the historian apparently did? If they were permitted to live in their familiar slave quarters and receive regular food, or if they received stipends and had families with which to live, they might have enjoyed freedom in their declining years. Considering the traditional Chinese attitude of respect and care for the aged, and government sensitivity to popular opinion, it is hard to believe that old slaves were simply turned out to beg. An analogous case in the Three Kingdoms period fortifies this view. In A.D. 239, Emperor Fei ordered all government male and female slaves over sixty to be freed and become "good people." Seven years later he had apparently been informed that aged government slaves were being sold on the market. He ordered his officials to inspect the markets to observe sales of discharged government male and female slaves over seventy, or infirm and crippled ones. "Forsooth," he said, "the government, considering their strength to be exhausted, resells them so they have no place to turn. Let all of them be freed and become 'good people,' and if there are those who cannot support

[1] Wei Hung states that kung-jen (Palace Women) were especially selected young slave girls, who were sent out to be married when they reached the age of thirty-five (91). But it is not certain that "kung-jen" was used only for slaves. Emperor Ch'eng's Palace Women were sent out if they were under thirty. Apparently the older ones, less likely to be married, had earned the right to stay in security. There are three analogous cases in the Former Han history. Emperor Wen provided in his testamentary decree that his Ladies and women of lower rank down to Junior Maids should be sent back to their families (HFHD, vol. I, p. 271). Emperor Ching likewise provided that his Palace Women should be sent home (op. cit., p. 332). There is no other report of this practice down to 7 B.C., but when Emperor P'ing died early in A.D. 6, Wang Mang ordered that women who had accompanied his Empress into the palace should be sent home and be allowed to marry (CHS, 12, 4b, and notes by Wang Hsien-Ch'ien in HSPC, 12, 10a). There were kung-jen of Emperor Chao still in the palace when Liu Ho came in as Emperor, for he had sexual relations with some of them (69).

[2] Emperor Shang's edict cited above probably meant that old and sick slaves would be freed. In A.D. 518 Emperor Wu of Liang freed all (government?) male slaves more than sixty years old and female slaves more than fifty years old. Cf. Ch'eng Shu-te, Chiu ch'ao lü k'ao, ch. 4 ("Liang lü k'ao"), p. 382. A decree of A.D. 566 freed all government slaves over sixty-five from Chiang-ling, and another of A.D. 657 freed all government slaves who were over sixty or invalids. Cf. Liang Ch'i-ch'ao, op. cit., p. 549.

themselves, let the commanderies and prefectures relieve and support them." [1]

Emperor Ai did not state in his edict the kind of care that should be given to those who could not support themselves. While the spirit of the edict appears to be humanitarian, the possibility cannot be excluded that it was an economy measure disguised as a benevolent act.[2]

A large proportion of government slaves were non-productive, and a great expense to the treasury. Slaves over fifty would be nearly worthless in heavy labor and not very useful in service capacities. It is worth noting, therefore, that about a generation earlier Kung Yü seriously proposed freeing all government slaves in order to cut down expenses. He argued that it would be cheaper to feed them from the government granaries than to keep them as slaves (89). Kung Yü knew about state finance from the inside, having just been treasurer of one of the palaces.

This raises a question about Emperor Wen's reason (in the second case) for freeing government slaves near the end of his reign. The act is recorded just after a general amnesty and may have been part of it. Emperor Wen, the most economical and socially minded of all the Han rulers, several times cut government expenses and reduced taxes and labor duties specifically to lighten the burdens on the populace. It is therefore possible that economy was one of his motives in liberating government slaves. This was the only decreed manumission of public or private slaves during both the Former and Latter Han periods not limited to some specified group. Does it follow that all the government slaves were actually freed? Realistically speaking, this is unlikely. Perhaps Emperor Wen meant to authorize a general weeding out of slaves with the dual motives of benevolence and economy.

Manumission of Private Slaves

Masters could naturally free their own slaves, but we do not know the legal procedure necessary to make the act binding. In T'ang times, as shown above, a slave freed by a master was given a document co-signed by the master's oldest son and other presump-

---

[1] *San kuo chih, Wei chih,* 4, 1a and 2b, under years A.D. 239 and A.D. 246. It is a real puzzle as to who might be in the market for aged or sick slaves, unless it might be their free relatives or humanitarian folk. There is no evidence that the Buddhists performed this good work as early as this date.

[2] Ma Fei-pai ("Source material on the economic history of Ch'in and Han," pt. 6, "The slavery system," p. 399) holds this view.

tive heirs, and a similar document was validated and filed in the local government office. Whether the act was equally formalized in Han times is not clear, for original manumission records, so valuable in the study of Greek and Roman slavery, are still lacking for China of the Han period.

The King of Ch'ang-i freed a number of his male slaves and made them Gentlemen and officials (69). Three slave women of the marquises of Ch'eng-tu and Ping-a and of the Noblewoman Hsü were freed and became commoners. They may have been freed by wills, for their masters died in 12, 17 or 16, and 8 B.C., respectively. It is more likely that the one who had belonged to Noblewoman Hsü was freed in some other way, perhaps when her mistress was deposed as Empress in 17 B.C. The three ex-slave women were later simply commanded to enter the palace as private slaves of the imperial concubine née Chao. Later she presumably freed the three women again, for she presented each with ten slave women as a bribe to keep quiet about her evil practices.[1]

The manner in which Luan Pu won his freedom is not stated. Purchased specifically to do a deed of revenge for his master, he later rose to be a commandant and then a general (5). Probably he was freed as a reward for having successfully performed the deed.[2] There is likewise no specific statement about the manumission of Tou Kuang-kuo and the several children of Dame Wei, who suddenly rose to prominence as relatives of empresses. Affinal relationship made their freedom automatic.[3]

The most interesting document on manumission is one recording a slave woman's purchase of her own freedom. Her owner, the Marquis of P'u, kidnaped and re-enslaved her. For this he was brought to trial and deposed (102). This case proves that freedom by purchase was legally recognized even at the expense of a member of the nobility. It also raises the question of peculium, discussed later (pp. 219-220).

Paralleling the series of edicts which freed groups of government slaves is another series which freed specified types of private slaves.

---

[1] Document 107; see especially footnotes 20 and 21.

[2] Precedent for this assumption is found in a case reported in the *Tso chuan*, Duke Hsiang, 23rd year (James Legge, *The Chinese classics*, 2nd ed., 5 vols., Oxford, 1893–95, vol. 5, pt. 2, pp. 497, 501), in which the slave Fei Pao agreed to kill a man in exchange for his freedom. To validate his manumission the "red book," obviously a record of enslavement, was to be burned.

[3] *14; 26, 27,* and *29.* See discussion of the Wei family, pp. 160–161, below.

One of these edicts dates from early in the reign of Emperor Kao and five from that of Emperor Kuang-wu, early in the Latter Han.

First.—In 202 B.C. Kao-tsu ordered that people who had sold themselves because of famine were all to be freed and become commoners (*9*).

Second.—In A.D. 26 Emperor Kuang-wu ordered that plebeians' wives and children who had been married off or sold should, if they wished, be allowed to return to their parents (*134*).

Third.—In 31 the Emperor ordered that officials or commoners who had become slaves or lesser wives through famine and turmoil, or kidnaping by the eastern robbers, should, if they wished, be allowed to go free (*136*).

Fourth.—In 36 an edict freed and made commoners of people in Kansu and Szechwan who had been kidnaped into slavery and had reported to the judiciary but had not been requited.

Fifth.—In 37 an edict freed and made commoners of people in Yunnan who had been kidnaped into slavery after A.D. 32.

Sixth.—In 39 an edict freed and made commoners of male and female slaves in Yunnan and Kansu who had pled their cases to the local government after A.D. 32. The sellers were not compelled to return the purchase price.[1]

These government orders to free private slaves all occurred during the first few years of the Former and Latter Han periods, and were attempts to correct injustices or irregularities that had occurred during the upheaval of founding a dynasty. More than two centuries elapsed between the first and second edicts, and there is no recorded edict that freed private slaves after either dynasty was soundly established. In other words, the government apparently did not interfere with private ownership of slaves properly acquired during normal times.

Several close parallels mark the first two manumissions. Both were promulgated almost immediately after the founder of the dynasty had achieved preliminary control, but before he had quelled opposition and established the machinery of civil administration. Both freed people who had sunk into slavery because of economic distress brought on by the chaos of war. Neither indicated how the edict was to be enforced.

---

[1] For the last three edicts see *136*, footnote 3.

Consider the manumission of famine victims in 202 B.C. The same edict that freed the slaves directed officials to take up their duties, ordered refugees to return home, and granted honorary rewards and exemption from taxation to people who had distinguished themselves as Kao-tsu's followers. It was merely a proclamation for the world to return from war to peace.

Could this manumission have been enforced?

Kao-tsu had killed Hiang Yü only a few months before his edict of 202 B.C., and had just established his first capital at Lo-yang. Although he had ordered the demobilization of troops, the country was still filled with private armies. Under these circumstances he lacked the machinery and power to enforce the manumission. It is doubtful that he even meant to enforce it. What would have happened? Wealthy and powerful people would have been robbed of their property. Kao-tsu could not have had the stomach to antagonize them and to threaten his precarious supremacy. Who, moreover, were to go free? A group of helpless folk, sunk into slavery to save themselves from famine. How could they profit his dynasty, and how would his order profit them? For many of them slavery in a well-to-do household must have been preferable to freedom in a war-torn world. If the decree had come ten years later, when the empire was firmly established, it might have been put into effect regardless of opposition. In view of the date, this manumission looks like a humanitarian gesture, placed on record for effect, a plea for public approval neither intended nor capable of being enforced.[1]

As pointed out, Emperor Kuang-wu's first edict freeing private slaves was closely parallel to Kao-tsu's. His later edicts were more realistic. Limited to particular areas recently conquered, they

---

[1] Chinese students of slavery seem not to have considered this manumission in its historical setting. Since it was an imperial edict it is simply assumed to have been carried out in full.

Ma Fei-pai (op. cit., pp. 399–400) even deduces shrewd economic motives for it. He argues that Kao-tsu and Kuang-wu, also, represented the landlords in opposition to the newly rising commercial class. Before Emperor Ching, government policy aided agriculture at the expense of commercialism. Since private slaves were one of the most profitable instruments of commercial capitalism and were linked to it much more closely than to landlordism, freeing of private slaves was an attack on commercial capitalism. Such is Ma's thesis.

Government economic policies early in the Han period seem to have encouraged agriculture and demeaned commerce, but there is little indication of a struggle between two hostile economic groups. Furthermore, there is no shred of evidence that slavery was linked more closely to the commercial class than to the landlord class during any part of the Han period. Indeed, for the whole of Han history, there is far more evidence that large landowners were also large slave owners than that merchants were; and while people deriving their wealth

ordered civil authorities to use specified laws against recalcitrant owners. He may have meant to enforce these edicts, but the normally close connection between officials and the slave-owning class probably thwarted his intention in many cases.

A fact about the eleven recorded edicts ordering manumission is worth noting: Only one contains evidence that slaves were actually freed. This does not mean that the edicts were disregarded; it is simply a caution against assuming immediate liberation of all slaves in the groups specified. We do not know how faithfully and thoroughly orders were carried out, or how many slaves were affected. Imperial orders to free government slaves could be carried out through regular administrative channels within the closed system of the imperial government; but orders to the populace to free its slaves at personal economic loss would be vastly more difficult to enforce.

On the other hand it cannot be assumed that the eleven edicts represent the only government manumissions of groups during two and one-half centuries. It is only the manumission of larger groups or of important people like Chin Jih-ti or Tse (important for the narrative) that were worth recording. Probably many minor manumissions, involving individuals or small groups, were overlooked.

Every reference to manumission specifying the status of the freed slaves uses the term "commoner" or "common people" [1] except when the slave rose immediately to some honorary rank. This is significant. The terms refer to the vast mass of the Chinese people. Kings, marquises, and the highest ministers of state tumbled to the very same rank when they committed crimes requiring their expulsion from the ruling class. There was an unrestricted transition from slave to commoner status, and a quick transition from plebeian to noble rank in cases of talent or fortunate marriage. On the other hand, there was an equally easy descent from noble to plebeian rank through crime, and from commoner to slave status through economic distress or "rebellion." T'ang law reflects a certain rigidity of status. Government slaves had to pass through two higher stages,

from either or both sources did own slaves as a result of that wealth, there is little to prove that slaves were important as producers of wealth. Evidence that slaves contributed to wealth of merchants is scanty for the whole Han period and only one or two items even close to 202 B.C. can be cited. Finally, there is no way of knowing who had bought famine victims or which group might have been harder hit by having its slaves freed. If the manumission was not widely enforced, as I believe, then the latter uncertainty is, of course, beside the point.

[1] Documents *9, 24, 80, 89, 92, 102, 107, 110, 135, 138*, and HHS, 1B, 3b, 4b, and 5b; 4, 9a; 5, 4a.

with separate pardons, before they became *liang-jen*, "good people."
Later still, freed slaves and their descendants were prohibited from
taking civil service examinations, the normal road to office.[1]

In Former Han times, however, slavery was not caste-bound
although slaves possessed a definite ascribed status. The next
problem is to determine the nature of that status.

[1] Cf. Wang Shih-chieh, op. cit., p. 325 (Pippon, op. cit., pp. 128–129), and
his whole discussion of legal slave status.

VI. STATUS OF SLAVES

"Status" is the position or standing of individuals in relation to other individuals, groups, or the state. It is manifested by prerogatives or limitations, rights or duties, enjoyed by or imposed upon individuals in correspondence to their membership in recognized social groups. It is usually characterized by accepted modes of reciprocal behavior between persons of different status. Differences may be formally defined or they may be merely implied by systems of classification according to sex, age, kinship, rank, caste, occupation, membership in special associations, and so forth. The status of an individual may be ascribed to him automatically because of his membership in these groups, or he may achieve certain types by special accomplishments and skills. Servile status is ascribed.

When status is determined by social custom and maintained by moral, religious, or social sanctions in various degrees of rigidity it is "customary" status. But certain types of status are codified. Legal status represents the standing of a person before the law, or his relation toward others and the state in matters such as citizenship, property rights, marriage, infancy, and majority. If slaves were a well-defined class in Han society we should expect to find them endowed with a particular status in reference to members of other groups or classes; and conversely, if slaves had status different from that of people in all other classes, it would indicate a formal distinction between slaves and other people in the social structure.

Historical literature reflects social custom only vaguely. Yet the thoughts of historians and philosophers, and the attitudes of free people toward slaves do reveal something of customary slave status in China during the period here studied. Fortunately, well-codified T'ang and post-T'ang legal materials illuminate the fragmentary evidences of legal slave status in the Former Han period. Distinct in their degree of formalization, and reconstructed from differing kinds of sources, these two types of status need to be examined separately.

CUSTOMARY ATTITUDE TOWARD SLAVES

Han statesmen and writers considered slave status base, but fail to explain in what respects it was demeaning. Apparently they accepted it as a matter of course, and not a subject for speculation. Thus, the historian Pan Ku listed men of humble origin who rose

to greatness: Pu Shih, the shepherd; Sang Hung-yang, the lowly
tradesman; Wei Ch'ing, the slave; and Chin Jih-ti, the surrendered
captive (*26*, footnote 12). Ssu-ma Ch'ien defended Chi Pu's voluntary
enslavement to avoid capture as if it were the depth of disgrace,
by pointing out that it was at least more noble than suicide, the
recourse of slave women, concubines and other mean people (*56*).
He, or some earlier writer from whom he copied, employed slave
status as a simile for baseness and ill-treatment in the statement
that the daughter of the rich man of Wai-huang looked upon her
husband as a hired laborer or male slave (*A2*), and similarly in the
remark that Wang Wen-shu skilfully served those in power, but
looked upon them as though they were slaves as soon as they lost
their power (*A9*). Pao Hsüan, a Grandee Censor at the end of the
Former Han period, protested that it was against Heaven's intention
for the slaves of Tung Hsien to be liberally rewarded, officially
employed, and consequently become rich (*118*).

Any personal relation between rulers and slaves was considered
vastly demeaning. The contemporaries of Liu Ho, King of Ch'ang-i
till 74 B.C., severely censured him for having slaves as friends. This
impropriety was one excuse for his impeachment after he became
Emperor, and his adviser, Kung Sui, was spared execution primarily
because he had protested against it (*67*, *69*). Wang Yin, Liu Hsiang,
and Ku Yung all criticized Emperor Ch'eng for taking incognito
journeys in the intimate company of male slaves, and for keeping
private slaves in his palace (*104*).

Some moralists considered it highly improper for slaves, or even
common free folk, to wear fine clothes, especially any bit of costume
emblematic of noble or official status. This attitude had a philosophic background, strongly Confucian but inherent in other schools
of thought as well. Ranks, functions, duties, and prerogatives of
various members of a family group, of classes in society, and of
strata in the political organization had to be distinctly and properly
differentiated. Likewise the symbols of rank—both physical and
abstract—had to correspond. When such distinctions were upheld,
when all realms of social and political organization were in proper
harmonious relationship, nature too would be harmonious. But
defiance of proper differentiation could violently upset natural
phenomena and cause physical disasters. According to this school,
if slaves were allowed to wear costumes reserved for or symbolic
of the highest ranks, the ethical impropriety created an actual
physical menace.

Chia Yi criticized the practice of dressing slaves in beautiful clothes reserved in antiquity for emperors and empresses, and the custom of using stuffs, once reserved for the service of an emperor and his empress, to decorate the walls of rich people's homes. In a memorial to Emperor Wen, he asked: "How can there be no danger that the world will be unsubmissive [to the Emperor] if now the walls of the rooms of commoners may be done with an emperor's clothes; if singers and entertainers [and other] mean people may have the ornaments of an empress?" (*16*.)

The ceremonial cap was the most distinctive emblem of the upper class. When Liu Ho conferred this cap upon a male slave he horrified his contemporaries and shocked later commentators. Kung Sui, his righteous adviser, saw in such acts a veritable peril to the kingdom's gods of the soil and grain (*67*, footnote 5). Liu Hsiang considered it as approaching "heterodoxy in clothing." Ching Fang, a specialist on disasters and unnatural phenomena, is quoted as having said: "His conduct was not compliant [with natural law]; it brought disaster on the man. A male slave was capped; and the world was [thrown into] anarchy." An unknown writer whose words are now part of the chapter on "Unnatural Phenomena" in the *Ch'ien Han shu*, said of the act: "A ceremonial cap is honorable clothing; a male slave is a mean person. [The way Liu] Ho enjoyed conferring uncustomary ceremonial cappings without reason, was a symbol of [the way he] regarded honors. Ceremonially capping a male slave is equivalent to making the height of honor fall down to the extreme of meanness." (*67*.)[1]

This belief that servile status was demeaning is not supported by any theoretic discussion on the nature of slavery, nor is it mixed with any antagonism toward aliens, for there is no evidence of a marked non-Chinese element in the slave population. It was accepted as self-evident, and the point of view reflected what "everyone" thought at the time. A few Han documents picture this general attitude.

The *Shih chi* and *Ch'ien Han shu* both tell that in the State of Ch'i "it was customary to look down upon male slave captives." (*17*.) Early in the Han period Wei Pao refused to rejoin Emperor Kao, saying: "Now the King of Han insults people. He curses

---

[1] This quotation sounds like a commentary. It may have been copied by the authors into the *Ch'ien Han shu* from some such writer as Liu Hsiang or Ching Fang; but it might be a later commentary which has slipped into the body of the text. The attitude expressed appears, however, to be typical of the common attitude in Former Han times.

and scolds the nobles and ministers just as [one curses] male slaves, only!" (*A3*.) Wei Ch'ing's two proud but penniless retainers, Jen An and T'ien Jen, refused to eat at the same mat with the male cavalry slaves of the Princess of P'ing-yang. They cut the mat in two with their knives and sat apart (*39*). The fact that Wei Ch'ing himself had been a male slave and cavalry man in the same household only a few years earlier lends an ironic touch to the situation. We even have a report of Wei Ch'ing's own attitude toward his slave status when a physiognomist told him that he would become a marquis. To this prediction he is said to have replied, skeptically: "Born as another's male slave, it is sufficient not to be beaten and cursed. How could I get appointed a marquis!" (*26*.)

Thus slaves were apparently considered to be on the lowest level of the social scale. But slave status is only one of the innumerable kinds of status. An individual does not have a single and permanently fixed customary status, but many, deriving from such factors as sex, age, kinship, occupation, political position, and nationality. In some fields status may change gradually, as with age, or quickly, with accomplishment. The standing of Tou Kuang-kuo before and after he established his identity as the brother of an empress is an example of rapid change. Furthermore, status does not operate abstractly, but concretely, in the relations of individuals each having a combination of statuses.

Within the slave group itself there were marked differences in status. Among government slaves, for example, there must have been differences between enslaved families of criminals—wearing felon's dress, their heads shaved, and perhaps even permanently disfigured by tattoo marks around the eyes—and private slaves given to the government or seized by it.

The work done by a government slave must itself have determined his status within the slave group, but it is not easy to distinguish the personal qualities, or the circumstances in a slave's acquisition that determined the type of occupation to which he was assigned. Some toiled at hard labor transporting grain, or in the government mint. Others, more skilled and clever, manufactured implements or prepared the palace banquets. Some among them even rose to be "senior slaves," in charge of their lesser fellows. They must have had a customary status above that of the toilers; and as government employees, knowing the ropes, familiar with bureau affairs, they doubtless enjoyed a commanding position among the common folk who were actually free.

The *élite* among the government slaves were probably those who worked in imperial palaces. Most palace slaves were women; many worked in the Concubines' Quarter as servants of palace ladies, though some were in other parts of the palaces, too. Some, like Ts'ao Kung, unwittingly became involved in palace intrigue.

The attractive daughter of a government slave woman, Ts'ao Kung was a student clerk attached to the Empress. Although she had a homosexual attachment with another slave girl named Tao Fang, she was "favored" by Emperor Ch'eng and conceived. She boasted to Tao Fang and her mother about her great good fortune. Her prestige was growing rapidly. The child she bore was a boy, the presumptive heir to the throne. Six slave women were placed at her disposal. Had the boy been made Heir-apparent, Ts'ao Kung would probably have become Empress; yet she was legally a slave and theoretically that was still her status. Because of the wild jealousy of the favorite imperial concubine, the Emperor commanded Ts'ao Kung to take poison. Her son was slain, and the six slave women who attended her were compelled to hang themselves. Cheng Ch'i, another slave woman who had nursed the babe for eleven days, lived to tell her side of the story to the investigating commission, as did Ts'ao Kung's mother and the friend, Tao Fang (*107*).

This document reveals some aspects of the life of palace slave women. The violent and most dramatic scenes may not be typical of the life of such women, but intrigue was always current in the palace. The slaves saw much and knew the gossip of the court. When freed, or when mixing with other slaves and commoners, they had much to hint at or tell. They enjoyed a customary status loftier than that of most government bondsmen, and far above that theoretically ascribed them as slaves. The humble palace slave woman Tse— whose surname is not even reported, but who had an audience with the Emperor and received a gift that to her was fabulous—must have enjoyed far greater customary status amongst her neighbors because of her former position in the palace than she possessed, after emancipation, from her rank as a commoner (*80*).

The toiler slaves, the servile bureaucrats, and the palace slaves may all have been equal before the law. Certainly they were different from commoners, and were considered beneath them. But within this common status there must have been marked degrees of difference. If a single principle defines that difference it is function. Information about government slavery in Former Han times is too scanty to allow an arrangement of various slave occupations in a series of increasing importance. Yet the principle of relationship between the function of individuals and their customary status is applicable also to private slaves.

Some of Tiao Chien's slaves associated with generals, administrators of commanderies, and chancellors of kingdoms. Tiao Chien trusted them so completely that they preferred their status as his slaves to freedom and noble rank (*17*). Likewise, the male slaves Feng Tzu-tou and Wang Tzu-fang, Ho Kuang's confidential advisers, who were regarded by officialdom as more important than the Chancellor (*66*, and footnote 3), had a status on the basis of function beyond that of his ordinary slaves. Feng Tzu-tou even had his name listed along with several nobles and high officials in an imperial edict about the conspirators of the Ho family clique,[1] a dubious honor made possible primarily because of his importance in the business affairs of the family (*72*, and footnote 3).

So, too, the status of other private slaves probably varied; a servant girl must have been lower in status—both among her fellows and in the social scale—than a female chamberlain slave, who had personal charge of her master's wardrobe and bed. Male slaves who did manual work could hardly have enjoyed the prestige of their fellows who were cavalry escorts and personal guards for their masters.

The actual customary status of private slaves was affected also by the status of their masters. The best documented example of this modification of status concerns the slaves of Ho Kuang. His two confidential slaves ranked above their fellows because of their special position, but their status with officialdom arose from the fact that they were the key for access to Ho Kuang. Yet all his slaves enjoyed special prestige. In Ho Kuang's native seat, the male slaves and retainers of the family would go armed into town, fighting and brawling, and no official dared to stop them except Yin Weng-kuei, who, as the historian admiringly reports, enforced the laws impartially (*65*). Shortly after Ho Kuang's death one of his grand-nephews had the audacity to send a slave in his stead to attend the imperial court. Certainly it was no ordinary slave who could appear before the Emperor at formal assembly, but a top slave of the most powerful family in the realm. Even after their master was dead the Ho family slaves were exceedingly arrogant. Once a party of them disputed the right of way with the slaves of Wei Hsiang, who was Grandee Secretary. Here was a clash between slaves over

[1] CHS, 8, 5a.

their relative status. To avenge the insult to their prestige, the Ho slaves invaded Wei Hsiang's residency and made him knock his head upon the ground and apologize to them! (*72*.) This humiliation was partly responsible for Wei Hsiang's prosecution and final destruction of the Ho clan when he became Chancellor. Similarly, the slaves of Tung Hsien, Emperor Ai's favorite, received rich gifts from various officials (*117*), and "looked on wine as though it were soup, and meat as though it were beans." (*118*.)

Wang Shih-chieh, in a very interesting article on Chinese slavery,[1] devotes a section to a discussion of the legal position of slaves, under six headings: limitation of rights of marriage; limitation on right of examination and official position; punishment of slaves for crimes; crimes against slaves; limitation of rights in law suit; and manumission. Drawing on laws, edicts, and cases from all Chinese history, but especially from T'ang times on, he is able to formulate several important generalizations concerning slave status. For the Han period, however, his information is scanty because of the paucity of extant legal material.

From T'ang times down to the end of the nineteenth century the legal status of slaves was definitely inferior to that of the free. Slaves who committed crimes of violence, sex, or abuse against their masters or against other free people were much more severely punished than free people who committed the same crimes against each other. On the other hand, masters or other free people who committed these crimes against slaves were lightly punished. Male slaves could not legally marry free women; nor could slaves accuse their masters in court (except in crimes of high treason), even for redress against personal wrong.[2]

SLAVES IN CRIMINAL LAW

Because the law code of the Han dynasty has been lost since the sixth century we must go on the one hand to edicts or recorded cases, and on the other to later codes based upon it in order to formulate an opinion regarding the legal status of slaves prior to the

---

[1] Wang Shih-chieh, "The Chinese slavery system" (translated by Toni Pippon, "Beitrag zum Chinesischen Sklavensystem"). On legal aspects see especially pp. 315–325 (Pippon, pp. 113–129).

[2] The legal documentation on these points may be found in Wang Shih-chieh, op. cit., pp. 319–322, 316–318, and 322, respectively. See also Shen Chia-pen, *Li tai hsing fa k'ao*, "Fen k'ao," ch. 15, pp. 10a–11b, and 29b, and Liang Ch'i-ch'ao, "System of slavery in China," pp. 547–549.

first century of our era. Yet it is clear that slaves had an inferior position in criminal law as compared with free people not their masters. This generalization is based upon two edicts by the first Emperor of the Latter Han dynasty, referring to legal matters during the preceding period.

In A.D. 35 Emperor Kuang-wu revoked the law of public execution for male and female slaves who shot and wounded people (*138*). No such law is elsewhere recorded for the Former Han period, but an imperial edict revoking such a law is evidence of its earlier existence. The edict does not specify whether "people" means any free person or the master. The phrasing is also vague on the point of accidental or purposeful wounding. Apparently the circumstances in such cases were of no concern; a slave who shot and wounded a free man intentionally, or possibly even accidentally, could legally be executed in public. Was this inequitably severe?

Ch'en Lung, a Commandant of Justice in A.D. 94, reported to the throne that there were 610 listed crimes involving the death penalty.[1] In Han times the death sentence was applied in three ways, which differed in degree of severity. The worst penalty was to behead the criminal and exhibit his head in a public place. The second was to cut the criminal in two at the waist. The least severe was public execution (lit., "casting on the market place"), since this did not involve dismemberment of the body.[2] The severity of each penalty could be increased by extending the sentence to various relatives of the criminal. In practice, and in theory also, the degree of the punishment was conditioned by the rank and social status of the criminal; punishment was not decreed objectively as a pre-established sentence for a specific crime.[3]

When a slave shot and wounded a free man the proper sentence was public execution. This was excessively severe treatment judged either by comparison with crimes of free people which resulted in their being publicly executed, or by comparison with the punishments legally applied to free people who merely wounded other free people.

[1] HHS, 76, 4b.

[2] In 148 B.C. Emperor Ching abolished the punishment of "quartering" and substituted public execution. See HFHD, vol. I, p. 319, especially the important footnote 6.4. Beheading and cutting in two at the waist continued to be practiced, as is shown by cases during the rest of the dynasty.

[3] Cf., for example, cases incidentally reported in documents *44, 52, 64, 98, 103, 113.* Cf. also HFHD, vol. I, pp. 176–177.

Analyzing a considerable number of cases in which criminals were actually publicly executed, and examining known laws concerning this punishment, we find that this third form of execution was applied in general to four classes of very serious crimes. These classes were: (1) crimes against the Emperor or imperial prerogatives; (2) murder; (3) violation of fundamental morality; and (4) serious corruption or crime by high officials.[1] This shows not only that the law applied to slaves was discriminatingly severe, but also points to a formalized differentiation in Han criminal law between crimes committed by slaves and by free people.[2]

[1] This classification certainly does not accurately represent the Chinese conceptual background in which ethics, morality, and law are mingled in a way which defies classification in western terms. The difficulty is immediately apparent in the number of cases which might fall in two or more of these categories. In compiling the following list, items were taken from the first six chapters of Ch'eng Shu-te, *Chiu ch'ao lü k'ao* ("Han lü k'ao"). In general only items of the Former Han period referring specifically to public execution, and quoted from the SC or CHS, were taken. The pages referred to are in the one-volume edition of 1935.

Class 1

Page
75: Father, mother, wife, children, brothers and sisters should be publicly executed in cases of treason and inhumanity (also class 3).
77: Forging imperial edicts and disregarding imperial orders.
127: Divulging conversations held in the imperial palace.
145: Entering the imperial audience hall without a pass.
176, 184, 185: Criticizing the imperial family.
102, 180: Counterfeiting, or making false gold.

Class 2

131: Murder (2 cases).
133: Having a person murdered by another (5 cases).
135: Wounding a person who then died within a short time.

Class 3

115: Inhumanity—an official bearing a grudge against and slandering a member of the government.
117: Unfilial conduct—a son bringing public accusation against his father (cf. also pp. 114–118 *passim*).

Class 4

119: Wilful negligence—a Commandant of Justice failing to punish a capital crime.
120: The same—a Prefect failing to prosecute a conspiracy of rebellion (also class 1).
123: Concealing criminals—a marquis concealing a gang of robbers; a Commandant of Justice concealing conspirators of rebellion (also class 1).
127, 157: False accusation of innocent people—by a Commandant of Justice, by a marquis.
160: Officials mutually recommending each other for advancement.
163: Being disrespectful about ceremonial purification.

[2] Wu Ching-ch'ao ("The slavery system of the Western Han," p. 267) says that this punishment for slaves was one degree more severe than if the guilty person were free. He does not document his statement, but his opinion may be based on an analogous law of T'ang times which specified that male or female slaves who beat "good people" were to receive a punishment two degrees more severe than would be applied to free culprits (*T'ang lü su i*, ch. 22. Cf. Shen

In determining the normal punishment for a free person who merely wounded another free person, we arrive at the same conclusion. A basic principle of Han law was the famous declaration of Emperor Kao after he entered the Ch'in capital in 207 B.C.: "He who kills a person will die; he who wounds a person or robs [will be punished] according to the offense." [1]

There are few recorded cases of free people punished for wounding others because such matters were not generally of serious state concern. Two cases involving noblemen and officials happen to be recorded, and are valuable for comparison. In one, a marquis was tried for wounding a man under circumstances which are not reported, and was dismissed.[2] The other is the case in which Hsüeh K'uang hired a man to attack and horribly disfigure an enemy, for which he was only banished to Tun-huang. During the official debate concerning the crime, which was complicated by a number of interesting factors, the Commandant of Justice enunciated an important legal principle and quoted a significant law. First, "The universal principle of the past and present, unaltered during the Three Dynasties, is that 'murderers die, and wounders [are punished with] mutilation.' " The law he cited was: "[One who] wounds another with a bladed weapon while fighting will be left whole [i.e., unmutilated] and will [be sentenced to] work on [frontier] fortifications and patrol; one who purposely attacks [and wounds another will receive] a punishment increased by one degree; one who plotted with [the actual attacker will receive] the same punishment." [3]

Chia-pen, op. cit., p. 29b; Wang Shih-chieh, op. cit., p. 320). In T'ang times there was a special class, called *pu ch'ü*, whose status was between that of slaves and free people. Punishments for *pu ch'ü* were one degree more severe than for free people, and one degree less severe than for slaves.

[1] Cf. CHS, 1A, 7a, and HFHD, vol. I, p. 58. Wang Shih-chieh (op. cit., p. 320) emphasizes the fundamental difference between this principle and the law regarding slaves who wounded people.

[2] Ch'eng Shu-te, op. cit., p. 76. Another case is there reported of a marquis who was tried for premeditated attack and murder, and was dismissed.

[3] The word translated as "left whole" refers to those who escaped mutilation after Emperor Wen abolished that form of punishment (cf. HFHD, vol. I, p. 255, and Ch'eng Shu-te, op. cit., pp. 44–45, 178). The increase of punishment by one degree would here probably have involved tattooing on the face as well as frontier service, or increase from four to five years' servitude (ibid., pp. 51–52). This complex case occurred in 7 B.C., and is reported in detail in CHS, 83, 3b–4b. An official named Shen Hsien was slandering a fellow official, Hsüeh Hsüan, for lack of loyalty and filial piety. Hsüeh K'uang, the son of Hsüeh Hsüan, feared that Shen Hsien would make an official accusation against his father, and therefore plotted to hire a retainer, Yang Ming, to disfigure Shen Hsien so that he could not appear at court. Learning that Shen Hsien was about to be made Colonel over the Retainers, Hsüeh K'uang ordered Yang Ming to go ahead

We thus have a dual contrast. On the one hand, free people were publicly executed only for very serious crimes; yet slaves could be publicly executed merely for wounding free people. On the other hand, if free people wounded other free people they were punished in some equivalent or proportionate degree; but slaves who wounded free people could be punished far beyond the degree of the actual crime itself. In cases involving slaves the punishment was obviously not balanced to equal the criminal act alone, but was determined on the basis of status as well.

There is no further documentation in Former Han records about slaves who wounded free people. But the discussion cannot end there. Emperor Kuang-wu revoked a particular law which harshly discriminated against slaves who committed a particular crime. While no other similar specific laws still exist it is almost beyond the realm of possibility that the very elaborate Han code contained an isolated law to deal exclusively with slaves who shot and wounded

with the deed. Yang Ming and some others attacked Shen Hsien on the great road in front of the palace gate, cut off his nose and lips, and hacked his body in eight places. In the discussion among the officials as to proper punishment, two opinions developed.

The first maintained that Hsüeh Hsüan and his son were both officials; that Hsüeh Hsüan's lack of filial piety was common knowledge and should have been officially known; that the attack on an official by the agent of another official had been made in front of the palace, and in public, so that it had a very bad effect on public morals. Thus the crime was *ta pu ching* ("great disrespect for the Emperor"), and therefore both Hsüeh K'uang and Yang Ming ought to be publicly executed.

The second opinion, advanced by the Commandant of Justice, starts with the quotation of the Code about wounding in fighting, etc. (translated above), and maintained that Shen Hsien was not justified in constantly speaking of Hsüeh Hsüan's bad conduct; that it was a private fight and not different from fights between ordinary civilians simply because it occurred outside the palace gate. The Commandant then cited the unalterable ancient principle that "murderers die, and wounders [are punished by] mutilation." This fundamental principle, a quid pro quo, may be contrasted with the law of public execution as punishment for slaves who wounded free people! Continuing, he contended that to treat Hsüeh K'uang and Yang Ming as being guilty of *ta pu ching* because they were officials was a violation of the principle of the *Ch'un ch'iu* that there was no difference between public and private matters; that, considering the original impulse of the crime, Hsüeh K'uang was violently angered by observing a person slandering his father, and was guilty of no other great crime. He believed that Yang Ming and Hsüeh K'uang ought to be sentenced respectively according to the law pertaining to the premeditated attack and wounding of a person, and to plotting with the attacker. But, since both had honorary titles, the sentence ought to be reduced to working on frontier fortifications and patrol, without mutilation. (Yen Shih-ku explains that if a person had honorary rank he received a reduced sentence and was not mutilated. Thus, these men, by getting a reduction, would be given the punishment due for wounding another in an *un*premeditated fight.)

Emperor Ai then put the question for discussion among the high ministers. The Chancellor, K'ung Kuang, and the Grandee Secretary, Shih Tan, agreed with the first decision, while all the other ministers agreed with the second. In the end, Hsüeh K'uang had his sentence reduced one degree, and was banished to Tun-huang. What happened to Yang Ming is, characteristically, not told.

free people; that it had no other laws of this class; and, finally, that this one law happened to be preserved among the relatively few Han laws known to this day. In other words, this law was probably typical rather than unique. It must have been one of a class of laws which discriminated against slaves by condemning them to more severe punishments than those applied to free people guilty of the same or similar crimes.

There was a group of laws discriminating against slaves in the T'ang code, and T'ang law was based upon the Han law indirectly through intervening codes, and probably even directly. Moreover, the principle of inequality was carried on in all the later great codes based on T'ang. These codes, in fact, did not even alter many of the details.[1] The general continuity of Chinese law is a fact not to be minimized when a principle rather than a particular point is in question.

If slaves were in general punished more severely for crimes against free people than were free people themselves, then were free people punished less severely for crimes against slaves than for similar crimes against other free people? This reverse side of the question is suggested by another edict of Emperor Kuang-wu. In A.D. 35 he proclaimed: "In the nature of heaven and earth, man is most important. He who kills a male or female slave will not receive a reduction in punishment." (*137.*)

This imperial edict lays down the principle that, under law, the murder of a slave is no less serious than the murder of a free person; or, more specifically, that the murderer of a slave could not thereafter be sentenced to a lighter penalty than the murderer of a free man. Does this not mean that before A.D. 35 the murderer of a slave properly received a reduced penalty? Modern Chinese writers on slavery conclude that it does.[2] Analogy with the T'ang code suggests the same conclusion. According to T'ang law, "those 'good

---

[1] Wang Shih-chieh, op. cit., p. 320. For example, the T'ang law (p. 148, footnote 2) which specified two extra degrees of punishment for slaves who beat and wounded "good people," is only part of the law. Thus, if a slave beat "a good person" and broke a limb or a bone in his body, or blinded one eye, he would be strangled; if the slave beat the "good person" to death he would be beheaded (*T'ang lü su i*, ch. 22). Again, a male slave who had peaceable sexual relations with a free woman would be punished with two and a half years' servitude; if he raped her he would be banished; if he injured her during rape he would be strangled (ibid., ch. 24). Crimes by slaves against their masters or their masters' relatives were even more severely punished.

[2] Wu Ching-ch'ao (op. cit., p. 267) uses the edict as direct evidence concerning the legal position of slaves in Former Han times, as does Liang Ch'i-ch'ao (op. cit., p. 546). The belief is implied also by Ma Fei-pai ("Source material on the economic history of Ch'in and Han," pt. 6, "The slavery system," p. 395).

people' who beat and wound other people's *pu ch'ü* [shall receive sentences] reduced by one degree [from the sentence for beating and wounding] ordinary people. [Those who beat and wound] male or female slaves [shall receive sentences] further reduced by one degree. Those who purposely kill *pu ch'ü* [shall be] strangled; [those who purposely kill] male or female slaves [shall be] banished 3,000 *li*." [1]

Emperor Kuang-wu's edict did not differentiate between people who killed slaves belonging to the government or to other people, and masters who killed their own slaves.

LEGAL RIGHTS OF MASTERS OVER SLAVES

Apparently masters had the right to kill their slaves, but under certain conditions only. Even then they were held legally accountable to the government. Just before the beginning of the dynasty one of the rebels against Ch'in used the following stratagem to gain access to the Prefect of Ti in order to murder him. T'ien Tan "deceivingly bound up his male slave, and escorted by [a group of] young bloods, went to the court [of the Prefect of Ti, as though] wishing an interview to [announce his intention to] kill the male slave." He was successful in this stratagem, and having been admitted to court, he killed the Prefect (4). This passage must have seemed intelligible to the authors of the *Shih chi* when they composed or copied it toward the end of the second century B.C. Today, however, its implications are revealed only through the commentators. Fu Ch'ien, writing toward the end of the Latter Han period, explains that formerly anyone killing a male or female slave had to announce it to the government; and that T'ien Tan, wishing to kill the Prefect, bound up his male slave in order to get an interview. Yen Shih-ku adds that he fraudulently bound up his male slave to create the appearance of killing the slave (4, footnote 4).

In later histories, this law or usage becomes clearer, and the right of masters to kill their slaves is more strictly defined. In the *History of the Chin dynasty*, A.D. 265–419,[2] a statement in the

---

[1] *T'ang lü su i*, ch. 22 (cf. Wang Shih-chieh, op. cit., p. 321; Liang Ch'i-ch'ao, op. cit., p. 547).

Wang Shih-chieh says that the Sung law was the same as T'ang, while those of the Yüan, Ming and Ch'ing periods were modified only in detail. The principle was apparently the same. He also cites equally discriminatory T'ang and later laws concerning sexual relations between "good people" and public or private slaves.

[2] *Chin shu*, ch. 30 (Hsing fa chih), 7b, quoted by Ch'eng Shu-te (op. cit. [Chin lü k'ao], p. 275), Liang Ch'i-ch'ao (op. cit., p. 547), and Shen Chia-pen (op. cit., p. 29a).

section on law says that if a male or female slave resists his master, the master may pay a visit (to an official) and then kill the slave. Early in the T'ang period the law read: "When various male or female slaves commit crimes, those of their masters who kill them without requesting [permission of] the government officials shall be basti-nadoed one hundred strokes." [1] The element which these later laws had in common with the situation in 209 B.C. is the master's right to kill his slaves after receiving permission from the government. In the earliest case it is not stated on what grounds permission would be granted.

Tung Chung-shu, one of the foremost Han social philosophers, implied that in practice masters often killed slaves on their own authority, and advocated that Emperor Wu abolish slavery in order to eliminate the terror of autocratic execution (35). Since masters were supposed to obtain permission from the government, were they punished if they neglected to do so?

Known cases of masters (or presumed masters) who auto-cratically executed slaves indicate at the outset that such acts were treated as criminal. In most of these cases the master committed other serious crimes as well, so that it is not possible to assess the relative gravity of the slave murder and of the other crimes in terms of the punishment. For example, when the Marquis of Chao was tried for murdering sixteen men, some of whom were slaves (52), the brief report does not differentiate the crimes or tell how many were slaves and how many free. Three out of sixteen people foully murdered by the King of Kuang-ch'uan at the instigation of his Queen were slaves (64). But in the trial the sixteen murders were treated together. Likewise, Liu Li, the King of Liang, ordered a slave to murder two officials, and then murdered the slave to silence

---

[1] *T'ang lü su i*, ch. 22. The law continues: "Those [masters] who kill innocent [slaves] shall [be punished by] one year of servitude; those who accidentally kill [their slaves] shall not be tried." Wang Shih-chieh (op. cit., p. 321) states that the Yüan, Ming and Ch'ing codes copied the T'ang law either entirely or in general.

In contrast to these light punishments for masters who killed their slaves, is the reverse situation, in which slaves harmed their masters. The T'ang law does not even specify a punishment for slaves who purposely killed their masters, but "all those *pu ch'ü* or male and female slaves who plot to kill their masters shall be decapitated. Those who plot to kill the masters' relatives or mothers' parents shall be strangled; those who [plot to kill and] actually wound [such relatives] shall all be decapitated." Furthermore, "All those *pu ch'ü* or male and female slaves who accidentally kill their masters shall be strangled. Those who beat their masters' relatives or mothers' parents shall be strangled; those who [thus] actually wound [the masters' relatives] shall all be beheaded. Those who curse [their masters or masters' relatives(?)] shall be [punished by] two years servitude." (*T'ang lü su i*, ch. 17 and 22.) See also Liang Ch'i-ch'ao (ibid.), Wang Shih-chieh (op. cit., p. 319) and R. Deloustal ("La justice dans l'ancien Annam," BEFEO, vol. 11, 1911, p. 318, footnote 2).

him (*106*). He was officially accused of three murders, as well as of other crimes.

After the death of Liu Yüan, King Miu of Chao, the Grand Herald memorialized the throne about his former criminal acts, accusing him of killing slaves and of ordering others to be killed after his death. The wording is important. "[Liu] Yüan formerly *illicitly* killed male and female slaves with a sword." Does this not mean that he killed when he did not have the right to kill? Later, when the King was mortally ill he made a will commanding that his entertainer slaves be buried with him. After his death sixteen of them were compelled to commit suicide. Only the fact that his son had killed an internuncio complicates this case, preventing it from being a clear example of punishment for the illegal killing of slaves. The earlier illegal killing of slaves, the son's killing of the inter- nuncio, and the enforced suicide of sixteen entertainer slaves were equally recorded in the memorial as grounds for abolishing the kingdom (*84*).

This lumping together of murders of free people and slaves owned by the murderer is significant. It indicates that the wanton killing of a slave was itself a serious crime. The facts in each of the above cases are on record primarily because the murderer was an important nobleman and a member of the imperial clan, so that the punishment vitally affected an hereditary line and a political unit. Yet in each case the fact that some of the victims were slaves was of enough additional importance in the total picture to be reported specifically. Thus, even in cases where nobles were guilty of ruth- lessly murdering free people, the official records of the cases include the fact that they also murdered their own slaves.

The wife of the Marquis of Chiang-ling was so uncontrollably jealous of other women in the household that she murdered forty or more female serving slaves. She was publicly executed for these and other crimes, but the case was so extreme that it does not serve as a good test (*82*). A decisive one is the matter of Chancellor Wei Hsiang.

Two separate reports of the suspicious death of Chancellor Wei Hsiang's female slave chamberlain prove unequivocally that masters could not freely kill innocent slaves. The *Ch'ien Han shu* relates that Chao Kuang-han, Administrator of the Capital District, feared that Chancellor Wei Hsiang was about to accuse him of past crimes. Through a spy he learned that the Chancellor's female slave chamber- lain had died violently some time before, and suspected that the

Chancellor's wife had killed her out of jealousy. Armed with this information, he tried to frighten the Chancellor into dropping his charges, but when this failed he sent up a document reporting the crime. The case was referred back to him, as Administrator of the Capital District, to prosecute. Seizing this opportunity, he invaded the chancellery, cross-questioned the wife, took witnesses, and charged the wife with murdering the slave. Chancellor Wei Hsiang was thus driven to submit a document personally affirming his wife's innocence and requesting an imperial commission to investigate the slave's death. The Commandant of Justice determined that the Chancellor himself had scolded and beaten the slave because of her faults, and that she had gone to an outside mansion and died, i.e., by suicide. The Chancellor and his wife were thus absolved; but Chao Kuang-han was tried and executed for slandering a high official as well as for his other earlier crimes (76).

The account in the present *Shih chi*, appended by Ch'u Shao-sun, who lived at the very time, is less complete but adds certain valuable details. Regarding Chao Kuang-han's attempt to dissuade the Chancellor from accusing him, it states that he "again sent someone to coerce and frighten Chancellor Wei concerning the matter of his wife's *illicit* killing of a serving female slave; while [at the same time] he secretly and individually presented a memorial requesting a thorough judicial investigation into it." It also says that "in fact [the female slave] had not been killed with a weapon." The Chancellor's counter-accusation charged Chao Kuang-han with the iniquity of making "a false accusation of his wife's *illicit* killing of a female slave." (77.)

It is not known what punishment the Chancellor and his wife would have received, or should legally have been sentenced to, if Chao Kuang-han had been able to prove that the wife had murdered the female slave. But it is quite clear that Chao Kuang-han, who knew the law, pressed his suspicion in an official accusation in order to prevent the Chancellor from accusing him of serious crimes. It is equally clear that the Chancellor was thereby placed in such a dangerous situation that he had to request an impartial judicial investigation to establish his wife's innocence. One could hardly demand from the available historical sources more conclusive evidence that in Former Han times masters could not legally or securely kill slaves who were innocent of any crime. This is a good and necessary corrective for some modern Chinese writers who assert that masters had absolute and unlimited rights over their slaves.

Yet Emperor Kuang-wu's edict—"he who kills a male or female slave will not receive a reduction in punishment"—makes it clear that when masters did kill their slaves illegally during the previous part of the dynasty they were punished less severely than they would have been for killing free people. On the other hand, masters seem to have had the right to kill slaves guilty of certain crimes, not now known, provided they first reported to the proper government authorities. The second and third of these conclusions indicate the inferior legal status of slaves, while the first shows that they had some legal protection.

SLAVES IN THE COURTS OF LAW

The rights of slaves to make accusations or act as witnesses in law courts also illuminate this question of slave status. Under T'ang law a slave could not accuse his master except in cases of rebellion and high treason. A slave who reported other crimes was strangled whether the accusation was true or false, while the master was treated as if he had voluntarily confessed, and was thus excused from punishment or received a reduction in it. Furthermore, slaves who accused their masters' relatives were punished by banishment even if the charge was true. The codes from Sung through Ming followed the T'ang code with little change.[1]

The principle underlying these laws seems to be part of the larger and fundamental Chinese principle that within a family group—as well as within certain other more extended groups—persons of inferior rank or age could not accuse their superiors or elders. Such accusations profoundly violated the fundamental ethical and moral values which constituted the framework of Chinese society.

Now this moral principle was already well entrenched in Former Han times. There are clear records showing that sons who accused their fathers could be punished by execution. For example, the Heir-apparent of the King of Heng-shan submitted a document to court accusing his father of plotting rebellion. Although this was true, and the King was therefore executed, the Heir-apparent was also executed on the grounds of unfilially (*pu hsiao*) accusing his father. In another instance, an eclipse of the sun was blamed upon the immorality of Chancellor Wang Shang. One of the charges was that his son, Wang Chün, had actually prepared a document

---

[1] *T'ang lü su i*, ch. 24. See also Wang Shih-chieh (op. cit., p. 322) and Deloustal (BEFEO, vol. 8, 1908, pp. 191–192).

accusing his father [of murder and incest(?)]. Wang Chün's wife seized the document to show it to her father, Shih Tan, who was so disgusted by this family schism that he made her leave Wang Shang's house. This family disharmony was listed as one of the reasons why the Chancellor was unfit for his post. He was dismissed.[1]

There is no direct evidence that in Han times prohibitions which forbade people of lesser rank in a family to accuse their superiors were extended to slaves accusing their masters. Yet slaves were included within the incest group to the extent that a son might not have relations with a female slave who had been favored by his father.[2] There is, furthermore, a censorious and possibly significant statement by the historian concerning Wang Mang's confiscation of illegal profits: "This opened [the way for] officers to inform on their generals, and male and female slaves to inform on their masters." (128.) Though this remark proves nothing concerning laws against accusations by slaves, it does indicate the historian's belief that such conduct was reprehensible.

The testimony of slaves was admitted as evidence against their masters in cases already under judicial investigation. This is quite different from an accusation brought by a slave in the first instance. Liu Ch'ü, the unspeakably cruel King of Kuang-ch'uan, was finally brought to justice because a slave who murdered a woman on his orders was apprehended and confessed. An imperial decree ordered that the Queen, concubines, male and female slaves, and other witnesses be put in prison, and their testimony about the sixteen murders formed the basis for the King's banishment (64). Chao Kuang-han seized the slaves of Chancellor Wei Hsiang as witnesses against their master (76, 77). Six government slave women are listed among the chief witnesses against the imperial concubine née Chao in the important investigation of the murder of two imperial sons (107).

One document indicates that government slaves could bring accusations against free men. In this case the older slave brother of a government slave woman reported that his sister had been debauched by a Gentleman. It is interesting that the slave's accusation actually reached Chang An-shih, the Superintendent of the Gentlemen of the Palace, even though he suppressed the matter and punished the slave. The historian made an approving comment

---

[1] CHS, 44, 7a; and CHS, 82, 2a, respectively. Cf. documents 37 and 98 for more complete details on the background of both cases.

[2] Cf. 37 and 48 for cases punished, and 59 and 98 for cases reported with censure.

that Chang An-shih "always concealed others' misdoings in this manner." (*63*.)

"MIXED MARRIAGES," AND STATUS OF CHILDREN

In the matured slavery system of T'ang times intermarriage between slaves and free people was legally restricted. Free women, especially, could not marry male slaves. If they did, the girl and the slave were separated, and the master, his slave, and the girl's family all were punished. If male or female slaves passed themselves off, or were passed off, as "good people" and became the husbands or wives of "good people," they were punished by two years of penal servitude, and each member of the marriage was returned to his former status.[1]

There is no record of such legal restrictions on marriage between slaves and free people earlier than T'ang times. Even the class of laws on marriages, under which these restrictions fall in the T'ang law, was not instituted before the Northern Wei period.[2] It seems unlikely, in fact, that such alliances were forbidden in Han law.

Early in the Han period, Ch'ao Ts'o memorialized Emperor Wen about the problems of frontier defense, and suggested that male and female criminals, private male and female slaves contributed to the government, and civilian volunteers be sent to establish permanent agricultural garrisons. He also proposed that the government should buy mates for those migrants who were single (*19*). The plan to set up colonies received imperial approval but it is not told whether all details suggested by Ch'ao Ts'o were adopted. All we know, therefore, is Ch'ao Ts'o's proposal that unmarried male and female criminals, slaves, and plebeians be provided with mates who had been purchased and therefore presumably were slaves. After establishing colonies all of them would probably have been freed.

The palace slave woman named Tse had a free husband. She worked in the Palace of the Imperial Concubines in 63 B.C., but was in contact with her commoner husband, for she had him submit

---

[1] *T'ang lü su i*, ch. 14. Cf. Liang Ch'i-ch'ao, op. cit., p. 548, and Wang Shih-chieh, op. cit., pp. 316–317. Liang Ch'i-ch'ao points out that if a male slave tried to elevate his status by marriage he was punished, but if a free woman lowered her status by marrying a slave she (or her family) was much more severely punished.

[2] Cf. Ch'eng Shu-te, op. cit. ("Hou Wei lü k'ao"), p. 413, and ("Pei Ch'i lü k'ao"), p. 468. Evidence of earlier legal restrictions may exist, although Shen Chia-pen (op. cit., p. 15a) starts his citations on this subject with the *Chin History* (i.e., after A.D. 1115).

for her a memorandum claiming special merit because, some twenty
years before, she had nursed the infant who eventually became
Emperor Hsüan.   Yen Shih-ku's comment about her matrimonial
status actually befogs the situation: "It means that at the time when
she had not yet become a palace slave woman she had had a former
husband, who at this time was among the populace." Does he mean
that formerly she had been a free person married to a free man,
and then became a palace slave, while her husband remained free?
Or was she previously a government or private slave married to
a free man, and then became a palace slave?   Or was she previously
a government or private slave married to a slave who later became
free?   All that is certain on the basis of the historical text is that she
was a palace slave woman with a free husband (80).

Wang Lin-ch'ing killed the lover, or husband, of one of his female
slaves about 7 B.C.   Yen Shih-ku says that the man was an outsider
who had had illicit relations with the slave, but the additional commentary, also quoted by Wang Hsien-ch'ien, says that he was the
husband to whom the serving girl was married.   The term hsü
(a son-in-law), which is used to designate the man, makes the second
interpretation seem more likely, especially as it is used in the Fang
yen for the act in which commoners mated female slaves (11, and
footnote 4).   Wang Lin-ch'ing should have been prosecuted for this
murder, but the official who knew all about the case did not think
the time was appropriate, especially in view of the fact that Wang
Lin-ch'ing had just been dismissed from court (112).

There is no recorded instance of a free woman married to a male
slave.   This was the type of alliance most rigorously forbidden in
T'ang times.   Yet a social stigma against such marriages is perhaps
reflected in the great reluctance of the Elder-Princess of Yang-hsin
to marry Wei Ch'ing, the most eligible of the marquises, because
he had once been a slave in her household.   His later position, rather
than the earlier status, decided the issue, and the Princess arranged
the marriage through the Empress née Wei and Emperor Wu, as
intermediaries (26, and footnote 12).   Further evidence of a social
stigma against mixed marriages resides in the Fang yen definition
of the terms tsang and huo, always used demeaningly: "In the northern outskirts of Shantung, and in the northern countryside of Hopei
all plebeian males who mate with female slaves are called tsang;
[plebeian] women who become wives of male slaves are called
huo."   A variant meaning of these terms, given by the third century
writer, Wei Shao, carries the same connotation: "When a good man

takes a female slave as wife and she bears a child, [the child] is called a *huo;* when a male slave takes a good woman as wife and she bears a child, [the child] is called a *tsang*." [1]

Thus there is nothing to indicate a legal restriction against marriages between slaves and free people, and there is some reason to believe that in practice they occurred. What was the status of the children of such marriages?

No cases reveal the status of children born of a free mother and a slave father. Actual marriages of that sort must have been rare, at least among the classes of society that appear in history.[2] On this point no conclusion can be squeezed from the available texts.

Children of slave women by free men not their masters were probably slaves. The chief evidence for this concerns the children of "old lady" Wei, who was a slave in the household of the Marquis of P'ing-yang. He was the husband of Emperor Wu's older sister, the Elder-Princess of Yang-hsin. "Old lady" Wei had six children, probably in the following order: A boy named Wei Chang-chün, three girls named Chün-ju, Shao-erh, and Tzu-fu, and then two boys named Ch'ing and Pu-kuang. She may have been "married" to a man named Wei, who fathered the first boy and Tzu-fu. Whether he was father of the two other girls is uncertain. Ch'ing was the son of a prefectural clerk named Cheng Chi, who had relations with Dame Wei while serving in the marquis' household. Pu-kuang's father is not specified. Ch'ing and Pu-kuang adopted the surname Wei when their older sister became important. All the children grew up in the household of the marquis, and three of them were almost certainly slaves, as the following biographical items reveal.

When Wei Ch'ing was still young he went to live with his father, who employed him as a sheep herder. He considered himself a slave, and his father's other children by the real wife "treated him as a male slave and did not count him as a brother." When he grew up he was a cavalry man in the household of the marquis as an attendant for the Princess (*26*). Cavalry escorts of this sort were frequently slaves (see p. 179).

The girl Shao-erh was a "serving one" in the household of the same marquis. The term applied to her was often used as a functional

---

[1] Document *11*, and footnote 5. See also discussion of terminology, pp. 68–69, above.

[2] Three instances of sexual relations between free women and male slaves are recorded but these were not marriages, and only one resulted in offspring (*37, 72, 85*). This last was a case of general promiscuity so that the paternity of the child could not be determined and the child was done away with.

designation of female slaves. Furthermore, she had a child by secret relations with Ho Chung-ju, who, like Wei Ch'ing's father, was a prefectural official serving a term in the marquis' household. This child was Ho Ch'ü-ping. He, too, grew up in the marquis' household and did not see his father till twenty years later (29).

Wei Tzu-fu was a chorus singer for the Princess of P'ing-yang (27). Comely slave children were regularly trained as entertainers in the great households.

Because of her great good fortune we know these details about the family, and its subsequent rise to glory. Shortly after Emperor Wu ascended the throne he visited his older sister. There he saw Wei Tzu-fu singing and dancing in the chorus and was delighted with her. He presented his sister with a thousand catties of gold, and she accordingly memorialized that Wei Tzu-fu should be sent to the Emperor's palace. She bore Emperor Wu three daughters, and finally, in 128, his first son. Thus she became Empress. The family fortunes began rising as soon as she conceived her first child. Wei Chang-chün was called to the palace but died before his sister became Empress. Chün-ju married Emperor Wu's boyhood retainer, Chief of Stud Kung-sun Ho, who later became Chancellor. Shao-erh apparently married Ch'en Chang (a great-grandson of Ch'en P'ing), with whom she had formerly had relations. Wei Ch'ing was made a Grand Palace Grandee, and then so distinguished himself as a general that he won a marquisate and later became General-in-Chief. Nothing is said about the youngest boy, Pu-kuang, but Ho Ch'ü-ping, the son of Shao-erh by a secret intimacy, arose from the marquis' household to be an even greater general than his uncle. Ho Ch'ü-ping's younger half-brother by his father's real wife also came to court. This was Ho Kuang, the maker of emperors, who dominated China for two decades after the death of Emperor Wu.

The interesting details of this family history should not obscure the point of primary interest—that the children of this slave woman retained their mother's status, or at least grew up in her master's household, until an unexpected event entirely changed their position in society. Unfortunately, it is a unique case in early records; there is no other specific evidence from Han times to support the belief that children by slave women and men not their masters were slaves.

There is yet a third combination. A master had sexual rights over his slave woman provided she had not been used by his father. The child of a slave woman and her master might be free, especially if it were a boy. This situation is closely related to concubinage.

The terms "female slave" and "concubine" sometimes appear together as though there were no great distinction between the two
(*26*, footnote 5; *56; 60*, footnote 4; *72; 106*), and there are references
to selling children and marrying off wives (*A13, 134*), and to women
becoming slaves or "lesser wives" (*136*). Favored female slaves were
within the same incest group, with reference to sons, as the principal
wife and concubines.

Formal distinctions between the principal wife and all other
women, and between various ranks among concubines were probably
established by marriage contracts between the man's family and the
respective families of the women. Yet the terminology applied to
a woman may conceal as much as it reveals, because it indicates her
status only at a particular time. In the imperial household, about
which information is fullest, the mother of the boy selected as Heir-
apparent generally became Empress—if she was lucky enough not
to be murdered by a rival—even though she had been only a
concubine.[1] Even the son of a slave woman might become Emperor.
This happened in the case of Emperor Hsüan (*55*) and might have
happened to Emperor Wu's first Heir-apparent (*27*) and to the son
of Emperor Ch'eng by the palace slave Ts'ao Kung (*107*). Wang
Li tried to promote a boy that he claimed was the son of the Emperor
Ai by the slave Yang Chi (*A18*). Superficially the issue in this
last case hinged on a question of fact—whether the Emperor was
indeed the father—though the matter was probably decided according to the relative power among aspirants for the regency.

When a woman became a favorite her status changed, and this
change might be made official by granting her an established rank
in the imperial household. Wei Tzu-fu became a *fu-jen* after she had
conceived her first child, and later became Empress. The onetime
slave Chao Fei-yen became a *chieh-yü*, then Empress, even though
she had no children. Wang Weng-hsü was scorned by the wives
and concubines of the imperial grandson Shih; they called her a
"householder," properly considering her a slave. But because she
bore a son she became a *fu-jen*, and when the boy became Emperor
she was posthumously called "Empress." Both Ts'ao Kung and
Yang Hui could have become empresses, though perhaps fictitiously,
had their sons been put on the throne.

[1] Cf., for example, document *31*, and HFHD, vol. I, pp. 229–300, as well as
Dubs's introductions to other reigns, in this and succeeding volumes. For similar
situations of inheritance and intrigue, cf. documents *37* and *64* and the revealing
article by Wu Ching-ch'ao, "Liang Han to-ch'i ti chia-t'ing (The polygamous
family of the Han dynasty)," CLHP, vol. 1, 1931, pp. 47–57.

The important point in regard to status of children is this: The originally humble position of the mother was no bar to the child's advancement if there was some good reason for his selection.

Similarly, in private households—patterned after, or more probably the model for, the imperial system—when the principal wife bore no son the male child of a slave girl might become heir and his mother at least a concubine. The case of Chu Po, who had no son, is a good example. Wang Mang bought a supposedly fertile slave girl and gave her to Chu Po, hoping that she would bear him a son (*108*). Had this happened there can be no doubt that the child would have had the status of his father. In spite of the attempt, Chu Po had the calamitous Chinese misfortune to die without a son, and had only a daughter by his real wife.

Yüan Shao, a leading general in the wars which finally divided China into the Three Kingdoms, was the eldest son of Yüan Feng, but not by the principal wife. His mother's rank is not stated specifically in his two official biographies, but one commentary says that he was the "commoner son" of Feng; another that he was the son of a concubine. The most specific statement comes in a speech of his enemy Kung-sun Tsan, who, recalling the principle of the *Ch'un-ch'iu*—that a son takes his rank from that of his *mother*—said that Shao's mother was a chamberlain slave so that his station was really base and lowly. The mother's original status is confirmed by an angry remark of Yüan Shu, Shao's younger half-brother by their father's principal wife. The two men were rival generals, but Shao was far more successful in acquiring allies. Furious at this situation, Shu said: "Why does the crowd not follow me, but instead follows my family's male slave?" He wrote to Kung-sun Tsan that "Shao is not a son of the Yüan family." [1]

Putting the facts together it is safe to deduce that Yüan Shao's mother was, in fact, a female slave chamberlain. When she bore Shao, the first male child, she became a concubine, and the boy was recognized as a member of the family. Then the principal wife belatedly bore Shu, who was the natural heir. Shao's position was less secure. Long after, when the half-brothers were rivals, Shu tried to claim that Shao was really his family slave and had no

---

[1] Biographies of Yüan Shao: HHS, 104A, and *San kuo chih, Wei chih*, 6, 6b–13a; ref. 1a and 6b, respectively. For statements of Kung-sun Tsan and Yüan Shu: HHS, 103, 4a, and 105, 3b.

There is reason to believe that Ho Kuang's second wife, Hsien, the mother of Ho Yü, was originally a slave, though this is only the assertion of a second century commentator. Certainly there was nothing inherently improbable in his statement (*72*, footnote 3).

right to the family surname. While this happened some time before
A.D. 192, long after the end of the Former Han, it indicates for its
own period how the problem was handled when a female slave bore
a son to her master.

The casual intimacies between masters and their slave women
must have resulted in innumerable children who never achieved free
status, but naturally we know nothing of them.

————————

Regarding slave status there are other legal questions which
remain unanswered. Was there a conflict between the legal concepts
of slaves as property and as human beings? The only suggestions of
this are imperial decrees which cited the Confucian precept and
principle that "in the nature of heaven and earth, man is most important." (*122, 137*.) It was this principle which Emperor Kuang-
wu adduced as the basis of his law that people who killed slaves
would not receive reduction of punishment. It is not clear to what
legal protection or redress slaves were entitled when people other
than their masters committed crimes of violence or lust against them,
or whether, in such cases, their masters could sue for damages.

To summarize the legal aspects of slave status during the Former
Han period: slaves appear to have had a definitely inferior position
in criminal law. They were punished for crimes against free people
more severely than free people who committed similar crimes against
their fellows. A free person received lighter punishment for killing
a slave than for killing a free person. But he could expect to be
punished. Masters who killed their innocent slaves were punished,
though they could apparently kill slaves guilty of certain crimes
provided they received permission from the government first.
Probably slaves could not bring legal suit against their masters, but
their testimony was accepted in court if a case was already under
investigation. There is no evidence that laws forbade slaves to
marry free people. Probably children of slave women by men not
their masters were normally slaves; but sons by the master might
attain full family status.

VII. SLAVE OWNERS AND NUMBERS OF SLAVES

A knowledge of slave owners is more important for an understanding of the function of slavery in Chinese economics and social structure than an acquaintance with slaves themselves. When we know what sorts of people owned slaves we can begin to ask why the slaves were owned, and to what distinctive use they were put.

Glancing through the translated documents one might gain the impression that all sorts of people owned slaves, and accordingly that the slave population of the Former Han period was very large. How should we classify the following slave owners: The scholar-poet Wang Pao (*83*); the squire of the Chancellor of Ch'i, who had a male slave attendant (*22*); leaders of the robber gangs of Ch'ang-an, who used "youth" escorts to give the appearance of being solid citizens (*81*); the redresser of wrongs, Yüan She, whose male slave involved him in a nasty mess with the local official (*125*); a former wet-nurse of Emperor Wu (*A6*); a rich widow (*A20*); the charcoal-burner who owned Tou Kuang-kuo (*14*); several knights fighting against the army of Wu in the Rebellion of the Seven States (*25*); and three slave women each given ten slaves by the Brilliant Companion *née* Chao (*107*)? The only common characteristic of these owners is that they were important enough in their own right, or indirectly, to be mentioned with their slaves in literature and history.

Yet this characteristic is exceedingly important. It is the nub of the whole question of classifying slave owners. Ownership *per se* was of no special interest to the Han historians except to illustrate the wealth of an individual, his imperial favor, or some other notable matter in which slaves had to be mentioned to make the facts intelligible. Items about slaves have a certain random and incidental quality, but it is no accident that only certain sorts of owners were granted space in the enduring chronicles. They were people who were for some other reason important historically. This situation colors the whole picture of slave ownership, but does not distort it entirely. The ability to own slaves depended largely upon wealth, and there is a real though rough correspondence between wealth and historical importance. Political or military ability and noble status, which made men historically significant, also usually led to riches. Wealth, on the other hand, often opened the way to political or social dominance, and also was occasionally an independent criterion of importance. Yet historical importance and wealth could

be entirely distinct.   Many of the scholars and writers accorded
significant space in the histories of the Han dynasty were poor men.
Thus the gross correlation between historical importance, wealth,
and large-scale ownership helps to correct historical bias, while
importance dissociated from wealth offers a means to check that
bias by presenting a diversity of "important people" among whom
to look for types of owners.   Furthermore, we are not entirely dependent upon analyses of individual owners, for edicts and memorials
often indicate the types of people that owned slaves without reference
to individuals.

Types of Slave Owners

Edicts of Emperors Ch'eng and Ai emphasized members of the
nobility and high officials as extensive slave owners (*105, 110*).
More than twice as many Former Han documents mentioning specific
owners refer to noblemen as to untitled officials and plebeians.   Thus
the nobility constituted an important slaveholding class.   Probably
every nobleman of any consequence owned slaves.

It is curious that some emperors, empresses, and imperial concubines owned private slaves, even though they had an almost unlimited number of government slaves at their disposal.   Emperor
Ch'eng was severely censured by his high ministers for keeping
private male slaves in the palace and taking them as companions
on his incognito journeys (*104*).   The Empress *née* Shang-kuan sent
her private male and female slaves to guard the graves of her father
and grandfather who had been executed for treason (*62*).   Since
she was only eight years old it may be assumed that the slaves were
sent on her behalf by some minister.   Presumably these slaves had
belonged to the Shang-kuan family; some of them may have accompanied the child Empress into the palace as her personal servants
and guards.   The imperial concubine *née* Chao was given three
women as her private slaves (*107*), and the Empress Dowager *née*
Fu, who must have been surrounded by palace slaves, nevertheless
bought a number from various government bureaus (*116*).

Because kings had royal governments which were replicas of the
imperial government early in the Han period, they controlled their
government slaves as well as household ones.   Yet it appears that
private slaves are referred to in the frequent textual association of
kings and slaves unless government slaves are specified.[1]   The King
of Ch'i-pei certainly owned the four entertainers he bought in the

[1] As in *A8* and *69*.   King's household slaves are specified in *12* and probably *75*.
Other references: *21, 37, 38, 44, 64, 67, 68, 84, 85, 106, 109, 110,* and *113*.

common people's market (21), and Emperor Ai was referring to privately owned ones when he limited kings to two hundred adults (110). Princesses, mentioned in the previous chapter as owners, were given slaves when they set up independent households. For them Emperor Ai thought a hundred male and female slaves should suffice.

An impressive number of documents mention marquises as slave owners.[1] They were the most numerous group in the nobility, usually wealthy from the fixed incomes of their estates, special government grants, and investments in private land. Many maintained expensive households and needed slaves as servants and for social display.

The nobility form a natural category easy to isolate as a class in society and clearly identified by contemporary writers as a slave-owning class. Other groups are much more difficult to classify. We have to decide which system will be significant from the viewpoint of economics and social structure. Three groupings, on the basis of occupation or sources of income, appear valid: officials, merchants or manufacturers, and owners of large amounts of land. Noblemen cannot be excluded from any of these groups, nor are the groups entirely distinct from one another. The occupations and sources of income of owners were diversified. Both officials and merchants were frequently landlords; nobles were generally landlords, often officials, and sometimes merchants. Yet many masters seem to have belonged primarily to one of the three groups, and the groups were recognized in Han times as a way of classifying the people of substance.

An imperial decree of 13 B.C. chid lesser officials for emulating the nobility and great ministers in slave-owning and other extravagances (105). At the end of the Former Han, out of 130,285 officials probably only a small proportion received enough salary to maintain slaves.[2] The vast majority were petty clerks and minor

---

[1] Or presumed owners. The documents are not always specific. Marquises, sons of kings: 51, 52, 115, A11; marquises by affinal connection: 59, 61, 62, 82, 98, 99, 100, 108, 109, 111, 114, 119, 120; marquises for military merit (other than in group two): 26, 48, 49, 71, 76, 87, 102, 103. Distinctions between the second and third group are not as clear-cut as appears from their separate listing in CHS, 18, and 16–17. I attempted here, perhaps unwisely, to make distinctions that did not always follow the CHS system.

[2] The figure comes from CHS, 19A, 8a. Wu Po-lun ("An investigation of slavery in the Western Han," p. 279) makes the wild estimate that officials averaged a hundred slaves each, thus alone counting some 13,000,000 slaves! Wu Ching-ch'ao ("The slavery system of the Western Han," p. 270) compares salaries of lesser officials with normal living costs to show that most officials lived very unpretentiously. See also Ma Ch'eng-feng (An economic history of China, vol. 2, p. 245) for further refutation.

bureaucrats who could do little more than support their families on their modest incomes from salary and petty graft. But well-to-do officials, especially those seeking to climb by social means, probably maintained as many slaves as they could afford. Lu Chia was given a hundred, together with considerable sums of money, precisely so he could mingle in official society at the court (*15*). A few of the great officials known to be slave owners are Shang-kuan Chieh and Shang-kuan An (*59, 61*), Ho Kuang (*65*), Chang An-shih (*71*), Wei Hsiang (*76*), Shih Tan (*97*), Wang Shang (*98*), Wang Ch'ung (*120*), and the various relatives of Empress Dowager *née* Wang, who one after another controlled the empire (*99*). These men formed the pattern of society, and though they were noblemen also, they and their kind must have set the pace for official life. Yüan Ang (*23*), Shih Fen (*A5*), and Wang Tsun (*A15*) were middling important officials probably representative of the lesser slave-owning officialdom. Emperor Ai considered thirty slaves adequate for any official not a nobleman, and probably few were able to maintain that number on their salaries alone.

The first requirement of the new dynasty was to revive agriculture and place it on a productive, that is to say, tax-paying basis. Attempts were made to prevent business men from investing their profits in farm land, thereby dispossessing independent small farmers who were the backbone of the tax-paying peasantry. Passages dealing with this policy show substantial merchants and manufacturers to have been a slave-owning class. A recommendation presented to Emperor Wu by his high ministers in 119 B.C. suggested that any merchant who owned private fields should have his land and his slaves confiscated (*45*). Between 119 and 113 B.C. the government acquired thousands of slaves, together with fields, houses, and money, by confiscating the accumulated fortunes of well-to-do business men and merchants (*46*). Chang Shou-chieh, an important eighth century commentator, states in this connection that merchants were taxed double for their slaves and other property (*127*, footnote 1). Besides these general indications we have specific cases of merchants or manufacturers who were owners: the Cho family of Szechwan, wealthy from iron-smelting and trade, who had hundreds of "youths" (*2*); Tiao Chien of Shantung, who used slaves in salt-refining, fishing, and as his traveling and resident agents (*17*); and, finally, Marquis Chang An-shih, a manufacturer who, during the reign of Emperor Hsüan, became fabulously wealthy from the sale of products turned out by his seven hundred household "youths" (*71*).

Land was the indestructible foundation of any "permanent" fortune, and the most common investment. Probably all wealthy people put their excess capital into land; even merchants, stringently restricted by early laws, could not be effectively prevented from acquiring it. Therefore, the classification of landlords is practically synonymous with the classification of wealth. It embraces nobility, officialdom, and business. It also covers a class of owners who were almost exclusively landowners, never acquiring noble or official status and indulging in little trade beyond disposing of the harvests derived from their tenants. The subject of landlordism and slavery is discussed at length in a later section on slaves in agriculture (pp. 195 ff.); suffice it here to mention Cho Wen-chün, who was given a hundred "youths" and a hundred myriad cash by her father and immediately bought fields and houses (28); and the edict of Wang Mang, forbidding people to buy or sell lands and slaves (122).

Among the groups thus segregated it is difficult to determine which was numerically largest or which owned the most slaves. Yet in spite of the historical bias it is logical to believe that the nobility were the distinctive owner class, possessing more slaves on an average than any other group.

The nobility had among all classes the freest access to wealth: through fixed incomes from estates, rents from private farm land, special grants from the treasury, official salary, graft, appropriation under the cloak of imperial favor, and, to a certain extent, the profits of trade. Not all noblemen enjoyed all these sources of wealth, but no other group had access to more than a few of them. Moreover, because of their position in society the nobility organized their mode of living most closely on the pattern of the imperial household, in which slaves played a prominent part. No other group had such a conspicuous need for numerous slaves employed for luxurious living, entertainment, and display. Their mansions, particularly those of the kings, princesses, and marquises through affinal connection, were run like little imperial palaces, and fixed the pattern to be aped by officialdom as well as by powerful local gentry who derived their wealth from land and trade.

NUMBERS OF SLAVES INDIVIDUALLY OWNED

Chinese students of Han slavery frequently present lists of owners recorded as having many slaves, and use the lists to create the impression that many people owned large groups of slaves, or that the slave population was indeed considerable. Among the

translated documents the list of owners of many slaves, arranged
chronologically, runs as follows:

(1) After 228 B.C.: The Cho family owned 800 (variant, 1,000) "youths." (*2*.)

(2) 181–180: Lu Chia was given 100 male and female slaves (*15*).

(3) 144: Cho Wang-sun owned 800 "youths" and guests (or "youth-guests";
SC gives "household 'youths' "), and gave his daughter 100 "youths."
(*28*.)

(4) 144: Cheng Ch'eng also owned several hundred ("youths" and guests; as
in No. 3) (*28*).

(5) Ca. 140: Emperor Wu gave his half-sister 300 male and female slaves (*31*).

(6) 113: Emperor Wu gave Luan Ta 1,000 "youths." (*49*.)

(7) Ca. 87–68: Imperial grants totaling 170 male and female slaves were given
to Ho Kuang (*70*).

(8) 74–62: Chang An-shih owned 700 household "youths." (*71*.)

(9) 67: Liu Ho, ex-King of Ch'ang-i, owned 183 male and female slaves (*75*).

(10) 33–15: Imperial grants of "youths" and male slaves to Shih Tan were numbered by the hundred (*97*).

(11) Before 25: Wang Shang's whole clan owned private male slaves numbered
by the thousand (*98*).

(12) Ca. 23: The brothers of the Empress Dowager *née* Wang owned "youths"
and male slaves numbered by the thousand or hundred (*99*).[1]

A few points about this list are worth emphasizing. Only two
of the twelve items employ specific figures; all the rest are round
numbers in terms of hundreds or thousands. Thus, most of them
are symbolic; they are rough estimates and probably not reports
of known numbers. Seven use the term "youth" for either the whole
figure or part of it. As shown in the discussion of terminology (p. 67),
this term does not mean slaves exclusively; it often means children.
While in the above passages the term probably does refer to slaves,
we may note in passing that Chang An-shih used his 700 "youths"
in household manufacturing, where free child-labor would be just
as useful as, and probably less expensive than, slave labor. Also
some of Cho Wang-sun's total includes guests, which he had "num-

---

[1] Shortly before Han times, Chang Liang inherited 300 household "youths."
(*A1*.) Two other pre-Han numbers may be relegated to the obscurity of a footnote as merited by their extreme unreliability: Lü Pu-wei had a myriad household
"youths"; Liao Tu had several thousand household "youths." (SC, 85, 2b;
and 3a.) The list can also be projected into the Latter Han period with the
following references: Before A.D. 59, the family of Tou Jung had male and female
slaves numbered by the thousand (HHS, 53, 5a); in 64 the King of Tung-p'ing
received an imperial grant of 500 Palace Women and male and female slaves (72,
5b); in 83 the King of Chi-nan had 1,400 male and female slaves (72, 4a); about
92 the King of Ch'ing-ho was given an imperial grant of 300 male and female
slaves (85, 2a); before 93 the King of Liang-chieh had been given imperial grants
of 200 male and female slaves, and other male and female slaves and "green-heads"
from government offices (78, 4a); about 150 Liang Chi took several thousand "good
people" and made them male and female slaves (64, 6b); undated, Che Kuo had
800 household "youths" (112A, 6b). These statements, while perhaps indicating
a trend toward increase in private slave numbers, need to be judged by the same
criteria as are applied below to the Former Han documents.

bered by the hundred." [1] At any rate there is a correspondence between large, vague figures and use of the term "youth"; the eleventh item alone mentions a really large number of slaves (*nu*) only.

Finally, in every case but one these figures are given expressly to portray the wealth, power, or imperial favor enjoyed by the owners. Consider the reasons for mentioning slaves in the items not already familiar from the previous discussion. Cho Wang-sun and Cheng Ch'eng were two of the wealthiest men in Szechwan. Emperor Wu was very liberal to his long-lost half-sister, and extraordinarily so to the magician Luan Ta, whom he loaded with riches. This latter account is suspect because it may be meant to illustrate the extent of Emperor Wu's gullibility and superstition. Shih Tan's wealth measures the extent of imperial gratitude for the part his family played in rearing the orphan who became Emperor Hsüan.

The statement concerning male slaves owned by Wang Shang's clan appeared in a memorial by the spokesman of the rival clan, designed to show that Wang Shang was a potential menace to the throne. Exaggeration of numbers would seem to be the very essence of such a memorial. Further, it referred to the holdings of the Wang clan, at the apex of its power. The report of slaves owned by Wang Mang's uncles figures in the picture of their enormous wealth and luxury wherein exaggeration might be expected even if it were not written during the dynasty which overthrew Wang Mang, the "usurper."

If these figures were recorded as measures of wealth then they cannot be taken as a common measure of slaves individually owned. They represent the unusual, in some instances the phenomenal and amazing, cases. Therefore, the two documents giving specific numbers are worth considering carefully.

The first casually mentions 183 slaves owned by Liu Ho, the former King of Ch'ang-i (75). It is part of an exact and detailed eyewitness description of the living conditions of the former King, made by Chang Ch'ang, an experienced and trusted administrator, at the specific command of Emperor Hsüan. He accompanied his description with an invoice of the male and female slaves and other property of the former King, who, together with his sisters, had been given the entire household wealth of his kingdom.

---

[1] Unless we take the *Shih chi* reading of "household youths," or assume that "youth-guest" is a compound term for a type of slave, which may be correct.

Slaves were part of that wealth, and the number 183 could be checked against the invoice. It is true that Liu Ho was somewhat hard-pressed financially at the time of the investigation; nevertheless, this document must be used as a primary point of reference regarding numbers of slaves owned by single individuals.

The second document is equally important as a point reference for reports of large imperial *gifts* of slaves. During his entire lifetime Ho Kuang received 170 male and female slaves by imperial grant. The figure is revealing for two reasons: Ho Kuang was one of the most important political figures during the entire Han period; and it is possible to compare the gifts of slaves with gifts of other sorts which he received. He was indirectly related to, and directly sponsored by, the family of the Empress *née* Wei. Emperor Wu publicly honored him as his most loyal and trustworthy minister, and on his deathbed appointed Ho Kuang one of three regents for young Emperor Chao. His granddaughter became the new Empress, and he became virtual ruler. When Emperor Chao died in 74 B.C. without heirs, Ho Kuang determined the selection of his successor, Liu Ho, and then after twenty-seven days deposed him. He next selected a great-grandson of Emperor Wu to become Emperor Hsüan, and thus continued the dominant figure at court until he died in 68 B.C. Probably few men received richer rewards than he. Among the totals mentioned are fiefs, with the income from an aggregate of 20,000 households, 7,000 catties (about 55,000 troy ounces) of gold, 60,000,000 cash, 30,000 pieces of silk, 170 male and female slaves, 2,000 horses, and a first-grade mansion (*70*). Taken in conjunction with these other gifts, whether exaggerated or not, the 170 slaves must have been considered a lavish and unusual imperial gift at that time. This document compels suspicion about statements of even larger imperial gifts of slaves, especially since each of them uses vague round numbers.

Two other documents, one near the beginning and the other toward the close of the Former Han period, support the belief that from one hundred to two hundred slaves constituted a large number for any private owner. The first (No. 2 in the list above) tells of 100 male and female slaves, 50 outfits of carriages and horses, and 5,000,000 cash largess that were sent to Lu Chia for his expenses in helping to engineer the destruction of the house of Lü. Because of this wealth Lu Chia was able to mingle at the Han court on an equal footing with dukes and ministers, and he achieved a bad reputation for extravagance (*15*).

The documents regarding Liu Ho and Ho Kuang, coming near the middle of the period, probably indicate an advance in numbers privately owned as the dynasty progressed. The trend is further suggested by the following occurrence in 7 B.C.

When Emperor Ai came to the throne his former tutor, Shih Tan, memorialized concerning the dangerous contrasts between the wealth of the upper classes and the poverty of the masses. His suggestion that wealth be restricted was handed down for discussion, and the Chancellor and Grandee Secretary, both marquises, proposed specific limits on the extent of land and number of slaves which various grades of the nobility, officials, and common people might own. For slaves more than ten and less than sixty years of age these limits were 200 for kings, 100 for marquises and princesses, and 30 for *kuan-nei* marquises, officials, and commoners (*109, 110*).

Since this was a reform we must assume that some individuals owned more slaves than allowed in the various classes. This is confirmed by the statement that the price of fields, houses, and slaves immediately depreciated. On the other hand, the Chancellor and Grandee Secretary were both noblemen, and they apparently made their proposal seriously, believing that the limits were reasonable and that the law could be enforced. As it turned out, the law was too drastic. It was "inconvenient" for members of the Ting and Fu families, who were affinally related to Emperor Ai, and for his favorite, Tung Hsien. The Emperor ordered it to be deferred "temporarily." But note this: The principal objectors were in the groups limited to 30 *ch'ing* (340 acres) of land, and to either 100 or to 30 slaves.

The total impression created by this document is that while some members of the nobility may have had upwards of 200 slaves the statesmen of the time believed that 200 for kings and 100 for regular marquises were adequate and feasible numbers. They miscalculated the opposition of Emperor Ai's affinal relatives, who were marquises, and of the imperial catamite, Tung Hsien, and various relatives not ennobled, who would have been limited to thirty slaves. Since this was the end of a cycle, a period of extreme luxury, the event strengthens the deduction that throughout the Han period private ownership of 100 or 200 slaves was unusual.

Probably a few score made a respectable showing for most people, especially since many slaves were used almost exclusively in non-productive capacities. The number "forty or more" is twice mentioned for slaves of one or the other sex, owned by men who were marquises through imperial affinal connection, in a way that might indicate that the number represented approximately the total number of males or females owned. Some time about 64–58 B.C. the pathologically jealous wife of the Marquis of Chiang-ling strangled to death more than forty serving female slaves (*82*). Likewise, shortly before 15 B.C. the imperial favorite, Chang Fang, who was exceedingly wealthy, sent his senior male slave, Chün, and forty or more others to invade a government bureau and square a personal grudge (*100*). It is probable that for this job he mustered all or most of the male slaves available.

Total Number of Slaves

In attempting to reckon slave numbers during the Former Han period we work in such a vacuum that estimates by Chinese students have ranged as wildly as from 600,000 to between twenty and thirty millions![1] And this disparity figures in a total population given as 59,594,978 at A.D. 2.[2] Is there any way honestly to estimate the maximum slave population during Former Han times? Only a very vague way.

The starting point for any such attempt is document *89*, where Kung Yü, in a memorial dated 44 B.C., speaks of the ten myriad and more government slaves. The possible accuracy of this statement is discussed extensively in a footnote to that document where it was concluded that Kung Yü was a man of the highest reputation for integrity, and with full access to such facts as were known. If he erred it was probably on the side of exaggeration. The figure is in reasonable accord with other independent figures of special groups in the population.

Before 44 B.C. government slaves were probably less numerous. Kung Yü was about eighty years old, and had held several government offices earlier in his career before he went into retirement.

---

[1] Wu Ching-ch'ao, op. cit., pp. 269–270; and Wu Po-lun, op. cit., pp. 278–279, respectively.

[2] CHS, 28B, 9a. The figure derives from imperial censuses made from time to time for tax purposes, as discussed in *89*, footnote 3. Wu Ching-ch'ao (op. cit., p. 270, footnote 6) believes that the actual population was larger, on the assumption of deception to avoid taxation, a regular Chinese practice. On Han population, see also Ma Fei-pai ("Source material on the economic history of Ch'in and Han," pt. 5, "Jen-k'ou chi t'u-ti [Population and land]," *Shih Huo*, vol. 3, No. 3, Jan. 1, 1936, pp. 102–132), and Lao Kan ("Liang Han hu-chi yü ti-li chih kuan-hsi [Population and geography in the two Han dynasties]," Academia Sinica, *Bulletin of the Institute of History and Philology*, vol. 5, pt. 2, Dec., 1935, pp. 179–214 and 215–240). All Chinese population figures are highly suspect; they must be used as rough approximations, indicating trends in growth and decline, and not as accurately determined numbers, even though solemnly recorded down to the last unit.

Possibly he noted, during his second period of office, from 48 to 44 B.C., that the government slave population had grown during his lifetime, for his memorial emphasized the magnitude of the figures. Independently of this deduction, it appears evident that the government owned many fewer slaves during the reign of Emperor Wu, for when it confiscated from a thousand to a myriad private slaves between 119 and 113 B.C. it was simply embarrassed by the superfluity (*46*), which indicates a rather low "absorption point" for new slaves. Wei Hung, living in the first years of the Latter Han dynasty, mentions 30,000 slaves tending horses on 36 government ranches during the previous epoch (*93*). His figure, for one of the most extensive occupations of government slaves, is not startlingly large. Unfortunately it is undated and may apply only to the closing years of the period.

It is not known whether the number of government slaves increased in the half century between 44 B.C. and A.D. 2, or if it did, by how much. Emperor Ai ordered all government slaves over fifty years of age to be freed, but it is not certain how thoroughly the order was carried out. Probably it did not reduce the totals greatly if we assume for China then, as in recent times, a low percentage in the higher age levels of the population. Even a 50 per cent growth in government slave numbers would only bring the total to 150,000 or so, which is suggested as a liberal estimate.

Apparently Chinese students have found no more accurate way of determining the private slave population than to multiply Kung Yü's figure for government slaves by some arbitrarily selected multiple. No one has approached the subject by estimating the number of slaves owned by the nobility, who were the most important group of private owners. Chapters 14 to 18 of the *Ch'ien Han shu* give fairly complete lists of the nobility under various classifications, emphasizing original ennoblement but carrying each line down until it ran out or was dropped from the record. The longer a noble line lasted, the scantier becomes the information about it, especially in regard to the date when it died out. Therefore it is not easy to determine how many noblemen there were at any given period; often it is necessary to guess whether a noble line still existed by counting the number of generations after the last specific date entered. Giving the benefit of the doubt to all uncertain cases, we arrive at a figure not only probably too large, but also including many people who were noblemen in title only, neither prominent nor wealthy.

On the basis of a careful count there were 17 kings and 206 full marquises (including 77 doubtful cases) in 7 B.C., when Emperor Ai made his famous restrictions on slave-owning.[1] The tables do not list princesses for they did not establish independent lines. Only the sisters of Emperor Ch'eng, and the sisters and aunts of Emperor Ai need be counted. They could hardly have totaled more than ten, for Emperors Yüan and Ch'eng and the father of Emperor Ai were not prolific.

Using Emperor Ai's proposed law of 200 adult slaves as a maximum for kings and princesses, and 100 for full marquises (certainly generous for an average), we arrive at surprisingly low figures: 3,400 for kings, ±2,000 for princesses, and 20,600 for full marquises—a total of not more than 26,000. Suppose that the restrictions reduced by an average of one hundred the number of slaves owned by each nobleman. This allows 300 slaves for kings and princesses, and 200 for marquises, and gives a total of only 49,300. Perhaps the fifteen listed *kuan-nei* marquises should be counted as full marquises even though the Emperor restricted them to 30 slaves each, since these particular marquises were probably wealthy. This would add another 3,000 or 4,500, giving top figures of 29,000 or 53,800 slaves owned by noblemen.

By comparison the same calculations were made for the year 44 B.C., when Kung Yü mentioned 100,000 or more government slaves. There are listed for that time 18 kings and 169 marquises, including doubtful cases. Adding a possible 15 princesses, and using the alternative sets of multiples, we arrive at 23,500 or 43,700.

Maximum figures were used through every step of these calculations. Kung Yü's estimate of 100,000 or more government slaves was probably a maximum and possibly an exaggeration. All doubtful cases were counted in, listed *kuan-nei* marquises were treated as full marquises, and the average number of slaves assigned to each group of nobles was probably high even for the richest of them. But there were at least some basic records as points of departure. Any estimate of the remaining slave population is a pure guess—simply a matter of selecting some multiple to apply to the estimated number of slaves owned by nobles.

Taking the top figures and multiplying by ten, officials, rich people, and those of moderate means all together owned 437,000

[1] The count excludes descendants of all those honorary noblemen who were granted titles in 62 B.C. as collateral descendants of early Han noble lines that had long since run out. They were mostly petty officials or gentry, given titles for sentimental reasons, but neither active nor wealthy.

slaves in 44, and 538,000 in 7 B.C.   It would have taken some 22,000 owners in 44, or 27,000 owners in 7 B.C., each able to support a score of slaves, to total those figures.   This seems very high when we recall that "itinerant traders and resident merchants, and [people of] middling [wealth] and up were generally ruined" in the great confiscation of land, money, and slaves throughout the empire in 119–113 B.C.   Yet they produced only a myriad, or at most a few myriads of slaves! (46.)   If recorded figures, estimates, and guesses are combined the grand total of government slaves and those of noble and non-noble owners would have been roughly 580,000 in 44 B.C. and 741,000 in 7 B.C.   The Chinese population figure of roughly 60,000,000 in A.D. 2 is not exact; the population was probably not less than 50,000,000 and not more than 70,000,000.   In the same sense, estimates of the slave population are not accurate; they indicate only that the number was probably less than a million and probably more than 300,000.

These calculations, neither scientific nor soundly historic, can be assailed at every step; and yet they portray in a shadowy way the proportion of the total population that was enslaved.   It may have been under 1 per cent.   This bears upon the heated discussion among Chinese economic historians whether China during the Han period was a "slavery society" or "slave economy society" (*nu-li she-hui* or *nu-li ching-chi she-hui*).   While their discussion is somewhat sterile in the sense that there seems to be no agreement upon the meaning of the terms, and no accepted criteria by which known facts should be judged, it has had the stimulating effect of focusing attention away from pure description to an analysis of the function of slavery in Chinese economy and of slaves in the social structure. These are the subjects of primary interest in the succeeding chapters.

VIII. SERVICE FUNCTIONS OF PRIVATE SLAVES

The most important thing about slavery is the way in which slaves were used—their function. When we know the function of slaves it is easier to understand the significance of the slavery system itself and to acquire a clearer picture of the social and economic organization of which slavery was a part.

In the succeeding discussion two major headings are useful: services and production. The first term covers occupations contributing to the comfort, pleasure, or prestige of the private owner, and services for the government. "Production" refers to the production and processing of goods for sale or use by the master or the government, to merchandising, and to other sorts of activity that increased the owner's wealth. These categories are purely schematic. Owners employed slaves in both ways, and individual slaves worked in both capacities.

The first category, services, bears more closely upon society, while the second, production, has more to do with economics. This division clarifies the extent to which slaves participated in the process of production, on the one hand, and the extent to which they were wealth-consuming luxuries, on the other. These two main categories help to explain why the government and private individuals owned slaves at all.

DUTIES OF DOMESTIC SLAVES

One of the principal occupations of household slaves was general servant's work, which is essentially the same throughout the world. Formal histories, recording events of great importance to the state, or presenting biographies of men of affairs, tell little about the work of menials. Casual references mention specific duties, but the mass of routine work—cleaning, washing, cooking, serving, repairing, errand-running and the like—is referred to only in the semi-humorous but very enlightening slave contract by Wang Pao.[1] The amount and diversity of work listed in this contract is amazing. On top of multifarious productive duties to be mentioned below, the slave Pien-liao was expected to cook, serve, wash dishes, clean house,

[1] The semi-humorous nature of the document does not invalidate it. Even if it were imaginative it would still necessarily be based upon experience and fact, as is pointed out by Ma Fei-pai ("Source material on the economic history of Ch'in and Han, " pt. 6, "The slavery system," p. 393). Whether the account is autobiographical or purely fictitious, Wang Pao, the author, pictures himself as thinking of all the work which might need to be done and of trying to cover every eventuality.

MORTUARY FIGURINE OF A SERVANT OR SLAVE OF THE HAN PERIOD

Pien-liao, the slave of Wang Pao, may have worn a similar hat and coat and carried such a broom and dustpan. Collected by D. C. Graham in a cave-tomb near Kiating, Szechwan, and now in the United States National Museum

tend the barnyard, wash clothes, help in making wine, run errands, and guard the house (*83*). In other documents we read of a male slave attending his master at the imperial court (*22*); of another being dispatched to buy meat from a butcher (*125*); of male slaves caring for horses in the stable at night (*74*); and of ten courtiers becoming slaves to the ex-King of Chao, Chang Ao, so they could follow him to prison (*12*), undoubtedly to wait upon him. In contrast with such slaves-of-all-work, domestic slaves in the grander households were highly specialized.

Male slaves regularly acted as bodyguards and outriding escorts; they constituted a special class, mounted and armed, who rode with their masters on trips and excursions—in fact, whenever they left the house. Wei Ch'ing as a slave in the household of the Marquis of P'ing-yang was a horseman and attendant for the Princess (*26*), and we read later of other cavalry slaves in the same household (*39*). When Emperor Ch'eng went on incognito journeys he was attended by a small group of gentlemen, male slaves, and guests. All were dressed in plain clothes and carried swords, and rode either in small chariots or on horseback (*104*). Wang Lin-ch'ing, a relative of an empress, traveled in a carriage escorted by armed and mounted slaves (*112*); even the leaders of thieving gangs at Ch'ang-an went about escorted by "youth horsemen," which created the impression that they were fine gentlemen (*81*).

On at least one occasion, which may be representative of a common practice, cavalry slaves went into battle with their masters. During the Rebellion of the Seven States, in 154 B.C., Kuan Fu wanted to avenge the death of his father by a private sortie into the Wu encampment. He called for volunteers among the hardy men of the army who loved him and were willing to follow him. When it came time for the foray, however, the venture was so risky that only two friends dared to go with him. Yet they were unhesitatingly followed into battle by their attendant male slaves. The ten or more horsemen galloped into the Wu army to the very foot of the general's standard, killing and wounding several tens of the enemy (*25*).

Many Latter Han bas-reliefs, sometimes presumably depicting scenes from the lives of the dead, show processions of chariots and cavalry escorts. Some of these outriders may well be slaves occupying positions like those of the cavalry slaves in the previous period.[1]

---

[1] Cf. Edouard Chavannes, *Mission archéologique dans la Chine septentrionale*, Plates, pt. 1, pls. XXIV, XXV, XLIV, L, LII, LV, LVI, LIX, and *passim*.

Female slaves, especially young girls, performed intimate services for their masters and mistresses and their guests. Wei Tzu-fu, belonging to the Princess of P'ing-yang, helped young Emperor Wu change clothes when he was a house guest (*27*). A "serving female slave" (*shih-pei*) of the rich widow Tso A-chün helped a drunken guest to bed (*A20*), and another such girl died of a disease just as she was following the King of Chi-pei to carry his sword when he went out to the toilet (*21*). Ho Kuang's widow enjoyed being trundled through her elaborate mansion by "serving female slaves" dressed in many-colored silks (*72*). Wei Shao-erh, the older sister of Wei Ch'ing, and mother of Ho Ch'ü-ping, was a "serving one" in the household of the Marquis of P'ing-yang (*29*). When Yüan Ang was Chancellor of Wu State he had a "serving child" (*23*); and Wang Mang once secretly bought a "serving female slave," and gave her to General Chu Tzu-yüan (*108*).

·The term *fu* or *fu-pei*, translated "chamberlain," or "female slave chamberlain," is explained by Yen Shih-ku as always referring to those who attended to their master's clothes and bed, and he further states that another character *fu*, meaning "a close favorite," may be used interchangeably (*120*, footnote 2). Wang Wu's "chamberlain" must have been considerably younger than he, for his son Wang Shang had sexual relations with her (*98*). When the female slave chamberlain of Wei Hsiang died suddenly, Administrator of the Capital District Chao Kuang-han suspected the Chancellor's wife of killing her out of jealousy (*76*). Wang Ch'ung was poisoned by his female slave chamberlain and died (*120*).[1]

People of fashion in Han times employed musicians, dancers, singers, acrobats, and jugglers to entertain at their banquets. Graphic illustrations of feasts and entertainments also preserved

---

[1] The term *fu-pei* appears several times in the HHS in ways which also indicate a close relationship between master and female slave chamberlain. In A.D. 95 the Chancellor of the Kingdom of Lo-ch'eng reported two matters against his King, Liu Tang. In violation of an old prohibition that Palace Women sent out to be married could not go to any of the kingdoms (i.e. into a royal palace), Liu Tang commanded a former musician of the imperial Concubines' Quarter to enter his palace, and had relations with her although she was already married to a commoner. He had her husband killed to silence him, and also killed three inner "serving" (slave?) girls to prevent them from talking. Also he took as lesser wife the *fu-pei* of the late King of Chung-shan (HHS, 80, 2b). Some time after A.D. 162 Fen K'un was memorialized against by a military inspector for going out in uniform accompanied by two *fu-pei*. No law was found applicable and the charge was dropped (HHS, 68, 4a). The estrangement between Lü Pu and Tung Cho, two of the leading figures at the end of the Latter Han, started because Lü Pu had relations with Tung Cho's *fu-pei* (HHS, 105, 5b). Yüan Shao was said to have been the son of his father's *fu-pei*, which cast doubt on his right to the family surname (HHS, 103, 3b–4a, biography of Kung-sun Tsan; see also pp. 163–164, above).

in bas-reliefs of the Latter Han period probably reflect closely the general conditions only a century or two earlier.[1] On these reliefs, dancers, both male and female, some with elongated sleeves, posture in their dances, while drummers beat time on enormous drums. Musicians, pictured individually or in groups, play various wind, string, and percussion instruments. Jugglers nimbly keep three, seven, and even nine balls flying in the air at one time. Acrobats walk on their hands and do cartwheels; in one scene a man supports a pyramid of four balancing children, while another precariously keeps his balance treading on a ball.

It is in just such occupations that young slaves are regularly mentioned in Former Han documents, and perhaps some of the entertainers pictured in the Latter Han bas-reliefs are actually talented slaves.[2] The long and careful training necessary for these arts must have begun when they were quite young, and surely enhanced their value greatly.

About 175 B.C., Chia Yi protested in a memorial to Emperor Wen about the lavish customs of the day, and he referred in passing to the sale and treatment of young slaves that were probably of the entertainer type. These youths were dressed in "embroidered clothes and silken shoes with the edges all embellished." (16.) The King of Chi-pei explained his lavish payment for four girls by calling attention to their skill at doing tricks (21).

Wang Weng-hsü was just such an entertainer. Her training under Liu Chung-ch'ing started when she was only eight or nine years old. Later a merchant from Han-tan came looking for singers and dancers, and Liu Chung-ch'ing sold her in spite of her mother's claim (the father may have been cheating!) that the parents had never been paid a cent for her. The merchant kept her with a group of five entertainers and later probably sold the quintet to the representative of Emperor Wu's ill-starred Heir-apparent, who came from Ch'ang-an looking for singers and dancers for his patron's palace (55). Before he sold them the merchant presumably hired the girls

---

[1] See Chavannes, op. cit., plates, pt. 1, text, t. 1: pl. XXVIII, No. 49, text, p. 86; pl. XLIX, No. 104, pp. 184–185; pl. LIX, No. 122, p. 201; pl. LXXVIII, No. 149, pp. 226–227; pl. LXXXV, No. 158, p. 232; pl. LXXXVI, No. 160, p. 232; pl. LXXXVII, No. 163, p. 233; pl. XCVII, No. 182, p. 247 (sic); and t. 1, pl. DXLI, No. 1270, p. 277. Cf. also Chao Pang-yen, "Han hua so chien yu-hsi [Sports as seen in Han drawings]," Academia Sinica, *Studies presented to Ts'ai Yuan-p'ei on his sixty-fifth birthday*, 2 vols., Peking, 1933–35, pt. 1, pp. 325–338.

[2] Probably some of the mortuary figurines of musicians and dancers, dating from Han through T'ang times, represent slaves, who were used as entertainers in those epochs.

out for feasts and parties. Emperor Hsüan's great-grandmother was that chorus singer Wei Tzu-fu, who infatuated young Emperor Wu so that he had no eyes for any of the girls of good family who had been assembled and especially groomed for his inspection (27). Emperor Ch'eng's second Empress, whose sobriquet was "Flying Swallow," was once a slave dancing-girl in the household of the Princess of Yang-a, where the Emperor first saw and fell in love with her (101). His passion for her was so overwhelming that he deposed the Empress née Hsü, and made "Flying Swallow" his consort.

The "serving one" of the Queen of Heng-shan was a fine dancer (37); the infamous King of Kuang-ch'uan made his singing girls and entertainers play about naked among the guests at banquets (64). When the King of Chao was ill he made a will commanding that those of his male and female slaves who could make music should follow him in death, and sixteen were compelled to commit suicide (84). In contrast to this dark incident there is a pleasant passage in a letter from Yang Yün to a friend describing the pleasures of rural retirement (87): "My home was originally in Ch'in, so I can play Ch'in music; my wife is a girl from Chao, quite good on the drum and lute; and there are several male and female slave singers. After the wine has begun to warm my ears, I gaze up to heaven and beat my pottery drum and sing wu, wu."

Girls trained as entertainers were obviously chosen for their natural grace and beauty, and probably received instruction in seductive arts. Numerous references to sexual relations between slave girls and their masters, or to illicit relations with other men, indicate another important "service" function of private female slaves. The term yü, used in combination with shih or pei, appears to indicate a sexual relationship with the master which should be reserved to him alone. For example, the scheming Queen of Heng-shan tried to create a schism between the King and one of his sons (the child of another woman) by inducing the boy to have relations with her own "serving one," already favored by the King. Later the boy was tried and executed for having had relations with the King's "personal female slave." Obviously his relations were incestuous (37, and footnote 4). In another case a son who had relations with his late father's "personal female slave" was tried, committed suicide, and his marquisate was abolished (48). Shang-kuan An had incestuous relations with his stepmother and various of his father's ladies and "serving personal ones." (59.) Again, a king allowed his favorite male slaves to have relations with his palace ladies and "personal female slaves." For this and other abnormal acts his kingdom was reduced by four prefectures (*85*). A number of other cases indicate that masters had sexual rights to their slave women, though these rights were often violated by other men.[1] The relationship between concubinage and slavery stands out clearly. Concubinage is often a criterion of a domestic type of slavery. As shown in the discussion of status, the crucial factors in the imperial household were winning the Emperor's "favors," bearing children, and, above all, bearing a son. In the palace, change in rank was complicated by the bitter struggles for power between various consort families. Such struggles undoubtedly occurred also in private families, but much less was at stake. By analogy with cases in the imperial household where considerable details are known, it would seem that slave women not infrequently became concubines "legally," or were concubines in fact.

Private slaves sometimes served as guards for the tombs of their dead masters. This service was naturally confined to rich families with extensive burial grounds. Only two documents report it, yet rather casually. After Ho Kuang's death, his widow elaborately expanded and improved the buildings and grounds of the cemetery and secluded there "Sweet Ladies," slave women, and concubines to guard it (*72*). When Shang-kuan Chieh and his son An were executed, the child Empress *née* Shang-kuan sent her private male and female slaves to guard the graves of her father and grandfather (*62*). Clearly, the slaves were domiciled in the cemeteries, which were isolated regions well outside the city, and they were probably self-sustaining groups that stayed at their posts without constraint. Their duties included guarding and tending the grounds, grave mounds, and temples, and performing periodic ceremonies to the dead; probably these duties were hereditary as long as the family continued important or its memory was strong enough to protect the tomb.[2]

---

[1] *23, 26, 29, 98, 108, 112.* *A16* reports the case of a marquis who was deposed for daring to have adulterous relations with a female slave in the presence of his wife, the Princess of Yang-i, and for drunkenly cursing her. It must have been his effrontery to the daughter of an Emperor which caused him to be deposed, rather than the fact that he had relations with another woman.

[2] Judging by analogy with documents *55, 58,* and *62,* see also HFHD, vol. I, p. 140. Speculating further, but without specific proof, it seems likely that such grave-watchers eventually became either free people or hereditary families of nominal slaves or serfs bound only in a special legal or customary way to the memory of those masters whom their ancestors had once served. So long as the descendants continued to care for the graves, their right to use land about the graves would probably have been validated by law or customary usage.

At least one master used his trusted male slave to manage his financial interests. Ho Kuang loved and favored his "supervising male slave," Feng Tzu-tou, and always consulted with him on business (72). Yen Shih-ku explains the term as meaning a slave who supervises and is familiar with the household business. Feng Tzu-tou's responsibilities must have been great, for, as already shown, Ho Kuang received annually the tax income from 20,000 households, and during his lifetime acquired enormous gifts (70), many of which he probably sold. Feng Tzu-tou was no ordinary slave. Not only did Ho Kuang always consult with him on business, but also he was recognized by the officialdom as being the key for access to Ho Kuang in political matters. "All the officials and lesser people only served Feng Tzu-tou and Wang Tzu-fang, and regarded the Chancellor as less important." (66.) Although legally a slave, Feng Tzu-tou was virtually free. After Ho Kuang's death he had relations with the widow, and is described as often breaking the law. In the annals of Emperor Hsüan he is referred to as a commoner from Ch'ang-an and listed as one of the important rebels against the throne in 66 B.C. (72, and footnote 3). One of the few slaves known by his full name, he even had a courtesy name, which might be translated "Adonis." [1]

TREATMENT AND POSITION OF DOMESTIC SLAVES

Several observations arise from a study of documents that mention domestic slaves. They were in a certain sense members of the family, well clothed, fed, and housed, and many of them showed a strong personal loyalty towards their masters. Slaves that carried

---

[1] Two passages in the *Hou Han shu* mention supervising slaves and contain important supplementary information. The first is dated about A.D. 150, and concerns a slave of Liang Chi, the powerful affinal relative of the imperial house who established two emperors on the throne and from whose family came seven marquises, three empresses, six imperial concubines, two generals-in-chief, three princesses, and fifty-seven various officials. Liang Chi's "beloved" supervising male slave, Ch'ing Kung, rose in office to the position of Superintendent of Public Granaries. He also had relations with his master's wife. His power was so great that censors and commandery officials all came to visit and consult with him (HHS, 64, 5b).

The second instance is that of the supervising male slave of the eunuch Chang Jang, an influential official and marquis during the reign of Emperor Ling (A.D. 168–188). This supervising slave was entrusted with and controlled his master's household affairs, and was intermediary for bribes in goods and money. His power and authority were well known. Meng T'o, an aspirant for office, once succeeded in getting to the master by becoming a close friend of the slave and getting him in debt. Thus, when Meng T'o wanted an interview with the eunuch Chang Jang, the supervising slave welcomed him ostentatiously and escorted him into the gate past a crowd of other aspirants who were waiting outside. The other aspirants immediately assumed that Meng T'o was a close friend of the eunuch

weapons and rode horseback must already have achieved, in fact,
a semi-free status. When generations of slaves served in the same
household, their relations to the family must have been very close.
Young Liu Ho, King of Ch'ang-i, was intimate and companionable
with his male slaves and servants (67). This is represented as an
objectionable quirk in his character, but later, when he had been
deprived of his kingdom, and lived, half-demented, in the seclusion
of his palace, his slaves took care of him (75). The slaves of Tung
Hsien were treated like members of his family when it came to gifts;
officials and Emperor Ai both gave generous amounts of money
and valuable presents to them all (117, 119). Ho Kuang's slaves
identified themselves closely with their master's importance. When
he was at the height of his power they were arrogant and lawless
(65), and after his death, when the power of the family was challenged
by the Emperor through Grandee Secretary Wei Hsiang, they undertook to humiliate Wei Hsiang—with disastrous results (72). The
gossiping of a group of slaves about the rebellion being plotted
by the Ho family was overheard by a man trying to sleep in the
stable, and was revealed by him (74). Even the grooms knew of
the plot before it was fully matured!

The fact that the famous redresser of wrongs, Yüan She, was
held directly responsible for the conduct of his slave also indicates
a legal conception of slaves as family members. His slave quarreled
with the butcher, chopped him very badly, and then ran away.
When the slave did not show up by the next day the officials were
about to execute Yüan She on the spot. His friends intervened in
the nick of time, and arranged a face-saving device for the magistrate
in which Yüan She took on the outer appearance of a slave or
criminal, apologized humbly, and was absolved (125).

These are but a few specific cases. More general indications of
standing in the family are the fact that certain female slaves were
counted in the incest group, and the use of the term k'o, "guest"
or "retainer," in combination with "male slave" or "youth."[1]

and therefore gave him bribes. He divided the bribes with the eunuch, who was
very pleased and got him appointed Censor of Liang Chou (HHS, 108, 9b–10a).

In both these passages the supervising slaves were similar to Feng Tzu-tou
in that they occupied positions of confidence with their influential masters, and
were accorded great respect by officials or aspirants. One rose to high office,
while the other was in charge of his master's business affairs and acted as intermediary in matters involving bribes.

[1] For passages using "slave" and "guest" together see 28, 37, 61, 65, 104, 118.
It is not clear whether nu-k'o and t'ung-k'o should be translated as compounds
("male slave-guest," "youth-guest") or as separate terms. The institution of
"guests" or "retainers" was well established in Chan-kuo times. "Guests"

"Guests" were not part of the blood family but were closely associated economically and socially. On the other hand, slaves had
their own surnames, which differed from those of their masters.
Here Chinese familism showed its great strength, over-riding
economic considerations.

Details about the living conditions of domestic slaves are hap-
hazard, but aside from several specific cases of ill-treatment, the
accounts indicate that they were physically well cared for. This
would be especially true of slaves in noble or wealthy households,
who probably fared better than most plebeians. Tung Hsien's slaves
ate so well that they looked upon wine as though it were soup and
meat as though it were beans (118); and two of Wei Ch'ing's squires,
guests with him in the home of a princess, were invited to eat with
cavalry slaves of the family (39). The squires thought this was a
disgrace, but apparently the hostess considered her slaves' food
quite good enough for poor men of the Gentleman class. It was
fashionable to dress slaves in fancy silks (16, 72, 105), and a memorial
praising Wang Mang's frugality and modesty signalized the fact
that his slaves wore coarse clothes, as though such costume were
unusual in his day (A19). We read twice about the famous court
physician Shun-yü Yi examining slaves for their masters (21, 22).
On the other hand, some private slaves were apparently branded,
though there may have been a Former Han law against it (138).

The personal loyalty of slaves to their masters was marked.
The male slaves who galloped with Kuan Fu and his two companions
into hopeless battle were all killed after fighting valiantly and taking
a heavy toll of the enemy (25). When Emperor Kao uncovered a
plot on his life he ordered the King of Chao and his rebellious
ministers to be arrested and brought to the capital, and warned
that anyone in Chao daring to follow the King to Ch'ang-an would
be punished by death and the extermination of his three sets of
relatives. T'ien Shu, Meng Shu, and some eight others shaved their
heads, put on russet clothes and iron collars, and thus disguised
as slaves could follow the King to prison (12). Several versions
of this story stress the great loyalty of the King's retainers. The
interesting thing is that it was considered natural for slaves to
follow their masters to prison.

attached themselves as advisers, and usually as loyal followers, to important
political and military men. Translating the terms separately, in accordance with
their separate historical backgrounds, should not obscure the fact that during
Han times "attendant slaves" and "guests" had a functional similarity. On
"guests," cf. T'ao Hsi-sheng, "Hsi Han ti k'o ['Guests' in the Western Han period],"
Shih Huo, vol. 5, No. 1, Jan. 1, 1937, pp. 1–6.

Anthropology, Vol. 34, Plate 2

SCENES OF UPPER-CLASS LIFE DURING THE HAN PERIOD, SHOWING SERVICES OFTEN PERFORMED BY SLAVES

Above, an entertainment with acrobats and musicians; below, chariots and outriders

Restoration by Wilma C. Fairbank of a rubbing from a bas-relief in the mortuary shrine of the Wu family. Shantung Province, ca. A.D. 150

The loyalty of female slaves to their mistresses sometimes made them dangerous to rival ladies. The King of Kuang-ch'uan had two concubines *née* Wang, both of whom he promised to make his Queen. Another woman, *née* Yang-ch'eng, won his affection, and the two disappointed candidates planned to kill her. When the King discovered this he assembled all his ladies, and in their presence he and his favorite slowly hacked the Wangs to death. Lady Yang-ch'eng then pointed out to the King that the slave women of the two concubines might let the matter leak out. The Wangs' three attendant female slaves were therefore strangled (*64*). Probably the three "attendant" female slaves had come from the Wang family into the King's palace as personal servants for their mistresses. For that reason the King feared that they alone of all the women would reveal the murder.[1] Later Yang-ch'eng Chao-hsin, wanting to monopolize the King's affection, persuaded him to use her elder slave woman as gate guard over the Concubines' Quarter, to prevent the other ladies from "licentious promiscuity." Apparently she trusted her elder slave women to protect her interests!

Loyalty of slaves to their masters was not, however, an absolute quality; in two cases masters killed slaves to prevent them from letting the facts of a crime leak out (*106*, *129*), and, as mentioned before, the imperial concubine *née* Chao tried to bribe three of her private female slaves not to reveal her mountainous sins. She had good reason to suspect their loyalty. Formerly household slaves of the rival Wang and Hsü families, and freed by them, the three women had simply been commanded to enter the palace and become her private slaves (*107*).

All these occupations of private slaves—general servants' work, armed escort, entertaining, personal attendance and sexual relations, tomb-watching, and managerial work—were "non-productive" in the sense that they added nothing to the master's wealth. They were luxury occupations, promoting the owner's comfort, pleasure, or prestige. Without these aids to gracious living, noble and wealthy people probably told one another they "simply could not endure."

SLAVES AS INSTRUMENTS OF POWER

There was yet another "service" function of private slaves, and it has a sinister aspect. This was the use of slaves as instruments of

---

[1] Every upper-class woman may have taken with her a few family slaves as personal servants when she was married. Quite probably the "private" male and female slaves of the child Empress *née* Shang-kuan were simply her family slaves who went into the palace to wait on her and protect her from rivals (*62*).

power.   Because this subject has been generally neglected by
previous writers it merits careful analysis.   It demonstrates more
clearly than any of the previously mentioned service occupations
the relationship between private slavery and the societal structure
of the Former Han period.

Nobles and landed gentry were the actual rulers of their local
areas whether political control was vested in them or not.   They
forced their will upon the common people through political connection and economic power; they appropriated land by illegal or
shifty means, laid tribute, and extorted extra corvée labor for their
personal ends.   Social philosophers inveighed against these practices
over and over again.

Part of the phenomenon was the use of armed male slaves—an
inevitable development, since the principal duty of a special class
of male slaves was to bear arms and ride escort with their masters.
Trained as fighters, they were personally loyal to one man, obeying
his commands alone.   Cases in which masters used their slave
retainers to enforce their will on others and to obstruct justice are
so common and so flagrant as to indicate that private slavery had
a special function in maintaining and extending the power of the
slave-owning class.

Slaves were the principal or accessory agents in several cases of
terrorism.   The most notorious concerned a cousin of Emperor Wu,
Liu P'eng-li, King of Chi-tung.   In the years before 116 B.C. the King
made a practice of going out at dusk with several tens of his male
slaves and lawless young bloods, plundering and assassinating people
"all for sport."   More than a hundred cases of people killed were
actually divulged.   No one dared travel at night in the kingdom.
Finally the sons of people killed sent a statement to the imperial
court reporting the facts, and the officials begged the Emperor to
have the King executed.   Emperor Wu "could not bear" to do that;
instead he deposed Liu P'eng-li, made him a commoner, and banished
him to northwestern Hupei (44).

Seven other judicial cases reveal that slaves murdered people
at their masters' command.   In 110 B.C. Liu Lung, the Marquis
of Fu, was tried for causing a male slave to kill a man.   The marquisate was abolished and the marquis was thrown into prison, where
he wasted and died (51).

When Liu Ch'ü, the infamous King of Kuang-ch'uan, was a
boy he had a teacher who criticized and disciplined him.   When
Liu Ch'ü grew older he drove the teacher out, but some time after-

wards the latter was appointed an official of the kingdom, and several times got restrictions placed upon the King's household. Liu Ch'ü ordered a male slave to kill the official and his son. Later two of his concubines, the sisters *née* T'ao, were killed. Completely destroying the corpse of one girl, Liu Ch'ü delivered to the mother a substitute corpse with the body of the sister. The mother was not deceived, however. She "howled and lamented," demanding the real corpse of her daughter. Queen Yang-ch'eng Chao-hsin ordered a male slave to murder her. The slave was caught, and his confession started an investigation which revealed sixteen murders by the King and his jealous Queen. Though the judicial commission recommended public execution, Emperor Wu demanded some other punishment. The King was deposed and banished with his wife to northern Hupei, where he was promised a small estate. On the way he committed suicide and only then was the Queen publicly executed. The kingdom was abolished (*64*).

Chi Tang, Baron of Chou-tzu-nan, was tried in 67 B.C. for causing a male slave to kill his household manager. He was publicly executed and the barony abolished (*73*).

Among the accusations against Chancellor Wang Shang, Marquis of Lo-ch'ang, was the suspicion that he had had a male slave murder his sister's lover. Because Wang Shang was a cousin of Emperor Hsüan his crimes were pardoned but he was removed from office and noble position (25 B.C.). Three days later he "fell sick, spat blood, and died." (*98*.)

Hsiao Huo, a seventh generation descendant of Hsiao Ho, was tried in 16 B.C. because he had ordered a male slave to kill a man. The marquisate was abolished, but his sentence was reduced from execution to "guarding the frontier." (*103*.)

A male slave owned by the King of Liang assassinated two high officials on his master's order because they had enraged the King on matters of public business. Then the King killed the slave to silence him. For these and other crimes the judicial officials begged for his execution, but Emperor Ch'eng only reduced his kingdom by five prefectures (*106*).

The Marquis of Wu-an was deposed in 3 B.C. for having caused a male slave to kill a man (*115*).

Eight cases of slaves employed to murder during a period of more than two centuries may appear insignificant. On the contrary, they probably exemplify the importance of slaves as instruments of power. This does not mean that the original archivists or the authors of the *Shih chi* and *Ch'ien Han shu* recorded the cases to illustrate that phenomenon.   From their point of view the fact that slaves were involved was purely incidental; nothing is said of what happened to the actual murderers, the slaves.   The important fact, naturally, was that noblemen were tried, with the result that five political units were abolished, a kingdom reduced, a marquis deposed, and a chancellor dismissed.   Personal punishments included execution, reduction of sentence from execution to guarding the frontier, banishment, and imprisonment resulting in death.

Each case concerned (1) a capital crime, which (2) involved a nobleman, who (3) was actually brought to justice.   They were all matters of imperial and historical concern.   It is, therefore, legitimate to make three corresponding assumptions: (1) Less serious illegal uses of slaves happened frequently, but were not recorded because the consequences were not important matters of state. (2) Similar capital cases occurred, involving slave-owning commoners who were tried, but the cases were not of enough historical importance to be reported.   (3) Other cases of murder by slaves at the behest of their noble masters probably occurred but are not recorded because they were not revealed, were suppressed, were not the principal or most serious charges against the nobleman, or were simply forgotten.   It cannot be assumed that every such murder was revealed, tried, punished, recorded, and finally included in the histories.   In all probability the eight recorded cases were a mere fraction of the total.   If this reasoning is correct, it is justifiable to assume that they typify a general phenomenon.

A few more historical tidbits fall into the above category.   Luan Pu was purchased for the specific purpose of doing a deed of revenge for his master (5), but only because he later became famous do we know even that much about his enslavement.   The King of Huai-nan used a government slave (or slaves) to forge imperial seals and all sorts of official insignia in preparation for rebellion (*A8*).   Private slave women were twice ordered to invoke magic curses against emperors in the hope of causing death.   In each instance a king and his queen conspired in the witchcraft, and it happens that both kings committed suicide and both queens were executed (*38, 113*). Another queen was executed for having ordered a female slave to kill her predecessor by magic poison (*37*).   The last four items concern kings and queens who were actually brought to justice for using slaves in the crimes of rebellion and murder; they fit the formula established for the eight cases just cited.

Two cases where masters used their slaves to enforce their will against common people happen to be recorded. When Liu Ho, the King of Ch'ang-i, was rushing to the capital to be made Emperor in 74 B.C. he had his senior male slave kidnap girls and load them into a screened carriage to take along with him. Since he was quite close to the capital an official sent out to meet him was able to have the slave arrested and turned over to the guard for punishment in spite of Liu Ho's objections. There is no indication that the girls were set free, but the incident was one of the grounds for deposing Liu Ho after a brief period as Emperor (*68*, and footnote 3).

Chang Fang was Emperor Ch'eng's cousin and catamite; his wife was the Empress' niece. The Emperor called him his son, and gave him a mansion, chariots, clothes, and jewelry; when he was married the Empress presented him with girls, probably slaves, from her private bureau. He accompanied the Emperor on his famous incognito journeys, and was a cock-fighting and horse-racing "fan," generally arrogant, self-indulgent, prodigal, and debauched. Finally, the Chancellor and Grandee Secretary memorialized the Emperor, revealing some of the crimes of Chang Fang and insisting that he be sent away from the capital. One complaint was that when he learned that a certain commoner was planning to give his daughter to the imperial seraglio, he sent the Inspector of Musicians in the Bureau of Music to get her (for himself) by force. Unsuccessful in this, Chang Fang sent his male slaves to the commoner's home. They broke in and wounded three people (*100*). This happened in the capital and was perpetrated by the Emperor's personal favorite.

Slaves were used not only to enforce the master's will against other people, but also to oppose the government and obstruct justice in cases where proper judicial procedure endangered the owner or his interests. The acts of Princess Kai, the older sister of Emperor Chao, are a clear example. Her lover, a commoner named Ting "Wai-jen," hated the former Prefect of the Capital and sent a "guest" (*k'o*) to slay him. Because the retainer hid in the Princess' house the officials did not dare arrest him. Hu Chien, Prefect of the city where she lived, boldly surrounded the house with his officers and soldiers, placing it under guard. When the Princess learned about it she assembled her lover and her friend General Shang-kuan An, father of the Empress, and the three galloped up, accompanied by a large number of male slaves and guests who shot at the officials and chased them off. There was some fighting, for one of the Princess's slaves was wounded. This enraged her. She sent her chief gate guard to impeach Hu Chien's subordinate, the Police Chief of the district, for wounding a slave of her household. Hu Chien protected his subordinate by reporting back that he was not guilty. Furious at this, the Princess submitted a letter to court, accusing Hu Chien of having invaded and insulted a Grand Princess, and of shielding an officer who he knew had outrageously wounded her slave. Ho Kuang was able to table her memorial, but later fell ill. Thus co-regent Shang-kuan Chieh, the father of Shang-kuan An, had a chance to take over the case. He sent an official to arrest Hu Chien, who committed suicide. This was recognized by everyone as a great injustice (*61*).

A similar case concerned the same Chang Fang who tried to kidnap the commoner's daughter. Officials ordered to his house to arrest a known thief were locked out and shot at with military crossbows by Chang Fang's slaves under his orders. Again, because he was angered at the Police Chief of the Bureau of Music about some governmental affair, he sent his senior male slave and a gang of forty or more, all armed with military crossbows, to invade the bureau in broad daylight. They shot up the offices, wrecked the furnishings, tied up the children of the chief official, and would not stop until the police chief and his assistants, dressed in the costume of convicts, apologized to Chang Fang personally (*100*).

If some of the flower of the nobility used their slaves to terrorize officials in the capital one may imagine how they lorded it over administrators in the provinces. After Wang Lin-ch'ing had been dismissed from court on the death of his sponsor, one of the Empresses *née* Wang, he returned to his native seat, where he and his ruffian associates continued to flout the law. He was advised officially to move on to the next prefecture, but as a last defiant gesture sent back a slave to beat on the assembly drum standing before the prefectural offices. Ho Ping, who was Prefect of the district, set out with officers to arrest Wang Lin-ch'ing, and toward sundown was hot on the trail. In these straits, Wang Lin-ch'ing made one of his cavalry slaves exchange clothes with him and take his place in the carriage, while he galloped off in disguise and escaped. When Ho Ping overtook the party he realized he had lost his man; but he pretended that the slave was the master and had him beheaded on the spot. The slave's head was publicly exhibited with a label proclaiming it to be Wang Lin-ch'ing. Thus the master lost his official identity and the populace believed him dead. When the facts were learned at court another Dowager Empress, grieving for a relative of the late Empress Dowager *née* Wang, reported to Emperor Ai. Far from being angry, the Emperor upheld Ho Ping and advanced him in position (*112*, and footnotes).

The Ho family slaves and guests living at P'ing-yang, the family's native seat, would carry weapons and go into town fighting and brawling, and the officials could not prevent them. It is specially noted to the credit of Yin Weng-kuei that when he became an official in the town no one—not even the Ho family slaves and guests—dared to break the laws (*65*). Both these incidents were recorded to illustrate the character and administration of particularly fearless and aggressive officials. This is both a backhand commentary on the average local official, and an unconscious indication of the way powerful individuals probably used their slaves to dominate local areas.

Dangers inherent in the lawless use of slaves did not escape the notice of a few high officials in the government, but there is no evidence that they were concerned with the matter as a general phenomenon.[1] Specific crimes were specifically punished, the master being charged with the crime committed by the slave under order. Two memorials show, however, that certain owners of numerous male slaves were considered a menace to the government. Chancellor Wang Shang, leader of the clan of Emperor Hsüan's mother, was accused of controlling the palace and embittering the whole empire by his ruthless acts. Supported by a powerful clan whose combined capital was reckoned by the hundred million cash and whose private male slaves were said to be numbered by the thousand, Wang Shang was accused of being a potential threat to the throne. The memorialist considered him much more dangerous than Chü Meng, who, as a lone wolf with many independent braves for followers, held the balance of power during the Rebellion of the Seven States (*98*). The other memorial criticized the political power and private conduct of Wang Ken, half-brother of Emperor Yüan's consort, and leader of the other Wang family from which Wang Mang sprang. Immediately after pointing out how he had infringed upon imperial prerogatives it disclosed that he made his male slave attendants wear armor, carry bows and crossbows, and deploy like infantry (*111*).

[1] Unless we assume that one reason for repeated attempts to limit numbers of slaves individually owned was to prevent accumulation of too much terroristic power. There is no textual evidence for this assumption, and none of the restrictions specifies a limit to the number of *male* slaves a family could own.

The fear that private slaves of these powerful consort families might be employed against the imperial house was not imaginary. Throughout the Former Han period consort families frequently acquired so much power that they might have menaced the House of Liu. Between the never-forgotten attempted revolution by the Lü family near the beginning of the dynasty and the successful one by Wang Mang at the end, the clan of nearly every Empress became so dominant that it had to be quelled. If open revolt had broken out, instead of mere political intrigue, private male slaves, loyal and armed, could have been used as shock troops in the fighting.

IX. PRODUCTIVE EMPLOYMENT OF PRIVATE SLAVES

There is far more evidence that private slaves were used in service capacities, including maintenance of power, than as producers of wealth. How much "productive" work, therefore, did slaves do? What kind of work was it? How important was slave labor in the total process of production during Han times?

In a country with an agrarian economy such as China had during the Former Han period, the really basic problem in regard to productive employment of slaves is their use in agriculture. Most slave owners, and probably all large slave holders, also owned agricultural land. Indeed, land was primary; slaves were secondary. There is no reason to doubt that masters who directed their tenants or managed their own farms used some of their male slaves to work during those crucial periods of planting, cultivating, and especially harvesting when all hands were mustered to help. Some masters, likewise, may have kept small groups of unfree cultivators for the regular farm work, and used hired labor at crucial periods. The fundamental question is not, however, whether slaves worked on farms, but whether slave labor was an important form of agricultural labor during the Former Han period. If there is any indication that it may have been important, then the problem is to compare slave labor with other types of agricultural labor existing during the epoch. If slave labor was an important part of agricultural labor, then slavery was correspondingly important to Chinese economy in general. The subject is at the very center of the controversy whether Chinese society was a "slavery society" and whether the economy of Han times was a "slavery economy." It is therefore essential to subject to the sharpest scrutiny those texts which suggest a relationship between slaves and farming.

EVIDENCE AND PRESUMPTION OF SLAVES IN AGRICULTURE

There is an initial enigma: only two documents speak definitely of slaves working on farms, and in each only a single slave is mentioned.

Chu Chia, the buyer and protector of Chi Pu, hid him in a house in the fields, and instructed his son to be lenient with the slave in the field work and to share his own food with him (8).[1]

[1] Chu Chia's instructions to his son are not in the CHS, but come from the SC. There is a possibility that the SC text is secondary, which would lessen its importance in regard to agriculture.

Chu Chia's son may have been manager of the farm. Since Chi Pu was in disguise as a slave it must have been quite natural for him to be working as a farm hand. Obviously there were other workers in the same fields, but not necessarily slaves, for Chu Chia had innumerable hired (or indentured) laborers, but was not noted as a slave owner.[1]

In 59 B.C., Wang Pao wrote into his purchase contract the specifications for agricultural work to be done by his slave. Pien-liao was to hoe the garden, and plant ginger, melons, eggplant, and onions. At the time of the vernal equinox he was to repair the ditches, dikes, and boundary walls of the fields, fertilize the land and prepare it for planting; in the fourth month to transplant; in the ninth to harvest; and in the tenth to gather in the beans. He also had to prune mulberry trees (used for production of silk), and tend an extensive orchard of peach, plum, pear and persimmon trees (*83*). This interesting document gives insight into work on a farm managed by the owner where the products were for sale and home consumption. But it was certainly not a plantation, for Pien-liao appears to have been the only male slave owned by Wang Pao.

There are two groups of documents which, by mentioning fields and slaves in close proximity, suggest a functional connection; i.e. that some of the slaves worked in the fields. The first group reports wealth of certain individuals, or gifts to them, in terms of fields and slaves. The case of Ho Ch'ü-ping, who liberally bought fields, houses, and slaves for his father, merits attention. It seems obvious that the slaves were producers of wealth, and not mere consumers, because the father was a humble man who certainly could not support luxury slaves (*42*). Likewise, the daughter of Cho Wang-sun was given a large sum of money and a hundred "youths" by her father. She immediately invested in farm land and houses and became a rich person (*28*). Is it justifiable to assume that the slaves in these and certain similar cases[2] were agricultural slaves? It may be; and yet the assumption is an arbitrary one. There are similar documents which report wealth in terms of slaves and other goods without mentioning farm land, and furthermore these other types of wealth, such as mansions, carriages, horses, furniture, silks, gold,

---

[1] See pp. 122–123 and footnote.

[2] Emperor Wu's gift of 1,000,000 cash, 300 slaves, 100 *ch'ing* of fields, and a mansion to his half-sister (*31*), and the reward of a princess' fields, houses, and slaves granted to the Chinese lady who had been sent as bride to a Wu-sun king, when she returned to China (*88*).

and money, have no functional connection with land.[1] Thus it may be an error to pick out farm land and slaves and assume that they belong together. They may merely have been two of the standard indices of wealth.

The second group of documents includes ministerial protests against extensive owning of fields and slaves, and imperial edicts or laws restricting such ownership. This group merits close study since the documents appear more definitely to imply a functional connection.[2]

Tung Chung-shu, the outstanding social reformer of the Han period before Wang Mang, was deeply concerned with economic problems besetting the empire during the early years of Emperor Wu's reign. Especially was he the champion of the common people, the great peasant group whose toil he considered the real basis of national wealth. In a speech to Emperor Wu he complained about the way in which nobles and high officials, enjoying big incomes, took advantage of their wealth and position to compete for profits with the common people who could not possibly match them. "Therefore," said Tung Chung-shu, "[the influential people] multiply their male and female slaves, increase their [herds of] cattle and sheep, enlarge their fields and houses, broaden their fixed property, and accumulate goods. Busily engaged in these pursuits without end, they thereby oppress and trample on the common people. The common people are daily pared down and monthly squeezed, gradually becoming greatly impoverished." He urged the Emperor to prevent households that received official income from competing with the people (34).

Does this imply that slaves were an instrument of this competition? Were they used in the fields to produce crops sold in compe-

---

[1] As in the cases of Ch'en P'ing (15), Luan Ta (49), the grandaunt of Emperor Chao (58), Ho Kuang (70), Shih Tan (97), Wang Mang's uncles (99), and the family of his second Empress (133).

[2] Documents of the kind to be discussed have been quoted by Chinese writers as proof or strong presumption that the slaves were used in the fields, but they have been cited without careful analysis, so far as I have read. Tai Chen-hui ("Liang Han nu-li chih-tu [The slavery system of the two Han dynasties]," *Shih Huo*, vol. 1, No. 7, March 1, 1935, pp. 286–291 [hereafter cited by translated title], see p. 287) uses the association as definite proof. Wu Po-lun ("An investigation of slavery in the Western Han," p. 282) says that the association suggests that slaves were used in agriculture, though he believes that the system of share-crop farming made slaves unimportant. Ma Ch'eng-feng (*An economic history of China*, vol. 2, pp. 269–271) quotes the passages I am citing and similar HHS ones as proof, though he concludes that in the nation's agriculture, slave labor was not important. Presumably Liang Ch'i-ch'ao ("System of slavery in China," p. 552) had the same sources in mind in his discussion of large-scale landowning and use of slaves in agriculture.

tition with those of the small farmer? This possibility cannot be ignored, but the development of ideas in the memorial implies that the successful business enterprises of people enjoying government income and personal power as officials or noblemen *resulted* in the accumulation of slaves, herds, farms, real estate, and other kinds of wealth. In another memorial, closely similar, Tung Chung-shu also mentioned both fields and slaves, but treated them as distinct problems. He urged the Emperor to limit the amount of private farm land any individual could own, "in order to assist those in want." After suggesting two other reforms, the second of which had no connection with land, he urged the abolition of slavery, in order to eliminate the fear of autocratic execution. Then he recommended reduction in taxation and corvée duties (*35*). There is certainly no suggestion here that slaves were employed in agriculture or that their employment created an economic problem.

In 119 B.C. other ministers urged Emperor Wu to forbid resident merchants to own fields. Their recommendation is phrased as though it were an administrative order: "[If anyone] dares to violate this order, confiscate his fields and youths." (*45*.) Why should merchants illegally owning fields have their fields *and* "youths" confiscated? Does this mean that the "youths" (probably slaves) worked in the fields? The *Ch'ien Han shu* variant of the passage uses the term "goods" in place of the *Shih chi* "youths," thus creating doubt as to which reading is correct. It gives the impression that merchants would have their illegally owned fields confiscated, and as punishment lose their other wealth as well, and makes no hint of a functional connection between fields and slaves. Incidentally, during the next seven years when the government confiscated large amounts of farm land and thousands of slaves it did not use them on this land, as it presumably would have done had they been agricultural slaves (*46*).

The next protest against extensive ownership of fields and slaves, a protest of the same textual order as earlier and later ones, dates a century later. Emperor Ch'eng was censured by his high officials for privately owning both. But the land and slaves were not connected. The fields were scattered among those of the people while the private male slaves lived with the Emperor in the Northern Palace to be his companions on his incognito journeys (*104*).

The famous attempt by ministers of Emperor Ai to set limits to ownership of land and slaves, reported both in the "Treatise on Economics" and in the "Imperial Annals," is exceedingly suggestive. When Emperor Ai was given the throne in 7 B.C., his former tutor,

Shih Tan, delivered a lecture on economic conditions. He recalled the ancient *ching-t'ien* system of land division, and the fact that early in the Han period Emperor Wen had emphasized agriculture and sericulture, and set an example of thrift. Therefore, said Shih Tan, the people had an abundance, and the accumulation of land, offices, and other sources of income did not occur. Wherefore Emperor Wen *"did not set limits on people's fields and male and female slaves."* Shih Tan emphasized that now, in contrast to conditions in that day, the overbearing officials and rich plebeians had riches counted by the hundred millions while the poor and weak were increasingly distressed. He recommended that general restrictions be ordered (*109*).

The Emperor then discussed the problem in an edict:[1]

> Now the vassal kings, the ranking marquises, the princesses, the officials [receiving a salary of] two thousand piculs, and the overbearing, rich people *herd many male and female slaves, and fields and residences without limit. They compete with the common people for profit, and the people have lost their occupations*, and are heavily distressed and in want. Let limitations and regulations be discussed [*110*].

Shih Tan's statement that it was unnecessary for Emperor Wen to set limits on fields and slaves, and Emperor Ai's complaint that nobles, high officials, and rich plebeians accumulated slaves and fields and competed with the commoners for profit, would both seem to be prima-facie evidence that fields and slaves were considered in 7 B.C. to be instruments of competition, and that accumulation of them by the powerful minority created an unfavorable economic situation.

Chancellor K'ung Kuang and Grandee Secretary Ho Wu proposed the following restrictions: Vassal kings and marquises should be allowed to own fields in their own states; it is not clear whether they could possess unlimited amounts or were restricted to thirty *ch'ing* (about 340 acres). Marquises who lived at the capital, and princesses likewise, should be limited to thirty *ch'ing* in prefectures and border marches outside their states. *Kuan-nei* marquises, who alone had incomes from estates near the capital, and officials and plebeians should all be limited to thirty *ch'ing*. No merchant could own private fields or become an official. As to male and female slaves between the ages of ten and sixty, vassal kings were to be

---

[1] That is to say, the next step in the development of the law was an edict by the Emperor. We do not know who wrote the edict for young Emperor Ai, or exactly whose ideas he was expressing, though Shih Tan, K'ung Kuang, and Ho Wu were the moving spirits in the reform.

allowed two hundred, marquises and princesses one hundred, and *kuan-nei* marquises, officials, and plebeians thirty. All private fields and slaves exceeding the areas or numbers allowed in each category were to be confiscated after a three-year period (*109, 110*).

In considering this law it is assumed to have been seriously proposed by officials who looked upon it as a necessary corrective for social and economic problems of the day. K'ung Kuang, Ho Wu, and other high officials charged with writing the terms of the ordinance, were thoroughly conversant with conditions of land- and slave-owning, and settled upon limits that they believed were equitable. Even though opposition from powerful affinal relatives of the Emperor and from his favorite Tung Hsien prevented the law from going into effect, the high ministers must have believed it could be put into operation within the three years allowed for liquidating excess holdings.

It must be observed that the numbers of slaves allowed did not depend upon the amount of land owned, but upon the social position of the master. Kings, having the most elaborate palaces, holding court in imitation of the imperial pattern, and by 7 B.C. possessing the forms but not the power of rule, were considered to need no more than two hundred adult slaves of both sexes. Marquises, whether they lived at their estates or in the capital, needed a maximum of one hundred, as did princesses. Thirty slaves sufficed for lesser ranks of nobility, non-noble officials, and all plebeians.[1]

---

[1] An even stronger case develops if, as Dubs states ("Wang Mang and his economic reforms," TP, vol. 35, 1940, p. 246), ". . . kings and marquises should be allowed unrestricted amounts of private land within their kingdoms and marquisates; outside those areas they should be restricted to 3,000 *mou* (140 acres)." According to this interpretation, instead of everyone being limited to 340 acres of private land, except merchants, who could have none, we find different amounts of land determined by the location of the fields, and by the dwelling place, rank, or occupation of the owner; while slave numbers depended upon the owner's status only.

Rank or class	Land	Slaves
Kings	Unlimited in own state?	200
Marquises	Unlimited in own state?	100
Marquises living at the capital	30 *ch'ing*	100
	(plus unlimited in own state?)	
Princesses	30 *ch'ing*	100
Kuan-nei marquises	30 *ch'ing*	30
Non-noble officials	30 *ch'ing*	30
Plebeians	30 *ch'ing*	30
Merchants	None	30

I place this interpretation, which I consider correct, in a footnote because the general argument does not depend upon which particular interpretation of the passage is accepted. In the other reading also, amounts of farm land and numbers of slaves are unrelated.

Restrictions on slave-owning seem to have been based, not upon economic considerations, but rather upon the precedent of general sumptuary laws already well established early in the Han period. Slave-owning was the subject of purely sumptuary legislation only six years before and ten years after 7 B.C. In 13 B.C. Emperor Ch'eng delivered an edict censuring the nobility and high officials for their lavish style of living:

> Some among them are extravagant and neglectful; busy with expanding their mansions and houses, setting out gardens and pools, accumulating numerous male and female slaves, dressing them in fancy silks, setting out bells and drums, providing female orchestras, carriages, clothing, marriages, and funerals and tombs beyond the regulations.
>
> Lesser officials and common people admire and emulate them [until such extravagance] gradually becomes the custom .... Let it be announced to the proper officials to prohibit gradually [the above offenses] .... Let the marquises and close ministers examine themselves and mend their conduct. Let the Colonel over the Retainers judicially investigate those who do not change [105].

In A.D. 3 Wang Mang presented a memorial to regulate among various classes of officials and plebeians, styles of carriages and clothing, expenditures for celebrating births, weddings, and funerals, and possession of fields, male and female slaves, houses, utensils, and implements (121).

When Wang Mang assumed the throne six years later he introduced very far-reaching economic and humanitarian reforms which bear closely upon our problem. He ordered that all land should be called "the King's fields," changed the name for male and female slaves to "private retainers," and decreed that neither could be bought or sold! The historian reports that innumerable people were tried and punished for selling and buying fields, residences, male and female slaves, and for coining money. Three years later, in A.D. 12, discontent was so great that Wang Mang had to repeal his prohibition and to allow the sale of both fields and slaves (124). As late as A.D. 21 this discontent was still evident in a plot against Wang Mang in which a conspirator, in listing grievances against the usurper, said: "Since the house of Hsin came to the throne, common people's fields and male and female slaves can not be sold or bought." (A22).[1]

---

[1] The phrasing of this complaint, and also the passage A23, suggests that Wang Mang did not entirely relax his restrictions on fields and slaves in A.D. 12. In 17 he levied a tax of 3,600 cash per slave on all slave owners. This was apparently only a revenue-raising device, and had no specific relation to landowners. Ying Shao tells that there was a double poll-tax on slaves, but the date of that tax is uncertain. A T'ang dynasty commentator mentions taxes on slaves about 120 B.C. as a money-raising scheme (127, and footnote 1).

The prohibition against selling and buying land or slaves apparently stands at the heart of this initial reform. Did Wang Mang consider land and slaves to be functionally connected? His edict offers no hint that he did. There he treated them as individual problems. In giving his reasons for reform, Wang Mang described the evils of the Ch'in administration: heavy taxation and destruction of the system of communal agriculture, which resulted in greed for wealth, annexation of land by the strong, and landlessness of the poor. Next he discussed the evils of slavery: sale of people like cattle and horses, and kidnaping and selling women and children for profit. He denounced slavery as a violation of Heaven's intention, a perversion of human relationships, and a negation of the basic principle that in the nature of heaven and earth man is most important. He cited the *Shu ching* for proof that in antiquity enslavement was confined to punishment for crime.

Then he turned his attention to contemporary economic problems. He admitted that Han rulers had reduced the tax on farm produce from the former one-tenth to one-thirtieth, but pointed out that there were always extra taxes. He described how the powerful encroached upon and oppressed the weak, "dividing the fields out at usurious rentals," so that in name the tax on produce was one-thirtieth, but in reality it was five parts in ten. Wang Mang was clearly speaking of a tenancy system. Yen Shih-ku so explains it: " 'Dividing the fields' means that poor people, having no fields, take the fields of rich people, plowing and planting them, and dividing the produce [with the owner]. 'Lending' also means that poor people rent rich people's fields . . . ." No commentary could be more explicit. Modern Chinese writers on the economics of the Han dynasty constantly use this passage as basic evidence for tenant farming. They regularly point out that the landlords, collecting half the produce but paying only one-thirtieth in taxes, were the real beneficiaries of the tax reduction.

In Wang Mang's words the evil results of this tenancy system were:

> Fathers and sons, husbands and wives plow and cultivate the whole year long, yet what they receive is insufficient to support themselves. Therefore the rich, whose dogs and horses have a surplus of beans and grain, are haughty and become depraved. The poor, who do not feel full on dregs and husks, are exhausted and become villainous. Both fall into crime; punishments are employed and not set aside.

Here again it is clear that Wang Mang referred to tenants, not slaves. He recalled that his earlier order that the public lands of the empire be divided into sections on the basis of population figures had resulted in auspicious omens.

Apparently Wang Mang saw two problems: slavery; and excessive accumulation of farm land by wealthy landlords, which resulted in an oppressed, land-hungry peasantry. By decree he proclaimed that all fields in the empire were to be called "the King's fields"; private slaves were to be called "private retainers"; and neither henceforth could be bought or sold. The rest of the decree exclusively concerns the establishment of the *ching-t'ien* system of communal farming and the redistribution of land so that those who formerly had no fields were now to receive them. There is no suggestion that slaves were to be actually freed; but land owners possessing more than the specified areas of fields were ordered to divide the excess land among their clansmen, neighbors, and fellow villagers (*122*).

These are the documents most suggestive of slaves in agriculture. Two refer definitely to individuals so used, while a series of passages, by mentioning fields and slaves in close proximity, make it appear that the two were part of the same problem, a problem not now clearly understood. Examined closely, however, these documents fail to prove what they first suggest, that slavery was a part of the Chinese system of agricultural production of that day. If it was, it is strange that the evidence for it should be so ambiguous. It remains a presumption; a presumption so persistent, however, as to demand a closer study of the agricultural labor forms of the time.

RELATION BETWEEN SLAVE AND FREE LABOR

The nature and use of slave labor can be understood only in reference to the corresponding nature and use of free labor. Slave and free labor compete, not necessarily with any consciousness of competing, but nevertheless quite directly affecting each other where profits are concerned. An abundant supply of cheap and docile free labor may discourage large-scale use of slaves for productive purposes, for free labor has certain definite advantages. It can be paid by the productive hour, day, or week and be discharged when work is slack. Wages can be scaled as low as demand for work allows. Slaves "eat their heads off" when no work needs to be done. The owner has an investment which is idle when the slave is sick, disabled, or otherwise non-productive. Slave labor must be worked at optimum rather than maximum intensity, unless there is an unlimited supply of cheap slaves, for if slaves die or successfully revolt, the investment is wiped out and must be replaced. Investment and upkeep of the human machine are a definite part of the cost of producing goods and may be a determining factor in the success of a competitive enterprise. Highly skilled slave labor, on the other hand, has the advantage of permanency, which is not guaranteed by free labor.

This preliminary generalization is subject to all sorts of modifications arising from the nature of the free and slave labor reservoirs, the types of industry involved, and the social and economic forms of the society in question. Here it is merely introduced to clarify the need for examining labor conditions in relation to agriculture during the Han age. The subject is exceedingly difficult because there is even less systematic historical material about free labor in the period than about slavery. The study of free labor in agriculture must be approached from a wider perspective than a mere examination of passages which describe agricultural labor *per se*.

Factors That Produced Landless Free Labor

Three interdependent factors, population growth, landlordism, and famine, operating at an increasing intensity as the dynasty progressed, helped produce a great supply of free but landless agricultural labor.

The Ch'in dynasty confirmed and spread a trend toward private ownership of land by farmers, and the Han extended it. But the Han period began with a population greatly reduced and dispersed by seven years of bitter fighting and by famines which in some regions had cut the populace in half. Ssu-ma Ch'ien remarks that if a count had been made, only one or two tenths of the original population would have been found. Liang Ch'i-ch'ao has estimated the early Han population at five or six millions, though this may be too low. There was, on the other hand, an abundance of potentially good arable land. The basic problem was to get farmers back onto the soil, and to make it useful by water conservancy and irrigation. An edict of Emperor Wen in 163 B.C. indicates that even after forty years of peace the population had not grown to pre-Han figures. But it was growing and continued to grow until some time in the reign of Emperor Wu. Then the trend was checked and even reversed because of incessant warfare, economic depletion, and famine. Apparently losses were made up during the last years of his reign and during the peaceful era of Emperor Chao when Ho Kuang wisely reduced forced labor and taxes in order to "give the people a rest." From then on the populace gradually multiplied.

The "Treatise on Economics," describing the period just before Wang Mang, says specifically that "although the wealth of the masses did not come up to [what it had been during the time of] Emperors Wen and Ching, yet the population of the empire was exceedingly abundant." This remark is borne out by the census of A.D. 2, recorded in the "Treatise on Geography." That census was chosen for record, according to Yen Shih-ku, because at that time "the Han population . . . had reached the utmost abundance." After many decades of peace it was roughly 60,000,000. The intensity of the land problem at the close of the Former Han suggests strongly that enlargement of the empire, opening of new land, extension of irrigation, and improvement in agricultural techniques combined had not compensated for population growth. With the agricultural methods in practice there was too little land for the increased numbers of peasants.[1]

Early in the Han period most of the farm land was owned in small tracts by the families who cultivated it. At the end of the Former Han large amounts of land, perhaps most of the land strategically placed in relation to public irrigation works, was owned by landlords. Landlordism, the second factor influencing free agricultural labor, began at the very outset of the period. The story of Hsiao Ho, Kao-tsu's first Chancellor, is particularly revealing. Several revolts in 197 and 196 B.C. made the Emperor suspicious of Hsiao Ho's loyalty. An adviser suggested to Hsiao Ho that he buy large amounts of farm land to prove his trustworthiness; that is, to establish an obvious stake in the empire as it was. Hsiao Ho followed this advice so energetically that someone presented to the Emperor a document accusing his Chancellor of forcibly buying lands and houses at cheap prices from thousands of people. Kao-tsu was delighted with Hsiao Ho's demonstration of loyalty and jested with him about profiting from the people! Later, however, when

---

[1] No figures exist for the Ch'in and early Han periods so that it is impossible to calculate numerically the decrease in population. Ssu-ma Ch'ien's estimate is in his preface to SC, 18; cf. MH, vol. III, pp. 123–124. In the somewhat similar period between the two Hans there is a drop in the recorded figures from approximately 60,000,000 in A.D. 2 (20 years before the revolt) to 21,000,000 in A.D. 57 (about twenty years after consolidation); then a slow rise to 49,000,000 in A.D. 140. Cf. Wan Kwoh-ting, *An agrarian history of China*, vol. 1, pp. 124–125, where also Liang Ch'i-ch'ao's estimate is quoted. See *15*, footnote 4, concerning a city that had numbered 30,000 households under Ch'in but had only 5,000 at the beginning of Han. Emperor Wen's edict is in HFHD, vol. I, pp. 261–263. Decline under Emperor Wu and recovery under Emperor Chao is reported in the eulogy of the latter, CHS, 7, 5a; statement in the "Treatise on Economics," 24A, 8a; Yen Shih-ku's remark, 28A, 5b. The total given in 28B, 9a, for A.D. 2 is 59,594,978, but Chinese population figures are only estimates at best.

Hsiao Ho was out of office he made his home and bought fields in obscure places so that in future days if his descendants were no longer powerful all the land would not be appropriated by some other more dominant family.[1]

Though landlordism commenced at the beginning of the dynasty it had not begun to create an acute situation, so far as can be judged from extant documents, until sixty or seventy years later. Even then nothing was really done to check it. Farmers who sold part of their produce, usually in a buyer's market, were regularly cheated by dealers, and they paid disproportionately high prices for essential commodities, especially salt and iron. After successive bad years farmers lacking adequate reserves had to borrow grain evaluated at scarcity prices and had to pay the dealers high rates of interest. When driven to the wall by drought and debt they had to sell their land or become tenants of their creditors. This process, by which small farmers were dispossessed, was clearly described by several Han memorialists.

The phenomenon of landlordism had a positive side also. Unification of the empire, elimination of internal customs barriers, and the growing use of coined money all favored the growth of commerce, though inter-regional trade was limited to a few goods not everywhere produced, such as salt, iron, lacquer, silk, furs, and goods made of bamboo. Political stability, development of water conservancy, and long periods of peace created great reserves of taxes, allowing regular and liberal salaries for higher officials and a generous income for nobles, together with rich graft and numerous special gifts to imperial favorites. But there was almost no place to invest the profits from manufacturing, trade, grain-dealing, and money-lending, or the surpluses from official and noble income, except in farm land. Land was especially valuable because the government policy of encouraging agriculture kept the tax on it low; Emperor Ching finally settled the tax on agricultural produce at one-thirtieth of the harvests.

Landlordism became most intensive in areas of densest population: the best irrigated regions, in the neighborhood of big cities, and particularly around the capital. Imperial favorites and high officials were able by shady means to acquire land favored by abundant water. The wealth concentrated in cities naturally went into nearby

---

[1] SC, 53, 2b–3a, and CHS, 39, 2b–3b. T'ao Hsi-sheng (*An economic history of Western Han*, p. 32) and Ma Ch'eng-feng (op. cit., p. 276), who also quotes another article by T'ao, agree that early in the Han period most farmers owned their land, though they disagree fundamentally on many other economic questions.

farm land while the profits flowed back into the cities. It may have been around the capital that landlordism was at first most apparent. Tung Chung-shu's statement that fields of the rich extended in every direction while the poor did not have enough land on which to stand a needle, probably described conditions near the capital. He urged Emperor Wu to make decrees compelling those who received government income to stop competing with the people (*34*); specifically on behalf of the farmers he urged limitations on the amount of land that could be individually owned, "in order to assist those in want." (*35*.)[1]

The first harsh restrictions were placed on merchants during the reign of Emperor Wu. Formerly they were not allowed to wear certain types of costumes or become palace officials, and they paid a double poll-tax. In 119 B.C. high officials proposed special taxes on the instruments of trade, and a prohibition against merchants or their relatives owning agricultural land. This prohibition was made specifically for the benefit of the agricultural class. Between 119 and 113 the government stripped the merchant and business class of its investments in land, so that people of middling wealth and up were generally ruined. But this was a temporary measure to refill the depleted treasury, and the rule against merchants owning land, though not reported as being rescinded, could not be effectively enforced. During the long period of relative peace after Emperor Wu's death landlordism increased steadily until it was recognized as a major economic problem.[2] Emperor Ch'eng inveighed against it; Emperor Ai attempted unsuccessfully to limit amounts of land that could be individually owned; and Wang Mang tried nationaliza-

---

[1] The problem of landlordism is emphasized by nearly every modern Chinese historian; see particularly Ch'en Po-yin (*An investigation of the Chinese land system*, pp. 51–55), Wan Kwoh-ting (op. cit., pp. 82–88), T'ao Hsi-sheng (op. cit., *passim*, especially chap. 3, pp. 43–73), Ma Ch'eng-feng (op. cit., vol. 2, pp. 255, 277–278). R. H. Tawney (*Land and labour in China*, London, 1932, pp. 54–63) gives the clearest exposition I know concerning the disadvantages of Chinese farmers in their business dealings. Although describing recent conditions, his discussion could apply almost verbatim to analogous conditions described unsystematically in Han histories. Cf., for example, the business methods of Pai Kuei in SC, 129, 2b, and CHS, 91, 2b; and the memorials of Chia Yi, Ch'ao Ts'o, and Tung Chung-shu, CHS, 24A, 4a–7a. On concentration of landlordism around the capital, see Homer H. Dubs ("Wang Mang and his economic reforms," pp. 249–250). On land tenure and Chinese agriculture in general during Han times, see W. Eberhard ("Zur Landwirtschaft der Han-Zeit," MSOS, vol. 35, 1932, pp. 74–105) and Mabel Ping-hua Lee (*The economic history of China, with special reference to agriculture*, New York, 1921, pp. 56–63, 147–187).

[2] For early restrictions on merchants, cf. HFHD, vol. I, pp. 120, 184, 331; under Emperor Wu, SC, 30, 4b (MH, vol. III, pp. 572–575), and CHS, 24B, 5a; also documents *45* and *46*.

tion, prohibition of sale, and redistribution (see pp. 198–203). But landlordism could not be stopped.

The third factor helping to produce a great supply of free but landless agricultural labor was recurrent and widespread famine, a particularly grievous problem throughout the dynasty. Famine is not an independent phenomenon; often it is the symptom of many underlying causes. Some natural disasters produce widespread famine only because the majority of the affected population has no reserves on which to subsist, and because methods of communication are too poorly developed to transport adequate surpluses from other areas. But these aspects are not here in question. In general, the historical records of famine merely note the date and the area affected; yet some do give revealing details about numbers of victims and about government measures for relief. A few of these may be paraphrased.[1]

202 B.C.—There was a great famine in Shensi in which "half the population" died. Emperor Kao permitted people to sell their children and migrate to Szechwan in search of food.

157 B.C.—An edict of Emperor Ching discussed the problem of successive bad harvests in unfavored and crowded regions, and granted permission for people to migrate to fertile and undeveloped regions.

119 B.C.—In a period of flood and great starvation east of the mountains, the government attempted to feed the people from public granaries. When this attempt and private relief measures failed, more than 700,000 people, it is said, were removed to the northwest and colonized under government supervision.

107 B.C.—East of the pass there were 2,000,000 refugees and an estimated 400,000 unregistered people. The officials recommended a plan to transfer them to the frontiers.

67 B.C.—In a single kingdom in Shantung there were 80,000 squatters and refugees.

46 B.C.—Chia Chüan-chih described severe famines in eastern China which for years in succession sent people drifting from their homes and living along the highways.

[1] See respectively CHS, 24A, 3b–4a, and document 7; 5, 1b (HFHD, vol. I, pp. 309–310); 24B, 4a–b; 46, 2a (biography of Wan Shih-chün); 89, 2a (biography of Wang Ch'eng); 64B, 7b (biography of Chia Chüan-chih); 85, 6a (biography of Ku Yung); 81, 9b (biography of K'ung Kuang). For other similar items see *Hsi Han hui yao*, ch. 48, last section. Dubs (op. cit., p. 243) says that "a famine

15 B.C.—Ku Yung noted recently frequent natural disasters which caused famines during which refugees died on the roads "by the million."

After *6 B.C.* K'ung Kuang spoke of refugees counted by the hundred thousand along the roads and highways.

Throughout most of the Former Han epoch the government was unable to solve in any basic way the economic problems of the peasantry who made up the bulk of the population, and the tax on whose produce was the main source of revenue both for the state and for the governing class. It is impossible to know how intense and extensive the problems were, since historical records usually apply only to specific times and certain regions. But measures taken to meet them indicate at least an endemic maladjustment. Reign by reign the "Imperial Annals" contain edict after edict concerning agriculture. The low taxes on farm produce were in many years remitted entirely. Tax exemptions and honors went to "vigorous cultivators." Through conservancy works and irrigation canals the government extended cultivable land. It lent grain to farmers; it dabbled in price-fixing to prevent wild fluctuations between bad and good years; it distributed improved tools and gave instruction in better methods of cultivation. To alleviate the condition of landless peasants and to care for the hordes of refugees, myriads of people were transported to more favored or less densely populated regions, colonized in new territories on the extending frontiers, or allowed to cultivate imperial preserves and other government lands, often without rent or taxes during the initial years.[1]

This digression into agricultural conditions, with special reference to population growth, landlordism, and famines, supports the belief that during the last century and a half of the Former Han period there was an abundance of free farm labor struggling for land

year inevitably produced great hordes of vagrants, who died on the roads and thronged into regions where there was food. Since the government levied poll-taxes upon adults and children, besides the land-tax, this vagrancy meant not only human suffering but also a great loss of income."

[1] Edicts on agriculture and orders to remit taxes are conveniently assembled in the *Hsi Han hui yao*, ch. 50. On irrigation works, see Chi Ch'ao-ting, *Key economic areas in Chinese history* . . . , pp. 78–93; and SC, 29 (MH, vol. III, pp. 520–537), CHS, 29. The materials in these basic chapters have been analyzed by M. S. Bates, "Problems of rivers and canals under Han Wu Ti (140–87 B.C.)." For price fixing, cf. Dubs, op. cit., pp. 258–259. On training in agricultural techniques, see CHS, 24A, 7a, of which part is translated in document 57. See Wan Kwoh-ting (op. cit., pp. 115–119) for citations on government policies for aiding landless farmers by colonization, etc.

and a chance to work. Ma Ch'eng-feng has analyzed, with many historical references, the various ways in which dispossessed free farmers and the victims of famine found subsistence and employment during the Former and Latter Han periods. First, they could migrate, and sometimes could take up new land under government supervision. Second, when they could not get new land of their own they might become tenants of private landlords or of the government. Third, they could become hired or indentured farm laborers. And finally, as a last resort, they might sell themselves into slavery.[1]

USE OF LAND OWNED AS INVESTMENT

So far this discussion has avoided the problem of how landlords used their agricultural land to produce revenue. Did profits come from tenancy? Was land used under a managerial system approximating plantations? If so, did free or slave labor prevail?

There is no adequate description of tenant farming in Former Han literature. Modern Chinese students are compelled to revert to two brief accounts in the "Treatise on Economics" of the *Ch'ien Han shu*. The first is in the address by Tung Chung-shu to Emperor Wu. Ostensibly he was describing conditions under the Ch'in rulers, but since he says that the Han dynasty followed the Ch'in without change, he must also have been describing conditions in his own day, probably from personal observation. After lauding the practices of antiquity, Tung Chung-shu said:

> Coming [to the period of] Ch'in it was otherwise. It used the methods of Shang Yang, altered the institutions of [ancient] rulers, and abolished the *ching-t'ien* [system]. Commoners could buy and sell [fields]. The fields of the rich were connected path and furrow, while the poor were without land on which to stand a needle .... Some cultivated the fields of overbearing [officials] and commoners, undergoing a produce tax of five parts in ten ....

Yen Shih-ku explains: "It means that the lower households and poor people, themselves having no fields, cultivated imperial, overbearing [officials'] and rich families' fields. Among ten parts [of the produce] they took five to submit to the original landlord." [2]

---

[1] Ma Ch'eng-feng, op. cit., pp. 280–287. Ma is careless in his citation of historical texts, and must be constantly checked, but he is thoughtful in his deductions. Actually there is not much documentary evidence that farmers sold themselves. Most passages refer to sale of children and "marrying off of wives." See pp. 85–88, above.

[2] CHS, 24A, 6b. Parts of Tung Chung-shu's address are translated by J. J. L. Duyvendak (*The book of Lord Shang*, pp. 45, 55–56) and Derk Bodde (*China's first unifier*, pp. 172–173). His recommendations are translated in part in *35*.

The second account of tenancy comes in the edict of Wang Mang, translated in document *122* and discussed above (p. 202). That passage also described the rich dividing out the fields to the poor and getting a return of half the produce.

To these classic passages may be added a few others. At least twice when the word *chia* appears in connection with fields, Yen Shih-ku defines it as meaning "to rent." [1] "*Chia* also means that poor people rented rich people's fields." His second note "*Chia* means 'to rent,'" is in the chapter on rich people in connection with the exploit of Ning Ch'eng, who, during the reign of Emperor Wu, "borrowed on credit more than a thousand *ch'ing* [over 11,400 acres] of ruined fields and *lent* [i.e. rented] them to poor people, employing the services of several thousand families. After several years . . . he had achieved an estate [worth] several ten million [cash]." [2]

These few references to the system of tenancy give no adequate idea of the details, which must have varied widely in different parts of the country, nor do they allow us to judge what proportion of landlords parcelled their holdings into small farms worked by tenants. Yet modern Chinese scholars of all shades of economic opinion consistently hold to the view that tenant farming was widespread in Former Han times. Perhaps they better understand indefinite references in the light of the prevalence of tenancy throughout many later and more fully documented periods of Chinese history, as well as in the light of widespread tenancy today. Certain considerations

---

[1] CHS, 24A, 8b: 假亦謂貧人賃富人之田也. CHS, 90, 2a: 假謂雇賃也. The first is in connection with Wang Mang's decree, translated in document *122*.

[2] Biography of Ning Ch'eng, CHS, 90, 2a–b. The expression *ch'ien-wan* is taken as "thousand times myriad" in view of figures of wealth at this time. To read it as "several thousand up to a myriad," or "several thousands and myriads," would mean that he had profited less than ten cash, or some score cash, per tenant family during several years in business.

The same sense is perhaps applicable to several passages telling of the government's lending imperial or public lands to the poor in times of special distress. In 69 B.C. there was an order to lend fields to the poor in commanderies and kingdoms (CHS, 8, 4a). In 67 it was ordered that plebeians who had drifted away and would return should be lent public fields, seed-grain, and food, at interest (8, 4b). In 43 B.C. there was an amnesty and order for pardoned convicts to devote themselves to agriculture. All those without fields were to be lent them and be lent seed-grain and food at interest like poor commoners (9, 3b). All these are special cases, but criticism of the way the government used its land indicates that it regularly rented much of it to tenants, obtaining direct revenue to supplement tax income. See *Yen t'ieh lun*, ch. 3, sec. 13, trans. by Esson M. Gale, *Discourses on salt and iron*, pp. 81–84. See other references in *Hsi Han hui yao*, ch. 50, section on "lending the plebeians public fields"; also CHS, 75, 6b (biography of Yi Feng).

support their view. The normal farm owned by the family that worked it was apparently small; a hundred *mou*, equivalent to 11.4 acres, is usually given as standard by Han writers, though that figure has no statistical value. If individual farm holdings were similar to modern ones as described in recent agricultural surveys sampling many different regions, then they consisted of open fields, in small, non-contiguous plots, rather than of compact units. Small farms operated by owners, part-owners, and tenants fit together naturally into an agricultural-economic pattern. In so far as the process of acquiring large amounts of land consisted of accumulating many small farms taken one by one from scattered bankrupt owners, tenancy would be the natural result, since such scattered holdings could be made immediately profitable only through renting to tenants. They could not be consolidated into unified plantations until non-contiguous plots and farms were all assembled under single ownership. The process of reorganization would be slow and certainly would run counter to the prevalent system of small units worked by individual families.

There are no exact lines between small farms worked by the owner and his family, larger farms on which the working owner permanently employed extra labor, and big estates managed by the landlord or his agents and using gang labor. Wang Pao's farm would seem to fall into the second category, and perhaps Yang Yün's also. Chu Chia, early in Han, appears to have had a large farm run by his son as manager and using hired or indentured laborers among whom a man disguised as a slave could mingle unnoticed. Theoretically, plantations could develop most easily in regions newly opened to farming by state-directed irrigation works, or on large tracts of land given to favorites by the government. The first possibility is nearly fulfilled in the case of Chang Yü, an important government official under Emperors Yüan and Ch'eng. Chang Yü eventually became Chancellor. His family made agriculture its profession, and when Chang Yü became rich and noble he bought 400 *ch'ing* (4,560 acres) of the best land, watered by the Ching and Wei rivers. The outstanding case fulfilling the second possibility was Emperor Ai's gift to Tung Hsien of 2,000 *ch'ing* (22,800 acres) from an abolished imperial park. In neither of these reports is there any mention of whether income was secured by renting, or by operating the land in big units with managed labor.

Fan Chung, the uncle of Emperor Kuang-wu, the first Latter Han ruler, came from several generations of expert agriculturalists who were also good at business. For three generations Fan Chung's family had managed its property without waste. All their "youth-servants" (*t'ung-li*) were trained and employed according to their abilities, so that by a united effort wealth and profit yearly doubled. Eventually the family acquired over 300 *ch'ing* (3,420 acres) of land, which it irrigated with water from dams. Along with farming, the family also raised fish, herded livestock, and grew lacquer-producing trees. From these combined enterprises the Fans became exceedingly wealthy. This account of a family which specialized in agriculture, seemingly maintained its own irrigation works, and employed slave or hired labor on a permanent basis, suggests, more clearly than any other account I have been able to find, some sort of plantation system. Yet it is only presumptive evidence. All in all, there seems to be little deviation from what was apparently the Chinese norm of owner-farming mixed with tenant-farming.[1]

Wherever slave labor could be used on farms, hired labor could be used also. When farm families grew too large to subsist off paternal holdings and when farmers were dispossessed through debt or driven away by flood and drought, they could seek new land or become tenants. But as the population grew and most of the land was taken up there must have been an increasing amount of free agricultural labor for hire. References already cited indicate conclusively that this labor reservoir existed. In 62 B.C. Emperor Hsüan even ordered his officials to search for descendants of early Han noblemen who were so impoverished that they had to go out and work among indentured laborers. One classic example of hired laborers working on farms concerns Ch'en She, an early rebel against Ch'in. As a young man he was one of a group of hired plowmen (*yung keng*). Yen Shih-ku explains this term as "receiving someone's hire price and plowing for him, which is called 'selling one's labor.'" When in 83 B.C. young Emperor Chao had an edict delivered in his name deploring the fact that due to successive bad harvests plebeians had drifted away and hired or indentured themselves out, the edict must have referred primarily to migrant farm laborers. K'uang Heng is a good example of presumptive evidence of the same thing. He came from a family that had for generations been farmers, and as an ambitious but poor young man hired himself out in order to study. Considering his background it seems a fair assumption that he worked as a farm hand. A number of other

---

[1] For Wang Pao, Yang Yün, and Chu Chia, see documents *83*, *87*, and *8*. On Chang Yü, Tung Hsien, and Fan Chung, see CHS, 81, 6a; 86, 5b (document *117*); and HHS, 62, 1a.

references to hired or indentured labor in non-agricultural work show that there were other fields of employment but do not weaken the contention that most landless peasants could have hoped to find employment only as farm workers.[1]

Theoretically, the extensive use of slaves in agriculture should have occurred under conditions exactly opposite to those of the last half century of the dynasty when the slave population was at its apex and when restrictive legislation occurred. Slaves in agriculture would seem more likely when the population was small and the land abundant and accessible to free farmers, thus compelling landlords to develop plantations by using enforced labor, slave or indentured, in place of the free labor they could not attract under tenancy or hire. Liang Ch'i-ch'ao makes a historical generalization which accords with this theoretic view, stating that after periods of up-heaval and war the slavery system in China suddenly flourished because land was extensive and the population depleted. The "tyrannical gentry" then appropriated land and used slave labor to exploit it. He believes slave labor was useful in large- but not in small-scale farming.[2] It is interesting to note in this connection that

[1] Report of Emperor Hsüan's edict, CHS, 16 (introduction), 1b. Ch'en She (or Shen), SC, 48, 1a, and CHS, 31, 1a. Edict of Emperor Chao, CHS, 7, 2a. K'uang Heng, CHS, 81, 1a. Cf. HHS, 106, 6b, for a story of how Meng Ch'ang became a hired plowman.

Just before the Han period Luan Pu and P'eng Yüeh hired themselves out to serve a wine-shop keeper (5). CHS, 40, 12b, relates how hired laborers working for Chou Ya-fu, apparently building his father's tomb, became bitter at him for not paying them and exposed his purchase of armor from the arsenal. CHS, 57A, 1b, tells of Ssu-ma Hsiang-ju putting on "calf-nose" drawers and washing utensils in the market, with hired or indentured laborers. Lao Kan ("The system of slavery during the two Han dynasties," pp. 10–11) has an interesting discussion of hired and indentured labor, but many of the references he cites are characteristi-cally vague concerning type of occupation. Ma Ch'eng-feng (op. cit., pp. 285–286) discusses hired farm labor but most of his citations do not specify agricultural work.

The reason for using the expression "indentured labor" for *yung* 傭 and especially for *yung-pao* 保 is that there is a persistent sense of enslavement about these terms, but at the same time a distinct difference between *nu* and *yung* which is well covered by the term "indenture." Cf. the commentary to the passage about Ssu-ma Hsiang-ju in SC, 117, 1b, which tells that in southern regions *pao-yung* is a demeaning appellation for slaves (quoting the *Fang yen*, ch. 3, 1a). The term is frequently treated under the general category of slaves, in Chinese encyclopaedias. Cf. *Yüan chien lei han*, ch. 258 (*jen pu* 17); and *Wen hsien t'ung k'ao*, ch. 3.

[2] Liang Ch'i-ch'ao, op. cit., p. 551. He advances this generalization to explain the decline of slavery during the Manchu dynasty when a great increase in popula-tion made slavery unnecessary in agriculture.

One of the best-documented instances of slaves used in farming is in the Northern Wei dynasty (A.D. 386–534) when exactly these conditions existed. After several centuries of civil and foreign war, southward migration, famine, and

the only Former Han reference to large-scale farming with slave labor dates from 202 B.C. when the population was greatly reduced and arable land was extensive (8).

PROBABLE UNIMPORTANCE OF SLAVES IN AGRICULTURE

In summary, slaves were indeed used in farming, but a real obscurity surrounds the connection between landlordism and large-scale slave-owning. A functional connection, in the sense that numerous slaves were used to cultivate extensive land, cannot be proved, and scrutiny of each reference makes it appear dubious. Landlordism and large-scale slave-owning may have been individual aspects of wealth, land being the outstanding form of investment (producing more wealth), while slaves were the most conspicuous form of expenditure for displaying wealth.

Han China was a broad country with many different types of terrain and climate favoring different crops and agricultural systems. Methods of using land must have varied from region to region as they do today. Furthermore, there is a time-span of more than two centuries, with a continuous development away from pre-Ch'in feudalism, a slow development in agricultural techniques, and in general a steady growth in population from scarcity to superabundance. Some regions were progressive, while others doubtless clung tenaciously to serfdom or to antiquated methods in agricultural economy. This means that generalizing for the whole country and the entire period is dangerous.

Even if we assume that some big landlords used most of their slaves in agriculture and that slaves were frequently used in a supplementary way, there arises another question. What was the probable relative importance of slave labor as against that of free labor in

pestilence, there were idle farm lands and a reduced population in north China. A type of serfdom had previously grown up in which weaker families took refuge under the protection of the strong, and also escaped government taxation and corvée duty by deeding their land over to their protectors while reserving the use of it. There had been several attempts to redistribute land, and especially to grant idle land to the poor. Among the redistribution laws of Emperor Wen (A.D. 471–499) there are several references to male slaves who have the duty of plowing, and owners were allowed extra land in proportion to the number of their agricultural slaves. The basic texts are in the *Wei shu*, or *History of the (Northern or Latter) Wei dynasty*, ch. 110 ("Treatise on Economics"), 3a–4a, under the years 485 and 486; also biographies of Li An-shih and Li Chung, ch. 53, 4b–5a, and 6b. Cf. also Ch'eng Shu-te, *Chiu ch'ao lü k'ao*, ch. 5 ("Hou Wei lü k'ao"), pp. 450 and 460; Shen Chia-pen, *Li-tai hsing fa k'ao*, "Fen k'ao," ch. 15, 12a; Ch'en Po-yin, op. cit., pp. 91 ff.; and especially Wan Kwoh-ting, op. cit., pp. 163 ff.

Perhaps this is the period referred to by Dubs ("Wang Mang and his economic reforms," p. 247) when he boldly asserts that "except for one brief interval in later times, slavery has never been used for agricultural work [in China]."(!)

agricultural production?   Much too little is known about the management of land in Former Han times to allow a categorical pronouncement, but slave labor seems to have been relatively unimportant.   In the first place, slaves apparently constituted a small part of the total population—probably well under 5 and not even 1 per cent.   An important proportion of all slaves was employed most of the time in non-productive activities.   On the other hand, most of the free population, the great peasant group, worked at farming.   What proportion owned the land it worked and what proportion were tenants or hired laborers cannot possibly be estimated; but considering only the land owned for investment, the tenant system would seem to have been most prevalent.   If there was any form of plantation system, cheap free labor, of which there was an abundance, must have been an important alternative to slave labor.

Use of Slaves in Manufactures and Commerce

I have assumed that slave and free labor competed in production for profit.   Production of certain goods for the owner's use was, however, a distinct function of slaves.   Females doubtless spun, wove and dyed cloth, made clothes and bedding, and embroidered. Men made everyday utensils, tools, and furniture, and performed all sorts of duties required in nearly self-sufficient households.   The degree of specialization was probably in direct proportion to the number of slaves owned by a single master.   Wang Pao specified in his purchase contract many types of handicraft and processing work for his lone slave.   Aside from the long list of products the slave was expected to supply by his work in garden, field, orchard, barnyard and fishpond, and from hunting and fishing. the luckless Pien-liao was supposed to weave shoes, hew out cart shafts, make sacrificial stands, benches, wooden shoes, and food pans, whittle writing tablets, gather wood, burn charcoal, make rope, and weave mats (83).   Most of the products of his toil were for household consumption.   Only knives and bows are mentioned as articles for sale, but Wang Pao could not have known when he made the contract that the slave would be adept at this sort of work.   A casual reference speaks of young Tou Kuang-kuo, who was employed by his owner as a charcoal burner, but leaves us uninformed whether the rest of the gang, numbering about a hundred, were slaves or hired free laborers (14).

Did manufacturers train slaves in processing and handicraft, and did merchants use them as agents in commerce?   The obvious place to seek an answer to these questions would appear to be the chapters on rich merchants in the *Shih chi* and *Ch'ien Han shu*.[1] Both chapters have sections describing general economic conditions in late Chou and Former Han times, with special reference to manufacture and trade. Together they also contain biographies or brief notices of forty-one individuals who became wealthy from industry or commerce. It seems significant, therefore, that the general discussions do not mention slaves as wealth producers, though they do speak of slaves—that is, "youths"—once as articles of commerce, and once in a list of commodities annually "consumed" in an average trade center of the period.[2] Slaves are mentioned with only three of the forty-one manufacturers and merchants, and of these only Tiao Chien is said to have used his slaves as producers of wealth.[3]

Rather indefinite in time, this case may indeed refer to the end of the Chou rather than to the Han period. Opening with the statement that in Ch'i it was customary to look down upon male slave captives, the biography reports that Tiao Chien *alone* appreciated and valued them. He used them for profits to be had in fishing and salt-refining, and as resident and traveling merchants, gave them great freedom, and entrusted them the more when they were able to associate intimately with generals and high officials. By their help he finally became very rich (*17*).

Salt and iron were basic commodities in Han times. Salt-refining, and mining and smelting of iron became government monopolies in 119 B.C. Before that time business men made large fortunes in those fields. Ch'i in Shantung was famous for the production of salt, and Tiao Chien employed slaves in that work.

---

[1] Ch. 129 and 91 respectively. For an analysis of the structure and contents of these monographs, and a discussion of their differences, cf. Nancy Lee Swann, "A woman among the rich merchants . . . ," JAOS, vol. 54, 1934, pp. 186–193.

[2] Cf. SC, 129, 7a, and document *53*. The list mentions "a thousand fingers of 'youths.'" "Fingers" as a numerical classifier is explained by the commentator Meng K'ang (ca. A.D. 180–260) thus: "*T'ung* are male and female slaves. In early times there were no unemployed [slaves]: all had manual duties. Manual duties require the fingers, wherefore it speaks of fingers in contradistinction to the hoofs and horns of horses and cattle." Yen Shih-ku adds: "The fingers refer to those who are skilful . . . ." It is only in the explanation of the commentators that we have a suggestion of the use of slaves in production of goods. Those modern Chinese students of Han slavery who emphasize its economic importance quote this passage as important proof. Another evidence, which is only inferential, is the T'ang dynasty commentator's statement that in Emperor Wu's day slaves of merchants were taxed double (*127*, footnote 1).

[3] The other cases are Pai Kuei, a dealer in grain, silk, and lacquer, living early in the fourth century B.C., who "shared misery and happiness with the youth-servants he employed"; and the Cho family, which became rich to the extent of possessing 800 youths (*2*).

There is no mention of private slave labor in mining and smelting. The only document even hinting at it is the biography of the Cho family, rich iron-smelters of Chao state, deported after 228 B.C. to Szechwan. There the family again took up smelting at "iron mountain," and traded with regions to the south. It became so rich that it possessed 800 "youths" and the pleasures of fields, ponds, and hunting preserves comparable to those of a prince (2). This passage is frequently cited as proof that slaves were used in mining and metallurgy, but its structure shows clearly that the author listed "youths" and other items as measures of the profits *derived* from smelting and trade; that is, the Cho family became so wealthy that it could afford to own a magnificent establishment. While it may be justifiable to assume that a great metallurgist and merchant owning numerous "youths" would employ many of them in his business—one cannot imagine hundreds of "youths" only for display —this is nothing more than a deduction unsupported by proof.

No other family which made its fortune out of salt and iron is mentioned as a slave owner. The *Discourses on salt and iron* does not mention slaves used in either field, and one passage describing conditions before the government monopoly speaks definitely of migrant plebeian labor:

> Formerly the overbearing and powerful great families, obtaining control of the profits of mountains and seas, mined iron at Shih-ku and smelted it, and evaporated salt. A single family would assemble a multitude, sometimes to the extent of a thousand or more men, most of them dispersed and migrant plebeians who had gone far from their native hamlets, abandoning the tombs [of their ancestors]. Attaching themselves to the great families, they assembled in the midst of deep mountains and barren marshes . . . .[1]

Only one other document in the *Ch'ien Han shu* reports private slaves used in large numbers to produce goods for profit. Dating near the middle of the Former Han period, it tells how Chang An-shih, a self-made man and close friend of Emperor Hsüan, became rich. He enjoyed the income from a marquisate of 10,000 households, "yet he dressed himself in coarse black cloth, and his wife herself spun and wove. His seven hundred household youths were all skilled in manufacturing; he produced goods within [his household] and saved up even the minutest things; wherefore he was able to produce commodities. He was richer than General-in-Chief [Ho] Kuang." (71.) Early literature on the Former Han period quotes many complaints against noblemen and officials—the outstanding

---

[1] *Yen t'ieh lun*, ch. 1, sec. 6, trans. also by Gale, op. cit., p. 35. Shih-ku was in Anhwei province.

slave-owning groups—for competing in business with commoners, but this is the only report of a nobleman's using his slaves in manufacturing. The tone of the historian is rather of admiration than censure. Was the fact that he used his slaves profitably the key to his wealth, or was it because he was so miserly? The number is remarkably large for Former Han times. The word *t'ung*, purposely translated by the indefinite term "youths," makes it allowable to suppose that many of his workers were children hired or indentured to him by their parents. Seven hundred slaves would constitute a huge investment if there were plenty of cheap child labor available. All the "youths" may, however, have been slaves; it is only a supposition that they were not.

In spite of qualifications concerning Tiao Chien and Chang An-shih, the main point must not be missed. Each document indicates that a business man was successful in using slave labor for profit. Where one was successful others would surely have followed. What cannot be determined is how widespread the following was, or what factors in manufacturing techniques and in the free labor market favored or hindered the use of slaves in production for profit.

As to merchandising, Wang Pao planned to intrust his slave with business duties involving extensive travel. Most of his commercial work, however, was rather petty; the slave would be classed as an itinerant peddler (*83*). Such work was probably not uncommon for slaves who were enterprising and trustworthy, but is not very important in the general economic picture.

Tiao Chien's use of slaves as resident and traveling merchants was of a different order. He allowed them great freedom of movement; some were important enough to associate with generals or be intimate with administrators of commanderies or chancellors of kingdoms, and "by their help he became [rich to the extent of] several thousand myriad [cash]." Therefore they preferred being his slaves to the chance of freedom and noble rank. "Which meant," says the writer, "that he could cause fierce male slaves [to feel] self-satisfied while exhausting their strength." (*17*.)

Several passages previously cited have indicated that both private and public slaves had money of their own. One woman was able to ransom herself; Tung Hsien's slaves received rich money gifts from Emperor Ai and from officials; Ho Kuang's confidential adviser helped him run his affairs and was certainly placed strategically to exact bribes. Wang Pao wrote into his semi-humorous purchase contract, which was disciplinary in intent, the stipulation that the unruly Pien-liao could have no private savings except gifts from the master or guests (*83*). These facts indicate that slaves of the period could own peculium, even though we are left ignorant about the legal aspects of such ownership.

This raises interesting questions. Did masters train slaves in crafts and professions, and hire them out to work for others? Did owners, especially noblemen and officials who were not supposed to indulge in private business, set some of their slaves up in money-making enterprises? In other words, were slaves used in China during the two centuries before our era in the way they were so extensively used in Greece and Rome at precisely the same time? Were slaves a form of capital investment, and were some masters merely collectors of rent on or from their slaves? Han literature is silent on these points. Yet the way Tiao Chien is reported to have used his slaves suggests a fairly sophisticated employment of them which was certainly in advance of his contemporaries at the very beginning of the Han period, or perhaps even earlier. It may be that the writer from whom Ssu-ma Ch'ien copied this passage was describing something he did not understand, something very like the system here in question. But this is merely inference.

To conclude, as some modern Chinese writers do, that slaves were extensively used in manufactures and commerce goes far beyond the evidence of the few extant documents scattered over several centuries. On the other hand, absence of evidence is no proof that slaves were unimportant in those fields. There may have been innumerable small workshops, each employing a few skilled slaves. Some masters may have used their slaves almost exclusively to make and sell goods, and if so, the slaves were naturally important to them economically. We happen to know of only two who did. It is the extra factor of abundant and cheap free labor during at least the second half of the period, which—by the same process of reasoning used in reference to agriculture—points to the conclusion that private slaves were relatively unimportant in the industry and trade of the nation as a whole.

X. FUNCTIONS OF GOVERNMENT SLAVES

The government owned "ten myriad and more" male and female slaves toward the close of the Former Han period. Since there were few attempts during the dynasty to diminish numbers by manumissions of large groups, they were apparently considered usefully employed in spite of Kung Yü's opposite opinion. No Han writer gives a list of the duties of government slaves, and the random character of available documents precludes a clear picture of them. In this dilemma we are thrown back upon oblique approaches to the question of the general functions of government slaves. One method is to generalize from similarities with the more fully documented duties of private slaves, bearing in mind, however, certain basic differences. Another is to establish a hypothesis about the types of work the Han government would have been most likely to demand of its slaves, and then attempt to test the hypothesis by the scattered documents available.

Differences between government and private ownership, and between government and private slaves, suggest certain differences in employment. In the first place, who owned government slaves? The people who ruled and administered the state under a body of laws and traditions did not individually own the government property they managed. Even the Emperor, as head of the state, did not personally own all government slaves. The slaves, on the other hand, were true government property within whatever definition, actual or implied, the government itself established and society accepted.

Slaves assigned to various bureaus presumably long outlasted their chief officials. When performing government work they were part of the government in the same sense that petty officers were. Bureau chiefs were responsible for the well-being of slaves just as they were for the good management of other government property (*78*). Prices at which slaves were sold from their bureaus were an important concern, as shown by the protest of one bureau chief against the cheap price paid for eight of his girls (*116*). Direction of bureau slaves was more an aspect of stewardship than ownership. Administrators may have been held accountable for definite quotas of work by their slaves.

A proportion of all government slaves differed from private ones in their mode of acquisition. Families of criminals, and possibly some criminals themselves, were forced into government slavery.

Other slaves were confiscated from law-breaking private owners. Some may have been prisoners of war. The members of these groups were not hand-picked for special jobs, but had to be given work appropriate to their crimes, suitable to their abilities, or conforming to the requirements of close guarding, in cases when that was necessary.

The enormous difference between the number of government slaves and those of any private owner is also important. Although divided into groups for administrative purposes, government slaves often worked in larger aggregations than private ones, and certain officials controlled many more than did any private owner. This suggests less personal treatment and less freedom of action, also more specialization among groups and individuals, than among private slaves. Only a small proportion of all government slaves was needed for display and entertainment; none as instruments of power. Finally, the government employed several other numerous groups: the bureaucracy, the standing army, and convicts.

In order to get a clearer picture of particular fields of slave work, as distinguished from governmental work of non-slave groups, there must be first a list of government labor-consuming enterprises; second, an examination of the non-slave labor the government commanded; and third, an analysis of the characteristics of government slaves to find what they could do best.

Government Enterprises and Labor Supply

Public works included building dams and repairing dikes, principally along the Yellow River; digging transportation and irrigation canals; making and keeping up important roads and post stations; and erecting frontier fortifications and extending the Great Wall. Together, the imperial and national governments owned vast areas of the land, including forests, game preserves, cemeteries, horse ranches, waste land and marshes, and an abundance of farm land. All of this had to be tended, and much of it was made to produce income for the imperial and national treasuries. Collecting taxes, especially bulky grain and other produce taxes, transporting and storing them, and distributing them to the army, to workers, and to government bureaus for salaries all involved heavy labor, together with extensive clerical work. During most of the dynasty the government monopolized salt-refining, mining and smelting of iron, and minting, employing thousands and myriads of workers. There was always construction and repair work on palaces, residencies, bureaus, granaries, barracks, imperial tombs, and ancestral temples. Arsenals turned out weapons for the armies; imperial ateliers, working in bronze, iron, wood, lacquer, pottery, and jade, made furniture, utensils, and mortuary objects, while special bureaus spun, wove, dyed, and embroidered silks of all descriptions, and fabricated garments. Managing all these enterprises and attending the multifarious other duties of administration were dozens of departments, scores of bureaus, and innumerable local offices connected with the imperial court, the central government, the capital district, kingdoms, commanderies, and prefectures. They were staffed with thousands of petty officials, clerks, and servants. The number in the bureaucracy, presumably during the reign of Emperor Ai, is given as 130,285, counting assistant clerks and up.[1]

Besides salaried officials, hired workmen, and slaves, the government commanded an inexhaustible supply of forced labor, corvée and convict. Every male commoner between the ages of 20 (or 23) and 56 years was liable to one month of labor service a year, unless he was a member of some select exempted group. Corvée labor was usually directed by local governments for local enterprises, but sometimes large levies were sent away from home for special tasks. Types of work that happen to be listed are building city walls, repairing dikes, digging canals, erecting imperial tombs and government buildings, transporting military supplies, and toiling in government salt refineries and iron mines. Exemption from service could be arranged by paying 2,000 cash, ostensibly used to hire a substitute. The amount of corvée labor assembled for certain projects is indicated by the following reports: 146,000 men and women (145,000 two years later) levied for a month at a time from the region within 600 *li* of the capital to build the city wall of Ch'ang-an during the reign of Emperor Hui; 20,000 men to build the tomb of Emperor Chao's mother in 87 B.C.; and 50,000 to dig and cover an imperial tomb during the reign of Emperor Ai. Then there were myriads of plebeian conscripts employed on large conservancy and irrigation works.[2]

---

[1] The primary source for information on government organization is CHS, 19A, introduction (abstracted in MH, vol. II, pp. 513–533); but important materials are scattered throughout the CHS; cf. *Hsi Han hui yao*, ch. 31–43, covering 162 pages in the Commercial Press one volume edition. Chü Ch'ing-yüan ("Han tai ti kuan-fu kung-yeh [Government industry in the Han period]," *Shih Huo*, vol. 1, No. 1, Dec. 1, 1934, pp. 1–5) assembles historical texts and inscriptions dealing with various government factories.

[2] References to corvée labor are assembled in the *Hsi Han hui yao*, ch. 47. On numbers employed, cf. CHS, 2, 2a (192 B.C.) and 2b (190 B.C.); 97A, 7b (87 B.C.); 11, 2b (5 B.C.). On conservancy and irrigation cf. CHS, 29, *passim;* MH, vol. III, pp. 520–537.

The number of convicts was constantly large enough so that the government relied on them to accomplish many projects entailing heavy gang labor. Many convicts served sentences varying from one to five years only; this, at least, was the codified term. Aside from criminals banished to the frontiers and those used as soldiers and commissaries, great numbers toiled on imperial tombs, walls, roads, and dikes. Evidence that criminals worked on tombs is revealed by the amnesties in 146, 57, and 20 B.C., which pardoned them. In 192 B.C., 20,000 "criminals and servitors" sent from the states of kings and marquises worked with corvée laborers to build the city wall of Ch'ang-an, and in 75 B.C. convicts, mobilized in various commanderies, built walls in Manchuria and Korea. Before 32 B.C. convicts in the imperial prison at Shang-lin, the largest imperial park, cared for game and worked on palaces and lodges. Kung Yü, in a memorial dated 44 B.C., speaks of more than a hundred thousand people, including convicts, who were mining copper and iron from the mountains, while the *Discourses on salt and iron*, of 81 B.C., mentions convicts who were employed in casting iron implements in the government monopoly.[1]

Convicts (*t'u*) started three serious revolts during the reign of Emperor Ch'eng. During 22 B.C. a convict named Shen T'u-sheng led in revolt 180 of his fellows working in the Iron Bureau at Ying-ch'uan near present Kaifeng, Honan. They killed their officials, stole arsenal weapons, and crossed through nine prefectures before being overcome. Ch'eng Kung and some sixty other "shackled men" attacked the government officers of Kuang-han in Szechwan, freed convicts, and stole weapons from the arsenal in 18 B.C. By the next winter they had ravaged four prefectures and assembled "a myriad" of followers. Finally, Chao Hu with an army of 30,000 from two commanderies defeated them, and for this was advanced and richly rewarded. Su Ling, a convict working in another Iron Bureau at Shan-yang, near present Chinhsiang in Shantung, and 228 of his fellows attacked and killed the officials of the bureau in

---

[1] Amnesties of convicts: CHS, 5, 3b; 8, 8b; and 10, 4b, respectively. Wall-building: CHS, 2, 2b; and 7, 4b. On roads and dikes see Lao Kan ("The system of slavery during the two Han dynasties," p. 8), citing HHS and commentaries to the *Chou-li*. CHS, 29, on "Rivers and Canals," seems only to mention conscripted labor and "soldiers." In 32 B.C. the prison in Shang-lin was abolished; cf. CHS, 10, 1b. There Yen Shih-ku quotes the *Han chiu i* as saying: "The imperial prison at Shang-lin managed and directed work [connected with] birds and beasts, and palaces and lodges within the park . . . ." The prisoners must have done all sorts of work on grounds and buildings. Kung Yü's memorial: CHS, 72, 6b. The number he mentions refers to officials, conscripts, and convicts, but we do not know how many there were of each. *Yen t'ieh lun*, ch. 1, sec. 6, trans. by Esson M. Gale, *Discourses on salt and iron*, p. 34.

14 B.C. Stealing weapons from the arsenal, they traversed nineteen kingdoms and commanderies and succeeded in killing a commandery administrator and a chief commandant. Su Ling was finally killed and the revolt quelled by Yen Hsin, Administrator of Ju-nan, who also was richly rewarded and advanced.[1]

Two observations need to be made before analyzing the characteristics of government slaves which may have determined the types of work they did in contradistinction to the work of convicts, conscripted plebeians, hired laborers, and salaried officials. First, any list of government works is only a catalogue of labor-consuming enterprises, giving no impression of the variety of occupations each enterprise entailed. For example, a statement in the chapter on rivers and canals that several myriad workers constructed a certain canal does not indicate the complexity of work involved. Naturally, most of the men would have been diggers and dirt carriers —gang laborers conscripted from neighboring commanderies and prefectures. But thousands of workers would have needed to be organized, with straw-bosses and foremen, "timekeepers," tool-checkers, clerks, recorders, police, and commissaries. It takes engineers, surveyors, cartographers, masons, and carpenters to plan and put through a canal, to build sluice gates and bridges. Likewise, workers in an Iron Bureau, whether convicts, conscripts, slaves, hired workmen, or officials, must have done all sorts of specific jobs: digging and reinforcing shafts and tunnels, mining, sifting, grading and transporting ore, burning charcoal, tending furnaces, smelting, designing products and making molds, casting, finishing, polishing, and so forth, almost without end. As in any large factory, office-workers and executives must have managed the plant, made contracts and planned work. Historical texts do not report details of that sort, and there are no archival "rubbish heaps," such as Sir Aurel Stein and others have found in abandoned guard stations of Chinese Turkestan, to fill the gaps in our knowledge. Yet government

---

[1] Revolt of 22 B.C.: CHS, 10, 4a. Revolt of 18 B.C.: CHS, 10, 5a; 27A, 8b; and 83, 3a (biography of Hsüeh Hsüan). The second reference speaks of the original attackers as being "men with iron collars," which is explained by Yen Shih-ku as meaning convicts wearing iron collars. Revolt of 14 B.C.: CHS, 10, 6a; 27A, 8b–9a; and 67, 4b (biography of Mei Fu). The second reference says they traversed more than *forty* kingdoms and commanderies. Ma Fei-pai ("Source material on the economic history of Ch'in and Han," pt. 6, "The slavery system," pp. 396–397) treats these events as slave revolts, and compares them to the Spartacus rebellion. He views them as indications of a sharpening of the "class struggle." Wu Po-lun ("An investigation of slavery in the Western Han," p. 285) also calls them slave revolts, and thinks many slaves must have participated in the revolution of the "Red Eyebrows" and other societies during Wang Mang's reign. Both authors class convicts as slaves by definition.

bureaus and works projects must always be visualized as organic enterprises in which all kinds of people worked at all kinds of jobs.

The second observation is that such terms as convict, slave, commoner, and official designate legal status. Theoretically they are mutually exclusive terms to classify units of the total population according to a single system of reference. They do not describe the components of the groups any more precisely than do such terms as "alien," "war veteran," or "relief-worker," which emphasize one characteristic to the exclusion of all others. But convicts were people. They came from all sorts of backgrounds, possessed different temperaments and skills, and varied in age. The principal thing they had in common was a criminal sentence, though their individual crimes ranged over the entire penal code. Conscripted commoners differed among themselves as widely as do the army conscripts of a modern nation at war. Likewise, government slaves were of all sorts: male and female, young and old; intelligent, attractive, and ambitious, or dull and coarse. They had been enslaved in different fashions; some were educated or trained in crafts, while others were fit only for toil and sweat.

Thus, when we read of convicts working on an imperial tomb, conscripted commoners building a wall, or slaves serving on frontier ranches, we deal with compound abstractions. We only know the legal status of the workers and the general nature of the work. Convicts did not do one kind of work only, slaves another, and conscripts a third; nor did Iron Bureaus or the Shang-lin park employ one or another status-group exclusively.

HYPOTHETICAL SPHERES OF GOVERNMENT SLAVE WORK

The government could draw upon an inexhaustible supply of corvée labor, and thousands of slaves and convicts, as well as hired laborers and salaried officials. It must have effected an intelligent distribution of functions not only according to individual abilities, but also according to characteristics which members of various groups had in common because they were members of those groups. This assumes that certain characteristics were shared by enough members of each group so that a natural correlation existed between types of work to be done and groups of workers available. In other words, we suggest the working hypothesis that slaves resembled each other in certain fundamental respects as slaves, and differed from conscripts and convicts; further, that these characteristics may have determined to a considerable degree the way in which slaves were used by the government. This shifts emphasis from individual differences to group characteristics.

Slaves served for life. Individuals or groups might be freed or transferred to private owners, but such events were not predictable, nor were they essential characteristics of slavery. Plebeians and convicts, on the other hand, served respectively for intermittent brief periods and for terms less than six years. Thus, slaves would be most useful in work where long experience was valuable. In this respect they were like hired workers or salaried officials. Many government slaves were born into that status or became slaves as children, whereas conscripted plebeians and convicts were usually adults. Young slaves could be trained as entertainers or for highly skilled crafts, or could be educated for clerical or servants' work. The government could plan their careers earlier than those of individuals in any other group, and could retain them as long as it wished.

Finally, government slaves appear to have been a docile group. This is a generalization only more or less true. Many of them knew no other life, and in slavery they had the security of regular food, clothing, and shelter. In these respects their life was better than that of "average" commoners. Some, of course, were unruly; many were held under compulsion. Those who were docile were suited to minor positions of trust and individual jobs without close supervision. Convicts were just the opposite. All guilty of crimes and serving sentences under compulsion, but used to plebeian or official life, many if not most of them had to be closely watched. To make escape difficult they were often fettered with iron collars, dressed in russet clothes, and had their heads shaven. Most convicts were probably worked in gangs under armed guards. There are reports of convict revolts; there is no record of a revolt of government slaves.

From these considerations it seems likely that government slaves would have been employed primarily in service capacities and in skilled work, though certainly a proportion of them, being unskilled or untrustworthy, worked in labor gangs. If we bear in mind that slaves differed as individuals, and recognize that details of work in various bureaus or government projects are not revealed, do the documents support the hypothesis that government slaves were used chiefly in positions of trust as servants or skilled workers?

SERVICE DUTIES OF GOVERNMENT SLAVES

Two general criticisms of government slaves indicate that much of their work was not visibly productive. The *Discourses on salt and iron*, reporting a great debate on state policy in 81 B.C., attributes the following remarks to the Worthies, who opposed much of the government's economic activity:

> Now the government accumulates numerous male and female slaves who sit and are stipended with clothes and food. Privately they create estates and make evil profits. Their strength and labor are not used up [so that] the government loses the reality [of the slaves]. Some of the people do not have in store a peck or a basket [of grain, yet] government male slaves accumulate a hundred [catties] of gold. From dawn to dusk the common people are not free from work, [yet] male and female slaves idle about with folded hands [60].

Kung Yü made a very similar criticism in 44 B.C. when suggesting various methods of reducing government expenses:

> The ten myriad and more male and female slaves of the various government bureaus loaf about without work, [while the government] taxes the good people to support them, at an annual expense of five or six hundred million [cash]. It would be proper to dismiss them and make them commoners, and feed them from the granaries; and command them to take the place of the garrison soldiers east of the [Han-ku] Pass, or to mount the guard towers and Barrier on the northern frontier and stand watch [89].

These quotations might describe petty government officials in any land at any time. Slaves appear as minor bureaucrats, indolent, regularly fed, sometimes indulging in graft; what modern Chinese would call "rats under the altar." These criticisms must have had a foundation in truth. How much better to put them on the dole, as Kung Yü suggested? In spite of his disparagement, however, the management of each palace and of every bureau required a great amount of routine servants' and clerical work. This is exactly the type of service that slaves of both sexes are mentioned as giving.

Work in the imperial palaces, which were simply grander private residences, must have been much like that described for domestic slaves. The official report of a judicial commission which investigated the infanticide of two sons of Emperor Ch'eng supplies an intimate and first-hand glimpse, based upon testimony given by palace officials, eunuchs, and female slaves. The young slave girl Ts'ao Kung was a student clerk in the Middle Palace, competent in reciting poetry, which she taught the Empress. In this work she had evidently been educated from childhood. After bearing a son from a casual intimacy with Emperor Ch'eng, she was confined to prison in the Concubines' Quarter and supplied with six female slaves to attend her needs. The child was taken from her, but before being killed was turned over to another slave woman chosen as its wet-nurse. Yü K'o-tzu, Wang P'ien, and Tsang Chien were three other female slaves, personal attendants (*yü-che*) to the perfidious favorite *née* Chao. Posted in her rooms to be on hand for errand-running and all sorts of little tasks, they were able to overhear several damaging and highly revealing conversations between their mistress and Emperor Ch'eng. They acted as messengers during the murder of Beauty Hsü's child (*107*).

Yen Shih-ku explains, in connection with the Empress *née* Chao, that "Palace Woman" was the name for government slave women who were servants in the forbidden parts of the palaces, and cites in substantiation the *Han chiu i* by Wei Hung of the first century A.D. He adds that Chao Fei-yen was called a Ch'ang-an Palace Woman to indicate that she lived in a palace there, rather than at the Kan-ch'üan or some other forbidden palace (*101*, and footnote 3). The government slave woman Tse worked in the Palace of Imperial Concubines during the reign of Emperor Hsüan, and the fact that she was middle-aged suggests that she did menial work (*80*).

Aside from such indirect historical testimony there is rich descriptive material about palace slaves in Wei Hung's *Han chiu i*, a book prepared specifically to record government practices of the Former Han period only a few decades after the fall of the dynasty. "Palace Women," says Wei Hung, "were selected from among palace female slaves in their eighth year or over. They waited upon [ladies of the palace from] the Empress on down." (*91*.) Again, "In the Inner Apartments [of the palace], Maidservants and Orderlies were all government female slaves selected in their eighth year or over. They were dressed in green and were called 'Palace Women.' They were not allowed to go outside the gates of the Inner Apartments .... Elderly ones ... taught Palace Women how to serve." (*92*.) As to the wet-nurses, such as the one who cared for Ts'ao Kung's child, Wei Hung says that they were women chosen from the government female slaves (*91*).

Male slaves were probably excluded from the inner parts of palaces, which were the domain of eunuchs, but they served in sections where government business was conducted. Thus we read of a high official waiting impatiently for an audience and ordering a senior government male slave to inquire about the state of the imperial progress. The slave returned from the audience hall and reported that the water-clock had risen to the fourteenth mark, and that the imperial progress had almost arrived (*A14*). Wei Hung relates that in the audience halls of the palaces, Eunuch's Assistants and Gentlemen's Assistants were all government male and female slaves who transmitted verbal messages in a loud, chanting voice. They were called "Executors." [1]

During great palace banquets the male and female slaves of the Grand Provisioner and the Bakery wore pale red silk garments down to the knee, and green turbans. Each of these departments employed three thousand slaves to keep the palace supplied with food and drink (94).

The green turban became a sort of insigne for more important male slaves, both government and private, and explanations of the nickname "green-head" afford the best descriptions of service duties in various government bureaus. "Government male slaves were selected to give [service] as writers and accountants. Those of [the rank of] Attaché and below were 'green-heads,' [wearing] blue-green turbans. They were given to the 'hundred' government bureaus to assist [officials] and escort them into the halls of the palace." (92.) The Ch'ien Han shu animates for us Wei Hung's later statement by describing how Ho Kuang's protégé, Imperial Household Grandee Wang Chung-weng, bustled importantly in and out of the palace attended by "green-heads" and "hut-dwellers." (A12.) When he descended from his carriage and hastened up to a gate the repeated shouting of his name from one attendant to the next echoed most impressively.

In the residency of the Chancellor, government male and female slaves kept track of time by the water-clock, and shouted the hours from one to the next in order to keep the daily schedule running smoothly. They beat the drum that summoned officials to early morning court at the residency. Certain of their number had charge of the small gate through which officials came to report individual business to the Chancellor. When officials were first appointed they became acquainted with these gate slaves, so that when they came again and knocked for admission they could be identified (90).

Each of the numerous government bureaus apparently had its corps of slaves of both sexes to work as attendants, servants, and clerks. When the Colonel over the Retainers was reduced in authority and his bureau made into an inspectorate, the government

---

[1] 92. An unidentified commentary, perhaps by Wei Hung himself, adds that others swept and kept the palaces tidy (ibid., footnote 6). The "Treatise on the Bureaucracy" in the Hou Han shu (ch. 36, 3a), listing a eunuch in charge of the Jung-hsiang, has an author's commentary that this eunuch had charge of government female slaves and maidservants. The same source says the Chief of the Yü-fu (Imperial Storehouse?) had charge of government female slaves who made, repaired, and washed clothes for the palaces.

took twelve hundred convicts and male slaves from bureaus in the capital city and attached them to the inspectorate (*95*). Almost any office would seem a more likely place than the Bureau of the Chief of Palace Police for female slaves to work! They must have been servants, and since the Empress Dowager wanted some of them they were surely efficient or attractive (*116*).

As a diplomatic measure the government decided in 64 B.C. to send a Chinese princess to marry the Heir-apparent of the Wu-sun Kingdom, in Central Asia. As the first step in preparing for this embassy, Emperor Hsüan ordered more than a hundred serving attendants (*shih-yü*) belonging to the government to be lodged in Shang-lin park to study the Wu-sun language (*79*). These serving attendants were rather definitely slave girls, going to live in virtual exile as servants and companions of the princess. Introductory training in the Wu-sun language would therefore have been indispensable.

Most of the government slaves described above were servants doing the work of maids, waiters, messengers, and doormen. Others were clerks and accountants. There was some system by which talented slaves or those with potentialities were selected for special service. In the palace, elder slave women coached the girls chosen to be servants of the Emperor's ladies. Education of those picked to be clerks and accountants must have begun when they were very young. Some slaves held responsible positions in charge of their lesser fellows. They understood the routine of the palace and how business should be transacted in each of the bureaus.

Thus, in the life of the court and in the functioning of government, slaves were important. Those working in or near the capital, and not specifically associated with criminals in hard labor, were apparently well treated. Nothing is known of their living conditions except that special quarters were erected for them in the administrative area probably not far from the palace (*A10*). That they were normally well fed and cared for is shown by the indictment of Tu Yen-nien, in which an investigator charged that the male and female slaves of his bureau were in want of food and clothing. The charge was evidently trumped up,[1] but it indicates that such an accusation was a satisfactory basis for dismissing an unwanted official, and furthermore that treatment of slaves in a bureau was a proper subject for judicial investigation. Slaves in key positions probably had chances to earn a little "wine money" by doing special favors

[1] Cf. *78*, footnote 4.

for officials. Some undoubtedly grafted, just as the Worthies complained that they did.

Productive Employment of Government Slaves

Kung Yü and the Worthies portrayed government slaves as a useless extravagance, but critics of an institution do not give the entire picture. Other documents show conclusively that they did "productive" jobs which could never have been accomplished with conscript or criminal labor alone. Only hired or salaried workers could have competed.

One of these jobs was horse-tending. The Hsiung-nu prince Chin Jih-ti, enslaved at the age of fourteen, was set to work tending horses inside one of the palace areas under the supervision of eunuchs. As a groom he was very proficient (41). It was work exactly suited to a Hsiung-nu lad, raised from infancy to handle horses, and his assignment cannot have been an accident. Some of the thousands of male and female slaves confiscated between 119 and 113 B.C. were distributed to various parks to care for dogs, horses, birds and wild beasts (46). These slaves had belonged to private owners; presumably they knew how to care for estates and animals. Game-keeping may not seem very productive work; and the mention of dogs with horses gives the impression of imperial kennels and stables in hunting parks such as the Shang-lin. Yet we know from Wei Hung that slaves tended horses on a grand scale. According to the *Han chiu i* the Chief of Stud and his herdsmen had charge of thirty-six ranches distributed over the north and west frontiers where 30,000 government male and female slaves cared for 300,000 horses. After these horses had been assorted and trained they were turned over to various government stables. Innumerable cattle and sheep were also reared on the ranches for state sacrifices (93). Supplying mounts for the cavalry was an important enterprise throughout the Han period. Wei Hung's description is not dated, but we know that the Chief of Stud employed male and female slaves at least as early as 65 B.C., for it was in that year that Tu Yen-nien was dismissed because "most of the ranch horses had died, and the bureau's male and female slaves were in want of food and clothing." (78.)

Three of these passages mention female as well as male slaves engaged in ranching or similar enterprises. Wei Hung's inclusion of female slaves on distant ranches suggests that slaves were domiciled as families of horse-tenders. Now, it could hardly be said that ranching on distant frontiers was a suitable occupation for people who had to be closely guarded![1] Unlike the system of fenced pasture and stabled horses, ranching demands great freedom of movement for the workers. Ranch hands wanting to escape not only have plenty of opportunity but also can always pick out a fast mount for flight. These ranches, furthermore, were on the frontier, which was easily penetrated in spite of the Great Wall. If we assume that Wei Hung accurately described conditions with which he was familiar, then the Han government used an average of 800 slaves on its various frontier ranches, with a proportion of ten horses to each male and female slave. Interesting as horse-tending is as a type of productive activity, it is much more interesting as evidence about the nature of Han slavery, for it dramatically confirms the presumption that an important number of government slaves were trustworthy and satisfied with their lot.

The Shang-lin was a vast preserve near the capital which supplied quantities of game for the imperial table and contained seventy scattered hostels. Here the Emperor relaxed after a strenuous day's sport. Male and female slaves tended the game in this and other parks during Emperor Wu's day (46). The slaves at the Shang-lin, as well as poor plebeians rehabilitated there, collected deer manure. They must have sold it, for they paid five cash a day for the privilege. By the time of Emperor Yüan the accumulation of their payments had reached an enormous figure, and was used to finance an army fighting in Central Asia (47).

The Han government owned large amounts of farm land. Since slaves were successfully used in ranching and park-tending, were they employed in farming? Presumption that they were not comes from the report about the confiscation of "accumulated fortunes," adopted as an emergency measure to refill the depleted treasury in 119 B.C. During the next seven years the government

> ... acquired people's property reckoned by the hundred million [cash]; male and female slaves numbered by the thousand [even to] a myriad; fields, in large prefectures by the several hundred *ch'ing*, in small prefectures by the hundred and more *ch'ing;* and houses in proportion .... Then the accumulated fortunes were distributed among various bureaus, while the [Chief Commandant of] Public Lands, [the Treasurer of] the Privy Purse, the Chief of Stud, and the Grand [Minister of] Agriculture each established agricultural bureaus [whose officials] constantly went to commanderies and prefectures, continually confiscating fields and putting them into cultivation.

[1] According to the same *Han chiu i* the prison at Shang-lin had charge of palaces, lodges, and "birds and beasts." This, of course, refers to the work of the convicts in the prison, and it is possibly significant that horse-tending was not one of their listed duties (see p. 224, footnote).

If the government had normally used slaves to farm its land it would seem only natural for it to have placed some of its newly acquired ones on its new land. It did not. Rather,

> ... the confiscated male and female slaves were distributed among various parks ... and were given to various bureaus. The bureaus enlarged or miscellaneously established were numerous. The convicts and male and female slaves were a multitude, and were sent down the river to transport four million piculs [of grain].[1]

Indeed, there is no direct evidence that the government ever used its extensive lands and slaves together in farming. Such of its fields as were not given to found taxable yeoman families, were apparently rented to tenants by the share-crop system.[2]

The use of slaves to manufacture agricultural implements has a special interest. During the last years of Emperor Wu's reign the government tried to increase national production by improving techniques of farming. Commissary Commandant Chao Kuo, an expert on crop rotation, taught his methods on land belonging to various government bureaus at the capital. The Grand Minister of Agriculture "set skilled and clever male slaves with assistants to manufacture agricultural implements" of improved types especially adapted for plowing, planting, and hoeing. Administrators of commanderies and chancellors of kingdoms sent prefects, chiefs, san-lao, and "vigorous cultivators" to the capital where they received these implements, learned to use them, and studied crop rotation in the demonstration places. According to the plan, these students would spread a knowledge of new methods and specialized tools throughout their native districts. The result was that farmers in frontier colonies and in commanderies near the capital all took advantage of rotation of crops, and got increased yields by less labor.[3]

Rural officials and outstanding farmers were all to receive sample tools. Therefore many slaves must have been required to make a great number of sets. Those chosen to make the tools were known to be "skilled and clever." This can only mean that they

---

[1] Document 46 and notes. Ma Ch'eng-feng (An economic history of China, vol. 2, p. 250) uses this passage as initial proof that government slaves had no important place in the process of production. In this he goes a little too far. T'ao Hsi-sheng (An economic history of Western Han, p. 60), on the other hand, states categorically that these confiscated slaves were distributed to the Departments of the Privy Purse, Public Lands, and Agriculture to cultivate government land, which is not what the text says.

[2] Cf. p. 211, footnote 2.

[3] Document 57, and footnotes. Consult the whole passage, CHS, 24A, 7a–7b, for a more complete exposition of the reform than is given in the section translated.

were skilful in manufacturing iron or bronze objects. We know of thousands of slaves doing the skilled work of the Grand Provisioner and the Bakery (*94*), but there seems to be no historical confirmation of the deduction that the "skilled and clever" slaves in the present text normally worked in imperial ateliers, foundries, and arsenals. Inscriptions on Han bronzes and lacquers are often signed with the names of local bureau officials and even with the names of individual "workmen," but fail to tell whether the workmen were hired or slave. Historical references to various government workshops seldom mention the workers, and those which do generally fail to specify their status. Exceptions are the previously mentioned statement by Kung Yü about workers, including convicts mining copper and iron, the passage in the *Discourses on salt and iron* which mentions convicts casting iron implements, and reports of convicts revolting in Iron Bureaus. Yet we do not know whether their work was skilled or heavy labor.

Convicts and slaves are associated in several documents. During the preceding Ch'in dynasty, men born into slavery worked with convicts at Li Mountain probably erecting and extending the tombs of the Ch'in emperors (*3*). Only convict and corvée labor is mentioned for tomb-building during the Former Han dynasty. Whether this indicates a historical change, or is simply an accident of the texts, cannot be inferred.

The organization by which taxes collected in grain were transported to the capital was a cornerstone of imperial power, supplying provisions for the army and salaries for the bureaucracy. By 119 B.C. the supply of grain coming to the capital from the fertile granary of central Shensi and adjacent areas was totally inadequate. It could no longer support wars on the northern and northwestern frontiers, liberal rewards to victorious armies, subsidies to surrendered enemies, including some 40,000 followers of the King of Hunhsieh, relief of famine victims, and an expensive colonization scheme. Among the slaves confiscated during the next few years there must have been hundreds, perhaps thousands, unfit for menial work and tending animals. A "multitude" of convicts and slaves was sent down the Yellow River to transport an extra five million bushels of grain (annually?), and this "was enough." (*46*.) It was an emergency measure. Characteristically, we are left in the dark whether slaves continued to be so used thereafter.

Employment of slaves with convicts in the rough labor of transporting grain—which presumably included hauling it to barges, loading and unloading it, towing barges, etc.—does not invalidate the hypothesis that slaves were most useful in services and skilled labor. These were newly acquired slaves, mostly adults. There were doubtless always many slaves fit only for unskilled manual labor, just as there must have been convicts capable of doing skilled work in shops and factories. Equally significant in regard to the hypothesis is the fact that many of the slaves acquired during these years were sent to parks or distributed to "various bureaus," even when there was an emergency in the vital grain transport.

The remaining report of slaves doing productive work illustrates the importance of the background of enslavement. The myriad of counterfeiters and mutually implicated groups of families enslaved in A.D. 21 were sent to Ch'ang-an to work in the Bureau of Mint.[1] Occurring so near the end of the period under consideration, this event has a suggestive rather than an informational value. Wang Mang's dynasty was overthrown within two years, and those of the slaves who did not escape during the turmoil of founding the new dynasty were freed ten years later. These people were not only slaves, they were also convicted criminals. Forced into servitude against their will, they could not be trusted like government slaves of long standing, or even like confiscated private slaves. After arrest and trial they walked to the capital in chains or were transported in prison carts, and were so harshly treated that many died on the way. In their work they must have been heavily guarded. On the other hand, they were considered to be slaves and were called *nu-pei*. Unable to foresee the success of the revolution only two years later, the government probably expected to be able to use them the rest of their lives, and put them to work accordingly.

---

[1] Documents *131* and *132*. See also discussion in chapter on enslavement (pp. 76–79). The historian reports that those confiscated were "in the number of ten myriad," which includes women and children, but that "six or seven out of every ten died of the grief and suffering." Even if both these statements were true it is inconceivable that the Bureau of Mint could suddenly absorb thirty or forty thousand additional workers among whom were women and children. Probably the truth lies somewhere between; the number enslaved may be an exaggeration, and only those actually useful worked in the bureau.

XI. SYNTHESIS

During the Former Han period the percentage of China's population that was enslaved appears to have been greater than at any other time, and the slavery system seems to have reached its economic peak. Pre-Han data on real slavery are so scarce and fragmentary, and so indecisive as to create the impression of a weak and underdeveloped system, a situation to be expected in an economy based upon serfdom. This suggests that a considerable maturing of the institution occurred between the end of the third century B.C. and the beginning of the first century of our era, when, after two and a quarter centuries, China had made great strides in political, social, and economic development.

EVIDENCES OF HISTORICAL DEVELOPMENT

Except for the clear-cut phenomenon of legislation on slavery concentrated in the last half-century of the period there are actually very few decisive evidences of a maturing process, and trends are portrayed only in a shadowy way. Some of the early references to slaves suggest archaic methods of treatment which may have been abandoned as time passed. Early texts refer to pre-Han slavery as though enslavement to the government for crime were the primary form, and private slavery a later and secondary development. Datable associations of government slaves with convicts occur early in the period or in the previous Ch'in dynasty. Though private ownership was already well established at the beginning of the dynasty, the only reports of private slaves being dressed in the costume of convicts—shackles, coarse or russet clothes, and the shaven head—date from the first decade of the period (*8* and *12*). About twenty years later the noted scholar Chia Yi described the sale of slaves in markets and the dressing of them in fancy clothes as something novel (*16*). There is some evidence of maturing methods of selling, but no direct proof of increased kidnaping and debtor slavery as the dynasty progressed, although an increase may have occurred in connection with over-population and a lower standard of living among common people, both of which are well documented.

Public "viewing with alarm" shows that increase in numbers of slaves owned by individual masters was a distinct trend during the period. But the first protest does not appear until the dynasty was seventy years old (*34*). The first protest against large numbers

237

of government slaves is not reported until 81 B.C. (*60*), and the second, which actually reports the total number, comes in 44 B.C., after a century and a half of Han rule (*89*). In this connection it may be significant that the only edict for a general manumission was in 160 B.C., at a time when government slaves were fewer. Kung Yü's suggestion that Emperor Yüan free all government slaves in 44 B.C., when the total number was really great, came to nothing. These late protests against government slave-owning also indicate an increasing use of slaves in service capacities, understandably viewed as "loafing," but hardly applicable as a description of the gang labor of criminal slaves. Apparently hereditary bondsmen became more and more like permanent "government servants." Reports about private slaves toward the end of the dynasty emphasize their use for the conspicuous display of wealth (*97, 99, 105, 111*).

The sequence of protests and legislation against large-scale slave-owning is as follows:

Shortly after 140 B.C.—Tung Chung-shu protested against the way in which influential people multiplied the numbers of their slaves (*34*).

81 B.C.—The Worthies objected to the government's policy of "accumulating numerous slaves." (*60*.)

44 B.C.—Kung Yü suggested that the ten myriad or more government slaves be freed to reduce tax burdens (*89*).

13 B.C.—Emperor Ch'eng disapproved of the accumulation of slaves by the ruling class, and ordered appropriate officials gradually to prohibit such offenses (*105*).

7 B.C.—Ministers of Emperor Ai proposed restrictions on the numbers of adult slaves to be allowed to members of each class in society (*109* and *110*).

A.D. 3.—Wang Mang presented a memorial regulating the scale of slave-owning and other sumptuary matters (*121*).

The striking fact about this sequence is that all but one of the items occur before, or more than half a century after, the time when Chinese troops were extensively capturing prisoners of war on the various frontiers. This makes it appear that enslavement of captives was not practiced on such a scale that it greatly increased the slave population in the way that it did, for example, during the last two centuries of the Roman Republic. The only protest coming anywhere near the period of expansion by conquest was that lodged by the Worthies in 81 B.C., and the government slaves there described could not possibly have been to any extent non-Chinese.

All recorded restrictive legislation in regard to slave-owning is concentrated at the end of the dynasty. This indicates clearly that slavery had become a problem. The nature of the problem is not so clear. Ma Ch'eng-feng, who accepts the association of land and slaves in various texts as proof of slave labor in agriculture, but who does not believe that such labor was important on a national scale during most of the dynasty, deduces from the concentration of slavery legislation just before and during Wang Mang's reign that the problem had to do with agricultural slavery and a competition between slave-owning landlords and the free peasants. He believes, however, that escape of slaves during the "peasant uprisings" at the end of the dynasty, Emperor Kuang-wu's several manumissions of private slaves, depopulation, and the destruction of landed estates due to civil war, stopped the development just before it reached a crisis.[1]

My previous section on slaves in agriculture analyzed this legislation as presumptive evidence for that type of employment, but established no definite proof. There it was suggested that fields and slaves are frequently mentioned together because land was the principal source of wealth while slaves were the outstanding means of displaying wealth. This is not entirely convincing. It is somewhat more impressive when it is understood that many private slaves were used primarily for luxury purposes and were an expensive part of the princely establishments maintained by the upper classes. To run these establishments, and to feed unproductive domestic slaves, the owners laid heavier and heavier burdens on their tenants, secured larger and larger grants from the government, indulged in business competition, and grafted viciously. By restricting slave numbers, by fixing limits to the styles of houses, carriages, clothes, and furniture used by various ranks in society, as well as by specifying amounts of money that could be spent in celebrating births, weddings, and funerals, the government hoped to cut down competitive extravagance and upper-class living costs, which had to be paid ultimately by the economically depressed.

Even this explanation, which treats slaves as a symptom of economic decline, or at most as an indirect cause, does not dissolve the strong impression that slaves were indeed instruments of com-

---

[1] Ma Ch'eng-feng, *An economic history of China*, vol. 2, pp. 290–291. This argument runs counter to the theory of Liang Ch'i-ch'ao (see above, p. 214).

petition and therefore one of the factors producing the decline. Probably no single explanation of this concentrated legislation suffices. For example, the ascendancy of humanistic Confucian philosophy among statesmen after Emperor Wu's day bears upon the question. The cardinal point in regard to historical development is that legislation occurred or was proposed during the reigns of five successive rulers, Emperors Ch'eng, Ai, P'ing, Wang Mang, and Kuang-wu. Legislation before Wang Mang was concerned with reducing numbers individually owned. Wang Mang attempted to abolish slavery by forbidding sale and by changing the name, that is, the status of slaves (*122*). Later he levied a tax of 3,600 cash on each slave (*127*), but this may have been merely a revenue device which would have tended to discourage ownership only if enforced for several years. After nearly two decades of destructive civil war, which must have altered the entire problem of slave numbers, Emperor Kuang-wu introduced three humanitarian reforms: that people who killed slaves would not be allowed a reduction in punishment (*137*); that branded slaves would be freed; and that slaves who shot and wounded people would not be publicly executed (*138*). The remainder of the Latter Han dynasty has nothing to correspond with this phenomenon; indeed, there is nothing like it until the end of the Manchu dynasty, when slavery was already dying out.

Former Han Slavery Generalized

Chinese slavery was well developed in its general aspects during the Former Han period. It displayed most of the characteristics found in the system in other complex civilizations. The right of ownership, as shown by free sale of people already enslaved, was recognized by law during the entire period except for three years, A.D. 9-12. Slaves had a special status, both customary and legal, which made them inferior members of society, with restricted rights and definite disabilities.

Most of the important kinds of enslavement were practiced: self-sale, sale of women and children, debtor slavery, and probably rescue of exposed infants, as well as kidnaping, slave-raiding, and capture in war. Enslavement as punishment for crime was modified in accordance with the Chinese family system so that it primarily involved the relatives of major criminals who were themselves executed. Hereditary slavery, inheritance, manumission, government and private ownership, and foreign- and native-born slaves were all general phenomena. Slave-trading included government and private selling, markets, and possibly specialized dealers, import and probably export, and fluctuations in prices due to legislation and economic factors.

Slaves were employed in many different ways: in farming, food and handicraft industries, commerce, and perhaps in mining; as business managers, bodyguards, fighters, tomb watchers, servants, grooms, singers, dancers, and acrobats; in concubinage, luxury and display, and in reinforcing the master's power. Government bondsmen worked as servants, retainers, clerks, accountants, and petty bureaucrats; in skilled crafts, game-keeping, ranching, and to some extent in heavy gang labor.

On the other hand, Chinese slavery shows marked truncation in comparison with the institution in Greece from about 500 B.C. into Hellenistic times, and especially in comparison with Roman slavery in the period contemporary with the Former Han dynasty when analogies between the two civilizations in other respects abound. This appearance of underdevelopment could be due merely to inadequacies of the source materials, but the available facts all converge to the same conclusion—that it did not develop into an industrial system.

In the first place, slaves seem to have made up not more than 1 per cent of the total population even at the time when the institution was most fully developed. Evidences about the sources of slaves also indicate an arrested growth. Enslavement of prisoners of war, slave-hunting, and importation of foreigners were apparently practiced to a limited extent only. Certainly there is no manifestation of a large demand for foreign slaves. Kidnaping of native-born into slavery was, of course, outlawed. Reports of the practice are frequent only for the chaotic periods at the end of the Ch'in and beginning of the Han, or at the end of the Former Han dynasty. Famine victims and children of poor families were probably the chief source of native slaves, if we may generalize from later Chinese history, but this source was apparently extra-legal. Hereditary slavery supplied a good proportion of both government and private bondsmen.

The government created some slaves by legal processes, but reports of actual cases are infrequent and there is no way to judge the prevalence or numbers involved. Conviction for a limited period of penal labor is reported much more frequently. The state also acquired slaves by confiscation and by gift from private owners.

Confiscation was a technique that would have been peculiarly useful whenever the government needed to increase its slave holdings, yet there is only one report of its having been resorted to for that purpose by a preconceived plan. This was when the treasury was depleted by foreign wars. It was only one of many revenue-raising schemes, the slaves were only part of the loot, and their number was an embarrassment. The government appealed for gifts of slaves only twice, so far as we know. Once they were to be used as colonists, and in the second instance perhaps for sale. This plan appears to have been dropped within four years in favor of selling honorary titles of "military merit."

On the basis of the source material it is impossible to visualize any demand for slaves on a national scale at any time during the period, even though a continuous market did encourage some kidnaping and importation. On the economic side of the question, there is a deficiency of evidence that slaves were used for production.

The most suggestive indications that they were extensively used in that way are two complaints that slave owners competed with commoners for profits (*34, 110*). The implication of the first complaint is that the privileged class, because of its special advantages, was able to compete unfairly with commoners, and therefore (as a result?) acquired large numbers of slaves and other valuables. Slaves were certainly used in farming, but to an unknown extent; there is no clear indication of a plantation system. They are mentioned infrequently in connection with manufacturing and merchandising, but may have been used more in those fields than the texts reveal. Business men were not restrained from owning or using them, although impediments of other sorts, especially laws against investing profits in farm land, were a feature of the policy of hindering "secondary occupations."

Certain other negative factors lessen the belief that slaves were extensively exploited. There is no convincing evidence of general callous treatment. There are no reports of slave revolts, nor even of concern with the danger of revolts—in contrast with positive evidence of violent convict revolts. There is no indication that slaves were a self-conscious group with interests in opposition to those of their masters or other free classes.

There are several suggestive points about slave status. It had no racial character, as it might have had if a considerable element of the slave population had consisted of the despised Hsiung-nu or other foreign groups. It shows no semblance of having been a caste system, and there seem to have been no types of work which slaves were forbidden to perform. They probably even participated in the ancestral ceremonies of their masters. Manumission brought full commoner rank in one step, and apparently carried no disabilities, though it did from T'ang times on.

In general, the system remained at the level of domestic slavery in spite of the fact that it had the potentialities for development into an industrial system. It is sometimes difficult to distinguish between this domestic slavery and the system of clientage which also flourished among the upper classes in Former Han times. Unless the historical sources badly distort the picture, the most important functions of private slaves were in the category of household services, contributing to the owner's comfort and prestige. One important service was reinforcement of the master's economic power and local influence. But power and influence were not based upon slave labor primarily, but upon such other factors as land-owning, political position or connections, intra- and extra-family relationships, etc., which were all very important in China then as now. Slaves were a subsidiary part of the economic family, participating in its benefits, contributing to general comfort, but not creating wealth on an important scale. This domestic slavery was a rather mild form of the system, as it is everywhere. Private slaves—so far as we know anything about them—may be suspected of having enjoyed a better standard of living than "average" common folk.[1]

The same conclusions stand in regard to government slavery. State-owned slaves did not create wealth in an important way, and probably cost more than they contributed. They were most useful in service capacities, in certain types of skilled labor, and in ranching. Except in regard to penal slaves of the first generation, treatment of them was also mild. They were unimportant in upholding dynastic power. That function was lodged in the two pillars of the state, the bureaucracy, and the army and palace guard. Government slaves were a subsidiary element of the bureaucracy.

This synthesis, with the preceding chapters on which it is based, contributes to a solution of the dispute among Chinese historians as to whether Chinese society during the Han period was a "slavery society," and whether in the economic field it was a "slavery economy

---

[1] This opinion reverses the one which the writer held during most of the time this study was in progress. The study was originally conceived of as one way to learn more about the condition of the lower classes in Han times, but it now appears to reveal much more about the ruling group, and to contribute only indirectly to a knowledge of the common people.

society." [1]   These concepts are very vague. Only the broadest
definition of them, allowing the inclusion of many types of forced
labor besides actual slavery, could make them applicable to China
in the Han period. Unless a great deal more evidence, particularly
from excavated records, can be produced to show greater numbers
of slaves and much fuller productive employment of them, it is
unwarranted to consider slaves a crucial part of Han society, or
slavery an important factor in Han economy.

This is not merely a negative conclusion.

It indicates that China had a different sort of society and economy
from that of other advanced civilizations in which slavery became
fundamentally important. What factors in Chinese culture stunted
Han slavery so that it did not become economically important, even
though it had the potentialities for such a development?

REASONS FOR ARRESTED GROWTH

There is no one answer to this question. It reaches back into
the very essentials of Chinese civilization. Since the problem presents
itself most clearly as an economic one, having to do with the nature

---

[1] *Nu-li she-hui* 奴隸社會 and *nu-li ching-chi* 經濟 *she-hui*.

The literature is much more extensive than the writer has been able to cover.
Articles read which arrive at a positive conclusion are the following: Tai Chen-hui,
"The slavery system of the two Han dynasties." The author believes that Chinese
society during the Han dynasty was a "slavery economy society," and that without
slavery there could not have been a Han dynasty, or at least it would have been
much smaller. Fu An-hua, "Kuan yü nu-li she-hui li-lun ti chi-ko wen-t'i [Questions
regarding the slavery society theory]," *Shih Huo*, vol. 5, No. 5, March 1, 1937,
pp. 246–257. The writer states that T'ao Hsi-sheng was one of the first to propose that the society of the Ch'in and Han periods might be called a slavery
society, and attempts by purely theoretic arguments deriving from recent Russian
dialectics to prove that it must have been.

Opposed to these views are the following: Wu Ching-ch'ao ("The slavery
system of the Western Han") concludes (p. 270) that although the Western Han
had a slave class it did not have a slavery society. Wu Po-lun ("An investigation of
slavery in the Western Han") reaches an amazing conclusion. He figures the
total slave population to have been between 20,000,000 and 30,000,000 (p. 279)
but says (p. 283) that slaves were unimportant in agriculture and therefore Han
society cannot be called a slavery society. Liu Hsing-t'ang ("Nu-li she-hui ti cheng-
chieh [The obstinate problem of a slavery society]," *Shih Huo*, vol. 5, No. 11,
June 1, 1937, pp. 460–463) discusses the background of the dispute and the various
schools of thought, and gives his own conclusion (p. 462) that slavery did not
have a basic position in the economic organization of Chinese society, and therefore that there is no period which may be described as possessing a slavery society.

Ma Ch'eng-feng (op. cit., vol. 2, pp. 229–332) goes into the question much
more thoroughly than any other writer, and his whole study is essentially a refutation of the idea that Han economy and society were based upon slavery. In his
first section (pp. 232–236) he lists advocates and opponents of the idea that
China during any of the periods of its development possessed a slavery society.
Advocates whom he lists are Kuo Mo-jo 郭沫若, Wang I-ch'ang 王宜昌, T'ao

of human exploitation in China, economic factors must be given the greatest weight even though many of the prime causes underlying the Han economic pattern are understood only obscurely.[1]

The aboriginal people within China who became distinctively "the" Chinese developed a bent toward intensive agriculture, which in time became one of the most characteristic features of Chinese civilization. This bent may have been stimulated by the combination of loess soil, an invigorating climate and undependable rainfall, and the flora and fauna characteristic of the middle reaches of the Yellow River, China's cradle area. An emphasis on artificial irrigation seems to have been present early in China's historical period. Chinese culture spread wherever it could bring new land into cultivation with the already established techniques, but stopped spreading in areas that could not be used with those techniques. Water-control was the most important of these techniques. In the loess region the chief concern was to conduct water to the inexhaustibly fertile soil. The problem in the great plain was to prevent the Yellow River from flooding the land, watered mainly by rainfall and wells. Drainage, storage, and proper distribution of abundant water were the chief requisites of the rice-culture area.

Even at its most primitive level, artificial irrigation and water-control pre-suppose a food production beyond the requirements of subsistence that would allow some of the population to be free for work on conservancy projects not immediately beneficial. Whether the toilers would be slaves, working all of the time, or conscripted plebians working in constant rotation, is a matter of cultural selec-

Hsi-sheng 陶希聖, and Yeh Ch'ing 葉青. Opponents are Li Chi 李季, Tu Wei-chih 杜畏之, Wang Li-hsi 王禮錫, Hu Ch'iu-yüan 胡秋原, Wang Po-p'ing 王伯平, Hsiung Te-shan 熊得山, Ch'en Hsiao-chiang 陳嘯江, Wang Hsing-jui 王興瑞, and Wu Po-lun 武伯綸. The importance of some of the writers on each side of the question indicates that it is not one to be dismissed lightly. For a summary of the views of most of these authors about China's economic history, see Wang Yü-ch'üan, "The development of modern social sciences in China," *Pacific Affairs*, vol. 11, 1938, pp. 345–362 (pp. 357–359).

[1] The following discussion is the broadest kind of generalization, and there is no attempt at documentation. Detailed substantiation and systematic exposition would require a book of such scope as the forthcoming publication *Economic and social history of China*, by K. A. Wittfogel. I have not seen this work, but some of my concepts stem indirectly from Dr. Wittfogel's study. In addition to original Han sources, four works have influenced the concepts set forth below: Owen Lattimore, *Inner Asian frontiers of China;* Chi Ch'ao-ting, *Key economic areas in Chinese history as revealed in the development of public works for water-control;* Ma Ch'eng-feng, *An economic history of China* (in Chinese); and W. L. Westermann, "Sklaverei," in *Paulys Realenzyklopädie der klassischen Altertums-Wissenschaft*, supplement, vol. 6, 1935, col. 893–1068, which I was privileged to read in the original English manuscript also.

tion. In China the latter alternative was the more common, perhaps because the fertile soil, once irrigated, created a sudden abundance which encouraged the growth of the rural population. Free labor was always available, and, being conscripted, was just as cheap as slave labor. The massing of labor drawn from the general population to work on water control for specified periods in rotation is an early and constant characteristic of the Chinese economic system. Increased production from one project allowed a further stored margin to support bigger concentrations of man-power that were used to improve old land or to bring new territory under cultivation.

What was at first only a trend in specialization toward intensive, irrigated agriculture became a characteristic, developing ultimately into hypnosis. It caused, or was at least accompanied by, a disregard for labor-saving devices other than animal power in farming, and a negativistic attitude toward economic pursuits of a "secondary" nature such as mining, manufacture, commerce, and even extensive farming, or mixed farming and husbandry. The basis of China's economy during most of its history has been land, labor, and grain. The ability to organize and direct man-power beyond the extent of the family or village group has been the basis for rule and for wealth. Government may have originated in this function. The need to control large areas because of long dykes and canals probably contributed to unification. It has always been a duty of the Chinese state to plan and direct large-scale water conservancy works, and because of the low development of private capitalism even small irrigation works were usually the responsibility of district governments. As important as owning land was the power to see that it was irrigated from the public system. The power to be in on the planning of water conservancy, or to acquire land properly watered, is virtually a guarantee of wealth in China.

Intensive agriculture and water-control helped to form China's cultural landscape, with its cellular structure of nucleus towns each surrounded by tributary farming terrain. The walled town was the storage place for tax grain, part of which was used to feed gangs of plebeian laborers recruited in the surrounding district. Civil administration centered in the town, and had charge of those parts of canals and dykes passing through the district. It also directed local projects, determined water rights, and collected taxes. District government was reinforced when necessary by provincial garrisons that subsisted on tax-grain contributed by all the districts in the province. The provincial governments merely linked up the separate but similar *hsien* "cells," while the national government tied the provinces together.

The imperial government in Han times was a tax-collecting, labor-directing organization, resting upon the broad base of a peasant population. Its chief revenue was the produce tax, supplemented, it is true, by money taxes, rent, income from monopolies, and tribute. This income richly supported the rulers and a small upper class, and paid for the bureaucracy and the army. A flourishing and moderately well-fed peasantry, able to pay one-fifteenth or one-thirtieth of its produce besides various other taxes and exactions, and to serve one month a year in corvée, was recognized as essential to the well-being of the state. The government was vitally interested in increased agricultural production, that is, revenue, provided this revenue could be transported to the capital or effectively used elsewhere. It concentrated first on improving water transport and increasing production in the Shensi region which was its economic base. When this "key economic area" had been developed to maximum productivity within the limits of known techniques, the central government attended to developing such other areas as could be tapped by water transport. Its attitude toward improving inaccessible regions was negative except in the case of frontier colonies where strategic considerations were uppermost.

Normal increase of the rural population was probably encouraged by the productivity of a fertile soil, properly watered and tirelessly cultivated. Need for labor on farms put a premium on large peasant families, while the combination of free land-owning and low taxation allowed a substantial margin of food for growth of the population. The insistence upon male descendants which was part of the ancestor-worship complex may have encouraged large families, but it is debatable whether this actually increased population, and it is not clear how universal this originally patrician religion had become by Han times. The parallel doctrine of "filial piety," which included the idea of submission to more remote vested authority than the family, may have encouraged docility to corvée labor, but on the other hand the doctrine may have been the rationalization and systematization of a social attitude already long established from economic necessity. Whatever may explain the facts, it seems evident that during most of the Former Han period the state ruled over an extensive peasant population with a tradition of corvée labor.

Universal compulsory labor provided not only for water conservancy, but also for building of walls, roads, tombs, and government buildings, and much of the work in state monopolies and the grain transport. The peasantry also supplied plenty of tenant-farmers for state lands; indeed, the pressure exerted by landless farmers on the government to throw open its preserves to tenants exceeded the government's desire for rental income. The labor of criminals was an adjunct to corvée labor, used particularly where the system of compulsory short-term shifts of workers was unsatisfactory. Convicts were transported to the frontiers where colonies had been established by the inducement of tax and labor exemption for specified periods, or they were used in gang labor suitable to close surveillance. This system of corvée and convict labor made slaves economically unimportant as far as the government was concerned, and tended to limit to services and skilled labor those who were not first generation slaves of the criminal class.

It might be said as a generalization that the wealth of the dynasty and state was based, both in revenue and labor, upon moderate exploitation of all the people rather than heavy exploitation of a minority.

The channelization of Chinese economy into intensive agriculture, the underdevelopment of industry and commerce, and the interests of the Han state also aided in retarding the development of private slavery into an exploiting system.

Factors acting against extensive use of Chinese slaves in agriculture have already been discussed: small-patch farming which approached gardening in its intensiveness, the tenancy system, and the excess peasant population during the first century B.C., when slaves were apparently most numerous. Even though Chinese agriculture was not then as intensive as it later became, the skill and industry of Chinese farmers in comparison with all surrounding peoples must have discouraged the use of foreign slaves for cultivation. Native slaves could have been used, provided they would work with the same industry as free Chinese farmers. There is no evidence that China's foreign wars created among free Chinese peasants a labor shortage that encouraged either foreign or native slave labor as Greek and Roman wars did. China's expansion during the Former Han period compares in extent with that of Rome during the last two centuries of the Republic and the first century of the Empire. But it does not compare in the relative proportion of new territory added to the original nucleus, or in the proportion of the original population kept under arms. The real burden on the Chinese peasantry arose from increased indirect taxation to finance the wars, and extra corvée labor in transporting supplies. These lowered the living standards and created more tenant and migratory labor. There was a great increase of landless peasants in eastern China at the very height of Emperor Wu's wars, which was one of the reasons for colonizing hundreds of thousands of them in the newly conquered northwest territory. Increased landlordism paralleled the growth of the peasant population and the decline in its living standard. It is axiomatic that the farms acquired for investment by nobles, officials, and the "tyrannical gentry" were the best-watered ones, exactly the land for which there would be the keenest competition among tenants. Not only is there no convincing evidence of large-scale slave labor in agriculture, but also there appears to have been no imperative reason for it within the Chinese economic system except at the beginning of the Han dynasty.

The end period of Chou feudalism and the first imperial age witnessed a development of manufacturing and commerce that was something new in China. During most of the first millennium B.C. these things had had a negligible importance. The development was concurrent with, and partly the result of, the introduction of coined money, which allowed a new kind and source of wealth. It resulted in a competition between money economy and the feudal economy based upon land, labor, and grain. Political unification of the country, external expansion, improved internal communications, destruction of many trade barriers, and a more numerous wealthy class also contributed to this new element. In general, however, manufactures and trade remained at a low level of capitalistic development and failed to achieve more than a minor rôle in the national economy. Even today industry and commerce are just emerging from a pre-industrial stage. Compared with Greece from the sixth century B.C., and with Rome during the two centuries before and after Christ, Han China was unsophisticated in the development and relative importance of merchant capital. Why?

Geography furnishes one answer. The Han empire was a continental empire. In terms of China today, the political and economic center was then in the northwest, far inland and remote from the sea. Even if all the area between the Yangtze and the Wall be considered as the important part of the empire, still that was the region where water-transport is least possible. Communications were mostly by land. Routes followed valleys of rivers, on most of which boats could be used only to a restricted extent. Development of transport canals and full use of the navigable portions of rivers modified, but did not fundamentally alter, this geographic fact. The eastern Mediterranean and Black Sea, into which flow several important navigable rivers, were an ideal setting for international trade. Whereas the factories and ateliers of Greek and Roman cities poured out wares that could easily be distributed all over the classical world, Chinese cities were in no such strategic position with regard to either domestic or foreign trade. Even the Shantung peninsula was not favored with much maritime commerce, and the north China rivers were less useful than the Nile, Tigris, Euphrates, and Danube.

The man-made geography also retarded the development of commercial capital. In a country made up of nearly identical politico-economic cells, each virtually self-sufficient in agriculture, handicraft industry, and trade, there was little need for exchange between neighboring districts. Under a land-labor-grain economy, inter-regional commerce was restricted to such essentials as were not everywhere produced—salt, metals, wool, leather, and bamboo—and to luxury items. Land transport—and north China roads are phenomenally bad—limited distant trade to goods of small bulk and high value.

A strong cultural tradition also acted against the development of commercial capital. The Chinese were and are tenaciously provincial. Merchants were cosmopolitan. They brought in strange goods and new ideas, which may be a vice or a virtue depending upon the cultural bias. In China it was a vice. Merchants were a *luan* force; they "stirred things up." Under feudalism there was little place or opportunity for independent merchants. When, coincidental with the decline of feudalism, they began to grow numerous and wealthy, they were recognized as a disruptive influence. Difficult to control and tax, they challenged the economic system of which they were no integral part. Almost unanimously the late Chou philosophers attacked merchants, making a dogma of the antagonism of the ruling class toward them. Farming was the fundamental pursuit, enriching rulers and nourishing the masses. Business men were looked upon as parasites who profited from "secondary" occupations at the expense of those who practiced the fundamental one. The anti-feudal Ch'in state as well as the empire was most vigorously opposed to merchants, although it was unable effectively to prevent their increasing and profiting from the changing conditions.

The policy-making statesmen of the Han dynasty inherited and reinforced this attitude. But it was not a mere prejudice, even though there was an active hostility among the scholar-gentry class toward the merchants. The introductory chapter noted some of the economic reasons for the attitude, namely, the fact that merchants, and particularly grain dealers, fleeced the farmers, and the more important fact that both the state and the ruling class subsisted directly on the produce taxes and rent of the peasantry. Not only did the government try to uphold the tax-paying and labor-giving potential of the peasants; it also put certain encumbrances on the merchants, such as forbidding them to own farms or become palace officials. Although it charged them double poll-taxes, heavy market dues, and at one time introduced a capital levy, and although it must have realized considerable income from these sources, it did nothing to encourage private industry and commerce as an extra source of revenue. The state had the machinery to channelize the benefits of agriculture toward the dynasty and ruling group through control of irrigation, but to drain off the profits of commerce was much more difficult. Taxes on merchants were essentially repressive. Most of the furnishings and weapons needed for palaces, bureaus, tombs, and the army were produced in government ateliers and arsenals. The government eventually took control of the two essential commodities, salt and iron, from which private enterprise profited most abundantly. At the same time, however, it found that it had to employ business men to run these enterprises and the many other financial schemes concurrently introduced. This only sharpened the antagonism of the scholar-gentry class, which looked upon the civil government as its exclusive preserve, as indicated by protests in the *Discourses on salt and iron*.

Neither the overwhelming bent of the Chinese toward intensive agriculture, nor the strong geographic handicaps, nor political-cultural antagonism prevented the establishment of commercial capitalism during the Former Han period. But they certainly retarded its full development. This helps to explain why Chinese slavery did not mature into a system of exploitation in the industrial and commercial fields, if that conclusion is correct. The law forbidding merchants to possess farm land may not have been enforced all the time, but its existence on the statutes as a constant menace must have added to the difficulty of investing profits. Both discriminatory taxation and, after 119 B.C., the threat that excess profits and capital assets would be confiscated, must have discouraged manufacturers and merchants from investing in machinery—that is, slaves—for business purposes, the more so since taxes were levied on slaves and slaves were specifically subject to confiscation. It may be significant that the only manufacturer known to have used slave (lit. "youth") labor extensively was a nobleman, who was further secured by being an imperial favorite, more deep in the affection of Emperor Hsüan than was Ho Kuang. The only producer-merchant reported to have used slaves profitably in commercial work lived at the very beginning of the Han period or perhaps earlier. Since specific Han laws against merchants cannot be traced continuously after their promulgation, nor can their effect be tested, it is impossible to know the extent to which repression was a factor, throughout the dynasty, in discouraging industrial slavery. But the existence of an abundant free labor supply during the time when the laws may have been in disuse argues to the same end from the opposite point of view. Industrial slavery under such conditions would probably not have been economical.

This discussion is not in the least an argument that Han China was characterized by a mildness in human exploitation. Within the limits of social tolerance, no people have exploited peasants and laborers more bitterly than the Chinese landlord and business class, then and today. But also, no people have been shrewder to recognize the system of exploitation in which the maximum immediate profits lay.

SLAVERY IN CHINA DURING THE FORMER HAN DYNASTY

PART II

NOTATION AND METHODS OF TRANSLATION

The following translations are arranged in chronological order. The first number appearing in the caption is the number of the document, as referred to in italics throughout the work. The date refers to the time when the event relating to slavery occurred, and not to the date when the text was written. The next item is the citation of the passage translated, as in the following example: CHS, 24A, 6b (17a). CHS means *Ch'ien Han shu;* 24A represents *chüan* 24 上 (capital letters stand for sections of a single *chüan* when the sections are *separately* paged. In some *chüan* there are more than two parts. In every instance B stands for the second separately paged section, C for the third, etc.); 6b means page 6 verso. The numbers in parentheses refer to the page numbers in Wang Hsien-ch'ien's *Han shu pu chu*, published in Changsha in 1900. When a passage has been broken, as indicated by three dots in the transcript and the translation, a semicolon represents the point of break.

The translation is as literal as is consistent with good English. Additions necessary for clarity are placed in brackets, as in Dubs's translation. Names of offices are translated as in HFHD, vol. I, when found there; for unfamiliar terminology Dubs's *system* is used.

For footnotes see following list of abbreviations of reference works. In biographical notes the most important SC or CHS reference is given first (usually it is the one containing the formal biography). All references are separated by semicolons, but SC or CHS is not repeated in case of several references to those texts.

ABBREVIATIONS USED IN PART II

AAs	*Artibus Asiae*
BEFEO	*Bulletin de l'Ecole Française d'Extrême-Orient*
BMFEA	*Bulletin of the Museum of Far Eastern Antiquities*
BSOS	*Bulletin of the School of Oriental Studies*
CHHP	*Ch'ing Hua hsüeh pao (Tsing Hua journal)*
CHS	*Ch'ien Han shu*
CJ	*China journal of science and arts*
CLHP	*Chin Ling hsüeh pao (Nanking journal)*
DC	Couvreur, F. Séraphin. *Dictionnaire classique de la langue chinoise*
Giles B	Giles, Herbert A. *A Chinese biographical dictionary* (Numbers are biography numbers)
Giles D	Giles, Herbert A. *A Chinese-English dictionary* (Numbers are numbers of characters)
HCI	*Han chiu i*
HCIPI	*Han chiu i pu i*
HFHD	*The history of the Former Han dynasty by Pan Ku*, translated by Homer H. Dubs
HJAS	*Harvard journal of Asiatic studies*
HHS	*Hou Han shu*
HSPC	*Han shu pu chu*
HTT	*Chung-hua min-kuo hsin ti t'u* (References to longitude and latitude may be located on corresponding maps)
HY7	Harvard-Yenching Institute. Sinological index series, No. 7: *Index to the Ssu k'u ch'üan shu tsung mu and Wei shou shu mu* (Roman numerals I and II are divisions on titles and authors respectively; numbers are pages under main divisions)
HY10	Ibid., No. 10: *Combined indices to twenty historical bibliographies* (Roman numerals I to V are five main divisions according to indexing system; numbers are pages under main divisions)
HY36	Ibid., No. 36: *Combined indices to Han shu and the notes of Yen Shih-ku and Wang Hsien-ch'ien*
JA	*Journal asiatique*
JAI	*Journal of the Anthropological Institute of Great Britain and Ireland*
JAOS	*Journal of the American Oriental Society*
JMT	*Chung-kuo jen ming ta tz'u-tien*
JNCBRAS	*Journal of the North China Branch of the Royal Asiatic Society*
KCT	*Chung-kuo ku chin ti ming ta tz'u-tien*
LTM	*Li tai ming jen sheng tsu nien piao*
MH	*Les mémoires historiques de Se-ma Ts'ien*, translated by Edouard Chavannes
MRDTB	*Memoirs of the Research Department of the Toyo Bunko*
MS	*Monumenta serica*
MSOS	*Mitteilungen des Seminars für orientalische Sprachen*
RAA	*Revue des arts asiatiques*
SC	*Shih chi*
SKC	*Ssu k'u ch'üan shu tsung mu* (References to *chüan* and page, using *a* and *b* for recto and verso)

TB	Teng Ssu-yü and Knight Biggerstaff. *An annotated bibliography of selected Chinese reference works*
TH	Wieger, L. *Textes historiques*
TMT	*Chung-kuo ti ming ta tz'u-tien*
TP	*T'oung pao*
TT	*Tz'u t'ung*
25S	*Erh-shih-wu shih jen ming so-yin*
TY	*Tz'u yüan*
WHC	*Chung-kuo wen-hsüeh-chia ta tz'u tien* (Numbers refer to biography numbers)
YCHP	*Yen Ching hsüeh pao* (*Yenching journal of Chinese studies*)
YCLH	*Yüan chien lei han*
YTL	*Yen t'ieh lun*

1. Ca. 350 B.C.?[1] CHS, 23, 4b (9b)

其奴男子入于罪隸女子入舂槁凡有爵者與七十者
與未齔者皆不爲奴

[Describing criminal laws of the Chou period]: As to slaves,[2] males went into criminal servitude;[3] females went into pounding dried grain.[4] No one who had noble title, or was seventy, or had not yet lost the milk teeth became a slave.

[1] This passage also appears in the *Chou li* (cf. Edouard Biot, trans., *Le Tcheou-li ou rites des Tcheou*, t. 2, pp. 363–364), and the date of composition of that work is not precisely known, though it may have been written some time in the fourth century B.C. The *Chou li* was suppressed in 213 B.C., then rediscovered in its archaic script some time between 155 and 130 B.C., and published by Liu Hsin about the time of Wang Mang. The author of the *Ch'ien Han shu* presumably copied this passage from the *Chou li*, and the practice described is set down as being a Chou practice. On the authenticity of the *Chou li*, cf. Bernhard Karlgren, "The early history of the Chou Li and Tso Chuan texts," BMFEA, vol. 3, 1931, pp. 1–59; and references noted by Charles S. Gardner, *Chinese traditional histori-ography*, p. 30, footnote 28, and index under *Jou li*.

[2] Li Chi (fl. ca. A.D. 200) here comments: "A general term for male and female convicts was *nu* 男女徒總名爲奴."

[3] *Tsui-li* is defined two ways in TY: (1) "Like government male slaves. The families and dependents of criminals, enslaved by the government." (2) "The name of a bureau. Listed in the *Chou li* under the Autumn Bureau, which had charge of petty servitors."

[4] *Ch'ung-kao* is defined in TY by quoting a commentary to the *Chou li*: "In Chou times the *ch'ung-jen* and *kao-jen* were names of two bureaus. The wives and children of criminals, enslaved by the government, did fatiguing work, and women went into these two bureaus." Apparently the work was to pound (i.e. hull) grain for sacrifices, and other menial labor. Cf. HFHD, vol. I, p. 177, footnote 1, for fuller details on Han punishments.

2.   After 228 B.C.[1]   CHS, 91, 4a (8b)

蜀卓氏之先趙人也用鐵冶富秦破趙遷卓氏之蜀夫
妻推輦行諸遷虜少有餘財爭與吏求近處處葭萌唯卓
氏曰此地陜薄吾聞岷山之下沃壄下有蹲鴟至死不饑
民工作布易賈乃求遠遷致之臨邛大憙即鐵山鼓鑄運
籌算賈滇蜀民富至僮八百人田池射獵之樂擬於人君

In Shu,[2] the Cho[3] family's ancestors were natives of Chao. They were rich from iron-smelting. When Ch'in defeated Chao, [Ch'in] deported the Cho family[4] to Shu. The husband and wife [alone] went pushing a cart. [When the party was going toward the deportation place[5]], all the deported captives who had a little extra wealth competed in begging for a nearer place from the officials. They were placed at Chia-meng. Only Mr. Cho said: "This land is restricted and poor. I have heard that below Min Mountain there are *chün-ch'ih* [tubers[6]] under the rich soil, so that during a whole lifetime there will be no starving. The people skillfully make cloth[7] for barter and trade." Thereupon he requested to be deported farther, arrived at Lin-ch'iung, and was greatly delighted. He went to Iron Mountain, smelted and coined, manipulated tallies, and traded with the people of T'ien and Shu. He became rich to the extent of [possessing] eight hundred[8] youths and the pleasures of fields, ponds, and hunting [preserves] comparable to [those of] a prince.

[1] The year when Ch'in conquered Chao.

[2] Shu was the region of west-central Szechwan, around the present Chengtu. Other places mentioned in this passage are as follows (the route of the journey may be followed on page 20 of Herrmann's *Atlas*): Chao was a late Chou feudal state in eastern Shansi, southern Hopei, and northern Honan. The last capital was at Han-tan, southwest of present Han-tan hsien in Hopei Province. It was just east of a great iron-smelting district in Shansi. Chia-meng, a prefecture in Han times, was southwest of modern Chao-hua hsien in Szechwan. Lin-ch'iung was in present Ch'iung-hsia hsien, some 30 or 40 miles southwest of Chengtu. Among the various Iron Mountains listed in KCT, p. 1381, the most probable one is that about 25 miles west of Yung hsien in Szechwan (HTT, map 34: 104° 22'; 29° 29'). This is spoken of as producing very hard iron, from which weapons were made. This mountain would be 75 or 100 miles south of Lin-ch'iung in the direction of Yunnan. T'ien, the place where the Cho family traded, was that part of Yunnan centering around modern Kunming or Yunnanfu.

[3] The whole biography is here translated. It is a typical example of the biographies of the rich people. The same passage is found in SC, 129, 7a–b, with

minor variations, some of which are noted below.   Cho Wang-sun, the father-in-law of Ssu-ma Hsiang-ju, was probably a third or fourth generation descendant of this man of the same surname.   Cf. *28*.

[4] SC differs slightly here: "When Ch'in defeated Chao, [Ch'in] deported the Cho family.   The Cho family was captured.   The husband and wife alone [of all the party] went pushing a cart."

[5] From SC.

[6] SC writes the name of the plant with slight differences.   It is defined in the commentaries as a kind of tuber.

[7] SC and HSPC use *shih* (market) in place of *pu* (cloth) in CHS.

[8] SC here has one thousand.

3. 209 B.C. CHS, 31, 2a (4b)

秦令少府章邯免驪山徒人奴產子悉發以擊楚軍大
敗之

[In 209 B.C. Chou Chang, a general under the Ch'u rebel Ch'en
She, had organized an army of a thousand chariots and 100,000
infantry, had got through Han-ku Pass, and was ready to attack
the Ch'in armies at Hsi[1]]. Ch'in ordered the Treasurer of the
Privy Purse, Chang Han,[2] to free the Li Mountain[3] convicts and born
male slaves.[4] They were all sent forth to attack the army of Ch'u.
They badly defeated it.[5]

[1] Chou Chang or Chou Wen (CHS, 31, 2a; JMT, p. 525) was a diviner of lucky
days, who said he was practiced with troops but was not much of a general. Ch'en
She or Ch'en Shen (CHS, 31, 1a–3b; SC, 48, 1a–4a; JMT, p. 1088) was one of the
original rebels against Ch'in. He was killed by his charioteer shortly after this
defeat. Hsi, the theatre of the battle, was on Hsi River, a southern tributary
of the Wei River, between Han-ku Pass and Ch'ang-an (HFHD, vol. I, map).

[2] Chang Han (SC, 7, 3b–5b *passim;* CHS, 31, 2a ff.) was one of the outstanding
generals of Ch'in. He defeated Hsiang Liang, but then deserted with his army
to Hsiang Yü.

[3] Li Mountain (HFHD, vol. I, map) is in Shensi, southeast of the present
Lin-t'ung hsien. It was not far south of Hsi. The convicts may have been work-
ing on the tomb of the First Ch'in Emperor (cf. MH, vol. II, p. 330, footnote 4).
When Kao-tsu first rebelled he was escorting convicts to work at Li Mountain
(HFHD, vol. I, p. 34, and footnote 1).

[4] The commentator Fu Ch'ien (ca. A.D. 125–195) says these were slaves born
to domestics. Yen Shih-ku (A.D. 581–645) says: "The *nu ch'an tzu* are like what
people now call 'houseborn slaves.'" Interesting light is thrown on the term
家生奴, "house-born slave," employed by Yen Shih-ku to explain *nu ch'an tzu*
in the present text, by a T'ang will written two centuries after Yen Shih-ku's
death. This manuscript, dated A.D. 865, was discovered by Sir Aurel Stein at
Tun-huang. It was published by Lionel Giles ("Dated Chinese manuscripts in
the Stein collection, IV," BSOS, vol. 9, 1939, pp. 1029–30). A nun bequeaths
her only property, a house-born female slave named Wei-niang, to her niece
P'an-niang. Giles translates *pei* as servant-girl, but it is quite obvious from the
context that female slave is meant.

The account of the freeing of the convicts of Li Mountain given in SC, 6,
14a (MH, vol. II, p. 205) says: "Chang Han said, 'The convicts of Li Mountain
are numerous. I beg they be freed and receive arms in order to attack [the enemy.'
Emperor] Erh Shih thereupon amnestied the empire, sending Chang Han as
general, who defeated the army of Chou Chang." The slaves are not mentioned,
but are perhaps suggested in the general amnesty.

[5] The battle is merely mentioned in CHS, 1A, 3b (HFHD, vol. I, pp. 41–42).
The SC and CHS chronologies do not agree as to the time of the battle, the first
putting it in the second year of Emperor Erh Shih, the latter in the end of his
first year. It was October, 209 B.C. (HFHD, vol. I, pp. 41 and 42, footnote 2),
rather than 208 B.C., as Chavannes gives it (MH, vol. II, p. 205).

4. 209 B.C.[1] CHS, 33, 1b (2a)

田儋狄人也故齊王田氏之族也儋從弟榮榮弟橫皆
豪桀宗彊能得人陳涉使周市略地北至狄狄城守儋陽
爲縛其奴從少年之廷欲謁殺奴見狄令因擊殺令

T'ien Tan[2] was a man from Ti, of the clan of the former kings of Ch'i, named T'ien. [T'ien] Tan's cousin was [T'ien] Jung, whose younger brother was [T'ien] Heng; all were braves, forceful and able to win followers. When Ch'en She dispatched Chou Shih to overrun the territories to the north as far as Ti, Ti [manned] the walls and went on guard. [T'ien] Tan deceivingly[3] bound up his male slave, and escorted by [a group of] young bloods, went to the court [of the Prefect of Ti, as though] wishing an interview to [announce his intention to] kill the male slave.[4] [When he got to] see the Prefect of Ti he took advantage [of the opportunity] to attack and kill the Prefect.

[1] This occurred just before T'ien Tan established himself as King of Ch'i at the end of 209 or early in 208 B.C.

[2] T'ien Tan (SC, 94; CHS, 33, 1b–3a; JMT, p. 202) was one of the early rebels against Ch'in. After this incident he set himself up as King of Ch'i, defeated Chou Shih, but was slain in battle by the Ch'in general Chang Han within a year, in July, 208 B.C. (HFHD, vol. I, p. 45).

Ti was a city in Ch'i State, northwest of the present Kao-yüan hsien in Shantung.

[3] SC here uses 詳 for CHS 陽; both have the sense of 佯, "to feign," "to pretend."

[4] The commentator Fu Ch'ien (ca. A.D. 125–195) says: "Formerly anyone killing a male or female slave had to announce it to the government. [T'ien] Tan, wishing to kill the Prefect, deceivingly bound up his male slave in order to get an interview." Yen Shih-ku (A.D. 581–645) says: "He fraudulently bound up his male slave to create the appearance of killing the male slave...."

5. Before 207 B.C.[1] CHS, 37, 2a (3b)

欒布梁人也彭越爲家人時嘗與布游窮困賣庸於齊
爲酒家保數歲別去而布爲人所略賣爲奴於燕爲其主
家報仇燕將臧荼舉以爲都尉荼爲燕王布爲將

Luan Pu[2] was a Liang man. When P'eng Yüeh[3] was a house-holder, he was a companion of [Luan] Pu. Being poor and in distress they hired themselves out in Ch'i to serve a wine [-shop] keeper. When after several years they separated, [Luan] Pu was kidnaped by someone and sold as a male slave at Yen[4] to [do a deed of] revenge for his master. The Yen general Tsang T'u[5] raised him to be a commandant. [When Tsang] T'u became King of Yen, [Luan] Pu became a general.[6]

[1] This event occurred before General Tsang T'u became King of Yen in 207 B.C., but it could not have been long before, because Luan Pu lived to about 145 B.C. See footnote 2.

[2] Luan Pu (SC, 100, 2a–b; CHS, 37, 2a–b, and 17, 1b; JMT, p. 1805). When Tsang T'u rebelled in 202 B.C. he was defeated by Kao-tsu, and Luan Pu was captured, but released on the plea of his old friend P'eng Yüeh, now King of Liang. He rose to high office. In 151 B.C. he became Marquis of Yü because of his part in putting down the Rebellion of the Seven States; his heir was appointed in 144 B.C., presumably the year after his death (CHS, 17, 1b). Thus he must have been quite young when he was kidnaped some 63 years earlier, yet already old enough to do a deed of revenge.

[3] P'eng Yüeh (SC, 90, 1b–2b; CHS, 34, 6a–7a; JMT, p. 1153) was a general who rose up in the rebellion against Ch'in, but fought both for and against Hsiang Yü and Kao-tsu, finally being made King of Liang by Kao-tsu. In 196 B.C. he rebelled and was executed by Kao-tsu (MH, vol. II, p. 395; HFHD, vol. I, p. 132).

[4] Ch'i was an important state in Shantung, with its capital near the present Lin-tzu hsien. Yen was the area of northern Hopei, with its center around Peking. The direct distance between Ch'i and Yen, capital to capital, is about 200 miles.

[5] Tsang T'u (JMT, p. 1373; MH, vol. II, index, p. 2357) was a general in the Kingdom of Yen, and joined Hsiang Yü in the revolt against Ch'in. Hsiang Yü made him King of Yen in 206 B.C. He rebelled against Kao-tsu in 202 B.C. and was captured and killed.

[6] This passage appears with little difference in SC, 100, 2a.

6. 207–206 B.C. CHS, 31, 7a (16b)

異時諸侯吏卒徭役屯戍過秦中秦中遇之多亡狀及
秦軍降諸侯諸侯吏卒乘勝奴虜使之輕重折辱秦吏卒
吏卒多竊言曰章將軍等詐吾屬降諸侯今能入關破秦
大善卽不能諸侯虜吾屬而東秦又盡誅吾父母妻子諸
將微聞其計以告羽羽迺召英布蒲將軍計曰秦吏卒尚
衆其心不服至關不聽事必危不如擊之獨與章邯長史
欣都尉翳入秦於是夜擊阬秦軍二十餘萬人

Previously when the officers and soldiers of the Nobles had crossed Ch'in-chung[1] while on conscript labor or agricultural garrison [duty, the officers and soldiers of[2]] Ch'in-chung received them most uncivilly. Later when the Ch'in army surrendered to the Nobles, the officers and soldiers of the Nobles took advantage of their victory to treat [the members of the Ch'in army like] slave captives, and to slight and insult the officers and soldiers of Ch'in.

The officers and soldiers [of Ch'in] often secretly conferred, saying: "General Chang[3] and the others treacherously made us surrender to the Nobles, who now may enter the pass and defeat Ch'in. If, by great good luck,[4] they are not able to, the Nobles will make captives of us [and take us] east. Ch'in, moreover, will completely slaughter our parents, wives, and children."

The generals heard rumors of their consultations and reported to [Hsiang] Yü.[5] [Hsiang] Yü thereupon summoned Ying Pu and General P'u[6] to consult. They said: "The officers and soldiers of Ch'in are still numerous, and their hearts are not submissive. When we get to the pass[7] they will not obey orders, and matters are sure to be dangerous. It would be better to attack them and enter Ch'in with only Chang Han, Chief Official [Ssu-ma] Hsin, and Commandant [Tung] Yi."[8]

Therefore in the night they attacked and buried the Ch'in army, more than 200,000 men.[9]

---

[1] Yen Shih-ku (A.D. 581–645) says: "Ch'in-chung is Kuan-chung [i.e., west of the Han-ku Pass] in Ch'in territory." TY equates it with the present Shensi Province.

[2] From SC, 7, 5b.

[3] Cf. *3*, footnote 2. He surrendered to the Nobles in August/September, 207 B.C. Some time between then and January/February, 206, occurred the events here recorded (cf. HFHD, vol. I, pp. 54, 59–60).

[4] My edition here has 書 for *shan*, a typographical mistake.

[5] Hsiang Yü or Hsiang Chi (SC, 7; CHS, 31, 4a–11a; JMT, pp. 1216–17) was the superior and then chief rival of Kao-tsu in the rebellion against Ch'in. He almost won the throne, but Kao-tsu finally defeated him and founded the new Han dynasty.

[6] Ying Pu or Ch'ing Pu (CHS, 34, 7a–10a; JMT, p. 704) was one of the leading rebels against Ch'in, serving under Hsiang Yü. He later joined Kao-tsu and was made a king. In early life he was a convict working on Li Mountain.

General P'u (MH, vol. II, p. 254, footnote 1; mentioned in SC, 7, and CHS, 31). Little is known of him.

[7] This means the Han-ku Pass. Cf. HFHD, vol. I, p. 42, footnote 1. SC has: "When we arrive at Kuan-chung," i.e., within or west of the pass. At this time Hsiang Yü and the Nobles were east of the pass at Hsin-an in Honan, while Kao-tsu was inside the pass.

[8] Chang Han, Ssu-ma Hsin, and Tung Yi, three generals of Ch'in, were later rewarded by Hsiang Yü by each being made king of one of the three parts into which Kuan-chung (Ch'in-chung) was divided (cf. HFHD, vol. I, pp. 66–67).

[9] CHS, 1A, 7b (HFHD, vol. I, p. 61), states that at this time Hsiang Yü's troops numbered 400,000, though they were asserted to be a million. An army of that size could hardly have suddenly slain more than 200,000 men. A note in HJAS, vol. 2, 1937, p. 28, reports Miyazaki's observation that during the epoch of the Three Kingdoms (A.D. 220–265) statistics of defeated or decapitated enemies were recorded as ten times their actual number. While the number is incredible, the fact of the treachery and slaughter is probably authentic. Kao-tsu made it the sixth point in his famous denunciation of Hsiang Yü (cf. HFHD, vol. I, p. 90, and footnote 3).

7. Ca. 205 B.C.   CHS, 24A, 3b (9b)

漢興接秦之敝諸侯並起民失作業而大饑饉凡米石
五千人相食死者過半高祖乃令民得賣子就食蜀漢

When the Han dynasty arose, it inherited the corruption of
Ch'in.   The Nobles simultaneously rose up [in strife] and the people
lost their economic occupations, so that there was a great famine
in which all grain [cost] five thousand [cash] the picul.[1]   People
ate each other, and over half the population died.   Kao-tsu thereupon
ordered that people might sell their children and migrate to Shu
and Han for food.[2]

[1] The term *tan*, translated picul, equaled about 64 pounds 8.8 ounces avoir.,
or 29.3 kilograms, according to HFHD, vol. I, p. 280.

[2] This may be the famine in Kuan-chung of June/July, 205 B.C.   It is reported
(CHS, 1A, 11b; HFHD, vol. I, p. 82) that "in Kuan-chung there was a great
famine; a *hu* of rice [or hulled millet cost] ten thousand cash [and] people ate
each other.   [The King of Han (later Emperor Kao)] ordered people to go to Shu
and Han to eat."   The *T'u shu chi ch'eng*, sec. IV, ch. 107, pp. 2b–3a, connects
the events.

Cf. *9* for an edict by Kao-tsu in 202 B.C., freeing all who had sold themselves
into slavery because of famine.

8. 202 B.C.[1] CHS, 37, 1a (1a)

季布楚人也爲任俠有名項籍使將兵數窘漢王項籍
滅高祖購求布千金敢有舍匿罪三族布匿濮陽周氏周
氏曰漢求將軍急迹且至臣家能聽臣臣敢進計卽否願
先自剄布許之迺髡鉗布衣褐置廣柳車中幷與其家僮
數十人之魯朱家所賣之朱家心知其季布也買置田舍

Chi Pu[2] was a man from Ch'u, who became famous as a trusty stalwart. Hsiang Chi[3] employed him to lead troops, and he often harassed the King of Han.[4] When Hsiang Chi had been destroyed, Kao-tsu offered a thousand [catties of] gold as a reward for the capture of [Chi] Pu, [warning that] anyone daring to entertain or secrete him would be punished [by death and the extermination of his] three [sets of] relatives.[5] [Chi] Pu hid at Pu-yang with a Mr. Chou.[6]

Mr. Chou said: "[The King of] Han is urgently seeking you, General, and the trail will soon lead to your servant's house. If you can listen to your servant, your servant presumes to advance a plan; but if not, I would like to cut my throat beforehand." [Chi] Pu assented to the plan.

Thereupon [Mr. Chou] shaved [Chi] Pu's head, put an iron collar on him, dressed him in coarse clothes, and put him in a broad willow-cart[7] together with several tens of his household youths, sending them to Chu Chia[8] of Lu to sell. Chu Chia recognized him to be Chi Pu. He bought him and put him in a house among the fields. [Then he enjoined his son, saying: "In the field work be lenient with this male slave; you must eat together."][9]

[1] Hsiang Yü was defeated in December/January, 203/202 B.C. This event happened shortly after.

[2] Chi Pu (SC, 100, 1a–2a; CHS, 37, 1a–2a; JMT, pp. 556–557). After the events recorded here he was pardoned by Kao-tsu at the suggestion of Chu Chia made through the Lord of Teng, Hsia-hou Ying. He rose to be Administrator of the Ho-tung Commandery under Emperor Hui, and almost became Grandee Secretary under Emperor Wen. If it is true that he was one of the generals of Hsiang Yü, and often harassed Kao-tsu it is curious that he is not mentioned in SC, 7 and 8, or CHS, 1.

At the end of his biography appears a eulogy, presumably by Ssu-ma Ch'ien, which has been translated (cf. 56).

Several manuscript copies of a popular ballad about Chi Pu were discovered by Stein and Pelliot in the Tun-huang library. One, dated as of A.D. 939, is described by Lionel Giles in BSOS, vol. 10, 1940, pp. 337–339. This ballad goes far beyond the sober historical facts, but in the part translated by Giles there is no mention of the enslavement of Chi Pu.

[3] I.e., Hsiang Yü (cf. *6*, footnote 5).

[4] I.e., Kao-tsu.

[5] This was a punishment for crimes of high treason. According to one explanation, all the relatives of the guilty person's father, mother, and wife were executed; but according to another, it was (1) the generation above that of the criminal (his parents, uncles, and aunts); (2) the same generation (brothers, sisters, cousins, and wife); (3) the next generation (sons and daughters, nephews and nieces). This, according to a communication from Dr. H. H. Dubs, included all those required by the custom of the blood feud to revenge a death in the clan.

[6] There are two places possible for this: Pu hsien, in western Shantung, and Pu-yang hsien in southern Hopei. They are close together, just north of the Yellow River.
Mr. Chou (SC, 100, 1a; CHS, 37, 1a) is unknown other than here.

[7] Or "willow-covered ox-cart." Long commentaries both in SC and CHS at this point discuss whether this "willow-cart" was a funeral cart, used for disguise, or just a cart with willow sides. Only Fu Ch'ien and Teng Chan note the important fact that Chi Pu was being hidden. Both conclude, therefore, that it was a funeral cart. But if Chi Pu were hidden inside a funeral cart why should he have his head shaved, be shackled, and dressed in coarse clothes? He would have to be fed and could only leave the cart with great secrecy. Furthermore, would not a funeral cart escorted by several tens of slaves marching off to be sold be much more suspicious than a cart in which the slaves were riding? Probably Chi Pu simply rode to Lu with a score of slaves or more, all dressed and shackled alike.

[8] Chu Chia (SC, 124, 2a; CHS, 92, 1b–2a; JMT, p. 257) was a famous "knight-errant" with many retainers and innumerable hired workers 庸. His service for Chi Pu is mentioned in his SC and CHS biography. He lived at Lu, the old Confucian state, which was in the present Ch'ü-fu hsien, Shantung. It is something less than 100 miles almost directly east of Pu-yang. That would be a number of days' journey by cart.

[9] Taken from SC, 100, 1a, a similar biography of Chi Pu: 誠其子曰田事聽此奴必與同食.

---

9.   202 B.C.   CHS, 1B, 2b (4b)

民以饑餓自賣爲人奴婢者皆免爲庶人

[In May/June, 202 B.C., an imperial edict said]: "Those common people who because of famine have sold themselves to be people's male and female slaves are all to be freed and become commoners." [1]

[1] The passage is not in SC, 8.

10.   Ca. 200 B.C.   CHS, 95, 1b (2a)

十餘歲秦滅及漢興皆棄此國而開蜀故徼巴蜀民或
竊出商賈取其筰馬僰僮旄牛以此巴蜀殷富

After ten or more years when Ch'in was destroyed and Han arose, [Han] abandoned all these states and opened the ancient frontiers of Shu.[1] Some of the people of Pa and Shu went out clandestinely for trade, taking their horses from Tse, and youths[2] and yaks from P'o;[3] and because of this [trade] the people of Pa and Shu became prosperous and wealthy.[4]

[1] The states of Ch'ien and T'ien, in the present regions of Kweichow and Yunnan, came under the nominal control of Ch'in when it defeated the Kingdom of Ch'u in 223 B.C., but could not be held by Han during the period of internal warfare by which the Han dynasty was established. Whether the frontiers were between the territories of Shu (cf. *2*, footnote 2) and the rest of north China, or were the southern frontiers of Shu is not clear. Probably the first is meant because Shu was incorporated in the Han territory in contrast with the states farther south which were abandoned.

[2] Fu Ch'ien (ca. A.D. 125–195) makes an exceedingly interesting statement in the commentary to this same passage in SC (116, 1b): "In the former capital [i.e., the Ch'ang-an of Fu Ch'ien's day] there are female slaves from P'o." Does not his statement indicate that the trade was still going on in his day? It is interesting that he specifies female slaves from P'o, because the term always used for these slaves of P'o is *t'ung* 僮 or 童, "youths." This more often means boy slaves, though it definitely means girl slave in *26*.

[3] Pa was a state in eastern Szechwan, with its center near modern Chungking. Tse was a state in southwestern Szechwan, with its center southwest of present Han-yüan hsien. P'o was in extreme south-central Szechwan, with its center in present I-pin hsien, at the juncture of the Yangtze and Min rivers.

[4] Other references to this trade in youths from the region of southern Szechwan and Yunnan are equally laconic: CHS, 28B, 10a; SC, 116, 1b, and 129, 3b. The first, in describing the great natural wealth of Pa, Shu, and Kuang-han commandcries, particularly calls attention to this trade, mentioning T'ien (the Kunming region) as well as P'o.

11. Ca. 200 B.C.[1] *Fang yen*, 3, 1a

臧甬侮獲奴婢賤稱也荊淮海岱雜齊之間罵奴曰臧
罵婢曰獲齊之北鄙燕之北郊凡民男而聟婢謂之臧女
而婦奴謂之獲亡奴謂之臧亡婢謂之獲皆異方罵奴婢
之醜稱也自關而東陳魏宋楚之間保庸謂之甬秦晉之
間罵奴婢曰侮

Tsang, yung, wu, and *huo* are degrading terms for male and
female slaves. In the regions of the central Yangtze Valley, the
Huai River Valley, the sea coast, T'ai shan, and uncultured parts
of Shantung,[2] when cursing a male slave, one says *"tsang"*; when
cursing a female slave, one says *"huo."* In the northern outskirts
of Shantung, and in the northern[3] countryside of Hopei, all plebeian
males who mate[4] with female slaves are called *tsang*; [plebeian]
females who become wives of male slaves are called *huo*. Runaway
male slaves are called *tsang*; runaway female slaves are called *huo*.
They are all abusive terms of diverse regions for cursing male and
female slaves. From the pass eastward, in the region of Honan,
west Shantung, and Hupei, indentured laborers are called *yung*.
In the regions of Shensi and Shansi, in cursing male and female slaves
one says *"wu."* [5]

[1] It is obviously impossible to date such a passage as this. The terminology
may be that of late Chou times rather than Han, but the expressions probably
continued in use, though they are met only infrequently in Han literature. Here
the interest is primarily in the social attitudes implied, and not in the terms
themselves.

The *Fang yen* is a dictionary of dialectical variants probably dating from
the first century of our era. Its attribution to Yang Hsiung (53 B.C.–A.D. 18) is
very suspect; cf. SKC, 40, 2a–3a, and Pelliot, *Encyclopaedia Sinica*, p. 299. The
text here used comes from an edition of the *Han Wei ts'ung-shu* published in 1894
by the Hunan I wen shu chü with a preface by Yang T'ing-jui dated 1894. The
passage has been checked with quotations in the *Yüan chien lei han*, ch. 258
(*jen pu*, 17), 2a; the *Chin ting ku chin t'u shu chi ch'eng*, sec. XII (*chia fan tien*),
ch. 113, 1a; the *Tz'u t'ung*, p. 2595; and the *Tz'u yüan*. There are few differences,
and none significant for this study.

[2] These locations are only approximations. Cf. Herrmann, *Atlas*, pp. 15, 16,
for various regions mentioned, as they existed toward the close of the Chou epoch.

[3] The *Yüan chien lei han* here has "southern."

[4] The YCLH, and *Tz'u yüan* here give a variant form with the meaning "a son-
in-law." It sometimes has the extra connotation of a man who goes to live in the
wife's family, which is especially significant here. For the term used in commentaries to explain a somewhat similar expression, cf. *33*.

⁵ The terms *tsang* and *huo*, or *tsang-huo*, do not appear elsewhere in the translated documents, though they occur occasionally in literature referring to the Former Han period in the probable sense of slave; cf., for example, the *Yen t'ieh lun*, ch. 4 (sec. 19) (Esson M. Gale, trans., *Discourses on salt and iron*, p. 122), and CHS, 62, 9a. This latter reference, in the biography of Ssu-ma Ch'ien, is in the letter he is supposed to have written to Jen An. But this letter may be a forgery introduced into the CHS; it is certainly suspect (cf. Pelliot, RAA, vol. 6, 1929–30, p. 115, and TP, vol. 29, 1932, p. 132; and Duyvendak, JAOS, vol. 55, 1935, pp. 332–333). Chavannes translates the letter in MH, vol. I, pp. ccxxvi–ccxxxviii; cf. also, ibid., p. xlii, footnote 1. The letter, whoever wrote it, also appears as a piece of outstanding literature in the *Wen hsüan*, ch. 41, as the "Pao Jen An shu."

In the CHS reference (62, 9a) there are commentaries explaining the term *tsang-huo*, which are not themselves discredited by doubt as to the authorship of the letter. Ying Shao (ca. A.D. 140–206) cites the *Fang yen* meanings about cursing male and female slaves, and plebeians who marry slaves, and his explanation is approved by Yen Shih-ku. Chin Shao (fl. ca. A.D. 275) offers an entirely new meaning: "*Tsang-huo* are those defeated enemy who have been captured and made slaves 敗敵所被虜獲爲奴隸者." Wei Shao (A.D. 204–273) in a commentary to the *Wen hsüan*, quoted by the *Tz'u yüan*, gives a variant of the second *Fang yen* meaning: "When a good man takes a female slave as wife and she bears a child, [the child] is called a *huo;* when a male slave takes a good woman as wife and she bears a child, [the child] is called a *tsang* 善人以婢爲妻生子曰獲奴以善人爲妻生子曰臧." This reverses the terminology applied to plebeians who mate with slaves, but follows the use of *huo* for female slaves and *tsang* for male slaves.

Finally, another meaning is attributed to Ying Shao, or at least is quoted from the *Feng su t'ung i*. The YCLH, loc. cit., quotes the following: "In the ancient institutes there were originally no male and female slaves, and then those who committed offenses were the origin of it. *Tsang-che* are those [males] who have undergone the punishment of *tsang*, being seized and becoming government slaves. *Huo-che* are [female] runaways who have been recaptured and become slaves 古制本無奴婢卽犯事者原之臧者被罪沒入爲官奴獲者逃亡復得爲婢." I have not found this passage in the *Feng su t'ung i* in the *Han Wei ts'ung-shu*. It is quoted, however, from the *Ch'u hsüeh chi* compiled in 724, in the *Shuo wen chieh tzu i teng*, photolithographed in the *Shuo wen chieh tzu ku lin* under *nu*, pp. 5554–56. This has several differences: After *fan shih che* it introduces the word 或, "perhaps"; and in the second sentence it uses *nu-pei* instead of *nu* in the first phrase and *pei* in the second.

十二月行如雒陽貫高等謀逆發覺逮捕高等幷捕趙
王敖下獄詔敢有隨王罪三族郎中田叔孟舒等十人自
髡鉗爲王家奴從王就獄王實不知其謀春正月廢趙王
敖爲宣平侯徙代王如意爲趙王王趙國丙寅前有罪殊
死已下皆赦之二月行自雒陽至賢趙臣田叔孟舒等十
人召見與語漢廷臣無能出其右者上說盡拜爲郡守諸
侯相

In the twelfth month [the Emperor] went to Lo-yang. Kuan Kao[2] and others had plotted rebellion. This was discovered and [Kuan] Kao and the others were arrested. At the same time the King of Chao, [Chang] Ao,[3] was captured and sent to prison, and an imperial edict [proclaimed that] anyone daring to accompany the King would be punished by [death and the extermination of his] three [sets of] relatives. [Nevertheless, his] Gentlemen of the Palace, T'ien Shu, Meng Shu[4] and others, in all ten people, personally shaved their heads, put on iron collars, and became the King's household male slaves, and followed the King to prison. The King had really not known of the plot. In the spring, the first month, [the Emperor] freed the King of Chao, [Chang] Ao, and made him Marquis of Hsüan P'ing, and shifted the King of Tai, [Liu] Ju-i, to be King of Chao, ruling over the State of Chao. Those who, before the day *ping-yin*, had committed crimes not punishable by death were all pardoned. In the second month [the Emperor] went from Lo-yang to [the capital]. He esteemed the ten ministers of Chao, T'ien Shu, Meng Shu, and the others, summoned them for an audience, and talked with them. None of the ministers of the Han court could surpass them. The Emperor was pleased, and appointed them all Administrators of commanderies or Chancellors to the Nobles.[5]

---

[1] The whole incident occurred between January and April. The day *ping-yin* was March 11.

[2] Kuan Kao (SC, 89, 4b–5b, and 104, 1b; CHS, 32, 4a, and 37, 3a; JMT, p. 1041) was the Chancellor of the King of Chao, Chang Ao. Kao-tsu passed through Chao and slighted the King, because of which Kuan Kao wished to assassinate him. The King refused to allow it, but Kuan Kao and some others

went ahead with a plot, which was unsuccessful (HFHD, vol. I, p. 119). The plot was then reported to Kao-tsu by an enemy of Kuan Kao. After capture, and under cross-examination, Kuan Kao took the whole responsibility upon himself, saying that the King of Chao had not known of the plot.

[3] Chang Ao (SC, 89, 4b–5b; CHS, 32, 4a–b; JMT, p. 952) was the son of Chang Erh, and was married to the eldest daughter of Kao-tsu. After his pardon he was made Marquis of Hsüan P'ing. He died in 182 B.C.

[4] T'ien Shu (SC, 104, 1a–2a; CHS, 37, 2b–3b; JMT, p. 199) was a man from Chao and a member of the clan of the former kings of Ch'i. He became a Gentleman of the Palace to the King of Chao on the recommendation of Kuan Kao. After this affair he was appointed Administrator of Han-chung, then Chancellor of Lu.

Meng Shu (ibid.; JMT, p. 555). Little is known of him except in this connection. He was appointed Administrator of Yün-chung, was dismissed, but was later reappointed by Emperor Wen on the recommendation of T'ien Shu.

[5] This famous incident is also recorded in (1) CHS, 37, 3a; (2) SC, 104, 1b (biographies of T'ien Shu); and (3) SC, 89, 5a–b (biographies of Chang Erh and Ch'en Yü). The first adds that the "guests" put on russet clothes (the costume of convicts) as well as shaving and shackling themselves; the second adds that they called themselves, or feigned to be 稱, the King's household slaves. The third account closes with the statement that the Emperor esteemed King Chang's guests, who as shackled male slaves had followed King Chang through the pass.

13. 197 B.C. CHS, 34, 5b (12b)

漢十年豨果反高帝自將而往信病不從陰使人之豨
所而與家臣謀夜詐赦諸官徒奴欲發兵襲呂后太子

In the tenth year of Han, [Ch'en] Hsi[1] really did revolt. Emperor Kao personally took command and went forth [to battle. Han] Hsin[2] [pretended to be] sick and did not accompany him, but secretly sent a man to [Ch'en] Hsi's place and plotted with his household minister that in the night they would forge [an imperial edict[3]] to pardon the convicts and male slaves[4] of the various bureaus, with the plan to send them out as soldiers and stealthily attack the Empress [*née*] Lü[5] and the Heir-apparent.

[1] Ch'en Hsi (CHS, 1B, 6b; JMT, p. 1098) was Chancellor of State in Tai, which was in the present Hopei Province north of the Great Wall; the old city was 25 *li* east of the present Yü hsien (Yü chou). For details of the revolt cf. MH, vol. II, pp. 393–395; HFHD, vol. I, pp. 125–128.

[2] Han Hsin (SC, 92; CHS, 34, 1a–5a; JMT, p. 1698) was one of the greatest generals of Kao-tsu, who made him Marquis of Huai-yin. He was killed in February/March, 196 B.C., for his part in this revolt (HFHD, vol. I, p. 128 and footnote 4). The above incident is also recorded in SC, 92, 7b.

[3] From SC, 92, 7b.

[4] *T'u nu* might be translated as a single term: "convict-slaves."

[5] The Empress *née* Lü (SC, 8 *passim;* and 9; CHS, 1–3 *passim;* and 97A, 1b–2b; JMT, pp. 336–337) was Kao-tsu's Empress. She was the real ruler for 15 years from his death to hers in 180 B.C. Her death was the signal for a general revolt against her family by the loyal followers of the Emperor. The Lü family was stamped out. In the present case it was the Empress herself who foiled Han Hsin's plot and tricked him to his death.

14. Ca. 190–179 B.C.[1] CHS, 97A, 3b (7b)

竇后兄長君弟廣國字少君年四五歲時家貧爲人所
略賣其家不知處傳十餘家至宜陽爲其主人入山作炭
暮臥岸下百餘人岸崩盡厭殺臥者少君獨脫不死自卜
數日當爲侯從其家之長安聞皇后新立家在觀津姓竇
氏廣國去時雖少識其縣名及姓又嘗與其姊采桑墮用
爲符信上書自陳皇后言帝召見問之具言其故果是復
問其所識曰姊去我西時與我決傳舍中勾沐沐我已飯
我乃去於是竇皇后持之而泣侍御左右皆悲迺厚賜之
家於長安

The older brother of the Empress [*née*] Tou[2] was [Tou] Chang-chün;[3] her younger brother was [Tou] Kuang-kuo,[4] whose style name was Shao-chün.   When [the latter was] four or five years old the family was poor[5] and he was kidnaped and sold by someone, and his family did not know his whereabouts.   He was passed along through ten or more families[6] till he arrived at I-yang[7] and went into the mountains to make charcoal for his master.   One evening more than a hundred people were sleeping under a cliff.   The cliff slid and completely buried and killed the sleepers.   [Tou] Shao-chün alone escaped and did not die.

He cast his divination [and learned that] in a few days[8] he should become a marquis.   He followed his master and went to Ch'ang-an[9] where he heard that the Empress had newly been established, that her home was in Kuan-chin,[10] and that her surname was Tou. Although [Tou] Kuang-kuo had been young at the time he left home he still remembered the name of his prefecture and his surname, and also that once he had tumbled when picking mulberry leaves with his older sister.   Using [this incident] as a mark of evidence he sent up a letter reporting himself.

The Empress told the Emperor.[11]   They summoned [Tou Kuang-kuo] for an audience and questioned him.   He told his whole past. It proved to be true [that he was her brother.   She] again asked what he remembered.[12]   He said: "At the time sister left me [to go]

275

west she parted with me in the transfer house,[13] called for bathing things, bathed me, and having fed me,[14] then left."

At this the Empress [*née*] Tou embraced him and wept. The attendants[15] and people about were all deeply touched. She thereupon liberally rewarded him[16] and housed him at Ch'ang-an.[17]

[1] The latter date is the time when the concubine *née* Tou was made Empress, shortly after which Tou Kuang-kuo's slavery ended. The earlier date is uncertain. Tou Kuang-kuo was sold into slavery when he was four or five, probably only shortly after his sister went into the palace, for he remembered some of the details long after. It is not stated when she left her family. The first date given is 188 B.C. when she bore the child who became Emperor Ching. She had already borne a daughter. Thus she must have left home at least two years earlier, and probably more.

[2] The Empress *née* Tou (SC, 49, 2b–3b; CHS, 97A, 3b; JMT, p. 1771) was born in Kuan-chin prefecture in Ch'ing-ho Commandery (see footnote 10) and was chosen to go into the palace to wait on the Empress Dowager *née* Lü. She was one of the girls presented by the Empress Dowager to the King of Tai, who granted her his favors. She bore him a daughter and then a son, who later became Emperor Ching. In 180 B.C. the King of Tai was chosen to become Emperor Wen, and in 179 his oldest surviving son, by his concubine *née* Tou, was established as Heir-apparent, and she was made Empress. She was a stanch advocate of Taoism. Three of her relatives became marquises. She died in 135 B.C.

[3] Tou Chang-chün (SC, 49, 3a; CHS, 97A, 3b). Little is known of him, except that he was an older brother of the Empress *née* Tou and died before 157 B.C. His son, Tou P'eng-tsu, was made a marquis.

[4] Tou Kuang-kuo (SC, 49, 3a–b; CHS, 97A, 3b–4a; 18, 5a; JMT, p. 1773). The first part of his biography is here translated. In 157 B.C. he was made Marquis of Ch'ang-wu with an income from a thousand households. He died in 151 B.C.

[5] The fact that the family was poor when Tou Kuang-kuo was sold might suggest that he was forcibly sold to cover a debt. Yet this passage is cited as *locus classicus* for the term *lüeh mai*, "to kidnap and sell." Cf. TY; DC, p. 600. It is interesting that the family was poor, for it had only recently sent a daughter to the palace. Obviously she was still in such an inconspicuous position that she could not help her family financially.

[6] I.e., he was sold and resold. Cf. also the phrase in the *Lun heng*, footnote 17, below.

[7] I-yang was in present northwestern Honan Province, some 17 miles west of the present I-yang hsien, and not far from Lo-yang. Thus in being owned by several successive masters young Tou Kuang-kuo went from Kuan-chin several hundred miles southwestward.

[8] HSPC here quotes Chou Shou-ch'ang, who quotes the remark of Liu Ch'ang (1019–68) that "day" should probably be "said." For it was actually many years before Tou Kuang-kuo became a marquis, in 157, on the accession of his nephew Emperor Ching. This reading makes *pu-shu* the name of a particular kind of divination, and Chou Shou-ch'ang cites the term so used in CHS, 98. With this correction the passage reads: "He cast his divination, which said . . . ."

[9] Following the commentary of Yen Shih-ku and the more explicit *So-yin* commentary in SC, 49, 3a.

[10] Kuan-chin, in Ch'ing-ho Commandery, was in present southeastern Hopei Province, about eight miles southeast of Wu-i hsien, near the Shantung border.

[11] SC says: "Empress Tou discussed it with Emperor Wen."

[12] SC says: "She also again asked what he could give as further evidence."

[13] The *So-yin* commentary to SC explains this as a house in the imperial dispatch system, and that when Empress Tou was first entering the palace she parted from her younger brother in the transfer house.

[14] SC says: ". . . begged to give food to me, and then left."

[15] This may mean attendant slave-girls (cf. *59*, footnote 3) but here the question is irrelevant.

[16] SC here adds: ". . . with fields, houses, money, and she ennobled her duke cousin . . . ." The *So-yin* commentary explains this latter as referring to Tou Ying, the son of her cousin on her father's side.

[17] The story of Tou Kuang-kuo also appears in the *Lun heng* by Wang Ch'ung, a philosopher who lived ca. A.D. 27–97 (*Han Wei ts'ung-shu*, *Lun heng*, ch. 2, 22a. Cf. Alfred Forke, trans., *Lun-Hêng*, pt. I, p. 179). Forke translates:

"A younger brother of the Empress Dowager Tou, of the name of *Kuang Kuo*, was, at the age of 4 or 5 years, robbed from his poor family, and sold, his people not knowing his whereabouts. More than ten times he was sold again to other families, till he came to I-yang. There he went on the hills for his master to make charcoal:—When it grew cold at night, over a hundred people lay down under the coal. The coal collapsed, and all were crushed to death, save *Kuang Kuo*, who managed to escape. He then divined himself, and ascertained that, after a certain number of days, he would be made a marquis. He left his home, and betook himself to *Chang-an*. There he learned that the Empress *Tou* had lately settled her family at *Kuan-chin* in *Ch'ing-ho*. He reported himself to the Emperor. The Empress Dowager prevailed upon *Ching Ti* to grant him an audience. What he replied to the questions about his origin proved true, and the Emperor made him rich presents. At the accession of *Wen Ti*, *Kuang Kuo* was created a marquis of *Chang Wu* . . . ."

Two points regarding slavery are of interest: (1) The *Lun heng* says: "His family was poor and he was *robbed and sold* 掠賣." This confirms the SC and CHS story. (2) "He was *sold and resold* 傳賣 through ten or more families." This is more explicit than the SC and CHS versions.

The statement that it was charcoal which buried the sleepers is probably a typographical error of 炭 instead of the SC and CHS 岸. It is certainly an error that the Empress Dowager (sic) told Emperor Ching about her brother. That would place the event about 157 B.C., twenty-two years after she became Empress. It is also a glaring error that Tou Kuang-kuo was made a marquis at the accession of Emperor Wen. That was in 180 B.C. CHS, 18, 5a, says explicitly that he was made a marquis in 157 B.C. at the accession of Emperor Ching (cf. also SC, 19, 16b).

By comparison with the SC and CHS versions it is clear that in one or two places Forke has punctuated wrongly, and therefore mistranslated. In several points the *Lun heng* version is closer to the present CHS than to the present SC, which may be secondary here. Wang Ch'ung was a disciple of Pan Ku's father, Pan Piao, and knew his preliminary version of the Han history, but not the CHS itself.

15. 181–180 B.C.[1] CHS, 43, 4a (8b)

陳平乃以奴婢百人車馬五十乘錢五百萬遺買爲食
飲費買以此游漢廷公卿間名聲籍甚

Ch'en P'ing[2] thereupon bestowed on [Lu] Chia[3] one hundred male and female slaves, fifty sets of carriages and horses, and five million cash for his entertaining expenses.[4] Because of this, [Lu] Chia mingled at the Han court among dukes and ministers, and his reputation was very bad.[5]

[1] This event occurred shortly before the destruction of the Lü family in August/September, 180 B.C.

[2] Ch'en P'ing (SC, 56, 1a–4b; CHS, 40, 5b–8a; JMT, p. 1067) was at first a follower of Hsiang Yü, but joined Kao-tsu and was perhaps his most valuable adviser, several times solving difficult state problems, and once in 200 B.C. saving him from defeat by the Huns (HFHD, vol. I, p. 116 and footnote 2). He was made a marquis as a reward. He was Lieutenant Chancellor at the time of the present incident, and guided the revolt which quashed the Lü family (HFHD, vol. I, pp. 201–210), then helped put Emperor Wen on the throne.

[3] Lu Chia (SC, 97, 3a–4a; CHS, 43, 2b–4a; JMT, p. 1122) was a personal retainer of Kao-tsu, best known in connection with his missions to the Kingdom of Nan Yüeh (see Léonard Aurousseau, "La première conquête chinoise des pays annamites," pp. 184, 188–195). In the present situation his job was to act as personal emissary and assistant to Ch'en P'ing in lining up the powerful nobles to combat the plot of the Empress née Lü to establish her family in power.

[4] Whether the slaves, carriages and horses, and money were the personal property of Ch'en P'ing, or whether as Lieutenant Chancellor he was able to give them from the government, is not clear; neither the word "public" nor "private" modifies "slaves," nor is the source of the other property stated. Ch'en P'ing was probably wealthy. He had the income from a city which was estimated at 5,000 households when it was given to him twenty years before this time, but which had numbered approximately 30,000 before the devastating wars of the establishment of Han (CHS, 40, 7b). From the wording of the text it is assumed that Ch'en P'ing was to receive the income from the entire city no matter how great it grew, for the grant was of a special nature. If this gift to Lu Chia was given by Ch'en P'ing personally, it sounds amazing. It put Lu Chia on an equal social footing with dukes and ministers. On the other hand, there seems to be no way of knowing whether a Lieutenant Chancellor had the legal power or some illegal means of giving government property.

[5] The last four words are thus translated by Couvreur (DC, p. 688). The expression seems to connote primarily a bad reputation for extravagance and dispersing largess.

16.   177–174 B.C.[1]   CHS, 48, 6b (17b)

今民賣僮者爲之繡衣絲履偏諸緣內之閑中是古天
子后服所以廟而不宴者也而庶人得以衣婢妾白穀之
表薄紈之裏緁以偏諸美者黼繡是古天子之服今富人
大賈嘉會召客者以被牆古者以奉一帝一后而節適今
庶人屋壁得爲帝服倡優下賤得爲后飾然而天下不屈
者殆未有也

[Chia Yi[2] said in memorials to Emperor Wen]: "Nowadays people who sell youths[3] dress them up in embroidered clothes and silken shoes with the edges all embellished, and put them into pens.[4] These [clothes] are what ancient empresses wore at the ancestral temples and not [even] for feasts. And common people are allowed, in dressing their female slaves and concubines, to use white silk gauze outside and thin white silk underneath, with braid on the hem—the most beautiful, painted and embroidered. These are the ancient emperors' clothes. Nowadays rich men and great merchants, when inviting guests for a great feast, use to cover the walls what the ancients used for the service of one emperor and one empress, and in moderation. How can there be no danger that the world will be unsubmissive [to the Emperor] if now the walls of the rooms of commoners may be done with an emperor's clothes; if singers and entertainers, [and other] mean people may have the ornaments of an empress?"

[1] This passage comes from a summary of various memorials by Chia Yi, some eight pages of text: CHS, 48, 3a–11a. Just before it begins, several events are mentioned: The incursion of the Huns, probably that of June/July, 177 (HFHD, vol. I, p. 246); the rebellion and death of the King of Huai-nan, December/January, 175/174 (ibid., p. 250); and the rebellion and death of the King of Chi-pei, September/October, 177 B.C. (ibid., p. 248). At the end of the passage it says that at this time the Chancellor Chou P'o had been dismissed and had returned to his state, then had been accused of rebellion and tried but found innocent. These events occurred in 176 B.C. (ibid., pp. 246, 249). The speeches of Chia Yi, from which this passage is an abstract, were thus probably made during the years 177–174 B.C.

[2] Chia Yi (SC, 84, 3b–6b; CHS, 48; JMT, p. 1332) lived ca. 201–165 B.C. He was one of the greatest literary figures of the Han period, and one of its first statesmen. He was the author of the *Hsin shu*, of which a part is the *Kuo Ch'in lun*, or "Discourse on the faults of Ch'in," which makes up part of SC, 6.

[3] Ju Shun (fl. ca. A.D. 189–265) comments: "僮謂隸妾也 *T'ung* means menials and concubines." This passage is important evidence that *t'ung* were

sold, and that the term sometimes means slaves. From the description of their costume it may be assumed that these *t'ung* were for the luxury trade—if males, perhaps for pederasty, and if females, for concubinage or prostitution. If the last line translated refers back to this—as the reference to the ornaments of an empress suggests—it suggests that the *t'ung* were trained and used as professional entertainers, which also implies prostitution.

[4] Fu Ch'ien (ca. A.D. 125–195) defines "pen" as an enclosure for selling male and female slaves.

17. Ca. 200–150 B.C.[1] CHS, 91, 4b (9b)

齊俗賤奴虜而刁閒獨愛貴之桀黠奴人之所患唯刁
閒收取使之逐魚鹽商買之利或連車騎交守相然愈益
任之終得其力起數千萬故曰寧爵無刁言能使豪奴自
饒而盡其力也

In Ch'i[2] it was customary to look down upon male slave captives,[3] but Tiao Chien[4] alone appreciated and valued them. Rascally and crafty male slaves are what men suffer from. But Tiao Chien alone gathered and employed them to go after the profits of fishing, salt [refining], and itinerant and resident merchandising. Some [among them even] associated with [generals of] chariots and cavalry, and were intimate with administrators [of commanderies] and chancellors [of kingdoms], yet he entrusted them the more. Eventually by their help he became [rich[5] to the extent of] several thousand myriad[6] [cash]. Therefore [his slaves] said: "Rather no noble rank [than to be] without Tiao."[7] Which meant that he was able to cause fierce male slaves [to feel] self-satisfied while exhausting their strength.[8]

[1] There seems to be no way of precisely fixing the date of this passage. Presumably it was copied by Pan Ku from Ssu-ma Ch'ien, who wrote or copied it about 100 B.C. Tiao Chien may have lived any time before that. The CHS passage takes up immediately after Tiao Chien, and in the same section, one Sheng Wei, who flourished toward the end of the Former Han. JMT, p. 10, calls Tiao Chien a Han man. Perhaps second century B.C. is a conservative estimate.

[2] Ch'i is equivalent to much of modern Shantung Province. The reference seems to refer to the region rather than to the period before 221 B.C. when Ch'i was an independent state.

[3] It may mean male slaves and captives (of war). The close association of the terms is interesting.

[4] Tiao Chien. His complete biography is here translated. The passage in SC, 129, 7b, is identical save for one word.

[5] From SC.

[6] I.e., several ten-million. This might be read, "several thousand up to a myriad [cash]," *wan* being the terminal figure. The term *ch'ien wan* certainly at times means thousand times myriad (cf. DC, p. 106), and here must mean that, for several thousand or a myriad is not a large figure for money in Han times, and certainly could not have been the extent of Tiao Chien's riches.

[7] This very terse sentence is explained by Meng K'ang (ca. A.D. 180–260): "Tiao Chien was able to keep fierce male slaves. Some of the slaves associated with [generals of] chariots and cavalry, and were intimate with administrators and chancellors. The slaves said to themselves: 'Would we want to be freed and become plebeians with honorary rank if we had to stop being Tiao Chien's slaves?' " The phrasing is rhetorical; the answer is "no." Chou Shou-ch'ang's interpreta-

tion (HSPC) is radically different. According to him the sentence means: "We would rather have the honor of a title, but if not, then the abundance of Tiao."

⁸ This last sentence might be translated: "He was able to employ fierce male slaves to enrich himself, while [making them] put forth all their effort."

---

18.   178–165 B.C.¹   CHS, 24A, 5a (13b)

有者半買而賣亡者取倍稱之息於是有賣田宅鬻子
孫以償責者矣

[In an address to Emperor Wen on the hardships of the agri-cultural classes, Ch'ao Ts'o² said]: "Those who have [grain] sell at half price, and those who have none get respite by borrowing, to be repaid double; and therefore there are those who sell their lands and houses, and sell their children and grandchildren in order to repay their creditors."

¹ This date is selected on the following grounds: The discourse is treated immediately after one by Chia Yi for which the date 178 B.C. has been proposed. Other discourses by Ch'ao Ts'o on similar subjects appear in his biography before a statement which says: "Chia Yi was at this time already dead." (CHS, 49, 9b.) Chia Yi died at the latest in 165 B.C., perhaps as early as 169 (WHC, 28). In 165 Ch'ao Ts'o was in high favor with Emperor Wen, who accepted a proposal by him for examinations of people who thought they could assist in government (CHS, 4, 7a; HFHD, vol. I, p. 259 and footnote 1).

² Ch'ao Ts'o (SC, 101, 3b–4a; CHS, 49, 3b–11a; JMT, p. 1744) was an influential official under Emperor Wen, Tutor to the Heir-apparent, and later Grandee Secretary under Emperor Ching. He was a brilliant literary figure, noted for his well-phrased memorials, which occupy most of his biographical memoir. Several of them have been translated into western languages. He was executed in 154 B.C. in an attempt by Emperor Ching to appease the leaders of the Rebellion of the Seven States (cf. HFHD, vol. I, pp. 294–295).

19.　Ca. 167 B.C.[1]　CHS, 49, 6a (14b)

先爲室屋具田器迺募辠人及免徒復作令居之不足
募以丁奴婢贖辠及輸奴婢欲以拜爵者不足迺募民之
欲往者皆賜高爵復其家予冬夏衣廩食能自給而止郡
縣之民得買其爵以自增至卿其亡夫若妻者縣官買予
之人情非有匹敵不能久安其處塞下之民祿利不厚不
可使久居危難之地胡人入驅而能止其所驅者以其半
予之縣官爲贖其民如是則邑里相救助赴胡不避死非

[Ch'ao Ts'o[2] in an address to Emperor Wen again discussed the two most urgent problems of the day—guarding the frontier and encouraging agriculture. Advising the establishment of frontier colonies, he said]: "First make habitations and prepare agricultural implements. Then enlist[3] condemned people together with pardoned convicts working out their sentences,[4] and order them to settle there. [If their number is] insufficient, invite [people] to atone for their crimes by means of [giving] adult male and female slaves, and [invite] those who wish to be granted noble ranks [to earn them] by presenting male and female slaves.[5] [If the number is still] insufficient, then enlist those common people who desire to go, granting them all high noble rank, and exempting their families [from taxation]. Give them winter and summer clothes and food from the granaries; when they are self-supporting, stop [giving the stake]. People of the commanderies and prefectures will thus be able to buy noble rank in order to raise themselves to [the level of honorary] minister.

"As for those without husbands or wives, let the imperial government buy and give them [mates, for] it is man's nature that without a mate he cannot long be satisfied in such a place. The people living along the Barrier, if their salaries and profits are not generous, cannot be made to stay long in such a dangerous and difficult region.

"If the Huns invade and plunder, and there are those who can recover what has been plundered, give them half [of what they recover[6]], the imperial government making restitution [to the original owner[7]].

283

以德上也欲全親戚而利其財也此與東方之戍卒不習
地執而心畏胡者功相萬也以陛下之時徙民實邊使遠
方亡屯戍之事塞下之民父子相保亡係虜之患利施後
世名稱聖明其與秦之行怨民相去遠矣上從其言募民
徙塞下

"If people are like this [i.e., vigorous to stop the Huns], then cities
and hamlets will mutually rescue and help each other, standing up
to the Huns, and not shunning death—not in order to show gratitude
to the Emperor, but with the wish to preserve their kinsfolk, and
to take advantage of the wealth [they can thus acquire].   The
efficacy of this [system] will be ten thousand times [as much as
the efficacy of] those military garrisons of the eastern regions, which
are not familiar with local conditions and heartily fear the Huns.
[Now] by Your Majesty's timely colonizing, the people will fructify
the borders, allowing the distant regions to be without the annoyance
of military garrisons.   With the people beneath the Barrier, fathers
and sons mutually protecting each other, freed from the fear of
captivity; with benefits spreading to later generations, and [Your]
fame being praised as sage and brilliant—far indeed will be the
divergence of this [method] from the practices of Ch'in, which embittered the people!"

The Emperor followed his counsel and enlisted people to remove
to beneath the Barrier.[8]

[1] The date is indefinite.   The speech was given during the reign of Emperor
Wen (180–157 B.C.), and though we are told that the Emperor followed the counsel
and enlisted people to remove to beneath the Barrier, there is no record of this
in the Annals of Emperor Wen.   In 167, however, occurred the greatest of the
Hun raids, and "the Emperor himself inquired about the army's welfare and
aroused the troops by reiterated instructions and orders and by making grants
to the officers and soldiers.   He himself wanted to make the expedition against
the Huns." (HFHD, vol. I, p. 256.)   Thus, the question was greatly on the Emperor's
mind, and it seems likely that Ch'ao Ts'o presented his scheme at this time.
    Broader dates might be 177–165 B.C.   In 177 the Huns resumed their raids
(ibid., p. 246), breaking the peace treaty which had been reaffirmed when Emperor
Wen took the throne.   Raids and diplomatic representations followed periodically
until 167, when the trouble was really serious.   The date 165 is probably the
terminus, for three pages after this passage it says that Chia Yi had already died
(CHS, 49, 9b).   The latest date for his death is 165, but he may have died as
early as 169 (WHC, 28).

[2] Cf. *18*, footnote 2.

[3] *Mu* has the sense of "to solicit," "to enlist soldiers," or "to invite," i.e.,
a voluntary enlistment.

[4] The expression *fu-tso* offers certain perplexities, and the commentators have
two explanations: that the term stands for (1) female convicts lightly sentenced;

(2) amnestied convicts who must, however, serve out their sentences. Li Chi (ca. A.D. 200) says that the expression *nu t'u fu-tso*, "female convict *fu-tso*," in CHS, 8, 1a, refers to one who commits a minor crime which would be punished by a year's frontier guard duty if committed by a man. Since women are weak, such a female convict would be allowed to work out her sentence in a government bureau. This interpretation is supported by a quotation from the *Han chiu i* cited by Ch'eng Shu-te (*Chiu ch'ao lü k'ao*, p. 54). But if *fu-tso* is by definition a female convict, why the redundant expression "female convict *fu-tso*"?

The other explanation, adopted here, is proposed by Meng K'ang (A.D. 180–260) in CHS, 8, 1a, also. He says that *fu-tso* is a convict whose punishment has been relaxed. There having been an amnesty and an imperial edict, his iron collar, iron leg rings, and russet clothes are removed, and he is no longer considered a convict but is a plebeian, though he must still work out the term of his sentence with the government. This explanation is approved by Yen Shih-ku, and is substantially the same as one proposed by Fu Tsan (ca. A.D. 285). Cf. HFHD, vol. II, chap. 8, footnote 1.4.

[5] It is certainly implied that the private slaves secured in these two ways would be sent to the frontier as colonists.

[6] The commentators disagree on the meaning of this passage. Meng K'ang says: "When the Huns invade to plunder and carry off, give half [the captives] to those Chinese who can capture them." Yen Shih-ku (A.D. 581–645) says: "What Meng [K'ang] says is incorrect. It means when the Huns invade to plunder, and kidnap Chinese and [their] live stock, and others are able to stop [them] and get [back] what they have plundered, order the original owner to give half [to the recoverer] as a reward." This reading is confirmed by the next sentence as Yen Shih-ku points out, and I have followed it.

[7] Here Chang Yen (third century) says: "[If they] get [back] Chinese, the government will redeem them." Yen Shih-ku says: "This [phrase in the text], following the phrase above, merely means that the government will provide [the owners] the cost to compensate them [the rescuers]. What Chang [Yen] says is incorrect."

By a different punctuation the last phrase may read: ". . . the government making restitution for [recovered] people." In this reading, the first words of the next sentence (*ch'i min*) become the last words of this one. Liu Feng-shih and Wang Hsien-ch'ien argue for this reading in HSPC.

[8] This passage does not appear in the biography of Ch'ao Ts'o in SC, 101. In CHS, 24A, 6a, there is a statement that Emperor Wen agreed to memorials of Ch'ao Ts'o regarding the giving of grain for frontier defense, in order to obtain titles. This is mentioned also in SC, 30 (MH, vol. III, p. 543). This is probably closely connected with the memorial above quoted. No date is given.

齊太倉令淳于公有罪當刑防獄逮繫長安淳于公無
男有五女當行會逮罵其女曰生子不生男緩急非有益
也其少女緹縈自傷悲泣迺隨其父至長安上書曰妾父
爲吏齊中皆稱其廉平今坐法當刑妾傷夫死者不可復
生刑者不可復屬雖後欲改過自新其道亡繇也妾願没
入爲官婢以贖父刑罪使得自新書奏天子

[In May/June, 167 B.C.] His Excellency Shun-yü [Yi],[1] Super-intendent of the Great Granaries in Ch'i, committed a crime deserving punishment [by mutilation[2]]. Prison guards[3] sent him bound to Ch'ang-an. His Excellency Shun-yü [Yi] had no sons, but five daughters. When about to start out he cursed his daughters, saying: "When one has children but no sons, they are of no use either in prosperity or adversity."

His youngest daughter, T'i-ying,[4] blamed herself and wept. She thereupon followed her father to Ch'ang-an and sent up a letter [to court], saying: "As an official, Your servant's father is considered incorruptible and just by every one in Ch'i. Now he has been tried and is about to be punished. Your servant grieves. Verily, when one is dead he cannot be reborn; when one is punished [by mutilation] he cannot attach [the lost member] again. Although he may later wish to reform and start himself afresh there is no way to follow. Your servant desires to be seized and become a government slave, in order to ransom her father from his punishment, and allow him to start afresh."

The letter was presented as a memorial to the Emperor.[5]

[1] Shun-yü Yi (SC, 105, 3b–5a; JMT, p. 1009) was a noted physician attached to the court in 180 B.C. Much of SC, 105, is devoted to medical cases and diagnoses attributed to him. See the two following documents.

[2] Legal punishment usually involved some sort of mutilation: tattooing the face, amputation of nose or feet, castration, or capital punishment. Cf. CHS, 23, 4b; HFHD, vol. I, p. 118, footnote 1; p. 177, footnote 1.

[3] HSPC here has "The Imperial Judge . . . ."

[4] Shun-yü T'i-ying (JMT, pp. 1525–26; Giles B, 1912) has become a famous filial example because of this incident, her story being transmitted in the *Lieh nu chuan* by Liu Hsiang. In modern editions it appears in ch. 6, under "Ch'i t'ai ts'ang nu," "The daughter of the Superintendent of Granaries of Ch'i."

[5] It is told in the following passage that Emperor Wen was so moved by her plea that he abolished the law of punishment by mutilation (also CHS, 4, 6b; HFHD, vol. I, p. 255). The whole story appears with slight modifications in SC, 10, 5b (MH, vol. II, pp. 474–476), and in SC, 105, 4a, where, however, it is dated 176 B.C.

濟北王召意診脈諸女子侍者至女子豎豎無病臣意
告永巷長曰豎傷脾不可勞法當春嘔血死臣意言王曰
才人女子豎何能王曰是好爲方多伎能爲所是案法新
往年市之民所四百七十萬曹偶四人王曰得毋有病乎
臣意對曰豎病重在死法中王召視之其顏色不變以爲
不然不賣諸侯所至春豎奉劍從王之廁王去豎後王令
人召之即仆於廁嘔血死

The King of Chi-pei[2] summoned [Shun-yü] Yi[3] to examine the pulse of all his girls and serving ones.[4] [When the examination] reached a girl page,[5] the page had no [apparent] sickness. Your servant, Yi, informed the Chief of the women's quarter, saying: "The page has injured her spleen; she cannot be worked hard. [According to my medical] rules she should spit blood and die in the spring."

Your servant, Yi, said to the King: "What abilities have these 'talented persons' and girl pages?"

The King said: "They are good at doing tricks, and have many skills. They do things according to new methods.[6] Formerly I bought them in the common people's [market[7]] place, for 4,700,000 [cash[8]] for the group of four." Then the King said: "Are they sick?"

Your servant, Yi, replied, saying: "The page is seriously sick and will die."

The King summoned and looked at her. Her complexion was unchanged, and he considered [the diagnosis] untrue. [Therefore] he did not sell her at the [market] place for nobles.

When spring came, the page was [one time] following the King to the toilet, carrying his sword. When the King left, the page remained behind. The King ordered someone to summon her. Just then she fell over flat by the toilet, spat blood, and died.[9]

[1] The dating of this and the following passage can only be solved by a study of the interlocking dates of various individuals mentioned in the different medical case-records copied by the authors of the SC into this chapter. The memoir itself consists of three parts: a brief biography, about twenty cases, and a group of medical questions and answers. The second and third were copied from a

memorial written by Shun-yü Yi in response to an inquiry from court. Two fixed dates appear in the biography. The eighth year of the Empress Dowager *née* Lü, 180 B.C., is mentioned twice as the year when Shun-yü Yi began his medical studies with Yang Ch'ing, who was then over seventy years old. The commentator Hsü Kuang (ca. A.D. 352–425) states that Shun-yü Yi was then twenty-six. This figure may have been derived from the statement that he was thirty-nine after he had studied for three years with Yang Ch'ing, and then for ten more years after Yang Ch'ing's death (cf. also *k'ao-teng* commentary by Ku Yen-wu). If this reasoning be correct, then Shun-yü Yi was born about 206 B.C. The second fixed date is when Shun-yü Yi was taken to Ch'ang-an for mutilation in 167 B.C. (cf. *20;* SC, 105, gives the date 176, but in SC, 10, 5b, and CHS, 23, 5b, the date 167 is given, and linked with Emperor Wen's edict revoking punishment by mutilation).

Interlocking dates for the professional period of Shun-yü Yi's life come from the nobles mentioned in the medical records. None of the other individuals mentioned is important enough to appear elsewhere in historical context. The pivotal reference is to the Chancellor of the Marquis of Yang-hsü. This marquisate only existed between 176 and 164 B.C. (SC, 19, 12b; CHS, 15A, 3b; MH, vol. III, p. 154, No. 25; HFHD, vol. 1, pp. 249 and 259). In 164 the Marquis of Yang-hsü, Liu Chiang-lü, was made King of Ch'i, and he died in 154 B.C. (MH, vol. III, p. 112, No. 5). Liu Chiang-lü is referred to in another case-record, not by name, but as "the King of Ch'i, formerly the Marquis of Yang-hsü." On page 10a it is said that Shun-yü Yi lived with the Marquis of Yang-hsü, and followed him to the court at Ch'ang-an, where he had a chance to practice. This must have been before 164, and may have been before 167 when Shun-yü Yi was found guilty of a crime.

In four cases the King of Chi-pei is mentioned. This kingdom was founded in 178 and abolished the next year, when Liu Hsing-chü revolted and was killed (MH, vol. III, p. 110, No. 1. This King is probably the one referred to, posthumously, in the phrase: "The wet-nurse of the former King of Chi-pei," p. 7a). The kingdom was not re-established until 164. It was held by Liu Chih till 154, when he became King of Tzu-ch'uan (MH, vol. III, p. 110, No. 2). He is probably the King of Chi-pei referred to in the present passage. The kingdom continued for many years under the new line, but these later kings seem too late to be involved.

The King of Tzu-ch'uan is mentioned once. This kingdom was founded in 164 and held by Liu Hsien until the Seven States Rebellion, in 154, when the King revolted and was killed. The kingdom continued under the above Liu Chih, formerly King of Chi-pei, who died in 130. The reference to the King of Tzu-ch'uan is probably to the first king, Liu Hsien, who reigned 164–154. If the second king, Liu Chih, had been meant it is likely that he would have been spoken of as the former King of Chi-pei, especially since that person is mentioned in several previous cases.

On page 9b the sickness of King Wen is mentioned, though Shun-yü Yi was not called into consultation. At that time his family was poor, and he wanted to practice medicine. The commentator Hsü Kuang says that this was King Wen of Ch'i (Liu Tse), who died in 165 B.C. Hsü Kuang is certainly right, for the only other kings named Wen (MH, vol. III, pp. 93–114) were the Kings of Ch'ang-sha (202 B.C.), Ch'u (153–151), and Ho-chien (178–166). Shun-yü Yi did not practice in those regions as far as the records show.

In the same passage it is stated that the kings of Chao, Chiao-hsi, Chi-nan, and Wu all summoned Shun-yü Yi, but he did not dare to go. Of these states three are helpful. Chiao-hsi was not founded until 164 B.C.; Chi-nan lasted only between 164 and 154; Wu was called by that name only between 196 and 154 (MH, vol. III, pp. 97, 98, 110).

With this evidence, I think the dates 167–154, or perhaps 170–150, would cover the period of Shun-yü Yi's medical practice.

[2] Probably Liu Chih, son of Liu Fei, the King of Ch'i. Cf. footnote 1 above. Chi-pei was one of the kingdoms into which the Kingdom of Ch'i was divided. Its capital was in Shantung, south of the present Ch'ang-ch'ing hsien.

[3] Cf. *20,* footnote 1.

[4] Probably they were slave-girls; cf. *29, 37, 59*.

[5] She was a slave, for she was purchased, and the King had the power to sell her.

[6] The text is difficult. My reading follows the *So-yin* commentary.

[7] The text says "common people's place," and later mentions a "nobles' place." The context indicates that these "places" were market places. I have found no other examples of this usage.

[8] The *So-yin* commentary says: "This equals 4,700 *kuan* of today." A *kuan* was a string of 1,000 cash. In most Han texts where figures of money are quoted without designating the unit, cash (*ch'ien*) are meant.

[9] The passage concludes with diagnostic information on the case.

齊丞相舍人奴從朝入宮臣意見之食閨門外望其色
有病氣臣意卽告宦者平平好爲脈學臣意所臣意卽示
之舍人奴病告之曰此傷脾氣也當至春鬲塞不通不能
食飲法至夏泄血死宦者平卽往告相曰君之舍人奴有
病病重死期有日相君曰卿何以知之曰君朝時入宮君
之舍人奴盡食閨門外平與倉公立卽示平曰病如是者
死相卽召舍人奴而謂之曰公奴有病不舍人曰奴無病
身無痛者至春果病至四月泄血死

A male slave of the *she-jen*[2] of the Chancellor[3] of [the Kingdom] of Ch'i followed [his master to] court and entered the palace. Your servant, [Shun-yü] Yi observed him eating outside the *kuei-men*[4] and noticed that his complexion had a sickly emanation. Your servant, Yi, immediately informed eunuch P'ing. P'ing was good at taking the pulse, and had studied at Your servant Yi's establishment. Your servant, Yi, forthwith pointed out to him [the features of] the illness of the male slave of the *she-jen*, and instructed him, saying: "This is the emanation of an injured spleen. In spring he will be stopped up and [the organs] will not intercommunicate, so that he will not be able to eat or drink. [According to my medical] rules, when summer comes he will pass blood and die."

Eunuch P'ing immediately went and informed the Chancellor, saying: "The male slave of Your Excellency's *she-jen* is sick, and the sickness is serious. The period of his death is fixed."

His Excellency the Chancellor said: "Sir, how did you learn that?"

[The eunuch] said: "Since Your Excellency came to court and entered the palace, the male slave of Your Excellency's *she-jen* has always eaten outside the *kuei-men*. P'ing was standing there with the Superintendent of the Granary, [Shun-yü Yi, who] explained [the slave's sickness to] P'ing, saying: 'One who is sick like this will die.'"

The Chancellor immediately summoned the male slave of his *she-jen*, and spoke [to the latter], saying: "Is Your Excellency's male slave sick or not?"

The *she-jen* said: "The male slave is not sick, and he has no pain in his body."

When spring came he really was sick, and in the fourth month he passed blood and died.[5]

[1] See preceding document for dating. The fact that Shun-yü Yi is spoken of in this passage as Superintendent of the Granary might indicate that the event occurred before 167 B.C., at which time he was found guilty of a crime deserving mutilation (cf. *20*). Yet it is not clearly stated that he held that position when he was condemned or if he did that he lost it thereby.

It is stated on page 10a that he accompanied the Marquis of Yang-hsü to Ch'ang-an, where he was able to practice at court. That occasion must have been between 176 and 164—probably near 164. However, it is not certain that this was the only time Shun-yü Yi was at Ch'ang-an as a physician.

[2] *She-jen;* cf. *39*, footnote 3.

[3] In 145 B.C. the term *ch'eng-hsiang* for chancellors of states was changed to simple *hsiang.* Cf. HFHD, vol. I, p. 322.

[4] According to TY, the *kuei-men* was the gate to the inner quarters, where the women lived. The significance of the fact that the slave always ate outside the *kuei-men* is not clear. Was he eating women's food because he was sick?

[5] The passage concludes with a long diagnostic discussion, which indicates that the slave had often toasted himself before the fire and then gone out into strong winds.

23. Ca. 165–157 B.C.[1] CHS, 49, 3a (6a)

初盎爲吳相時從史盜私盎侍兒盎知之弗泄遇之如
故人有告從史君知女與侍者通迺亡去盎驅自追之遂
以侍者賜之復爲從史

Formerly when [Yüan] Ang[2] was Chancellor of Wu [State] his Attendant Secretary had secret relations with [Yüan] Ang's serving child.[3] [Yüan] Ang learned of it but did not reveal [that he knew], and treated him as usual. Someone informed the Attendant Secretary, [saying]: "His Excellency knows that you and the serving one are having relations." Thereupon he fled. [Yüan] Ang immediately pursued him personally, then presented him with the serving one, and made him his Attendant Secretary again.[4]

[1] Yüan Ang was made Chancellor of Wu State toward the end of the reign of Emperor Wen, and held the office until 157 B.C. The event probably happened a few years before.

[2] Yüan Ang (SC, 101, 1a–3b; CHS, 49, 1a–3b; JMT, p. 847) was a Gentleman of the Household under Emperor Wen, and a great favorite. Famous for his free criticism, he once went too far, and was transferred to the position of Commandant of Lung-hsi, then was made Chancellor of Ch'i. Again transferred to the position of Chancellor of Wu State, he was accused by Ch'ao Ts'o of taking bribes from the King of Wu, whom he was supposed to watch for the Emperor. For this he was dismissed. In 154 B.C. he reported the rebellion planned by the King of Wu, and suggested that Ch'ao Ts'o, one of the greatest Han ministers, whose policy was endangering the various kings, be executed to appease the kings of the Seven States who were planning to rebel. This was done (cf. HFHD, vol. I, pp. 292–297), but it did not stop the rebellion. Later Yüan Ang was assassinated. He is not listed as a marquis.

[3] Wen Ying (fl. ca. A.D. 196–220) states that she was a female slave. TY quotes this passage as evidence that the term shih-erh means "female slave."

[4] The story was recorded because the Attendant Secretary was later able to save Yüan Ang's life. The passage appears with only minor variations in SC, 101, 3a, with Wen Ying's commentary also given.

---

24. 160 B.C. CHS, 4, 7b (17b)

五月赦天下免官奴婢爲庶人

[In the latter part of his reign, the fourth year], the fifth month, [Emperor Wen proclaimed] a general amnesty and [also] freed the government male and female slaves to become commoners.[1]

[1] This amnesty is not recorded in SC, since this is one of the years not mentioned there. Cf. HFHD, vol. I, p. 265.

25.   154 B.C.   CHS, 52, 2b (6b)

夫不肯隨喪歸奮曰願取吳王若將軍頭以報父仇於
是夫被甲持戟募軍中壯士所善願從數十人及出壁門
莫敢前獨兩人及從奴十餘騎馳入吳軍至戲下所殺傷
數十人不得前復還走漢壁亡其奴獨與一騎歸夫身中
大創十餘適有萬金良藥故得無死

[During the Rebellion of the Seven States, Kuan Fu[1] and his father Kuan Meng were fighting on the Han side. The father was killed, and according to Han law Kuan Fu could have returned home with the body. But Kuan] Fu was unwilling to follow the coffin home. He spiritedly said: "I wish to take the head of the King of Wu, or that of a general, to avenge my father."

Therefore [Kuan] Fu donned his armor, grasped his halberd, and asked for several tens of volunteers from among those hardy men of the army who loved him and wanted to follow him. When they were about to sally out the gate of the [Han] ramparts none dared to advance except two men. With their attendant male slaves, [in all] ten or more horsemen, they galloped into the Wu army to the very foot of the [general's] standard, killing and wounding several tens of people. Unable to go forward, they rushed back to the Han ramparts. Their male slaves were lost,[2] and only one of the [free] horsemen returned with [Kuan] Fu, who had ten or more great wounds in his body. Opportunely there was some precious and good medicine, and therefore he did not die.

[1] Kuan Fu (SC, 107, 3a–6a; CHS, 52, 2b–5b; JMT, p. 1786) was the son of Chang Meng, who was a retainer of Kuan Ying, and therefore changed his surname to Kuan. After the famous event recorded here, Kuan Fu became Administrator of Huai-yang, then in 140 B.C. was appointed Chief of the Stud, then Chancellor of the State of Yen. Considerably later, about 122 B.C., he fell into disgrace and was executed.

[2] It is not certain whether the slaves were killed in battle or escaped, perhaps by surrender. The first interpretation seems more likely, because the ten or more horsemen (three leaders, and over seven slaves) killed and wounded several tens of the enemy. Obviously the slaves were fighting, too. Also it is not likely that Kuan Fu and his friends would have taken mounted and armed slaves into battle unless they could be trusted not to desert.

衞青字仲卿其父鄭季河東平陽人也以縣史給事侯
家平陽侯曹壽尙武帝姊陽信長公主季與主家僮衞媼
通生靑靑有同母兄衞長君及姊子夫子夫自平陽公主
家得幸武帝故靑冒姓爲衞氏衞媼長女君孺次女少兒
次女則子夫子夫男弟步廣皆冒衞氏靑爲侯家人少時
歸其父父使牧羊民母之子皆奴畜之不以爲兄弟數靑
嘗從人至甘泉居室有一鉗徒相靑曰貴人也官至封侯
靑笑曰人奴之生得無笞罵卽足矣安得封侯事乎靑壯
爲侯家騎從平陽主建元二年春靑姊子夫得入宮幸上

Wei Ch'ing;[2] his style name was Chung-ch'ing. His father was Cheng Chi, a man from P'ing-yang in Ho-tung. As a prefectural clerk[3] [the father] served in the household of a marquis, Ts'ao Shou,[4] the Marquis of P'ing-yang, who had married an elder sister of Emperor Wu, the Elder-Princess of Yang-hsin. [Cheng] Chi had relations with the Princess' household maiden, Dame Wei,[5] and she begat Ch'ing. By the same mother [but a different father] Ch'ing had an elder brother, Wei Chang-chün, and an elder sister, [Wei] Tzu-fu. [Wei] Tzu-fu, coming from the household of the Princess of P'ing-yang, obtained the favors of Emperor Wu.[6] Therefore Ch'ing adopted the surname Wei. Dame Wei's eldest daughter was Chün-ju; the next daughter was Shao-erh;[7] and the next daughter, then, was [Wei] Tzu-fu. [Wei] Tzu-fu's younger brother was Pu-kuang. Both [boys] adopted the surname Wei.[8]

[Wei] Ch'ing was the marquis' householder. When still young he returned to his father. His father employed him as a sheep herder, and the children by the plebeian mother[9] all treated him as a male slave and did not count him as a brother.

Once [Wei] Ch'ing went with someone to the Kan-ch'üan [palace] guard house[10] where an iron-collared convict physiognomized [Wei] Ch'ing and said: "[You have] a nobleman's [features]; your official positions will go so far as enfoeffment as a marquis." [Wei] Ch'ing laughed and replied: "Born as another's male slave, it is sufficient not to be beaten and cursed.   How could I get appointed a marquis!" [11]

When [Wei] Ch'ing grew up he was a horseman in the marquis' household, escorting the Princess of P'ing-yang.[12] In the spring of 139 B.C. [Wei] Ch'ing's elder sister [Wei] Tzu-fu succeeded in entering the palace and received the Emperor's favors.

[1] The dates when the Marquis of P'ing-yang was first appointed (see footnote 4) and when Wei Ch'ing was made Grand Palace Grandee.

[2] Wei Ch'ing (SC, 111, 1a–6b; CHS, 55, 1a–3a; JMT, p. 1603) was one of the greatest Han generals. In 139 B.C. he was made Grand Palace Grandee when his elder sister, Wei Tzu-fu, was taken into Emperor Wu's harem; later she became Empress in 128. The year before, Wei Ch'ing had been made General of Chariots and Cavalry. In 127 he became Marquis of Ch'ang-p'ing. He conducted seven great campaigns against the Hsiung-nu before he died in 106 B.C. See also footnote 12.

[3] SC and HSPC here have li, "a minor official," for shih, "clerk." P'ing-yang, in Ho-tung Commandery, was in present Shansi, southwest of Lin-fen hsien.

[4] Ts'ao Shou is not listed as Marquis of P'ing-yang in SC, 18, 2b (MH, vol. III, p. 139), or CHS, 16, 2b. In the SC account, however, Yen Shih-ku points out that Ts'ao Shih must be the same as Ts'ao Shou. SC, 54, 3b, substantiates this, for it says that Ts'ao Shih married the Princess of P'ing-yang. (CHS, 39, 5b, skips Ts'ao Shih.) He was marquis from 153 to 132 B.C. (CHS, 16, 2b; MH, vol. III, p. 139). Assuming that Wei Ch'ing was conceived in 153, the first year of Marquis Ts'ao Shou (or Shih), he would have been only 14 or 15 when made Grand Palace Grandee.

[5] Yen Shih-ku says: "The word t'ung is a general term for female slave-concubines. The word Ao ["dame"] was her appellation later when she was old, and not what she was called at that time. The name Wei was her husband's surname." SC calls her the marquis' concubine 侯妾, instead of chu chia t'ung. The So-yin commentary, after a long discussion about the term Dame Wei, says that a ch'ieh would probably not have a husband other than the marquis. But it points out that later on it is said that Wei Ch'ing's older brother, Wei Chang-tzu (sic), and his older sister, Wei Tzu-fu, by the same mother, both adopted the surname Wei, which makes it appear as if she did have a husband. The commentary concludes that it is not clear whether the surname they adopted was that of either the father or the mother.

In the light of the SC and CHS texts, which differ on the matter of which children falsely adopted the surname Wei, it might be safely concluded that the mother, being a slave-girl, had no special surname. When Tzu-fu was taken into the Emperor's harem all the children and the mother adopted the surname Wei. Wei was the surname of the father of Wei Chang-chün, the oldest boy, and/or of the father of Tzu-fu, the child who was really important.

[6] For this story, see the next document.

[7] She was the mother of Ho Ch'ü-ping, whose father was Ho Chung-ju (CHS, 55, 3a). Their relations were apparently out of wedlock. There is no indication in CHS, 55, that Shao-erh was considered a slave-girl, but she is called a shih-che ("serving one") in 29, and the term seems to indicate slavery in that instance. About 128 B.C. Wei Shao-erh married an official named Ch'en Chang.

[8] Yen Shih-ku says: "It means that Pu-kuang and Ch'ing, two people, neither having the surname Wei, adopted it."

In all there were six children of Dame Wei. Three were older than Wei Tzu-fu: the boy, Wei Chang-chün, and the two girls, Chün-ju and Shao-erh. The two younger children were boys, [Wei] Ch'ing and [Wei] Pu-kuang.

⁹ I.e., Wei Ch'ing's half-brothers and half-sisters by Cheng Chi and his real wife. Fu Ch'ien (ca. A.D. 125–195) says: "The *min mu* ["plebeian mother"] was the real wife." Yen Shih-ku says: "It means Cheng Chi's principal [or real] wife, who was originally [registered] in the census of households, as distinguished from [the other woman in] the house of the Princess. . . ."

Yen Shih-ku's distinction between a woman listed in the plebeian register, and a maiden (*t'ung*) in the household of the Princess is interesting. While not contemporary evidence, it suggests that a maiden in the household of a princess would not be listed in the register of common people, and if registered at all, would appear in a list of the nobility and its possessions.

¹⁰ Following Chang Yen (third–fourth centuries), who says it was a house for convicts at Kan-ch'üan; see also HSPC here.

¹¹ How did such an intimate detail get to the authors of the present SC and CHS? It may be apocryphal, as one would suspect about any such accurate prediction. If this is assumed, then it is the perpetrator of the tale and the historians who must be credited with believing that Wei Ch'ing considered himself a slave. Yet such an incident might have occurred; especially we cannot dismiss the idea that Wei Ch'ing did consider himself born a slave. For Wei Ch'ing was at the height of his fame during the life of Ssu-ma Tan, and died after Ssu-ma Ch'ien took over his father's historical work. In writing the biography of this great contemporary one or both of them probably sought and obtained first- or second-hand information about his boyhood.

The original biography was probably from the brush of Ssu-ma Tan or Ch'ien, but it cannot be asserted which of the present SC or CHS texts is the older— it is always possible that a passage in the present SC was copied back into it from the CHS after having been lost. Apparently the story was current in the first century A.D. (probably in the contemporary SC version or some other now lost) for the event is alluded to at least twice in the *Lun heng* by Wang Ch'ung (ca. A.D. 27–97) (Wang Ch'ung knew Pan Piao's version of the CHS, but not the final one). Cf. Alfred Forke, trans., *Lun-Hêng*, pt. I, pp. 169, 308.

The second reference is translated by Forke as follows: "The father of *Wei Ch'ing, Cheng Chi* had illicit intercourse with a maid of the princess *Yang Hsin, Wei. Wei Ch'ing* was born in the Chien-chang Palace. A convict read his destiny in his features and said: 'He is noble, and will be invested with the rank of a marquis.' *Wei Ch'ing* replied:—'For a slave it is quite enough not to be whipped or reviled. How could he dream of a marquisate?' " In the text (*Han Wei ts'ung-shu, Lun heng*, ch. 3, 7b), the first four words of Wei Ch'ing's reply are: 人奴之道 instead of the above *jen nu chih shong*. Thus it does not express the idea that he was born a slave as does CHS.

¹² At the end of the biography of Ho Ch'ü-ping, CHS, 55, 6b, there is a very interesting further point about Wei Ch'ing and the Elder-Princess of Yang-hsin, who was also called the Princess of P'ing-yang after her marriage to Ts'ao Shou, the Marquis of P'ing-yang (d. 132 B.C.): "When [Wei] Ch'ing was first honored and ennobled, Ts'ao Shou, the Marquis of P'ing-yang, had an incurable illness and returned to his state. The Elder-Princess [thought of marrying again and] inquired as to who among the marquises was the most worthy. Everyone about her spoke of the General-in-Chief [Wei Ch'ing]. The Princess laughed and said: 'He came out from my household and frequently escorted me as a cavalry man. How could it be?' Those about her said: 'At present none can compare to him in honor and nobility.' The Elder-Princess hinted about it to the Empress [*née* Wei Tzu-fu], and the Empress spoke of it to the Emperor. [The Emperor] thereupon summoned [Wei] Ch'ing and he married the Princess of P'ing-yang. He was buried together with the Princess. The tomb was erected at Hsiang-lu Mountain."

An author's eulogy in CHS, 58, 6b, lists Wei Ch'ing among a group of unusual men of lowly backgrounds: "Pu Shih, plucked up from being a shepherd; [Sang] Hung-yang, selected from the lowly tradesmen; Wei Ch'ing, roused up from slavery; and [Chin] Jih-ti, brought forth from being a surrendered captive." The same text occurs in SC, 112, 6b, but is an addition quoting CHS. The author of the sentiment is therefore probably Pan Ku.

孝武衞皇后字子夫生微也其家號曰衞氏出平陽侯
邑子夫爲平陽主謳者武帝即位數年無子平陽主求良
家女十餘人飾置家帝祓霸上還過平陽主主見所侍美
人帝不說既飲謳者進帝獨說子夫帝起更衣子夫侍尙
衣軒中得幸還坐驩甚賜平陽主金千斤主因奏子夫送
入宮子夫上車主拊其背曰行矣強飯勉之即貴願無忘
入宮歲餘不復幸武帝擇宮人不中用者斥出之子夫得
見涕泣請出上憐之復幸遂有身尊寵召其兄衞長君弟
青侍中而子夫生三女元朔元年生男據遂立爲皇后

Emperor Wu's Empress [*née*] Wei, whose style name was Tzu-fu, was of humble birth.   Her family[2] was called "the Wei family," and came from the fief-city of the Marquis of P'ing-yang.   [Wei] Tzu-fu was a chorus singer[3] for the Princess of P'ing-yang.

When Emperor Wu was on the throne several years and had no children, the Princess of P'ing-yang selected ten or more girls of good families, groomed them, and placed them in her household. The Emperor lustrated himself at Pa-shang,[4] and on his return visited the Princess of P'ing-yang.   The Princess introduced the Beauties who were in waiting, but the Emperor was not pleased.   During the drinking the chorus singers entered.   The Emperor was pleased only with [Wei] Tzu-fu.   The Emperor got up to change his clothes and [Wei] Tzu-fu attended him to care for his clothing.   She received his favors in the clothes carriage.   [The Emperor] returned to his seat profoundly satisfied.   He presented the Princess of P'ing-yang a thousand catties of gold, and the Princess accordingly memorialized that [Wei] Tzu-fu should be sent into the palace.

When [Wei] Tzu-fu mounted her carriage [to depart], the Princess patted her on the back and said: "Good luck.   Eat well and exert yourself.   When you have become noble I hope you will not forget me."

She entered the palace, but for a year or more was not favored again.   Emperor Wu was weeding out the Palace Women[5] who were no longer useful, and dismissing them. [Wei] Tzu-fu received an audience, wept, and begged to [be allowed to] go. The Emperor pitied her and again favored her. Then she conceived, and was honored and esteemed. [The Emperor] summoned her older brother Wei Chang-chün and her younger brother [Wei] Ch'ing to serve in the palace.

Thereafter [Wei] Tzu-fu bore three daughters. In 128 B.C. she bore a son, Chü.[6] Consequently she was made Empress.

[1] The period covered by the events in this passage while Wei Tzu-fu was a slave, and allowing her to be a year or two older than Wei Ch'ing. Cf. *26*.

[2] Cf. *26*, and footnotes, for general information on the family, places, and other people mentioned. The present passage appears also in SC, 49, 4b–5a, with occasional added information.

[3] She was also almost certainly a slave-girl, having been born of a slave woman and raised in her mistress' household. Her younger brother, Wei Ch'ing, was a slave, and probably her older sister, Shao-erh, was also.

[4] Pa-shang was a place on Pa River east of the capital (HFHD, vol. I, inset map). If the Emperor stopped at his sister's home on his way back to the capital, it must be assumed that she was then living at or near Ch'ang-an rather than at P'ing-yang in southwestern Shansi Province.

[5] According to Wei Hung (fl. ca. A.D. 25–57) *kung-jen* were government female slaves, chosen at the age of eight or older, to wait upon the Ladies of the Palace. Cf. *91* and *92*. Whether the term had this technical meaning in Emperor Wu's day and was so used by Ssu-ma Ch'ien and Pan Ku is uncertain. There may have been many *kung-jen* who were not slaves.

[6] This boy became Heir-apparent, but was executed in the scandalous witchcraft affair of 91 B.C. Cf. *80*, footnote 3, and *97*, footnote 2.

28.   144 B.C.[1]   CHS, 57A, 1a; 2a (1b; 3a)

臨邛多富人卓王孫僮客八百人程鄭亦數百人…卓
王孫不得已分與文君僮百人錢百萬及其嫁時衣被財
物文君乃與相如歸成都買田宅爲富人

Lin-ch'iung had many rich people. Cho Wang-sun[2] had eight hundred youths and guests,[3] while Cheng Ch'eng[4] also had several hundred ....

Cho Wang-sun had no alternative but to give a share [of his wealth to Cho] Wen-chün: a hundred youths, a hundred myriad cash, and the trousseau and dowry of her [former] marriage. [Cho] Wen-chün then returned with [Ssu-ma] Hsiang-ju to Ch'eng-tu, where they bought fields and houses, and were rich people.

[1] The passage refers to events in the life of Ssu-ma Hsiang-ju (SC, 117; CHS, 57; JMT, p. 184) just after the death of his patron, Liu Wu, King Hsiao of Liang, who died in May/June, 144 B.C. (HFHD, vol. I, p. 324).

Ssu-ma Hsiang-ju came to Lin-ch'iung, near the present Chengtu in Szechwan, where he met the widowed daughter of the town's richest man. The girl, Cho Wen-chün, fell in love with him, and they eloped. Being penniless, they set up a wine-shop in Lin-ch'iung, greatly shaming her rich father, Cho Wang-sun. After the event told here, Ssu-ma Hsiang-ju was called to court by Emperor Wu, and much of his biography is made up of his conversations and remonstrances with the Emperor. One of the greatest poets and literary figures of Han times, he died in 117 B.C.

[2] Cho Wang-sun is chiefly noted for his great wealth. The Mr. Cho mentioned in the Chapter on the Rich People (cf. 2), also lived in Lin-ch'iung some time after 228 B.C. and is said to have had 800 youths and other forms of wealth. He may have been an ancestor of Cho Wang-sun.

[3] Yen Shih-ku says: "Youths means male slaves 僮謂奴." SC, 117, 1b, here uses the term *chia t'ung*, "household youths," and does not mention the guests. Both texts say below, however, that Mr. Cho's guests were numbered by the hundred. In several other documents the term *nu k'o*, "male slaves [and?] guests," occurs: *37, 61, 65, 104*, but there is no decisive contextual evidence to prove whether the term is a compound or represents people in two distinct, but similar, forms of relationship with a master.

[4] Cheng Ch'eng (SC, 129, 7b; CHS, 91, 4a; JMT, p. 1191) is known only as a rich man of Szechwan.

29. Ca. 142 B.C.[1] CHS, 68, 1a (1a)

霍光字子孟票騎將軍去病弟也父中孺河東平陽人
也以縣吏給事平陽侯家與侍者衛少兒私通而生去病
中孺吏畢歸家娶婦生光因絕不相聞

Ho Kuang,[2] whose style name was Tzu-meng, was a younger [half-] brother of General of the Dashing Cavalry [Ho] Ch'ü-ping.[3] His father, Ho Chung-ju, was a man from P'ing-yang in Ho-tung, who, when serving as a minor prefectural official in the household of the Marquis of P'ing-yang, had secret relations with the serving one,[4] Wei Shao-erh, who bore [Ho] Ch'ü-ping. When [Ho] Chung-ju's official [duties] were finished he returned home, and took a wife who bore [Ho] Kuang. Being separated [the half-brothers] did not hear of each other.

---

[1] The approximate date of the conception of Ho Ch'ü-ping. See footnote 3.

[2] Ho Kuang (CHS, 68, 1a–8b; 7 passim; 8, 1a–4a passim; JMT, p. 1626) figures frequently in connection with slavery. He was one of the most powerful officials in the Han period, having been virtual ruler from 86 to 68 B.C. He was the half-brother of Ho Ch'ü-ping, who introduced him to court at the age of ten or more, some time shortly after 121 B.C. Thus he was born around 131 B.C. He died in 68 B.C.

Ho Kuang first became prominent in 91 B.C., when he was honored as Emperor Wu's most loyal and trustworthy minister. In the Emperor's last year, 87 B.C., he was appointed one of the three regents for the Heir-apparent, together with Shang-kuan Chieh and Chin Jih-ti. During the reign of Emperor Chao (87–74 B.C.) Ho Kuang became more and more dominant. His daughter had married Shang-kuan An, the son of Shang-kuan Chieh, and the child of that union was made Empress. In 80 B.C. Ho Kuang's power was threatened by a coalition of his enemies: Shang-kuan Chieh and An, Sang Hung-yang, Liu Tan the King of Yen, the Princess Kai of Ao-i (an older sister of the Emperor), and her lover, Ting Wai-jen. They plotted to kill Ho Kuang and the Emperor and then to put the King of Yen on the throne; the Shang-kuan family had a further secret plot to kill the King of Yen and put Shang-kuan Chieh on the throne. Through the unexpected support of the Emperor, Ho Kuang won out, and the plotters were exterminated.

When Emperor Chao died without heir in 74 B.C., Ho Kuang selected Liu Ho to the succession, but deposed him after 27 days. He then chose a great-grandson of Emperor Wu, who became Emperor Hsüan. Ho Kuang's power was now almost absolute. His son, Ho Yü, and his grandnephews, Ho Yün and Ho Shan, became marquises and held high official posts.

In 71 B.C. occurred an event which later caused the downfall of the Ho family. Hsien, the second wife of Ho Kuang, wished to get her own daughter (Ho Kuang's youngest) made Empress. She managed secretly to have Emperor Hsüan's consort, the Empress née Hsü, poisoned, and then persuaded Ho Kuang to have their daughter appointed the new Empress. (The surprising fact was that Ho Kuang's granddaughter, the Dowager Empress née Shang-kuan, was of the higher generation officially, while his daughter, the new Empress, was of the lower.) Someone then exposed the poisoning, and Ho Kuang, who learned the facts for the first time, succeeded in suppressing the scandal. After Ho Kuang's death, however, Emperor Hsüan personally took control of the government and began elevating officials opposed to the Ho faction. Wei Hsiang, for example, was made Chancellor; he had a particular hate for the Ho family because he had recently been terribly humiliated by the Ho family slaves (cf. *72*). The poisoning scandal was revealed to the Emperor in 66 B.C., and other accusations against the haughty Ho family were brought forward. All members of the family and numerous associates were either executed or committed suicide. Members of the Ho party were dismissed. For a complete account of Ho Kuang's life and times, see Arvid Jongchell, *Huo Kuang och Hans tid* (in Swedish).

³ Ho Ch'ü-ping (CHS, 55, 3a–6a; 18, 7a; JMT, p. 1626) was one of the greatest Han generals. He was born of a casual intimacy between Ho Chung-ju and Wei Shao-erh, an older sister of Wei Tzu-fu, who became Empress in 128 B.C. (cf. *26*). He was the nephew of General Wei Ch'ing. At the age of 14 he became an Attaché of the Emperor, probably in the same year as the appointment of his aunt as Empress. This would make his birth about 141 B.C. He followed his uncle Wei Ch'ing to the wars, and soon rose to high military command and became Marquis of Kuan-chün in 123 B.C. In 121 or 120 B.C. (the basic texts disagree) Emperor Wu created for him a new military title, General of the Dashing Cavalry. He died in 117 B.C., after a brilliant military career, including six great campaigns against the Hsiung-nu, at the age of 24!

There is an extensive western literature on the tomb of Ho Ch'ü-ping, erected at the command of the Emperor: Victor Segalen, Gilbert de Voisins, and Jean Lartigue (*Mission archaéologique en Chine.* Text vol. I, *L'art funéraire a l'époque des Han,* Paris, 1935, pp. 33–43), Carl Hentze ("Les influences etrangeres dans le monument de Houo-K'iu-Ping," AAs, 1925, No. 1, pp. 31–36), Jean Lartigue ("Au tombeau de Houo K'iu-Ping," AAs, 1927, No. 2, pp. 85–94), Carl Whiting Bishop ("Notes on the tomb of Ho Ch'u-ping," AAs, 1928, No. 1, pp. 34–46), John C. Ferguson ("Tomb of Ho Ch'ü-ping," AAs, 1928–29, No. 4, pp. 228–232), and Zoltan de Takacs ("On the Hsiung-nu figure at the tomb of Huo Ch'ü-ping," MS, vol. 3, 1938, pp. 275–277).

⁴ The term *shih-che,* "serving one," is used interchangeably with *yü-pei,* "personal female slave," in *37*. The term *shih-erh,* "serving child," is clearly used in the sense of *pei,* "female slave," in *23*. These uses, together with the fact that the mother of Wei Shao-erh was a *chia-t'ung,* "household maiden," and the fact that Wei Ch'ing, the younger brother of Wei Shao-erh, was treated as a slave and considered himself to be one (cf. *26*), all indicate that Wei Shao-erh was herself a serving slave-girl.

There is something curious and suspicious about the close similarity between the stories of the birth of Wei Ch'ing and of Ho Ch'ü-ping. Is one a copy of the other, or is there only a coincidence?

30. 140 B.C. CHS, 6, 1b (2b)

赦吳楚七國帑輸在官者

[In May/June, 140 B.C., Emperor Wu] pardoned the families of [the leaders of the rebellion of] Wu, Ch'u, the Seven States,[1] who had been condemned[2] to the government [as slaves[3]].

[1] For an account of this serious rebellion of 154 B.C. cf. HFHD, vol. I, pp. 292–297. Seven States rebelled; the leadership came from the states of Wu and Ch'u in the Yangtze Valley region; hence the name.

[2] Lit. "lost in," or "submitted to." The expression seems to be similar to 沒入, "submerged into," the usual term for confiscation of property, or seizure and enslavement of people.

[3] The commentary of Ying Shao (ca. A.D. 140–206) says: "At the time of the rebellion of Wu, Ch'u, the Seven States, the wives and children of the leaders had been seized and made government slaves. Emperor Wu, pitying them, pardoned them and sent them all away."

It is puzzling that no mention is made of the condemnation of these people in CHS, 5, or SC, 11, or in the biographies of the leaders of this great rebellion, viz., Liu P'i, the King of Wu; Liu Mou, the King of Ch'u; Liu Sui, the King of Chao; and the descendants of Liu Fei, the King of Ch'i (CHS, 35, 4a–7a; 36, 2a; 38, 1b–2a; and 4b–5b, respectively); or in SC, 106, another biography of the King of Wu, which is the most detailed account of the Rebellion.

31. Ca. 140 B.C. CHS, 97A, 5a (10a)

初皇太后微時所爲金王孫生女俗在民間蓋諱之也
武帝始立韓嫣白之帝曰何爲不蚤言乃車駕自往迎之
其家在長陵小市直至其門使左右入求之家人驚恐女
逃匿扶將出拜帝下車立曰大姊何臧之深也載至長樂
宮與俱謁太后太后垂涕女亦悲泣帝奉酒前爲壽錢千
萬奴婢三百人公田百頃甲第以賜姊太后謝曰爲帝費
因賜湯沐邑號修成君

The daughter whom the Empress Dowager [*née* Wang[1]] had borne to Chin Wang-sun when she was of humble station, lived as a commoner[2] among the people; [her identity] had simply been hushed up. When Emperor Wu first ascended the throne Han Yen[3] revealed it. The Emperor said: "Why was it not told earlier?"

Thereupon he went personally to welcome her with a carriage. Her home was in a small town in Ch'ang-ling.[4] He went right to her door and sent attendants to go in and seek her. The family was terrified; the girl ran off and hid. She was supported and led out to make obeisances. The Emperor got down from the carriage, stood [before her] and said: "Eldest sister, why are you hidden away so deep?"

He transported her to the Ch'ang-lo Palace, and called with her upon the Empress Dowager [*née* Wang]. The Empress Dowager wept and the girl also wept grievously. The Emperor offered her wine, and made her a toast. He bestowed on his sister a million cash, three hundred male and female slaves, a hundred *ch'ing* of public fields, and a first-class mansion. The Empress Dowager thanked him and said: "It causes the Emperor much trouble."

He furthermore bestowed [on his sister] a T'ang-mu estate, and she was called Baroness Hsiu-ch'eng.[5]

[1] The Empress Dowager *née* Wang (SC, 49, 3b–4a; CHS, 97A, 4a–5a; JMT, p. 88) was the mother of Emperor Wu. When he was made Heir-apparent in 150 B.C. she became Empress. She died in 126 B.C.

The story about her earlier life, and how she happened to have a daughter by Chin Wang-sun, is interesting and complicated. Her father was one Wang Chung. Her mother, Tsang Erh, was the granddaughter of the King of Yen, Tsang T'u, who was overthrown in 202 B.C. By this marriage there was a son,

Wang Hsin, and two daughters, one of whom was our lady *née* Wang. When Wang Chung died, Tsang Erh married a Mr. T'ien, and bore two sons, T'ien Feng and T'ien Sheng, both of whom later became famous because of their relationship to the lady *née* Wang.

The lady *née* Wang grew up and married Chin Wang-sun and bore him a daughter, the older half-sister of Emperor Wu in the present account. Tsang Erh consulted a necromancer who told her that her two daughters would become important people. She therefore tried to get her daughter (the lady *née* Wang) away from the Chin family. They would not consent to a divorce, so Tsang Erh got the lady *née* Wang sent into the palace of the Heir-apparent. The Heir-apparent, later Emperor Ching, fell in love with her. She bore him three daughters and a son, who later became Emperor Wu.

After Emperor Ching ascended the throne there was a complicated period of intrigue, but finally, in 150 B.C., the son of the lady *née* Wang was made Heir-apparent and she became Empress. In 141 B.C. when her son ascended the throne she became Empress Dowager. All this time the daughter borne by the lady *née* Wang to Chin Wang-sun had been kept in obscurity. Emperor Wu brought her to the palace as here related.

[2] Following Yen Shih-ku against Hsü Kuang (ca. A.D. 352–425), Ch'ien Ta-hsin and Wang Hsien-ch'ien, who would read *Su* as the girl's name. HY36 does not index it so.

[3] Han Yen (SC, 125, 2a; CHS, 93, 2a; JMT, p. 1705) was Emperor Wu's closest companion and personal confidant from boyhood days. He was a natural person to reveal the matter of the unknown half-sister.

[4] Ch'ang-ling in modern Shensi Province, east of Hsien-yang hsien, was the site of Kao-tsu's tomb.

[5] The same story is told in more detail in SC, 49, 5a–b, at the beginning of the section by Master Ch'u, or Ch'u Shao-sun (cf. *39*, footnote 7). He says that when he was a Gentleman he heard one Chung-li Sheng, who was an expert on anecdotes about the Han [i.e. Liu] family, say . . . . He then quotes this anecdote. After a brief introduction, which does not duplicate the background found in SC, 49, 3b (and summarized from the CHS text in footnote 1, above), he tells the story translated here. There are many vivid details, especially about the finding of the girl, and her introduction to her mother, which are not given in the more sober CHS passage. The part concerning the gift of money, slaves, fields, and a mansion is, however, word for word the same.

It seems quite possible that Master Ch'u's quotation of the anecdote, as it was told to him about a century after the event, is here the primary source for the CHS passage. The content of the passage does not seem to be the sort of thing which would be reported with such trifling details and filed in imperial archives, but is exactly what one would expect in verbally transmitted anecdotes. If this be a correct assumption, then it is likely that the authors of the CHS took Master Ch'u's passage, left out unnecessary details, and put it into their history. It is of course also possible that there was a common source, a book of anecdotes quoted both by Master Ch'u and the authors of the CHS.

32. 138 B.C. CHS, 61, 1a (1a)

漢方欲事滅胡聞此言欲通使道必更匈奴中迺募能
使者騫以郎應募使月氏與堂邑氏奴甘父

Han was just then planning to engage in destroying the Huns,
and hearing this information [about the defeat of the Yüeh-chih by
the Huns, the minister said that if Han] wanted to establish ambassa-
dorial relations [with the Yüeh-chih] the road would necessarily
have to lead through Hsiung-nu [territory]. Thereupon there was
an enlistment of those able [to undertake the task of] emissary.
[Chang] Ch'ien,[1] being a Gentleman, volunteered. He was sent to
the Yüeh-chih with a male slave of the T'ang-i family, Kan Fu.[2]

[1] Chang Ch'ien (SC, 123, 1a–2a; CHS, 61, 1a–4a; JMT, p. 978) was one of
China's great explorers. His biography is so well known that it does not need
repeating. See Chavannes (MH, vol. I, pp. lxxi ff.), F. Hirth ("The story of Chang
K'ién," JAOS, vol. 37, 1917, pp. 93–95), and A. Wylie ("Notes on the western
regions," JAI, vol. 10, 1880, pp. 66–73).

[2] Little is known about Kan Fu. Below (CHS, 61, 1b) it is definitely stated
that "T'ang-i Fu [a different name for Kan Fu] was a Hun [*Hu jen*], and an excellent archer, [so that when the expedition] was exhausted and in distress he shot
game to give [the expedition] food." The following commentaries discuss Kan Fu:

(1) Fu Ch'ien (ca. A.D. 125–195) says: "T'ang-i is a surname. He was a
Chinese. His male slave's given name was Kan-fu."

(2) Yen Shih-ku (A.D. 581–645) says: "Mr. T'ang-i's male slave was originally
a Hun, with the given name Kan-fu. Below, where it speaks of T'ang-i Fu, it
simply takes the master's surname as his family name [*shih*], and abbreviates
his given name to Fu."

(3) With these conclusions Liu Pin (A.D. 1022–88) disagrees. He says:
"[The three words] *nu kan fu* are simply this man's given name [and/or] appellation. It does not mean 'The T'ang-i family's male slave with the given name
Kan-fu.' According to the Hun [system of] given names and styles, they often
take *nu* as an appellation. Moreover, it later speaks of T'ang-i Fu, [so that we
even] more clearly know that this person's own family name was T'ang-i and his
given name was Nu-kan-fu."

(4) In SC, 123, 1a, the *Chi-chieh* commentary (by P'ei Yin, fl. A.D. 465–472)
says: "According to what the *Han shu yin i* [by Hsü Kuang] says, T'ang-i was
his family surname, and Hu-nu-kan-fu was his style."

(5) The *So-yin* commentary (by Ssu-ma Cheng, fl. A.D. 713–742) says:
"Kan-fu was the given name of a former Hun male slave in a family from T'ang-i
hsien. Where below it mentions T'ang-i Fu it is probably an abbreviation by a
later copyist who only wrote T'ang-i Fu, and left out the word Kan. Perhaps
Kan is his surname."

There is thus some question whether he was a slave or not. This depends upon
the proper interpretation of the last six words, *t'ang i shih nu kan fu*. The equivalent passage in SC, 123, 1a, gives the phrase *t'ang i shih ku hu nu kan fu*, adding
ku hu, "former Hun." The CHS phrase has been translated, "a male slave of
the T'ang-i family, Kan Fu." Wylie (op. cit., p. 66) agrees. The SC passage,
according to my interpretation, would be translated, "a former Hun male slave
of the T'ang-i family, Kan Fu." Hirth (op. cit., p. 94) renders it, "Kan Fu, a
Tartar, formerly a slave in the T'ang-i family." In support of the interpretation

that T'ang-i is the name of the owner, and that Kan Fu was a slave, there are the commentaries 1 and 2 above. Commentary 5 suggests that T'ang-i is the name of the place where the owner of Kan Fu lived, i.e., T'ang-i hsien in Shantung. Wang Hsien-ch'ien sides with Fu Ch'ien and Yen Shih-ku.

As opposed to the above interpretations there are the commentaries 3 and 4, which conclude that the whole phrase represents the name of one man. JMT, p. 897, subscribes to this interpretation. His name, being Hunnic, may be variously interpreted to conform to Chinese usage in naming. In this interpretation there is no suggestion of his former enslavement.

Dr. J. J. L. Duyvendak, in a personal communication, agrees with commentary 3, and suggests that Kan Fu might have been a sinicized Hun, possibly living in T'ang-i hsien and taking his name from it. He thinks a slave would not be specifically mentioned as his companion by Chang Ch'ien; such a slave would be more or less nameless and would simply follow him. A sinicized Hun, probably of chieftain rank or so, would be a proper companion and would be the right person to guide Chang Ch'ien. Dr. Duyvendak assumes that he was a friend of this Hun, who possibly encouraged him to the enterprise.

On the other hand, it should be pointed out that probably Kan Fu was mentioned at all only because he was the lone member of the original party of over a hundred who finally came back with Chang Ch'ien, for whom he was also useful in securing game. Thus, it is equally possible that Kan Fu was a slave, Hsiung-nu by race, who was inconspicuous when he left, but who proved his worth on the trip, and loyally stayed with Chang Ch'ien during thirteen years. Professor Duyvendak's suggestion seems to assume that the account of the start of the expedition was recorded at the time it left, and that only Chang Ch'ien and Kan Fu were then mentioned. It seems more likely, however, that while a list of the important people with Chang Ch'ien was compiled at the start, the two names now in the history are the only ones recorded because only those two came back. The names record the important people at the end of the trip, not at the beginning. After all, numerous embassies of which we do not now know the personnel went to and fro across Central Asia. Chang Ch'ien himself would probably never have found a niche in history had he not returned with startling new information.

Thus, the question whether Kan Fu was ever a slave remains, to me, uncertain, with the possibilities equal either way.

33.   135 B.C.[1]   CHS, 64A, 2a (3b)

且越人愚戇輕薄負約反覆其不用天子之法度非一
日之積也壹不奉詔舉兵誅之臣恐後兵革無時得息也
閒者數年歲比不登民待賣爵贅子以接衣食

[Liu An,[2] King of Huai-nan, in a long document to Emperor
Wu, criticizing a proposed expedition against the Kingdom of
Yüeh, said]: "Furthermore, the people of Yüeh are stupid and
flighty; they break contracts and vacillate. For a long, long time
they have not made use of the Emperors' laws and regulations.[3]
Your servant fears that hereafter military [expeditions] will be
endless if every time they did not respect [Your] imperial edicts
[You] were to levy troops to punish them. For several years the
harvests [in China] have successively not been abundant,[4] and people
have had to depend upon selling their honorary ranks and pawning
their children[5] in order to continue to clothe and feed themselves."

[1] The date is given in CHS, 64A, 1a and 1b.

[2] Liu An, King of Huai-nan (SC, 118, 3a–7b; CHS, 44, 4a–6b; JMT, p. 1441),
is also known as Huai-nan Wang or Huai-nan Tzu, and lived 178–122 B.C. He
was a grandson of Emperor Kao. He is known principally as a literary figure,
and in legend as a Taoist adept, who found the secret drug of immortality. The
Kingdom of Huai-nan was in the north-central part of present Anhwei, its center
at Shou hsien.

It is somewhat surprising to find a long letter (1b–4a) from Liu An to Emperor
Wu in the biography of Yen Chu. It is not quoted in the biography of Liu An
in SC, 118, 3a–7a. Cf. Pelliot, BEFEO, vol. 2, 1902, p. 332, where it is reported
that the imperial reply presumably to this letter may be found in the *Wen kuan
tz'u lin* of A.D. 658, fragments of which were preserved in Japan after having been
lost in China.

[3] Lit. "Their disuse of the laws and regulations of the emperors is not an
accumulation of a single day."

[4] A major famine in which people practiced cannibalism is recorded in the
reign of Emperor Wu before this date (cf. CHS, 6, 1b). The argument is that
conditions are so bad in China that it is ill-advised to send an expedition against
Yüeh.

[5] There is considerable discussion among the commentators as to the exact
meaning of *chui tzu* (here trans. "pawning their children"). Two principal ideas
are advanced.

Ju Shun (fl. A.D. 189–265) says (meaning 1): "It is the custom in Huai-nan
[for parents] to sell children to others to work [as] slaves, which is called *chui tzu*
["pawning children." If within] three years they cannot redeem them, [the
children] then become slaves."

Yen Shih-ku (A.D. 581–645) says: "*Chui* is [synonymous with] *chih* 質 ["to
pawn," "a hostage"]. Someone has said [meaning 2]: '*Chui tzu* means to command

a son to go out to his wife's family to be a *chui hsü* 贅壻 ["a pawned son-in-law"].' An explanation of *chui hsü* is in the biography of Chia Yi."

In the biography of Chia Yi (CHS, 48, 7a) appear the following commentaries explaining *chui hsü*. Ying Shao (ca. 140–206 A.D.) explains: "The son goes out to be a son-in-law living with his wife's family." Yen Shih-ku adds: "To say 'son-in-law living with his wife's family' is to say he was improperly sent to live in his wife's household, which is just like a tumor on a man's body. Some say that *chui* means to pawn; the family being poor and not having betrothal money [the groom] uses himself as collateral for borrowing [the money from the wife's family]."

From the HSPC, 64A, 4a, come further interpretations:

Shen Ch'in-han (A.D. 1775–1831) says: "In the epitaph to Liu Tzu-hou [i.e., Liu Tsung-yüan, or Liu Chou (A.D. 773–819), who lived at Liu chou], written by Han Yü [A.D. 768–824], it is recorded that 'it is the custom in Liu chou [present Ma-p'ing hsien, Kwangsi Province] to use boys and girls as collateral for borrowing money. If the contract is not redeemed in [the specified] time, or if the interest and principal have become equal, then [the children] will be seized and become slaves.' [Cf. TY, *yin*, p. 1, under *tzu-pen*, "interest and principal."] What Ju [Shun] says is right."

The *Huai nan pen ching hsün* (not listed in HY7, HY10) has the phrase: "*Chui* the wife and sell the children." The commentary there says: "*Chui* [means] to go into the wife's house. Perhaps [one could] use *lin ch'i* 賃妻 ["rent the wife" (for *chui* the wife)], which has the same meaning as *chui* the son."

The *Shuo wen* (by Hsü Shen; presented to the throne in A.D. 121) is cited as defining *chui* as "using goods as collateral for borrowing money." The etymology then given does not help in the present question.

Finally, Wang Hsien-ch'ien cites a passage in CHS, 4 (8a; HFHD, vol. I, p. 266), which is irrelevant. He concludes: "What someone says [i.e., meaning 2, in the first commentary by Yen Shih-ku, above] is incorrect."

What conclusions can be drawn from this array of commentaries? A system of pawning children may well have been practiced in Han times. Actually it is only a variation of the practice of outright sale of children, already used early in Han times, and a constant in Chinese history during famine. The pawning system had the mitigation of a contractual basis for redeeming the children within a specified time.

34. Ca. 140–128 B.C.[1]   CHS, 56, 8b (16b)

身寵而載高位家溫而食厚祿因乘富貴之資力以與
民爭利於下民安能如之哉是故眾其奴婢多其牛羊廣
其田宅博其產業畜其積委務此而亡已以迫蹴民民日
削月朘寖以大窮富者奢侈羨溢貧者窮急愁苦窮急愁
苦而上不救則民不樂生民不樂生尚不避死安能避罪
此刑罰之所以蕃而姦邪不可勝者也故受祿之家食祿
而已不與民爭業然後利可均布而民可家足此上天之
理而亦太古之道天子之所宜法以爲制大夫之所當循
以爲行也

[Tung Chung-shu[2] in an address to Emperor Wu said]: "People of honor and high office, with comfortable homes and enjoying large official salaries, take advantage of the capital and power of their wealth and position, to compete for profits with those below them. How can the people match them?

"Therefore, [the influential people] multiply their male and female slaves, increase their [herds of] cattle and sheep, enlarge their fields and houses, broaden their fixed property, and accumulate goods. Busily engaged in these pursuits without end, they thereby oppress and trample on the common people. The common people are daily pared down and monthly squeezed, gradually becoming greatly impoverished. The rich are extravagant and wasteful and fond of lavish display; the poor are impoverished and desperate, hateful and bitter. Impoverished and desperate, hateful and bitter, if the Emperor does not rescue them, then the common people will have no joy in living. When the common people have no joy in living, and also do not flinch at death, how can they shun crime? That is why, though punishments are made numerous, evil cannot be suppressed.

"Therefore, if those households which receive official salary would live off that salary merely, and not compete with the common people in their occupations, then profits could be spread equitably, and the common people would have enough for their homes. That is the fundamental principle of Heaven above, as well as the way of

310

antiquity; that is what the Emperor should properly take as his example in making decrees; and that is what the grandees should comply with and make their practice." [3]

[1] Probably nearer to 140, for the "additional commentary," *k'ao-teng*, 1a, emphasizes Tung Chung-shu's closeness to Emperor Wu early in his reign. At the end of the present passage (p. 9a) it says Emperor Wu made Tung Chung-shu Chancellor to the King of Chiang-tu, Liu Fei. The latter was King of Chiang-tu from 153 to 128 or 127 (CHS, 14, 13a; and 53, 2a–b). This gives the terminus for the passage.

[2] Tung Chung-shu (SC, 121, 4b–5a; CHS, 56; JMT, p. 1311) lived ca. 179–93 B.C. He was one of the great Confucian scholars at the court of Emperors Ching and Wu. His biography has been translated or abstracted several times into foreign languages; for a list, see John K. Shryock, *The origin and development of the state cult of Confucius*, p. 60, footnote 1.

[3] There is no record that Emperor Wu accepted this advice. However, the confiscations of accumulated fortunes, especially of rich and powerful merchants, in 119–113 B.C. (cf. 46) may be an indirect reflection of the ideas of Tung Chung-shu.

This passage seems to be the first statement of the policy of restricting ownership of lands and slaves by the nobility and officials.

35.   140–93 B.C.[1]   CHS, 24A, 6b (17a)

漢興循而未改古井田法雖難卒行宜少近古限民名
田以澹不足塞并兼之路鹽鐵皆歸於民去奴婢除專殺
之威薄賦斂省繇役以寬民力然後可善治也

[Tung Chung-shu[2] in an address to Emperor Wu described the evils of the policy of Ch'in, and then said]: "When Han arose to power it followed and did not alter [the Ch'in system]. Although it would be difficult abruptly to put into practice the ancient *ching-t'ien*[3] system, [still] it would be fitting to approach somewhat the ancient [practices]. Limit people's private fields in order to assist those in want. Stop up the way to simultaneous accumulation [of offices, land, and other sources of income[4]]. Salt and iron should both be returned to the people.[5] Abolish male and female slaves, [in order to] eliminate their fear of autocratic execution.[6] Lighten taxes and be lenient in corvée service, in order to extend the people's strength. After this, there can be good government!"

[1] This date is hard to fix. The event occurred during the reign of Emperor Wu, therefore after 141 B.C.; possibly only shortly after his accession to the throne when Tung Chung-shu was in high favor, and when he carried on the famous series of discourses on government with the Emperor. Cf. John K. Shryock, *The origin and development of the state cult of Confucius*, pp. 49–63. The suggestion that salt and iron should be given back to the people would date the passage after 119 B.C., when the monopolies were reinstituted.

[2] Cf. *34*, footnote 2.

[3] The *ching-t'ien* or well-field system of agriculture is a system of communal tenancy attributed to the Chou period, in which a group of eight farm families formed a unit, each family cultivating one-ninth of a square of land, and together cultivating the remaining ninth for the noble owner. It does not appear to have been practiced during the period covered by this study, except for a few years during the reign of Emperor Wang Mang as a retrospective reform (cf. *122*). The system has been much studied by sinologists, and there is no unanimity of opinion on the question whether it was in actual practice in ancient China, or was merely an imaginary system read back into the ancient literature by Chinese scholars as a utopianism. J. J. L. Duyvendak (*The Book of Lord Shang*, p. 42) and Henri Maspero (*La Chine antique*, pp. 108–110) view it as authentic though by no means universal. Chi Ch'ao-ting (*Key economic areas in Chinese history*, pp. 50–63) discusses the basic texts and offers a hypothesis as to how literally the system may be taken. See also K. A. Wittfogel ("The foundations and stages of Chinese economic history," pp. 42–45). Hu Shih (*Hu Shih wen ts'un*, ch. 2, pp. 247–284) and Wan Kwoh-ting (*An agrarian history of China, passim*) consider it merely a utopianism, never actually practiced. See also Chen Huan-chang (*The economic principles of Confucius and his school*, pp. 352–355) and Wolfram Eberhard ("Zur Landwirtschaft der Han-Zeit," pp. 78 ff.).

Whether or not the *ching-t'ien* system was ever practiced as described is a question outside the scope of this book. In discussions of the problem, questions of textual criticism and philology should not be allowed to obscure the probability that communal tenancy and various systems of labor rent on the noble's domain did exist in pre-Ch'in times, just as they have existed in various other societies, both primitive and complex.

⁴ The term *ping-chien* seems here to refer to a single person holding two or more different offices, or practicing more than one profession, or possessing government office together with private sources of income, such as land. It seems especially to apply to the accumulation of large areas of farm land, or many fields, in the hands of a single owner. There were laws to prevent merchants from owning private fields or from holding government office. Tung Chung-shu suggested restrictions to prevent people from accumulating wealth from several different sources.

⁵ On the Han dynasty state monopoly of salt and iron, see Esson M. Gale (*Discourses on salt and iron*) and C. M. Chang (*The genesis and meaning of Huan Kuan's "Discourses on salt and iron."*).

⁶ The commentator Fu Ch'ien (ca. A.D. 125–195) explains: "Prevent the autocratic execution of male and female slaves." However, the construction leaves some doubt whether the abolition of male and female slaves and the prevention of autocratic execution may not be two separate ideas.

---

36. 127 B.C.¹ CHS, 24B, 3b (7b)

府庫並虛迺募民能入奴婢得以終身復爲郎增秩及入羊爲郎始於此

The treasuries and arsenals simultaneously became empty, whereupon [Emperor Wu] appealed to plebeians [with the announcement that they] could contribute male and female slaves [to the government] and obtain thereby [tax or corvée] exemption for life; [those who already] had become Gentlemen [could by the same method receive] increase in rank.² Contributing sheep [in order] to become a Gentleman began at this time.³

¹ The next passage begins, "Four years later . . . ," which Chavannes dates 124 B.C.

² Yen Shih-ku explains: "Commoners who contributed male and female slaves would be exempted for life. Those who were already Gentlemen would have an increase in their rank. Someone has said: 'Those who contributed a few male and female slaves would be exempted for life; those who [contributed] many could become Gentlemen; those formerly Gentlemen would have an increase in rank.' "

³ Chavannes (MH, vol. III, p. 552, footnote 5) explains this last remark as a satirical comment by the historian Ssu-ma Ch'ien. Cf. *19* for a memorial suggesting even earlier than this that slaves be contributed in exchange for honorary rank. There it is only said that the Emperor followed the memorialist's counsel, but does not make clear whether the suggestion about slaves was adopted. The passage here translated also appears in SC, 30, 2b.

厥姬乃惡徐來於太子曰徐來使婢蠱殺太子母太子
心怨徐來徐來兄至衡山太子與飲以刃刑傷之后以此
怨太子數惡之於王女弟無采嫁棄歸與客姦太子數以
數讓之無采怒不與太子通…元朔四年中人有賊傷后
假母者王疑太子使人傷之笞太子後王病太子時稱病
不侍孝無采惡太子實不病自言有喜色王於是大怒欲
廢太子而立弟孝后知王決廢太子又欲并廢孝后有侍
者善舞王幸之后欲令與孝亂以污之欲并廢二子而以
己子廣代之太子知之念后數惡己無已時欲與亂以止
其口后飲太子太子前爲壽因據后股求與臥后怒以告
王王迺召欲縛笞之太子知王常欲廢己而立孝迺謂王
曰孝與王御者姦無采與奴姦…孝坐與王御婢姦及后
徐來坐蠱前后乘舒及太子爽坐告王父不孝皆棄市諸
坐與王謀反者皆誅國除爲郡

[Liu Szu,[1] King of Heng-shan, had three children by his Queen, Ch'eng-shu: the oldest was a boy named Shuang, who was established as Heir-apparent; the second was a girl named Wu-ts'ai; the youngest was a boy named Hsiao. He also had four children, boys and girls, by his concubine Hsü-lai, and two children by a Beauty named Chüeh-chi.

Some time between 129 and 125 B.C. the Queen died, and Hsü-lai was made Queen. Since Chüeh-chi had also enjoyed the King's favors the two women were mutually jealous]. Chüeh-chi thereupon slandered Hsü-lai to the Heir-apparent [Shuang], saying: "Hsü-lai caused a female slave to kill the Heir-apparent's mother by magic poison."[2] [Therefore] the Heir-apparent hated Hsü-lai.

The elder brother of Hsü-lai came to Heng-shan. The Heir-apparent, drinking with him, cut and wounded him with a knife. Because of this the Queen [Hsü-lai] hated the Heir-apparent, and several times slandered him to the King.

[The Heir-apparent's] younger sister, Wu-ts'ai, had been cast off by her husband and returned [to Heng-shan, and had relations with a male slave,[3] and also] had relations with a guest. The Heir-apparent several times reprimanded her. Wu-ts'ai resented this, and did not associate with the Heir-apparent. [Therefore she and the youngest son, Hsiao, who had been brought up by the new Queen, Hsü-lai, came under the Queen's influence and became party to her schemes] . . . .

In 125 B.C. someone stealthily wounded the stepmother of the Queen. The King suspected the Heir-apparent of ordering someone to wound her, and beat him.

Later the King was sick and the Heir-apparent promptly feigned sickness and did not wait upon him. Hsiao and Wu-ts'ai slandered the Heir-apparent [saying that he] really was not sick and had himself said he felt well. The King therefore became very angry and wanted to depose the Heir-apparent and establish the younger brother, Hsiao.

The Queen, learning that the King was definitely going to depose the Heir-apparent, also hoped to have Hsiao deposed simultaneously. The Queen had a serving one,[4] a fine dancer, to whom the King had granted his favors. The Queen wanted to make her have relations with Hsiao so as to besmirch him, desiring thus simultaneously to depose the two sons, and have her own son, Kuang, take their place.

The Heir-apparent [Shuang] learned this, and considering how the Queen slandered him endlessly, wished to have relations with her in order to silence her. [Therefore, one time when] the Queen was drinking with the Heir-apparent, the Heir-apparent came forward to offer a toast, and took the occasion to seize the Queen by the thighs, seeking to lie with her. The Queen was angry and told the King about it.

The King thereupon summoned him, intending to bind and beat him. The Heir-apparent knew that the King always wished to depose him and to establish Hsiao, so he spoke to the King, saying: "Hsiao had relations with the King's personal one,[4] and Wu-ts'ai had relations with a male slave . . . ."

[After all this Liu Szu, the King of Heng-shan, plotted rebellion, and then in 122 committed suicide to escape trial. Hsiao was acquitted of his connection with the rebellion, because he had been the first to confess it, but] Hsiao was tried for having had relations with the King's personal female slave;[4] Queen Hsü-lai was tried for poisoning the former Queen, Ch'eng-shu; and Heir-apparent

Shuang was tried for unfilially reporting on his father, the King. All were publicly executed. All those tried for plotting rebellion with the King were executed. The kingdom was abolished and made a commandery.

[1] Liu Szu, King of Heng-shan (SC, 118, 7b–8b; CHS, 44, 6a–7a; and 14, 6b), was a grandson of Emperor Kao. He was implicated with his brother Liu An, King of Huai-nan, in a rebellion in 123–122 B.C. Heng-shan was in the northeastern part of present Hupei Province.

[2] This magic was *ku*. Poisonous snakes and insects, etc., were placed in a kettle until only one survived. The supreme poison of this one was administered to the victim. See H. Y. Feng and J. K. Shryock, "The black magic in China known as *ku*," JAOS, vol. 55, 1935, pp. 1–30.

[3] Her relations with the male slave are left out of the CHS passage but appear in the SC account, which says that she also had relations with a guest. Below, however, both accounts mention her relations with the slave, only.

It is interesting that the relations between Wu-ts'ai and the slave did not constitute a crime for which she could be tried; at least no trial of her is mentioned. There is no indication that she had any part in the rebellion, and there is no record of what happened to her.

[4] Three terms seem to be equated in both the SC and the CHS accounts: *shih-che*, "serving one," *yü-che*, "personal one," and *yü-pei*, "personal female slave." *Shih* as female slave is noted in *23*. See *48*, footnote 2, for explanation of the term *yü*.

---

38.   123 B.C.[1]   CHS, 53, 3a (6a)

建恐誅心內不安與其后成光共使越婢下神祝詛上

[The King of Chiang-tu, Liu] Chien,[2] fearing execution and uneasy in heart, together with his Queen, Ch'eng-kuang, caused a female slave from Yüeh[3] to descend to the spirits and invoke curses on Emperor [Wu].

[1] This was just about the time of the rebellion of the Kings of Heng-shan and Huai-nan, Liu Szu and Liu An, in 123 B.C.

[2] Liu Chien (SC, 59, 2a; CHS, 53, 2b–3b) was a grandson of Emperor Ching, and became King of Chiang-tu in 127 B.C. He was incestuous, and unspeakably cruel and perverted, having in the few years before this incident murdered 35 people, often for pure sport, and forced palace ladies to practice bestiality. Realizing that his crimes were going to get him into trouble, he organized a rebellion, and when it was suppressed he committed suicide in 121 B.C. to escape punishment. His Queen, Ch'eng-kuang, was publicly executed and the kingdom abolished. Chiang-tu was in the present Kiangsu Province near Nanking.

[3] Yüeh was an ancient coastal state in the present Chekiang and northern Fukien region, having a strongly non-Chinese cultural element. The slave woman was quite possibly a special sorceress accomplished in Yüeh black arts.

39. 129–115 B.C.[1] SC, 104, 2b

乃爲衞將軍舍人與田仁會俱爲舍人居門下同心相
愛此二人家貧無錢用以事將軍家監家監使養惡齧馬
兩人同牀臥仁竊言曰不知人哉家監也任安曰將軍尚
不知人何乃家監也衞將軍從此兩人過平陽主主家令
兩人與騎奴同席而食此二子拔刀列斷席別坐主家皆
怪而惡之莫敢呵

Thereupon [Jen An[2]] became the *she-jen*[3] of General Wei [Ch'ing[4]] and became a close friend of T'ien Jen,[5] who just then likewise became a *she-jen* [of Wei Ch'ing] and lived in his house [also]. The families of these two men were poor and they had no money with which to bribe the manager of the General's household. The manager of the household ordered them to tend the vicious, biting horses. The two men slept in the same bed.

[T'ien] Jen confidentially said [to Jen An]: "The manager of the household certainly doesn't recognize [valuable] men!"

Jen An said: "Even the General doesn't recognize men [of value]. How then could the manager of his household!"

General Wei, accompanied by these two men, visited the Princess of P'ing-yang.[6] [Someone in] the Princess' household ordered the two men to eat at the same mat with the male cavalry slaves. These two fellows drew out their knives, cut the mat in two, and sat apart. All in the Princess' household were offended at this and despised them for it, but no one dared reprimand them.[7]

---

[1] The event must have occurred between the time Wei Ch'ing became a general in 129 and the period when Chao Yü was Treasurer of the Privy Purse. Chao Yü was appointed in 124 B.C. and is spoken of as the former Treasurer in 113. A man named Tang is mentioned as Treasurer in 115 (CHS, 19B, 16a, 18a, and 19a). Presumably 115 B.C. was the date when Chao Yü ceased being Treasurer.

[2] Jen An (SC, 104, 2a–3b; CHS, 66, 2a; JMT, p. 223), T. Shao-ch'ing, became an orphan when young and his first positions were as Assistant Thief-catcher, Chief of a *t'ing*, and *San-lao*. After he had entered Wei Ch'ing's service he was recommended to Emperor Wu and became Inspector of I-chou. In 91 B.C. he was an officer in the Northern Army at the capital during the tragic witchcraft scandal and uprising. He played a negative part in the affair, refusing to support the Heir-apparent Li, but also failing to arrest him. When, too late, Emperor Wu realized the innocence of his son, Jen An was executed for double-dealing and disloyalty.

317

Jen An is the person to whom was addressed a famous letter attributed to Ssu-ma Ch'ien. The circumstances are told by Chavannes (MH, vol. I, pp. xlii–xliii).

³ *She-jen* is defined in the *Chi-chieh* commentary in SC, 6, 1a, which quotes Wen Ying as saying: "It is the name of an official who oversees lesser officials in the stable. Some say that guests who serve and attend [their hosts, as opposed to real guests(?)] are called *she-jen*." TY gives a long set of definitions which show that the term changed meaning from late Chou through Ch'ing times. Chavannes (MH, vol. II, p. 101) translates "aventuriers"; Dubs (HFHD, vol. I, p. 174) uses "members of his suite." I would suggest the term "squire."

The present passage to page 3a affords the best contextual evidence on the meaning of the term that I have found. Herewith an abstract of the additional material:

Later there was an imperial edict for the selection of some of General Wei's *she-jen* to become Gentlemen. The General selected the rich ones among his *she-jen* and told them to equip themselves with saddles, horses, dark-red garments, jade *pei*, and swords, for the introduction to court. Just then Treasurer of the Privy Purse Chao Yü visited General Wei and the General assembled his *she-jen* for Chao Yü to inspect. Chao Yü questioned about ten of them one by one, and found not one possessed of talent. He advised the General against introducing them, saying that it would be a reflection on his own ability, and suggesting that the Emperor was probably really testing him out. He reproved him for selecting only rich men's sons, whom he characterized as wooden puppets dressed in fine silk. Then one by one Chao Yü questioned more than a hundred of General Wei's *she-jen*, and found only T'ien Jen and Jen An suitable for introduction to court. He told each to equip himself with saddle, horse, and new dark-red garments. The men replied that their families were poor and that they did not have such equipment. Though General Wei was loath to equip them himself there seemed to be no other way, and he sent up their names. They were summoned for an audience, were imperially questioned, and gave good answers. Both were given official positions.

This event is referred to in a commentary quoted by Dubs (HFHD, vol. I, p. 329, footnote 9.9).

⁴ Cf. *26*, footnote 2.

⁵ T'ien Jen (SC, 104, 2a–3b; CHS, 37, 3b; 66, 2b; JMT, p. 197) is said to have been the son of T'ien Shu (*12*, footnote 4). If this is true, father and son spanned at least 115 years, and probably more. His career began with his association with Wei Ch'ing, who presented him to court. He became a Gentleman of the Palace and then Chief Secretary to the Chancellor. He brought accusations against several commandery administrators and other officials closely related to Grandee Secretary Tu Chou (98–94 B.C.) and Chancellor Shih Ch'ing (112–103 B.C.), and for this fearlessness he won the praise of Emperor Wu, who appointed him Assistant to the Chancellor. In 91 B.C. he, too, was caught in the palace uprising. In command of one of the gates to the city, but siding with the Heir-apparent, he let him escape through the gate. For this he was executed before the Heir-apparent was vindicated.

⁶ Cf. *26*. Presumably she was the princess in whose household Wei Ch'ing had risen from slavery, and whom he later married.

⁷ This passage, though in the present SC, is ascribed to Master Ch'u, identified as Ch'u Shao-sun (CHS, 88, 8a; JMT, p. 1543; SKC, 45, 1b), a scholar who flourished during the latter half of the first century B.C. The CHS devotes only a few lines to him in the biography of Wang Shih: Some time after Wang Shih had been imprisoned in 74 B.C. for his connection with the King of Ch'ang-i (Liu Ho; cf. *67*, footnote 2), Ch'u Shao-sun from P'ei came to Wang Shih to study the classics. Later he rose to be an Erudit.

Such are the facts in the CHS. Though the authors knew of him they did not mention any connection between him and the SC text of their day, though they did mention that ten of the 130 chapters in the SC had titles but no texts (CHS, 30, 6a).

The whole problem of Ch'u Shao-sun or Master Ch'u and his share in the present SC text is brilliantly discussed by Chavannes (MH, vol. I, pp. cci–ccx). Supplementary information comes from Pelliot (BEFEO, vol. 2, 1902, pp. 334–335). The following brief review is abstracted from these authors and the basic commentaries (SC, 12, 1a; 130, 13b; CHS, 62, 6a–b).

The third century commentator Chang Yen named the ten missing chapters, and stated that Master Ch'u filled in this lacuna during the reigns of Emperors Yüan and Ch'eng (48–33; 33–7 B.C.), and wrote four of the chapters, which are named (SC, 130; CHS, 62; cf. MH, vol. I, pp. cci–ccii). Pelliot found the same statement (though apparently not the list of the four chapters) in the Shih lüeh 史略, part of which is preserved in the Ku i ts'ung-shu, a collection of early Chinese works preserved in Japan. The important point is that the Shih lüeh quoted the Wei Hung chiu i 衞宏舊儀 (i.e., the Han kuan 漢官 chiu i by Wei Hung). This places the authority back to Wei Hung, a well-known first century writer (fl. A.D. 25–57), and a contemporary of Pan Ku (A.D. 32–92), the main author of the CHS.

Chang Yen says further (SC, 12) that Master Ch'u was Ch'u Shao-sun, an Erudit in Han times. He is indirectly quoted as saying that Master Ch'u was a man from Ying-ch'uan and was an official during the reigns of Emperors Yüan and Ch'eng. The next item of information (also in SC, 12, 1a) is quoted from Wei Ling. Pelliot was able to add from the Shih lüeh what Chavannes did not know, that Wei Ling lived during the Liang dynasty (A.D. 502–555) and wrote the Han shu hsiu hsün. Wei Ling is indirectly quoted as saying that according to the Ch'u Yi chia chuan [The memoirs of the house of Ch'u Yi, first mentioned in the bibliography of a dynastic history in the Sui shu (HY10, V, p. 116)], Ch'u Shao-sun was a grandson of Ch'u Ta-ti, some time Chancellor of Liang; he was an Erudit during the reign of Emperor Hsüan (74–49 B.C.); while in P'ei he worked with Wang Shih and was therefore called the Master; and he continued the work of the Grand Astrologer (Ssu-ma Ch'ien). The cataloguers of the Ch'ien-lung imperial library (SKC, 45, 1b) note the discrepancy in reigns during which he is said to have been an Erudit, but point out that there were only 18 years between the end of the reign of Emperor Hsüan and the beginning of the reign of Emperor Ch'eng.

Wei Hung, Chang Yen, and the T'ang commentators who ascribed parts of the then extant SC to Ch'u Shao-sun undoubtedly had access to much information now lost. On the basis of information now at hand, however, it must be admitted that very little is known about him. All the parts attributed to him were probably not written by him, as Chavannes has pointed out.

What we know is that during the period between the death of Ssu-ma Ch'ien and the activity of the Pan family, historical records continued to be kept and many writers were active. Some historical material now attached to the SC is either absent from the SC and CHS (the present document is an example), or is in different form in the CHS (document 77, for instance). This material is attributed to Master Ch'u, also known as Ch'u Shao-sun. At least from T'ang times the writings of this man have been appended to the SC and have been accorded a rating higher than many other Han works—this in spite of the fact that T'ang commentators criticize the style as base.

In search of material on slavery during Han times, therefore, the writings of Master Ch'u cannot be discarded. Unfortunately we do not know where or how he got his information. Aside from the fact that he was an Erudit there is only internal evidence that he had access to records no longer extant elsewhere.

居無何匈奴渾邪王帥眾來降漢發車三萬乘縣官亡
錢從民貰馬民或匿馬馬不具上怒欲斬長安令黯曰長
安令亡罪獨斬臣黯民迺肯出馬且匈奴畔其主而降漢
徐以縣次傳之何至令天下騷動罷中國甘心夷狄之人
乎上默然後渾邪王至賈人與市者坐當死五百餘人黯
入請閒見高門曰夫匈奴攻當路塞絕和親中國舉兵誅
之死傷不可勝計而費以鉅萬百數臣愚以爲陛下得胡
人皆以爲奴婢賜從軍死者家鹵獲因與之以謝天下塞
百姓之心今縱不能渾邪帥數萬之眾來虛府庫賞賜發
良民侍養若奉驕子愚民安知市買長安中而文吏繩以
爲闌出財物如邊關乎陛下縱不能得匈奴之贏以謝天
下又以微文殺無知者五百餘人臣竊爲陛下弗取也上
弗許曰吾久不聞汲黯之言今又復妄發矣

Shortly after, the Hsiung-nu King of Hun-hsieh came to surrender, leading a multitude of followers.[1] The Han [government] issued thirty thousand[2] carts [to transport them, but] the imperial government lacked funds [and so tried] to buy horses from the people on credit. Some people hid their horses, [and enough] horses could not be assembled. The Emperor was furious and wished to behead the Prefect of Ch'ang-an.

[Chi] Yen[3] said: "The Prefect of Ch'ang-an is not at fault; just behead Your servant [Chi] Yen, and then the people may be willing to produce their horses. Furthermore, the Hsiung-nu, having rebelled against their ruler, are submitting to Han. [It would suffice] slowly to pass them on from one prefecture to the next. Why disturb the empire and exhaust the nation, just to pamper the barbarians?"

The Emperor said nothing.

Later when the King of Hun-hsieh arrived [at Ch'ang-an], merchants who traded with [his followers] were tried, and more than 500 were found guilty [and sentenced to] death.[4]

[Chi] Yen entered and asked for a private interview and was received at the High Gate [Hall]. He said: "Now, the Hsiung-nu, attacking and blocking the highways and barriers, broke the [treaty of] peace and friendship. China raised troops to punish them, and the [Chinese] killed and wounded were innumerable, while the expenses were counted by the ten billions [of cash]. Your servant foolishly thinks that when Your Majesty obtains northern barbarians they should all be made slaves and be granted to the families of those who died in the army; [also let (whatever[5])] is captured be given to them, in order to relieve the empire ['s distress[6]] and satisfy the hearts of the people.

"Now, supposing You cannot do that. The King of Hun-hsieh comes leading a horde of several myriad [to surrender. You] empty the treasury and reward them, and send forth good people to wait on them as though serving spoiled children. How can the ignorant people understand that because they traded [with the Hsiung-nu] in Ch'ang-an the civil officials arrest them for exporting goods as though at a frontier pass?[7] If Your Majesty cannot derive benefit out of the Hsiung-nu for relief of the empire, still more [how can You] execute more than 500 ignorant people because of a trifling law?[8] Your servant ventures to suggest that Your Majesty should not take [such a step]."

The Emperor did not assent. He said: "For a long time I have not heard Chi Yen. Now he is carelessly [speaking] out again!"

[1] The event is recorded in CHS, 6, 6a, as happening in the autumn of 121 B.C. The situation was as follows: The successes of General Ho Ch'ü-ping and other Han generals caused such slaughter of the western Hsiung-nu that the *Shan-yü* was going to punish the kings of Hun-hsieh and Hsiu-ch'u, whose lands were in western Kansu. Therefore they planned to submit to China, but at the last minute the King of Hsiu-ch'u wavered, and the King of Hun-hsieh killed him, united the two hordes, and surrendered to China. The cost of caring for this horde of four myriad strained the resources of the empire. Aspects of the situation are recorded in SC, 30 (MH, vol. III, p. 559); CHS, 24B, 4a; and 58, 4b; 59, 2a; 94A, 8b–9a (cf. also MH, vol. I, pp. lxviii, ciii; TH, vol. I, pp. 479–480; Alexander Wylie, "History of the Heung-noo in their relations with China," JAI, vol. 3, 1873, p. 427; and J. J. M. de Groot, *Die Hunnen der vorchristlichen Zeit*, Berlin, 1921, pp. 126 ff.). Dubs uses the variant readings, Kun-hsieh and Hsiu-t'u.

[2] SC, 120, 2b, gives twenty thousand.

[3] Chi Yen (SC, 120, 1a–3a; CHS, 50, 3b–5b; JMT, p. 485) had been an out-rider for Emperor Wu when he was still Heir-apparent. He rose through the ranks to be Administrator of Tung-hai, Commandant of Honorary Ranks, and Prefect of the western part of the capital district. He was noted for his outspoken criticism, and as a champion of the people.

[4] They were tried for violating laws which forbade trading with the Hsiung-nu or exporting certain goods *at the frontier passes*; see below, footnote 7. Chi Yen, a vigorous opponent of excessive legalism, sprang to the merchants' defense.

⁵ From SC, 120, 2b. In a personal communication Dr. Homer H. Dubs suggests that this phrase be read "... for (whoever) is captured is [ordinarily] given [to the families of those who have been killed] ...."

⁶ Ibid.

⁷ See footnote 4. Ying Shao (ca. A.D. 140–206) says that in trading with the Huns, officials and plebeians were not allowed export weapons or iron. Although the trade was done at the capital, the law was the same.

⁸ SC adds: "This is what may be called protecting the leaves and injuring the branches;" i.e., harming what is essential (Chinese) to save what is non-essential (the Hsiung-nu)—a common Chinese metaphor.

41. 121 B.C.[1] CHS, 68, 9a (18b)

日磾以父不降見殺與母閼氏弟倫俱没入官輸黃門
養馬時年十四矣久之武帝游宴見馬後宮滿側日磾等
數十人牽馬過殿下莫不竊視至日磾獨不敢日磾長八
尺二寸容貌甚嚴馬又肥好上異而問之具以本狀對上
奇焉即日賜湯沐衣冠拜爲馬監遷侍中駙馬都尉光祿
大夫

[Chin] Jih-ti,[2] whose father had been murdered for not surrendering [to Han], his mother the Queen, and his younger brother Lun, were all seized by the government. [Chin Jih-ti] was turned over to the Yellow Gate[3] [eunuchs] to care for horses. At that time he had reached his fourteenth year. Long afterward Emperor Wu was once amusing himself by inspecting his horses, with the ladies of his seraglio all about him. [Chin] Jih-ti and several tens of other [grooms] led the horses past the foot of the hall. None [of the other grooms] missed sneaking a look [at the ladies, but when] it came to [Chin] Jih-ti, he alone did not presume to. [Chin] Jih-ti was six feet two[4] inches tall, and very grave and dignified in appearance, and furthermore his horses were fat and in good condition. The Emperor was surprised and questioned him. In reply he stated his case from the beginning. The Emperor marveled, and that very day granted him a ceremonial bath, robe, and cap, and appointed him Superintendent of Horses. [He was successively] advanced to Attaché, Commandant of Imperial Equipage, and Imperial Household Grandee.

[1] The date when Chin Jih-ti was enslaved. No date is given for his freedom.

[2] Chin Jih-ti, or Mi-ti (CHS, 68, 8b–11a; 17, 18a; JMT, p. 607), was the Heir-apparent of the Hsiung-nu King of Hsiu-ch'u. His father planned to surrender to China, then lost heart and was killed by the King of Hun-hsieh, who did surrender, and handed over Chin Jih-ti and his mother and brother to the Chinese. Cf. 40.

After the incidents here translated, Chin Jih-ti became one of Emperor Wu's most trusted personal advisers. In 88 B.C. he saved the Emperor from an assassin, and in reward was made a marquis. Emperor Wu, on his deathbed, appointed Ho Kuang, Chin Jih-ti, and Shang-kuan Chieh as regents for young Emperor Chao. The next year, 86 B.C., Chin Jih-ti died.

[3] In CHS, 19A, 4b, the Yellow Gate eunuchs are listed under the Treasurer of the Privy Purse (*Shao fu*) (cf. MH, vol. II, pp. 519–521). According to TY they

served behind the Yellow Gate, i.e., within the inner palace. It says that in Han times the personnel consisted of Gentlemen (*shih-jen*) and eunuchs (Chavannes, op. cit., says they were all eunuchs), though later only Gentlemen were used. A quotation is given from CHS, "Withdraw [from] the Yellow Gate the chariots, carriages, dogs, and horses," which would seem to indicate that the Yellow Gate eunuchs had charge of these things. Chin Jih-ti was not made a eunuch; he later had two sons. His brother, who became a Huang-men Lang, also had a son.

⁴ Western measure; eight feet two inches in Han measure.

---

42.   Ca. 120 B.C.   CHS, 68 (1b)

去病大爲中孺買田宅奴婢而去

[After Ho Ch'ü-ping¹ had been made General of the Dashing Cavalry in 121 B.C., he was passing through Ho-tung Commandery and for the first time met his father, Ho Chung-ju. Ho] Ch'ü-ping liberally bought fields, houses, and male and female slaves for [Ho] Chung-ju, and then left.

¹ Cf. *29*, footnote 3.

43. 120 B.C.[1] CHS, 90, 4a (8a)

部吏如居廣平時方略捕郡中豪猾相連坐千餘家上
書請大者至族小者乃死家盡没入償臧奏行不過二日
得可事論報至流血十餘里

[After Wang Wen-shu[2] had been appointed Administrator of Ho-nei Commandery] his officers, just as [they had done] when stationed in Kuang-p'ing, forcibly arrested the tyrannical gentry of the commandery. More than a thousand families were mutually implicated and tried. He sent up a memorandum begging that for those [involved in] major [crimes the execution] should include all the relatives; and that those [involved in] small [crimes] should be executed [alone]—their household being entirely seized,[3] and restitution being made for plunder.[4]

The memorial had been sent not more than two days when he received authorization to act, sentence, and report. Blood flowed over ten or more *li*.[5]

[1] The year before Wang Wen-shu's appointment as Palace Military Commander (CHS, 19B, 17a).

[2] Wang Wen-shu (SC, 122, 6a; CHS, 90, 3b–4b; 19B, 17a–21b; JMT, p. 133), a vigorous but ruthless administrator, started his career as Chief of a *t'ing*, and then became a jailer for the Commandant of Justice, Chang T'ang. When the latter was appointed Grandee Secretary, Wang Wen-shu was made Commandant of Kuang-p'ing Commandery. His record in suppressing lawlessness quickly won him the position of Administrator of Ho-nei Commandery. The present incident occurred there. In 119 B.C. he was made Palace Military Commander. Thereafter he held the following administrative positions: Commandant of Justice (114), Palace Military Commander again (113–112), Treasurer of the Privy Purse (109–107), Senior Prefect of the Capital (107–105). He committed suicide in 104 B.C., after his grafting had been exposed.

[3] *Chia*, "household," might mean only household goods. Seizures were made of family members (*chia shu*) or of household goods (*chia ts'ai* or *chia wu*), or of both. The word *chin*, "entirely," seems to indicate that in this case both family members and goods were to be seized. Government seizure of people meant enslavement.

[4] Yen Shih-ku says: "Those proved guilty of plundering were immediately enslaved. Also they were made to produce double [the amount of their] plunder, some [i.e., one-half?] being taken by the government and some being returned to the original owner."

[5] This passage appears almost word for word the same in SC, 122, 6a.

44.   144–116 B.C.[1]   CHS, 47, 2b (6a)

濟東王彭離立二十九年彭離驕悍昏暮私與其奴亡
命少年數十人行剽殺人取財物以爲好所殺發覺者百
餘人國皆知之莫敢夜行所殺者子上書告言有司請誅
武帝弗忍廢爲庶人徙上庸國除爲大河郡

[Liu] P'eng-li,[2] King of Chi-tung, ruled twenty-nine years.
[Liu] P'eng-li was haughty and cruel. At dusk he would go out
secretly with several tens of his male slaves and lawless young bloods,
plundering and assassinating people, taking their valuables, all for
sport. Of those who were killed, more than a hundred [cases were
actually] divulged. Everyone in the kingdom knew about it and
no one dared travel at night. The sons of those killed sent up a
statement reporting [the facts]. The officials begged for his execution. Emperor Wu could not bear [that, but] deposed him, made
him a commoner, and removed him to Shang-yung. The kingdom
was abolished and made the Ta-ho Commandery.

[1] Probably near 116, for it is difficult to believe that the crimes went unreported during the whole period.

[2] Liu P'eng-li (SC, 58, 3b; CHS, 47, 2b–3a) was a grandson of Emperor Wen,
and a cousin of Emperor Wu. He was made King in 144 B.C., and was removed
in 116 B.C. (CHS, 6, 7b). The passage translated appears also in the SC, with
only minor variations. Chi-tung was in eastern Shantung near T'ai-an.

45.   119 B.C.   SC, 30, 5a

買人有市籍者及其家屬皆無得籍名田以便農敢犯令沒入田僮

[In a recommendation[1] presented to Emperor Wu by his high ministers, suggestions were made regarding taxes and restrictions against merchants. The concluding suggestion says]: "All those resident merchants who are on the market register, together with their family dependents, may not register[2] privately owned fields. [This suggestion is made] so as to benefit farmers.[3]   [If anyone] dares to violate this order, confiscate his fields and youths."[4]

[1] The entire passage is translated by Chavannes (MH, vol. III, pp. 572–575).

Since there is no definite statement that the Emperor agreed and put these suggestions into practice, it is not certain that they became law.   Two things indicate, however, that the recommendation was accepted at least in part.   The recommendation to tax the accumulated fortunes of merchants was instituted the same year (CHS, 6, 6b).   The passage ends with the statement, "[If anyone] dares to violate this order . . . ," which hints that the historian was using a document drawn up in the form of an order, or with an order appended.

[2] The nearly identical passage in CHS, 24B, 5b, leaves out the word "register," rendering the meaning, "may not have privately owned fields."   Yen Shih-ku there explains: "If a man has [i.e., is on] a market register, then he personally and those in his household, all may not have fields."   Cf. Chavannes (ibid., p. 575, footnote 3).

[3] Chavannes translates the phrase 以便農 as, "afin de profiter des (avantages accordés aux) agriculteurs."

[4] The So-yin commentary says: "If merchants in addition [to being merchants, try to] register fields, then confiscate their fields together with their servant-youths 僕僮, who will all be taken in by the government."

A crucial difference appears in the CHS text, which employs the term 貨, "goods," or "possessions," as the last word, instead of the SC t'ung, "youths." The texts throughout are so nearly identical that there seems to be no way of judging which, if either, of the present versions is primary.   Did the CHS broaden the SC statement, or did the present SC restrict the term used in the CHS?   The difference may be due merely to an early textual corruption.   Pelliot (BEFEO, vol. 2, 1902, p. 335) calls attention to a copy of a T'ang manuscript of CHS, 24, in the Ku i ts'ung-shu.   He states that a comparison of the T'ang text and the present one shows a hundred differences in characters, of which about twenty are useful corrections but not of great importance.   Pelliot failed to state that the manuscript is of the first half of CHS, 24 only.   The present passage does not occur in it.

46. 119–113 B.C.[1]   CHS, 24B, 6b (16a)

得民財物以億計奴婢以千萬數田大縣數百頃小縣
百餘頃宅亦如之於是商賈中家以上大氐破民媮甘食
好衣不事畜臧之業而縣官以鹽鐵緡錢之故用少饒矣
…廼分緡錢諸官而水衡少府太僕大農各置農官往往
卽郡縣比沒入田田之其沒入奴婢分諸苑養狗馬禽獸
及與諸官官益雜置多徒奴婢衆而下河漕度四百萬石
及官自糴廼足

[Emperor Wu, on the advice of his counselors, instituted a policy of confiscating accumulated fortunes, especially those of merchants.[2]   The government] acquired people's property reckoned by the hundred million[3] [cash]; male and female slaves numbered by the thousand [even to] a myriad;[4] fields, in large prefectures by the several hundred *ch'ing*, in small prefectures by the hundred and more *ch'ing*;[5] and houses in proportion.   Thereupon itinerant traders and resident merchants, and families of middling [wealth] and up were generally ruined.   The people wastefully indulged in eating, and liked fine clothes, and would not undertake the work of storing up property; while the imperial government, because of [income from the monopoly on] salt and iron, and [confiscations of] accumulated fortunes, had a small abundance . . . .[6]

Then the accumulated fortunes were distributed among various bureaus, while the [Chief Commandant of] Public Lands, [the Treasurer of] the Privy Purse, the Chief of Stud, and the Grand [Minister of] Agriculture[7] each established agricultural bureaus [whose officials] constantly went to commanderies and prefectures, continually confiscating fields and putting them into cultivation. The confiscated male and female slaves were distributed among various parks [and employed] to rear dogs, horses, birds, and beasts, and were given to the various bureaus.   The bureaus enlarged or miscellaneously established were numerous.   The convicts and male and female slaves were a multitude, and were sent down the river to transport four million piculs[8] [of grain, which] with [what] the bureaus themselves laid up, was enough.[9]

¹ It is between these dates that the events are mentioned (see MH, vol. III, pp. 572, 589).

² For an account of this confiscation policy, and the philosophy behind it, see MH, vol. III, pp. 572 ff.

³ According to TY, there are two ways to figure *i* 億, either as "ten myriad," or as "a myriad myriad." Since it refers to cash, the second is more likely here.

⁴ There are three ways to translate *ch'ien-wan* ("thousand-myriad"), depending upon the construction and context, though in each case the figure is symbolic rather than precise. (1) *From a thousand to a myriad.* Myriad is the terminal figure. (2) *By the thousand and the myriad.* This is simply a large number, but less than "several myriad," or "ten myriad," etc. (3) *Thousand times myriad.* This sense usually refers to large amounts of money (cash), and equals ten million, not an unusual figure for individual Han fortunes. An example is in the chapter on "Rich Merchants," biography of Ning Ch'eng (CHS, 90, 2a–b). During the reign of Emperor Wu, Ning Ch'eng borrowed more than a thousand *ch'ing* of ruined fields on credit, and rented them to several thousand poor families. After several years he had achieved an estate of several *ch'ien-wan.* Considering prices of grain and the fifty-fifty share crop system, this must mean several ten million (cash), corresponding to the several thousand families of tenants. If either the first or second of the above readings were taken it would mean that during several years he had only profited about one cash or some score cash per tenant family.

In translating the present passage I have adopted the first reading on the advice of Dr. J. J. L. Duyvendak. Exactly the same construction occurs in CHS, 24A, 6b, quoting a memorial in which Tung Chung-shu says that under the rule of Ch'in those condemned to prison were yearly numbered by the *ch'ien-wan.* While not to be taken literally anyway, this can hardly mean several myriad sentenced each year (cf. translation by Derk Bodde, *China's first unifier*, p. 173).

⁵ A *ch'ing* was 100 *mou.* According to calculations by Dr. H. H. Dubs (to appear in HFHD, trans., vol. III, ch. 99A, footnote 9.3) the Han *mou* contained 4,956 square feet English measure, or 0.114 acres. A hundred *ch'ing*, equaling 1,140 acres, does not seem a very large area even in a small prefecture, but it must have represented many small holdings.

⁶ The text digresses to discuss the government salt and iron monopoly, and a war with the people of Yüeh which necessitated expansion of an artificial lake and building of towered boats on which to train troops.

⁷ The Ta-nung was actually the State Treasurer, the principal source of state income being from the grain tax.

⁸ One picul equaled 64 pounds 8.8 ounces avoir. (HFHD, vol. I, p. 280), so that four million would equal 258,200,000 pounds of millet (the most important crop of north China, and also the basic standard for weights and measures; see ibid., pp. 276–278). This comes to 5,164,000 bushels (using U.S. standard weight for a bushel of millet, which is 50 pounds).

⁹ The bureaus presumably got their supplies of grain from the fertile Shensi region around the capital. Grain transported from the lower Yellow River would come from Shansi, Honan, and farther eastward. From the two sources there was enough to maintain the court, pay salaries in kind to the bureaucracy, and feed other government employees and the army around the capital—this may be what is meant by "was enough."

The same passage, with only minor variations, is in SC, 30, 6a–b (MH, vol. III, pp. 586–588).

47. Ca. 115 B.C. and after.[1] HCI, B, 8a

武帝時使上林苑中官奴婢及天下貧民貲不滿五千
徙置苑中養鹿因收撫鹿矢人日五錢到元帝時七十億
萬以給軍擊西域

In the time of Emperor Wu [the Emperor] used government male and female slaves who were in the Shang-lin park,[2] together with the poor people of the empire whose property did not equal five thousand [cash] and who were transported to and established in the park, to care for the deer.   They picked up and assembled deer manure, each person [paying] five cash per day [for the privilege[3]]. By the time of Emperor Yüan [the total income] had reached seventy billion [cash],[4] which was given to the army for attacks on the Western Regions.

[1] The midpoint of Emperor Wu's reign would be about 115 B.C., and it was about this time that we first read of government slaves sent to various parks. Cf. *46*.   This is the only dated passage dealing with slaves in the *Han chiu i*.   For the others see *90* ff.   Most of this passage is given in a commentary in HSPC, 24B, 17a.

[2] The Shang-lin park was a vast preserve west of the capital on the south side of the Wei River.   It contained seventy imperial hostels, and was used as an imperial hunting preserve and to supply all kinds of game in huge quantities for the palaces.   Established during the Ch'in, it was enlarged by Emperor Wu, who loved to retire there for vacations.

[3] This might mean that each person paid five cash per day for the privilege of gathering and selling manure; or the five cash might be an average received from sale by the government.

[4] This is arrived at by taking the lesser figure for *i*, that is, 100,000 (cf. *46*, footnote 3).   The figure is fantastic.   There could hardly have been seventy million strings of cash, a thousand to a string, in existence.   Of course the receipts could have been converted into stored gold, but consider Kung Yü's statement (*89*, footnote 2) that Emperor Yüan was so frugal that the reserves of the Treasury were four billion; of the Public Lands, two and a half billion; and of the Privy Purse, one billion eight hundred million cash.

48. 115 B.C. CHS, 41, 4b (11a)

傳至曾孫頗尚平陽公主坐與父御婢姦自殺國除

[The Marquisate of Ju-yin, first held by Hsia-hou Ying] was carried on to his great-grandson [Hsia-hou] P'o,[1] who married the Princess of P'ing-yang. He was tried for having had relations with his father's personal female slave,[2] and killed himself. The state was abolished.

[1] Hsia-hou P'o (SC, 18, 3b, and 95, 5a; CHS, 16, 3b, and 41, 4b) was the great-grandson of one of Kao-tsu's fellow townsmen and close companions in the rebellion against Ch'in. Nothing else seems to be recorded about Hsia-hou P'o or the Princess of P'ing-yang whom he married. Presumably she was a daughter of Emperor Wu; the question is extensively discussed by Wang Hsien-ch'ien.

[2] The term yü has the sense of imperial or royal, reserved for the use of an emperor or king, hence, "personal." The idea is that the woman was a personal attendant to, or was for the personal use of, the marquis.

The crime was not in the illicit relations, but in the fact that the woman was his father's personal slave woman, which connotes incest.

The terse account in CHS, 16, 3b, not separately translated, leaves out the word "female slave," but it occurs in the equivalent SC passage and in SC, 95, 5a. All three accounts give the date 115 B.C., which is left out here.

49.   113 B.C.   CHS, 25A, 10b (28b)

其以二千戶封地士將軍大爲樂通侯賜列侯甲第童
千人乘輿斥車馬帷帳器物以充其家又以衞長公主妻
之齎金十萬斤更名其邑曰當利公主

[Emperor Wu] enfeoffed [Luan] Ta,[1] General of Magicians of the Earth, with an income from two thousand households and with the title of Marquis Lo-t'ung. He presented him with the highest-class mansion for a marquis, a thousand youths, a princely chariot, extra carriages and horses, and curtains and furniture to fill his house. Further, he married him to the Grand Princess Wei,[2] presenting [her with a dowry of] ten myriads of metal,[3] and changing the name of her city to Tang Li Kung Chu.[4]

[1] Luan Ta (SC, 28, 11a; CHS, 25A, 10b; JMT, p. 1805; MH, vol. III, pp. 477–481) was one of the great magicians attached to the superstitious Emperor Wu, who lavishly favored him, then had him executed a year later. His appointment as Marquis Lo-t'ung (lit. "Happy Communication") is recorded in SC, 20, 14a; CHS, 6, 8a; and 18, 8a.

[2] The eldest daughter of the Emperor Wu and the Empress *née* Wei (Wei Tzu-fu; cf. *27*).

[3] Probably not gold, as translated by Chavannes. It would total 53,750 pounds avoir. (cf. HFHD, vol. I, p. 280), but the figure need not be taken literally; in fact, in two other places where the gift is recorded the word "ten" is left out. Cf. HSPC, 25A, 28b.

[4] Lit. "[The city] which should profit the Princess."

50. 113 B.C. CHS, 95, 6b (13b)

於是天子遣千秋與王太后弟摎樂將二千人往入粵
境呂嘉迺遂反下令國中曰王年少太后中國人又與使
者亂專欲內屬盡持先王寶入獻天子以自媚多從人行
至長安虜賣以爲僮奴自脫一時利亡顧趙氏社稷爲萬
世慮之意迺與其弟將卒攻殺太后王盡殺漢使者

Thereupon[1] Emperor [Wu] dispatched [Han] Ch'ien-ch'iu and
Chiu Lo, the younger brother of the Dowager Queen [of Nan Yüeh,
née Chiu], leading two thousand men to invade the boundaries of
Yüeh. Lü Chia thereupon immediately rebelled and issued a statement to the kingdom, saying: "The King is young and the Dowager
Queen is a Chinese. Moreover, she has intercourse with the emissary,
and intends on her own authority to incorporate [our kingdom with
China] and to take in the entire treasure of the late King as tribute
to the Emperor in order [to win] personal favor. With many attendants [she intends] to go to Ch'ang-an [where they] will be made
captives and sold to become youths and male slaves,[2] so that she
may take for herself a momentary profit. She does not consider the
Chao family's gods of the soil and grain, nor plan for the hopes of a
thousand future generations."

Then [Lü Chia], together with his younger brother, led troops
to attack and slay the Dowager Queen and the King, and killed all
the Han emissaries.

[1] The background of this incident was as follows (SC, 113, 2b–3a; CHS,
95, 5b–6a): The aged King of Yüeh (in modern Chekiang, Fukien, and Kwangtung
[cf. Herrmann, *Atlas*, p. 20]), named Chao T'o, died in 113 B.C. He was succeeded
by his grandson, Chao Hu, who in turn was succeeded by Chao Ying-ch'i. Before
he became King, Chao Ying-ch'i had lived as a hostage at the Han court and had
married a Chinese woman, *née* Chiu. She bore him an heir and became his Queen.
When Chao Ying-ch'i died, their young son Chao Hsing became King, and the
Queen became Dowager Queen. Before her marriage she had had sexual relations
with a Chinese named An-kuo Shao-chi. In 113 B.C. Emperor Wu sent this man
as emissary to order the Dowager Queen and young King to come to court. The
former lovers began to have secret relations again, causing a scandal in Yüeh. Also
the Dowager Queen hoped to bring the independent Kingdom of Yüeh into the
Han empire. This scheme was opposed by Lü Chia, who had been Chancellor
to the last three kings of Yüeh. In order to prevent the submission of Yüeh to
Han he plotted a rebellion which led to the event in the passage here translated.

As a result of the revolt Emperor Wu sent a great expedition against the
Yüeh Kingdom, and in 111 B.C. southeastern China was conquered and incorporated
into the Han empire. A good discussion of the early history of this region is

given by Léonard Aurousseau ("La première conquête chinoise des pays annamites," BEFEO, vol. 23, 1923, pp. 137–265).

[2] In the nearly identical passage in SC, 113, 3a, the term *t'ung p'u* 僮僕 is used for *t'ung nu*. HSPC leaves out *nu*, and begins the next phrase with 取, as in the SC. I have punctuated here according to the suggestion of Wang Hsien-ch'ien.

This mention of slaves is merely an accusation of what the Dowager Queen intended to do, and is not a historical fact. However, if the historicity of the passage itself is granted, it indicates that there would have been a market for slaves from Yüeh in Ch'ang-an, for Lü Chia would hardly have accused the Dowager Queen of planning an act outside the realm of possibility. From other references it is known that the regions south of China were sources for slaves. A female slave from Yüeh is mentioned in the year 123 B.C., ten years earlier (cf. *38*).

51. 110 B.C. CHS, 15A, 19b (27a)

元康元年坐使奴殺人下獄瘐死

In 110 B.C.[1] [Liu Lung,[2] the Marquis of Fu] was tried for causing a male slave to kill a man. He was thrown into prison where he wasted and died.

[1] The actual date given is 65 B.C., which is 63 years (Chinese count) after Liu Lung was appointed in 127 B.C. (CHS, 15A, 15b). However, the text says it was 16 years after his appointment that he was tried, or 111 B.C., perhaps early in 110 B.C.—the latter year is *"Yüan-feng* [rather than *Yüan-k'ang*] first year," and seems more reasonable as answering most problems. Wang Hsien-ch'ien makes the same correction.

[2] Liu Lung was one of the sons of the King of Chi-pei. SC, 21, 11b, says nothing of his trial.

---

52. 100 B.C. CHS, 15A, 20b (28a)

天漢元年坐殺人及奴凡十六人以捕匈奴千騎免

In 100 B.C. [Liu Shun[1] the Marquis of Chao] was tried for the murder of sixteen men and male slaves. Because he had captured a thousand Hsiung-nu cavalry he was [merely] deposed [from his marquisate].

[1] Liu Shun was one of the sons of King Kung of Tai. SC, 21, 13a (cf. MH, vol. III, p. 172) calls him Liu Shen, and does not tell of his being deposed.

53. Ca. 100 B.C.[1] CHS, 91, 3b (7a)

馬蹄躈千牛千足羊彘千雙童手指千

[Discussing the advantages of rich people during Han times, the author compares an average city with a medium-sized state in Chou times, and lists the commodities[2] annually consumed in a trade center or (commandery?) capital]—a thousand foot-mouth[3] of horses, a thousand foot[4] of oxen, a thousand brace of sheep and hogs, a thousand fingers[5] of youths . . . .

[1] Since this passage also appears in SC, 129, 7a, it is presumed to be by Ssu-ma Ch'ien. The date of the writing is indefinite.

[2] The list is interesting, though it has no statistical value, since nearly every item is listed by the thousand of its appropriate individual measure, and the modern equivalents of most of these measures are not known. The author is talking in round numbers, perhaps arrived at only by guess. A complete translation of the list would involve so many footnotes and calculations as to obscure entirely the reference to "youths," which is alone important here. The list includes the following items: wine, pickle, pickle juice, butchered cattle, sheep and hogs, grain, fuel, boats (by total length), planks of lumber, bamboo, light carriages, oxcarts, lacquered wood utensils, bronze utensils, plain wood and iron utensils, . . . delicate or colored cloth, thick cloth, lacquer, wine mash and salt beans, salt- and fresh-water fish, jujubes and chestnuts, furs of fox and sable, pelts of kid and lamb, mats, fruits . . . .

[3] Following the commentators here and in SC. I cannot agree, however, with Yen Shih-ku that, since the numerical classifier is made up of foot and mouth, the total should therefore be divided by five (each horse having four feet and one mouth), thereby giving a total of 200 horses. Such a conclusion is too academic. The numerical classifier must have sprung from popular usage, and no horse-trader would use a classifier which always had to be divided by five to get the total number of head in a transaction. See also footnote 5.

[4] Yen Shih-ku is silent as to whether this means 250 or 1,000 head of cattle.

[5] Meng K'ang (A.D. 180–260) says: "*T'ung* are male and female slaves. In early times there were none unemployed; all had manual duties. Manual duties require the fingers, wherefore it speaks of fingers in contradistinction to the hoofs and horns of horses and cattle."
Yen Shih-ku says: "The fingers refer to those who are skillful. The fingers being one thousand the individuals would be one hundred." This is just as unacceptable as the case above, footnote 3. Wang Hsien-ch'ien and Kametaro Takigawa, in their editions of CHS and SC, are silent on this point.

54. Ca. 100 B.C.[1] CHS, 94A, 4a (7b)

舉事常隨月盛壯以攻戰月虧則退兵其攻戰斬首虜
賜一卮酒而所得鹵獲因以予之得人以爲奴婢故其戰
人人自爲趨利善爲誘兵以包敵故其逐利如鳥之集其
困敗瓦解雲散矣戰而扶輿死者盡得死者家財

When starting a [military] affair [the Hsiung-nu] always follow [the phases of] the moon;[2] when it is waxing or full they attack; when it is waning they then withdraw their troops. In battle, he who cuts off a head or takes a captive is given a beaker of wine, and the loot and captives are likewise given to him; the people he gets become his male and female slaves. Therefore in war every man personally rushes in for profit. They are good at luring tactics to surround an enemy. Wherefore,[3] in their pursuit of profit they are like birds flocking on a tree; but distressed and in defeat [they are like] broken tiles and scattering clouds. [After] battle he who carries back the dead gets all the dead one's household wealth.

[1] This passage is placed in the chronological framework of the chapter (likewise in SC, 110, 4b–5a) just at the beginning of the Han period. It is probably an ethnographic report of a Chinese returned from residence among the Hsiung-nu, or of a Hsiung-nu living in China, and the conditions described cannot be fixed at any single year. The year 100 B.C., at the middle of the Former Han period, was also approximately the high point of Chinese–Hsiung-nu relations. The chapter on the Hsiung-nu, from which this passage comes, has been translated by Wylie (JAI, vol. 3, 1873, pp. 401–451, and vol. 5, 1875, pp. 41–80) and by de Groot (*Die Hunnen der vorchristlichen Zeit*, Berlin, 1921).

[2] SC here says: "In starting a [military] affair they await the stars and moon; when the moon is waxing full then they attack."

[3] SC inserts here: "When they see the enemy, then ...."

既得王媼令大中大夫任宣與丞相御史屬雜考問鄉
里識知者皆曰王媼嫗言名妄人家本涿郡蠡吾平鄉年
十四嫁爲同鄉王更得妻更得死嫁爲廣望王迺始婦產
子男無故武女翁須翁須年八九歲時寄居廣望節侯子
劉仲卿宅仲卿謂迺始曰予我翁須自養長之媼爲翁須
作繡單衣送仲卿家仲卿教翁須歌舞往來歸取冬夏衣
居四五歲翁須來言邯鄲賈長兒求歌舞者仲卿欲以我
與之媼即與翁須逃走之平鄉仲卿載迺始共求媼媼惶
急將翁須歸曰兒居君家非受一錢也奈何欲予它人仲
卿詐曰不也後數日翁須乘長兒車馬過門呼曰我果見
行當之柳宿媼與迺始之柳宿見翁須相對涕泣謂曰我
欲爲汝自言翁須曰毋置之何家不可以居自言無益也
媼與迺始還求錢用隨逐至中山盧奴見翁須與歌舞等
比五人同處媼與翁須共宿明日迺始留視翁須媼還求
錢欲隨至邯鄲媼歸羅買未具迺始來歸曰翁須已去我
無錢用隨也因絕至今不聞其問賈長兒妻貞及從者師

When [Emperor Hsüan's] commissioners found [his maternal grandmother] Dame Wang,[2] [the Emperor] ordered Grand Palace Grandee Jen Hsüan and subordinates of the Chancellor and [Grandee] Secretary to investigate and question those of her neighborhood who remembered [the circumstances]. They all said:[3]

"Dame Wang. The Dame said her name was Wang-jen. Her home was originally in Cho Commandery, Li-wu [Prefecture], P'ing District.[4] In her fourteenth year she was married to be the wife of Wang Keng-te, from the same district. Keng-te died and she was married to be the remarried wife of Wang Nai-shih from Kuang-wang [Prefecture]. She bore children, the sons, Wu-ku and Wu, and a daughter, Weng-hsü.

338

"When Weng-hsü was in her eighth or ninth year [the family] lodged in a house belonging to Liu Chung-ch'ing, the son of Marquis Chieh of Kuang-wang.[5] [Liu] Chung-ch'ing said to [Wang] Nai-shih: 'Give me Weng-hsü. I myself will feed and rear her.' Dame [Wang] made an unlined silk dress for Weng-hsü and took her to [Liu] Chung-ch'ing's home. [Liu] Chung-ch'ing taught Weng-hsü to sing and dance, and she went back and forth, returning home to get winter or summer clothes.

"[After having] lived there four or five years, Weng-hsü came [home] and said: 'Chang-erh, a merchant from Han-tan,[6] is looking for singers and dancers, and [Liu] Chung-ch'ing wants to give[7] me to him.' Dame [Wang] immediately ran away with Weng-hsü to P'ing District. [Liu] Chung-ch'ing loaded [Wang] Nai-shih into a cart and together they searched for Dame [Wang]. In great agitation, Dame [Wang] led Weng-hsü back, saying: 'The child lived in Your Excellency's house, but we have never received a single cash [for her]. How can you plan to give her to someone else?' [Liu] Chung-ch'ing falsely said: 'I don't.'

"Several days later, Weng-hsü, riding on Chang-erh's carriage horse, passed the gate and called out: 'I am being sent after all, and should go to Liu-hsiu.'[8] Dame [Wang] and [Wang] Nai-shih went to Liu-hsiu to see Weng-hsü, and when they met they wept. [Dame Wang] said to her: 'I want to plead your case for you.' Weng-hsü said: 'Mother, dismiss it. One can live anywhere. Pleading the case will be useless.' Dame [Wang] and [Wang] Nai-shih returned home to seek expense money, and then followed her to Lu-nu [Prefecture] in Chung-shan [Kingdom] where they saw Weng-hsü living as one of a quintet of singers and dancers. Dame [Wang] spent the night with Weng-hsü. Next day [Wang] Nai-shih stayed behind to watch over Weng-hsü while Dame [Wang] went back to find some money, planning to follow [Weng-hsü] to Han-tan. Dame [Wang] had returned home, but the transactions[9] were not yet completed when [Wang] Nai-shih came home, saying: 'Weng-hsü has already left. I had no money to follow her.' Thus they were separated and [Dame Wang] did not hear any rumor[10] of her till now.

"Chen, the wife of the merchant Chang-erh, together with her attendants and teacher, made the following testimony:

" 'Twenty[11] years before, Hou Ming, a member of the Heir-apparent's suite, came from Ch'ang-an looking for singers and dancers.

遂辭往二十歲太子舍人侯明從長安來求歌舞者請翁
須等五人長兒使遂送至長安皆入太子家及廣望三老
更始劉仲卿妻其等四十五人辭皆驗宣奏王媼悼后母
明白

He asked for Weng-hsü and the others of the quintet, and Chang-erh, induced to comply, brought [the girls] to Ch'ang-an. They all entered the Heir-apparent's household.' ''

With these [statements] the testimonies of Keng-shih, the *San-lao* of Kuang-wang, of Ch'i, the wife of Liu Chung-ch'ing, and of forty-five other people, all agreed. [Jen] Hsüan memorialized that it was clearly established that Dame Wang was the mother of the [late] Empress Tao.[12]

[1] These are roughly the dates when the girl Weng-hsü was being trained as a singer and dancer, was sold against her parents' wishes, practiced her trade, and then passed into the family of the Heir-apparent. The present investigation took place in 67 B.C. Weng-hsü bore Emperor Hsüan in 91 B.C. She passed into the Heir-apparent's household some time during the *T'ai-shih* period, 96–92 B.C. Events before that time are not precisely dated.

[2] The background, as given in the part preceding this passage and elsewhere, is abstracted as follows: Lady Wang, the Weng-hsü of the present story, was a favorite of the imperial grandson Shih, son of Heir-apparent Liu Chü, who was son of Emperor Wu by his Empress *née* Wei (cf. *27*). Some time between 96 and 92 B.C. she first received the imperial grandson's favors, but in spite of this, his wife and concubines all called her "the householder," 家人子, which appears to be one term for a slave, and conformed with the fact that she had once been sold. In 91 B.C. she bore the son who later became Emperor Hsüan. A few months later there occurred the great witchcraft scandal in which the Heir-apparent was falsely accused of conspiring to kill his father, Emperor Wu, by black magic. The Heir-apparent, his son, and all his family were slain except Weng-hsü's child. None received proper ceremonial burial. The child was saved by Ping Chi and reared in the family of his father's mother, *née* Shih (cf. *80*, footnote 3). When he became Emperor (74 B.C.) he retroactively conferred on his mother the post-humous title "Empress Tao," and on his grandmother the title "Empress Shih." Both were ceremonially reburied and garden cities were established to make offerings and guard their tombs forever (see CHS, 63, 1a–3a). In 67 B.C. Emperor Hsüan sought for and found his maternal grandmother, Dame Wang, and her sons Wu-ku and Wu. Several times before he had sent emissaries to search for his maternal relatives, and many people were found who appeared to be the right ones but really were not. Therefore the Emperor instituted a thorough investigation to be sure. It is the findings of the investigation which are here translated.

[3] In HSPC Chou Shou-ch'ang points out that from here to the end of the next-to-the-last paragraph is all Jen Hsüan's official report of the testimony of those questioned. To what extent the historian copied verbatim and to what extent he abstracted is not clear, just as it is not clear how much of the report itself is direct quotation of testimony and how much is an indirect abstract. Some of Dame Wang's testimony, for example, seems to be given in the first person, and some in the third. I have put her testimony in the third person, except where she quoted others, because a verbatim translation entirely in the first person proves exceedingly clumsy.

[4] P'ing-hsiang must mean P'ing District in Li-wu Prefecture, rather than P'ing-hsiang Prefecture, which was too far south to be part of Li-wu and Cho Commandery. The latter was near the present Cho hsien, southwest of Peking on the Peking-Hankow railway. Li-wu Prefecture was near present Po-yeh hsien in west-central Hopei, south of present Ch'ing-wan hsien or Paoting Fu. The next place mentioned, Kuang-wang Prefecture, was a marquisate 50 *li* southwest of Paoting Fu.

[5] Marquis Chieh of Kuang-wang (CHS, 15A, 14b) was enfeoffed in 127 B.C. and died 30 years later. A son, Liu Chung, inherited the marquisate in 97. Liu Chung-ch'ing must have been a younger son of Marquis Chieh, and the event probably occurred before 97 B.C.

[6] Han-tan was an important commercial and manufacturing center (see Map) in southwestern Hopei, probably not far from present Han-tan on the Peking-Hankow line.

[7] I.e., sell.

[8] Liu-hsiu was southeast of present Wang-tu hsien, the first hsien south of Paoting Fu on the railway. It was also the seat of a marquisate. In a commentary, Su Lin says it was 30 *li* northeast of Lu-nu in Chung-shan, the next place mentioned. Lu-nu was a prefecture near present Ting hsien, the next stop on the railway. It had been made the center of Chung-shan Kingdom.

[9] She was apparently selling off her possessions in order either to buy back her daughter or at least to follow her to Han-tan.

[10] Following Wang Hsien-ch'ien's punctuation and comment here. This is necessary unless we assume that the historian here stops quoting and starts a new passage with *ch'i wen:* "They [i.e., the commission] questioned . . . ," etc.

[11] This must be an error for thirty. The investigation was in 67 B.C. and Weng-hsü was already dead in 91 B.C.

[12] Herewith an abstract of what followed: Emperor Hsüan called Dame Wang and her sons, Wu-ku and Wu, for an audience, and made both men *kuan-nei* marquises. Shortly after, he gave them gifts reckoned by the hundred million cash. By imperial edict he then made his maternal grandmother the Baroness of Po-p'ing and gave her 11,000 households in Po-p'ing and Li-wu prefectures as her estate; he enfeoffed Wu-ku as Marquis of P'ing-ch'ang, and Wu as Marquis of Lo-ch'ang, each with estates of 6,000 households. Wang Nai-shih had already died in 70 B.C., but he was posthumously ennobled as Marquis of Ssu-ch'eng, and Cho Commandery was ordered to erect a grave mound and shrine and establish a garden city of 400 households to make offerings and guard his tomb forever. Shortly after, the Baroness of Po-p'ing died and she and her late husband were buried together in a new spot with its garden city. Of the two Marquises Wang, Wu-ku's son, Chieh, became Grand Minister of Agriculture and General of Cavalry and Chariots, while Wu's son, Wang Shang, rose to be Chancellor, and has his own biography (cf. CHS, 82, 1a–2b; and *98*, footnote 3).

56. Ca. 98 B.C.[1] CHS, 37, 3b (6a)

贊曰以項羽之氣而季布以勇顯名楚身履軍搴旗者
數矣可謂壯士及至困厄奴僇苟活而不變何也彼自負
其材受辱不羞欲有所用其未足也故終爲漢名將賢者
誠重其死夫婢妾賤人感慨而自殺非能勇也其畫無俚
之至耳

In eulogy we say: "Having the animus of a Hsiang Yü, Chi Pu[2] was famous in Ch'u for bravery and eminence. [The instances] in which he personally stepped into the army and captured the [enemy] flag were numerous. It may be said that he was valorous. Why, when he arrived at adversity, did he become a slave, improperly [clinging to] life rather than steadfastly [holding to his principles]?[3] This disdain of his own abilities, acceptance of disgrace without shame, and the desire to have someone employ him [even as a slave, was due to the fact that] his [career] was not yet complete. Therefore, when he finally became a famous general of Han, the men of worth considered his death an important matter. Now if slave women, concubines, and [other] mean people commit suicide under emotion, it can not be called brave—such a plan is the extremity of resourcelessness."

[1] This dating derives from the assumption that the original author of this eulogy was Ssu-ma Ch'ien. The passage is also found in SC, 100, 2b–3a. The text there may have been copied into the present SC from the CHS, but the sentiment sounds like an example of Ssu-ma Ch'ien's defense of his own willingness to suffer the disgrace of castration so that he could complete his historical work. The disgrace occurred in 98 and Ssu-ma Ch'ien died about 86 B.C.

[2] Cf. *8* for the incident here referred to.

[3] SC writes: 被刑戮爲人奴而不死何其下也. This is the only important deviation between the two texts.

342

57.   Ca. 87 B.C.   CHS, 24A, 7a (18a)

過使敎田太常三輔大農置工巧奴與從事爲作田器
二千石遺令長三老力田及里父老善田者受田器學耕
種養苗狀

[Commissary Commandant Chao] Kuo[1] caused instruction in agriculture [to be given in lands under] the Grand Ceremonialist and the Three Adjuncts.[2]   The Grand [Minister of] Agriculture[3] set skilled and clever male slaves with assistants to manufacture agricultural implements.   The [officials of the rank of] two thousand piculs[4] dispatched prefects, chiefs, *san-lao*, and vigorous cultivators,[5] together with hamlet elders who were excellent cultivators, to receive these agricultural implements and to study the conditions of plowing, planting, and raising plants.

[1] Chao Kuo has no biography and is mentioned here only.   At the beginning of the section of which the present passage is a part, it says that in the last years of his reign Emperor Wu regretted his warlike activities, ennobled his Chancellor (Ch'e Ch'ien-ch'iu) as the Marquis Enriching the People, and issued an imperial edict, saying: "The present most important task is to strengthen agriculture." Ch'e Ch'ien-ch'iu became marquis in 89 B.C. (CHS, 18, 8b).   The text then says that Chao Kuo was appointed Commissary Commandant (*Sou su tou wei*).   This was a military position under the Minister of Agriculture, with the duty of provisioning the army (CHS, 19A, 4a; MH, vol. II, p. 519, and vol. III, p. 597, footnote 1).   Sang Hung-yang held the position between 97 and 87 B.C. (CHS, 19B, 22b and 26a).   Thus, Chao Kuo was probably appointed to fill his place in 87 when Sang Hung-yang became Grandee Secretary.   We are told that Chao Kuo was able to rotate the fields by using three ditches (or furrows [strips?]) in a field and each year changing their location.   The text then devotes a number of lines to methods of agriculture, notes the advantages of having special implements for plowing, hoeing, and planting, and discusses the increase in harvests that is obtainable by using ox-plows.   The portion translated follows here, and is better understood against this background.

[2] The Grand Ceremonialist had charge of rites and ceremonies in the imperial ancestral temple (MH, vol. II, p. 514), and according to a commentary by Su Lin (fl. A.D. 196–227) he had charge of imperial grave mounds and was therefore responsible for the planting of the fields there.

The Three Adjuncts were the three officers governing the three commanderies of the Capital District (MH, vol. II, p. 524; HFHD, vol. I, p. 325, footnote 8.3).

[3] The Grand Minister of Agriculture was in charge of taxes from agriculture and commerce of the empire (MH, vol. II, p. 519).

[4] According to Ch'ien Ta-chao (1744–1813), officials having this rank were administrators of commanderies and chancellors of kingdoms (HFHD, vol. I, p. 193, footnote 3).   They were the ones who selected "vigorous cultivators" and other commoners given rank (ibid.).   They would be the proper ones to send key people to the capital to receive implements and study improved agricultural methods.

343

[5] The *san-lao* ("thrice venerable") were commoners over fifty years old who were selected one in each district. One district *San-lao* was chosen to be prefectural *San-lao* to act as consultant to the Prefect, Assistant Prefect, and Chief of Police (cf. HFHD, vol. I, p. 75).

The "vigorous cultivators" apparently were commoners who had distinguished themselves for success in farming. They were recommended by the officials with rank of two thousand piculs, and were honored with low official rank (cf. HFHD, vol. I, p. 193 and footnote 3, and p. 253).

58.   87 B.C.   CHS, 97A, 7b (17a)

昭帝即位追尊鉤弋倢伃爲皇太后發卒二萬人起雲
陵邑三千戶追尊外祖趙父爲順成侯詔右扶風置園邑
二百家長丞奉守如法須成侯有姊君姁賜錢二百萬奴
婢第宅以充實焉

When Emperor Chao ascended the throne he retroactively honored the Kou-i [Palace] *Chieh-yü*[1] [his late mother *née* Chao[2]] as Empress Dowager, and sent 20,000 conscripts to erect the Yün-ling [tumulus], with a fief-city of 3,000 households [to maintain it. He also] retroactively honored his late maternal grandfather, Chao,[3] as Marquis of Shün-ch'eng.   There was an imperial edict to the [Administrator of] Yu-fu-feng to establish a garden fief-city of 200 families to make offerings to and guard [his tomb] according to the law, forever.   The Marquis of Shün-ch'eng had an older sister, [Chao] Chün-hsü.[4]   She was given two million cash, male and female slaves, and a mansion and houses in order [to give her] abundance.

[1] The Kou-i Palace, according to Yen Shih-ku (CHS, 97A, 7a), who quotes the *San fu Huang t'u* and the *Han Wu ku shih,* was outside the city (of Ch'ang-an), south of the Chih men.   *Chieh-yü* (TY; MH, vol. II, p. 533) were the highest class of concubines, just below the Empress.

[2] Chao *Chieh-yü* (CHS, 97A, 7a–b; 7, 1a).   It is told that when Emperor Wu was passing through Ho-chien, where she lived, she was called to his attention because of a deformity of her hands which kept them tightly shut.   Emperor Wu miraculously cured her by a touch, and then granted her his favors.   She was brought into the palace, and conceived a child who was in her womb to the four-teenth lunar month.   Emperor Wu was very fond of the boy, who was sturdy and bright, and who bore a close resemblance to him.   After the great witchcraft scandal of 91 B.C., in which the Heir-apparent was executed, Emperor Wu con-sidered making the child the Heir-apparent.   The chief obstacle was the extreme youth of its mother; Emperor Wu feared she would be able to dominate the court for many years.   He debated the matter for some time.   Then it is starkly related that Chao *Chieh-yü* committed a fault, was scolded, and died of grief.   She was buried at Yün-yang.   Emperor Wu, on his deathbed, appointed the eight-year-old boy Heir-apparent, with Ho Kuang, Chin Jih-ti, and Shang-kuan Chieh as regents. The boy became Emperor Chao, and the acts here detailed were obviously done for the child and merely ascribed to him.

[3] Mr. Chao (CHS, 97A, 7a), whose personal name is not even given, had formerly committed a crime, been castrated, and been a Yellow Gate eunuch. He had died at Ch'ang-an and been buried northwest of the city.   For that reason it was the Administrator of Yu-fu-feng, in control of the western part of the Capital District, who was ordered to attend to his tomb.

[4] Nothing else is known of her.   She was Emperor Chao's maternal grandaunt.

59. 82 B.C. CHS, 97A, 8a (18a)

安醉則裸行內與後母及父諸良人侍御皆亂

When [Shang-kuan] An[1] was drunk he would go naked into the inner apartments and have incestuous relations with his stepmother and various of his father's Ladies[2] and serving personal [female slaves[3]].

[1] Shang-kuan An (CHS, 97A, 7b–8b; 7, 3a–b; 18, 9a; 67, 2a–b; 68, 2a–b; JMT, p. 12) was the son of Shang-kuan Chieh (ibid.), who, together with Ho Kuang and Chin Jih-ti, was regent for Emperor Chao. Shang-kuan An was married to a daughter of Ho Kuang. The daughter of that marriage was made Empress (August 3, 82 B.C.) at the age of five or six—Emperor Chao was only twelve or thirteen. Shang-kuan An, because he was father of the Empress, was made Marquis of Shang-lo, with an income from 1,500 households, and was appointed General of Chariots and Cavalry. He was excessively haughty and licentious, and almost childishly proud of his new honors and gifts. The present passage is one of the evidences cited in his biography to illustrate his character.

In 80 B.C. the Shang-kuan family entered into a plot with Princess Kai of Ao-i, Liu Tan the King of Yen, and Sang Hung-yang to kill Ho Kuang and Emperor Chao and put the King of Yen on the throne. The plot was discovered, and Shang-kuan Chieh and An were executed, while Princess Kai and the King of Yen committed suicide (October/November, 80 B.C.).

[2] Among the women of the imperial palace, the *liang-jen* (Sweet Ladies) were of third rank below the Empress (HFHD, vol. I, p. 271, footnote 1; MH, vol. II, p. 533). In the present instance, which did not involve the imperial palace but rather a rich and powerful nobleman, the term probably means concubine, as Yen Shih-ku says.

[3] Yen Shih-ku makes the important statement: *"Liang-jen* means concubine. The *shih-yü* were at the same time female slaves."

60. 81 B.C.[1] YTL, 6 (sec. 29), 8a

今縣官多畜奴婢坐稟衣食私作產業爲姦利力作不
盡縣官失實百生或無斗筲之儲官奴累百金黎民昏晨
不釋事奴婢垂拱遨遊也

[The Worthies[2] said]: "Now the government[3] accumulates
numerous male and female slaves who sit and are stipended with
clothes and food. Privately they create estates and make evil
profits. Their strength and labor are not used up [so that] the government loses the reality [of the slaves]. Some of the people do not have
in store a peck or a basket [of grain, yet] government male slaves
accumulate a hundred [catties] of gold. From dawn to dusk the
common people are not free from work, [yet] male and female slaves
idle about with folded hands." [4]

[1] This was the year in which the great debate on government economic policies
was held (CHS, 7, 2b; YTL, 1a). This passage comes from the *Yen t'ieh lun*,
written by Huan K'uan during the reign of Emperor Hsüan (74–49 B.C.) to record
the arguments advanced by each side. The text used comes from an edition of
the *Han Wei ts'ung-shu* published in 1894 by the Hunan I wen shu chü, with a
preface by Yang T'ing-jui of Shan-hua, dated 1894.

On the circumstances of the debate, and textual criticism of the *Yen t'ieh lun*
see C. M. Chang ("The genesis and meaning of Huan Kuan's 'Discourses on salt
and iron,' " *The Chinese Social and Political Science Review*, vol. 18, 1934, pp. 1–52)
and Esson M. Gale, trans. (*Discourses on salt and iron, a debate on state control of
commerce and industry in ancient China*, chapters I–XIX, translated from the
Chinese of Huan K'uan, Leiden, 1931, pp. xvii–lvi). The *Yen t'ieh lun* is not, of
course, a stenographic report of the debate, but appears rather to be a literary
version of it, edited from archives.

Now arranged in 10 *chüan* and 60 sections, about half the text (5 *chüan* and
28 sections) has been translated by Gale (op. cit.), and by him and his collaborators,
Peter A. Boodberg and T. C. Lin ("Discourses on salt and iron [*Yen t'ieh lun:*
chaps. XX–XXVIII]," JNCBRAS, vol. 65, 1934, pp. 73–110). The present
passage, from *chüan* 6 (sec. [their chapter] 29), falls in the part not yet published
by them.

[2] Who opposed the government's economic policy.

[3] Cf. HFHD, vol. I, p. 311, footnote 3.5.

[4] This is the only YTL reference to slaves included in the documents. Other
references occur, but the present one alone seemed to merit independent translation. Gale and his collaborators obscured two references by not using the word
"slave." The references are:

YTL, 2 (sec. 9), 8a: Gale, op. cit., p. 56. *Read* "female slaves and concubines"
for "maids and concubines."

YTL, 4 (sec. 19), 10b: Gale, op. cit., p. 122. The word translated "slave"
is *tsang-huo*, for which cf. *11*.

YTL, 5 (sec. 28), 22b: Gale, Boodberg and Lin, op. cit., p. 109. *Read* "female
slaves and concubines" *for* "servant wenches."

YTL, 5 (sec. 29), 8b: mentions female slaves and concubines.

後爲渭城令治甚有聲值昭帝幼皇后父上官將軍安
與帝姊蓋主私夫丁外人相善外人驕忿怨故京兆尹樊
福使客射殺之客藏公主廬吏不敢捕渭城令建將吏卒
圍捕蓋主聞之與外人上官將軍多從奴客往犇射迫吏
吏散走主使僕射劾渭城令游徼傷主家奴建報亡它坐
蓋主怒使人上書告建侵辱長公主射甲舍門知吏賊傷
奴辟報故不窮審大將軍霍光寢其奏後光病上官氏代
聽事下吏捕建建自殺吏民稱冤至今渭城立其祠

Later [Hu Chien²] became Prefect of Wei-ch'eng³ and his ad-ministration was very famous. At that time Emperor Chao was young. The Empress' father, General Shang-kuan An,⁴ was a close friend of Ting Wai-jen,⁵ the lover of the Emperor's older sister, the Princess Kai.⁶ [Ting] Wai-jen was haughty and unrestrained, and he hated the former Prefect of the Capital District, Fan Fu.⁷ He sent a guest to shoot and slay him. The guest hid in the house of the Princess, and the officials did not dare arrest him. The Prefect of Wei-ch'eng, [Hu] Chien led his officials and soldiers and surrounded [the house] and placed it under guard. The Princess Kai heard of it, and with [Ting] Wai-jen and General Shang-kuan [An], accompanied by numerous male slaves and guests, rushed up and shot at the officials to chase them off. The officials dispersed.

[Then] the Princess sent the Chief Gate Guard to impeach the Police Chief of the Prefect of Wei-ch'eng for wounding a household male slave of the Princess. [Hu] Chien reported back [that the Police Chief was found] guiltless. The Princess Kai was furious, and sent someone to submit a letter to court accusing [Hu] Chien of invading and insulting a Grand Princess by shooting at the gate of her mansion; and of not holding a thorough judicial investigation in order to shield an officer [whom he] knew had outrageously wounded her male slave. General-in-Chief Ho Kuang⁸ tabled her memorial.

Later when [Ho] Kuang was ill and Shang-kuan [Chieh] was administering affairs as a substitute, [the latter] sent an official to arrest [Hu] Chien. [Hu] Chien killed himself. Officials and commoners all called it a great injustice. Up to the present Wei-ch'eng still maintains his memorial shrine.

1 Fan Fu was Prefect of the Capital District in 81 B.C. This event must have occurred the next year but before the conspiracy against Ho Kuang was discovered in October/November, 80 B.C.

2 Hu Chien (CHS, 67, 1b–2b; JMT, p. 693), whose T. was Tzu-meng, was a man from Ho-tung. Only two incidents are related about him, both of which illustrate his upright character and fearlessness in office. In the period 100–97 B.C., when he was an assistant to a First Assistant [in the Army Inspectorate(?)] he discovered that the Inspecting Secretary of the Army was grafting, and personally denounced him and led troops to execute him. This act was praised in an imperial decree. The other event is here translated.

3 Wei-ch'eng was another name for Hsien-yang, the Ch'in capital, a city west of the Han capital but within the Capital District. According to Ch'i Shao-nan (A.D. 1703–68), the mansion of the Princess Kai was in Wei-ch'eng.

4 Shang-kuan An; cf. 59, footnote 1.

5 Ting Wai-jen (CHS, 67, 2a–b; 97A, 7b–8b; JMT, p. 2) was the lover (lit. "secret husband") of the Princess Kai. The adamant refusal of Ho Kuang to make him a marquis or to give him an office was partly responsible for the plot against Ho Kuang during this year.

6 The Princess Kai (CHS, 7, 1a–3a; 63, 4b–5a; 67, 2a–b; 68, 2a–b; 97A, 7b–8a) was a daughter of Emperor Wu, and an older sister of Emperor Chao. She had an income from Ao-i, and was married to the Marquis of Kai, hence her title 鄂邑蓋長公主 (cf. CHS, 63, 4b, commentary). She committed suicide in 80 B.C.

7 Fan Fu. This seems to be the only reference to him except CHS, 19B, 27b, which says he was Prefect of the Capital District in 81 B.C.

8 Ho Kuang and Shang-kuan Chieh were co-regents.

62. 79 B.C. CHS, 97A, 8b (19a)

桀安宗族既滅皇后以年少不與謀亦光外孫故得不
廢皇后母前死葬茂陵郭東追尊曰敬夫人置園邑二百
家長丞奉守如法皇后自使私奴婢守桀安家

[Shang-kuan] Chieh and [his son Shang-kuan] An[1] and the whole clan were completely stamped out, [but] the Empress [née Shang-kuan[2]] was not deposed because, being young, she had not been in the plot, and also because she was a grandchild of [Ho] Kuang. The mother of the Empress had already died and was buried east of the Mao-ling suburbs. She was retroactively honored and called Lady Ching.[3] There was established a garden fief-city of 200 families to make offerings to and guard [her tomb] according to the law, forever. The Empress personally sent her private male and female slaves to guard the graves of [Shang-kuan] Chieh and [Shang-kuan] An.[4]

[1] Cf. *59*, footnote 1.

[2] The Empress *née* Shang-kuan (CHS, 97A, 7b–8b; JMT, p. 12) was the child of Shang-kuan An by a daughter of Ho Kuang. In 74, after the death of Emperor Chao, she became Empress Dowager at the age of fourteen or fifteen. Since she had no child, the King of Ch'ang-i, Liu Ho, was called to the throne. It was she to whom 38 high ministers addressed their petition for the deposing of Liu Ho, who stood in a fictitious relationship of son to her, and she was the instrument through which he was deposed (cf. *69*). On the accession of Emperor Hsüan she became Grand Empress Dowager. She died in 37 B.C. at the age of fifty-two.

[3] Lit. "The Revered Lady."

[4] According to Yen Shih-ku their tombs were east of Ho Kuang's tomb. The latter was at Mao-ling, the site of the tomb of Emperor Wu, a little east of modern Hsin-p'ing hsien in Shensi. It was some twenty to thirty miles west of the capital. Obviously the slaves were to make their homes there.

63.   86–68 B.C.[1]   CHS, 59, 4b (9b)

郎淫官婢婢兄自言安世曰奴以忿怒誣汙衣冠告署
適奴其隱人過失皆此類也

[When Chang An-shih[2] was Superintendent of Gentlemen of the Palace], a Gentleman debauched a government slave woman. The older brother of the slave woman reported it himself.[3] [Chang] An-shih said: "The male slave, because of his rage and anger, falsely smirched the cap and gown."[4]   He instructed the office to punish the male slave.   He always concealed others' misdoings in this manner.

[1] The dates when Chang An-shih was Superintendent of Gentlemen of the Palace (CHS, 19B, 29a–b).

[2] Chang An-shih (CHS, 59, 3b–5a; JMT, p. 931) was the son of Chang T'ang, and came to the attention of Emperor Wu because of his literary gifts.   He was made Keeper of Documents, then Superintendent of Gentlemen of the Palace. Under Emperor Chao he was Junior Commander and was appointed Marquis of Fu-p'ing.   He was associated with Ho Kuang in deposing Liu Ho in 74 B.C., and under Emperor Hsüan became Grand Marshal.   A man of very great wealth, he was also a close friend of the Emperor (cf. *70*).   He died in 62 B.C.

[3] I.e., without any outside verification.

[4] Referring to the Gentleman.

有幸姬王昭平王地餘許以爲后去嘗疾姬陽成昭信
侍視甚謹更愛之去與地餘戲得褒中刀笞問狀服欲與
昭平共殺昭信笞問昭平不服以鐵鍼鍼之彊服乃會諸
姬去以劍自擊地餘令昭信擊昭平皆死昭信曰兩姬婢
且泄口復絞殺從婢三人後昭信病夢見昭平等以狀告
去去曰虜乃復見畏我獨可燔燒耳掘出尸皆燒爲灰…
昭信欲擅愛曰王使明貞夫人主諸姬淫亂難禁請閉諸
姬舍門無令出敕使其大婢爲僕射主永巷盡封閉諸舍
上籥於后非大置酒召不得見…獨昭信兄子初爲乘華
夫人得朝夕見昭信與去從十餘奴博飲游敕初去年十
四五事師受易師數諫正去去益大逐之內史請以爲掾
師數令內史禁切王家去使奴殺師父子不發覺後去數
置酒令倡俳贏戲坐中以爲樂相彊劾繫倡闌入殿門奏
狀事下考案倡辭本爲王敎脩靡夫人莖卿弟都歌舞使
者召莖卿都去對皆淫亂自殺會赦不治莖卿前亨賁卽
取他死人與都死幷付其母母曰都是莖卿非也數號哭

[The King of Kuang-ch'uan, Liu Ch'ü[2]] had favored the concubines Wang Chao-p'ing and Wang Ti-yü, and promised [each
that she] would be made Queen. [Liu] Ch'ü happened to be sick,
and [another] concubine, Yang-ch'eng Chao-hsin, tended him so very
carefully that he loved her more. [Shortly after, Liu] Ch'ü was
romping with [Wang] Ti-yü and discovered a knife in her sleeve.
Beaten and questioned, she confessed that she was planning with
[Wang] Chao-p'ing to kill [Yang-ch'eng] Chao-hsin. [When Wang]
Chao-p'ing was beaten and questioned she would not confess.
Jabbed with an iron needle, she was forced to confess. Then having
assembled all the concubines, [Liu] Ch'ü personally hacked [Wang]
Ti-yü with his sword, and had [Yang-ch'eng] Chao-hsin hack [Wang]

Chao-p'ing, [till] both died. [Yang-ch'eng] Chao-hsin said: "The slave women of the two concubines might [let the matter] leak out." [So they] also strangled to death their three attendant female slaves.

Later [Yang-ch'eng] Chao-hsin was sick and dreamed she saw [Wang] Chao-p'ing and the others, and reported it to [Liu] Ch'ü. [Liu] Ch'ü said: "Those captives will appear again to terrify me; [we can] only burn them up." They dug up the corpses and burned them to ashes . . . .[3]

[Yang-ch'eng] Chao-hsin wanted to monopolize [the King's] affection, and said: "The King uses the *Ming-chen* Lady [Ho Hsiu-ch'eng] to oversee the concubines and it is difficult to prevent them from licentious promiscuity." She begged to lock the doors of the concubines' rooms, not letting them out to roam; to use her elder[4] slave woman as chief gate guard to oversee the Concubines' Quarter; to have their rooms completely sealed and locked and the key given to the Queen [i.e., herself]; and not to allow them to see [the King] except when summoned to great feasts . . . .[5] Only [Yang-ch'eng] Chao-hsin's niece, Ch'u, who became *Ch'eng-hua* Lady, could see him morning and evening. [Yang-ch'eng] Chao-hsin and [Liu] Ch'ü, attended by ten or more male slaves, gambled, drank, and idly roamed about.

Formerly, when [Liu] Ch'ü was fourteen or fifteen he was under a teacher, studying the [Book of] Changes. The teacher several times criticized and disciplined [Liu] Ch'ü. When [Liu] Ch'ü grew older he drove him out. The Prefect of the Capital[6] requested [the Emperor] to have [the teacher] made a principal official. Several times the teacher got the Prefect of the Capital to make restrictions on the King's household. [Liu] Ch'ü had a male slave kill the teacher and his son. This was not discovered.

Later [Liu] Ch'ü several times had banquets, and made the singing girls and entertainers go naked and play about among the guests for sport. [Finally] his Chancellor, Ch'iang,[7] accused and tied up the singing girls, penning them into the doorway of the audience chamber. He memorialized about the situation, and the matter was handed down [for investigation]. After questioning, it was determined that the singing girls' libretto was what the King had originally taught the *Hsiu-mi* Lady [T'ao] Wang-ch'ing and her younger sister [T'ao] Tu to sing and dance to. The [judicial] emissaries called for [T'ao] Wang-ch'ing and [T'ao] Tu. [Liu] Ch'ü replied that both had been licentiously promiscuous and had com-

求死昭信令奴殺之奴得辭服本始三年相内史奏狀具
言赦前所犯天子遣大鴻臚丞相長史御史丞廷尉正雜
治鉅鹿詔獄奏請逮捕去及后昭信制曰王后昭信諸姬
奴婢證者皆下獄辭服有司復請誅王制曰與列侯中二
千石二千石博士議議者皆以爲去悖虐聽后昭信讒言
燔燒亨煮生割剝人距師之諫殺其父子凡殺無辜十六
人至一家母子三人逆節絕理其十五人在赦前大惡仍
重當伏顯戮以示衆制曰朕不忍致王於法議其罰有司
請廢勿王與妻子徙上庸奏可與湯沐邑百戶去道自殺
昭信棄市立二十二年國除

mitted suicide.[8] Just then there was an amnesty[9] and the case was
not prosecuted.

[At the time of her murder, T'ao] Wang-ch'ing had been boiled
and pulverized, and immediately [the King] had taken a different
corpse and the corpse of [T'ao] Tu and delivered them together to
the mother. The mother had said: "Tu[s' corpse] is right but
Wang-ch'ing's is not [the real one]." Several times she howled and
lamented, demanding the [real] corpse. [Yang-ch'eng] Chao-hsin
ordered a male slave to murder her. The male slave was caught
and confessed.

In 71 B.C. the Chancellor and the Prefect of the Capital memorialized about the situation, presenting also a statement about the
crimes committed before the amnesty. The Emperor dispatched
the Grand Herald, the Chancellor's Chief Official, the assistant to
the [Grandee] Secretary, and the Commandant of Justice to form a
mixed court at the imperial jail at Chü-lu.[10] They memorialized,
requesting the arrest of [Liu] Ch'ü and Queen [Yang-ch'eng] Chao-
hsin. An imperial decree said: "Put Queen [Yang-ch'eng] Chao-hsin,
all the concubines, the male and female slaves, and [other] witnesses
into prison." They confessed.

The officials concerned begged again for the execution of the
King. An imperial decree said: "Let it be given to the marquises,
[officials with the rank of] Real Two Thousand Piculs and Two
Thousand Piculs, and the Erudits for discussion." All who dis-

cussed it considered that [Liu] Ch'ü had been indecent and cruel; he had listened to the false accusations of Queen [Yang-ch'eng] Chao-hsin, and had roasted and boiled [T'ao Wang-ch'ing], and sliced and skinned a person alive; he had rejected his teacher's advice, and killed him and his son.   In all he had killed sixteen innocent people, including three people in one family, a mother and her daughters. [These acts were] a violation of propriety and disruption of the principles of human behavior.   The great wickedness of [killing] those fifteen people,[11] though happening before the amnesty, is still heavy. [The King and Queen] ought to suffer public execution as an example to the populace.

An imperial decree said: "We cannot bear to send the King to [execution under] the law.   Consider other punishments."   The officials concerned begged to depose him and to banish him with his wife to Shang-yung.   This memorial was granted.   He was given a T'ang-mu estate of a hundred households.

[Liu] Ch'ü committed suicide on the way, and [Yang-ch'eng] Chao-hsin was publicly executed.   He had ruled 22 years.   The state was abolished.

[1] The date of the first incident, the strangling of three female slaves, is indefinite, but was some time after 91 B.C.   All other incidents concerning slaves probably occurred not long before 71 B.C.

[2] Liu Ch'ü (CHS, 53, 6a–7b; and 14, 15b) was a great-grandson of Emperor Ching.   He came to the throne in 91 B.C. and died in 70 B.C.   Most of his biography is here translated.   His banishment and death are recorded in CHS, 8, 3b.   The Kingdom of Kuang-ch'uan was in the present Hopei Province in Chi chou.   The old city was 30 *li* east of Chi-ch'iang hsien.

[3] Abstracting the text here: Liu Ch'ü then made Yang-ch'eng Chao-hsin his Queen.   She was jealous of all the other women, and slandered T'ao Wang-ch'ing in particular, till the King killed her most cruelly, and then mutilated, burned and dissolved the corpse, and also killed her sister, T'ao Tu.   Another concubine named Jung Ai was burned and sliced alive.   In all, fourteen people were murdered at the Queen's instigation and buried in the grounds of her palace, so that all the palace ladies were terrified of her.

[4] Following the explanation of Yen Shih-ku.

[5] Abstracting: The King granted her request, but he pitied the concubines, and made up a dolorous song for them to sing nightly before being locked up, the Queen beating time for them on a drum.   The song is quoted.

[6] Before 135 B.C. the *nei-shih* was Prefect of the Capital (MH, vol. II, p. 524). After that the term referred to similar officials in each kingdom, who governed the people of the kingdom (TY).   Here it means the Prefect of the Capital of the Kingdom of Kuang-ch'uan.

[7] Ju Shun (A.D. 189–265) says: "Ch'iang was the Chancellor's given name." His surname is not mentioned.

[8] See footnote 3 for what really happened.

⁹ Amnesties are recorded for July/August, 80 B.C., July/August, 79, summer of 75, October/November, 74, and June/July, 73 (CHS, 7 and 8, *passim*). It might have been any of these.

¹⁰ Chü-lu was a prefectural city in southern Hopei, in the present P'ing-hsiang hsien. It was about 100 *li* southwest of the capital of Kuang-ch'uan.

¹¹ On page 7a (see footnote 3) the historian reports that fourteen people were killed at the Queen's instigation. This must include the mother of the T'ao sisters, although she was actually killed after the amnesty. The fifteen killed before the amnesty were the five concubines, the three slave women, the teacher and his son, and five others not mentioned.

---

65.   80–68 B.C.¹   CHS, 76, 3a (6a)

是時大將軍霍光秉政諸霍在平陽奴客持刀兵入市
鬬變吏不能禁及翁歸爲市吏莫敢犯者

At this time General-in-Chief Ho Kuang controlled the government, and all the Ho [family's] male slaves and guests at P'ing-yang² would carry weapons and go into town fighting and brawling, and the officials could not prevent them. But when [Yin] Weng-kuei³ became an official of the town no one dared to break the laws.

¹ The period when Ho Kuang was at the height of his power (cf. *29*, footnote 2).

² P'ing-yang in present Shansi Province, south of Lin-feng hsien, was Ho Kuang's native seat.

³ Yin Weng-kuei (CHS, 76, 3a–4a; JMT, p. 50), T. Tzu-hsiung, was first a petty official in the jail at P'ing-yang. He was so expert with the sword that no one dared oppose him. The present incident is brought in to illustrate his prowess and courage. Later he became Administrator of several important commanderies, and was famous for his ability and justice.

66. Ca. 80–68 B.C.[1] CHS, 68, 7a (15a)

將軍至九卿封侯百官以下但事馮子都王子方等視
丞相亡如也

[Jen Hsüan,[2] a former Chief Official of Ho Yü, was telling him about conditions under his father, Ho Kuang, in order to explain the natural reaction against the Ho family after Ho Kuang's death in 68 B.C. Among other things he said]: "When the General became [one of the highest] nine ministers and was enfeoffed as a marquis, all the officials and lesser people only served Feng Tzu-tou and Wang Tzu-fang,[3] and regarded the Chancellor as less important [than they]."

[1] The period when the condition here described probably obtained. This is not the date of the conversation.

[2] Jen Hsüan is not accorded a biography but is mentioned several times in CHS, 68, and in 88, 4b. Yen Shih-ku says that in the biography of Ho Kuang he is called a son-in-law (I cannot find such a statement in CHS, 68). Piecing together available information: he was related to Ho Kuang by marriage, and was once Ho Yü's Chief Official. At the time of Ho Kuang's death he was a Grand Palace Grandee, and was then made Administrator of Tai Commandery. He was executed in the general destruction of the Ho family and associates.

The question naturally arises: How did the author of CHS know of a private conversation which happened more than a century earlier? It is possible that Jen Hsüan quoted the conversation during his trial. It is exactly the kind of evidence a man would adduce to prove that he had tried to prevent the rebellion, for the tenor of his advice was that Ho Yü should accept as inevitable the turn of events against the Ho family.

[3] Fu Ch'ien says: "They were both male slaves of [Ho] Kuang." Nothing else is known of Wang Tzu-fang, but Feng Tzu-tou (or Feng Yin) was Ho Kuang's "favorite supervising male slave . . . with whom he always consulted on business." Cf. *72* for more facts about him.

Thus, Jen Hsüan was pointing out that Ho Kuang's power was so absolute that officials found his confidential slaves more influential in government affairs than the Chancellor (Ho Kuang himself was never Chancellor).

67.   Ca. 74 B.C.[1]   CHS, 27B, 4b (10b)

昭帝時昌邑王賀遣中大夫之長安多治仄注冠以賜
大臣又以冠奴劉向以爲近服妖也時王賀狂悖聞天子
不豫弋獵馳騁如故與騶奴宰人游居娛戲驕嫚不敬冠
者尊服奴者賤人賀無故好作非常之冠暴尊象也以冠
奴者當自至尊墜至賤也…京房易傳曰行不順厥咎人
奴冠天下亂辟無適妾子拜

During the reign of Emperor Chao, the King of Ch'ang-i, [Liu] Ho,[2] dispatched his Palace Grandee to Ch'ang-an to direct [the making of] more "sidewise drooping ceremonial caps"[3] to present to his great ministers.   He also used one to cap a male slave.   Liu Hsiang[4] considered that as approaching heterodoxy in clothing.   At this time King [Liu] Ho was eccentric and perverse.   Hearing that the Emperor was ill he [nevertheless] hunted and rode as usual, associating and joking with grooms, male slaves and cooks, and being haughtily contemptuous and disrespectful [of the Emperor's condition].[5]

A ceremonial cap is honorable clothing; a male slave is a mean person.   [The way Liu] Ho enjoyed conferring uncustomary ceremonial cappings without reason, was a symbol of [the way he] regarded honors.   Ceremonially capping a male slave is equivalent to making the height of honor fall down to the extreme of meanness . . . .[6]

The *Ching Fang i chuan*[7] says: "His conduct was not compliant [with natural law]; it brought disaster on the man.   A male slave was ceremonially capped; and the world was [thrown into] anarchy.   The ruler had no heir, and a concubine's son was appointed [Emperor]."

[1] The events connected with slaves probably occurred only shortly before Liu Ho was made Emperor in 74 B.C., for he was only about twenty years old at that time.

[2] Liu Ho (CHS, 63, 7a–9a; and 8, 2a; 68, 2b–5a; 72, 2a–3a; 89, 5b; JMT, p. 1358) was the grandson of Emperor Wu and the son of King Ai of Ch'ang-i, Liu Po.   Since he appears frequently in this study, a rather full biography is here given, taken from the various CHS sources.

In 86 B.C. Liu Ho succeeded to the throne of Ch'ang-i at the age of six or seven (document 75 speaks of him as 26 or 27 years old in 66 B.C.).   The State of Ch'ang-i was in the present southwestern Shantung, with its capital 40 *li* northwest of the present Chin-hsiang hsien. The reports of his life at this period are bad. He associated with low characters, was most disrespectful of ceremonial usage, and often saw visions portentous of his unhappy end. His ministers were an unscrupulous lot, excepting Kung Sui, who attempted to correct the young King. When Emperor Chao was on his deathbed the King was particularly disrespectful of the grave situation.

Liu Ho came into prominence in 74 B.C. On July 3, Emperor Chao died without heir. The great regent, Commander-in-Chief Ho Kuang, selected Liu Ho for the imperial succession. He was sent for, and while rushing west to take the throne committed several high-handed acts and haughtily neglected to show the proper grief for the death of the Emperor. Nevertheless, he received the Emperor's seal on July 16.

For 27 days he was Emperor of China. During that time he committed many acts disrespectful to the late Emperor, behaved frivolously, and lavished indecent favors on his personal retainers and slaves. T'ien Yen-nien urged Ho Kuang to depose the Emperor, and Chang An-shih was brought into consultation to help form the plans. Then all the important ministers and high officials were assembled in secret conference. At first they were afraid to commit themselves, but T'ien Yen-nien threatened the life of any who dared oppose Ho Kuang, and all agreed. The whole body then conferred with the Empress Dowager *née* Shang-kuan, relating to her all the new Emperor's indecencies. The Emperor was summoned, and none of his retainers was allowed to accompany him. In the presence of the Empress Dowager and all the high ministers, the Keeper of Documents read to the Emperor the memorial which the 36 ministers had signed and presented to the Empress Dowager. It detailed all his evil acts since the death of Emperor Chao. This memorial (CHS, 68, 3b–5b) is a fascinating state document (cf. *69*). Ho Kuang then stripped the Emperor of his insignia and deposed him (August 3, 74 B.C.).

Although the ministers had begged that he be sent to exile in Han-chung, the Empress Dowager is credited with having allowed him to return home. His kingdom was abolished and made the Shan-yang Commandery. He and his sisters were allowed to keep all the possessions of the King's household, and he was given the income from 2,000 households. More than two hundred of his former ministers and associates were executed, though Kung Sui was spared.

Of his life in retirement some details are known from the report of Chang Ch'ang, made in 64 B.C. at the request of the new Emperor, Hsüan (cf. *75*). Liu Ho seems to have gone nearly insane. He lived in seclusion in the former palace, surrounded by his wives, children, and slaves. In 63 B.C. (CHS, 15B, 9, gives 64 B.C.) he was appointed Marquis of Hai-hun with an income from 4,000 households. He died in 59 B.C. No heir was set up until 48 B.C. The line continued to his great-grandson at the beginning of the Latter Han.

[3] The commentators disagree as to the appearance of this cap. The ceremonial cap was a mark of nobility during Chou times, and capping, conferred when a noble youth reached majority, corresponds roughly to knighting. The Confucian official class jealously guarded the emblems of rank, so that Liu Ho's act was scandalous and degrading in their eyes.

[4] Liu Hsiang (CHS, 36, 3a–14a; JMT, p. 1440) was one of the greatest literary figures of the Han period, and also a high official under Emperors Hsüan, Yüan, and Ch'eng. With his son, Liu Hsin, he had the task of working through the imperial archives. On his literary work, and especially for a defense of his son Liu Hsin on the charge of being a forger, see Bernhard Karlgren ("The early history of the Chou li and Tso chuan texts," pp. 1–2, 59, and *passim*) and Charles S. Gardner (*Chinese traditional historiography*, pp. 33–37, and *passim*).

[5] CHS, 89, 5a, tells how the upright minister Kung Sui protested against the King's behavior in "wandering, sporting, drinking, and eating with grooms, male slaves, and cooks, and bestowing unlimited gifts on them." During an audience Kung Sui wept and sighed, and said to the King: "Your servant grieves at the peril to [Your kingdom's] gods of the soil and grain."

Regarding the capping of the slave, Shen Ch'in-han is quoted in the HSPC, 68, 8b, as quoting the *T'ai p'ing yü lan*, ch. 500, which in turn quotes the *Hsin hsü* by Liu Hsiang, as follows: "The King of Ch'ang-i made ten sidewise-drooping ceremonial caps with which to cap his teachers, friends, and scholars.   Later he took a cap and capped a male slave.   Kung Sui removed his cap and returned it to the King, saying: 'Your presentation of caps to the scholars extended down to me.   Now, in using an extra cap to cap a slave-captive 奴虜, You are [symbolically] enslaving [*nu-lo*] and herding Your ministers.' "   I do not find this in the present *Hsin hsü* of the *Han Wei ts'ung-shu*.

⁶ In a personal communication Dr. J. J. L. Duyvendak indicates his opinion that this paragraph is a commentary.

⁷ Or, *The commentary on the [Book of] Changes*, by Ching Fang.   The book is described in SKC, 109, 4b, and is recorded under various names in many dynastic collections of literature (HY10, III, pp. 21–22).   Ching Fang (CHS, 75, 3a–5a, and 88, 5a; JMT, p. 519) was a specialist on disasters and unnatural phenomena. He lived in the latter half of the first century B.C.

68. 74 B.C. CHS, 63, 7b (18a)

過弘農使大奴善以衣車載女子至湖使者以讓相安
樂安樂告遂遂入問賀賀曰無有遂曰即無有何愛一善
以毀行義請收屬吏以湔洒大王即捽善屬衞士長行法

[When Liu Ho,[1] King of Ch'ang-i, was hastening to Ch'ang-an
to be made Emperor], he passed through Hung-nung,[2] and ordered
Shan, his senior male slave,[3] to load up the screened carts with
girls. When he reached Hu [hsien[4]] the emissary [from the capital]
reproved An-lo, his Chancellor. An-lo told Kung Sui.[5] [Kung]
Sui went to ask [Liu] Ho. [Liu] Ho said: "No such thing." [Kung] Sui
said: "Even if it is 'no such thing' why do You love one [person]
Shan to the injury of righteous conduct? I beg to arrest [Shan]
and turn him over to the officials in order to cleanse Your Majesty."

He immediately seized Shan and turned him over to the Captain
of the Guard for punishment.

[1] Cf. *67*, footnote 2.

[2] Hung-nung was a commandery in present Honan Province, 40 *li* south of
Lin-pao hsien, which is some 75 miles directly west of Lo-yang.

[3] The term *ta-nu* (or *pei*) occurs several times in CHS. Here Yen Shih-ku
lays down the principle: "Whenever it says *ta-nu* it means eldest slave." In
HSPC, however, Chou Shou-ch'ang cites other passages to show that a *ta-nu* was
the chief of a group of slaves. Wang Hsien-ch'ien agrees with this interpretation.
It is of interest that in CHS, 68, 3b, in the official accusation against Liu Ho,
on the basis of which he was deposed, it says: "He ordered his attendant officials
to kidnap girls and put them into screened carts." From what document did the
author of CHS learn, more than a century and a half later, that it was a slave,
and his name? Perhaps there were full records of Liu Ho's conduct, the primary
sources on the basis of which the official accusation was drawn up.

[4] Hu hsien was a prefecture in present Honan Province, 40 *li* east of Wen-
hsiang hsien. It must have been only a short distance beyond Hung-nung. It
was still about 100 miles east of the capital.

[5] Kung Sui (CHS, 89, 5a–6b; JMT, p. 1804) was Liu Ho's adviser while Liu Ho
was King of Ch'ang-i. Because he acted as a minister should in trying to divert his
ruler from evil conduct, he was not executed along with the faithless ministers and
associates of Liu Ho when the latter was deposed. Later Kung Sui held important
positions under Emperor Hsüan.

69. 74 B.C. CHS, 68, 4a; 4b (7b; 8b)

從官更持節引內昌邑從官駃宰官奴二百餘人常與
居禁闥內敖戲⋯使官奴騎乘遊戲掖庭中與孝昭皇帝
宮人蒙等淫亂詔掖庭令敢泄言要斬⋯取諸侯王列侯
二千石綬及墨綬黃綬以幷佩昌邑郎官者免奴變易節
上黃旄以赤發御府金錢刀劍玉器采繪賞賜所與遊戲
者與從官官奴夜飲湛沔於酒

[In the accusation against Liu Ho,[1] signed by 36 high ministers, detailing all his crimes and indecencies during his 27 days as Emperor, and read to him before the Empress Dowager *née* Shang-kuan[2] and all the ministers, there are the following[3] statements: "He commanded] the attendant officials [of the palace] to hand over the credentials they carried, and to induct [into the palace] more than two hundred attendant officials, grooms, and government male slaves from Ch'ang-i, who thereafter constantly lived with him inside the forbidden quarters in idleness and sport ....[4] He used the government male slaves in horseback and chariot riding and in playing about in the Concubines' Quarter. He had indecent relations with the late Emperor Chao's Palace Woman, Meng, and others, and decreed that the Chief of the Concubines' Quarter should be executed if he dared to let the facts leak out ....[5] He took the seal cords [reserved for] kings, marquises, and [officials with the rank of] Two Thousand Piculs, together with the black seal cords and the yellow seal cords, in order simultaneously to girdle the emancipated male slaves[6] who were his Ch'ang-i Gentlemen and Officials. He changed the yellow hair plumes on credentials to red. He issued money, knives and swords, jade objects, and colored embroideries from the Emperor's Treasury and gave them to those who played around with him. With his attendant officials and government male slaves he nightly soaked himself in wine ....."[7]

[1] Cf. *67*, footnote 2.

[2] Cf. *62*, footnote 2. She was only thirteen or fourteen, but was fictitiously the mother of the Emperor, Liu Ho.

[3] Abstracting the statement about his behavior just before he was made Emperor: He showed no respect or ceremonial grief for the dead Emperor. He ordered his attendant officials to kidnap girls (cf. *68*). After being made Heir-

362

apparent he secretly bought chicken and pork to eat. When he received the imperial seals in front of the coffin of the late Emperor Chao, he immediately sealed something, and did not cover up [the seal, so that all could see it].

⁴ There follows a recital of his frivolous behavior, of his acts lacking in honor for the late Emperor, and of the things he did in violation of ceremonial usage: He sent an imperially sealed document to ask after the health of a minor official in Ch'ang-i. He withdrew from the audience chamber the wives of the late Emperor who were mourning there, and put his musicians and entertainers in their place. He offered the sacrificial oxen at some place where they should not have been sacrificed, and then ate and drank (of the sacrificial food?) with his attendant officials. He rode and raced in the confines of the palace, and watched wild boar and tiger fights.

⁵ The reading of the accusation was here stopped by the Empress Dowager, who reviled Liu Ho. Then the reading continued.

⁶ Yen Shih-ku says: "Emancipated male slaves means those who have been freed and made good people."

⁷ There follow more recitals of his frivolities. The interesting statement is made that in 27 days the new Emperor issued 1,127 orders, edicts, etc., creating a great confusion. It relates his treatment of two officials, Hsia-hou Sheng and Fu Chia, who dared to reprove him. Finally, the accusation closes with generalizations on Liu Ho's unsuitability, cites passages from the *Odes* and the *Spring and Autumn Annals*, and recommends that the imperial ancestors be informed of his deposition. The Dowager Empress agreed to the memorial, and Ho Kuang stripped Liu Ho of his imperial seal.

70.   73 B.C.   CHS, 68, 5a (10b)

明年下詔曰夫襃有德賞元功古今通誼也大司馬大
將軍光宿衞忠正宣德明恩守節秉誼以安宗廟其以河
北東武陽益封光萬七千戶與故所食凡二萬戶賞賜前
後黃金七千斤錢六千萬雜繒三萬疋奴婢百七十人馬
二千疋甲第一區

The next year [the newly appointed Emperor Hsüan] issued an imperial edict which said: "The requiting of [people of] virtue and the rewarding of the most meritorious have always been fitting. The Grand Marshal and Commander-in-Chief [Ho] Kuang[1] has long been the guardian, loyal and upright; spreading the [imperial] virtue and illuminating the [imperial] grace; protecting propriety and upholding righteousness; thereby preserving in tranquillity the ancestral temples. Let there be granted to [Ho] Kuang additional estates in Ho-pei [Commandery], Tung [Commandery], and Wu-yang [Prefecture][2] of 17,000 households." [These], together with his former livings, totaled 20,000 households. From first to last his presents and grants [totaled] 7,000 catties of gold,[3] 60,000,000 cash, 30,000 pieces of various silks, 170 male and female slaves, 2,000 horses, and one first-class mansion.[4]

[1] Cf. 29, footnote 2.

[2] Or equally possible: "In Ho-pei [Commandery], and Tung-wu-yang [hsien]." For the location, see KCT, pp. 484, 489, 508, and 513, and MH, vol. II, pp. 534 ff.

[3] A catty came to 7.84 Troy ounces, according to Dr. Homer H. Dubs. Thus, Ho Kuang received 54,880 ounces, which at $35.00 an ounce would be worth $1,920,800. How much it was worth in purchasing power or prestige in Han times is unknown.

[4] Dr. Dubs suggests that this last phrase be read, "the first ranking mansion [in the capital]."

A similar list of valuables appears in the *Hsi ching tsa chi*, 1, 4a (cf. also HSPC, 97A, 22a, where it is quoted by Shen Ch'in-han) in a passage describing the rewards which Ho Kuang's wife, Hsien, gave to Shun-yü Yen, the female physician who poisoned Emperor Hsüan's first Empress *née* Hsü, at Hsien's instigation (cf. 29, footnote 2). The gift included 24 rolls of grape (pattern?) brocade, 25 rolls of scattered-flower silk gauze (especially woven in the Ho mansion by an expert who took 60 days to weave a roll; each roll valued at 10,000 cash), a string (supposedly numbering 500) of "traveling" pearls, 100 lengths of green silk gauze, 1,000,000 cash, 100 taels of gold, a mansion, and "innumerable" male and female slaves.

This circumstantial list would be more useful if the *Hsi ching tsa chi* were reliable, but it is a late compilation (sixth century) containing a great variety of traditions about the Han capital, some ancient, some purely legendary. Its attribution to Liu Hsin is false; cf. SKC, 140, 1a; Chavannes, TP, 1906, p. 102; Pelliot, TP, vol. 22, 1923, p. 220. The grape pattern brocade and the flowered silk gauze are particularly interesting in view of the purported date. The mention of "innumerable" slaves is unconvincing, and sounds gossipy when set beside the precise 170 given by imperial grants to Ho Kuang during his entire lifetime.

---

71. 74–62 B.C.[1] CHS, 59, 5a (10b)

安世尊爲公侯食邑萬戶然身衣弋綈夫人自紡績家
僮七百人皆有手技作事內治產業累積纖微是以能殖
其貨富於大將軍光天子甚尊憚大將軍然內親安世心
密於光焉

[Chang] An-shih[2] was honored among the nobility, and had the income from 10,000 households, yet he dressed himself in coarse black cloth and his wife, herself, spun and wove. His 700 household youths[3] were all skilled in manufacturing; he produced goods within [his household] and saved up even the minutest things; wherefore he was able to produce commodities. He was richer than General-in-Chief [Ho] Kuang. Emperor [Hsüan] deeply honored and feared the General-in-Chief, but in his inner affections [Chang] An-shih was closer than [Ho] Kuang.

[1] The first date is when Chang An-shih became Marquis of Fu-p'ing (CHS, 18, 9b); the second is the year of his death.

[2] Chang An-shih (cf. *63*) did not inherit his wealth from his father Chang T'ang, whose estate did not exceed 500 (ounces?) of metal (gold?) in total value (CHS, 59, 3b). Chang An-shih seems to have made his fortune from his offices and estates. His great-great-grandson, Chang Fang, was enormously wealthy, owning many slaves (cf. *100*).

[3] The word *t'ung* often means "slave." There is no proof, however, that here the term means "slave" exclusively.

太夫人顯改光時所自造塋制而侈大之起三出闕築
神道北臨昭靈南出承恩盛飾祠室輦閣通屬永巷而幽
良人婢妾守之廣治第室作乘輿輦加畫繡絪馮黃金塗
韋絮薦輪侍婢以五采絲輓顯游戲第中初光愛幸監奴
馮子都常與計事及顯寡居與子都亂而禹山亦並繕治
第宅走馬馳逐平樂館雲當朝請數稱病私出多從賓客
張圍獵黃山苑中使蒼頭奴上朝謁莫敢譴者而顯及諸
女晝夜出入長信宮殿中亡期度宣帝自在民間聞知霍
氏尊盛日久內不能善光薨上始躬親朝政御史大夫魏
相給事中顯謂禹雲山女曹不務奉大將軍餘業今大夫
給事中他人壹間女能復自救邪後兩家奴爭道霍氏奴
入御史府欲蹋大夫門御史為叩頭謝迺去人以謂霍氏
顯等始知憂

[After the death of Ho Kuang] his widow, Hsien,[1] altered the tumulus system [which Ho] Kuang himself had created during his lifetime, and extravagantly enlarged it. She erected three exit towers, and built a spirit road which approached the Chao-ling [temple] on the north and went out [near] the Ch'eng-en[2] [temple] on the south. She elaborately decorated the rooms of the memorial temple; a covered carriage way connected it with a concubines' prison. And she secluded there Sweet Ladies, slave women, and concubines to guard it.

She extensively remodeled her mansion and houses, and had princely chariots and trundle carriages made, adding paint and embroidered cushions, daubing them with gold wash, and tiring their wheels with leather and lint. Serving female slaves, in many-colored silks, trundled Hsien through the mansion for her amusement.

Formerly [Ho] Kuang had loved and favored a supervising male slave, Feng Tzu-tou, and had always consulted with him on business; and Hsien, living as a widow, had indecent relations with [Feng] Tzu-tou.[3]

And further, [Ho Kuang's son, Ho] Yü, and [his grandnephew, Ho] Shan, likewise both repaired their mansions and houses, rode horseback, and loitered about at the P'ing-lo lodge. [When Ho Kuang's other grandnephew, Ho] Yün should have been attending the court assembly he several times pretended to be sick and secretly went out to drive game and hunt in Huang-shan park, attended by many retainers and guests, sending a "green-head"[4] male slave up to court to pay the visit [in his stead]. There were none who dared to reprove him.

And further, [the widow] Hsien and all the girls, disregarding the regulations about fixed times, went in and out of the Ch'ang-hsin Palace [of the Empress Dowager Shang-kuan] and the palace halls by day or by night.

While Emperor Hsüan himself was one of the populace[5] he had learned of the long dominance of the Ho family, and when he was installed [as Emperor] he was unable to improve [the situation. When Ho] Kuang died, the Emperor for the first time personally controlled national politics. When Grandee Secretary Wei Hsiang[6] was Chargé d'Affaires in the palace, [the widow] Hsien said to [Ho] Yü, Yün, and Shan: "You fellows haven't carefully attended to the legacy of the Commander-in-Chief [Ho Kuang]. Now that the Grandee [Secretary Wei Hsiang] is Chargé d'Affaires in the palace, if someone once isolated you from him could you save yourselves?"

Later, the male slaves of the two families [Ho and Wei] disputed the highway, and the Ho family male slaves entered the residency of the [Grandee] Secretary planning to batter down his door. The [Grandee] Secretary knocked his head on the ground and apologized, whereupon they left. Someone told the Ho family about it, and Hsien and the others for the first time knew anxiety.

[1] For Ho Kuang, cf. *29*, footnote 2. Hsien, whose maiden name is curiously lacking, was the second wife, the first having been a lady *née* Tung-lu whose daughter married Shang-kuan An and was the mother of Emperor Chao's Empress *née* Shang-kuan. A commentary quoted below says Hsien was at one time a female slave. She it was who caused Emperor Hsüan's Empress *née* Hsü to be poisoned so that her own daughter could become Empress. The revelation of this deed, after Ho Kuang's death, brought on the destruction of the family.

[2] The commentators disagree on the meanings of these names. Fu Ch'ien (ca. A.D. 125–195) says they were *kuan* (i.e., clubs or lodges for the nobility), and Yen Shih-ku agrees; Li Chi (fl. ca. A.D. 200) says the first was the tumulus of Kao-tsu's mother; Wen Ying (fl. A.D. 196–220) says the second was the tumulus of the Marquis of Hsüan-p'ing (Chang Ao?). They must have been well outside the city of Ch'ang-an.

³ The following interesting commentaries appear at this point. Chin Shao (fl. ca. A.D. 275) says: "The *Han yü* [(by Hsün Shuang, A.D. 128–190) states that when Ho Kuang's first wife, the lady] *née* Tung-lu died, Hsien, being a female slave, was established in her stead. She had had illicit relations with Feng Yin." Yen Shih-ku says: "A *chien-nu* designates a male slave who supervises and is familiar with the household business. Yin was Tzu-tou's personal name." The HSPC here adds the commentary of Chou Shou-ch'ang (1814–84) in regard to the *Han yü* statement above: "Deducing from the sense of the situation, I suspect that [the lady] *née* Tung-lu had no sons, but only one daughter, who became the wife of Shang-kuan An. Hsien bore a son, Yü, and therefore Ho Kuang made her his second wife."

In the "Annals of Emperor Hsüan," under the year 66 B.C., the slave is cited as "the *nan-tzu*, Feng Yin," in an imperial edict that listed the major culprits in the Ho family rebellion. The term *nan-tzu* indicated a person not holding government office. HSPC, 8, 10b, here has a long note by Chou Shou-ch'ang, which starts with a quotation from the poem, "The Yü-lin lang," by a Han writer, Hsin Yen-nien: "There was formerly a Ho household slave whose surname was Feng, and whose personal name was Tzu-tou." In a note on the poem a certain Chin Wu-tzu has said: "The position of Yü-lin lang [Gentleman of the Yü-lin (guard)] was the post which Feng held." Chou Shou-ch'ang then goes on to speculate whether Feng Tzu-tou would be called a *nan-tzu* if he held such a post, and cites examples of others called by that term who did hold office. He also wonders whether a slave could hold the post of Yü-lin lang, but concludes that it would not have been strange for a slave of Feng Yin's high standing.

Feng Tzu-tou, or Feng Yin, is also mentioned in *66* as being more influential than the Chancellor; he is mentioned in CHS, 68, 7b, as often breaking the law. His position as supervising slave for Ho Kuang's household was important, for Ho Kuang was enormously wealthy and influential (cf. *70*). His courtesy name, Tzu-tou, might be translated "Adonis." The name appears in Mencius, Bk. VI, pt. 1, 8 (cf. Legge, *Chinese classics*, vol. 2, p. 406), as the courtesy name of Kung-sun O, who was a very handsome man. Cf. also TY, which explicitly mentions the same sense. This nickname seems to have suited Feng Yin, for he enjoyed the favors of both his master and his mistress. I am indebted to Dr. J. J. L. Duyvendak for calling the significance of the name to my attention.

⁴ On the term "green-head" cf. *118*, footnote 4.

⁵ Emperor Hsüan (Liu Hsün) was the grandson of Emperor Wu's first Heir-apparent, Liu Chü, who was slain in 91 B.C. on the false charge of rebellion and witchcraft. The child was saved from the general execution of the Heir-apparent's family, and was secretly reared as a commoner (cf. *80*, footnote 2). After Liu Ho had been deposed, Liu Hsün was discovered and installed as Emperor by Ho Kuang.

⁶ Wei Hsiang (CHS, 74, 1a–3b; 18, 11b; JMT, p. 1738) became Grandee Secretary in 71 B.C. and became Chancellor in 67 B.C., when he received a marquisate. He had a grudge against Ho Kuang from early in his career, and his advancement to the position of Chancellor after the death of Ho Kuang when Emperor Hsüan was beginning to take control of the government, marked the beginning of the decline of the Ho family. The humiliation of Wei Hsiang by the slaves of the Ho family occurred in 68 or 67 B.C. (between the death of Ho Kuang, and Wei Hsiang's appointment as Chancellor) and must have greatly intensified Wei Hsiang's hatred of the Ho family.

73. 67 B.C. CHS, 18, 7b (9b)

始元四年君當嗣十六年地節三年坐使奴殺家丞棄市

In 83 B.C. Baron [Chi] Tang[1] became heir [to the Barony of Chou-tzu-nan]. In the sixteenth year, in 67 B.C., he was tried for causing a male slave to kill his household manager. He was publicly executed.

[1] Chi Tang was the grandson of Chi Chia (CHS, 6, 8a; 18, 7b; 67, 6a), who was granted title in 113 B.C. as a descendant of the House of Chou.

---

74. 66 B.C. SC, 20, 25b

張章父故潁川人爲長安亭長失官之北闕上書寄宿
霍氏第舍臥馬櫪間夜聞養馬奴相與語言諸霍氏子孫
欲謀反狀因上書告反爲侯封三千戶

Chang Chang,[1] whose father was formerly a man from Ying-ch'uan, became Chief of a *t'ing* in Ch'ang-an. He lost his position and was going to the northern lookout tower. He sent up a document [stating that] he had spent the night in a shed of the Ho family mansion, sleeping in the horse stable. In the night he overheard the male slaves who took care of the horses talking together about the circumstances of the rebellion being plotted by all the descendants of Ho [Kuang]. Accordingly he sent up the document denouncing the rebellion. He became a marquis, enfeoffed with 3,000 households.

[1] This passage gives most of the information available about Chang Chang, who was given his marquisate in 66 B.C. and died in 58; cf. CHS, 17, 12a. The plot of the Ho family after Ho Kuang's death is told in CHS, 68, 7a–8a, where Chang Chang is mentioned. His son married a princess. The present passage comes from the addition to the *Shih chi* by Ch'u Shao-sun, who was living when the event occurred; cf. *39*, footnote 7. It is also quoted in a commentary in HSPC, 68, 16a.

元康二年遣使者賜山陽太守張敞璽書曰制詔山陽
太守其謹備盜賊察往來過客毋下所賜書敞於是條奏
賀居處著其廢亡之效曰臣敞地節三年五月視事故昌
邑王居故宮奴婢在中者百八十三人閉大門開小門廉
吏一人爲領錢物市買朝內食物它不得出入督盜一人
別主微循察往來者以王家錢取卒迹官清中備盜賊臣
敞數遣丞吏行察四年九月中臣敞入視居處狀故王年
二十六七爲人青黑色小目鼻末銳卑少須眉身體長大
疾痿行步不便衣短衣大絝冠惠文冠佩玉環簪筆持牘
趨謁臣敞與坐語中庭閱妻子奴婢臣敞欲動觀其意卽
以惡鳥感之曰昌邑多梟故王應曰然前賀西至長安殊
無梟復來東至濟陽迺復聞梟聲臣敞閱至子女持彎故
王跪曰持彎母嚴長孫女也臣敞故知執金吾嚴延年字
長孫女羅紨前爲故王妻察故王衣服言語跪起清狂不
惠妻十六人子二十二人其十一人男十一人女眛死奏
名籍及奴婢財物簿

In 64 B.C. [Emperor Hsüan] sent an emissary to bestow on Chang Ch'ang,[1] the Administrator of Shan-yang [Commandery], an imperially sealed letter, which said: "An imperial edict of decree. Let the Administrator of Shan-yang carefully guard against robbers and thieves and scrutinize visitors and guests who come and go. Do not hand down [to an assistant] this bestowed letter."

[Chang] Ch'ang therefore submitted an itemized report on the [activities of the] household of [Liu] Ho, making clear the results of [the former King's] deposition, saying: "In May/June of 67 B.C. Your servant Ch'ang inspected conditions in the former palace where the former King of Ch'ang-i resides. The male and female slaves within [numbered] 183 persons. The main gate was locked, and [only] a small gate was opened. A single incorruptible official took money and goods, marketed, and each morning brought in provisions; nothing else could go out or come in. There was a single police officer whose special duty was to patrol [the palace] and to scrutinize those who came and went. Using royal household money,[2] he hired soldiers to protect the palace, keep it clear [of undesirable people], and guard against robbers. Your servant Ch'ang several times sent his Assistant and lesser officials to investigate.

"During October/November of 66 B.C. Your servant Ch'ang went in and inspected conditions in the residence. The former King was in his twenty-sixth or -seventh year, a man of dark complexion, with small eyes, the tip of his nose sharp and beaked, with slight beard and eyebrows, and of large stature, [but] infirm, [so that] his steps were uncertain. He wore a short coat, large trousers, and was capped with a *hui-wen* cap.[3] He wore a jade circlet at his waist, had a pen stuck in his hair, and hastened to greet me holding a wooden writing tablet.

"Your servant Ch'ang sat and talked with him in the middle court and reviewed his wives and children and his male and female slaves. Your servant Ch'ang, wishing to sound out his ideas, stirred him up with the [matter of the] evil bird, saying: 'There are many owls in Ch'ang-i.' The former King replied: 'But formerly when I, Ho, went west to Ch'ang-an there were definitely no owls. When I returned east and arrived at Chi-yang, then I again heard the sound of owls.'[4]

"When Your servant Ch'ang's inspection reached the daughter Ch'ih-pei, the former King knelt and said: 'Ch'ih-pei's mother was the daughter of Yen Ch'ang-sun.' Your servant Ch'ang had formerly known that Lo-fu, the daughter of the Chief of Palace Police, Yen Yen-nien (whose style name was Ch'ang-sun), had previously become the wife of the former King.

"Observing the former King's clothes, conversation, and manner of kneeling and rising, [he seems] rational but unstable[5] and irresponsible. He has sixteen wives and twenty-two children, of whom eleven are boys and eleven girls. Risking death, I submit a register of their names, together with an invoice of the male and female slaves and [other] property."[6]

---

[1] Chang Ch'ang (CHS, 76, 6a–9a; JMT, p. 955) was the author of the report here quoted. What kind of an official and investigator was he? His father and grandfather had both been important officials. Prior to this time he had been appointed Inspector of Yü chou, in reward for his protests against the conduct of Liu Ho (cf. *67*, footnote 2) during his brief period as Emperor in 74 B.C. He

was soon advanced to the position of Grand Palace Grandee. After Liu Ho had been deposed and sent back to Ch'ang-i, Emperor Hsüan appointed Chang Ch'ang the Administrator of Shan-yang Commandery, into which the former Kingdom of Ch'ang-i had been converted. Its center was at the former capital city, about 40 *li* northwest of Chin-hsiang hsien in present Shantung Province. Apparently his chief responsibility was to keep his eye on Liu Ho, and he understood that the Emperor's letter instructed him to be particularly alert for signs of rebellion.

Because he had presented a memorial warning against the plot of rebellion among the members of the Ho family, he was next appointed Chancellor to the King of Chiao-tung. There he had great success in suppressing bandits, and was accordingly advanced to the position of Administrator of the Capital District. He made a famous record for maintaining order, and when he was dismissed from that position there were so many disturbances in the capital that he had to be called back hastily. He died about 48 B.C.

² When Liu Ho was deposed from the imperial throne he was sent back to Ch'ang-i where he had previously been King. But the kingdom had been abolished and he had been granted an estate enjoying an income from 2,000 households. The property of the former royal household was, however, all given to him and his four sisters, each of whom also received an estate of 1,000 households. Thus, it was money from the royal estate that was drawn upon to pay for police protection of the former royal palace. See CHS, 63, 7b.

³ The commentators disagree on the appearance of this cap. It is variously identified as the cap of a jailer, a waiter, or a military cap from Chou times. Liu Ho was noted for his disregard of conventional usage in ceremonial caps.

⁴ The owl was considered an evil bird because it is said to eat its mother. The history fails to tell how owls concerned Liu Ho.

⁵ As explained in the commentaries.

⁶ On the basis of this report, Emperor Hsüan no longer considered Liu Ho a threat. The next year he made him Marquis of Hai-hun, with the income from 4,000 households.

This is one of the most accurate and circumstantial of passages dealing with slaves, and its chances of authenticity are good. In answer to an imperial edict of decree, Chang Ch'ang, a noted administrator, sent a detailed statement of his personal investigations of Liu Ho, and included a list of the names of members of the former King's household, together with an invoice of his male and female slaves and other property. No doubt this report was filed away and was still preserved when Pan Ku worked through the documents for his history a little more than a century later. The report was excellent "primary source material" for the biography of Liu Ho during that obscure period after his deposition. As it appears here it may be abbreviated but is probably accurate.

Therefore, the figure 183, given as the number of slaves owned by the former King, is credible—allowing, of course, for the peculiar danger in Chinese that figures may be miscopied in transmission.

地節三年七月中丞相傅婢有過自絞死廣漢聞之疑
丞相夫人妒殺之府舍而丞相奉齋酎入廟祠廣漢得此
使中郎趙奉壽風曉丞相欲以脅之毋令窮正己事丞相
不聽案驗愈急廣漢欲告之先問太史知星氣者言今年
當有戮死大臣廣漢卽上書告丞相罪制曰下京兆尹治
廣漢知事迫切遂自將吏卒突入丞相府召其夫人跪庭
下受辭收奴婢十餘人去責以殺婢事丞相魏相上書自

In July/August, 67 B.C., a female slave chamberlain[2] of Chancellor [Wei Hsiang[3]] had done something wrong and strangled herself to death. [Chao] Kuang-han[4] learned about it and suspected that the Chancellor's wife had killed her out of jealousy in the residency mansion. Then [it happened that] the Chancellor, having prepared sacrifices and wine, entered the ancestral temple. [Chao] Kuang-han, taking advantage of this [occasion], sent a Gentleman of the Household, Chao Feng-shou, to hint to the Chancellor, hoping thereby to coerce him not to make an exhaustive examination of [Chao Kuang-han's] own affairs. The Chancellor did not comply, but pressed his investigation the more strictly.

[Chao] Kuang-han wanted to accuse him, but first consulted the Grand Astrologer, who understood the influence of the stars. [The Grand Astrologer] said that during this year there would occur the execution of a great minister.[5] [Hearing this, Chao] Kuang-han immediately sent up a document reporting the Chancellor's crime. An imperial decree said: "Refer the case to the Administrator of the Capital District[6] to administer."

[Chao] Kuang-han knew the matter was pressing, and accordingly he personally led his officers and soldiers, burst into the Chancellor's residency, and commanded the [Chancellor's] wife to kneel in the hall and undergo questioning. He collected more than ten male and female slaves and left, accusing her of having murdered the female slave.

Chancellor Wei Hsiang submitted a document [to the Emperor] stating his case: "My wife really did not murder the female slave.

373

陳妻實不殺婢廣漢數犯罪法不伏辜以詐巧迫脅臣相
幸臣相寬不奏願下明使者治廣漢所驗臣相家事事下
廷尉治罪實丞相自以過譴笞傅婢出至外第乃死不如
廣漢言

[Chao] Kuang-han has several times committed crimes but has not
undergone legal punishment. By falseness and trickery [he has
tried] to coerce Your servant Hsiang, but luckily [for him] Your
servant Hsiang has been generous and not memorialized [the facts].
I request the delegation of an impartial commissioner to investigate
those family affairs of Your servant Hsiang, which Chao Kuang-han
has pried into."

The matter was delegated to the Commandant of Justice to
administer.[7] In reality, the Chancellor himself had scolded and
beaten his female slave chamberlain because of her fault, and she
had gone to an outside mansion and died. It was not as [Chao]
Kuang-han had said.

[1] The period between the death of the slave and the execution of Chao Kuang-han. The first event had apparently occurred about two years before Chao Kuang-han learned of it.

[2] The term *fu-pei* is explained in *120*, footnote 3. In *77* the term *shih-pei*, "serving female slave," is used.

[3] Cf. *72*, footnote 6.

[4] Chao Kuang-han (CHS, 78, 1a–3a; JMT, p. 1418) held several important positions before he became Administrator of the Capital District in 71 B.C. In this office he had a brilliant record for suppressing robbers and maintaining peace. He worked closely with Ho Kuang, but after his death, when Emperor Hsüan personally took control of the government, Chao Kuang-han co-operated in the suppression of the Ho clan and the curtailment of power wielded by affinal relatives of the imperial family.

A series of incidents led up to the present situation. Earlier, one of Chao Kuang-han's guests was privately selling wine in Ch'ang-an market and was driven off by officers of the Chancellor. In retaliation Chao Kuang-han obtained the dishonorable discharge of one Su Hsien, a former cavalry officer, whom he suspected of reporting the matter. In a counter suit Chao Kuang-han's official tool, one Yü, was tried and executed. Though Chao Kuang-han was implicated he was pardoned and only reduced one degree in rank. In revenge he obtained the execution of a certain Yung Shu, who he thought had instigated the counter suit. The family of Yung Shu sent up a document accusing Chao Kuang-han; the matter was referred to the Chancellor and Grandee Secretary for investigation.

In this dangerous pass Chao Kuang-han tried to cover himself by sending a confidant to act as a gate guard at the Chancellor's residency to watch for any irregularities in the Chancellor's household. It was thus that he learned of the violent death of the female slave, which had occurred some time earlier. Using this intelligence Chao Kuang-han tried to blackmail Chancellor Wei Hsiang, as told in the present passage. Cf. *77* for a different account of the same event. The result was disastrous. Chao Kuang-han was sentenced and executed.

[5] The astrologer's prediction was ironically fulfilled by the death of Chao Kuang-han himself.

[6] I.e., to Chao Kuang-han himself!

[7] Omitting *tsui*, as Wang Hsien-ch'ien and others advocate in HSPC.

---

77. 67–64 B.C.[1] SC, 96, 4b

其時京兆尹趙君丞相奏以免罪使人執魏丞相欲求
脫罪而不聽復使人脅恐魏丞相以夫人賊殺侍婢事而
私獨奏請驗之發吏卒至丞相舍捕奴婢笞擊問之實不
以兵刃殺也而丞相司直繁君奏京兆尹趙君迫脅丞相
誣以夫人賊殺婢發吏卒圍捕丞相舍不道又得擅屏騎
士事趙京兆坐要斬

At this time the Administrator of the Capital District was Chao [Kuang-han]. Chancellor [Wei Hsiang] memorialized that he should be punished by dismissal. [Chao Kuang-han] sent someone to get in touch with Chancellor Wei, hoping to escape punishment, but [the Chancellor] did not comply. [Chao Kuang-han] again sent someone to coerce and frighten Chancellor Wei concerning the matter of his wife's illicit killing of a serving female slave, while [at the same time] he secretly and individually presented a memorial requesting a thorough judicial investigation into it. He dispatched officers and soldiers to the Chancellor's house, arrested his male and female slaves, and beat and cross-questioned them.

In fact [the female slave] had not been killed with a weapon. This being so, the Chancellor's Assistant, P'o, memorialized about the iniquity of Administrator of the Capital District Chao in coercing the Chancellor, in making a false accusation of his wife's illicit killing of a female slave, and in dispatching officers and troops to surround and put the house of the Chancellor under guard. The matter of his arbitrary discharge of the cavalry officer [Su Hsien[2]] was also learned. [Administrator of the] Capital District Chao was tried and executed by being cut in two at the waist.

[1] See *76* for date and notes on this incident. This passage is in an addition to the SC of Ssu-ma Ch'ien, by Ch'u Shao-sun, for whom cf. *39*, footnote 7.

[2] Cf. *76*, footnote 4.

78. 65 B.C. CHS, 60, 2b (5b)

霍光薨後子禹與宗族謀反誅上以延年霍氏舊人欲
退之而丞相魏相奏延年素貴用事官職多姦遣吏考案
但得苑馬多死官奴婢乏衣食延年坐免官削戶二千

After the death of Ho Kuang, his son [Ho] Yü and the [Ho] clan plotted rebellion and were put to death.[1] Emperor [Hsüan], considering that [Tu] Yen-nien[2] was a close associate of the Ho family, wished to retire him. This being so, Chancellor Wei Hsiang[3] memorialized that [Tu] Yen-nien had long been important in government affairs, but that there were many corruptions in his official administration. An official was sent to investigate, and simply found that most of the ranch horses had died, and that the bureau's male and female slaves were in want of food and clothing. [Tu] Yen-nien was tried, dismissed from office, and was cut off [from the income of] 2,000 households.[4]

[1] Ho Kuang died in April, 68 B.C., and his clan was exterminated in the autumn of 66. Cf. *29*, footnote 2.

[2] Tu Yen-nien (CHS, 60, 1b–3a; and 17, 18a; JMT, p. 462) was the son of Tu Chou. When Emperor Chao came to the throne in 87 B.C., the regent, Ho Kuang, appointed Tu Yen-nien an inspector in the army. Because he did good work in discovering crimes and graft he was successively appointed Grandee Censor and Junior Commander in 83 B.C., and Marquis of Chien-p'ing and Chief of Stud in 80 B.C. (CHS, 19B, 28a). He held the office of Chief of Stud until 65 B.C., when the present incident occurred. After his dismissal he was appointed Administrator of Pei-ti Commandery. A few years later he was given twenty catties of gold by Emperor Hsüan, and transferred to the position of Administrator of Hsi-ho Commandery. In 55 B.C. he became Grandee Secretary. He died in 52 B.C.

[3] Cf. *72*, footnote 6.

[4] His income had been from 2,360 households (CHS, 17, 18a).

From the complete biography it appears that Tu Yen-nien was an upright official who was never completely out of favor. Even after he had been dismissed in 65 B.C. on the charge of corruption and laxity in office, he was given important administrative positions and was financially rewarded by the Emperor. What, then, of the accusation that most of the ranch horses had died and the bureau slaves were in want of clothing and food?

The charge is completely out of character and looks very much trumped up. Emperor Hsüan and his ministers were nervous about the plot of rebellion by the Ho family. Tu Yen-nien had been a protégé and close associate of Ho Kuang, and was suspected by the Emperor, who "wished to retire him." The accusation by Wei Hsiang, therefore, may have been a routine memorandum for dismissing an officer in disfavor. Also, in the sentence which says, "An official was sent to investigate, and *simply* found . . . ," the word *tan*, "simply," or "merely," gives the impression in Chinese that the investigation was a hasty routine.

Although the facts in the case are dubious, it is still of interest that neglect of ranch horses and slaves was a passable excuse for dismissing an officer.

79.   64 B.C.   CHS, 96B, 2b (6b)

上迺以烏孫主解憂弟子相夫爲公主置官屬侍御百
餘人舍上林中學烏孫言

Emperor [Hsüan] thereupon[1] selected [Liu] Hsiang-fu, the child
of the younger brother of the Wu-sun Princess [*née* Liu] Chieh-yü,[2]
to become a princess [and bride of the Wu-sun Heir-apparent, Yüan-
kuei-mi], and established more than a hundred officers and serving
attendants,[3] who were housed in Shang-lin [park] to study the Wu-sun
language.[4]

[1] The ruler of the Wu-sun, a people living in the Ili River Valley and allied
with the Chinese against the Hsiung-nu, had requested a Chinese bride for his
son and heir, named Yüan-kuei-mi. This boy was half Chinese, for his mother
was the Chinese Princess Liu Chieh-yü. Emperor Hsüan welcomed this opportunity to strengthen and perpetuate Chinese influence among the Wu-sun, and
agreed to the request.

[2] Cf. *88*, footnote 1. She was Chinese by birth, but married to the Wu-sun
ruler. The alliance was to be a cross-cousin marriage; her son was to marry her
brother's daughter.

[3] The term *shih-yü* 侍御 may not exclusively mean slave-girls, but seems
to have that meaning here. They belonged to the government and were being
prepared to be sent to the distant Wu-sun country to live. Yen Shih-ku makes
an equation of *shih-yü* and *pei* 婢 in his commentary to CHS, 97A, 8a; cf. *59*,
footnote 3. Instances where *shih* and *yü* definitely refer to female slaves can be
found in *23*, *37*, *48*.

[4] The casual statement that Chinese who were part of the entourage were
made to study the Wu-sun language is interesting. Such training would be
necessary since they were to live out their lives among the Wu-sun, probably
intermarrying with them. There is little information regarding the study of
foreign languages by Chinese during the Han period. The *Chou Li* contains
a section on interpreters (cf. Biot, *Le Tcheou-li*, vol. II, pp. 435–437) but the
authenticity of this text is in some doubt. During the Former Han there were
Interpreters 譯官 under the Grand Herald (*Ta hung lu*: CHS, 19A, 4a; MH,
vol. II, p. 518), but their duties are not described. Similar references for later
periods are conveniently assembled in the *Ku chin t'u shu chi ch'eng*, sec. XI
(*Kuan ch'ang*), ch. 380. The Translation Bureau of Ming and Ch'ing times has
received considerable attention, but the subject is beyond the scope of this book.
Cf. Pelliot (JA, sér. 11, No. 4, 1914, pp. 177–191, and TP, vol. 26, 1929, pp. 53–61),
Maspero (BEFEO, vol. 12, No. 1, 1912, pp. 7–9), Aurousseau (BEFEO, vol. 12,
No. 9, 1912, pp. 198–201), and Fuchs (*Bulletin of the Catholic University of Peking*,
vol. 8, 1931). These also indicate many earlier studies.

80.　63 B.C.[1]　CHS, 74, 4b (8a)

是時掖庭宮婢則令民夫上書自陳嘗有阿保之功章
下掖庭令考問則辭引使者丙吉知狀掖庭令將則詣御
史府以視吉吉識謂則曰汝嘗坐養皇曾孫不謹督笞汝
安得有功獨渭城胡組淮陽郭徵卿有恩耳分別奏組等
共養勞苦狀詔吉求組徵卿已死有子孫皆受厚賞詔免
則爲庶人賜錢十萬上親見問然後知吉有舊恩而終不
言上大賢之

At this time, Tse, a palace slave woman in the Concubines' Quarter, caused her commoner husband[2] to send up a document in which she claimed for herself special merit for having formerly nourished and protected [Emperor Hsüan]. The statement was sent down to the Chief Official of the Concubines' Quarter. He cross-questioned Tse, and her statement involved the one who had employed her, Ping Chi,[3] who knew about the circumstances. The Chief Official of the Concubines' Quarter took Tse to the residency of the Grandee Secretary to show her to [Ping] Chi. [Ping] Chi recognized Tse and said to her: "You were once tried for being careless in tending the Imperial Great-Grandson. You were bastinadoed. How do you have any special merit? Only Hu Tsu of Wei-ch'eng and Kuo Cheng-ch'ing of Huai-yang showed any compassion." He presented a particularized memorial on the difficult conditions [under which Hu] Tsu and the others had jointly nourished [the young Emperor].

An imperial edict [ordered Ping] Chi to search for [Hu] Tsu and [Kuo] Cheng-ch'ing. They were already dead but had descendants who all received liberal rewards. An imperial edict freed Tse and made her a commoner, with a gift of ten myriad cash, and the Emperor personally interviewed and questioned her. Only then did he learn of [Ping] Chi's former compassion, which all this time he had not mentioned. The Emperor greatly venerated him.

[1] The rewards were given in April/May, 63 B.C. (CHS, 8, 6b–7a), probably only shortly after the other events here described.

[2] Yen Shih-ku says: "It means that at the time when she had not yet become a palace slave woman she had had a former husband who was at this time among

378

the populace." The text itself, however, gives no grounds for the idea that this was a former marriage, or that her status had changed. At any rate it was the free husband outside the palace, and not the slave woman inside, who presented the document. Since the incident for which she claimed merit had occurred 27 years earlier, she must have been middle-aged when she made her claim. Thus, her work in the palace was probably that of a servant.

³ Ping Chi (CHS, 74, 3b–5b; 8, 1a–b; JMT, p. 166), T. Shao-ch'ing. An important incident early in his career must be told to explain the present passage. In 91 B.C., toward the close of the reign of Emperor Wu, there occurred a great palace intrigue against the Heir-apparent, who was charged with performing black magic against the Emperor. The Heir-apparent and his whole family were exterminated except for a baby grandson, Liu Hsün. He was saved by Ping Chi, then an officer in the prison. He rescued the child and employed two wet-nurses named Hu Tsu and Kuo (or Chao) Cheng-ch'ing. Apparently a woman named Tse also helped care for the child. When the infant was sick, Ping Chi got him medicine, and also paid for his food and clothes. Thus the young scion of the imperial house grew up as a commoner, though not in Ping Chi's own household. The story is told in CHS, 8, 1a–b; 63, 1a–3a; and 74, 3a–4b.

Ping Chi held several positions as an army official and was admired by Ho Kuang. On the deposition of Liu Ho in 74 B.C., Ping Chi suggested to Ho Kuang that the unknown great-grandson of Emperor Wu be appointed to the succession. This was done and Liu Hsün became Emperor Hsüan. Ping Chi was rewarded by being made a *kuan-nei* marquis.

The next incident in his biography is the one related here. When the Emperor learned the whole story he made Ping Chi the Marquis of Po-yang with an estate of 1,300 households. He succeeded Wei Hsiang as Chancellor in 59 and died in 55 B.C.

81.　61 B.C.　CHS, 76, 7b (16a)

敞旣視事求問長安父老偷盜酋長數人居皆溫厚出
從童騎閭里以爲長者

When [Chang] Ch'ang[1] took charge of affairs [as Administrator of the Capital District] he sought out and questioned the elders of Ch'ang-an, [who told him that] the several gang-leaders of the thieves and robbers were all prosperous in everyday life; when they went out they were escorted by youth horsemen,[2] and the villagers all considered them to be fine gentlemen.[3]

[1] Cf. *75*, footnote 1. After the execution of Chao Kuang-han in 64 B.C. several men in turn were appointed to the position of Administrator of the Capital District, but were so inefficient that there were many robberies, and merchants in the capital suffered greatly. Therefore Chang Ch'ang, a noted administrator, was appointed in 61 B.C. He was a great success. This event (see footnote 3) is given in his biography as an example of his methods.

[2] Yen Shih-ku explains "youth horsemen," saying: "[The gang-leaders] made cavalry men of their *t'ung-nu* ["youth male slaves"] to escort them."

[3] After learning who the gang-leaders were, Chang Ch'ang called them together and allowed them to redeem themselves by turning state's evidence and helping to capture all the lesser thieves. The following trick was played: The gang-leaders gave a great feast for all the small thieves. When the latter were drunk the gang-leaders smeared red pigment on their coat tails. The police were then able to round them all up by means of the telltale red smears.

82. 64–58 B.C.[1] SC, 20, 25b

史子囘以宣帝大母家封爲侯二千六百戶與平臺侯
昆弟行也子囘妻宜君故成王孫嫉妬絞殺侍婢四十餘
人盜斷婦人初產子臂膝以爲媚道爲人所上書言論棄
市子囘以外家故不失侯

Shih Tzu-hui,[2] because he was of the family of Emperor Hsüan's
grandmother, was enfeoffed as Marquis [of Chiang-ling] with 2,600
households, advancing together with his brother, the Marquis of
P'ing-t'ai. [Shih] Tzu-hui's wife, I-chün, the granddaughter of the
former King Ch'eng, was terribly jealous and strangled to death
more than forty serving female slaves, and forcibly cut off the fore-
arms and lower legs of women's first-born children as a form of
magic curse.[3] She was reported on by someone who sent up a document, and was sentenced to public execution. Because [Shih] Tzu-
hui was an affinal relative [of the imperial house], he did not lose his
marquisate.[4]

[1] It was between these dates that Shih Tzu-hui was a marquis (cf. CHS,
18, 13a).

[2] Shih Tseng (CHS, 97A, 8b; 18, 13a), T. Tzu-hui, was the second son of
Shih Kung, who was the older brother of the girl who became a concubine of
Emperor Wu's first Heir-apparent. She was the mother of the Imperial Grandson, Shih, who was the father of Emperor Hsüan (cf. 55, footnote 2, and 97, footnote 2). After 91 B.C. the infant who later became Emperor Hsüan was reared
by Shih Kung and his mother. After he had been made Emperor he ennobled
Shih Kung's oldest son, Shih Kao, as Marquis of Lo-ling in 66 B.C., and then in
64 ennobled two other sons, the present Shih Tseng and Shih Hsüan.

[3] Cf. TY under mei-tao.

[4] This passage comes from an addition to the Shih chi by Ch'u Shao-sun, who
was living when this event occurred (cf. 39, footnote 7).

漢王褒僮約

蜀郡王子淵以事到煎上寡婦楊惠舍
有一奴名便了倩行酤酒便提大杖上
冢巔曰大夫買便了時但約守冢不約為他家男子
酤酒子淵大怒曰奴寧欲賣耶惠曰奴父許人人無
欲者子即決賣券云奴復曰欲使皆上券不上券便
不能為也子淵曰諾券文曰神爵三年正月十五
日資巾男子王淵從成都安志里女子楊惠買天
時戶下髯奴便了決賣萬五千奴從百役使不得有
二言晨起早歸食了洗滌居當穿臼縛帚裁盂鑿井
浚渠縛落鈕園斫陌杜坤音胛地刻大枷屈竹作把
削治鹿盧出入不得騎馬載車跼坐大呶下床振頭
垂釣刈芻結葦臚爐汲水酪佐酲音徂釀音莫織履
作鹿黏雀張鳥結網捕魚緣鴉彈兒登山射鹿入水
捕龜浚園縱魚鴈鶩百餘駈逐鴟烏持捎牧豬種薑

382

83. 59 B.C. THE CONTRACT FOR A YOUTH

by WANG PAO OF THE HAN[1]

Wang Tzu-yüan of Shu Commandery[2] went to the Chien [River] on business, and went up to the home of the widow Yang Hui, who had a male slave[3] named Pien-liao. [Wang Tzu-yüan] requested him to go and buy some wine. Picking up a big stick, Pien [-liao] climbed to the top of the grave mound and said: "When my master bought me, Pien-liao, he only contracted for me to care for the grave[4] and did not contract for me to buy wine for some other gentleman."

[Wang] Tzu-yüan was furious and said [to the widow]: "Wouldn't you prefer to sell this slave?"

[Yang] Hui said: "The slave's father offered him to people,[5] but no one wanted him."

[Wang] Tzu [-yüan] immediately settled on the sale contract, etc.

The slave again said: "Enter in the contract everything you wish to order me to do. I, Pien-liao, will not do anything not in the contract."

[Wang] Tzu-yüan said: "Agreed!"

The text of the contract said:

Third year of *Shen-chiao*, the first month, the fifteenth day,[6] the gentleman Wang Tzu-yüan, of Tzu-chung, purchases from the lady Yang Hui of An-chih village in Chengtu, the bearded male slave, Pien-liao, of her husband's[7] household. The fixed sale [price] is 15,000 [cash]. The slave shall obey orders about all kinds of work and may not argue.

He shall rise at dawn and do an early sweeping.[8] After eating he shall wash up. Ordinarily he should pound the grain mortar, tie up broom straws, carve bowls and bore wells,[9] scoop out ditches, tie up fallen [fences[10]], hoe the garden, trim up paths and dike up plats of land, cut big flails, bend bamboos to make rakes, and scrape and fix the well pulley.[11] In going and coming he may not ride horseback or in the cart, [nor may he] sit crosslegged or make a hubbub. When he gets out of bed he shall shake his head [to wake up], fish, cut forage, plait reeds and card hemp, draw water for gruel, and help in making *tsu-mo* [drink[12]]. He shall weave shoes and make [other] coarse things, catch birds on a gummed pole, knot nets and catch fish, shoot wild geese with arrows

養羊長育，豚駒糞除，常潔餧食（音伺），馬牛鼓四起坐

夜半益芻，二月春分，陂隄杜疆，落桑披穮，種瓜作（音）

昨瓠，別茄披葱，焚挭發疇，壟集破封，日中早蕢（音衛）

鷄鳴起舂，調治馬驢，兼落三重，舍中有客，攝壺行酤

汲水作鋪（音甫），滌（音）園中拔蒜，斷蘇切脯，築肉

膲芋膽魚，包鼈烹茶，盡具餔巳，而蓋藏關門塞竇餧

初學記〈卷之十九〉

豬縱犬，勿與隣里爭鬭，奴但當飲豆水，不得嗜酒欲

飲美酒，唯得染脣漬口，不得傾盂覆斗，不得晨出夜

入交關，伴偶舍後有樹，當裁作船，下至江州，上到煎

主為府掾，求用錢，推訪惡敗，緂索綿亭買席，往來都

洛，當為婦女求脂澤，販於小市，歸都擔枲，轉出略嵯

牽犬販鵝，武陽買茶，楊氏池中擔荷，往來市聚慎護

行偷入市，不得夷蹲夗卧，惡言醜罵，日作刀引持入

益州貨易牛羊，奴自交精慧，不得癡愚，持斧入山斷

on a string,[13] and shoot wild ducks with a pellet bow. He shall ascend the mountains to shoot deer, and go into the waters to catch turtles. He shall dig [a pond] in the garden to raise fish[14] and a hundred or so geese and ducks; and shall drive away owls and hawks. Holding a stick, he shall herd the pigs. He shall plant ginger and rear sheep; rear the shotes and colts; remove manure and always keep things clean; and feed the horses and cattle. When the drum sounds four he shall arise [and give them] a midnight addition of fodder.

In the second month at the vernal equinox he shall bank[15] the dikes and repair the boundary walls [of the fields]; prune the mulberry trees, skin the palm trees, plant melons to make gourd [utensils], select eggplant [seeds for planting], and transplant onion sets;[16] burn plant remains to generate the fields, pile up refuse and break up lumps [in the soil]. At mid-day he shall dry out things in the sun.[17] At cockcrow he shall rise and pound grain in the mortar, exercise and curry the horses, the donkeys, and likewise the mules—three classes.[18]

When there are guests in the house he shall carry a kettle and go after wine; draw water and prepare the evening meal; wash bowls and arrange food trays; pluck garlic from the garden; chop vegetables and slice meat; pound meat and make soup of tubers; stew fish and roast turtle; boil tea and fill the utensils.[19] When the dinner is over he shall cover and put away [leftovers]; shut the gates and close up the passageways for dogs; feed the pigs and air the dogs.

He shall not argue or fight with the neighbors. The slave should only drink bean water[20] and may not be greedy for wine. If he wishes to drink good wine he may only wet the lips and rinse the mouth; he may not empty the dipper or drain the cup. He may not go out at dawn and return at night, or have dealings with close chums.

Behind the house there are trees. He should hew them and make a boat, going down [river] as far as Chiang-chou and up to Chien-chu. On behalf of the officials he shall seek spending money, rejecting the strings [of cash] which are defective.[21] He shall buy mats at Mien-t'ing, and when traveling between Tu and Lo he should trade in the small markets to get powder [money] for the ladies. When he returns to Tu he shall carry hemp about on his pole, trans-

斬裁轅若殘當作俎機木殳及彖盤焚薪作炭屭屭力

罪切石薄岸治合蓋屋書削代牘日暮以歸當送乾

薪二三束四月當披五月當穫十月收豆多取蒲芋

音竹益作繩索雨墮無所爲當編蔣織箔植種菰李

梨挓柘桑三丈一樹八尺爲行果類相從縱橫相當

果熟收斂不得吮嘗犬吠當起驚告隣里振門柱戶

上樓擊鼓荷盾曳尋還落三周勤心疾作不得遨遊

奴老力索種莞織席事訖欲休當春一石夜半無事

浣衣當白若有私歛當笞一百讀券文偏訖詞窮咋索仡

關白奴不聽教當笞主給賓客奴不得有新私事當

仡扣頭兩手自縛目淚下落鼻涕長一尺當如王大

夫言不如早歸黃土陌蚯蚓鑽額早知當爾爲王大

夫酤酒不敢作惡此文

相傳多誤庶不遺漏

porting it out to the side markets. He shall lead dogs [for sale], and peddle geese. At Wu-yang he shall buy tea, and he shall carry lotus on his pole from the Yang family pool. When he travels to market assemblies he shall carefully guard against the practice[22] of theft. When he enters the market he may not squat like a barbarian, loll about, or [indulge in] evil talk and cursing. He shall make many[23] knives and bows, and take them into I-chou to barter for oxen and sheep. The slave shall teach[24] himself to be smart and clever, and may not be silly and stupid.

He shall take an axe and go into the mountains; cut memorandum tablets[25] and hew cart shafts; if there are leftovers he should make sacrificial stands, benches,[26] and wooden shoes, as well as food pans for pigs. He shall burn wood to make charcoal; collect stones and heap them into retaining walls;[27] make huts and roof houses; and whittle books[28] to take the place of [commercially prepared] writing tablets. On his return at dusk he should bring two or three bundles of dry wood.

In the fourth month he should transplant; in the ninth[29] month he should reap; and in the tenth month gather in the beans.[30] He shall gather quantities of hemp and rushes and stretch them into rope.

When it rains and there is nothing to do, he should plait grass and weave reeds. He shall plant and cultivate peach, plum, pear, and persimmon trees. He shall set out mulberry trees, one every thirty feet in rows eight feet apart, and fruit trees in corresponding sequence with the rows and intervals matching. When the fruit is ripe and is being picked or stored he may not suck or taste it.

[At night] if the dogs bark he should arise and warn the neighbors, block the gate and bar the doors, mount the tower and beat the drum, don his shield and grasp his spear. Returning down he shall make three circuits [of inspection].

He shall be industrious and quick-working, and he may not idle and loaf. When the slave is old and his strength spent, he shall plant marsh grass and weave mats. When his work is over and he wishes to rest he should pound a picul [of grain]. Late at night when there is no work he shall wash clothes really white. If he has private savings[31] they shall be the master's gift, or from guests. The slave may not have evil secrets; affairs should be open and reported. If the slave does not heed instructions, he shall be bastinadoed a hundred strokes.

The reading of the text of the contract came to an end. [The slave] was speechless and his lips were tied. Wildly he beat his head on the ground, and beat himself with his hands;[32] from his eyes the tears streamed down, and the drivel from his nose hung a foot long.

[He said]: "If it is to be exactly as master Wang says, I would rather return soon along the yellow-soil road, with the grave worms boring through my head. Had I known before I would have bought the wine for master Wang. I would not have dared to do that wrong."[33]

[1] Wang Pao (CHS, 64B, 4a–6a; JMT, p. 154; WHC, 70), T. Tzu-yüan. The dates of his birth and death are unknown, and the CHS biography gives few facts. He was a man from Shu (Szechwan, the Chengtu region). During the *Shen-chiao* and *Wu-feng* periods (61-54 B.C.) Emperor Hsüan desired to promote poetry; therefore the Inspector of I-chou, Wang Hsiang, called Wang Pao and had him compose three poems. Ho Wu and a certain Yang Fu-chung from Chengtu, who were young court singers, practiced these poems, which were thus brought to the attention of the Emperor (CHS, 86, 1a). Wang Pao was immediately recommended to him by Wang Hsiang. The Emperor summoned Wang Pao and had him compose a eulogy entitled *Shen chu te hsien ch'en* ("The saintly ruler acquires worthy ministers"). It is apparently the text of this eulogy which comprises most of Wang Pao's biography. He was made an attendant, and shortly thereafter was appointed a Grandee Censor. When the Heir-apparent was ill he was sent to entertain him; the Heir-apparent admired his compositions and had the court ladies and attendants recite them. Later, magicians reported that in I-chou there were the (spirits of?) the "golden horse and green-jade chicken" (cf. TY) which could be secured by sacrifice. Emperor Hsüan sent Wang Pao to sacrifice for them. He died on the way.

According to a commentary in text G (see below) the *T'ung chien (kang mu)* records this event in 61 B.C., which may be the source for the date of Wang Pao's death given in WHC. Considering the rest of the biography, however, I believe this to be an error. A number of Wang Pao's compositions have been preserved in the *Wen hsüan*, and he is ranked as one of the great writers of his day. For what is probably a curious error about Wang Pao, see TP, vol. 27, 1930, p. 387.

There are a number of works which contain the verse essay here translated. I have compared seven texts word by word. Each text differs from every other in minor ways, and texts C and D both lack entire, but different, passages. Commentaries in C and G have been helpful in interpreting some obscure passages. The text chosen for reproduction is found in the *Ch'u hsüeh chi*, an encyclopaedia compiled by Hsü Chien in A.D. 724 (cf. Pelliot, BEFEO, vol. 9, 1909, pp. 443–444; SKC, 135, 2b–3a), and one of the oldest of such works extant. The edition is dated 1598, but has no place of publication. It has an undated preface by the editor, Ch'en Ta-k'o 陳大科, 1534–1601, who was then Vice-president of the Board of Censors and concurrently President of the Board of War, according to information kindly supplied by Dr. A. W. Hummel, Chief of the Division of Orientalia, Library of Congress. This text was studied from a photostat of the passage in the copy of the *Ch'u hsüeh chi* in the Library of Congress. The passage appears in ch. 19, pp. 16a–18a, and is reproduced on pages 382, 384, and 386 of this volume. This is text A.

An earlier edition of the *Ch'u hsüeh chi* was also consulted in a photostat taken from the Library of Congress copy of the An Kuo edition, printed from movable type early in the Chia-ching period, presumably about 1531. This is text Aa. It is virtually the same as the edition used, except for a few different characters or variations. Because it was poorly printed and would not reproduce well it was not used as the basic text. It is nevertheless valuable as a check on text A.

The other texts consulted are as follows:

B. *Ku chin t'u shu chi ch'eng*, Shanghai edition of 1888, sec. XII (*Chia fan tien*), ch. 113, *i-wen*, pp. 1b–2b. On this work see Lionel Giles, *An alphabetical index to the Chinese encyclopaedia*, London, 1911, introduction; TB, p. 107.

C. *T'ai p'ing yü lan*, Commercial Press *Ssu pu ts'ung k'an* edition, 1935–36, ch. 598 (*wen pu*, 14), pp. 4a–5b. Cf. Wylie, *Notes on Chinese literature*, p. 183; SKC, 135, 5a–b; TB, p. 92. The Commercial Press states that it used a Sung edition, borrowed from several libraries in Japan, for its photolithographic reproduction. The *T'ai p'ing yü lan*, completed in A.D. 983, has a great reputation, but was disappointing for this text. Some of the passages were mixed up, violating both rhyme and sequence of ideas, and it contained only 610 characters as compared with 778 in the *Ch'u hsüeh chi*, or a possible maximum of 805 found in text F. I also compared the text in the 1572 movable type edition but found numerous typographical errors in addition to the poor text.

D. *I wen lei chü*, edition of Hua yang tang ta t'ang chung k'an, 1879, ch. 35 (*jen pu*, 19), pp. 32b–33b. Cf. Wylie, *Notes ...*, p. 182; SKC, 135, 1b–2a; TB, p. 88. This is a T'ang encyclopaedia compiled in the seventh century, even before the *Ch'u hsüeh chi*. What there is of the text is good, but it only contains 432 characters, or a little over half the text. Furthermore, it lacks the bill of sale, which is the most important part of the present document.

E. *Yüan chien lei han*, edition of 1710(?), ch. 258 (*jen pu*, 17), pp. 21b–23b. Cf. Wylie, *Notes...*, p. 188; SKC, 136, 4b–5a; TB, p. 106. This text is more like text A than any other, having the same number of characters, the same pronunciation notes but one, and agreeing on most important points where other texts differ. There are, however, some twenty-five differences. I suspect that its ultimate source was the *Ch'u hsüeh chi*, though not the edition here used. It is correct in several places where text A is obviously wrong, but it has an equal number of "errors" not in A.

F. *Ch'üan Han wen*, ch. 42, pp. 11b–12b. This comes from the *Ch'üan shang ku san-tai Ch'in Han San-kuo Liu-ch'ao wen* ("Complete collection of literature from remote antiquity, the Ch'in, Han, Three Kingdoms and Six Dynasties") by Yen K'o-chün, edition of 1894. Cf. Arthur W. Hummel, in *Library of Congress: Annual Report for 1932–33*, pp. 116–117; TB, p. 107. This is the longest of all the texts (805 characters) and in many ways the best. For a long time I planned to use it as the basic text, since it offers numerous good solutions for textual problems found in other works. At the end the author cites texts A, C, D, and G as sources. Probably Yen K'o-chün corrected the text where it seemed wise (as I have done, but usually in the footnotes). This suspicion, together with the fact that it is the latest of all works and editions consulted, led me to reject it. Though it certainly makes translation more easy, it seems too smooth to be an unedited early version.

G. *Ku wen yüan*, ch. 17, pp. 1b–4a. Cf. Wylie, *Notes...*, p. 239. This is taken from the *Shou shan ko ts'ung-shu*, published by the Hung wen shu chü in 1889, pt. 4 (*chi pu*). Cf. Wylie, *Notes...*, pp. 270–271. This text is also very similar to text A, having 779 characters, and differing in only thirty-five. However, it seems to introduce a few more "errors" than it corrects. It is especially valuable for long and sometimes thoughtful commentaries, though its identification of place names seems often not to be historically correct.

The translation which follows has been made as literal as possible except in cases of obvious typographical error as shown by all the other texts. Basic variant readings found in several other texts have been indicated in footnotes when of any intrinsic interest. A poetic text sometimes requires certain poetic license in choice of words. I have tried, therefore, to translate the common-sense meaning of the text at the expense of the poetic flavor of the Chinese. Division into paragraphs is made on the basis of grouping of ideas.

[2] A number of place names occur in the text. To avoid additional footnotes, these localities are all identified here:

Chien, written 湔 in C and F, is a river in Szechwan which starts west of Kuan hsien (about 35 miles northwest of Chengtu) and flows into the T'o River. The commentary in G identifies it thus, but would make 上 part of the name rather than a verb, saying that places through which the Chien River flows are called Chien-shang. In place of *shang*, texts D and F use 止, so that this construction could not apply in those texts.

Tzu-chung was a hsien in Han times north of present Tzu-yang hsien in Szechwan on the T'o River about 50 miles southwest of Chengtu. It is not the present Tzu-chung hsien.

Chiang-chou was a hsien corresponding to modern Chiang-pei hsien, across the river from Chungking. All other texts speak of going *up* to Chiang-chou and *down* to Chien-chu, which is geographically incorrect.

Chien-chu is not listed in KCT, TMT, or HTT. It is probably on the Chien River. The commentary in G, which is not very reliable in its geographical information, says that in Shu Commandery there was a Chien tao 道 of which Chien-chu was the administrative hsien. According to CHS, 28A, 17b, there was a Chien-ti 氐 tao in Shu; it was northwest of the present Sung-p'an hsien, which is far north of Chengtu, near the headwaters of the Min River.

Mien-t'ing is not listed. The commentary in G merely says it is the name of a place which produces mats. Possibly either Mien-chu in Kuang-han Commandery, north of present Tê-yang hsien, or Mien-ssu in Shu Commandery, west of Wen-ch'uan hsien may be meant (cf. CHS, 28A, 17b).

Tu and Lo are rather indefinite. The first would seem to be Chengtu. Should it mean the capital, Ch'ang-an, Lo would mean Lo-yang. This seems unlikely. The commentary in G says that in the *Ti li chih*, under Kuang-han Commandery, the commentary says that "Chang Mountain is the place from which the Lo River starts [and flows] southward to Hsin-tu where it enters the Chien River." In the *Ti li chih* of the *Ch'ien Han shu* (28A, 17b) this statement is different in that it gives the Mien River for Lo River.

Wu-yang was a hsien a few miles east of present P'eng-shan hsien in Szechwan, south of Chengtu on the Min River. C and F give Wu-tu 都, which was both a commandery and a hsien in Han times. It was in present southern Kansu Province west of Ch'eng hsien.

I-chou (CHS, 28A, 18a) was a commandery with its center near present Kunming in Yunnan.

Nan-an was a marquisal fief-city, later a hsien, northwest of present Chia-chiang hsien in Szechwan on the Ch'ing-i River above its juncture with the Min.

³ C and F state that the slave was from her husband's time.

⁴ F says *chia*, "house," which seems more likely. The two characters are almost identical. B, F, and G agree with A that the master contracted or agreed with the slave, while C and F say the master "wanted" 要. D uses "contracted" in the second phrase. That five texts indicate a contract or agreement between the master and slave, made at the time of purchase, and defining the slave's duties, is interesting, for later the slave demands that his duties with his new master be specified in the new contract.

⁵ F alone says, "When the slave grew older he was intractable toward others." 大忤人. This makes better sense, but may be a guess. Mr. C. C. Wang believes, however, that it must be the correct text. Does the present text mean that the slave's father offered him for sale, indentured servitude, or marriage, but no one wanted him?

⁶ February 18, 59 B.C.

⁷ Text A here has a typographical error. C and F add *late* husband. In the next sentence C and F say "price" for "sale."

[8] Only E agrees in the verb *kuei*, "return." The others say "sweep." This must be correct.

[9] B, E, and G agree. C says "cut tubers and bore out *tou* cups." D says "*bowls* and *tou* cups." F says "cut poles and bore out *tou* cups." The last is the most sensible. It must be of the same text family as C, either from a different edition or a correction.

[10] According to commentary in G.

[11] *Lu-lu*, which may be written in several forms, is defined as a water-wheel or well pulley in TT, pp. 369–370, and in commentary to G. Berthold Laufer (*Chinese pottery of the Han dynasty*, p. 72) gives the meaning "winch" or "windlass."

[12] The commentary in G explains that *tsu-mo* is also a fine brew of the type of *t'i-hu*. This is apparently a drink made from the skimmings of boiled butter; cf. Giles D, 11,008 and 4,940.

[13] An illustration of this hunting technique may be seen in a drawing taken from a late Chou bronze (RAA, vol. 12, No. 4, Dec., 1938, p. 137, fig. 4). From this it appears that the arrow does not hit the flying goose, but is shot across its outstretched neck so that when the arrow drops it tangles the cord around the bird's neck. The term is explained in the commentary to G.

[14] G agrees. B, D, and F say, "In the back yard there are a hundred or so free raised geese and ducks." In the next phrase the first word is an unusual form of 驅, given in the other texts.

[15] E also uses radical 170 in this word. C uses rad. 64, meaning "to open," "to unroll." B, F, and G use rad. 145, with the sense "to prepare." I think the idea is that in the spring the dikes and boundaries of the fields are to be repaired in preparation for flooding and rice planting.

[16] The preceding phrase is explained in the commentary in G.

[17] This rare character I have found only in the K'ang-hsi dictionary under rad. 86, 13 strokes. A commentary in G explains the term.

[18] The last three words make no sense as they stand. Dr. L. C. Goodrich suggests the possibility that *lo* may be a corruption of 驟, making the phrase "horses, asses and likewise mules—three classes." This seems a likely solution. The commentary in G offers an explanation which is here translated for what it may be worth: "*Lo* should be written 烙 ["to brand," "to burn"]. It means to heat an iron and burn the horse's hoof, making it hard so that it can endure to walk." 落當作烙謂燒鐵烙蹄令堅而耐踏. The commentary then quotes the well-known phrase from the "Ma-ti p'ien" of Chuang-tzu about Pai-lo, the horse tamer who branded, clipped, pared (the hoofs of), and haltered horses. There can be no question, I believe, that horses were shod at this early date, though the commentator might be right in thinking that the words *lo san ch'ung* have something to do with toughening the horses' hoofs.

[19] In B, F, and G, the only other texts which have this word, it is written 具, which seems more correct. G writes 茶 for tea, and the commentary explains it as a bitter sauce. There is some doubt whether the Chinese knew tea this early; cf. JAOS, vol. 62, 1942, pp. 74–76, 195–197. On the other hand, we may here have an earlier reference or an anachronism.

[20] G agrees. B, D, E, and F all say "eat beans and drink water," which is a little more rhythmic in the Chinese.

[21] The preceding 12 characters are among the most difficult to make sense in the entire text. The present interpretation depends on treating 訪 as 放, as suggested in commentary to G, which I have followed here. It reads: 府掾

郡之吏胥用錢庸直也檄索所以串錢紡 (also read 訪) 卽放字損敗者推 棄之. "The *fu-yüan* are the officials of the commandery. It is necessary to use money [(or give them) spending money] to hire [i.e., bribe] justice. The hemp cord is that on which cash are strung. *Fang* [is the same as] the character *fang* ["to let go," i.e., "reject"(?). He should] push and throw aside the defective ones." The idea seems to be that the slave should act as an intermediary for officials in getting bribes for them, and be careful not to accept any bad strings of cash. This does not sound very logical, and does not fit into this part of the text, which deals with the slave's business activities on behalf of his master. It may be that the text is too corrupt here to make sense.

The eighth, ninth, and tenth characters vary in different texts. *Fang* is the same in E and F, and is written 紡 in B, C, and G. *O* is written the same in B, E, and G, but is written 墍 in C and F. *Pai* is written the same in B, C, E, and G, but is written 敗 in F. Furthermore, C lacks the first four characters of the twelve entirely, making it impossible to divide the sentence six and six. If the sentence is divided into three phrases of four, and we read 訪墍敗 as in F, sense can be made: "He will seek [favors] of [or for] the officials; use money to investigate and inquire; bleach and peddle hemp cord." However . . . .

²² B, E, F, and G here have 姦. Read: "corruption and theft."

²³ All other texts (save D which lacks this section) use 多, which must be correct here. He could not daily make knives and bows and take them to I-chou.

²⁴ C and F have 教, which makes better sense.

²⁵ B, E, and G agree. C and F have 輮 "wheel rims," which goes better with cart shafts, but is not necessarily correct.

²⁶ All texts (save D) write 几 or 机, which seems more correct than looms.

²⁷ Commentary in C says this means to pile stones in a bamboo framework to repair banks.

²⁸ The two words are reversed in F, which makes better sense than to treat *shu* as a verb, or both as nouns. Note the commentary in G.

²⁹ C and F say ninth month, which seems more likely as a harvest month.

³⁰ C and F here have fourteen characters missing from other texts: 檜麥窖 芋南安拾栗採橘持車載轅. "Plant wheat and store tubers in the cellar. In Nan-an [hsien] pick up chestnuts and pluck oranges. Pull the cart with the axles loaded." The commentary in C says that during the tenth month people paid taxes. When the axles were loaded it meant that there was a profit.

³¹ C, D, E, and F all say "money."

³² E and F use 博, which would give better sense.

³³ This text (as well as Aa) ends with a statement written in the same size of type, but obviously an addition. It reads: "This text has many corruptions from continued transmission. I have not missed or omitted [anything]." Who wrote this remark is not known, but custom would seem to dictate that if it were some editor later than Hsü Chien, the compiler of the *Ch'u hsüeh chi*, it would be set in small type.

84. Ca. 56 B.C. CHS, 53, 4b (9b)

子繆王元嗣二十五年薨大鴻臚禹奏元前以刃賊殺
奴婢子男殺謁者爲刺史所舉奏罪名明白病先令令能
爲樂奴婢從死迫脅自殺者凡十六人暴虐不道故春秋
之義誅君之子不宜立元雖未伏誅不宜立嗣奏可國除

[After the death of Liu Yen, King P'ing-yü of Chao,] his son King Miu, [named Liu] Yüan,[1] inherited [the throne. After] twenty-five years he died. The Grand Herald, [Wang] Yü[2] memorialized [saying: "Liu] Yüan formerly illicitly killed male and female slaves with a sword. His son Nan killed an Internuncio,[3] as has been memorialized by the Inspector. His criminal record is clearly proved. When ill he made his will, commanding those male and female slaves who could make music[4] to follow him to death. Those who were compelled and coerced to commit suicide [in order to be buried with him] totaled sixteen persons. He was cruel and inhuman. Therefore the principle of the *Spring and Autumn Annals*—that the son of an executed ruler is not suitable to be invested—[is applicable, for] although [Liu] Yüan did not [actually] undergo execution, it is not suitable to invest his heir." The memorial was granted, and the kingdom was abolished.

[1] Liu Yüan, King Miu of Chao (CHS, 53, 4b; and 14, 13b) was a great-grandson of Emperor Ching. He came to the throne in 80 B.C. and died in 56 B.C. His whole biography is here translated. Chao was in Hopei Province, in Kuanp'ing fu.

[2] Wang Yü (CHS, 19B, 33a, 34a, 36a; JMT, p. 109) was Grand Herald from 57 B.C. to 48 B.C. Before that he had been Junior Major in 61 B.C. He is not listed in 25S, so apparently there is no biography of him.

[3] The son is not mentioned elsewhere. According to CHS, 14, 13b, Liu Yüan himself was tried for killing the Internuncio. He died during the trial.

[4] This probably also has the meaning "to make pleasure," i.e., to entertain him.

85. 57–53 B.C. CHS, 38, 5b (10a)

五鳳中青州刺史奏終古使所愛奴與八子及諸御婢
姦終古或參與被席…產子輒曰亂不可知使去其子

During the Wu-feng period the Inspector of Ch'ing chou[1] memorialized that [Liu] Chung-ku[2] caused his beloved male slaves to
commit adultery with his Eighth [Rank] Ladies[3] and personal
female slaves, [Liu] Chung-ku sometimes making a third with them
on the same mat . . . . When a son was born he would say, "[Its
paternity] is confused and cannot be known," and would order the
son to be removed.[4]

[1] The Shantung region.

[2] Liu Chung-ku (CHS, 38, 5b) was a sixth generation descendant from Emperor
Kao. He inherited the Kingdom of Ch'i, in Shantung, in 74 B.C. Little is known
of him except what is given here. Because of his bestial conduct four prefectures
were sliced off his kingdom. He died in 47 B.C. He had a legitimate heir, and the
line continued till the time of Wang Mang.

[3] For ranks of ladies in the harem see MH, vol. II, p. 533; HFHD, vol. I,
p. 271, footnote 1.

[4] Yen Shih-ku's commentary suggests that the child was killed.

---

86. 54 B.C. CHS, 17, 12a (17b)

五鳳四年坐爲九眞太守盜使人出買犀奴婢臧百萬
以上不道誅

In 54 B.C. [Chü] I-ch'ang[1] was tried because, in the position of
Governor of Chiu-chen he secretly caused people to buy and take
out rhinoceroses[2] and male and female slaves and treasures, [in value
totaling] more than ten myriad [cash. The verdict was]: immorality!
He was executed.

[1] Chü I-ch'ang, the Marquis of Hsiang-ch'eng, was the son of Chu Weng
(SC, 20, 17b; CHS, 17, 12a; JMT, pp. 568 and 1365), who had been Superintendent
of the city of Kuei-lin in the Kingdom of Nan Yüeh (present Kwangtung-Kwangsi
area). Chiu-chen corresponded to the present northern Annam.

[2] On the rhinoceros in China, cf. Laufer (*Chinese clay figures*, pt. 1, 1914,
pp. 73–173) and C. W. Bishop ("Rhinoceros and wild ox in ancient China,"
CJ, vol. 18, 1933, pp. 322–330). Here the term may mean rhinoceros horn;
cf. Léonard Aurousseau ("La première conquête chinoise . . . ," BEFEO, vol. 23,
1923, p. 172), where rhinoceros horn is specifically mentioned in a text from
Huai-nan-tzu dealing with the country of Yüeh.

87. 55–54 B.C. CHS, 66, 6b (12a)

田家作苦歲時伏臘烹羊炰羔斗酒自勞家本秦也能
爲秦聲婦趙女也雅善皷瑟奴婢歌者數人酒後耳熱仰
天拊缶而呼烏烏其詩曰田彼南山蕪穢不治種一頃豆
落而爲萁人生行樂耳須富貴何時是日也拂衣而喜奮
襃低卬頓足起舞誠淫荒無度不知其不可也

[In a letter to Sun Hui-tsung, explaining his reasons for retiring
into private life after his dismissal by Emperor Hsüan, Yang Yün[1]
says]: "In my house in the fields I have worked hard, involved
the year long in seasonal [matters such as] boiling mutton, roasting
lamb, and making my own barrel of wine. My home was originally
in Ch'in, so I can play Ch'in music; my wife is a girl from Chao,
quite good on the drum and lute; and there are several male and
female slave singers. After the wine has begun to warm my ears,
I gaze up to heaven and beat my pottery drum and sing *wu, wu*.
The verses go:

> The fields there in the southern mountains
> Are full of weeds and unkempt.
> I plant a section of beans,
> But sparse are the stalks.
> A man's life is only for enjoyment;
> Why wait for wealth and acclaim?[2]

On such occasions I hitch up my clothes and am happy; I wave
my sleeves and nod my head and tap my feet and break into a
dance. It is really licentious and uncontrolled, but I forget that it
is wrong."

[1] Yang Yün (CHS, 66, 4b–7a; 17, 20b; 19B, 33a; JMT, p. 1275) was a son of
Yang Ch'ang, the Chancellor at the time of the deposition of Liu Ho. His mother
was the daughter of Ssu-ma Ch'ien, the great historian and author of the *Shih
chi*. In 66 B.C., because he denounced the rebellion plotted by the Ho family he was
made Marquis of P'ing-t'ung and given the position of General of the Gentlemen
of the Household. Later he was advanced to the position of Superintendent of
Gentlemen of the Palace. He was incorrupt and exacting in office, and thereby
made enemies. Thus he got into a quarrel with Chief of Stud Tai Ch'ang-lo, a
personal friend of Emperor Hsüan. After a great deal of public accusation and
countercharge both men were dismissed and made commoners in January/Feb-
ruary, 55 B.C. Yang Yün immediately retired into private life, apparently as
a gentleman farmer, and amused himself with making money. A year or more
later, his friend Sun Hui-tsung wrote him a letter criticizing him for spending his
time on business affairs and high living. Yang Yün's letter of reply is a real bit
of bucolic literature, of which the section translated is a good example.

In May/June, 54 B.C., there was an eclipse of the sun, which was blamed on Yang Yün's arrogance and lavishness. His letter to Sun Hui-tsung fell into the hands of Emperor Hsüan, who was enraged by it. Yang Yün was executed and several of his friends were disgraced.

² The verse is a satirical comment on the imperial court.

---

88. 51 B.C. CHS, 96B, 3a (8b)

公主上書言年老土思願得歸骸骨葬漢地天子閔而
迎之公主與烏孫男女三人俱來至京師是歲甘露三年
也時年且七十賜以公主田宅奴婢奉養甚厚朝見儀比
公主後二歲卒三孫因留守墳墓云

The Princess [*née* Liu Chieh-yü¹] sent a letter [to Emperor Hsüan] saying she was old, her thoughts were of the home land, and she wished to be allowed to bring back her bones to be buried in China. The Emperor pitied her and welcomed her back. The Princess and her three Wu-sun male and female [grandchildren] all returned to the capital. This was in 51 B.C. and at this time her years were just seventy. She was rewarded with a princess' fields, houses, and male and female slaves.² She was treated and cared for very liberally, and the ceremony of her audiences at court was comparable to that of a [real] princess. Two years later she died and her three grandchildren accordingly remained [in China] to care for her grave.

¹ Liu Chieh-yü (CHS, 96B, 2a–3a) was the granddaughter of King Liu Wu of Ch'u, who was the grandson of Emperor Kao's younger half-brother. During the latter years of Emperor Wu's reign (some time between 100 and 87 B.C.?) she was made a princess and sent to marry the Wu-sun ruler. He died shortly after and she was married to his cousin, Weng-kuei-mi, who was to be regent during the minority of Ni-mi, the son of the deceased ruler and his Hsiung-nu wife. To Weng-kuei-mi she bore five children. The oldest son was named Yüan-kuei-mi. For several decades she played a very important part in Central Asian politics on behalf of the Chinese empire. When Weng-kuei-mi died (ca. 60 B.C.) she was married to the new ruler, Ni-mi, who was her stepson. Although at this time she must have been sixty, she is said to have borne a son to her third husband also. Later he was killed by a rival, and the Wu-sun territory was split into two parts. Her son Yüan-kuei-mi became ruler of the larger part. It was after his death that Liu Chieh-yü sent her request to be allowed to return to China. (For a correction of the confusion in Giles B, 2346, cf. TP, vol. 22, 1923, p. 219, footnote 2.)

² The commentator Sung Ch'i (A.D. 998–1061) says: "In the old edition [the word] *chu* [in *kung-chu*, meaning "princess"] is written *ti* ["mansion"]." This changes the meaning to "She was rewarded with a public [i.e., government] mansion, fields, and male and female slaves." That does not seem to be a plausible reading, especially in view of the next sentence.

89. 44 B.C. CHS, 72, 7a (14a)

又言諸離宮及長樂宮衞可減其太半以寬繇役又諸
官奴婢十萬餘人戲游亡事稅良民以給之歲費五六鉅
萬宜免爲庶人廩食令代關東戍卒乘北邊亭塞候望又
欲令近臣自諸曹侍中以上家亡得私販賣與民爭利犯
者輒免官削爵不得仕宦

[When Kung Yü[1] was Grandee Secretary, he] also said that the guards of the various separate palaces and of the Ch'ang-lo Palace might be reduced by more than half in order to moderate the corvée service. Also [he said that] the ten myriad and more[2] male and female slaves of the various government bureaus loaf about without work, [while the government] taxes the good people to support them, at an annual expense of 500,000,000 or 600,000,000 [cash].[3] It would be proper to dismiss them and make them commoners, and feed them from the granaries; and command them to take the place of the garrison soldiers east of the [Han-ku] Pass, or to mount the guard towers and Barrier on the northern frontier and stand watch. He also wanted [the Emperor] to command that his intimate courtiers [and their] families—from department heads and attachés on up—might not privately transact business and compete with the people for profit; and that violators should immediately be dismissed from office and stripped of titles and not be allowed to be officials thereafter.[4]

[1] Kung Yü (CHS, 72, 5a–8a; JMT, p. 853), T. Shao-weng, 123–44 B.C., was one of the most outspoken critics and fearless officials of the Han period. Most of his biography is composed of abstracts or quotations from his clear-cut and fluent memorials, largely on basic economic problems of the empire. Having become an Erudit, his first position was Inspector of Liang chou. He became Prefect of Ho-nan Commandery, but was accused of some misdeed and retired from public life. When Emperor Yüan ascended the throne in 48 B.C., Kung Yü was appointed Grandee Censor. A memorial he made at that time, vigorously protesting the lavish expense of government, is an important economic document. It is very roughly translated by Wieger (*China throughout the ages*, pp. 97–98; TH, vol. I, pp. 635–636). Kung Yü was next made Imperial Household Grandee, then Treasurer of the Privy Purse of Ch'ang-hsin Palace, and finally Grandee Secretary in 44 B.C. He died during the same year but had presented several tens of memorials, abstracts of which make up the bulk of his biography. This passage is taken from the abstract.

[2] Can there have been more than 100,000 government slaves, as Kung Yü says? The answer to this requires an appraisal of Kung Yü as a reporter, and a scrutiny of the figure itself.

The memorial presented by Kung Yü in 48 B.C. when he was Grandee Censor treated in detail those departments of the palace organization and of the imperial government which were excessively luxurious, or where expenses were too heavy. The Emperor, who was no infant but a man of 27 years, was enough impressed by his recommendations to issue an edict (CHS, 72, 6a; 9, 2a) which ordered the Chief of Stud to reduce the food for horses, and ordered the Commandant of Parks to reduce the food for wild beasts (i.e., to cut down on the number of animals?); and which turned over certain parks, marshes and waste lands to poor people (to cultivate or exploit), and abolished the bureaus for butting and other entertainments together with the *Ch'i-san-fu* (which had charge of making imperial textiles and clothing). The annals of the next four years show many imperial reforms which reflect Kung Yü's ideas. These facts indicate the importance attached by the Emperor and the government to Kung Yü's recommendations.

The positions to which he was appointed, especially the treasurership of the Privy Purse of Ch'ang-hsin Palace, where the Empress Dowager lived, and the second highest position in the realm, that of Grandee Secretary, indicate that he was a man of considerable experience and executive ability. Certainly he had access to information regarding the number of government slaves, if such a fact were known.

Nevertheless, Kung Yü's statement that there were more than 100,000 government slaves must excite suspicion. The term "ten myriad" is not very precise. Kung Yü had a special case to plead; he was describing to the Emperor the lavish expense of the court and central government in contrast to the poverty of the populace. Therefore, one must allow for exaggeration. By the same reasoning it is unlikely, on the other hand, that he would have understated the numbers. Thus, we can perhaps accept something more than 100,000 as an upper limit for the number of government slaves in 44 B.C.

Most population figures for antiquity are extremely dubious; those for China are no exception. While it is correct to maintain a skeptical attitude, it does not follow that we should therefore reject without examination the only figure in the CHS which points to a total of the number of government slaves.

Censuses were taken in Han times in connection with the poll-tax (cf. Kato Shigeru, "A study on the *suan-fu*, the poll tax of the Han dynasty," pp. 56–58; and HFHD, vol. I, p. 80 and footnote 2, also p. 312 and footnote 3.8. An official census for Tun-huang, dated 416 A.D., is among the Stein manuscripts; cf. Lionel Giles, "A census of Tun-huang," TP, vol. 16, 1915, pp. 468–488). Precise population figures are given in the CHS for each commandery and state. Now it cannot be known how accurate were the original censuses nor how factual are the figures reported; all Chinese censuses are generally believed to be inaccurate, and there is a further uncontrollable factor of possible error or falsification in so ancient a text. With these qualifications in mind it is nevertheless suggestive to compare Kung Yü's figure with other population figures given in the CHS, to determine whether, on the basis of proportion, his statement is within reason.

The total population of the Han Empire in A.D. 2 is given in CHS, 28B, 9a, as 12,233,062 households and 59,594,978 people. In Ssu-li Chou, the area under direct imperial control, the total population was 6,682,602 people. This area, the core of the empire, included the three commanderies of the Capital District, and Hung-nung, Ho-nei, Ho-nan, and Ho-tung. If we assume that all the government slaves were in Ssu-li chou, they would have made up less than one-sixtieth of the population. If we assume an even closer concentration the proportion of slaves to free is not fantastic. The Capital District (see HFHD, vol. I, inset map; Herrmann, Atlas, p. 22) consisted of 57 prefectures in the fertile Wei River Valley and contained most of the government bureaus. According to CHS, 28A, 5b–6a, the population in the three commanderies was as follows: Ching-chao-yin, 682,468; Tso-feng-i, 917,822; Yu-fu-feng, 836,070. If Kung Yü's 100,000 slaves had all been concentrated in the Capital District, with its population of 2,436,360, they would have numbered only one in twenty-four.

One obvious weakness in this reckoning is that we do not know how much the total population, or that of any particular region, grew between 44 B.C. and A.D. 2. If Ssu-li chou or the Capital District was less densely populated in Kung Yü's time, then the proportion of slaves to free would have been correspondingly higher.   On the other hand, it is by no means certain that all the government slaves were thus concentrated.   Many lived in parks and ranches near the frontier; some may have worked in government salt refineries, iron mines and foundries, and silk and lacquer bureaus in Shantung, Shansi, and Szechwan.

Comparable gross figures for people employed by the government are given in CHS, 2, 2a–b (HFHD, vol. I, pp. 181, 183).   There it is reported that in 192 B.C. 146,000 persons were sent from regions within six hundred *li* of Ch'ang-an (roughly 200 miles) to build the city wall; while in addition 20,000 criminals and retainers were sent from the states of the vassal kings and marquises (ibid., p. 181, footnote 3).   In the year 190 B.C. 145,000 persons, sent for the same purpose, completed the wall.

CHS, 19A, 8a, states that there were 130,285 officials counting all from assistant clerks to the Chancellor.   This was presumably at the end of the Former Han period, perhaps fifty years after Kung Yü's time.

Estimates of the numerical strength of ancient armies are necessarily very dubious.   On this point there is an interesting statement under the year 206 B.C. (CHS, 1A, 7a; HFHD, vol. I, p. 61): "At this time [Hsiang] Yü's troops [numbered] four hundred thousand and were asserted to be a million, [while] the Lord of P'ei's troops [numbered] a hundred thousand and were asserted to be two hundred thousand—his strength was not equal [to that of Hsiang Yü]."   This shows that falsification of figures was resorted to during civil war.   Reports of foreign campaigns may likewise have been falsified for other reasons, such as to allow for graft in requisitioning supplies.   It is a question for military historians to decide whether it would have been possible to provision the large armies reported for the wars of conquest under Emperor Wu.   The following are the wars listed in the Annals of Emperor Wu (CHS, 6), where figures are given.

B.C.	Number of troops	Campaign
133	300,000	Against Hsiung-nu, under Li Hsi.
124	Over 100,000	Against Hsiung-nu; six armies under Wei Ch'ing.
123	Over 100,000 cavalry	Against Hsiung-nu; led by Wei Ch'ing.
119	{ 50,000 cavalry / Several 100,000 foot }	Against Hsiung-nu; under Wei Ch'ing and Ho Ch'ü-ping.
112	100,000	Against southeast barbarians; combined river and land force.
111	100,000 cavalry and foot	Against the western Ch'iang.
110	180,000 cavalry	Against Hsiung-nu.
103	20,000 cavalry	Against Hsiung-nu.
99	30,000 cavalry	Against Hsiung-nu; 5,000 foot under Li Ling were defeated.
97	{ 70,000 cavalry / 130,000 foot }	Against Hsiung-nu; divided into four armies.
90	{ 40,000 cavalry / 90,000 unspecified }	Against Hsiung-nu; three armies.

These armies, which were on the most important campaigns, average nearly 130,000 men.   One campaign not specified above, namely, the expedition of Li Kuang-li against Ta Yüan in 102 B.C., may be cited to illuminate these figures. The year before, Li Kuang-li had been defeated and had not dared to re-enter China.   It is reported that the army sent to Tun-huang to supplement his troops numbered 60,000, not counting baggage carriers.   The supply trains consisted of 100,000 oxen, 30,000 horses, and myriads of donkeys, mules, and camels. Much of this supply train only went to the base at Tun-huang.   All parts of the empire contributed to the expedition.   A covering force of 180,000 frontier troops was stationed at Chü-yen, Hsiu-ch'u, Chiu-ch'uan, and Chang-yeh.   The army that finally attacked and defeated Ta Yüan numbered only 30,000 (cf. CHS, 61, 4b; SC, 123, 7b, and Friedrich Hirth, "The story of Chang K'ién," JAOS, vol. 37, 1917, pp. 111–112).

In summary, it is perhaps only admissible to say that Kung Yü, a man deeply interested in economic problems, highly respected by the Emperor and the bureaucracy, and holding the second highest office in the empire, presents a figure which is perfectly in accord with other figures seriously recorded in the history of the Former Han dynasty. His figure is not fantastic when compared with figures for Rome at about the same time (cf. W. L. Westermann, "Sklaverei," in *Paulys Realenzyklopädie der klassischen Altertums-Wissenschaft* . . . , supplement, vol. 6, 1935, *passim*, especially col. 954, line 6, concerning enslavement of 150,000 men from 70 towns of Epirus on direct order of the Roman Senate in 167 B.C.; col. 955, line 2, giving an estimate of 150,000 slave-prisoners as a result of Caesar's Gallic wars; and col. 958, line 14, the unsupported statement of Strabo that the slave market at Delos could handle 10,000 slaves in a day).

[3] Is 500,000,000 or 600,000,000 cash an excessively large figure for an annual government expenditure at this time? A rough idea of the fiscal situation during the reign of Emperor Yüan is given in a memorial presented to the throne in 4/3 B.C. by Chancellor Wang Chia (cf. *117*, footnote 2), who praised Emperor Yüan's governmental economy. "The late Emperor Yüan carefully attended to his rulership, and was mild and humble, and had few desires. In the capital [the reserves (according to Yen Shih-ku) of the treasury] were 4,000,000,000 cash; of the Public Lands were 2,500,000,000 cash; and of the Privy Purse were 1,800,-000,000 cash. . . . At that time there were few of his affinal relatives whose capital totaled 10,000,000 [cash], so that the [treasury of] the Public Lands and the Privy Purse had much cash on hand." (CHS, 86, 5a.) Yet it was this economical Emperor Yüan who, in 47 B.C. (CHS, 9, 2b), early in his reign, gave special rewards of 200,000 cash to all marquises (i.e., to the two highest ranks in the hierarchy), and 100,000 cash to all *Wu-ta-fu*. (It probably means all from *Wu-ta-fu* up to marquises, i.e., all of the second class, of which *Wu-ta-fu* were lowest, being ninth from the bottom of the hierarchy).

Using Kung Yü's statements of the number and cost of government slaves, the average annual upkeep of a slave would be 5,000 or 6,000 cash. Apparently Kung Yü thought this cost could be greatly reduced by simply feeding the slaves from the government granaries—the old discussion of work relief against the dole.

This annual cost of keeping a slave seems high when compared with the official income of a marquis, who was supposed to receive 200 cash annually from each household in his domain (SC, 129, 6a; CHS, 91, 3a). During the 25 years from 57–32 B.C., in which our date 44 B.C. falls in the middle, 85 new marquises were enfeoffed. In 24 instances it is stated how many households went with each fief (CHS, 15B, 11b–23b; 17, 20a–22a; 18, 14a–16a). An analysis of the incomes of these marquises bears on the present discussion. The 24 fiefs may be grouped as follows: 3 were fewer than 500 households (average 325, average theoretic income 65,000 cash); 6 between 500 and 1,000 (average 744.5, income 148,900); 6 between 1,000 and 1,500 (average 1296.5, income 259,300); 4 between 1,500 and 2,000 (average 1,705, income 341,000); 2 between 2,000 and 2,500 (average 2,375, income 475,000); 2 at 2,800 (income 560,000); one at 8,000 (income 1,600,000).

Thus, if it is correct that a marquis received 200 cash annually from each household in his domain (and assuming that this was his principal income), some of the marquises could have maintained only a very few non-productive slaves at the rate it cost the government.

What was the purchasing power of money at this time? Grain is a good commodity by which to judge prices, especially since official salaries were fixed in terms of grain, or grain and money. In 47 B.C. it is stated that because of a famine in Ch'i grain cost 300 cash a picul (*tan*. CHS, 9, 2b; and 24A, 8a). For the year 42 B.C. it is stated that, harvests having been bad for several years, grain cost 200 cash per picul at the capital; 400 cash in frontier commanderies; and 500 cash east of the pass (CHS, 79, 2a). A picul weighed approximately 64½ pounds avoir., as compared with 60 pounds for a U. S. bushel of wheat and 50 pounds for a bushel of millet. These statements, both about 44 B.C., give prices in bad years. At about Kung Yü's time, then, 6,000 cash would buy 30 piculs of grain at the capital. A very crude comparison with modern food consumption figures may be attempted. Among modern Chinese farm families, adult male units consume 1,002 grams of food per day in the "winter wheat–millet area" (in which the Han capital district lies) according to John L. Buck (*Land utilization in China*, vol. 1, p. 427, table 9). This represents 365.98 kilograms per year, which is equivalent to 12.49 Han piculs (HFHD, vol. I, p. 280; 1 *tan*=29.3 kg.). Of course it is really impossible to compare this 12.49 piculs of all foods with the 30 piculs of unspecified grain which 6,000 cash would buy in 44 B.C. Not only do we not know what proportion of the government outlay went for food, but also modern diet differs from ancient diet in at least the addition of New World foods such as maize and potatoes, etc. Furthermore, Buck gives no clear statement of the percentage of grains by bulk in the total modern diet, although he does emphasize the high proportion of grains measured by food energy. On the other hand, it probably can be assumed that the average annual consumption of food per slave for all government slaves (men, women, and children) was not considerably greater than that of an adult male unit farmer in the same region today.

The question of cost can be approached from another point of view. Official salaries were reckoned in piculs of grain, according to income brackets ranging from 2,000 piculs at the top to 100 piculs at the bottom. (An outline of the system is given in MH, vol. II, pp. 526–527, and Wu Ching-ch'ao, "The class system of the Western Han dynasty," pp. 613–614. Their lists differ slightly. The details of the system are drawn from HHS, 38, 6a, which describes the organization in later Han times, though this was patterned after the system of the Former Han.) Thus, the theoretic salary of the lowest-grade official would be only three times as much as it cost the government to maintain a slave, while that of the highest official, who probably owned many slaves and had a big household, would be only sixty-seven times as much.

If Kung Yü's figures were correct it would seem that an economy could have been effected by freeing the slaves and feeding them from the government granaries, as he suggested.

[4] Emperor Yüan is said to have been much impressed with Kung Yü's criticisms and to have attempted in several ways to reduce expenses. A number of reforms, which probably stemmed from Kung Yü, are listed in CHS, 9, 1b–3b; 24A, 8a; and 24B, 8b. For example, shortly before the present memorial the Emperor abolished the guards at Chien-ch'ang and Kan-ch'uan palaces, and reduced by half the guards at the ancestral temples of the vassal kings. There is no evidence in CHS, however, that the Emperor did anything about freeing or reducing the number of government slaves.

90.   Last decades B.C.[1]   HCI, A, 9b

丞相府官奴婢傳漏以起居不擊鼓官屬吏不朝旦白
錄而已諸吏初除謁視事間君侯應閤奴名白事以方尺
板叩閤大呼奴名君侯出入諸吏不得見見禮如師弟子
狀掾史有過君侯取錄推其錄三日白病去

The Chancellor's Residency.   Government male and female
slaves transmitted from one to another [the hours of the] water-
clock for [timing] the daily schedule.   If they did not beat the drum,
subordinate government officials did not assemble at dawn for
ceremonial court,[2] but merely made their reports in the morning.
When various officials were first appointed, they paid a visit [to
the Chancellor] to report for duty, and they asked for the name
of the Chancellor's[3] male slave who attended the small side gate.[4]
[When coming] to report affairs they beat on the small side gate with
an oblong, foot-long, wooden tablet, and loudly shouted the male
slave's name.   When the Chancellor went in or out, the various
officials were not allowed to see him.   If they did see him, they
performed the ceremony like that of student toward teacher.   If
his secretaries committed some error the Chancellor took their
report.   If he examined their report for three days, they announced
that they were sick, and departed.

[1] The following passages from the *Han chiu i* by Wei Hung describe practices
of the Former Han period, but are not precisely dated.   Presumably they refer
to conditions near the close of the period, but before Wang Mang made drastic
changes in official titles and government organization between A.D. 9 and 23.
Wei Hung lived ca. A.D. 25–57, and wrote the *Han chiu i* specifically "in order to
record the old affairs of the western capital," that is, of Ch'ang-an, which was
the Han capital only until the death of Wang Mang in A.D. 23.   (On Wei Hung and
the HCI, cf. HHS, 109B, 3b; SKC, 82, 1a and 83, 2a; and WHC, 109.)
   The text here used is part of the *Han kuan ch'i chung*, a collection of seven
Han works on government, assembled and edited by Sun Hsing-yen (1753–1818),
and found in the *P'ing chin kuan ts'ung-shu*.   Sun Hsing-yen states in his separate
preface to the *Han chiu i* that he used as his basis the text in the *Yung-lo ta tien*.
This contained only two *chüan* of the original four *chüan* by Wei Hung.   These
presumably make his sections *shang* and *hsia*, here called A and B.   Taking various
citations of the *Han chiu i* found scattered elsewhere, Sun Hsing-yen also composed
the *Han chiu i pu-i*, in another *chüan* of two parts.
   Sun Hsing-yen states that the *Han chiu i* originally had a commentary;
whether "originally" (*pen*) means that it was a commentary by Wei Hung, or
a commentary by another writer in some early edition, is not clear.   He further
states that writers of the Wei, Chin, and T'ang dynasties, quoting the *Han* [*chiu*]
i chu, are all referring to this latter book.   Nowadays they are not differentiated.
Only the *Yung-lo ta tien* preserves the original text, with the commentary printed
in small characters.

In the *Han chiu i* proper, Sun Hsing-yen gives in commentary form variant readings found in texts other than the *Yung-lo ta tien*. In the *Han chiu i pu-i* his commentary in the main merely lists the works in which he found the individual passages.

In captions for my documents, HCI means *Han chiu i* and HCIPI means *Han chiu i pu-i;* A and B refer to the sections *shang* and *hsia* in each.

[2] Or, "officials belonging to the bureau [of the Chancellor] did not assemble ...," etc. The term *chao* as a verb refers to the act of early morning court ceremony, and implies its extreme formality.

[3] The term *chün-hou* is here taken to refer to the Chancellor, rather than to high ministers and marquises in general.

[4] Proper translation of the last phrase is puzzling because of the lack of a verb other than *ying*, "ought," "should." It is clear from the next sentence why newly appointed officials should learn the name of the slave who attended the small side gate, for later when the officials came on business they had to summon the slave and identify themselves before they were admitted.

---

91. Last decades B.C. HCI, B, 2b

宮人擇官婢年八歲以上侍皇后以下年三十五出嫁乳母取官婢

Palace Women[1] were selected from among palace female slaves in their eighth year or over. They waited upon [ladies of the palace from] the Empress on down. At the age of thirty-five they were sent out to be married.[2] Wet-nurses were taken from among government female slaves.[3]

[1] The term *kung-jen* is explained by Yen Shih-ku (*101*, footnote 3), who refers to the *Han chiu i*, meaning presumably this and the next passage (which cf.). However, there is at least one instance in the CHS where the term is used for a man. Luan Ta, Emperor Wu's magician (cf. *49*), was at one time a *kung-jen* of the King of Chiao-tung; see HSPC, 25A, 27a, where Fu Ch'ien equates *kung-jen* with *chia-jen*, "householder," and where Chou Shou-ch'ang says: "Deducing from this, males could also be called *kung-jen*."

[2] Emperor Ai sent out to be married those Palace Women of the late Emperor Ch'eng's Concubines' Quarter who were *under* thirty (cf. *110*).

[3] We know of one such wet-nurse, Chang Ch'i, who suckled the child of Emperor Ch'eng by a slave girl (*107*). Note the distinction between palace female slaves and government female slaves. Chang Ch'i was a government slave. Were such women usually married?

官奴擇給書計從侍中以下爲倉頭青幘與百官從事
從入殿中省中待使令者皆官婢擇年八歲以上衣綠曰
宦人不得出省門置都監老者曰婢婢敎宦人給使尙書
侍中皆使官婢不得使宦人奴婢欲自贖錢千萬免爲庶
人宮殿中宦者署郞署皆官奴婢傳言曰作者歌傳以呼
召侍中以下署長

Government male slaves were selected to give [service] as writers and accountants. Those of [the rank of] Attaché and below were "green-heads," [wearing] blue-green turbans.[1] They were given to the "hundred" government bureaus to assist [officials] and escort them into the halls of the palace.

In the Inner Apartments [of the palace], Maidservants and Orderlies were all government female slaves selected in their eighth year or over. They dressed in green and were called "Palace[2] Women." They were not allowed to go outside the gates of the Inner Apartments. Supervisors were established for them. Elderly ones were called *"pei."*[3] The *pei* taught the Palace Women how to serve. Keepers of Documents and Attachés all employed government female slaves, but were not allowed to employ the Palace Women.

Male and female slaves who wished to buy their freedom [paid] a thousand myriad cash,[4] and were dismissed to become commoners.

In the palace and its halls, the offices of the Eunuchs and of the Gentlemen all [had] government male and female slaves. Those who transmitted verbal messages were called "Executors." They chanted from one to the next in shouting for office chiefs, from Attachés on down.[5]

[1] For explanations of the term "green-head," cf. *118*, footnote 4. In a commentary there, Fu Tsan quotes this sentence. His quotation lacks the verb "to select," and uses 巳 for 以.

[2] Sun Hsing-yen believes that *huan* should be written 宮, and cites the commentary of Yen Shih-ku based on this passage which uses *kung* (cf. *101*, footnote 3). I agree, and have made the correction in the translation here and twice below. In early script the two words were very similar. The description of Palace Women

in a passage two pages before (*91*) makes the correction essential. We cannot be sure the term *huan*, "eunuch," referred exclusively to eunuchs in Han times, but there is no evidence that it ever referred to female slaves.

[3] *Pei* is the term regularly translated "female slave." Here it seems to have the special meaning, "old female slaves who had once been Palace Women."

[4] Thousand times myriad is too great a figure to make sense. Lao Kan ("The system of slavery during the two Han dynasties," p. 5) suggests that thousand is a scribal error for ten, which is quite possible. The redemption price would then be 100,000 cash.

[5] The text of the last sentence seems corrupt. At this point there is an unidentified commentary, probably from the *Han i chu* as printed in small type in the *Yung-lo ta tien* edition, used by Sun Hsing-yen (cf. *90*, footnote 1): "The office chiefs of the Eunuchs and of the Gentlemen each watched a door, and were selected from government male slaves. [They wore] red turbans and assigned and led the Executors. Sweepers and removers were called 'Straighteners.' The method of chanting from one to the next was taken from the times of old Chou at Lo-yang, [where] transmission of shouts from one to the next was done in tunes."

---

93. Last decades B.C. HCIPI, A, 3b

太僕牧師諸苑三十六所分布北邊西邊以郎爲苑監
官奴婢三萬人分養馬三十萬頭擇取敎習給六廄牛羊
無數以給犧牲

The Chief of Stud and his Herdsmen [had charge of] thirty-six parks distributed and spread over the northern and western frontiers. Gentlemen were used as Park Superintendents. Thirty thousand government male and female slaves were distributed [in the parks] to care for 300,000 head of horses, which were selected and trained, and given to the six stables. There were cattle and sheep without number to be given as sacrificial animals.[1]

[1] This passage comes from the additional section to the *Han chiu i*, reconstructed by Sun Hsing-yen from various quotations of the now missing two *chüan*. He cites Ju Shun's commentary in CHS, 5, 4a (cf. HFHD, vol. I, p. 325, footnote 8.4); HHS, 4; the *San fu huang t'u*, 4; the *T'ang liu tien*, 17; the *I wen lei chü*, chih kuan pu; and the *T'ai-p'ing yü lan*, chih kuan pu.

94.   Last decades B.C.   HCIPI, A, 4a

太官主飲酒皆令丞治太官湯官奴婢各三千人置酒
皆緹襦蔽膝綠幘

The Grand Provisioner had charge of wine drinking.   Both a
Chief and an Assistant managed [the bureau].[1]   The Grand Provisioner and the Bakery[2] each had three thousand male and female
slaves.[3]   When serving banquets they all wore pale-red silk garments
down to the knee, and green turbans.[4]

[1] The structure of this sentence is not very clear.

[2] The *T'ai-kuan* and *T'ang-kuan* were both subordinate divisions of the
Privy Purse, which provided for the imperial needs.   Cf. CHS, 19A, 4b (MH,
vol. II, p. 520).   Yen Shih-ku there explains that the *T'ai-kuan* had charge of
delicacies and food while the *T'ang-kuan* had charge of cakes and pastries.   From
this passage the Grand Provisioner would seem also to have had supervision of
wine, and the passage immediately preceding it speaks of the Chief of the *T'ai-kuan* as being in charge of various drinking vessels as well as dishes.

[3] Or, "had male and female slaves, three thousand of each."

[4] Sun Hsing-yen cites the following sources: The *Pei t'ang shu*, ch'ao she
kuan pu; and the *T'ai p'ing yü lan*, chih kuan pu.

95. Last decades B.C.[1] HCIPI, A, 5b

司隸校尉武帝初置後諸侯王貴戚不服乃以中都中
官徒奴千二百人屬爲一校尉部刺史督二千石也

The Colonel over the Retainers[2] was first established by Emperor
Wu. Later, the vassal kings and noble relatives of the imperial
house by marriage would not submit [to his jurisdiction]. Thereupon [the government] took twelve hundred convicts[3] and male
slaves from bureaus within the capital city and subordinated them
to form a single inspectorate, [which had a] Divisional Inspector[4]
to supervise [officials with salaries of] two thousand piculs.[5]

[1] No close dating seems possible in spite of the several dates given in footnote 2,
from the passage in the "Table on the Bureaucracy," because the changes indicated
there do not tally with the "later" change noted in this text. Officials holding
the position of Colonel over the Retainers are mentioned in CHS, 19B, under
years 86, 28, 25, 13, and 6 B.C., and probably many others.

[2] Chavannes (MH, vol. II, p. 525) says: "Il paraît avoir été le chef de la brigade
des mœurs à la capital." The next passage in the HCIPI says: "The Colonel
over the Retainers controlled [all officials] below the Heir-apparent and the
Three Dukes. All provincial and commandery officials were controlled by him."
The "Table on the Bureaucracy," CHS, 19A, 6b–7a, has the following account
which I have divided into two paragraphs. The first seems to be a general statement, corresponding fairly closely to the account in this document. The second
notes the dates at which certain changes were made.

"The Colonel over the Retainers was a Chou [dynasty] office. Emperor Wu
first established [the office (for Han)] in the fourth year of Cheng-ho [89 B.C.].
Carrying credentials, [the Colonel over the Retainers] was escorted by twelve
hundred convicts [see footnote 3, below] from bureaus of the capital city [Yen
Shih-ku's commentary here is translated in footnote 3]. He arrested [those who
practiced] wu-ku [i.e., a form of witchcraft (the great witchcraft scandal had
occurred in 91 B.C., which accounts for the founding of this office two years later)],
and judicially investigated major [cases of] licentiousness and treachery. Later
his soldiers were abolished, and he made judicial investigations in the Capital
District [The San-fu, i.e., Ch'ang-an, Yu-fu-feng, and Tso-feng-i Commanderies],
the Three Ho [i.e., Ho-nei, Ho-nan, and Ho-tung Commanderies], and Hung-
nung [Commandery. (These seven commanderies made up the Ssu-li chou or
province directly governed from the capital.)].

"Emperor Yüan, in the fourth year of Ch'u-yüan [45 B.C.], removed his credentials. Emperor Ch'eng in the fourth year of Yüan-yen [9 B.C.] diminished
[his authority (CHS, 10, 7a, under that year, says the office was abolished)].
In the second year of Sui-ho [7 B.C.] Emperor Ai re-established [the office], but
made the ceremonial cap of the Colonel a chin-hsien ceremonial cap [i.e., of the
type worn by Ju (Confucian scholars); cf. TY]. He was under the Grandee Secretary [from 8 to 5 B.C., Ta ssu-k'ung was the title used for Yu-shih ta-fu] and approxi-
mated an Assistant to the Chancellor."

[3] This might mean convict male slaves. It is interesting that the CHS passage
translated in footnote 2 speaks of the same number but mentions only convicts,
then later says the soldiers 兵 were abolished. It is hard to understand why the
Colonel over the Retainers would be escorted only by convicts as the CHS has
it, but they may have been hereditary slaves descended from convicts. A passage

407

in CHS, 8, 7b, for the year 61 B.C. is especially interesting here: "The Western Ch'iang rebelled. [The government] dispatched the convicts of the San-fu and the capital city [*San-fu chung-tu kuan t'u*], relaxing their sentences." The commentary is significant. It speaks of 36 prisons of the various bureaus in Ch'ang-an. Yen Shih-ku there equates the *Chung-tu* [capital city] with the *Ching-shih*, as he does also in the CHS passage translated in footnote 2: "The *Chung-tu kuan* [were the] various bureaus and residencies [or treasuries (*fu*)] of the capital [*Ching-shih*]."

⁴ Divisional inspectors (*pu ts'e-shih*) were established in 106 B.C. (cf. CHS, 19A, 7b; MH, vol. II, p. 531; and CHS, 6, 11b). They traveled among the 13 provinces (*chou*) of the empire checking up on local officials. Thus, the Colonel over the Retainers was reduced from overseer of the nobility to a sort of censor to supervise officials with the salary of two thousand piculs.

⁵ Officials having the salary of two thousand piculs were Administrators of commanderies and Chancellors of kingdoms (cf. HFHD, vol. I, p. 193, footnote 3). This conforms with the CHS statement in footnote 2 that the Colonel over the Retainers in his reduced importance made judicial investigations in the seven commanderies of the province administered directly from the capital. In other words, he now was one of the regular inspectorate.

Sun Hsing-yen gives as his source for this passage the *Pei t'ang shu*, chao she kuan pu.

96.   33 B.C.   CHS, 94B, 4a (7a)

近西羌保塞與漢人交通吏民貪利侵盜其畜產妻子
以此怨恨起而背畔世世不絕今罷乘塞則生嫚易分爭
之漸五也⋯又邊人奴婢愁苦欲亡者多曰聞匈奴中樂
無奈候望急何然時有亡出塞者七也

[In the ten-point speech against turning over to the Hsiung-nu the guardianship of the northwestern sector of the Wall, Hou Ying[1] said]: "Recently the western Ch'iang[2] have protected the Barrier, and have had relations with the Chinese people. [Chinese] officials and commoners, greedy for profit, invade them and plunder their livestock, produce, and wives and children, because of which there is resentment and hatred. [The Ch'iang] rise up and rebel—generations will not end [the trouble]. Now, if we quit manning the Barrier it will produce [new] affronts and slights, gradually descending into strife. [That is] the fifth [point] . . . ." [3]

"Furthermore, the male and female slaves of the frontiersmen are melancholy and bitter. Those who want to escape are many. They say: 'We hear that [people living] among the Hsiung-nu are happy; yet the guard-watchers are oppressive—what can we do?' Yet occasionally there are those who do flee out the Barrier. [That is] the seventh [point]." [4]

[1] Hou Ying is apparently known only here; he is not mentioned in JMT, WHC, TY, or Giles B. The situation which brought up his speech was as follows: After the death in 36 B.C. of Chih-chih, the Hsiung-nu *Shan-yü*, his brother named Hu-han-hsieh, who was the *Shan-yü* of the eastern (or southern) Hsiung-nu, paid a visit to the Han court, and was richly rewarded with gifts. He requested an alliance by marriage, and Emperor Yüan gave him from his imperial seraglio a lady named Wang Ch'iang (T. Chao-chün)—the famous tragic lady of story and drama in "The sorrows of Han." Next Hu-han-hsieh proposed that he and his successors be allowed to take over the guarding of the Wall from Shang-ku west to Tun-huang, and that all Chinese troops be withdrawn from that frontier. The Emperor handed the matter down for debate. The officials agreed to the proposal, but a Gentleman of the Palace named Hou Ying made a ten-point rebuttal. Two points from his argument are here translated. As a result, Hu-han-hsieh's proposal was rejected, and the Chinese continued to man their own frontiers.

[2] The inhabitants of present eastern Tibet.

[3] The argument is that since only trouble has arisen from the use of Ch'iang people to guard the Wall, similar or worse trouble would arise from allowing the Hsiung-nu to take over a long sector.

⁴ I.e., if the Chinese soldiers do not continue to guard the Wall there will be no stopping male and female slaves of Chinese frontiersmen from escaping to the Hsiung-nu.

A peace treaty with the Hsiung-nu in A.D. 5 (CHS, 94B, 8a) stipulated as its first item that Chinese absconding to the Hsiung-nu should not be given asylum.

---

97.   33–15 B.C.¹   CHS, 82, 4a (7a)

丹爲人足知愷弟愛人貌若儻蕩不備然心甚謹密故
尤得信於上丹兄嗣父爵爲侯讓不受分丹盡得父財身
又食大國邑重以舊恩數見褒賞賞賜累千金僮奴以百
數後房妻妾數十人內奢淫好飮酒極滋味聲色之樂

As a man [Shih] Tan² was intelligent, kind, and friendly. His appearance seemed nonchalant and careless, but his mind was careful and precise; therefore he specially won the Emperor's confidence. [Shih] Tan's older brother inherited his father's rank as marquis, but yielded and did not take his portion, and [Shih] Tan received all his father's wealth. He himself also had the income from the cities of a big fief, and in addition, because of the earlier act of mercy [of his ancestors], he was several times praised and rewarded. His rewards and gifts totaled a thousand [weight] of gold, and youths and male slaves numbered by the hundred. In the women's quarters his wives and concubines numbered several tens. At home he was extravagant and indulgent; he liked to drink wine, and went to extremes in the pleasures of food, entertainment, and sex.

¹ The period during which Shih Tan probably received the gifts of slaves.

² Shih Tan (CHS, 82, 3a–4a; 18, 12b; 97A, 8b; JMT, p. 173) was the son of Shih Kao and grandson of Shih Kung. Shih Kung was the older brother of a girl who, in 113 B.C., became the concubine of Emperor Wu's first Heir-apparent, Liu Chü. They had a son, the Imperial Grandson Shih. This boy had a son by his Lady *née* Wang, who was named Liu Hsün, and who later became Emperor Hsüan. (Shih Kung was thus a great-uncle of Emperor Hsüan, and Shih Tan was the Emperor's second cousin on the distaff side.) In 91 B.C. after the execution of the Heir-apparent and his family, the babe Liu Hsün was rescued (cf. *80*, footnote 3) and was reared in the family of his grandmother, the concubine *née* Shih.

In 74 B.C. Liu Hsün was established as Emperor and the Shih family reaped its reward. When Emperor Yüan came to the throne in 48 B.C., Shih Tan was appointed Commandant of Imperial Equipage and became an Attaché in the Palace. Under Emperor Ch'eng he was made Ch'ang-lo Major and a *kuan-nei* marquis, with an income from 300 households; then Junior General (29 B.C.); and finally Senior General (26 B.C.) and Imperial Household Grandee. In 20 B.C. he was made Marquis of Wu-yang with the income from 1,100 households (CHS, 18, 12b, says 1,300). He had twenty children. He died in 14 B.C.

竊見丞相商作威作福從外制中取必於上性殘賊不
仁遣票輕吏微求人罪欲以立威天下患苦之前頻陽耿
定上書言商與父傅通及女弟淫亂奴殺其私夫疑商教
使章下有司商私怨懟…今商宗族權執合賞鉅萬計私
奴以千數非特劇孟匹夫之徒也且失道之至親戚畔之
閨門內亂父子相訐而欲使之宣明聖化調和海內豈不
繆哉…前商女弟內行不修奴賊殺人疑商教使爲商重

[At this time there was an eclipse of the sun and Chang K'uang[2] blamed it upon Wang Shang,[3] saying]: "I observe that Chancellor [Wang] Shang is autocratic, controls the palace from without,[4] and obtains from the Emperor whatever he wants. His temperament is ruthless and inhumane; he sends detectives secretly to seek out people's faults, desiring thereby to establish terror of himself—the whole empire suffers and is embittered by it.

"Formerly Keng Ting of P'in-yang submitted a document stating that [Wang] Shang had had intercourse with his father's [female slave] chamberlain,[5] and [yet when] his younger sister had improper sexual relations, a male slave murdered her lover. It is suspected that [Wang] Shang instructed [the slave to do it]. That document was sent down to those in authority, and [Wang] Shang was secretly [filled with] resentment and hatred . . . .[6]

"Now [Wang] Shang's whole clan is powerful. Their combined capital is reckoned by the hundred million [cash], and their private male slaves are numbered by the thousand. [Thus] he is not a fellow with Chü Meng,[7] who was a lone wolf; moreover, the extremity of his immorality [is such that] his relatives reject him, there is depravity in his women's apartments, and father and son mutually accuse each other. Under such circumstances to expect to use him to broadcast and illumine the saintly influence [of the Emperor] and to adjust and harmonize the world—is that not confused indeed? . . ." [8]

[The imperial edict of decree declared]: "Formerly the personal conduct of [Wang Shang's] younger sister had been improper; a male

411

臣故抑而不窮今或言商不以自悔而反怨懟朕甚傷之
惟商與先帝有外親未忍致于理其赦商罪使者收丞相
印綬商免相三日發病歐血薨

slave assassinated the man [in the case]. It is suspected that [Wang] Shang instructed [him to do it]. Because [Wang] Shang is an important minister We suppressed and did not investigate thoroughly [into the case]. Now some say that [Wang] Shang has not repented, but on the contrary is full of resentment and hatred [toward Us]. We are deeply wounded by this. But [Wang] Shang and the late Emperor were related, so that We cannot bear to go to the extreme of justice. Let [Wang] Shang's crimes be pardoned. An emissary shall take back his Chancellor's seal."

Three days after [Wang] Shang had been dismissed as Chancellor he fell sick, spat blood, and died.

[1] Chancellor Wang Shang was dismissed on June 5, 25 B.C. (CHS, 19B, 43a). Earlier that year there was an eclipse, and a flood in P'in River which was investigated by a commission. That may explain an accusation made by an otherwise unknown Keng Ting of P'in-yang. How much earlier than this occurred the incident of the slave murdering the lover is not stated.

[2] Chang K'uang, a man from Szechwan and a Grand Palace Grandee, is known only here and in CHS, 95, 3a, where he is mentioned by the same title.

[3] Wang Shang (CHS, 82, 1a–2b; 18, 12a; JMT, p. 118), T. Tzu-wei, must not be confused with the other Wang Shang, T. Tzu-hsia, Marquis of Ch'eng-tu, General-in-Chief (15–12 B.C.), and the uncle of Wang Mang. The present Wang Shang's father, Wang Wu, was a brother of the mother of Emperor Hsüan. After Liu Hsün had been brought from among the people and made Emperor Hsüan, Wang Wu, his uncle, was made Marquis of Lo-ch'ang in 66 B.C. (CHS, 18, 12a; 97A, 9a–b). In 52 B.C. Wang Shang inherited the marquisate of Lo-ch'ang. He was made Commander of Attachés and Gentlemen of the Household under Emperor Hsüan, and Imperial Household Grandee under Emperor Yüan, whose boyhood playmate he had been. Emperor Yüan's Empress née Wang was of a different clan from Wang Shang. When she bore the Heir-apparent, later Emperor Ch'eng, members of her family (the Wang Mang family) began to assume power.

In a public dispute Wang Shang bested the head of the other Wang clan, Wang Feng, who thereby lost face. The next year, 29 B.C., Wang Shang became Chancellor. An eclipse of the sun gave Wang Feng an opportunity for revenge by blaming it on Wang Shang. The present accusation was produced by an otherwise unimportant official. It does not necessarily follow from the background of intrigue that the charge was false in detail.

[4] Lit. "from the outside he controls the inside," i.e., as a maternal relation he dominates the Emperor within the palace.

[5] Yen Shih-ku says "fu means fu-pei." This term, translated "female slave chamberlain," is explained in 120, footnote 2.

[6] Abstracting from the accusation by Chang K'uang: Wang Shang's son, Wang Chün, wished to submit a document accusing his father. Wang Chün's wife, who was the daughter of General Shih Tan, took the document to her father, who was disgusted at this schism between father and son. The accusation states

that the eclipse of the sun is due to these irregularities in the family of the Chancellor, and argues from historical precedent that the Emperor should dismiss Wang Shang. A further part of the accusation continues as translated.

[7] Chü Meng (SC, 124, 2a; CHS, 92, 2a; JMT, p. 1429) was an independent chieftain with a considerable following during the Rebellion of the Seven States. His loyalty to the throne was won by Chou Ya-fu, who exclaimed that without this success the rebellion could not have been suppressed. The argument is that Wang Shang, with the backing of a powerful and rich family owning many male slaves, is much more dangerous to the Emperor than was Chü Meng, a pivotal character at the time of a serious rebellion against the imperial house.

[8] After this accusation had been heard by General Shih Tan, he and the others presented a memorial to the Emperor generalizing on Wang Shang's crimes and begging that he be sent to jail. The Emperor set the matter aside. General-in-Chief Wang Feng, who was the Emperor's uncle, strongly contested this decision, whereupon there was an imperial edict of decree condemning Wang Shang's disloyalty. The last half of the decree is here translated.

99.   Ca. 23 B.C.[1]   CHS, 98, 4a (7b)

又以侍中太僕音爲御史大夫列於三公而五侯羣弟
爭爲奢侈賂遺珍寶四面而至後庭姬妾各數十人僮奴
以千百數羅鐘磬舞鄭女作倡優狗馬馳逐大治第室起
土山漸臺洞門高廊閣道連屬彌望

Also [Wang Feng[2]] got Attaché and Chief of Stud [Wang] Yin[3] made Grandee Secretary, ranking among the three dukes, while the five marquises,[4] the group of younger brothers [of the Empress Dowager *née* Wang], competed in lavishness and luxury. Bribes and gifts of precious things came in from all sides. In their women's quarters each had several tens of concubines, and their youths and male slaves were numbered by the thousand or hundred. They collected drums and musical stones, had girls from Ch'en to dance, gave concerts and theatricals, and raced dogs and horses. They built grand mansions and houses, and erected artificial mountains with graduated terraces, grottoes, high porches and covered passage-ways—closely connected and filling the view.

[1] Wang Yin was made Grandee Secretary in 23 B.C., but the description of the wealth of the members of the Wang family could date for about two decades after 27 B.C.

[2] Wang Feng (CHS, 98, 1b–4b; 18, 14b; JMT, p. 143) was the brother of Emperor Yüan's Empress *née* Wang, who was the mother of Emperor Ch'eng. He succeeded to his father's Marquisate of Yang-p'ing in 42 B.C. Appointed Grand Marshal and Commander-in-Chief in 32 B.C., he was the first of the power-ful ministers of this Wang family in a succession that ended with Wang Mang. He had six brothers and half-brothers, a cousin, and a nephew who were made marquises. The following chart (based upon CHS, 18, 14b–16b; and 98) explains the relationship of the most important members of the family.

   A. Wang Chin: father of the Empress *née* Wang of Emperor Yüan. Marquis of Yang-p'ing in 48 B.C.; d. 42 B.C. He had eight sons in the following order:

   B1. Wang Feng: full brother of the Empress. Marquis of Yang-p'ing in 42 B.C.; d. 22 B.C.

   B2. Wang Man: half-brother of the Empress, and father of Wang Mang. Died before receiving a marquisate.

   B3. Wang T'an: half-brother of the Empress. Marquis of P'ing-a in 27 B.C.; d. 17 B.C.

   B4. Wang Ch'ung: full brother of the Empress. Marquis of An-ch'eng in 32 B.C.; d. 28 B.C.

   B5. Wang Shang: half-brother of the Empress. Marquis of Ch'eng-tu in 27 B.C.; d. 12 B.C.

   B6. Wang Li: half-brother of the Empress. Marquis of Hung-yang in 27 B.C.; d. A.D. 3.

B7. Wang Ken: half-brother of the Empress. Marquis of Ch'ü-yang in 27 B.C.; d. 6 B.C. or 2 B.C.

B8. Wang Feng-shih: half-brother of the Empress. Marquis of Kao-p'ing in 27 B.C.; d. 10 B.C.

BB. Wang Yin: cousin of the Empress. Marquis of An-yang in 20 B.C.; d. 15 B.C.

C. Wang Mang: son of Wang Man, nephew of the Empress. Marquis of Hsin-tu in 16 B.C.; d. A.D. 23.

[3] Wang Yin (CHS, 98, 4b–5a; 18, 26b; 19B, 44a; JMT, p. 111). When Wang Feng was dying he recommended to Emperor Ch'eng that he choose Wang Yin to succeed as Commander-in-Chief instead of any of the brothers. Wang Yin was thus the controlling member of the family from 23 B.C. until his death in 15 B.C.

[4] At this time the living half-brothers of the Empress Dowager were Wang T'an, Shang, Li, Ken, and Feng-shih. They were known as "the five marquises." (CHS, 98, 2b.)

時數有災異議者歸咎放等於是丞相宣御史大夫方
進奏放驕蹇縱恣奢淫不制前侍御史修等四人奉使至
放家逐名捕賊時放見在奴從者閉門設兵弩射吏距使
者不肯內知男子李游君欲獻女使樂府音監景武強求
不得使奴康等之其家賊傷三人又以縣官事怨樂府游
徼莽而使大奴駿等四十餘人羣黨盛兵弩白晝入樂府
攻射官寺縛束長吏子弟斫破器物官中皆犇走伏匿莽
自髡鉗衣赭衣及守令史調等皆徒跣叩頭謝放放乃止
奴從者支屬並乘權勢爲暴虐至求吏妻不得殺其夫或
恚一人妄殺其親屬輒亡入放第不得幸得勿治

At this time there were several calamities and wonders,[2] and those who deliberated about them put the blame on [Chang] Fang[3] and his like. Thereupon Chancellor [Hsieh] Hsüan and Grandee Secretary [Chai] Fang-chin memorialized [that Chang] Fang was arrogant, self-indulgent, prodigal and debauched without restraint.

Formerly Assistant Secretary Hsiu and others, four in all, had been commissioned to go to [Chang] Fang's house to arrest thieves wanted by name. [Chang] Fang was there at the time. The male slaves attending him locked the gates, set up military crossbows, shot at the officials, resisted the commissioners and would not permit them entrance.

When he learned that a commoner,[4] Li Yü-chün, planned to present his daughter [to court, Chang Fang] unsuccessfully sent Ching Wu, the Inspector of Musicians in the Bureau of Music, to get her by force [for himself]. He then sent a male slave, K'ang, and others, to his [Li Yü-chün's] house. They broke in and wounded three people.

Also, hating Mang, the Police Chief of the Bureau of Music, because of some governmental affair, he ordered his senior male slave, Chün, and forty or more others, a gang equipped with military crossbows, to enter the Bureau of Music in broad daylight. They attacked and shot up the offices, tied up the youngsters of the Chief

Official, and smashed the furnishings. All those in the women's quarters fled and hid. Mang personally shaved his head, put on an iron collar, and dressed himself in russet clothes,[5] and together with the administrator, assistant, and clerks, T'iao and others, all barefoot, knocked his head on the ground and asked forgiveness of [Chang] Fang. [Chang] Fang then stopped.

His male slave attendants and his dependents all took advantage of his power and influence to commit oppressive and ruthless acts, even going so far as to seek the wife of an official, and when they did not get her, to murder her husband. Once, bearing a grudge against one person, they madly murdered the whole family, and immediately hid in [Chang] Fang's mansion so they could not be caught. They were lucky to escape punishment.

[1] The first date is when Chang Fang inherited the marquisate (CHS, 18, 9b); 15 B.C. is the date of the memorial, for during only a few months of that year did the terms of office of Chancellor Hsieh Hsüan and Grandee Secretary Chai Fang-chin overlap (CHS, 19B, 46b).

[2] For the year 15 B.C., there is a record of meteorites falling like rain, and an eclipse of the sun, about which the Emperor made an edict (CHS, 10, 5b).

[3] Chang Fang (CHS, 59, 5b–6b; JMT, p. 939) was a fourth generation descendant of Chang An-shih (cf. 71 for an account of the latter's prestige, wealth, and many slaves). He was Emperor Ch'eng's cousin and catamite, and the Empress was his wife's aunt. The Emperor called him a son, and gave him a mansion, chariots, clothes, and jewelry. When he married, the Empress gave him girls (probably slaves) from the government and from her private bureau. He is said to have received as much as a thousand myriad cash in gifts. He was inseparable from the Emperor, accompanying him on his incognito journeys (cf. 104), and was enthusiastic about cock-fighting and horse-racing. These facts explain his arrogance and self-indulgence, and the power of his dependents.

Because of the opposition of the Empress Dowager, however, and because of the present memorial, which goes on to prove that his conduct upset the cosmic forces of yin and yang, thereby causing calamities and wonders, the Emperor had to send him away from the capital. During the next eight years he was several times called back and given high office, and then demoted because of the remonstrances of important ministers. When Emperor Ch'eng died Chang Fang died of grief.

[4] A commentary in HHS, 80, 2b, defines nan-tzu as a person without rank or office.

[5] The costume of a convict.

101. Ca. 20–18 B.C.[1] CHS, 97B, 5a (9a)

孝成趙皇后本長安官人初生時父母不舉三日不死
廼收養之及壯屬陽阿主家學歌舞號曰飛燕成帝嘗微
行出過陽阿主作樂上見飛燕而說之召入宮大幸

The Empress [*née*] Chao[2] of Emperor Ch'eng was originally a
Palace [slave[3]] Woman of Ch'ang-an. When she was born her father
and mother did not feed her, [but when after] three days she did not
die, they then took her and nourished her. When mature she
belonged to the household of the Princess of Yang-a.[4] She studied
singing and dancing and was called [Chao] Fei-yen. Once on an
incognito journey Emperor Ch'eng went to visit the Princess of
Yang-a. During the festivities the Emperor saw [Chao] Fei-yen
and was delighted with her. She was summoned into the palace,
and was greatly favored [by the Emperor].

[1] The date when Chao Fei-yen, a slave-girl entertainer in the household of
the Princess of Yang-a, was discovered by Emperor Ch'eng. His first incognito
journey was late in 20 B.C. (CHS, 10, 4b). The Empress *née* Hsü was deposed on
January 6, 17 B.C. (CHS, 10, 5a). This incident occurred between the two dates.

[2] The Empress *née* Chao (CHS, 97B, 5a–8a) is better known as Chao Fei-
yen (Chao "the Flying Swallow") (JMT, p. 1406; Giles B, 151—but very unre-
liable here). After the incidents in her life here translated, Chao Fei-yen and her
sister became Emperor Ch'eng's favorite concubines, and on July 12, 16 B.C.,
Chao Fei-yen was made Empress and her sister became the Brilliant Companion
(*Chao-i*). The palaces built for these sisters surpassed in lavishness anything
before known. The two women had a dominant control over the Emperor for
ten years, and although neither bore a son, the Brilliant Companion was instru-
mental in doing away with two sons born to the Emperor by other women. Since
the Emperor had no heir, the Empress Dowager *née* Fu bribed Chao Fei-yen
and her sister to have her grandson, Liu Hsin, chosen as Heir-apparent. The
next year Emperor Ch'eng died very suddenly under highly suspicious circumstances (April 15, 7 B.C.). Among the people there was great suspicion that
the Brilliant Companion was responsible for his death. The Grand Empress
Dowager *née* Wang commanded her nephew Wang Mang, Chancellor K'ung
Kuang, and Grandee Secretary Ho Wu, to assemble the Chief and Assistant Chiefs
of the Concubines' Quarter, servants in the Quarter, and the waiters at the last
feast. The Grandee Secretary, the Chancellor, and the Commandant of Justice
were then to hold an investigation concerning the late Emperor's habits and the
circumstances of his death. At this, the Brilliant Companion promptly committed
suicide. Part of the findings of this investigation is translated in *107*. In Feb-
ruary/March, 6 B.C., Chao Fei-yen's two brothers were dismissed from their
marquisates and banished. Chao Fei-yen was allowed to stay in the palace until
1 B.C., when by the order of Wang Mang she was demoted to the rank of commoner
and banished. She committed suicide.

[3] Yen Shih-ku says: "Originally a Palace Woman, she was presented to the
household of the Princess of Yang-a. The term *kung-jen* ["Palace Woman"] was
the name for government slave women who were servants in the forbidden parts
of the palaces. They were called *kung-jen* [because they] were not in the Emperor's

418

Concubines' Quarter. The matter is noted in the *Han chiu i*. [The text] says [she was a] Ch'ang-an [*kung-jen*] to differentiate [where she lived] from the Kan-ch'üan and various other forbidden palaces." (Cf. *91* and *92*.)

⁴ She was probably a sister or half-sister of Emperor Ch'eng, though there seems to be no biography of her.

---

102. 18 B.C. CHS, 17, 17b (25b)

侯夷吾嗣鴻嘉三年坐婢自贖爲民後略以爲婢免

Marquis [Su] I-wu¹ inherited [the Marquisate of P'u]. In 18 B.C. he was tried [in the following case]: A slave woman herself had purchased her freedom and become a commoner. Later he kidnaped her and made her his slave woman [again]. He was deposed.

¹ Su I-wu was the son of Su Ch'ang (CHS, 90, 6a), an official who co-operated in capturing Kung-sun Yung and Hu Ch'ien, who were fomenting rebellion in 90 B.C. As a reward Emperor Wu gave him the Marquisate of P'u (in P'u hsien, or P'u-tzu hsien, in Shansi), with the income from 1,026 households. Nothing else is known of the father, and all that is recorded of the son is here translated.

---

103. 16 B.C. CHS, 16, 9b (12b)

侯獲嗣永始元年坐使奴殺人減死完爲城旦

Marquis [Hsiao] Huo¹ inherited [the Marquisate of Tsan-wen-chung]. In 16 B.C. he was tried for causing a male slave to kill a man. His sentence was reduced from execution to guarding the frontier.

¹ Hsiao Huo (CHS, 39, 3b) was the seventh generation descendant of Hsiao Ho (SC, 53, 1a–3a; CHS, 39, 1a–3b; JMT, p. 1646), the great minister of Kao-tsu. CHS, 39, 3b, gives the same facts, and is not separately translated.

成帝鴻嘉永始之間好爲微行出游選從期門郎有材
力者及私奴客多至十餘少五六人皆白衣袒幘帶持刀
劍或乘小車御者在茵上或皆騎出入市里郊壄遠至旁
縣時大臣車騎將軍王音及劉向等數以切諫谷永曰易
稱得臣無家言王者臣天下無私家也今陛下棄萬乘之
至貴樂家人之賤事厭高美之尊稱好匹夫之卑字崇聚
票輕無誼之人以爲私客置私田於民間畜私奴車馬於
北宮

Emperor Ch'eng, during the period 20 to 12 B.C., liked to take incognito journeys.[1] Going out for sport, he chose as escort able and strong Gentlemen Gate Guards and some private male slaves and guests, at most ten or more men, or as few as five or six. All were in plain clothes, capless, and carrying swords in their girdles. Sometimes [Emperor Ch'eng] mounted a small carriage with the driver sitting on the [very same] cushion, sometimes all would ride horseback, going through markets and villages and into the country-side as far as the neighboring prefectures.

At this time the great ministers, General of Chariots and Cavalry Wang Yin[2] and Liu Hsiang[3] several times severely criticized this [behavior]. Ku Yung[4] said: "The *Yi* [*Ching*] says: 'Acquiring subjects one gives up household [affairs],' meaning that the ruler makes subjects of the whole empire and has no private household [affairs]. But now Your Majesty casts aside the most honorable [affairs of] state, and delights in the mean affairs of a householder;[5] wearied with the lofty beauty of Your honorable title, You adopt and enjoy the vulgar appellation of a common man.[6] You honor and assemble flighty and improper folk to be Your private guests, and set up private fields amidst those of the people, and accumulate private male slaves, carriages and horses within the Northern Palace."[7]

[1] CHS, 10, 4b, under the year 20 B.C., says: "The Emperor for the first time left on an incognito journey." The commentator Chang Yen (third century A.D.) says: "He went out of the rear gate escorted by ten or more Gentlemen Gate Guards and private male slaves and guests, in plain clothes and turbans, and riding horseback through markets and villages without having the roads cleared, as though

it were unimportant ordinary business.   Therefore it is called 'an incognito journey.' "

² Cf. *99*, footnote 3.   According to CHS, 19B, 44a, Wang Yin was General of Chariots and Cavalry from 22 to 15 B.C., when he died.   Thus the date is limited to the period between 20 and 15 B.C.

³ Cf. *67*, footnote 4.

⁴ Ku Yung (CHS, 85, 1a–9a; JMT, p. 506) was an important literary figure and associate of Ching Fang in studying calamities and unnatural phenomena, and frequently censured the Emperor and the court for causing calamities by their improper behavior.

⁵ Commenting on this phrase in CHS, 85, 6a, Yen Shih-ku says: "It means that he privately accumulated fields, together with male and female slaves, and goods."

⁶ Ju Shun (fl. ca. A.D. 189–265) says: "He called himself 'Chang Fang's house-holder.'   This was a lowly appellation."   Chang Fang was the favorite with whom he often took these journeys (cf. *100*).   Yen Shih-ku says: "Because he was making an incognito journey he changed his surname and name."   Meng K'ang, in CHS, 85, 6a, says: "Emperor Ch'eng liked incognito journeys, and, moreover, coined nicknames for [him and his friends] to call each other."

⁷ There follows a harangue on how the Emperor left the palace to carouse with low characters so that his ministers could not keep track of him.

Ku Yung's memorial is given more fully in his own biography (CHS, 85). He urged the Emperor, among other things (p. 6b), to "cut Yourself off from the crowd of base private guests, and dismiss those improperly decreed appointees; completely abolish from the Northern Palace Your private male slaves, carriages, and horses—the equipment for Your idle excursions; subdue Yourself and return to proper ceremonial behavior, and do not again commit the error of incognito journeys and drinking excursions—[do these things] in order to guard against imminent calamity . . . ."

又曰聖王明禮制以序尊卑異車服以章有德雖有其
財而無其尊不得踰制故民興行上義而下利方今世俗
奢僭罔極靡有厭足公卿列侯親屬近臣四方所則未聞
修身遵禮同心憂國者也或迺奢侈逸豫務廣第宅治園
池多畜奴婢被服綺縠設鐘鼓備女樂車服嫁娶葬埋過
制吏民慕效寖以成俗而欲望百姓儉節家給人足豈不
難哉詩不云乎赫赫師尹民具爾瞻其申敕有司以漸禁
之青綠民所常服且勿止列侯近臣各自省改司隸校尉
察不變者

[In July, 13 B.C., Emperor Ch'eng in a decree] further said: "The saint-kings clarified ceremonial conduct and official regulations in order to arrange into classes the noble and humble folk; they differentiated carriages and clothing in order to make manifest those with [noble] virtue. Although one had the corresponding wealth but lacked the proper noble rank, one could not overstep these regulations. Therefore the people prospered, emphasizing righteousness and belittling profit. Now social custom is extravagant without limit, there being no satisfaction with mere sufficiency. Among the dukes, ministers, imperial relatives, and close ministers, the very pattern of society, I do not hear of any who cultivate their persons, observe the rites, and are wholeheartedly exercised about [the condition of] the state. Some among them are extravagant and neglectful; busy with expanding their mansions and houses, setting out gardens and pools, accumulating numerous male and female slaves, dressing them in fancy silks, setting out bells and drums, providing female orchestras, carriages, clothing, marriages, and funerals and tombs beyond the regulations. Lesser officials and common people admire and emulate them [until such extravagance] gradually becomes the custom. But [under such conditions] to hope for the people to be temperate and frugal, with families self-sufficient and everyone satisfied—is this not difficult? Do not the *Odes* say:

Awe-inspiring are you, O [Grand-] master Yin,
And the people all look to you![1]

422

Let it be announced to the proper officials to prohibit gradually [the above offenses]. Let the people not stop wearing their regular clothing of blue and green. Let the marquises and close ministers examine themselves and mend their conduct. Let the Colonel over the Retainers judicially investigate those who do not change."

[1] Legge, *Chinese classics*, vol. IV, p. 309. The poem is "a lamentation over the miserable state of the kingdom, denouncing the injustice and carelessness of the Grand-master Yin as the cause of it . . . ." Thus, the quotation of this poem in the decree of Emperor Ch'eng is very apt.

---

106. 24–8 B.C.[1] CHS, 47, 4a; 4b (9b; 10b)

元延中立復以公事怨相掾及睢陽丞使奴殺之殺奴
以滅口凡殺三人傷五人手毆郎吏二十餘人上書不拜
奏謀篡死罪囚有司請誅上不忍削立五縣…立惶恐免
冠對曰立少失父母孤弱處深宮中獨與宦者婢妾居

Between 12 and 8 B.C. [Liu] Li,[2] [King of Liang,] was again angered at the officials of his chancery and at the Assistant [Prefect] of Sui-yang over public business, and caused a male slave to assassinate them. He killed the male slave to silence him. In all he killed three people and wounded five. With his fists he beat twenty or more Gentlemen and officials. When he sent up a document [to the Emperor] he did not prostrate himself in memorializing. He plotted [illegally] to take away prisoners sentenced to death.[3] The officials begged for his execution, but the Emperor could not bear to [consent, but only] reduced [the jurisdiction of Liu] Li by five prefectures . . . .

[A few years later when he was being tried for other crimes, Liu] Li became terrified, doffed his ceremonial cap, and replied: "When I was small I lost my father and mother. A weak orphan, I lived in the depths of the palace with only eunuchs, slave women, and concubines about me."

[1] The second paragraph refers to events after the death of Liu Li's father in 25 B.C.; the events of the first paragraph occurred between 12 and 8 B.C.

[2] Liu Li (CHS, 47, 3b–4b; and 14, 9b) was a descendant of Emperor Wen, eight generations removed. He inherited the Kingdom of Liang in 24 B.C. and was deposed in A.D. 3 and committed suicide. Liang was in present eastern Honan, with its capital at Sui-yang, south of present Shang-ch'iu hsien.

[3] The meaning of this sentence would be obscure but for the fact that it is used elsewhere in a way which shows that it had a special legal meaning (cf. Ch'eng Shu-te, *Chiu ch'ao lü k'ao*, "Han lü k'ao," p. 137).

後數月司隸解光奏言臣聞許美人及故中宮史曹宮
皆御幸孝成皇帝產子子隱不見臣遣從事掾業史塹驗
問知狀者掖庭獄丞籍武故中黃門王舜吳恭靳嚴官婢
曹曉道房張棄故趙昭儀御者于客子王偏臧兼等皆曰
宮卽曉子女前屬中宮爲學事史通詩授皇后房與宮對
食元延元年中宮語房曰陛下幸宮後數月曉入殿中見
宮腹大問宮宮曰御幸有身其十月中宮乳掖庭牛官令
舍有婢六人中黃門田客特詔記盛綠綈方底封御史中
丞印予武曰取牛官令舍婦人新產兒婢六人盡置暴室
獄母問兒男女誰兒也武迎置獄官曰善臧我兒胞丞知
是何等兒也後三日客持詔記與武問兒死未手書對牘
背武卽書對兒見在未死有頃客出曰上與昭儀大怒奈
何不殺武叩頭啼曰不殺兒自知當死殺之亦死卽因客
奏封事曰陛下未有繼嗣子無貴賤惟留意奏入客復持
詔記予武曰今夜漏上五刻持兒與舜會東交掖門武因
問客陛下得武書意何如曰憛也武以兒付舜舜受詔內

Several months later[2] Colonel over the Retainers Chieh Kuang[3] memorialized, saying:[4] Your servant has heard that Beauty Hsü[5] and the late Middle Palace clerk Ts'ao Kung[6] were both imperially favored by [the late] Emperor Hsiao-Ch'eng and bore sons. These sons were concealed and disappeared. Your servant dispatched his assistant official, Yeh, and his clerk, Wang,[7] to investigate and question those who know the circumstances. The assistant at the prison in the Concubines' Quarter, Chi Wu, the former inner Yellow Gate [Eunuchs], Wang Shun, Wu Kung, and Chin Yen, the government female slaves, Ts'ao Hsiao, Tao Fang, and Chang Ch'i, and the personal ones of the late Brilliant Companion [*née*] Chao,[8] Yü K'o-tzu, Wang P'ien, and Tsang Chien, and others all say:[9]

[Ts'ao] Kung, that is, [Ts'ao] Hsiao's daughter, was formerly attached to the Middle Palace as a student clerk, was competent in

poetry, and taught the Empress [*née* Chao. Tao] Fang and [Ts'ao]
Kung had a homosexual attachment.[10]   Around the middle of 12
B.C. [Ts'ao] Kung told [Tao] Fang: "His Majesty has favored me,
Kung."   Several months later [Ts'ao] Hsiao came into the Hall
and observed that [her daughter, Ts'ao] Kung was great with child,
and asked [Ts'ao] Kung about it.   [Ts'ao] Kung said: "I was imperially favored and have a child."

In the middle of her tenth month [Ts'ao] Kung gave birth [to
a son] in the house of the Chief of the Bureau of Oxen in the Concubines' Quarter.   She had six slave women [in attendance].   The
inner Yellow Gate [Eunuch] T'ien K'o[11] carried a personal edict[12]
contained in a heavy green silk, square-bottomed [envelope], and
sealed with the seal of the Assistant Palace Secretary, and gave it
to [Chi] Wu.   It said: "Take the woman in the house of the Chief
of the Bureau of Oxen, her newborn child, and the six slave women,
and place them all in the *Pao* house prison.[13]   Do not ask whether
the child is a boy or a girl, nor whose child it is."   [Chi] Wu received
[the group] and put it in the prison.   [Ts'ao] Kung said: "It would
be well to save my child's placenta.   You, Assistant, know what
rank of child this is!"

Three days later [T'ien] K'o carried a personal edict to [Chi]
Wu.   It asked: "Has the child died or not?   Answer in your own
handwriting on the back of this slip." [14]   [Chi] Wu immediately
wrote the reply: "The child is still here and has not died."   After
a moment [T'ien] K'o came out [of the Emperor's quarters] and said:
"The Emperor and the Brilliant Companion are very angry.   Why
did you not kill [the child]?"   [Chi] Wu kotowed and said weeping:
"If I did not kill the child I knew I should die; and if I killed it I
should also die."   By the agency of [T'ien] K'o he forthwith presented
a confidential memorial on the matter, saying: "Your Majesty has
no heir.   It is Your son irrespective of the nobility or humbleness
[of the mother].   Only consider it."   The memorial was taken in
[to the Emperor].

[T'ien] K'o again carried a personal edict and gave it to [Chi]
Wu.   It said: "Tonight when the water-clock reaches the fifth mark,
take the child and give it to [Wang] Shun.   Meet him at the side
gate of the eastern crossing."   [Chi] Wu inquired of [T'ien] K'o:
"When His Majesty received Wu's letter what appeared to be his
reaction?"   [T'ien K'o] said: "He stared." [15]

[Chi] Wu handed over the child to [Wang] Shun.   [Wang] Shun
received an imperial edict to put the child into one of the Halls, select

兒殿中爲擇乳母告善養兒且有賞母令漏泄舜擇棄爲
乳母時兒生八九日後三日客復持詔記封如前予武中
有封小綠篋記曰告武以篋中物書予獄中婦人武自臨
飲之武發篋中有裏藥二枚赫蹏書曰告偉能努力飲此
藥不可復入女自知之偉能即宮宮讀書已曰果也欲姊
弟擅天下我兒男也頷上有壯髮類孝元皇帝今兒安在
危殺之矣奈何令長信得聞之宮飲藥死後宮婢六人召
入出語武曰昭儀言女無過寧自殺邪若外家也我曹言
願自殺即自繆死武皆表奏狀棄所養兒十一日宮長李
南以詔書取兒去不知所置

　許美人前在上林涿沐館數召入飾室中若舍一歲再
三召留數月或半歲御幸元延二年褢子其十一月乳詔
使嚴持乳醫及五種和藥丸三送美人所後客子偏兼聞
昭儀謂成帝曰常紿我言從中宮來即從中宮來許美人
兒何從生中許氏竟當復立邪懟以手自擣以頭擊壁戶
柱從牀上自投地啼泣不肯食曰今當安置我欲歸耳帝
曰今故告之反怒爲殊不可曉也帝亦不食昭儀曰陛下

a wet-nurse for it, and to instruct her to nourish the child well, for
which there would be a reward, but not to let the matter leak out.
[Wang] Shun selected [Chang] Ch'i as its wet-nurse. At this time the
child had been born eight or nine days.

Three days later [T'ien] K'o again carried a personal edict,
sealed as before, and gave it to [Chi] Wu. Inside there was a small
green sealed container. The inscription said: "Tell [Chi] Wu to
take the things and the letter in the container and give them to
the woman in the prison. [Chi] Wu is personally to watch her drink
it." [Chi] Wu opened the container. Inside there were two packets
of wrapped medicine and a thin letter in red, which said: "I tell
you, Wei-nung, to drink this medicine with determination. You
may not enter [my presence] again. You yourself know why."
(Wei-nung was [Ts'ao] Kung.)

[Ts'ao] Kung read the letter to the end and said: "Just as I expected. [The Emperor] desires the sisters[16] to dominate the empire. My child is a boy; on his forehead there is stiff hair like that of [the late] Emperor Hsiao-Yüan. Now where is my child? He is in danger of being murdered. How can I let the Ch'ang-hsin [Palace, i.e., the Empress Dowager *née* Wang[17]] hear of it?" [Ts'ao] Kung drank the medicine and died.

Later [Ts'ao] Kung's six female slaves were summoned to enter [the palace]. When they came out they told [Chi] Wu: "The Brilliant Companion said: 'You are not to blame. Would you rather commit suicide or [go to some] outside house [to die[18]]?' We said: 'We choose to commit suicide.'" They forthwith strangled themselves and died.

[Chi] Wu stated the circumstances of each case in a memorial. [Chang] Ch'i nursed the child for eleven days. The Chief of the Palace, Li Nan, by [authority of] a personal edict, took the child away. It is not known where it was put.

The Beauty [*née*] Hsü was formerly at the Cho-mu lodge at Shang-lin [park], and was several times summoned to enter the Ornamented Chamber as though housed there. During a year she was summoned [to the Emperor] again and again, and stayed several months or half a year. She was imperially favored. In 11 B.C. she conceived, and in her eleventh month gave birth [to a son]. An imperial edict ordered [Chin] Yen to take a midwife and three pills of the five kinds of mixed medicine and deliver them to Beauty [Hsü's] place.

Later [Yü] K'o-tzu, [Wang] P'ien, and [Tsang] Chien overheard the Brilliant Companion say to Emperor Ch'eng: "You always deceived me in saying you had come from the Middle Palace. If you came from the Middle Palace how did Beauty Hsü's child come to be born in the palace?[19] Will [one of the] Hsü clan finally be established again [as Empress]?" She angrily beat herself with her fists, pounded her head against the door pillar, threw herself from the bed to the floor, howled and wept, and refused to eat. Then she said: "Now what are you going to do with me? I want to return home."

The Emperor said: "Now, I purposely told you about this [child], but in return you get angry. I simply cannot make you understand." The Emperor likewise would not eat.

自知是不食謂何陛下常自言約不負女今美人有子竟
負約謂何帝曰約以趙氏故不立許氏使天下無出趙氏
上者毋憂也後詔使嚴持綠囊書予許美人告嚴曰美人
當有以予女受來置飾室中簾南美人以葦篋一合盛所
生兒緘封及綠囊報書予嚴嚴持篋書置飾室簾南去帝
與昭儀坐使客子解篋緘未已帝使客子偏兼皆出自閉
戶獨與昭儀在須臾開戶漉客子偏兼使緘封篋及綠綈
方底推置屏風東恭受詔持篋方底予武皆封以御史中
丞印曰告武篋中有死兒理屏處勿令人知武穿獄樓垣
下為坎埋其中

故長定許貴人及故成都平阿侯家婢王業任孃公孫
習前免為庶人詔召入屬昭儀為私婢成帝崩未幸梓宮
倉卒悲哀之時昭儀自知罪惡大知業等故許氏王氏婢
恐事泄而以大婢羊子等賜予業等各且十人以慰其意
屬無道我家過失

The Brilliant Companion said: "Your Majesty yourself knows
[that you are in the wrong]. Why should you refuse to eat? Your
Majesty yourself has always said: 'I promise not to go back on you.'
But now that Beauty [Hsü] has a child, doesn't it mean that you
will finally go back on your promise?"

The Emperor said: "I promised for the sake of the Chao clan
not to establish [a member of] the Hsü clan [as Empress], or to
allow anyone in the empire to exceed the Chao clan. Do not worry."

Later an imperial edict ordered [Chin] Yen to carry a letter in
a green bag and give it to Beauty Hsü, and instructed [Chin] Yen,
saying: "The Beauty should give you something. Bring it back
and put it in the Ornamented Chamber, south of the screen." The
Beauty took a reed basket, put her child in it, tied and sealed it,
and gave it to [Chin] Yen with a return letter in the green bag.
[Chin] Yen carried the basket and the letter, put them south of the
screen in the Ornamented Chamber, and left.

The Emperor was sitting with the Brilliant Companion, and ordered [Yü] K'o-tzu to loosen the cords of the basket. Before she had finished, the Emperor ordered [Yü] K'o-tzu, [Wang] P'ien, and [Tsang] Chien all to go out, and personally closed the door. Only the Brilliant Companion was with him. After a moment he opened the door and called [Yü] K'o-tzu, [Wang] P'ien, and [Tsang] Chien, and ordered them to tie and seal the basket and a heavy green silk, square-bottomed [envelope], and to put them east of the door screen. They respectfully received an imperial edict, and took the basket and the square-bottomed [envelope] and gave them to [Chi] Wu. Both were sealed with the seal of the Assistant Palace Secretary, and [the edict] said: "Tell [Chi] Wu that in this basket there is a dead child. Bury it in a hidden place, and do not let anyone know."

[Chi] Wu dug a hole near the wall of the prison building and buried the child therein.

Wang Yeh, Jen Li, and Kung-sun Hsi, the household female slaves of the late Noblewoman Hsü of Ch'ang-ting [Palace], and of the late marquises of Ch'eng-tu and P'ing-a,[20] had formerly been freed and made commoners. An imperial edict had summoned them to enter [the palace] and be attached to the Brilliant Companion as her private female slaves.[21] When Emperor Ch'eng died but had not yet been placed in his coffin, during the unsettled time of mourning and grief, the Brilliant Companion herself knew that her crimes and wickedness were great. Knowing that [Wang] Yeh and the others had been the female slaves of the late [Noblewoman] Hsü and the Wangs, she feared her doings would leak out. So she presented her chief female slave, Yang-tzu, and others to [Wang] Yeh and the others—[giving] each of them about ten—in order to curb their intentions, and enjoined them: "Do not reveal the faults and failings of me [and my] family." [22]

[1] The dates of the two principal events involving slaves were 12 and 11 B.C. Some of the slaves acted as witnesses in 7 B.C.

[2] The background for this passage is as follows (cf. also *101*, footnote 2): On April 15, 7 B.C., Emperor Ch'eng died suddenly, under highly suspicious circumstances. The Chancellor, Grandee Secretary, and Commandant of Justice undertook an investigation, in the course of which they questioned the Chief and Assistant Chief of the Concubines' Quarter, servants in the Quarter, and the waiters at the last meal the Emperor had eaten before he died, concerning his living habits and the circumstances of his death. The investigation probably continued during most of the rest of the year, for final action was not taken until February/March, 6 B.C. It must have turned up a great deal of information. One group of facts revealed how the Emperor's favorite concubine, the Brilliant Companion *née* Chao, had persuaded the Emperor to do away with his two sons,

so that he died without an heir. This was very grave business indeed. The facts are gathered in this single memorial.

A document of such importance must have been carefully filed among the state archives, and when it came into the hands of the historians they recognized its value for the memoir on the Empress *née* Chao and her family. There is no reason to doubt the historicity of the incidental references to slaves contained in the memorial, and the information is of unusual value.

[3] Chieh Kuang is also mentioned in CHS, 75, 13a, and 98, 5b (cf. *111*). The Colonel over the Retainers seems to have been a censor of social custom at the capital (CHS, 19A, 6a–b; cf. *95*, footnote 2).

[4] From this point, everything is part of the memorial itself.

[5] Beauty Hsü was related to the Empress *née* Hsü, who had been deposed in 17 B.C. She was mother of the Emperor's son, as recounted in the second part of the memorial. The title *mei-jen*, "Beauty," was given to imperial concubines of second rank. It is not told what became of her after this incident, but she was apparently still living at the time of the memorial for she is not spoken of as the late Beauty Hsü.

[6] Ts'ao Kung was the mother of the Emperor's son, as told in the first part of the memorial. She was the daughter of the slave woman Ts'ao Hsiao, and was herself probably a slave, for she was attached to the Middle Palace, i.e., to the Empress *née* Chao. She had been trained as a clerk, and was competent in poetry (or the *Odes*). After she bore the Emperor's son she was forced to commit suicide.

[7] Yen Shih-ku says that these were their personal names, and that their surnames are not given.

[8] The Brilliant Companion *née* Chao (cf. *101*, footnote 2) was the younger sister of the Empress *née* Chao (Chao Fei-yen). When the investigation was started regarding the suspiciously sudden death of the Emperor she immediately committed suicide.

[9] From this point, the memorial presents in chronological order the two stories, assembled from the combined evidence given by the ten people mentioned. What follows is not a direct quotation from any one of these people. For convenience the two stories are separated, though there is no formal division in the text.

It is useful to identify these ten people and to distinguish the parts they played in the two stories, about which they were able to give evidence.

(1) Chi Wu was a principal character in both stories because of his position as Assistant at the Prison in the Concubines' Quarter. In the first story he had to lodge Ts'ao Kung in his prison and give an account of the child. He was brave enough to protest to the Emperor against slaying the child. He delivered it to Wang Shun. He had to carry to Ts'ao Kung her death sentence, and see that she committed suicide. He also heard from the six female slaves that they had been ordered to commit suicide, and reported on their death. In the second story he buried the dead child.

(2) Wang Shun was probably a palace eunuch, although the term "Yellow Gate" did not exclusively mean so in Han times (cf. *41*, footnote 3). He received Ts'ao Kung's child and was charged with selecting a wet-nurse for it.

(3) Wu Kung does not specifically figure in either story, but as a palace eunuch he probably played some minor part.

(4) Chin Yen, the third palace eunuch, figured in the second story. He took Beauty Hsü's child from her and delivered it to the Emperor.

(5) Ts'ao Hsiao, a government slave woman, was the mother of Ts'ao Kung, and was the first to notice her pregnancy. Ts'ao Kung told her mother that she was pregnant by the Emperor.

(6) Tao Fang, another government slave woman, was Ts'ao Kung's dearest friend, and was the first to hear that she had had relations with the Emperor.

(7) Chang Ch'i, a third government slave woman, was chosen by Wang Shun to be the wet-nurse of the child in the first story. She nursed the child for eleven days, and was the last, among those who gave evidence, to see the child alive.

(8–10) Yü K'o-tzu, Wang P'ien, and Tsang Chien were personal attendants of the Brilliant Companion *née* Chao, and were probably slaves. They overheard the quarrel between her and the Emperor concerning Beauty Hsü's child, and gave important circumstantial evidence that the Emperor himself had killed the child. They took the dead child to Chi Wu for burial.

[10] 食 is sometimes a euphemism for sexual intercourse. See a discussion on this point by Wen I-to ("Kao T'ang shen nu chuan shuo chih fen hsi," CHHP, 10, No. 4). Ying Shao (ca. 140–206 A.D.) says: "When palace women attach themselves as husband and wife it is called *tui shih*. They are intensely jealous of each other."

[11] T'ien K'o is not listed as one who gave evidence and may have died before the investigation. He figures in the first story only. He received orders directly from the Emperor, and had access to him, for he told Chi Wu how the Emperor looked when he read Chi Wu's remonstrance against killing the child.

[12] Wang Hsien-ch'ien says that the difference between a "personal edict" and a *chao-shu*, "edict-document," is that the first is in the Emperor's handwriting, while the other is written by a subordinate and has an imperial seal for authentication.

[13] Ying Shao (CHS, 8, 1b) defines the *Pao* house as the prison for Palace Women. According to Yen Shih-ku it got its name from the fact that it was the part of the Concubines' Quarter where silk was dried in the sun after it had been steamed or dyed.

Wang Hsien-ch'ien says that the next word, *mu*, "mother," is a mistake for *wu*, "do not," and that the error is found in all texts. A good translation can be made using *mu* ("The prison matron asked," etc. . . .), but considering the sequence of events, Wang Hsien-ch'ien's emendation is most sensible.

[14] Yen Shih-ku says it was a wooden memo slip. Probably the answer was to be in Chi Wu's own writing for future evidence.

[15] The implication seems to be that the Emperor was much upset but was helpless, and therefore simply stared straight ahead.

[16] I.e., the Empress *née* Chao (Chao Fei-yen) and her sister, the Brilliant Companion.

[17] The Ch'ang-hsin Palace was where the Empress Dowager lived. She was the Empress *née* Wang of the late Emperor Yüan, and was Emperor Ch'eng's mother.

[18] This is Chin Shao's explanation of a terse and rather puzzling sentence.

[19] Chin Shao and Yen Shih-ku give different explanations of this sentence. I have tried to follow Yen.

[20] Noblewoman Hsü was the former Empress, deposed by Emperor Ch'eng in 17 B.C. She died by suicide in December, 8 B.C. According to Wang Hsien-ch'ien, Ch'ang-ting was the name of the palace where she lived.

The late marquises, Wang Shang and Wang T'an, were half-brothers of the Dowager Empress of Emperor Yüan. Wang Shang had died in 12 B.C., Wang T'an in 17 B.C.

[21] Here is one of the few cases of manumitted Han slaves known by name. It is interesting that these ex-slaves were simply ordered to enter the palace and become private slaves of the imperial favorite. She did not trust their loyalty, and feared they would report her doings to the influential relatives of their former masters. Therefore she presented each of these slave women with ten slave women

of their own as a bribe to keep quiet.   Presumably she also gave them their freedom again.

²² The memorial continues with the recommendation that all members of the Chao family who had been advanced to important positions should be executed in spite of the fact that an intervening general amnesty would legally absolve them from the Brilliant Companion's crimes.   Historical precedents for this recommendation are cited.   The memorial recommends a complete judicial investigation, and a discussion by the high ministers of an appropriate punishment. In February/March, 6 B.C., Emperor Ai dismissed the two brothers of the Empress *née* Chao, the Marquis of Hsin-ch'eng, Chao Ch'in, and the Marquis of Ch'eng-yang, Chao Hsin, and sent them with all their family members and retainers into banishment.   In A.D. 1 the Empress *née* Chao, who was then Grand Empress Dowager, was deposed by Wang Mang and banished.   She committed suicide.

108.   10–8 B.C.[1]   CHS, 99A, 1b (2a)

嘗私買侍婢昆弟或頗聞知莽因曰後將軍朱子元無
子莽聞此兒種宜子爲買之卽日以婢奉子元其匿情求
名如此

[Wang Mang[2]] once privately bought a serving female slave.
Some of his cousins heard rumors of it.   [Wang] Mang thereupon
said: "The General of the Rear, Chu Tzu-yüan,[3] has no sons.   I
have heard that this child is of a fertile stock, and so I bought her
for him."   He immediately presented the female slave to [Chu]
Tzu-yüan.   His clandestine nature and seeking after reputation
were of such a nature.

[1] This passage is dated by the appointment of Chu Tzu-yüan as General of
the Rear in 10 B.C., and by Wang Mang's appointment as Grand Major in 8 B.C.

[2] Wang Mang (CHS, 99; 12; 98, 5b–8a; JMT, p. 129) is the central character
in Chinese history from this time till his death in A.D. 23.   In most of the following
passages he figures importantly.   His biography fills more than fifty double pages
in the edition of the Ch'ien Han shu used for this study.   A really adequate
biographical note is beyond the scope of this work; the reader's attention is directed
to the special bibliography here given.

Wang Mang was the nephew of the Empress née Wang of Emperor Yüan.
He was made Marquis of Hsin-tu in 16 B.C., and in 8 B.C. he succeeded his uncle,
Wang Ken, as leading member of the powerful Wang family.   He was then thirty-
eight years old.   In 7 B.C. Emperor Ch'eng died and the power of the Wang family
went into eclipse.   After the death of Emperor Ai in 1 B.C. Wang Mang and his
aunt, who was by then Great Grand Empress Dowager, began to rebuild the
family influence.   A child was placed on the throne as Emperor P'ing and Wang
Mang was made Imperial Tutor and was given the title An Han kung ("The Duke
Pacifying Han," or "The Duke Protector of Han").   Wang Mang steadily increased his popularity and his power.   After the death of Emperor P'ing early
in A.D. 6, he became regent for an infant, and in A.D. 9 he accepted the throne
and became Emperor.   His dynasty lasted only till his death in A.D. 23.

During his reign Wang Mang introduced many political, social, and economic
changes, but most of them were unsuccessful.   His reign was not officially recognized by later dynasties, and he has generally been treated as a usurper by Chinese
historians.   The author of his biography in the CHS is not entirely objective, and it
is difficult to get a clear impression of Wang Mang's social and economic policies
from a report which is essentially political.

Several biographies or biographical sketches of Wang Mang have appeared.
The following items are particularly useful: Clyde Bailey Sargent, Wang Mang:
A translation of the official account of his rise to power as given in the History of
the Former Han Dynasty (translation of CHS, 99A; in MSS.); Hans O. H. Stange,
Die Monographie über Wang Mang (Ts'ien-Han-shu Kap. 99), Kritisch bearbeitet,
übersetzt und erklärt, Leipzig, Deutsche Morgenländische Gesellschaft, 1939
(Abhandlungen für die Kunde des Morgenlandes, vol. XXIII, pt. 3, 1939); Hans
O. H. Stange, Leben, Persönlichkeit und Werk Wang Mang's, dargestellt nach dem
99. Kapitel der Han-Annalen, Berlin, 1934; Homer H. Dubs, "Wang Mang and
his economic reforms," TP, vol. 35, 1940, pp. 219–265; Léon Wieger, Textes
historiques, Ho-chien Fu, 1903–4, vol. 1, pp. 707–745; Hu Shih, "Wang Mang,

the socialist emperor of nineteen centuries ago," JNCBRAS, vol. 59, 1928, pp. 218–230; O. Franke, "Staatssocialistische Versuche im alten und mittelalterlichen China," *Sitzungsberichte der Preussischen Akademie der Wissenschaften, Phil.-Hist. Klasse*, Berlin, 1931, pp. 218–242. Dr. Dubs plans to publish a complete translation of CHS, 99, as vol. III of his *History of the Former Han Dynasty*.

[3] Chu Po, T. Tzu-yüan (CHS, 83, 5a–8b; 19B, 47a–51a; JMT, p. 260), was a protégé of Wang Feng, and was an important political figure with a good future at this time. He held the following positions and titles: Grand Minister of Agriculture (15 B.C.); Commandery Administrator (14 B.C.); Imperial Household Grandee; Commandant of Justice (11 B.C.); General of the Rear (10–8 B.C.); Administrator of the Capital District (7 B.C.); Grandee Secretary (6 B.C.); and Chancellor (5 B.C.). He was judged guilty of a political crime in 5 B.C., and committed suicide in 3 B.C. He never had a son, and only one daughter. It is somewhat ironic that only a few years after the present event it was Chancellor Chu Po who recommended that Wang Mang be stripped of his titles and made a commoner.

哀帝即位師丹輔政建言古之聖王莫不設井田然後
治迺可平孝文皇帝承亡周亂秦兵革之後天下空虛故
務勸農桑帥以節儉民始充實未有幷兼之害故不為民
田及奴婢為限今累世承平豪富吏民訾數鉅萬而貧弱
俞困蓋君子為政貴因循而重改作然所以有改者將以
救急也亦未可詳宜略為限天子下其議丞相孔光大司
空何武奏請諸侯王列侯皆得名田國中列侯在長安公

When Emperor Ai came to the throne, Shih Tan[1] assisted [the Emperor] in governing. He gave advice, saying: "Among the ancient sage-kings none did not set up the *ching-t'ien* [system of agriculture[2]], so that thereafter governing could be just. When Emperor Hsiao Wen inherited the disorders of the collapse of the Chou dynasty and the aftermath of the Ch'in dynasty wars, the empire was depopulated and desolate. Therefore he emphasized the encouragement of agriculture and sericulture, and led [the people] in temperance and thrift. The people for the first time had an abundance, and there was no evil of simultaneous accumulation [of offices, land, and other sources of income[3]]. Wherefore he did not set limits on people's fields and male and female slaves. Now for several generations there has been peace, and the property of the overbearing and rich officials and common people is counted by the hundred million, while the poor and weak are increasingly distressed. Now, when the princely man is governing he honors continuance and compliance [with antiquity], and seriously weighs instituting reforms; such reforms as are made are for the relief of urgent situations. Moreover it has not yet been possible to go into details; it would be suitable to make some generalized restrictions.

The Emperor referred his advice to the Chancellor, K'ung Kuang,[4] and the Grand Minister of Works, Ho Wu.[5] They memorialized: "We beg that vassal kings and ranking marquises all be allowed to name [i.e., to own] fields within their states; that ranking marquises living at Ch'ang-an, and princesses, who name fields in prefectures

435

主名田縣道及關內侯吏民名田皆毋過三十頃諸侯王
奴婢二百人列侯公主百人關內侯吏民三十人期盡三
年犯者没入官時田宅奴婢買爲減賤丁傅用事董賢隆
貴皆不便也詔書且須後遂寢不行

and border marches, together with *kuan-nei* marquises,[6] officials, and common people, who name fields, [should] all not [be allowed to] exceed thirty *ch'ing*.[7] Vassal kings [should be allowed] two hundred male and female slaves; ranking marquises and princesses [should be allowed] one hundred; *kuan-nei* marquises, officials, and common people [should be allowed] thirty. The time limit [for executing this should be] three years. Law breakers [should have their excess fields and slaves] confiscated by the government."

At this time the price of fields, residences, and male and female slaves depreciated. The Ting and Fu [clans[8]], who dominated affairs, and Tung Hsien,[9] the most eminently honored, were all inconvenienced.[10] An imperial edict temporarily deferred it. Consequently it was abandoned and not put into effect.

[1] Shih Tan (CHS, 86, 7b–10a; 19B, 50a; JMT, p. 773) had been the Grand Tutor of the Heir-apparent who became Emperor Ai, and he was at this time Grand Marshal. His surname was different from the Shih Tan in *97*.

[2] On this system, see *35*, footnote 3.

[3] Cf. *35*, footnote 4.

[4] K'ung Kuang (CHS, 81, 7b–11b; 19B, 46b–56a; JMT, p. 41), T. Tzu-hsia, was a fourteenth generation descendant of Confucius, and a scholar. In 33 B.C. he was made an Erudit, then an Imperial Household Grandee. In 15 B.C. he was appointed Superintendent of the Gentlemen of the Palace and Grandee Secretary in the same year. He held this position until 8 B.C., when he sponsored the unsuccessful candidate for appointment as Heir-apparent, and was accordingly demoted to Commandant of Justice. The next year, however, he became Chancellor and held the position till 5 B.C. when he was retired because of his opposition to the Empress Dowager *née* Fu. In 2 B.C. he became Grandee Secretary again and then Chancellor two months later. Because of his scholarship he was appointed Grand Tutor for young Emperor P'ing. He died in A.D. 5.

[5] Ho Wu (CHS, 86, 1a–3a; 19B, 49b; JMT, p. 289) held this position (which just at this time took the place of Grandee Secretary) for one year from 8 B.C.

[6] *Kuan-nei* marquises were of lower rank than full marquises; they alone had incomes from towns within the pass (HFHD, vol. I, p. 240, footnote 3).

[7] I have tried to translate this sentence very literally, and have left it crude in order to emphasize a point of uncertainty. Seven categories of people are differentiated: kings, marquises, marquises who lived at the capital, princesses, *kuan-nei* marquises, officials, and common people. The uncertainty is whether all seven were limited to 30 *ch'ing* (about 340 acres) of private fields, or whether kings and marquises could own unlimited amounts of land in their own states. Dubs ("Wang Mang and his economic reforms," TP, vol. 35, 1940, p. 246) says: "Kings

and marquises should be allowed unrestricted amounts of private land within their kingdoms and marquisates; outside those areas they should be restricted to 3,000 *mou* (140 acres)." (Note: Dr. Dubs has revised his calculation of the Han *mou* since this was written. For 140 acres, now read 342.) However, Ju Shun's commentary to the next document shows that he believed kings and marquises were also limited to 30 *ch'ing* in their own states. Wang Hsien-ch'ien's note is ambiguous (cf. *110*, footnote 2).

[8] Emperor Ai's mother had come from the Ting family; his grandmother and his Empress had come from the Fu family. Both families were powerful.

[9] Tung Hsien (CHS, 93, 4b–7a; JMT, p. 1318), T. Sheng-ch'ing, was Emperor Ai's catamite, and during a brief period was loaded with wealth and honors. He began his official career as a member of the Heir-apparent's suite in 8 B.C., and then became a Gentleman when Emperor Ai ascended the throne on May 5, 7 B.C. It was not till about two years later, however, that the Emperor first noticed his beauty and talked with him. He immediately won the Emperor's heart, lived with him, and started a meteoric rise. His sister was made an imperial concubine, and his father was accordingly appointed a *kuan-nei* marquis and given various official posts: successively Prefect, Imperial Household Grandee, Treasurer of the Privy Purse, and Commandant of the Palace Guard. His father-in-law was appointed Chief of the Bureau of Construction, and one of his first tasks was to erect a palace for Tung Hsien. The Emperor filled this palace with the most precious furnishings from the imperial storehouses, and gave great sums of money to various members of his family, his retainers, and even his slaves. The Emperor wanted to confer a marquisate on his favorite, but could find no excuse to do so. In September, 3 B.C., however, he enfeoffed him under the pretext that he had been one of those who had exposed the lèse majesté of the King of Tung-p'ing. When Chancellor Wang Chia opposed the appointment, and spoke out against the Emperor's favoritism, he was sent to jail where he died. Tung Hsien was also opposed by the uncle of the Emperor, the Grand Marshal Ting Ming, who was jealous for his family's prestige. In the struggle Ting Ming lost and was demoted, while Tung Hsien was appointed on June 20, 1 B.C., to the most influential post in the empire: he became Grand Marshal at the age of 22!

It was brief glory. Emperor Ai died on August 13, and the Grand Empress Dowager *née* Wang immediately dismissed Tung Hsien and appointed her nephew, Wang Mang, in his stead. Stripped of office and without a protector, Tung Hsien and his wife committed suicide. The rest of his family was banished, and his property was confiscated and sold by the government. The sale brought 4,300,000,000 cash! For other items about him, cf. *117–119*.

[10] If it is true that Tung Hsien was one of those "inconvenienced" by the law limiting amounts of land and numbers of slaves that might be owned, then the law must actually have been in effect for about two years, for, according to Tung Hsien's biography, he was not even noticed by the Emperor until some two years later, and there seems to be no earlier datable evidence of his rise than about 5 B.C. Did Pan Ku nod here?

又曰制節謹度以防奢淫爲政所先百王不易之道也
諸侯王列侯公主吏二千石及豪富民多畜奴婢田宅亡
限與民爭利百姓失職重困不足其議限列有司條奏諸
王列侯得名田國中列侯在長安及公主名田縣道關內
侯吏民名田皆無得過三十頃諸侯王奴婢二百人列侯
公主百人關內侯吏民三十人年六十以上十歲以下不
在數中買人皆不得名田爲吏犯者以律論諸名田畜奴
婢過品皆没入縣官…掖庭宫人年三十以下出嫁之
官奴婢五十以上免爲庶人

[In June/July, 7 B.C., an edict of Emperor Ai] also said:[1] "To govern by moderation and careful observance of law, in order to prevent extravagance and excess, has been the first principle of government, the unchanging way of the hundred benevolent kings. Now the vassal kings, the ranking marquises, the princesses, the officials [receiving a salary of] two thousand piculs, and the overbearing, rich people herd many male and female slaves, and fields and residences without limit. They compete with the common people for profit, and the people have lost their occupations, and are heavily distressed and in want. Let limitations and regulations be discussed."

The officials concerned submitted an itemized memorial: "Kings and ranking marquises [should] be allowed to name fields within their states; ranking marquises [living] at Ch'ang-an and also princesses, who name fields in prefectures and border marches, and *kuan-nei* marquises, officials, and common people who name fields, all [should] not be allowed to exceed thirty *ch'ing*.[2] Vassal kings [should be allowed] two hundred male and female slaves; ranking marquises and princesses [should be allowed] one hundred; *kuan-nei* marquises, officials, and common people [should be allowed] thirty. [Slaves] sixty years of age or older, or in their tenth year or younger, are not [counted] in these numbers. No merchants [should] be allowed to name fields or become an official. Law breakers [should] be sentenced according to the code. Named fields and herded male and female slaves exceeding the [number allowed to each] rank [should] all be confiscated by the imperial government."

... The Palace Women[3] of the Concubines' Quarter who were thirty years old or younger were sent out to be married. Government male and female slaves who were fifty years of age or older were dismissed and made commoners.

[1] Cf. *109*.

[2] For a discussion of the uncertainty about the exact meaning of this sentence, see *109*, footnote 7. Ju Shun has the following commentary here: " 'To name fields within their states' [refers to owning fields] in the states from which they derive income. In addition to receiving their land taxes and produce taxes, they also personally were allowed to have 30 *ch'ing* of private fields. As to 'naming fields in prefectures and border marches,' it was a primary order [of the dynasty] that nobles living in their states and naming fields in other prefectures would be fined two taels of gold. Now there were marquises who had not gone to their states. Although from a distance they derived income from the land taxes and produce taxes of their states, they were further personally allowed fields in other prefectures and border marches; princesses similarly. They were not to exceed 30 *ch'ing*."

Wang Hsien-ch'ien says: "To name fields is to claim [or occupy] fields. Each uses his name to claim them for himself. The kings and marquises each have states and therefore are allowed to name fields within their states. Ranking marquises living in Ch'ang-an who have not yet gone to their states, and also princesses, are only allowed to name fields in prefectures and border marches, and their limitation is the same as that for *kuan-nei* marquises, officials, and common people. [Where the] *T'ung chien* [*kang mu* by Ssu-ma Kuang] says, 'From vassal kings, ranking marquises, and princesses [on down?], who name fields, each has a limitation; *kuan-nei* marquises, officials, and common people shall all not exceed 30 *ch'ing*,' its structure seems somewhat erroneous. The *Hsün chi* statement, '[From] kings and marquises down to commoners, named fields are not allowed to exceed thirty *ch'ing*,' agrees with the text of the Annals [of Emperor Ai]."

[3] According to Wei Hung, who lived only shortly after the end of the Former Han dynasty, *kung-jen* were girls selected from among government female slaves eight years old or older, and trained to wait on the ladies of the palace. He says that those aged 35 and *older* were sent out to be married (cf. *91* and *92*). There is some doubt whether the term *kung-jen* meant slave girls exclusively.

111.   7 B.C.   CHS, 98, 5b (10b)

根行貪邪臧累鉅萬縱橫恣意大治室第第中起土山
立兩市殿上赤墀戶青瑣遊觀射獵使奴從者被甲持弓
弩陳爲步兵

[In a memorial criticizing the political power and private conduct of Wang Ken,[1] the Colonel over the Retainers, Chieh Kuang[2] said: "[Wang] Ken's conduct is greedy and corrupt; he has accumulated a hundred million [cash], and he indulges his desires in any direction. He built grand houses and a mansion, and in his mansion erected an artificial mountain and set up two markets.[3] His palace has crimson terraces and its doors are green and intricately carved.[4] He wanders about, watching shooting matches and hunting, and makes his male slave attendants wear armor and carry bows and crossbows and deploy like infantry."

[1] Wang Ken (CHS, 98, 5b–6a; JMT, p. 115; cf. *99*, footnote 2) was the half-brother of the Empress *née* Wang of Emperor Yüan, and the fourth member of the family to dominate the government through the position of Commander-in-Chief.   His marquisate had the income from 12,400 households.   As a result of this memorial Wang Ken was sent back to his estate, his nephew Wang K'uang, the Marquis of Ch'eng-tu, was deposed and made a commoner, and all the officials who had been sponsored by Wang Shang were dismissed.   When Wang Ken died in 6 or 2 B.C. (CHS, 18, 15b, and 98, 6a, disagree) his marquisate was abolished.

[2] Cf. *107*, footnote 3.

[3] This would seem clearly to indicate that he was in private business.   Officials were not supposed to compete with commoners in business, but many did.

[4] In thus decorating his palace he presumed on imperial prerogatives.   The identical accusation was made against him earlier (cf. CHS, 98, 5a, and commentary).

初邛成太后外家王氏貴而侍中王林卿通輕俠傾京
師後坐法免賓客愈盛歸長陵上冢因留飲連日並恐其
犯法自造門上謁謂林卿曰冢聞單外君宜以時歸林卿
曰諾先是林卿殺婢壻埋冢舍並具知之以非已時又見
其新免故不發舉欲無令留界中而已即且遣吏奉謁傳
送林卿素驕慚於賓客並度其爲變儲兵馬以待之林卿
既去北度涇橋令騎奴還至寺門拔刀剝其建鼓並自從

Earlier, when members of the Wang family, affinal relatives of the [Liu house through] Empress Dowager Ang-ch'eng,[1] had been influential, Attaché Wang Lin-ch'ing[2] associated with ruffians who flooded the capital. Later he was tried and dismissed. His retainers increased and he returned to Ch'ang-ling,[3] went up to [Kao-tsu's] tumulus, and made it a pretext to stay there and drink for several days. [Ho] Ping[4] [the Prefect of Ch'ang-ling], fearing he would violate the law, personally paid him a call and said to [Wang] Lin-ch'ing: "The precincts of the tumulus are outside the suburbs. Milord should return [to the city] at the proper time." [Wang] Lin-ch'ing assented.

Some time before this [Wang] Lin-ch'ing had killed the lover[5] of his female slave and buried [the corpse] in a guard house of the tomb. [Ho] Ping knew all about it, but thinking it was not an appropriate time, especially considering his recent dismissal, was not going to bring up the matter; he merely wanted to prevent him from remaining within the region [of his jurisdiction]. He forthwith sent officials to attend him and escort him on [to the next prefecture].

[Wang] Lin-ch'ing was by nature haughty, and he was mortified before his retainers. [Ho] Ping thought he might do something shifty, and so assembled troops and horses to await events. When [Wang] Lin-ch'ing had left and gone north over the Ch'ing River bridge he ordered a mounted male slave to go back to the gate of the [prefectural] offices, draw his sword, and beat on the drum set up on a stand.[6] [At this, Ho] Ping, escorted by his officers and

吏兵追林卿行數十里林卿迫窘迺令奴冠其冠被其襜褕自代乘車從童騎身變服從間徑馳去會日暮追及收縛冠奴奴曰我非侍中奴耳並心自知已失林卿迺曰王君困自稱奴得脫死邪吐吏斷頭持還縣所剟鼓置都亭下署曰故侍中王林卿坐殺人埋冢舍使奴剟寺門鼓吏民驚駭林卿因亡命眾庶讙譁以爲實死

soldiers, personally pursued [Wang] Lin-ch'ing, going several tens of *li*. Hotly pursued, [Wang] Lin-ch'ing thereupon ordered a male slave to put on his cap, don his big-sleeved coat, and take his own place in the carriage escorted by the youth horsemen.[7] Having changed clothes, [Wang Lin-ch'ing] himself galloped off on an unfrequented bypath.

At sundown the pursuers caught up. They seized and bound up the capped male slave. The male slave said: "I am not the Attaché, but merely a male slave." [Ho] Ping inwardly realized he had already lost [Wang] Lin-ch'ing, [but nevertheless] said: "Milord Wang is trapped. By calling yourself a male slave can you escape death?" He shouted to an officer to cut off his head, carry it back to the prefectural offices, beat the drum, and place [the head] on the tower in the [prefectural] capital with a label saying: "This is the former Attaché Wang Lin-ch'ing, tried for killing a man and burying him in a guard house of the tomb, and for sending a male slave to beat on the drum at the gate of the [prefectural] offices."

Officials and plebeians were alarmed and terrified. [Wang] Lin-ch'ing thereby having lost his official identity, the populace all babbled that he really was dead.

[1] Ying Shao (ca. A.D. 140–206) explains: "[Wang] Feng-k'uang, the father of Emperor Hsüan's Empress *née* Wang, was made the Marquis of Ang-ch'eng. The mother of Emperor Ch'eng was also surnamed Wang. Therefore the title of the [first woman's] father is used for differentiation." This method of differentiation is also pointed out in CHS, 97A, 11b.

The first family came from Ch'ang-ling, the scene of the present incident, and the place to which Wang Lin-ch'ing returned after his dismissal. Emperor Hsüan's Empress *née* Wang lived to be more than seventy years of age, and died in 16 B.C.

Wang Mang came from the other and greater Wang family, i.e., that of the mother of Emperor Ch'eng. Confusion arises unless the two families are kept separate.

[2] This event seems to be the only mention of Wang Lin-ch'ing in the CHS. He is not listed in JMT.

[3] Ch'ang-ling was a prefecture northeast of the present Hsien-yang hsien in Shensi. Emperor Kao was buried there.

[4] Ho Ping (CHS, 77, 7b–8a) was a grandson of a high official, and his first important office was Prefect of Ch'ang-ling. No date is recorded for this incident, but it occurred during the reign of Emperor Ai, hence the date for the passage. The biography tells that the Dowager Empress *née* Wang of Emperor Yüan (the mother of Emperor Ch'eng) grieved for a beloved relative of the Dowager Empress (also *née* Wang) of Emperor Hsüan, and told Emperor Ai about the above event. Far from being angry, Emperor Ai greatly admired Ho Ping, and advanced him to the position of Administrator of Lung-hsi Commandery, and then transferred him to be Administrator of Ying-ch'uan Commandery. Ho Ping died during the reign of Wang Mang.

[5] Yen Shih-ku says: "The *pei-hsü* 婢壻 was an outsider who had sexual relations with the female slave." *Hsü* is usually translated as "son-in-law." Wang Hsien-ch'ien, however, quotes the Additional Commentary of the Official Edition, and Wen Ying's commentary, to the effect that the man was the slave's husband.

[6] Cf. TY. In Ch'ing times such drums, set up before the office of the hsien magistrate, could be beaten by people having an accusation to make. This may also have been the practice in Han times, but not necessarily. In ordering his slave to beat the drum, Wang Lin-ch'ing was being defiant.

[7] Yen Shih-ku defines *t'ung-ch'i* as youthful male-slave horsemen; cf. his definition in *81*, footnote 2.

113.   4 B.C.[1]   CHS, 80, 5a (9a)

是時哀帝被疾多所惡事下有司逮王后謁下獄驗治
言使巫傅恭婢合歡等祠祭詛祝上爲雲求爲天子雲又
與知災異者高尚等指星宿言上疾必不愈雲當得天下
石立宣帝起之表也有司請誅王有詔廢徙房陵雲自殺
謁棄市立十七年國除

At this time Emperor Ai fell sick and there were many [signs] of malevolence [toward him]. The matter was sent down to the officials concerned, who arrested Queen Yeh[2] and threw her into prison. At the trial it was said that she had caused a witch, Fu Kung, and a female slave, Ho-huan, and others to offer sacrifices and implore calamities upon the Emperor, seeking that [Liu] Yün[3] should be made Emperor; [it was said] also that [Liu] Yün and a specialist in calamities and wonders, Kao Shang, and others had pointed at a constellation and had said: "The Emperor's sickness must be incurable; [Liu] Yün shall get the empire; the stone standing upright is a manifestation of the rise of Emperor Yüan ['s line]." [4]

The officials concerned begged for the execution of the King. There was an imperial edict to depose and banish him to Fan-ling. [Liu] Yün committed suicide, and [Queen] Yeh was publicly executed. [Liu Yün] had been on the throne 17 years. The state was abolished.

[1] The suicide and execution are recorded for December 22, 4 B.C. (cf. CHS, 11, 3a). The accusation was made during that year.

[2] The Queen of Liu Yün.

[3] Liu Yün (CHS, 80, 5a; 14, 20a) was the son of Liu Yü, King En of Tung-p'ing, who was the fourth son of Emperor Hsüan, by the concubine *née* Kung-sun. Liu Yü was King for 33 years. When he died Liu Yün became King Yang of Tung-p'ing (20 B.C.).

Some time between 7 and 4 B.C. there were several unusual phenomena; in particular a stone on Ku Mountain turned over and stood upright. Liu Yün and his Queen visited the place, worshiped, and then placed in their palace a replica of the mountain and stone to which they sacrificed. They seem to have seen in the stone a portent of a change of emperors, and Liu Yün hoped to succeed to the imperial throne, although he was of a generation higher than Emperor Ai. His disloyalty was denounced to the throne. The passage translated continues his biography from this point.

[4] The correct line of descent from Emperor Hsüan had run out with the death of his grandson, Emperor Ch'eng. Emperor Ai was descended through the concubine *née* Fu of Emperor Yüan.

114. 5–2 B.C.[1] CHS, 99A, 2a (3b)

莽杜門自守其中子獲殺奴莽切責獲令自殺

[Wang] Mang closed his doors and lived in retirement. His second son, Huo,[2] murdered a male slave. [Wang] Mang severely rebuked Huo, and commanded him to commit suicide.

[1] The years during which Wang Mang was in retirement.

[2] Wang Huo is apparently known only here. The text certainly means that Wang Mang commanded him to commit suicide and he did so.
Cf. *129* for another instance of Wang Mang's attitude toward the killing of slaves.

---

115. 3 B.C. CHS, 15B, 35a (51a)

元壽二年坐使奴殺人免元始元年復封八年免

In 3 B.C. [Liu Shou,[1] the Marquis of Wu-an] was tried for having caused a male slave to kill a man, and was deposed. In A.D. 1 he was reappointed, but in the eighth year he was deposed.

[1] Liu Shou was the son of King En of Ch'u (Liu Yen: CHS, 14, 21a) and a great-grandson of Emperor Hsüan. He does not seem to be mentioned elsewhere.

116. 3 B.C. CHS, 77, 7a (14b)

頃之傅太后使謁者買諸官婢賤取之復取執金吾官
婢八人隆奏言買賤請更平直

[Mu-chiang Lung,[1] Chief of the Palace Guard, had protested against Emperor Ai's gifts to his favorite Tung Hsien of goods taken from the public treasury and arsenal]. Shortly after, the Empress Dowager [née] Fu[2] sent an internuncio to buy female slaves from various government bureaus, taking them at a low price; and she also took eight female slaves from the Bureau of the Chief of the Palace Guard. [Mu-chiang] Lung memorialized, saying: "The price is too low. Please readjust it."[3]

[1] Mu-chiang Lung (CHS, 77, 7a–b; 19B, 5a–b) was a protégé of General-in-Chief Wang Yin, and after having been made a Gentleman of the Household, was appointed Grandee Censor. Toward the end of the reign of Emperor Ch'eng (d. 7 B.C.) he became a commandery Administrator. In 4 B.C. he was appointed Administrator of the Capital District, but a year later was made Chief of the Palace Guard, and the next year was transferred to Commandant of P'ei Commandery. This gives the date. Because of this incident he was demoted to the position of Administrator of P'ei Commandery, and was then shifted to Nan Commandery.

[2] Empress Dowager née Fu (CHS, 97B, 8a–9a; 11, 1a–b) should at this time have been called Grand Empress Dowager. She had been a favorite concubine of Emperor Yüan. Their son became a king, while the son of the Empress née Wang became Emperor Ch'eng. Since Emperor Ch'eng had no son, the grandson of the concubine née Fu was made Heir-apparent, and in 7 B.C. became Emperor Ai, while she became Grand Empress Dowager. She died in 2 B.C.

[3] The Emperor refused to enter the dispute against his grandmother, and censured Mu-chiang Lung for making a public case of a matter concerning only the imperial family.

117.   3 B.C.[1]   CHS, 86, 5b (11a)

賢家有賓婚及見親諸官並共賜及倉頭奴婢人十萬
錢使者護視發取市物百買震動道路讙譁羣臣惶惑詔
書罷苑而以賜賢二千餘頃均田之制從此墮壞奢僭放
縱變亂陰陽災異眾多

[Wang Chia[2] submitted a memorial to Emperor Ai, criticizing
his lavish expenses and attributing an eclipse of the sun to his
imperial grants to Tung Hsien[3]]: "When, in [Tung] Hsien's household
there was a marriage ceremony and a meeting of the relatives, the
various officials all made contributions; while the imperial gifts
extend [down even to Tung Hsien's] 'green-heads'[4] and male and
female slaves, ten myriad [cash] per person. With emissaries protecting and watching, [Tung Hsien's agents] confiscated goods from
the markets, which stirred up all the merchants, threw the highways
and streets into confusion, and terrified the ministers. [You] issued
an edict to abolish an imperial park, and from it gave [Tung] Hsien
more than 2,000 *ch'ing* of land. By this the system of equal fields
[for each official rank] was destroyed. Such extravagance, excess,
and lack of restraint have so upset [the cosmic forces of] *yin* and
yang that disasters and unnatural phenomena are numerous."

¹ The memorial was presented after, and as a result of, an eclipse of the sun,
which is recorded as of February 3, 2 B.C. The eclipse was associated with the
act of Emperor Ai in conferring marquisates on three of his favorites, Tung Hsien,
Sun Ch'ung, and Hsi-fu Kung, in September, 3 B.C. (CHS, 11, 3b; 18, 20a–b;
86, 4b). The matter relating to slaves seems to have occurred in 3 B.C. or perhaps
a little earlier.

² Wang Chia (CHS, 86, 3a–7b; 19B, 48b–52b; JMT, p. 138) had a brief
official career. Most of his biography is composed of memorials. After being
made a Grand Palace Grandee, he was appointed Administrator of Chiu-chiang
and Ho-nan Commanderies, where he earned a great reputation. In succession
he was appointed Grand Herald (10 B.C.); Administrator of the Capital District
(7 B.C.); Grandee Secretary (5 B.C.); and Chancellor (4 B.C.). Because of his
courageous opposition to the Emperor's favoritism of his distaff relatives and Tung
Hsien, Wang Chia was sent to jail and there died in March/April, 2 B.C.

³ Cf. *109*, footnote 9.

⁴ For definitions of *ts'ang-t'ou*, "green-head," cf. *118*, footnote 4.
Cf. *119* for another statement concerning gifts to Tung Hsien's slaves.

今貧民菜食不厭衣又穿空父子夫婦不能相保誠可
爲酸鼻陛下不救將安所歸命乎奈何獨私養外親與幸
臣董賢多賞賜以大萬數使奴從賓客漿酒霍肉蒼頭廬
兒皆用致富非天意也

[In a memorial addressed to Emperor Ai, Pao Hsüan[1] said]:
"Now the plain diet of the poor people is unsatisfying; their clothes
also are full of holes. Fathers and sons, and husbands and wives
cannot mutually care for each other. It honestly makes one weep.[2]
If Your Majesty does not succor them, then to whom may they
entrust their fate? How is it that [You, nevertheless,] only privately
care for Your affinal relatives and give to Your favorite Tung Hsien,[3]
liberally endowing them with many myriads [of cash, thus] causing
their male slave attendants and retainer-guests to [look on] wine
[as though it were] soup, and meat [as though it were] beans. That
the 'green-heads' and 'hut-dwellers'[4] should all be employed [as
officials] and become rich, is not Heaven's intention."

[1] Pao Hsüan (CHS, 72, 10a–13a; JMT, p. 1630), T. Tzu-tou. He was Grandee
Censor at the time he made this protest against the power of the relatives of the
Empress, and against the Emperor's favoritism of Tung Hsien. His biography
is largely composed of this and another memorial. Later he became involved in
a crime and was nearly executed, but on the plea of over a thousand scholars
the sentence was reduced to guarding the frontier. He committed suicide during
the reign of Emperor P'ing (A.D. 1–5).

[2] Lit. "sour nose."

[3] Cf. *109*, footnote 9.

[4] Meng K'ang (A.D. 180–260) says: "[In the expressions] *li-min* and *ch'ien
shou* [classical terms for the Chinese common people] *li* and *ch'ien* both mean 'black.'
The lower people are of the *yin* category, so 'black' is used to designate them.
[People of the] Han period named male slaves 'green-heads' (*ts'ang-t'ou*), [i.e.]
not pure black, in order to differentiate them from good people. The place where
all those who served in the halls [of a palace or residency] lived was a 'hut' (*lu*).
'Green-heads' who were serving attendants were therefore called 'hut-dwellers'
(*lu-erh*)."

Fu Tsan (ca. A.D. 285) quotes the *Han i chu* [i.e., the *Han (chiu) i* with com-
mentary] in regard to government male slaves working as writers and accountants.
See *92*.

TY quotes the *Li chi su* (by ?Chia Kung-yen, ca. A.D. 600, after K'ung Ying-
ta, A.D. 574–648) as saying that Han household menials were called *ts'ang-t'ou*,
"green-heads." They used green kerchiefs as adornment, to differentiate them
from commoners. Later generations likewise so differentiated them. Giles D,
1434, defines *ts'ang-t'ou* as "an old retainer, slave." Couvreur (DC, p. 791) gives
"a band of green or blue silk which soldiers bound around their heads; soldiers,

servants." C. C. Wang, however, thinks the relevant meaning of *ts'ang* in connection with slaves must be "hoary"; hence, an old slave or servant.

A Japanese study of "green-heads" has been translated into Chinese by Fu I-ling ("Han tai ts'ang-t'ou k'ao," *Shih huo*, vol. 4, No. 11, November 1, 1936, pp. 485–489). This indicates that in Chan Kuo times and at the beginning of Han, "green-heads" were actually private bodyguards or personal armies. The earliest Han reference to them as slaves is alleged to be that in CHS, 68, 6a (cf. *72*), dating about 68 B.C. A slightly earlier reference to government *ts'ang-t'ou*, however, is that cited in my appendix, from CHS, 78, 1b, dating some time between 80 and 70 B.C.

119.   Ca. 2 B.C.¹   CHS, 93, 4b (8b)

詔將作大匠爲賢起大第北闕下重殿洞門木土之功
窮極技巧柱檻衣以綈錦下至賢家僮僕皆受上賜及武
庫禁兵上方珍寶其選物上弟盡在董氏而乘輿所服迺
其副也

There was an imperial edict for the Chief of the Bureau of Con-
struction² to build a great mansion for Tung Hsien³ beneath the
Northern Portal,⁴ with a pair of main halls having connecting doors.⁵
The accomplishments of the carpenters and masons exhausted the
limits of talent and skill.   The pillars and balustrades were covered
with heavy embroidered silk.   All, right down to [Tung] Hsien's
household youths and servants, received imperial gifts, while forbidden weapons from the arsenal, and treasures from the imperial
atelier—select articles of the highest quality—were all [placed] in
the Tung family's [homes].   Their riding chariots and clothes
were commensurate.

¹ It is told just before this passage that Tung Kung, the father of Tung Hsien,
was made Treasurer of the Privy Purse, then advanced to Commandant of the
Palace Guard.   According to CHS, 19B, 52b, these appointments were made in
3 and 2 B.C., respectively.   In the second month of 2 B.C. (March/April) Tung
Kung was appointed Imperial Household Grandee and another man was made
Commandant of the Palace Guard; hence the date.   We cannot be certain, however,
that the historian paid strict attention to chronological details.

² This was Tung Hsien's father-in-law.   On the office see HJAS, vol. 2, 1937,
pp. 26–28.

³ Cf. *109*, footnote 9.

⁴ Translated thus by Dubs, HFHD, vol. I, p. 118 (cf. also MH, vol. II, p. 390).
TY says: "In antiquity there were constructed lookout portals at the north of
the palace, called the Northern Portal."   Would "Prospect Hill" just north
of the Forbidden City in modern Peking be a vestige of such lookout towers?

⁵ Tung Hsien's mansion was just north of the palace.   An explanation of the
"connecting doors" would seem to be that Tung Hsien's gate faced the north gate
of the palace.   The pair of halls would then be the Emperor's and Tung Hsien's.
Yen Shih-ku gives a different explanation: "The pair of halls means that there
were a front and a rear hall.   The connecting doors mean that the two doors
[of these halls] faced each other.   Both [the halls and the doors] usurped the
system [reserved] for the Emperor."   Thus, Yen Shih-ku's idea is simply that the
plan of Tung Hsien's house imitated that of the palace.
Cf. *117* for another statement concerning gifts to Tung Hsien's slaves.

120.   A.D. 3.   CHS, 72, 4b (9a)

莽遣就國歲餘爲傅婢所毒薨國除

[Wang] Mang sent [Wang Ch'ung[1]] back to his marquisate, where more than a year later he was poisoned by his female slave chamberlain,[2] and died.   His marquisate was abolished.

[1] Wang Ch'ung (CHS, 72, 4b; 18, 21a; JMT, p. 120) was the grandson of Wang Ch'i and son of Wang Chün, both of whom were high officials.   He held several important offices and finally became Grandee Secretary, even though he dared to criticize the powerful Wang family, of which he was not a member.   He gave up his post and retired in the second month of A.D. 2 (CHS, 19B, 55a), and was poisoned a little more than a year later.   The same statement about his death is given in CHS, 18, 21a, and is not separately translated.

[2] Yen Shih-ku says: "Whenever it says *fu-pei* ["female slave chamberlain,"] it means [one who] assists with the affairs of [her master's] clothes and bed.   *Fu* is also read *fu*, meaning a close favorite."   TY gives this passage as *locus classicus*, quoting Yen Shih-ku.   The term "chamberlain," in its archaic sense, conforms closely to Yen Shih-ku's explanation of *fu*.

---

121.   A.D. 3.   CHS, 12, 3a (6b)

夏安漢公奏車服制度吏民養生送終嫁娶奴婢田宅
器械之品

In the summer the Duke Protector of Han[1] presented a memorial on regulations concerning carriages and clothing, and on scales [of expenditure allowed to] officials and commoners [according to their ranks, for celebrating] births, funerals, and marriages, [and scales of their possession of] male and female slaves, fields, houses, utensils, and implements.

[1] I.e., Wang Mang (cf. *108*, footnote 2).

秦爲無道厚賦稅以自供奉罷民力以極欲壞聖制廢
井田是以兼幷起貪鄙生強者規田以千數弱者曾無立
錐之居又置奴婢之市與牛馬同蘭制於民臣顓斷其命
姦虐之人因緣爲利至略賣人妻子逆天心詩人倫繆於
天地之性人爲貴之義書曰予則奴戮女唯不用命者然
後被此皋矣漢氏減輕田租三十而稅一常有更賦罷癃
咸出而豪民侵陵分田刼假厥名三十稅一實什稅五也
父子夫婦終年耕芸所得不足以自存故富者犬馬餘菽
粟驕而爲邪貧者不厭糟糠窮而爲姦俱陷于辜刑用不
錯予前在大麓始令天下公田口井時則有嘉禾之祥遭
反虜逆賊且止今更名天下田曰王田奴婢曰私屬皆不
得賣買其男口不盈八而田過一井者分餘田予九族隣
里鄉黨故無田今當受田者如制度敢有非井田聖制無
法惑眾者投諸四裔以禦魑魅如皇始祖考虞帝故事是
時百姓便安漢五銖錢以莽錢大小兩行難知又數變改

[Wang Mang said[1]]: "The Ch'in dynasty was unprincipled. It increased the poll-tax and tax on produce in order to support itself; it exhausted the people's strength in order to fulfill its desires; it destroyed the institutions of the sages and abolished the *ching-t'ien* [system[2]]. For this reason, simultaneous accumulation [of offices, land, and other sources of income[3]] arose and avarice and vileness were born. The strong measured their fields by the thousand [*mu*], while the weak had no room even to stand an awl.

"Furthermore, [the Ch'in dynasty] established slave markets, [putting humans into] the same pens with cattle and horses. In its rule over the common people and subjects it arbitrarily cut short their lives. Wicked and cruel people took advantage of this to make profits, going so far as to kidnap and sell men's wives and children, violating Heaven's will, perverting natural human relationships, and

opposing the principle that, in the nature of heaven and earth, man
is most important. The *Book of History* says: 'I will then enslave
and dishonor you.'⁴   But only those who did not obey suffered
this punishment.

"The House of Han reduced and lightened the field tax, taxing
produce one part in thirty. But there were always the conscript
services and poll-taxes, which [even] the aged and sick all had to
produce. And powerful people encroached upon and oppressed [the
weak], dividing the fields out at usurious rentals.⁵ In name the
tax on produce was one-thirtieth; in reality the tax on produce was
five parts in ten.

"Fathers and sons, husbands and wives plow and cultivate the
whole year long, yet what they receive is insufficient to support
themselves. Therefore the rich, whose dogs and horses have a
surplus of beans and grain, are haughty and become depraved. The
poor, who do not feel full on dregs and husks, are exhausted and
become villainous. Both fall into crime; punishments are employed
and not set aside.⁶

"When I was formerly the chief director [of the administration],
I ordered the public lands of the empire [to be divided into] *ching*
[on the basis of a count of] the people.⁷ At that time, consequently,
there occurred the favorable omen of the Auspicious Grain. But
there were encounters with rebellion and treason, and [the plan]
was temporarily stopped.

"Now I change the name of the fields of the world, which shall
be called 'the King's fields';⁸ and of male and female slaves, which
shall be called 'private retainers.' Neither may be bought or sold.
Those [families] of less than eight males, whose fields exceed one
ching,⁹ shall divide the extra fields among their relatives and [people
in their] neighborhoods, hamlets, villages, and associations.¹⁰ Those
who formerly had no fields and should now receive fields [shall
receive them] according to the regulations. If there are any who
dare to oppose the holy *ching-t'ien* system, or lawlessly mislead
the masses, they shall be cast to the four boundaries of the empire
to ward off the hobgoblins—following the example of my imperial
first ancestor, the Lord of Yü, [Emperor Shun]."

At this time the people found convenient and were contented
with the Han five-*chu* cash, and considered the [Wang] Mang cash¹¹—
in two currencies, the large and the small—as hard to recognize and
also as untrustworthy because it was frequently changed; they all

不信皆私以五銖錢市買訛言大錢當罷莫肯挾莽患之
復下書挾五銖錢言大錢當罷者比非井田制投四裔於
是農商失業食貨俱廢民人至涕泣於市道及坐賣買田
宅奴婢鑄錢自諸侯卿大夫至于庶民抵罪者不可勝數

privately used the five-*chu* cash for market transactions, and falsely said that the large cash were going to be abolished. None was willing to keep them.

Wang Mang[12] was vexed at this, and again issued a document [which said]: "All those who hoard five-*chu* cash and say that the large cash are going to be abolished will be cast to the four boundaries, like those who oppose the *ching-t'ien* system."

Thereupon farmers and merchants lost their occupations, food and commodities both were ruined, and the people went so far as to weep in the markets and highways. Moreover, those who were tried for selling and buying fields, residences, and male and female slaves, and for coining money, and [actually] atoned for their crimes —from nobles, high ministers, and grandees down to commoners— were innumerable.

[1] This is actually an edict, a decree, or an order. Most of this statement from the third paragraph to the place indicated by footnote 10 is quoted in CHS, 24A, 8b, and begins: "下令曰 [Wang Mang] issued an order, saying...." Since the passage in Wang Mang's biography contains everything in the other passage and some extra phrases, the less complete passage is not translated.

[2] For a discussion of the *ching-t'ien* system cf. *35*, footnote 3.

[3] Cf. *35*, footnote 4.

[4] These are the last five words of the *Kan Shih*, a *chin wen* text of the *Book of History*. The phrase is variously translated by James Legge (*Chinese classics*, vol. III, p. 155), S. Couvreur (*Chou king*, pp. 78–79), and E. Chavannes (MH, vol. I, p. 165). For a discussion of its supposed Hsia date, see H. G. Creel, *Studies in early Chinese culture*, ser. 1, p. 97, footnote 2. The evidence points to its being later than Shang, and it may be post-Confucian.

[5] In the commentary to the passage in CHS, 24A, Yen Shih-ku says: " 'Dividing the fields' means that poor people, having no fields, take the fields of rich people, plowing and planting them, and dividing the produce [with the owners]. 'Lending' also means that poor people rent rich people's fields. The word *chieh* [(here translated "usurious")] means that] the rich people rob the tax on produce, taking it by fraud."

[6] Under a good administration it should not be necessary to employ punishments. The use of punishments is a sign that the government is bad.

[7] Following the explanation of Yen Shih-ku.

[8] Lit. "Wang's fields."

[9] The basic unit of the *ching-t'ien* system, supposed to equal 900 *mu*.

¹⁰ CHS, 24A, here concludes its quotation with the sentence: "Those who disobey this order shall be punished to the extent of death." It then states: "When the regulations [to cover this order] had not yet been fixed, officials made use of the situation to do evil; the whole country was filled with weeping, and multitudes fell into [the clutches of] the law."

¹¹ Wang Mang's various currency reforms are described in CHS, 24B, 8b–9a. See also Terrien de Lacouperie (*Catalogue of Chinese coins*, pp. 365, 381–383) and W. Vissering (*On Chinese currency*, pp. 49–50).

¹² The passage from here to the end also appears in abbreviated form in CHS, 24B, 9a.

123. A.D. 10. CHS, 99B, 7b (15a)

於是造寶貨五品語在食貨志百姓不從但行小大錢
二品而已盜鑄錢者不可禁迺重其法一家鑄錢五家坐
之沒入爲奴婢

Thereupon [Wang Mang] made five classes of "precious money," as told in the *Shih huo chih.*[1] The populace did not adopt [his monetary system, but] only circulated two classes, the large and the small cash. Counterfeiting of money could not be prevented.

Thereupon [Wang Mang] increased the severity of his laws; if one family coined money, the five [mutually responsible] families would be tried for it, and be seized and made slaves.

[1] CHS, 24B, 8b–9a. This details the 28 items of currency, made of five materials (bronze, gold, silver, tortoise shell, and cowrie) and having six names: cash (6 kinds), gold (1), silver (2), tortoise shell (4), cowrie (5), *pu* (lit. "cloth," but made of bronze, like cash, 10).

Cf. *131, 132* for a similar decree to enslave counterfeiters, and the report of a case where "ten myriad" counterfeiters and mutually responsible families were seized and enslaved by the government.

124. A.D. 12. CHS, 99B, 10a (20a)

莽知民怨迺下書曰諸名食王田皆得賣之勿拘以法
犯私買賣庶人者且一切勿治

[Wang] Mang realized[1] that the people were distressed [by his reforms], and thereupon handed down a document, saying: "Various [kinds of] fields—named, income, and 'the King's'—may all be sold without restraint of the law. Those who have violated [the law] and secretly bought or sold commoners,[2] now, in every case, will not be tried."

[1] Ou Po, a Gentleman of the Household, had presented a memorial criticizing Wang Mang's reforms, particularly the *ching-t'ien* system. He argued that such radical reforms could not be instituted suddenly, especially as the dynasty had just been established.

[2] The use of the term *shu-jen*, "commoners," here is very interesting. Superficially it would appear that Wang Mang was approving the sale of commoners into slavery. What he meant was only those commoners who had formerly been slaves. In A.D. 9 he had decreed that male and female slaves thereafter were to be called 私屬 "private retainers," and might not be bought or sold. These private retainers would then have had the status of commoners. Thus, three years later he speaks of them by their status. The formula of this passage is "commoner" = "private retainer" = former "slave." This is proved by the fact that in CHS, 24A, 8b, where the same decree is quoted, it is specified that "private retainers" may now be bought and sold. The edict said: "Various incomes and 'King's fields,' and 'private retainers' may all be bought and sold without restraint of the law." The author adds: "But the laws and punishments had cut deeply, and government affairs had been thrown into disorder."

涉欲上冢不欲會賓客密獨與故人期會涉單車歐上
茂陵投暮入其里宅因自匿不見人遣奴至市買肉奴乘
涉氣與屠爭言斫傷屠者亡是時茂陵守令尹公新視事
涉未謁也聞之大怒知涉名豪欲以示眾屬俗遣兩吏脅
守涉至日中奴不出吏欲便殺涉去涉迫窘不知所爲會
涉所與期上冢者車數十乘到皆諸豪也共說尹公尹公
不聽諸豪則曰原巨先奴犯法不得使肉袒自縛箭貫耳
詣廷門謝辜於君威亦足矣尹公許之涉如言謝復服遣
去

[Yüan] She² planned to visit the tumulus but did not want to meet his retainers, so he secretly made a date for a gathering of only his old friends. [Yüan] She drove up to Mao-ling³ in a lone carriage and at dusk slipped into his house in the village, where he secreted himself and would not see anyone. He sent a male slave to market to buy meat. The male slave, assuming his master's temperament, quarreled with the butcher, hacked and wounded him, and ran away.

At this time the Prefect of Mao-ling, His Excellency Yin, had newly taken office and [Yüan] She had not yet called on him. Hearing of this [act of the slave, the Prefect] was furious. Knowing that [Yüan] She was a famous brave, he wanted to make a disciplinary example of him for the multitude. He sent two officers to put [Yüan] She under compulsory guard. By noon [the next day] the male slave had not shown up, and the officials wished to kill [Yüan] She abruptly and leave. [Yüan] She was hard pressed and did not know what to do.

Just then ten or more carriages of those with whom [Yüan] She had made his appointment to visit the tomb arrived. They were all braves. In a body they argued with His Excellency Yin, [but] His Excellency Yin would not relent. Then the braves said: "Yüan Chü-hsien's⁴ male slave broke the law and was not caught. If we make [Yüan She] bare his shoulders, bind himself, put an arrow through his ear,⁵ and come to the gate of the court and apologize to Your Honor for the crime, your authority should then be satisfied."

His Excellency Yin consented to this. [Yüan] She apologized according to the agreement, [was told to] reclothe himself, and was sent away.

¹ Just before this, the historian mentions the death of the Empress Dowager, identified by the commentator as the Grand Empress Dowager Wen. This was Emperor Yüan's Empress *née* Wang. She died in A.D. 13, and was buried in Wei-ling.

² Yüan She (CHS, 92, 6a–7b; JMT, p. 733), T. Chü-hsien, was the grandson of a knight-errant of Emperor Wu's day. His father was a commandery administrator under Emperor Ai. Yüan She was a famous independent brave and redresser of wrongs—as is indicated by his inclusion in this chapter of the CHS. Because of his independent spirit and the lawlessness of his retainers Wang Mang had him arrested and desired to kill him, but finally granted him a pardon. In order to keep out of further trouble Yüan She gave up his offices and tried to be rid of all his retainers. About the time of the death of the Grand Empress Dowager *née* Wang, he returned home and was planning to visit some tomb, perhaps that of Emperor Wu. The event here translated then occurred. Later Wang Mang appointed him Administrator of a commandery. During the revolt in which Wang Mang was overthrown, Yüan She was executed by the victorious rebels.

³ Mao-ling was a prefecture northeast of Hsing-p'ing in Shensi Province. It was the site of the tomb of Emperor Wu, and was Yüan She's ancestral seat.

⁴ Yüan She's style-name.

⁵ Apparently these were acts symbolic of captivity.

126. A.D. 14. CHS, 99B, 12b (26a)

會匈奴使還單于知侍子登前誅死發兵寇邊莽復發
軍屯於是邊民流入內郡爲人奴婢迺禁吏民敢挾邊民
者棄市

Just then[1] the ambassador of the Hsiung-nu returned home and the *Shan-yü* learned that his hostage son, Teng, had been executed. He sent soldiers to invade the frontier. [Wang] Mang again sent armies and military colonists. Therefore, the frontier people poured into the interior commanderies, becoming people's male and female slaves. Thereupon [Wang Mang] imposed restrictions: "Those officials or plebeians who dare traffic in frontier people shall be publicly executed."

[1] In A.D. 12, Wang Mang had executed the Hsiung-nu hostage living at Ch'ang-an, a man named Teng, who was the son of Hsien, a younger brother of the *Shan-yü*. Wang Mang kept the matter secret. In 14 the *Shan-yü* died, and his younger brother Hsien became the new *Shan-yü*. He sought a new treaty of peace with China, and sent an envoy to arrange it. During this period there was serious famine in the frontier commanderies. Ju P'u was sent to inspect the region, and, in view of the new peace treaty, and because the garrisons had not been relieved in many years, he recommended the withdrawal of the Chinese frontier troops. An officer named Han Wei opposed this, and offered to take five thousand men and re-establish the frontier. Wang Mang assented to this plan, and made Han Wei a general. But at the same time he followed Ju P'u's suggestion and ordered back various frontier generals and abolished the military colonies at the four passes. Just at this critical time the new *Shan-yü* learned of the execution of his son two years before, and began his raids. The combination of famine and raids drove Chinese settlers back to the central commanderies.

127. A.D. 17. CHS, 99C, 1a (1b)

又一切調上公以下諸有奴婢者率一口出錢三千六
百天下愈愁盜賊起

Further, he levied a general tax on all those, from the highest
ministers on down, who owned male or female slaves, at a rate of
3,600 cash per head.[1] The empire became still more discontented,
and brigands arose.

[1] It is not indicated whether this tax was to be annual or a single levy, but
the latter seems more likely.

A commentary by Ying Shao (ca. A.D. 140–206) to a passage in CHS, 2, 2b,
regarding extra taxes for unmarried girls instituted in 190 B.C., mentions taxation
of slaves: "According to the Han code everybody paid one poll-tax. One poll-tax
equaled 120 cash. Only resident merchants and male and female slaves [were
charged] a double poll-tax. Now [unmarried girls] were caused [to pay] five [times
the] poll-tax, being punished for a crime." (HFHD, vol. I, p. 184, footnote 1;
Kato Shigeru, "A study on the *suan-fu*, the poll tax of the Han dynasty," MRDTB,
vol. 1, 1926, p. 51.) Ying Shao's statement appears to imply that the double
tax on merchants and slaves was in effect before this special tax on unmarried girls
was introduced. If this was his meaning, we cannot be sure he was right. Probably
he quoted from the Han Code in force in his day, or from the Code at the end of
the Former Han dynasty, and either would have been very different from the
Code of 190 B.C. Kato (op. cit., *passim*) shows that the system of poll-tax developed and changed considerably during Han times. It seems more likely that
the double tax on merchants was one of those special restrictions enforced against
merchants by Emperor Wu.

This conclusion is strengthened by a remark of Chang Shou-chieh (fl. 737) in
his Cheng-i commentary to the SC regarding the system of taxation and the denouncing of accumulated fortunes sponsored by Chang T'ang about 120 B.C. (SC,
122, 3b): "Emperor Wu fought the four barbarians and the national income was
insufficient. Therefore he taxed the people's fields, houses, boats, carts, livestock,
and male and female slaves. These were all appraised in terms of cash and every
thousand cash [worth of property] was one *suan* and paid one bracket. Resident
merchants [paid] double. If anyone concealed [his property] and did not pay the
tax, and someone reported it, one-half [the culprit's property] was given to the
informer and the other half was confiscated by the government . . . . The purpose
of the issuance of this order was to plow under and beat down the households of
overbearing gentry, [people practicing] simultaneous accumulation [of offices,
land, and other sources of income], wealthy traveling merchants, and great resident
merchants . . . ."

莽下詔曰詳考始建國二年胡虜猾夏以來諸軍吏及
緣邊吏大夫以上爲姦利增產致富者收其家所有財產
五分之四以助邊急公府士馳傳天下考覆貪饕開吏告
其將奴婢告其主幾以禁姦姦愈甚

[Because of famine and expenses for Hsiung-nu wars, official salaries could not be paid, and officials everywhere resorted to illegal profits. Therefore Wang] Mang issued an edict, saying: "I have considered carefully. All those from army officers, frontier officials, and grandees on up, who have made illicit profits, increased their property, and become rich since A.D. 10 when the Huns began to disturb China, shall have four-fifths of their family wealth confiscated for the aid of frontier urgencies."

Officers of the Public Treasury sped throughout the empire investigating and judging rapacious [officials. This] opened [the way for] officers to inform on their generals and male and female slaves to inform on their masters. [Wang Mang] had intended to prevent corruption, but corruption increased.

129.   A.D. 18.   CHS, 99C, 2a (3b)

宗姊妨爲衞將軍王興夫人祝詛姑殺婢以絕口事發
覺莽使中常侍𧨏惲責問妨幷以責興皆自殺事連及司
命孔仁妻亦自殺

[Wang] Tsung's sister [*née* Wang] Fang was the wife of General
of the Guard Wang Hsing.[1]   She put a supernatural curse on her
paternal aunt, and then murdered a female slave to silence her.
The matter was discovered.   [Wang] Mang sent a Palace Constant-
Attaché [named] Tai Yün[2] to rebuke and cross-examine [Wang]
Fang.   [Tai Yün] likewise rebuked and cross-examined [Wang] Hsing.
Both committed suicide.   The matter implicated [Military Police]
Commissioner K'ung Jen's[3] wife, who also committed suicide.[4]

[1] Wang Tsung (CHS, 99B, 1a; 99C, 2a) was the fourth son of the eldest son
of Wang Mang.   In A.D. 9 he was made a duke.   Nothing else is told of Wang Fang.

Wang Hsing (CHS, 99B, 1b; 99C, 2a) was apparently not related to Wang
Mang, though he had the same surname.   Once only a petty official, he was Prefect
of the Capital District in A.D. 9, when Wang Mang made him General of the Guard.
Nothing else is told of him except the circumstances of his death.   It is somewhat unusual for people of the same surname to be married.

[2] He was one of Wang Mang's most loyal followers, and is mentioned numerous
times in CHS, 99.   Officials with this title (cf. TY; MH, vol. II, p. 526) had access
to the forbidden palace; in the Latter Han period eunuchs were used.

[3] K'ung Jen (CHS, 99B, 13b; 99C, 2a) is mentioned in A.D. 15 as the Robber-
Catching General who successfully put down serious disturbances in Wu-yüan
and Tai Commanderies.   He appears several more times in CHS, 99C.

[4] Wang Mang once before showed similar severity when he ordered his own
son to commit suicide for slaying a slave.   Cf. *114.*

---

130.   A.D. 19.   CHS, 99C, 2b (4b)

而匈奴寇邊甚莽乃大募天下丁男及死罪囚吏民奴
名曰豬突豨勇以爲銳卒

And the Hsiung-nu invaded the frontiers seriously.   [Wang]
Mang thereupon widely enlisted the adult males of the empire as
well as prisoners sentenced to death and male slaves of officials and
commoners.   They were called "swine-rushers" and "boar-braves,"
and were used as shock troops.[1]

[1] This passage also appears in CHS, 24B, 11a, in somewhat abbreviated form.
It speaks only of the enlisting of imprisoned convicts and people's male slaves.

131. A.D. 20–21. CHS, 24B, 11a (26b)

迺更輕其法私鑄作泉布者與妻子没入爲官奴婢吏
及比伍知而不舉告與同罪非沮寶貨民罰作一歲吏免
官犯者俞衆及五人相坐皆没入郡國檻車鐵鎖傳送長
安鍾官愁苦死者什六七

[In A.D. 14 Wang Mang had again altered the currency, and given six years for its complete adoption. Innumerable people were executed for coining money, or sent to the bounds of the empire for opposing and stopping the "precious money." Wang] Mang thereupon changed and lightened the law: those who privately coined [*huo*] *ch'uan* and [*huo*] *pu* [money][1] would be seized with their wives and children and become government slaves. Officials and groups of [mutually responsible] five [families] who knew of and did not report [such counterfeiting] would be punished with them. Those who opposed and stopped the "precious money," [2] if common people, would be punished for one year; if officials, would be dismissed from office.

The offenders were increasingly numerous, and [they, together with the other mutually responsible] people [in the groups of] fives tried together with them, were all seized and enslaved in the commanderies and states and escorted along in cage-carts and with iron fetters to the Bureau of Mint at Ch'ang-an. Six or seven out of every ten of these died of grief and suffering.[3]

[1] The *huo ch'uan* and *huo pu* money are described in the text just above (10b).

[2] "Precious money" was the name for the gold, silver, tortoise shell, cowrie, and special cash introduced by Wang Mang (cf. CHS, 24B, 8b, and *123*, footnote 1).

[3] The law is also recorded in abbreviated form in CHS, 99C, 5b. It reports the total enslaved as being "in the number of ten myriad." Cf. *132* for a somewhat elaborated account of this mass enslavement.

132. A.D. 21. CHS, 99C, 6b (12b)

秋隕霜殺菽關東大饑蝗民犯鑄錢伍人相坐沒入爲
官奴婢其男子檻車兒女子步以鐵鎖琅當其頸傳詣鍾
官以十萬數到者易其夫婦愁苦死者什六七

In the autumn a fall of frost killed the beans. East of the pass[1]
there was a great famine and locusts. Plebeians illegally coined
money. [The mutually responsible groups of] five families were
tried together and were seized and became government slaves.
Males in cage-carts, children and women walking with iron fetters
jangling on their necks, were transported to the Bureau of Mint
[at Ch'ang-an] in the number of ten myriad. Those who arrived
had their husbands and wives exchanged. Six or seven out of every
ten died of grief and suffering.[2]

[1] I.e., Han-ku Pass; the regions affected by the famine were east of Shensi
Province.

[2] The same event is reported, with certain important differences, in CHS,
24B, 11a, and is translated in *131*.

---

133. A.D. 23. CHS, 99C, 10 (20a)

莽聞之愈恐欲外視自安迺染其須髮進所徵天下淑
女杜陵史氏女爲皇后聘黃金三萬斤車馬奴婢雜帛珍
寶以巨萬計

[Rebels were rising all about and could not be suppressed. One
group set up a man from the Liu family as Emperor, announced a
new reign period, and appointed officials. When Wang] Mang
heard of this he was even more afraid, but wanted to appear out-
wardly calm. Thereupon he dyed his beard and hair, and brought
forward [one of] the imperially selected virtuous girls of the empire,
the daughter of the Shih family of Tu-ling, to be made Empress.[1]
He gave marriage presents [to her family] of three myriad catties
of real gold,[2] carriages and horses, male and female slaves, various
silks, and precious things in enormous number.

[1] Wang Mang's wife had died in A.D. 21.

[2] This comes to 235,200 troy ounces, which if fine gold would be worth U.S.
$8,232,000 at $35.00 an ounce.

134. June 25, A.D. 26. HHS, 1A, 9a

癸未詔曰民有嫁妻賣子欲歸父母者恣聽之敢拘執論如律

[In the second year of the *chien-wu* period, the fifth month,] on the day *kuei-wei*, an imperial edict said: "If there are plebeians' wives married off and children sold, who wish to return to their parents, freely allow it. Deal according to the law[1] with those who dare restrain them."

[1] A discussion as to what law is meant here is found in the commentary to a similar edict of A.D. 31 (cf. *136*).

---

135. January 14, A.D. 31. HHS, 1B, 1b

十一月丁卯詔王莽時吏人没入爲奴婢不應舊法者皆免爲庶人

[In the sixth year of the *chien-wu* period,] in the eleventh month, the day *ting-mao*, an imperial edict [said]: "Those officials and people who, during Wang Mang's time, were seized and became slaves not in accordance with the former laws, are all to be freed and made commoners."

136. June 30, A.D. 31. HHS, 1B, 2a

甲寅詔吏人遭饑亂及爲青徐賊所略爲奴婢下妻欲
去留者恣聽之敢抱制不還以賣人法從事

[In the seventh year of the *chien-wu* period, the fifth month,] on the day *chia-yin,* an imperial edict [said]: "Those officials and people who encountered famine and turmoil, together with those who were kidnaped by the Ch'ing and Hsü[1] robbers, and thus became slaves or lesser wives, and now wish to leave but are detained— freely allow them [to go]. Try according to the law for selling people[2] those who dare to restrain and do not return them.[3]

[1] I.e., the provinces corresponding to Shantung, and northern Kiangsu and Anhwei, respectively.

[2] The commentary in Wang Hsien-ch'ien's edition, p. 4b, is as follows: "Hui Tung [1697–1758] says, 'The [Han?] law on robbery says, "Those who kidnap people, kidnap and sell people, sell people by persuasion, or buy people by persuasion, and make them slaves shall die." ' Ch'en Ch'ün [d. A.D. 236] in the preface to the *Hsin lü* [or New Code, prepared under his supervision for the Wei dynasty some time before A.D. 229] says, 'The law on robbery has [a provision covering] selling and buying people by persuasion.' According to this, then, the Section on Robbery in the Han law had an item on selling people. Two years earlier [HHS, 1A, 9a; cf. *134*] an imperial edict said: 'Deal according to the law with those who dare to restrain [their slaves from returning to their parents].' The law referred to was this law on selling people."

This last reference is actually to an edict dated five years earlier, on June 25, A.D. 26. A typographical error may have crept into the commentary.

The above commentary is very late, though it quotes Ch'en Ch'ün, who lived at the end of the Latter Han period. For items of the Han law on robbery, see Ch'eng Shu-te, *Chiu ch'ao lü k'ao,* "Han lü k'ao," pp. 65–68.

[3] There are from Emperor Kuang-wu several other edicts that freed slaves. One on April 23, A.D. 36, specifically relates to people in Kansu and Szechwan who had been kidnaped and made slaves (HHS, 1B, 3b). Another on November 25, A.D. 37, freed plebeians of Yunnan who had been kidnaped since A.D. 32 (HHS, 1B, 4b). A third, of January/February, A.D. 39, at one stroke freed and made commoners those male and female slaves in Yunnan and Kansu who had themselves pled their cases to their local governments since A.D. 32; the sellers did not have to return the purchase price (HHS, 1B, 5a). These appear to refer strictly to the Latter Han period and therefore are not separately translated.

137. March 6, A.D. 35. HHS, 1B, 3a

十一年春二月己卯詔曰天地之性人爲貴其殺奴婢
不得減罪

In the eleventh year [of the *chien-wu* period] in the spring, the second month, on the day *i-mao*, an imperial edict said: "In the nature of heaven and earth, mankind is most important. He who kills a male or female slave will not receive a reduction in punishment."

---

138. October 16, A.D. 35. HHS, 1B, 3b

癸亥詔曰敢炙灼奴婢論如律免所炙灼者爲庶民冬
十月壬午詔除奴婢射傷人棄市律

[In the eleventh year of the *chien-wu* period, the eighth month,] on the day *kuei-hai*, an imperial edict said: "[Anyone] daring to brand his male or female slaves shall be tried according to the law, and those branded shall be freed and made commoners."

In the winter, the tenth month, on the day *jen-wu*[1] an imperial edict revoked the law of public execution for male and female slaves who shot and wounded people.

[1] There is no such day in the tenth month. It would be November 4, if it were the ninth month; or January 3, A.D. 36, if the eleventh month. It was before the twelfth month.

APPENDIX: ABSTRACTS OF LESSER DOCUMENTS

A1. 230–218 B.C. CHS, 40, 1a (1a)

Chang Liang, descended from a line of chancellors of the State of Han, had three hundred household youths, but spent his entire inheritance seeking for people to assassinate the First Ch'in Emperor.

Also in SC, 55, 1a.

A2. Ca. 220 B.C. CHS, 32, 1a (1a)

The daughter of the rich man of Wai-huang [looked upon] her husband [as a] *yung-nu*. Later she married Chang Erh.

Yung appears to mean "indentured laborer." A textual problem is involved here, for SC, 89, 1a, says that she was married to a *yung-nu* and ran away from her husband. A study of the two passages makes it appear that the SC text is secondary.

A3. 205 B.C. CHS, 33, 1b (2a)

Wei Pao refused to rejoin Kao-tsu because "he insults people. He curses and scolds the nobles and ministers just as [one curses] male slaves only."

Also in SC, 90, 1b.

A4. 178 B.C. CHS, 24A, 4a (10b)

Chia Yi said that after forty years of Han rule the grain stores were still small, so that after bad harvests "pleadings to be allowed to sell titles and children have been heard."

A5. Ca. 156–139 B.C. CHS, 46, 1b (2a)

Describing the household of Shih Fen, a great stickler for propriety, it mentions that his youth-servants (*t'ung-p'u*) had to be bland and courteous.

Also in SC, 103, 1b.

A6. Ca. 140–120 B.C. SC, 126, 3b

The former wet-nurse of Emperor Wu was greatly favored by him, and the children and grandchildren and male slave escorts of her household oppressed the people of Ch'ang-an, beating people and halting their carriages and horses on the highways, and stealing people's clothing. Emperor Wu could not bear to apply the law to her.

A7.   128 B.C.   CHS, 57B, 3a (8b)

Ssu-ma Hsiang-ju, in a conversation with Emperor Wu about the barbarians in the southwest, mentions how children there were made slave captives, bound up and weeping.

In the same passage in SC, 117, 13b, the word "captive" is omitted.

A8.   123 B.C.   CHS, 44, 5b (12a)

Liu An, the King of Huai-nan, plotting a rebellion against Emperor Wu, ordered a government male slave [or slaves] to forge the Emperor's seal and the seals of various high civil and military officials.

Also in SC, 118, 6b.

A9.   119–104 B.C.   CHS, 90, 4a (9a)

Wang Wen-shu, one of Emperor Wu's ruthless administrators, was a great flatterer. "He skillfully served those in power, but as soon as they lost power he looked upon them as though they were slaves."

Also in SC, 122, 6b.

A10.   103–90 B.C.   CHS, 58, 4a (8a)

During this period the successive chancellors were of such inferior caliber that the guest-houses of the chancellery fell into disrepair and then were destroyed to make horse-stables, carriage-houses, and quarters for male and female slaves.

A11.   78 B.C.   CHS, 15A, 39a (56a)

Liu K'uan, the Marquis of Chang-pei and a grandson of Emperor Ching, was slain by a male slave.

A12.   80–70 B.C.   CHS, 78, 1b (2a)

Imperial Household Grandee Wang Chung-weng went in and out of the palace attended by green-heads and hut-dwellers.

This seems to be the earliest use in CHS of the term "ts'ang-t'ou" in the sense of government slave.   ·

A13.   46 B.C.   CHS, 64B, 7b (18a)

Chia Chüan-chih, attempting to dissuade Emperor Yüan from launching a punitive expedition against the inhabitants of Hainan Island, reported that great famines in eastern and central China had forced people to the extremity of marrying off their wives and selling their children.

A14. 33–30 B.C. CHS, 76, 11a (23b)

The Colonel over the Retainers, Wang Tsun, accused Chancellor K'uang Heng of disrespect for Emperor Ch'eng at the time of his accession. At the hour for the imperial procession, K'uang Heng had sent the senior male slave into the palace to inquire about the state of the imperial progress. Even though the slave had returned and reported that the procession had nearly arrived, K'uang Heng had sat at ease and displayed no evidence of awe and respect.

A15. 33–28 B.C. CHS, 76, 12a (26b)

Wang Tsun was being accused by the Grandee Secretary's assistant, Yang Fu, but was defended by a man named Hsing, who reported that Yang Fu had a grudge against Wang Tsun: Formerly, when Yang Fu had been a clerk for Wang Tsun he had often drunkenly offended Wang Tsun's senior male slave, Li Chia. Once Li Chia had slapped Yang Fu, and [Wang Tsun's] nephew, Hung, had drawn his sword to stab Yang Fu. This was the basis for the grudge.

A16. 29 B.C. CHS, 17, 20a (29a)

Chang Chien, the Marquis of Fu-ch'eng, was tried for being married to the Princess of Yang-i and yet having had, right in her presence, adulterous relations with a female slave, and for frequently having been drunk and cursing the Princess. He was deposed.

A17. 8 B.C. CHS, 99A, 1b (2a)

Once when Wang Mang's mother was sick, the high officials and noblemen sent their wives to call. Wang Mang's wife met them in a gown that did not trail the ground, and wearing an apron of common cloth. The ladies mistook her for a youth-servant, and were all amazed to learn that she was Wang Mang's wife.

A18. Ca. 1 B.C. CHS, 99A, 2b (4b)

Wang Mang induced K'ung Kuang to denounce Wang Mang's uncle, Wang Li. Wang Li was accused of having falsely announced that a secret child of a government slave woman named Yang Chi was the Emperor's son.

A19. Ca. A.D. 3. CHS, 99A, 6a (12a)

A memorial in praise of Wang Mang described his modesty and frugality and said: "His youths and male slaves are coarsely clothed and his horses are not foddered with grain. His uses of food and drink do not exceed those of the average commoner."

A20. Ca. A.D. 9. CHS, 92, 5a (10b)

Chen Tsun, a libertine, was officially accused of having visited a rich widow, Tso A-chün, just after his appointment to a government post. He had become drunk at the feast she provided, had danced and leaped, and then had fallen into a stupor. He had had to stay the night and had been helped to bed by a serving female slave.

A21. A.D. 11. CHS, 99B, 8b (17a)

Wang Mang issued a document in which he accused high civil and military officials of intimidating the people and of falsely putting seals upon people's necks and only taking them off on the payment of money.

Ju Shun explains that powerful ministers falsely used the law to force good people to become youth-servants, sealing their necks to differentiate them. If they received bribes, they removed the seals.

A22. A.D. 21. CHS, 99C, 6a (12a)

A diviner was inciting Li Yen to revolt against Wang Mang, and said: "Since the House of Hsin came to the throne, common people's fields and male and female slaves can not be sold or bought."

A23. A.D. 22. CHS, 99c, 9b (19a)

Wang Mang realized that his empire was falling apart and that some plan was urgent. He discussed the advisability of dispatching certain high officials throughout the empire to abolish the prohibitions dealing with the *ching-t'ien* system, male and female slaves, the resources from mountains and marshes, and the Six State Controls, and to revoke all his edicts and orders that were inconvenient to the people. But he waited to observe the outcome of events, and did not actually dispatch the officials.

BIBLIOGRAPHY

Primary sources are books which were written during the Former or Latter Han dynasties, or very shortly after. Everything else is secondary in regard to slavery in the Former Han period, even though some of the books are primary material for the later periods they cover.

The number of Chinese characters has been reduced to a minimum. Those who read Chinese will find no difficulty in locating books and articles mentioned, but as an aid I have added to each secondary reference book in Chinese a citation in brackets [TB], which tells the page on which the work is described in *An annotated bibliography of selected Chinese reference works*, by Teng Ssu-yü and Knight Biggerstaff. A complete list of abbreviations is given on pages 256 and 257.

PRIMARY SOURCES

Ch'ien Han shu [*History of the Former Han dynasty*], by Pan Ku. Imperial Ch'ien-lung edition of the twenty-four dynastic histories (1739–46). Chi ch'eng t'u shu kung ssu 集成圖書公司. Shanghai, 1908.

Fang yen 方言 [*Dialects*], attributed to Yang Hsiung. Edition of *Han Wei ts'ung-shu* (see below).

Feng su t'ung i 風俗通義 [*Rectification of customs*], by Ying Shao. Edition of *Han Wei ts'ung-shu* (see below).

Han [*kuan*] *chiu i* 漢[官]舊儀 [*The old ritual of the Han* (*government*)], by Wei Hung. Edited by Sun Hsing-yen 孫星衍 in *P'ing chin kuan ts'ung-shu* 平津館叢書.

Han [*kuan*] *chiu i pu-i* [*The old ritual of the Han* (*government, by Wei Hung*), reconstructed], by Sun Hsing-yen. Same edition as above.

Han shu pu-chu [*History of the* (*Former*) *Han dynasty, annotated*], by Wang Hsien-ch'ien 王先謙. Changsha, 1900.

Hou Han shu [*History of the Latter Han dynasty*], by Fan Yeh. Same edition as *Ch'ien Han shu.*

Lun heng 論衡 [*Philosophical essays*], by Wang Ch'ung. Edition of *Han Wei ts'ung-shu* (see below).

Shih chi [*Historical memoirs*], by Ssu-ma Ch'ien. Same edition as *Ch'ien Han shu.*

Shuo wen chieh tzu [*Etymological dictionary*], by Hsü Shen. *Shuo wen chieh tzu ku lin*, edited by Ting Fu-pao. Shanghai, 1930.

"*T'ung yüeh* [The contract for a youth]," by Wang Pao. Text from the *Ch'u hsüeh chi* (see below), compiled by Hsü Chien in 724. Edition of 1598, edited by Ch'en Ta-k'o. Ch. 19, pp. 16a–18a. For other editions consulted cf. document *83*, footnote 1.

Yen t'ieh lun [*Discourses on salt and iron*], by Huan K'uan. Edition of *Han Wei ts'ung-shu* (see below).

SECONDARY SOURCES

AUROUSSEAU, LÉONARD. "La première conquête chinoise des pays annamites." BEFEO, vol. 23, 1923, pp. 137–265.

BALAZS, STEFAN. "Beiträge zur Wirtschaftsgeschichte der T'ang-Zeit. II: Der Sklaverei." MSOS, vol. 35, 1932, pp. 2–14.

BATES, M. S. "Problems of rivers and canals under Han Wu Ti (140–87 B.C.)." JAOS, vol. 55, 1935, pp. 303–306.

BIOT, EDOUARD. "Mémoire sur la condition des esclaves et des serviteurs gagés en Chine." JA, ser. 3, t. 3, 1837, pp. 246–299. Translated into English: Canton Register, vol. 11, No. 8, 1838; and Chinese Repository, vol. 18, 1849, pp. 347–363.

BIOT, EDOUARD, translator. Le Tcheou-li ou rites des Tcheou. 2 vols., Paris, 1851.

BODDE, DERK. China's first unifier, a study of the Ch'in dynasty as seen in the life of Li Ssu (280?–208 B.C.). Sinica Leidensia, vol. 3, Leiden, 1938.

BODDE, DERK, translator. Statesman, patriot, and general in ancient China: Three Shih chi biographies of the Ch'in dynasty (255–206 B.C.). American Oriental Series, vol. 17, New Haven, 1940.

BUCK, JOHN LOSSING. Land utilization in China. 3 vols., Chicago, 1937.

CHANG, C. M. The genesis and meaning of Huan Kuan's "Discourses on salt and iron." Tientsin, 1934. Also published in the Chinese Social and Political Science Review, vol. 18, 1934, pp. 1–52.

CHANG, HSING-LANG. "The importation of negro slaves into China under the T'ang dynasty (A.D. 618–907)." Bulletin of the Catholic University of Peking, vol. 7, 1930, pp. 37–59.

CHANG, YIN-LIN 張蔭麟. "Chou tai ti feng-chien she-hui (Feudalism in the Chow dynasty)." CHHP, vol. 10, 1935, pp. 803–836.

CHAVANNES, EDOUARD. Les documents chinois découverts par Aurel Stein dans les sables du Turkestan oriental. Oxford, 1913.

    Mission archéologique dans la Chine septentrionale. 1 vol. (2 pts.) of pls., 1 vol. (2 pts.) of text, Paris, 1909, 1913, and 1915.

    "Trois généraux chinois de la dynastie des Han orientaux." TP, 2nd ser., vol. 7, 1906, pp. 210–269.

CHAVANNES, EDOUARD, translator. Les mémoires historiques de Se-ma Ts'ien. 5 vols., Paris, 1895–1905.

CHEN, HUAN-CHANG. The economic principles of Confucius and his school. 2 vols., New York, 1911.

CH'EN, HSIEN-HSÜAN 陳憲璇. "Ch'un-ch'iu ti nu-li [Slavery of the Ch'un-ch'iu period]." Shih Huo, vol. 2, No. 5, 1935, pp. 234–236.

CH'EN, PO-YIN 陳伯瀛. Chung-kuo t'ien chih ts'ung-k'ao [An investigation of the Chinese land system]. Revised edition, Shanghai, 1936.

CH'EN, S. C., translator. "Sang Hung-yang (143–80 B.C.)." JNCBRAS, vol. 67, 1936, pp. 160–170.

CH'ENG, SHU-TE 程樹德. Chiu ch'ao lü k'ao [An investigation of the legal codes of the nine dynasties (Han through Sui)]. Second edition (Commercial Press, one volume, western style), Shanghai, 1935.

CHI, CH'AO-TING. Key economic areas in Chinese history as revealed in the development of public works for water-control. London, 1936.

CH'I SSU-HO 齊思和. "Chan-kuo chih-tu k'ao (The institutions of the Chan-kuo period)." YCHP, No. 23, 1938, pp. 159–219.

Chin shu [History of the Chin dynasty (A.D. 265–419)], by Fang Ch'iao and others. Same edition as Ch'ien Han shu.

CHÔSEN-KOSEKI-KENKYU-KWAI. The tomb of the painted basket of Lo-lang. Detailed Report of Archaeological Research, vol. 1, Keijo, 1934.

Ch'u hsüeh chi [Encyclopaedia], compiled under imperial auspices by Hsü Chien (659–729), and others. Edition of Ch'en Ta-k'o, 1598. [TB, 89.]

CHÜ, CH'ING-YÜAN 鞠清遠. "Han tai ti kuan-fu kung-yeh [Government industry in the Han period]." Shih Huo, vol. 1, No. 1, 1934, pp. 1–5.

CH'Ü, TUI-CHIH 瞿兌之. "Hsi Han wu chia k'ao (Prices of commodities during the Western Han dynasty)." YCHP, 1929, pp. 877–881. Abstract by John C. Ferguson, China Journal, vol. 11, 1929, pp. 281–282.

Ch'üan shang ku san-tai Ch'in Han San-kuo Liu-ch'ao wen [Complete collection of the literature from remote antiquity, the Ch'in, Han, Three Kingdoms and Six Dynasties], collected by Yen K'o-chün (1762–1843). Kuang ya shu chü, 1894? [TB, 217.]

Chung-hua min-kuo hsin ti t'u [A new atlas of the Chinese Republic], compiled by V. K. Ting, Wong Wen-hao, and Tseng Shih-ying. Shanghai, 1934. [TB, 194.]

Chung-hua ta tzu-tien [Chinese great dictionary], compiled by Hsü Yüan-kao and others. 4 vols., fifth printing, Shanghai, Chung Hua Book Company, 1936. [TB, 162.]

Chung-kuo jen ming ta tz'u-tien [Chinese biographical dictionary], compiled by Fang Yi and others. Twelfth printing, Shanghai, 1933. [TB, 203.]

Chung-kuo ku chin ti ming ta tz'u-tien [Dictionary of Chinese ancient and modern place names], compiled by Tsang Li-ho and others. Reprinted, Shanghai, 1933. [TB, 189.]

Chung-kuo ti ming ta tz'u tien [Dictionary of Chinese place names], compiled by Liu Chün-jen. Peking, 1930. [TB, 188.]

Chung-kuo wen-hsüeh-chia ta tz'u-tien [Biographical dictionary of Chinese authors], compiled by T'an Cheng-pi. Shanghai, 1934. [TB, 204.]

CONRADY, AUGUST. Die chinesischen Handschriften und sonstigen Kleinfunde Sven Hedins in Lou-lan. Stockholm, 1920.

COULING, SAMUEL. See Encyclopaedia Sinica.

COUVREUR, F. SÉRAPHIN. Dictionnaire classique de la langue chinoise. Ho-kien Fou, 1904.

COUVREUR, F. SÉRAPHIN, translator. Chou king. Second edition, Hien Hien, 1919.

CREEL, HERRLEE GLESSNER. The birth of China: A survey of the formative period of Chinese civilization. London and New York, 1936.

"Soldier and scholar in ancient China." Pacific Affairs, vol. 7, 1935, pp. 336–343.

Studies in early Chinese culture. First series, Baltimore, 1937.

DUBS, HOMER H. "The 'golden man' of Former Han times." TP, vol. 33, 1937, pp. 1–14.

"Han Kao-tsu and Hsiang-Yü." JNCBRAS, vol. 67, 1936, pp. 58–80.

"The name and ancestry of Han Kao-tsu." TP, vol. 32, 1936, pp. 59–64.

"Wang Mang and his economic reforms." TP, vol. 35, 1940, pp. 219–265.

DUBS, HOMER H., translator. *The History of the Former Han dynasty by Pan Ku*. Translation, Volume One. *First division: The Imperial Annals, chapters I–V*. Baltimore, 1938.

DUYVENDAK, J. J. L., translator. *The book of Lord Shang, a classic of the Chinese school of law*. Probsthain's Oriental Series, vol. 17, London, 1928.

EBERHARD, WOLFRAM. "Zur Landwirtschaft der Han-Zeit (Im Anschluss an neuere Chinesische Arbeiten)." MSOS, vol. 35 (Abt. 1), 1932, pp. 74–105.

Encyclopaedia Sinica, edited by Samuel Couling. Shanghai, 1917.

Erh-shih-wu shih jen ming so-yin [Index to people's names in the twenty-five histories]. Shanghai, 1935. [TB, 214.]

ESCARRA, JEAN. *Le droit chinois: Conception et évolution, institutions législatives et judiciaires, science et enseignement*. Peking, 1936.

FENG, H. Y. and SHRYOCK, J. K. "The black magic in China known as *ku*." JAOS, vol. 55, 1935, pp. 1–30.

FORKE, ALFRED. "Das Chinesische Finanz- und Steuerwesen." MSOS, vol. 3, 1900, pp. 165–191; vol. 4, 1901, pp. 1–75.

FORKE, ALFRED, translator. *Lun-Hêng*. Part I: *Philosophical essays of Wang Ch'ung*. London, 1907. Part II: *Miscellaneous Essays of Wang Ch'ung*. Berlin, 1911.

FRANKE, O. "Staatssocialistische Versuche im alten und mittelalterlichen China." *Sitzungsberichte der Preussischen Akademie der Wissenschaften, Phil.-Hist. Kl.*, Berlin, 1931, vol. XIII, pp. 218–242.

FU, AN-HUA 傅安華. "Kuan yü nu-li she-hui li-lun ti chi-ko wen-t'i [Questions regarding the slavery society theory]." *Shih Huo*, vol. 5, No. 5, 1937.

GALE, ESSON M., translator. *Discourses on salt and iron, a debate on state control of commerce and industry in ancient China*. Chapters I–XIX, translated from the Chinese of Huan K'uan. Sinica Leidensia, vol. 2, Leiden, 1931. See also *Yen t'ieh lun*.

GALE, ESSON M., BOODBERG, PETER A. and LIN, T. C., translators. "Discourses on salt and iron (*Yen t'ieh lun*: chaps. XX–XXVIII)." JNCBRAS, vol. 65, 1934, pp. 73–110.

GARDNER, CHARLES S. *Chinese traditional historiography*. Harvard Historical Monographs, vol. XI, Cambridge, 1938.

GILES, HERBERT A. *A Chinese biographical dictionary*. Shanghai, 1898.

A Chinese-English dictionary. Second edition, London, 1912.

Gems of Chinese literature. Revised edition, Shanghai, 1922.

GILES, LIONEL. *An alphabetical index to the Chinese encyclopaedia: Ch'in ting ku chin t'u shu chi ch'eng*. London, British Museum, 1911.

"A census of Tun-huang." TP, vol. 16, 1915, pp. 468–488.

"Dated Chinese manuscripts in the Stein collection." BSOS, vol. 7, 1933–35, pp. 809–836; vol. 8, 1935–37, pp. 1–26; vol. 9, 1937–39, pp. 1–25, 1023–1046; vol. 10, 1940–, pp. 317–344.

GOODRICH, L. C. "Negroes in China." *Bulletin of the Catholic University of Peking*, vol. 8, 1931, pp. 137–139.

GROOT, J. J. M. DE. *Die Hunnen der vorchristlichen Zeit.* Vol. 1 of *Chinesische Urkunden zur Geschichte Asiens*, Berlin, 1921.

Han Wei ts'ung-shu [*Collection of books on the Han and Wei periods*], first assembled in the Ming period by Ch'eng Jung. Edition prefaced by Yang T'ing-jui 楊廷瑞 of Shan-hua (Changsha), and published by Hunan I wen shu chü 藝文書局 in 1894.

Harvard–Yenching Institute, Sinological index series, No. 7: *Index to Ssu k'u ch'üan shu tsung mu and Wei shou shu mu*, compiled by James R. Ware, revised by Weng Tu-chien. 2 vols., Peking, 1932. [TB, 26.]

No. 10: *I wen chih erh-shih chung tsung-ho yin-te* [*Combined indices to twenty historical bibliographies*], compiled by William Hung, Nieh Ch'ung-ch'i, and others. Peking, 1933. [TB, 12.]

No. 36: *Combined indices to Han shu and the notes of Yen Shih-ku and Wang Hsien-ch'ien.* Peking, 1940.

HERRMANN, ALBERT. *Historical and commercial atlas of China.* Harvard–Yenching Institute, Monograph Series, vol. 1, Cambridge, 1935.

HIRTH, FRIEDRICH. *The ancient history of China to the end of the Chóu dynasty.* New York, 1908.

HIRTH, FRIEDRICH, translator. "The story of Chang K'ién, China's pioneer in western Asia. Text and translation of chapter 123 of Ssï-ma Ts'ién's Shï-ki." JAOS, vol. 37, 1917, pp. 89–152.

Hsi Han hui yao [*A classified compendium on the Western Han dynasty*], by Hsü T'ien-lin, completed A.D. 1211. *Kuo-hsüeh chi-pen ts'ung-shu* edition (Commercial Press, one volume, western style). Shanghai, 1935. [TB, 139.]

HU, SHIH 胡適. *Hu Shih wen ts'un* [*The collected works of Hu Shih*]. 1st ser., 4 vols., Shanghai, 1921. (Reviewed by P. Demiéville, BEFEO, vol. 23, 1923, pp. 489–499.) 2nd ser., 4 vols., Shanghai, 1924.

"Wang Mang, the socialist emperor of nineteen centuries ago." JNCBRAS, vol. 59, 1928, pp. 218–230.

HUANG, HAN LIANG. *The land tax in China.* New York, 1918.

I wen lei chü [*Encyclopaedia*], compiled under imperial auspices by O-yang Hsün (557–641) and others. Edition of the Hua yang tang ta t'ang chung k'an, 1879. [TB, 88.]

JONGCHELL, ARVID. *Huo Kuang och Hans tid, täxter ur Pan Ku's Ch'ien Han shu.* Göteborg, 1930.

KAO, YÜN-HUI 高耘暉. "Chou tai t'u-ti chih-tu yü ching-t'ien [The Chou dynasty land system and *ching-t'ien*]." *Shih Huo*, vol. 1, 1935, pp. 264–274.

KARLGREN, BERNHARD. "The early history of the Chou li and Tso chuan texts." BMFEA, vol. 3, 1931, pp. 1–59.

KATO, SHIGERU. "A study on the *suan-fu*, the poll tax of the Han dynasty." MRDTB, vol. 1, 1926, pp. 51–68.

Ku chin t'u shu chi ch'eng [*Encyclopaedia*], compiled under imperial auspices by [Ch'en Meng-lei], Chiang T'ing-hsi, and others, and presented to the throne in 1725. Shanghai edition, 1888. [TB, 107.]

Ku wen yüan [*Garden of ancient literature*], compiler unknown; T'ang. Edition of the *Shou shan ko ts'ung-shu*, published by Hung wen shu chü, 1889.

LAO, KAN 勞榦. "Han tai nu-li chih-tu chi lüeh (The system of slavery during the two Han dynasties)." Academia Sinica: *Bulletin of the Institute of History and Philology*, vol. 5 (pt. 1), 1935, pp. 1–11.

"Liang Han hu-chi yü ti-li chih kuan-hsi (Population and geography in the two Han dynasties)." Ibid., vol. 5 (pt. 2), 1935, pp. 179–214 and 215–240.

LATTIMORE, OWEN. *Inner Asian frontiers of China.* American Geographical Society, Research Series, No. 21, New York, 1940.

LAUFER, BERTHOLD. *Chinese clay figures.* Part 1: *Prolegomena on the history of defensive armor.* Chicago, 1914.

Chinese pottery of the Han dynasty. Leiden, 1909.

LEE, MABEL PING-HUA. *The economic history of China, with special reference to agriculture.* New York, 1921.

LEGGE, JAMES, translator. *The Chinese classics.* Second edition, 5 vols. in 8, Oxford, 1893–95.

Li tai ming jen sheng tsu nien piao [*Table of birth and death dates of famous persons*], compiled by Liang T'ing-ts'an. Reprinted, Shanghai, 1935. [TB, 211.]

LIANG, CH'I-CH'AO 染啓超. "Chung-kuo nu-li chih-tu (System of slavery in China)." CHHP, vol. 2, 1925, pp. 527–553.

LIU, HSING-T'ANG 劉興唐. "Nu-li she-hui ti cheng-chieh [The obstinate problem of a slavery society]." *Shih Huo*, vol. 5, No. 11, 1937, pp. 460–463.

LO, TCHEN-YING. *Les formes et les méthodes historiques en Chine: Une famille d'historiens et son oeuvre.* Paris, 1931.

MA, CH'ENG-FENG 馬乘風. *Chung-kuo ching-chi shih* [*An economic history of China*]. Second edition, 2 vols., Shanghai, 1939.

"Ts'ung hsi Chou tao Sui ch'u chih i-ch'ien-ch'i-pai yü nien ti ching-chi chuan-i [Economic transition during the seventeen hundred years from Western Chou to the beginning of Sui]." *Shih Huo*, vol. 2, No. 9, 1935, pp. 400–410.

MA, FEI-PAI 馬非百. "Ch'in Han ching-chi shih tzu liao [Source material on the economic history of Ch'in and Han]." Part 5: "Jen-k'ou chi t'u-ti [Population and land]." *Shih Huo*, vol. 3, No. 3, 1936, pp. 102–132. Part 6: "Nu-li chih-tu [The slavery system]." Ibid., No. 8, 1936, pp. 385–400.

MARGOULIÈS, GEORGES. *Le Kou-wen chinois. Recueil de textes avec introduction et notes.* Paris, 1926.

MASPERO, HENRI. *La Chine antique.* Paris, 1927.

NIEBOER, H. J. *Slavery as an industrial system: Ethnological researches.* Second edition, The Hague, 1912.

NIIDA, NOBORU 仁井田陞. *To-rei shui* 唐令拾遺 [*T'ang ordinances reassembled*]. Tokyo, 1933.

PIPPON, TONI. "Beitrag zum Chinesischen Sklavensystem, nebst einer Ubersetzung des 'Chung kuo nu pei chih tu' (das Sklavensystem Chinas) von Wang Shih Chieh. Eine juristisch-soziologische Darstellung." *Mitteilungen der Deutschen Gesellschaft für Natur- und Volkerkunde Ostasiens*, Bd. 29, Teil B, Tokyo, 1936.

San kuo chih [History of the Three Kingdoms], by Ch'en Shou. Same edition as *Ch'ien Han shu.*

SARGENT, CLYDE BAILEY, translator. *Wang Mang: A translation of the official account of his rise to power as given in the History of the Former Han dynasty.* (In MS.)

SEGALEN, VICTOR, DE VOISINS, GILBERT, and LARTIGUE, JEAN. *Mission archéologique en Chine.* Text vol. 1: *L'Art funéraire a l'époque des Han.* Paris, 1935.

SEUFERT, WILHELM. "Urkunden zur staatlichen Neuordnung unter der Han-Dynastie." MSOS, vol. 23 (Abt. 1), 1922, pp. 1–50.

SHEN, CHIA-PEN 沈家本. *Li-tai hsing fa k'ao [An investigation into the history of the laws and punishments].* Part I of *Shen Chi-i hsien-sheng i shu*, a collection of his works printed in forty volumes (*ts'e*) after his death (1913) by the Shen family. n.d.

   Han lü chih i [The Han code assembled]. Part II of *Shen Chi-i hsien-sheng i shu.*

SHRYOCK, JOHN K. *The origin and development of the state cult of Confucius.* New York, 1932.

Ssu k'u ch'üan shu tsung mu [General table of contents to the complete works in the Imperial Library], compiled under imperial auspices by Chi Yün and others ca. 1790. Lithographic edition of Ta tung shu chü. Shanghai, 1930. [TB, 23.]

STANGE, HANS O. H. *Leben, Persönlichkeit und Werk Wang Mang's dargestellt nach dem 99. Kapitel der Han-Annalen.* Berlin, 1934.

STANGE, HANS O. H., translator. *Die Monographie über Wang Mang (Ts'ien-Han-shu Kap. 99), kritisch bearbeitet, übersetzt und erklärt.* Abhandlungen für die Kunde des Morgenlandes, vol. XXIII, pt. 3, Leipzig, 1938.

SWANN, NANCY LEE. *Pan Chao: Foremost woman scholar of China, first century A.D.* New York, 1932.

   "A woman among the rich merchants: The widow of Pa (3rd century B.C.)." JAOS, vol. 54, 1934, pp. 186–193.

SWANN, NANCY LEE, translator. "Biography of the Empress Têng, a translation from the Annals of the Later Han dynasty (Hou Han Shu, Chüan 10a)." JAOS, vol. 51, 1931, pp. 138–159.

TAI, CHEN-HUI 戴振輝. "Liang Han nu-li chih-tu [The slavery system of the two Han dynasties]." *Shih Huo*, vol. 1, No. 7, 1935, pp. 286–291.

T'ai p'ing yü lan [Encyclopaedia], compiled under imperial auspices by Li Fang (925–996) and others, completed in 983. Ssu pu ts'ung kan (Commercial Press). Shanghai, 1935–36. [TB, 92.]

T'ang lü su i [Commentary on the T'ang code], 唐律疏議, by Chang-sun Wu-ch'i, completed A.D. 653–654. *Kuo-hsüeh chi-pen ts'ung-shu* (Commercial Press). Shanghai, 1933.

T'AO, HSI-SHENG 陶希聖. *Hsi Han ching-chi shih* [*An economic history of Western Han*]. Shanghai, 1935.

"Hsi Han ti k'o ['Guests' in the Western Han period]." *Shih Huo*, vol. 5, No. 1, 1937, pp. 1–6.

TAWNEY, H. R. *Land and labour in China*. London, 1932.

TEGGART, FREDERICK J. *Rome and China: A study of correlations in historical events*. Berkeley, 1939.

TENG, SSU-YÜ and BIGGERSTAFF, KNIGHT. *An annotated bibliography of selected Chinese reference works*. Yenching Journal of Chinese Studies, Monograph No. 12, Peiping, 1936.

TERRIEN DE LACOUPERIE [A.E.J.B.]. *Catalogue of Chinese coins*. London, British Museum, 1892.

Tz'u t'ung [*Dictionary of variants*], compiled by Chu Ch'i-feng. 2 vols., Shanghai, 1934. [TB, 167.]

Tz'u yüan [*Dictionary*], compiled by Lu Erh-k'uei and others. Seventh printing, Shanghai (Commercial Press), 1921. [TB, 163.]

VISSERING, W. *On Chinese currency*. Leiden, Brill, 1877.

WAN, KWOH-TING 萬國鼎. *Chung-kuo t'ien chih shih* (*An agrarian history of China*). Vol. 1. Nanking, 1933.

"Han i ch'ien jen-k'ou chi t'u-ti li-yung chih i pan (Population and land utilization in China, 1400 B.C.–200 A.D.)." CLHP, vol. 1, 1931, pp. 133–150.

"Liang Han chih chün ch'an yün-tung (The movement for equal land holdings in the Han dynasty)." CLHP, vol. 1, 1931, pp. 1–25.

WANG, SHIH-CHIEH 王世杰. "Chung-kuo nu-pei chih-tu [The Chinese slavery system]." *She-hui k'e-hsüeh chi-kan* (*Social Science Quarterly*), vol. 3, 1925, pp. 303–328. Translated by PIPPON, TONI, pp. 93–113.

WANG, YÜ-CH'ÜAN. "The development of modern social sciences in China." *Pacific Affairs*, vol. 11, 1938, pp. 345–362.

WARE, JAMES R. "Once more the 'golden man.'" TP, vol. 34, 1938, pp. 174–178.

Wei shu [*History of the (Northern or Latter) Wei dynasty*], by Wei Shou. Same edition as *Ch'ien Han shu*.

Wen hsien t'ung k'ao [*Encyclopaedia on government, etc.*], compiled by Ma Tuan-lin, end of Sung or early in Yüan. Tien shu chai, Shanghai, 1899. [TB, 131.]

WESTERMANN, W. L. "Sklaverei." In *Paulys Realenzyklopädie der klassischen Altertums-Wissenschaft*, supplement, vol. 6, 1935, col. 893–1068.

WIEGER, LÉON. *China throughout the ages*, translated by Edward Chalmers Werner. Hsien Hsien, 1928.

WIEGER, LÉON, translator. *Textes historiques* (Rudiments, vols. 10–11). 2 vols., Ho-chien Fu, 1903–04.

WITTFOGEL, K. A. "The foundations and stages of Chinese economic history." *Zeitschrift für Sozialforschung*, Jahr. IV, Heft 1, 1935, pp. 26–58.

WU, CHING-CH'AO 吳景超. "Hsi Han nu-li chih-tu [The slavery system of the Western Han]." *Shih Huo*, vol. 2, No. 6, 1935, pp. 264–270.

"Hsi Han ti chieh-chi chih-tu (The class system of the Western Han dynasty)." CHHP, vol. 10, 1935, pp. 587–629.

"Liang Han to-ch'i ti chia-t'ing (The polygamous family of the Han dynasty)." CLHP, vol. 1, 1931, pp. 47–57.

WU, PO-LUN 武伯綸. "Hsi Han nu-li k'ao [An investigation of slavery in the Western Han]." *Shih Huo*, vol. 1, No. 7, pp. 275–285.

WYLIE, A. *Notes on Chinese literature.* Second edition, Shanghai, 1901.

WYLIE, A., translator. "History of the Heung-noo in their relations with China (translated from the Tseen-Han-shoo. Book 94, etc.)." JAI, vol. 3, 1873, pp. 401–451; vol. 5, 1875, pp. 41–80.

"History of the south-western barbarians and Chaou-sëen (translated from the 'Tseen Han Shoo,' Book 95)." JAI, vol. 9, 1879, pp. 53–96.

"Notes on the western regions. Translated from the 'Tseen Han Shoo,' Book 96." Part 1, JAI, vol. 10, 1880, pp. 20–73; Part 2, JAI, vol. 11, 1881, pp. 83–115.

Yüan chien lei han [*Encyclopaedia*], compiled under imperial auspices by Chang Ying and others, and presented to the throne in 1701; first printed 1710. Ku hsiang chai hsiu chen shih chung, 1876–84? [TB, 106.]

INDEX

482